Solutions to Unemployment

Solutions to Unemployment

EDITED BY

David C. Colander

HARCOURT BRACE JOVANOVICH, INC.

New York   San Diego   Chicago   San Francisco
Atlanta   London   Sydney   Toronto

Printed in the United States of America

Library of Congress Catalog Card Number: 80-83973

ISBN: 0-15-582456-2

CONTENTS

INTRODUCTION

The ideas of economists and political philosophers, both when they are right and when they are wrong, are more powerful than is commonly understood. Indeed the world is ruled by little else.

J. M. KEYNES

It all used to be so easy. Unemployment was bad, but if the government maintained a high level of aggregate demand through monetary and fiscal policy, it could achieve full employment, give or take 2–3 percent "frictional" unemployment. Unfortunately, the 2–3 percent began creeping upward, becoming 3 percent, 4 percent, 5 percent, 6 percent, and now some are even willing to argue that 8 percent or more is the "natural rate" of unemployment. If the government attempts to expand aggregate output beyond this, in order to provide for more jobs, it merely causes inflation.

As the numbers have risen, so too have the descriptions of its causes. Whereas once the "natural rate" of unemployment was associated with drunkards who couldn't work, hippies who wouldn't work, and a few individuals between jobs, it now has become associated with individuals searching for jobs (search unemployment), those waiting for better job offers (wait unemployment), or those making the transition from home or school to work (transition and new-entrant unemployment). In the "new" view, people are unemployed either because of structural problems or by choice. In either case, the resulting unemployment cannot be fought with aggregate demand policies; in fact, it is even questionable whether such unemployment should be called unemployment. According to this view, all the preoccupation with the unemployment rate is wrong; the unemployment rate is merely the *illusion* of a problem, and the macroeconomic fight against unemployment is a quixotic battle against windmills.

Others claim precisely the opposite—that the measured unemployment rate is merely the tip of an iceberg, which significantly understates the unemployment problem. Many workers are simply discouraged from even looking for a job: Since the search is hopeless, why bother? In this view, considering an 8 percent unemployment rate to be full employment is inhumane, inefficient, and unacceptable. Put simply, if frictional unemployment was once only 2 percent, it should still be 2 percent; any economy that cannot achieve "true full employment" is flawed. Leon Keyserling, one of the strongest advocates of this view, tells the following parable to make his point:

> A student when asked by his professor why so many men on the Titanic died, started into a long and complicated explanation about the division of lifeboats, how women and children were allocated to the boats first, how . . . . The professor, after listening patiently to the student, finally stopped him and pointed out that the complicated answer, while an impressive display of analytical virtuosity, was totally wrong. The men died simply because there weren't enough lifeboats.

Keyserling's point is clear. In his view, the problem with our economy is a shortage of jobs brought about by our failure to maintain adequate demand through planning. All these other "causes" are secondary, since they are only concerned with how the existing jobs are divided up.

WHERE THE TEXTBOOKS END

This book is designed, if not to eliminate the quandary presented by these opposing views, at least to put it in perspective. It begins where most textbooks end, providing insight into such questions as

What are the limits of aggregate demand policy?
What destroyed the trade-off between inflation and unemployment?
Are there alternative supply-side or microeconomic solutions to unemployment?

The first two sections, "The Death of Keynesian Macroeconomics" and "The Death of the Phillips Curve," explore the limits of aggregate demand management as a solution to unemployment; they provide a sense of what economists hoped for from aggregate policies and what they actually received. The historical foundation of the Phillips curve is presented along with the modern critiques of the trade-off, such as that made by proponents of rational expectations. Together, the articles provide a rather different view of the unemployment problem from that presented in most textbooks. Aggregate demand management is only the beginning of the battle against unemployment. If we are to win that battle we must be much more careful of the philosophical underpinnings of unemployment—making our welfare judgments about work and jobs more explicit.

The third section is designed to aid in this necessary task by providing a background into the meaning and history of full employment and full employment policy. In it you will see that the employment issue has never been as easy as it seemed. The issue of full employment is, and has always been, far more difficult than presented in the macroeconomic textbooks. And you will see how acceptance of the Keynesian view of macroeconomics merely swept these problems under the rug.

THE LIMITS OF FISCAL AND MONETARY POLICY

To understand what went wrong with the macroeconomic solution to unemployment, one must first examine that solution itself. Keynesian economics did not solve the employment problem, it solved the "effective nominal demand" problem. If there is a shortage of total spending, the government can make up that shortage. But a specific total nominal spending in an economy does not necessarily translate into a specific number of jobs—that depends on relative and nominal wages and prices in the economy. Increased nominal demand can merely lead to inflation, or to employment and high wages for some and unemployment for others. Macroeconomics pushed aside all such problems with an implicit assumption that a direct transition exists between aggregate demand and employment. Thus, if nominal income increases by 10 percent, employment is also expected to do so.

When economists first adopted macroeconomics, such a view was probably reasonable, as was its myopic focus on unemployment to the exclusion of other problems. Keynes was writing for a specific period in which the unemployment rate had risen to levels up to 25 percent. Many believed that if something were not done to control that rate and get people employed again, Western democracies did not have long to live. The severity of the problem called for an immediate solution, even though it might not be a long-run solution. In Keynes' writing it is not clear whether he meant his solution to be a long-run solution or merely a method of escaping from particular problems then existing in society. In the second view, Keynes is seen as the savior of the capitalist system, rather than a radical liberal introducing more and more government in everyday life. He found a way to patch capitalism together while maintaining minimal government interference with the internal relative pricing function of the market.

The old Keynesians never promised a rose garden. Policies that solve certain problems at one point are likely to cause others later, especially with the imperfect political system we must rely on to implement them. *Long-run costs of a policy do not mean we shouldn't use them.* That decision can only be made by comparing the costs of the program with the present benefits and judging those in relation to other possible policies, including the policy of having no policy. If the system's present problem is seen as sufficiently severe, even the fact that a solution will later present its own difficulties does not mean it should not be used. This may well have been the case with Keynesian macroeconomics.

INFLATION AND UNEMPLOYMENT

Keynesian or aggregate fiscal and monetary policies "solved" one type of unemployment but created new strains of unemployment that are immune to such solutions and left other types of unemployment untouched. Our present study of unemployment must not only consider aggregate demand but also the nominal/real split—how any increase in aggregate demand is divided into inflation and into more jobs. Thus, a major part of the unemployment debate concerns the relationship between inflation and unemployment in both the long and short run. Views of this relationship differ radically.

Some believe the existence of any unexpected inflation means the economy has exceeded the natural rate and excess demand exists. Such a level of aggregate demand can only be temporarily maintained. Unemployment below the natural rate exists only because the government fooled individuals into thinking that if they went to work, they would receive a higher real wage than they actually would get and thus tricked them into working more than they wanted. This view is called the *natural rate of unemployment hypothesis.*

A second view provides a quite different interpretation. Inflation does not imply excess demand but instead is caused by asymmetrical dynamic adjustment forces operating on the price level. Dynamic upward pressures on prices overwhelm downward pressures on them as soon as the economy approaches full employment, placing an upward push on prices *before* the natural rate is reached. Inflation, in this view, results from a failure of dynamic competitive forces to offset the upward push. A continual disequilibrium—in other words, unemployment—must be maintained to achieve this offset. If it is not, the inflation rate explodes. Thus, inflation is a type of dynamic externality to each individual. Since there is a difference between private and social costs of raising prices, room exists for potential government action in directly offsetting any upward push. If an independent method of restraining the inflationary forces or upward pressure can be found, unemployment can be significantly reduced. This view is called the NARU or *nonaccelerating rate of unemployment hypothesis.* It, the natural rate hypothesis, and the implications of both are explored in Section II.

BEYOND AGGREGATE DEMAND POLICY

Just because we have done all we can on the aggregate demand front does not mean we have done all in the battle against unemployment. Whether one believes in the natural rate or the NARU hypothesis, there are a variety of alternative policies that either reduce or eliminate unemployment. Programs such as structural reform of unemployment insurance, tax and market employment incentive plans, and guaranteed jobs proposals *will* eliminate unemployment. But before advocating any such proposals, we must determine their costs. If the costs are too high, we might decide that eliminating unemployment just is not worth it.

Alternatively, and more likely, we might decide to allow some types of unemployment and eliminate others.

It is likely some unemployment will remain because some types serve useful functions. The economy experiences both demand and supply shocks, and the adjustment to these shocks will cause changes in plans, which may well involve some unemployment. The relevant question is, How much, and who should bear the burden of these changes?

For some individuals, unemployment may be like a vacation. Of course, a vacation without money can be rather unpleasant. Thus an individual's ability to borrow, the fairness of the unemployment, and the fairness of the overall system become important parts of the welfare judgments about unemployment. Such welfare considerations should be made prior to those of any solution to unemployment. Yet in most macroeconomic literature, such considerations are totally lacking. In macroeconomics unemployment is considered bad—by assumption. Thus, macroeconomics provides little guidance in separating "good" from "bad" unemployment.

Unfortunately, most microeconomic literature also provides little help in approaching the unemployment problems. One of the assumptions of microeconomics is that individuals face the opportunities presented to them and choose the best possible alternatives. According to this psychological interpretation, "involuntary" unemployment is, by definition, impossible, since each individual puts his or her time to the best possible use. If individuals find that this best possible use of their time entails looking for a job, they are not really unemployed but are employed in looking for a job. Alternatively, if there are statistical irregularities in the employment offers, an individual may wait for an offer of a better-paying job rather than accept one currently available. Again, this type of individual is not truly unemployed, but merely employed in waiting. Both of these views about the unemployed are true by definition. However, it seems to be an easy transition for people to jump from these correct assumptions to incorrect ones stating no policies exist that can or should reduce unemployment and that such "voluntary" unemployment should not be the concern of government.

Economists have proven (subject to certain conditions) that if the economy has a "complete" set of markets, these second propositions follow from the first. However, our economy does not have a complete set of markets; for many activities, the transaction costs of setting up and using markets are too high. Therefore, in our economy the second propositions *do not* follow from the first. Since individuals do not take the unemployment consequences of their decisions into account, unemployment may be an externality that positive government actions can reduce. Whether it should or not depends only on the costs. Without a consideration of the relative cost of alternatives, microeconomics has no direct implications for policy.

Moreover, some of the key issues here are philosophical, not economic. What rights do people have to a job of their choice at a wage of their choice? Some believe the state owes an individual a job that meets his or her "reasonable" expectations. Others believe government only owes an individual a minimally satisfying job; still others believe the government owes an individual nothing. These differing beliefs about the role of the state in an individual's life are not based on economic analysis and so must be made prior to the analysis. Thus, the beliefs that we bring into an analysis of unemployment shape the conclusion we make and the policies we favor.

We must, of course, look at the costs of alternative policies in making decisions on government's role. The more for which we hold the state responsible, the higher the cost of achieving the goal. Higher costs mean higher taxes; stronger government policy means less freedom for individuals. These consequences counsel against a strong government role. On the other hand, the freedom to starve or the freedom to sleep under any available bridge is considered by some hardly a freedom. They view a certain equality of income and opportunity is necessary to guarantee an individual true freedom. Such beliefs have led conservatives and liberals alike to favor guaranteed minimum income proposals as a foundation for a fair economy.

Others argue that this belief is unjustified and misses a very real point. If the government guarantees an individual's income—even one based on a minimum wage—it has guaranteed too much. All the government should guarantee is a job, not a job of an individual's choice, but one that simply translates time into money. If the government takes the position that it will give individuals something for nothing, freedom is reduced because along with that gift comes a responisiblity to the ones who are footing the bill. Allowing some a free ride undermines the system and destroys the social consensus around which the society is built. Therefore the government should guarantee jobs, not income.

These philosophical disputes about the relationship of individuals to the state existed long before the development of macroeconomics. The widespread acceptance of Keynesian economics merely swept them under the rug, making the profession seem more united than it actually was. Many of the so-called theoretical debates about macroeconomics and microeconomics are actually philosophical debates about the meaning and purpose of freedom and liberty. Although these issues will likely never be settled, an understanding of them is necessary before we can consider alternative proposals. Section III fulfills this role, providing a brief history of full employment and an introduction to the debate.

NEW "SUPPLY-SIDE" APPROACHES TO UNEMPLOYMENT
Section IV discusses microeconomic or *incentive* policy options for dealing with unemployment. Four types of solutions to unemployment are

1. Modified solutions of existing incentive structures
2. Market incentive solutions
3. Tax incentive solutions
4. Direct regulatory solutions

All the above are *supply-side* solutions and do not rely on aggregate demand to solve unemployment. Instead these proposals work directly on unemployment, given the existing nominal demand. They redirect the total aggregate demand in an alternative way by structuring the *incentives* facing individuals. Since they work on incentives, they can be tailored to a variety of types of unemployment rather than affecting all unemployment.

Each of the proposals discussed will theoretically solve unemployment, but translating theory into practice is another story, and the solution may be worse than the problem. Some may even decide any approach is too costly and the problem should be allowed to take care of itself. Section IV includes a range of proposals that fall under these four headings. The reader is left to choose a solution from the various alternatives presented.

As will be apparent, disagreements concerning these proposals are substantial, which is to be expected. It is only natural that people differ in their assessments of the severity of a particular problem and of potential ones possibly developing from any given policy. However, once we understand the logic of the various arguments, we should reduce the differences to those of philosophy or of assessment of the relative costs. Once the arguments have been carried to this point, only empirical observation or an appeal to God can render a decision between the two. The final assessment on these solutions has not been made, and you will be hearing much more about them in the future.

I/THE DEATH OF KEYNESIAN MACROECONOMICS

Keynes said some things that were new and some things that were true. Unfortunately the things that were new weren't true and the things that were true weren't new.

FRANK KNIGHT

Life is tough. Any public policy not building this simple truth into its premise is guilty of deceptive advertising. Bargain solutions—those offering something for nothing—are almost never a bargain. Instead they are generally sleights of hand—a way of putting off today's problems until tomorrow and then hoping tomorrow never comes.

To a growing number of economists, macroeconomics, which promised prosperity and full employment, is precisely such a policy. Friedrich Hayek, the Nobel Prize-winning economist, is a leader among those who criticize macroeconomics and is probably one of its harshest critics. Comparing J. M. Keynes to John Law, a French scoundrel who caused massive inflation in France in the 1700s, he writes,

> Keynes could never free himself from the popular false belief that, as Law expressed it, "as the additional money will give work to people who were idle and enable those already working to earn more, the output will increase and industry will prosper." It is this work [of reeducating individuals to the falsity of macroeconomics] that we shall have to do again after the Keynesian flood.

As evidence of the death of macroeconomics, the present reality is offered: Inflation has become a chronic problem plaguing our society. And, according to this line of reasoning, we can directly attribute inflation to macroeconomic policies. Keynes said that in the long run we will all be dead yet the next generation will be very much alive and living in last generation's long run. In this view, Keynes and his generation gave us a legacy of inflation, our only escape being a return to the discipline of the market.

But Hayek later slightly modifies his condemnation of Keynes. He writes:

> It would be somewhat unfair to blame Lord Keynes too much for the developments after his death. I am certain that he would have been—whatever he said earlier—a leader in the fight against the present inflation. But the developments, at least in Britain, were also mainly determined by the version of Keynesianism published under the name of Lord Beveridge for which (since he himself understood no economics whatever) his scientific advisers must bear responsibility.

The first selection we read is from Lord Beveridge's famous book *Full Employment in a Free Society,* which bears the brunt of Hayek's scorn. In it Beveridge spells out his concept of a fully employed society and how and why to achieve it. Notice as you read that

Beveridge's view of full employment is independent of Keynesian macroeconomics. It is noneconomic because it is based on the labor market being in disequilibrium—a seller's rather than a buyer's market. Moreover, he foresees the possible inflationary consequence of Keynesian economics but argues that if Keynesian macroeconomics cannot reach that goal within a capitalist society, it is capitalism rather than the "full employment" goal that must be given up.

Despite the independence of full employment and Keynesian macroeconomics, the two are generally linked in everyone's mind. The achievement of full employment and the use of aggregate demand management have been treated as one. To support full employment has been to support the government running budget deficits to achieve full employment.

KEYNESIAN ECONOMICS AND THE ECONOMICS OF KEYNES

As Hayek mentioned in the above quote, Keynes had a somewhat different idea of the economic system than did Lord Beveridge. In the second selection, from Keynes' *General Theory,* we see his thoughts upon the implications of the "general theory" and the relationship between individual initiative and the social system. Judging from this selection it seems possible that Keynes might indeed have modified his views on macroeconomics, and may even have become a leader of the revolt against it.

Whatever Keynes may have believed, Keynesian macroeconomics prevailed, and, in macro, unemployment policy was aggregate demand policy in the 1950s and 1960s. In this view a shortage of aggregate demand caused unemployment, which expansionary policies could alleviate. Monetary and fiscal policy became *the tools* with which to fight unemployment.

The third reading provides a sense of the hope for and the belief in the Keynesian tools that existed in the 1950s and 1960s. Alvin Hansen, who has been called the dean of American Keynesians, in a selection from his book written in 1957, recounts the American "economic revolution," explaining how Keynes supplied the missing link. In this selection you can see the reason for his optimism: sixteen years of full employment and prosperity. Notice also as you read the piece this prophetic insight quoted by Hansen: "Facts alone can never destroy a theory. As James B. Conant has aptly put it, 'Men strive desperately to modify an old idea to make it accord with new experiments. An outworn theory will not be abandoned until it has been superseded by a better one.' " Hansen used the argument to explain why the Keynesian revolution was necessary; but it, better than anything else, also explains why the connection between Keynesian macroeconomics and full employment remained so closely entwined, even as the connection has become more and more tenuous.

Not all economists were optimistic about achieving full employment, however. Many feared and warned of the inflationary consequences, arguing against the government's continual deficit. The Depression was not a problem of secular stagnation; rather it was a temporary coordination problem, requiring only temporary deficits that temporary surpluses would offset. Thus, the concept of Keynesian economics developed from Hansen's *secular stagnation philosophy*—in which there is a chronic deficit of demand—to a *balanced wheel* philosophy—in which only temporary deficits exist and are offset by temporary surpluses. This balance wheel view forms the basis of modern stabilization theory. In the fourth reading Abba Lerner describes this balance wheel interpretation of Keynesian economics in a classic piece implicitly referred to in several later readings. Notice this theory of Keynesian economics offers no reason to expect government to run a continual deficit or to expect Keynesian economics to be associated with higher or lower government spending. But in fact it has been.

The reasons why Keynesian economics connect with government spending are sketched in the following two selections, the first from Milton Friedman's classic *Capitalism and Freedom* and the second from a recent assessment of macroeconomics by James Buchanan and Richard Wagner. In an ideal world a democratic government might be able to apply a balanced approach, offsetting booms and busts as they occur; but in the real world the process will likely involve a bias toward larger government spending and toward a perpetual boom, thus instilling an inflationary bias in the economy. Buchanan and Wagner's article updates the Friedman critique by concluding with a death knell for Keynesian macroeconomics. They write

Sober assessment suggests that, politically, Keynesianism represents a substantial disease that over the long run can prove fatal for the survival of democracy.

Many are still unwilling to accept this "sober assessment" and stand firm in their belief that macroeconomics, in some form, will rise again—although its new form will need to be altered to incorporate inflation. Thus, tomorrow's debate will likely be about the "rebirth of Keynesian economics"—which is not a bad title for my next collection of readings.

Full Employment in a Free Society

LORD WILLIAM BEVERIDGE

William H. Beveridge was a British social servant who gained fame as an authority on social problems. He was director of the London School of Economics until 1937 when he became master of University College, Oxford. His reports on social security and full employment (from which this article is excerpted) formed the basis of British economic policy and significantly increased the role of government. He died in 1963.

THE MEANING OF FULL EMPLOYMENT

What is meant by "full employment," and what is not meant by it? Full employment does not mean literally no unemployment; that is to say, it does not mean that every man and woman in the country who is fit and free for work is employed productively on every day of his or her working life. In every country with a variable climate there will be seasons when particular forms of work are impossible or difficult. In every progressive society there will be changes in the demand for labour, qualitatively if not quantitatively; that is to say, there will be periods during which particular individuals can no longer be advantageously employed in their former occupations and may be unemployed till they find and fit themselves for fresh occupations. Some frictional unemployment there will be in a progressive society however high the demand for labour. Full employment means that unemployment is reduced to short intervals of standing by, with the certainty that very soon one will be wanted in one's old job again or will be wanted in a new job that is within one's powers.

Full employment is sometimes defined as "a state of affairs in which the number of unfilled vacancies is not appreciably below the number of unemployed persons, so that unemployment at any time is due to the normal lag between a person losing one job and finding another."[1] Full employment in this Report means more than that in two ways. It means having always more vacant jobs than unemployed men, not slightly fewer jobs. It means that the jobs are at fair wages, of such a kind, and so located that the unemployed men can reasonably be expected to take them; it means, by consequence, that the normal lag between losing one job and finding another will be very short.

The proposition that there should always be more vacant jobs than unemployed men means that the labour market should always be a seller's market rather than a buyer's market. For this on the view of society underlying this Report—that society exists for the individual—there is a decisive reason of principle. The reason is that difficulty in selling labour has consequences of a

---

[1]This definition is taken from the Nuffield College Statement on *Employment Policy and Organization of Industry after the War*. The Statement adds that full employment in this sense "cannot be completely attained so long as there exist structural maladjustments needing to be put right."

Extracted from William Beveridge, *Full Employment in a Free Society* (New York: W. W. Norton, 1945), pp. 18–23. Reprinted by permission of George Allen & Unwin Publishers, Ltd.

different order of harmfulness from those associated with difficulty in buying labour. A person who has difficulty in buying the labour that he wants suffers inconvenience or reduction of profits. A person who cannot sell his labour is in effect told that he is of no use. The first difficulty causes annoyance or loss. The other is a personal catastrophe. This difference remains even if an adequate income is provided, by insurance or otherwise, during unemployment; idleness even on an income corrupts; the feeling of not being wanted demoralizes. The difference remains even if most people are unemployed only for relatively short periods. As long as there is any long-term unemployment not obviously due to personal deficiency, anybody who loses his job fears that he may be one of the unlucky ones who will not get another job quickly. The short-term unemployed do not know that they are short-term unemployed till their unemployment is over.

The human difference between failing to buy and failing to sell labour is the decisive reason for aiming to make the labour market a seller's rather than a buyer's market. There are other reasons, only slightly less important. One reason is that only if there is work for all is it fair to expect workpeople, individually and collectively in trade unions, to co-operate in making the most of all productive resources, including labour, and to forgo restrictionist prac-tices. Another reason, related to this, is that the character and duration of individual unemployment caused by structural and technical change in indus-try will depend on the strength of the demand for labour in the new forms required after the change. The greater the pace of the economic machine, the more rapidly will structural unemployment disappear, the less resistance of every kind will there be to progress. Yet another reason is the stimulus to technical advance that is given by shortage of labour. Where men are few, machines are used to save men for what men alone can do. Where labour is cheap it is often wasted in brainless, unassisted toil. The new lands empty of men are the homes of invention and business adventure in peace. Stimulus to labour saving of all kinds is one of the by-products of full employment in war.

The full employment that is the aim of this Report means more vacant jobs than unemployed men. It means something else as well. If there were 2 million chronically unemployed men in Britain and 2¼ million vacant jobs which they could not or would not fill, there would be more vacant jobs than unemployed men, but to call this state of affairs "full employment" would be mockery. It is not enough to say that there must be more vacant jobs than idle men—more or about as many. It is also necessary to be sure that the number unemployed, or rather the duration of unemployment in the individual case, is not excessive. Full employment, in any real sense, means that unemployment in the individual case need not last for a length of time exceeding that which can be covered by unemployment insurance without risk of demoralization. Those who lose jobs must be able to find new jobs at fair wages within their capacity, without delay. This means that the demand for labour and the supply of labour are related qualitatively as well as quantitatively. The demand must be adjusted to the kind of men available or the men must be capable of adjusting themselves to the demand. In the light of the facts of unemployment ... it is clear that the qualitative and local adjustment of demand for labour and supply of labour has to be approached from both ends, that of demand and that of supply. The demands must not only be sufficient in total but must be directed with regard to the quality and the location of the labour that is available. The labour supply must be capable of following the changes of demand that are inseparable from technical advance.

THE PURPOSE OF EMPLOYMENT

Idleness is not the same as Want, but a separate evil, which men do not escape by having an income. They must also have the chance of rendering useful service and of feeling that they are doing so. This means that employment is not wanted for the sake of employment, irrespective of what it produces. The material end of all human activity is consumption. Employment is wanted as a means to more consumption or more leisure, as a means to a higher standard of life. Employment which is merely time-wasting, equivalent to digging holes and filling them again, or merely destructive, like war and preparing for war, will not serve that purpose. Nor will it be felt worth while. It must be productive and progressive. The proposals of this Report are designed to preserve all the essential springs of material progress in the community, to leave to special efforts its rewards, to leave scope for change, invention, competition and initiative.

In so far as room is left for change and for freedom of movement from job to job, room is left for some unemployment. The aim of this Report . . . expressed in numerical terms [is] a reduction of unemployment to not more than 3 per cent, as compared with the 10 to 22 per cent experienced in Britain between the wars. But though the Report assumes the continuance of some unemployment and suggests a figure of 3 per cent, it is the essence of the proposals made in the Report that this 3 per cent should be unemployed only because there is industrial friction, and not because there are no vacant jobs. For men to have value and a sense of value there must always be useful things waiting to be done, with money to pay for doing them. Jobs, rather than men, should wait.

PRESERVATION OF ESSENTIAL LIBERTIES

The labour market in the past has invariably, or all but invariably, been a buyer's market rather than a seller's market, with more unemployed men— generally many more unemployed men—than unfilled jobs. To reverse this and make the labour market always a seller's rather than a buyer's market, to remove not only unemployment but the fear of unemployment, would affect the working of many existing institutions. It would change and is meant to change fundamentally the conditions of living and working in Britain, to make Britain again a land of opportunity for all. There are some things in Britain which neither full employment nor the means of achieving it should be allowed to change.

The Report, as its title indicates, is not concerned simply with the problem of full employment. It is concerned with the necessity, possibility and methods of achieving full employment in a free society, that is to say, subject to the proviso that all essential citizen liberties are preserved. The precise effect of the proviso depends on the list of essential citizen liberties. For the purpose of this Report they are taken as freedom of worship, speech, writing, study and teaching; freedom of assembly and of association for political and other purposes, including the bringing about of a peaceful change of the governing authority;

freedom in choice of occupation; and freedom in the management of a personal income. The proviso excludes the totalitarian solution of full employment in a society completely planned and regimented by an irremovable dictator. It makes the problem of full employment more complex in many ways, of which four call for special notice.

First, in a free society the governing authority is liable to be changed at short intervals by peaceful methods of political organization and voting. There must be reasonable continuity of economic policy in spite of such changes of government. The machinery of government, while responsive to general changes of opinion, must be resistant to "lobbies"—that is to say, organized sectional pressures.

Second, freedom of association for industrial purposes raises the issue of wage determination. Under conditions of full employment, can a rising spiral of wages and prices be prevented if collective bargaining, with the right to strike, remains absolutely free? Can the right to strike be limited generally in a free society in peace-time?

Third, freedom in choice of occupations makes it harder to ensure that all men at all times are occupied productively. It makes it impossible to retain men forcibly in particular work or to direct them to it with the threat of imprisonment if they refuse to go. One assumption underlying this Report is that neither the Essential Work Order nor the powers of industrial direction which have been found necessary in war should be continued when the war is over. In Britain at peace the supply of labour cannot be adjusted by decree to the demand for labour; it can only be guided by economic motives. From another angle, freedom in choice of occupation raises also the issue of industrial discipline. Under conditions of full employment, if men are free to move from one employment to another and do not fear dismissal, may not some of them at least become so irregular and undisciplined in their behaviour, as to lower appreciably the efficiency of industry?

Fourth, freedom in the management of a personal income complicates the problem of full employment from another side. If men cannot be forced to buy just what has been produced, this means that the demands for labour and its products cannot be fitted forcibly to the supply. There may be continual changes in the kinds of things on which consumers want to spend their money, that is to say, in the quality of consumers' outlay. There may be changes also in its quantity. For freedom in the management of a personal income includes freedom to decide between spending now and saving so as to have the power of spending later. A totalitarian regime, even if it used money and price and wage differentials to stimulate and guide individual activity, might abolish freedom of saving. It might retain from the national income of each year that portion which it needed for investment, i.e. for the sustenance of persons engaged in making instruments and materials of further production, and might issue to consumers money which, like ration coupons, could not be saved for spending later. In a free society individuals must be allowed to plan their spending over their lives as a whole. . . .

None of these freedoms can be exercised irresponsibly. Perpetual instability of economic or social policy would make full employment and any other social reforms futile or impossible. Bargaining for wages must be responsible, looking not to the snatching of short sectional advantages, but to the permanent good of the community. Choice of occupation means freedom in choosing between occupations which are available; it is not possible for an individual to choose to be an Archbishop of Canterbury, if that post is already filled by another. Work means doing what is wanted, not doing just what pleases one. All liberties carry their responsibilities. This does not mean that the liberties themselves must be surrendered. They must be retained.

In all the respects named, and possibly in some others, the problem of maintaining full employment is more complicated in a free society than it would be under a totalitarian regime. From one complication of some historic importance the problem, as posed here, is free. The list of essential liberties given above does not include liberty of a private citizen to own means of production and to employ other citizens in operating them at a wage. Whether private ownership of means of production to be operated by others is a good economic device or not, it must be judged as a device. It is not an essential citizen liberty in Britain, because it is not and never has been enjoyed by more than a very small proportion of the British people. It cannot even be suggested that any considerable proportion of the people have any lively hope of gaining such ownership later.

On the view taken in this Report, full employment is in fact attainable while leaving the conduct of industry in the main to private enterprise, and the proposals made in the Report are based on this view. But if, contrary to this view, it should be shown by experience or by argument that abolition of private property in the means of production was necessary for full employment, this abolition would have to be undertaken.

Concluding Notes on the Social Philosophy Towards Which the General Theory Might Lead

JOHN MAYNARD KEYNES

J. M. Keynes is probably the most famous economist of the twentieth century. His *General Theory* altered the way economics was done and created a new field—macroeconomics. His interests were extremely varied, and as part of the Bloomsbury society, he was involved in most of the important cultural affairs of his day. Additionally, as editor of the *Economic Journal* from 1912 to 1945, he had direct knowledge of most developments in economic theory. Although he died in 1946, the Keynesian legacy lives on. Thus, it seems only fitting to include Keynes' view on where Keynesian economics might lead.

THE GENERAL THEORY OF EMPLOYMENT

In some ... respects the foregoing theory is moderately conservative in its implications. For whilst it indicates the vital importance of establishing certain central controls in matters which are now left in the main to individual initiative, there are wide fields of activity which are unaffected. The State will have to exercise a guiding influence on the propensity to consume partly through its scheme of taxation, partly by fixing the rate of interest, and partly, perhaps, in other ways. Furthermore, it seems unlikely that the influence of banking policy on the rate of interest will be sufficient by itself to determine an optimum rate of investment. I conceive, therefore, that a somewhat comprehensive socialisation of investment will prove the only means of securing an approximation to full employment; though this need not exclude all manner of compromises and of devices by which public authority will co-operate with private initiative. But beyond this no obvious case is made out for a system of State Socialism which would embrace most of the economic life of the community. It is not the ownership of the instruments of production which it is important for the State to assume. If the State is able to determine the aggregate amount of resources devoted to augmenting the instruments and the basic rate of reward to those who own them, it will have accomplished all that is necessary. Moreover, the necessary measures of socialisation can be introduced gradually and without a break in the general traditions of society.

Our criticism of the accepted classical theory of economics has consisted not so much in finding logical flaws in its analysis as in pointing out that its tacit assumptions are seldom or never satisfied, with the result that it cannot solve the economic problems of the actual world. But if our central controls succeed in establishing an aggregate volume of output corresponding to full

Extracted from *The General Theory of Employment, Interest and Money* by John Maynard Keynes (New York: Harcourt, 1964), pp. 371–81, 383–84. Reprinted by permission of Harcourt Brace Jovanovich, Inc.

employment as nearly as is practicable, the classical theory comes into its own again from this point onwards. If we suppose the volume of output to be given, *i.e.* to be determined by forces outside the classical scheme of thought, then there is no objection to be raised against the classical analysis of the manner in which private self-interest will determine what in particular is produced, in what proportions the factors of production will be combined to produce it, and how the value of the final product will be distributed between them. Again, if we have dealt otherwise with the problem of thrift, there is no objection to be raised against the modern classical theory as to the degree of consilience between private and public advantage in conditions of perfect and imperfect competition respectively. Thus, apart from the necessity of central controls to bring about an adjustment between the propensity to consume and the inducement to invest, there is no more reason to socialise economic life than there was before.

To put the point concretely, I see no reason to suppose that the existing system seriously misemploys the factors of production which are in use. There are, of course, errors of foresight; but these would not be avoided by centralising decisions. When 9,000,000 men are employed out of 10,000,000 willing and able to work, there is evidence that the labour of these 9,000,000 men is misdirected. The complaint against the present system is not that these 9,000,000 men ought to be employed on different tasks, but that tasks should be available for the remaining 1,000,000 men. It is in determining the volume, not the direction, of actual employment that the existing system has broken down.

Thus I agree with Gesell that the result of filling in the gaps in the classical theory is not to dispose of the "Manchester System," but to indicate the nature of the environment which the free play of economic forces requires if it is to realise the full potentialities of production. The central controls necessary to ensure full employment will, of course, involve a large extension of the traditional functions of government. Furthermore, the modern classical theory has itself called attention to various conditions in which the free play of economic forces may need to be curbed or guided. But there will still remain a wide field for the exercise of private initiative and responsibility. Within this field the traditional advantages of individualism will still hold good.

Let us stop for a moment to remind ourselves what these advantages are. They are partly advantages of efficiency—the advantages of decentralisation and of the play of self-interest. The advantage to efficiency of the decentralisation of decisions and of individual responsiblity is even greater, perhaps, than the nineteenth century supposed; and the reaction against the appeal to self-interest may have gone too far. But, above all, individualism, if it can be purged of its defects and its abuses, is the best safeguard of personal liberty in the sense that, compared with any other system, it greatly widens the field for the exercise of personal choice. It is also the best safeguard of the variety of life, which emerges precisely from this extended field of personal choice, and the loss of which is the greatest of all the losses of the homogeneous or totalitarian state. For this variety preserves the traditions which embody the most secure and successful choices of former generations; it colours the present with the diversification of its fancy; and, being the handmaid of experiment as well as of tradition and of fancy, it is the most powerful instrument to better the future.

Whilst, therefore, the enlargement of the functions of government, involved in the task of adjusting to one another the propensity to consume and the inducement to invest, would seem to a nineteenth-century publicist or to a contemporary American financier to be a terrific encroachment on individualism, I defend it, on the contrary, both as the only practicable means of avoiding the destruction of existing economic forms in their entirety and as the condition of the successful functioning of individual initiative.

For if effective demand is deficient, not only is the public scandal of wasted resources intolerable, but the individual enterpriser who seeks to bring these resources into action is operating with the odds loaded against him. The game of hazard which he plays is furnished with many zeros, so that the players *as a whole* will lose if they have the energy and hope to deal all the cards. Hitherto the increment of the world's wealth has fallen short of the aggregate of positive individual savings; and the difference has been made up by the losses of those whose courage and initiative have not been supplemented by exceptional skill or unusual good fortune. But if effective demand is adequate, average skill and average good fortune will be enough.

The authoritarian state systems of to-day seem to solve the problem of unemployment at the expense of efficiency and of freedom. It is certain that the world will not much longer tolerate the unemployment which, apart from brief intervals of excitement, is associated—and, in my opinion, inevitably associated—with present-day capitalistic individualism. But it may be possible by a right analysis of the problem to cure the disease whilst preserving efficiency and freedom.

Is the fulfillment of these ideas a visionary hope? Have they insufficient roots in the motives which govern the evolution of political society? Are the interests which they will thwart stronger and more obvious than those which they will serve?

I do not attempt an answer in this place. It would need a volume of a different character from this one to indicate even in outline the practical measures in which they might be gradually clothed. But if the ideas are correct—an hypothesis on which the author himself must necessarily base what he writes—it would be a mistake, I predict, to dispute their potency over a period of time. At the present moment people are unusually expectant of a more fundamental diagnosis; more particularly ready to receive it; eager to try it out, if it should be even plausible. But apart from this contemporary mood, the ideas of economists and political philosophers, both when they are right and when they are wrong, are more powerful than is commonly understood. Indeed the world is ruled by little else. Practical men, who believe themselves to be quite exempt from any intellectual influences, are usually the slaves of some defunct economist. Madmen in authority, who hear voices in the air, are distilling their frenzy from some academic scribbler of a few years back. I am sure that the power of vested interests is vastly exaggerated compared with the gradual encroachment of ideas. Not, indeed, immediately, but after a certain interval; for in the field of economic and political philosophy there are not many who are influenced by new theories after they are twenty-five or thirty years of age, so that the ideas which civil servants and politicians and even agitators apply to current events are not likely to be the newest. But, soon or late, it is ideas, not vested interests, which are dangerous for good or evil.

The American Economy on the March

ALVIN H. HANSEN

Alvin Hansen was called the dean of American Keynesians, and his *Guide to Keynes* served as the introduction to Keynesian economics for millions of American economics students. As the Lucius N. Littaner Professor of Political Economy at Harvard University, he had a major effect on the economic policies of the 1950s and was the primary proponent of the secular stagnation theory. This selection, taken from his 1957 book, *The American Economy,* outlines the need for a highly expansionary fiscal policy.

A FULL-EMPLOYMENT ECONOMY

The American Economy has undergone a considerable remodeling during the last quarter-century. I begin with what I regard as by far the most important single factor. It is a new factor, never before experienced in American history. And it is this. We have not had a major depression since 1938. Nearly two decades without a serious downturn. We had, indeed, a minor dip in 1949 and again in 1954—light jolts but no serious depression. And we have had virtually continuous full employment since 1941, a period of fifteen years. Now this is something distinctly new, and we would do well to take a good look at this strange and quite novel experience.

I repeat, we have had virtually full employment and booming prosperity for sixteen years. Past experience has been quite different. Throughout our history every eight or nine years we have experienced serious depression and widespread unemployment. Indeed our economy was for a hundred years the most violently fluctuating economy in the world. And in the 1930s we had prolonged depression and seemingly endless stagnation.

THE MISSING LINK: ADEQUATE AGGREGATE DEMAND

What, then, is the essence of the American economic revolution of the last fifteen years? The miracle of production? The economy already had that *potential* back in the thirties, though the steam was unfortunately lacking. Now, however, we have seen what the economy can do under the pressure of *adequate aggregate demand.* We now have acquired at least some confidence in the government's responsibility for the maintenance of prosperity and full employment. When the British Conservative Government, under Churchill, announced its assumption of continuing responsibility for high employment in 1944, that Act was regarded as a new venture of government, and so indeed it was. The Employment Act of 1946 set much the same goal for the United States. But it was not until President Eisenhower's statement with respect to the firm determination of his Administration to use the full powers of the government to prevent depression that general bipartisan acceptance of this program was achieved. It is indeed a revolution in men's thinking. And this revolution is in no small part the result of the vigorous economic controversies which have filled the pages of economic journals, and from there spilled out into the public forums, during the last two decades.

The American economic revolution involves not only a high-employment policy but also the introduction of the "welfare state." Indeed the welfare state constitutes a solid foundation upon which to build a full-employment program. It is the welfare state which has furnished us with most of the so-called "built-in stabilizers"—the progressive income tax, social-security payments, farm-support programs, etc. It is the welfare state which provides the continuing support of governmentally sponsored housing programs, rural electrification, and lending and guaranteeing operations. The welfare state is not socialism. Socialism is government ownership and operation of productive enterprise. . . .

The welfare state does, however, involve government outlays large enough[1] to permit fiscal policy to play a controlling role in the adjustment of aggregate demand to the productive potential of which the private-enterprise economy is capable. The government makes large expenditures, but private enterprise does the job. It is this that distinguishes the welfare state from socialism.

Now someone will say that the miracle of production which we have witnessed during the upsurge of the last fifteen years could never have occurred without the resourcefulness of private enterprise, the technical know-how, the technological innovations, and the capital formation necessary to implement the new technique. This is indeed unquestionably true, and it is a fact that should be stressed again and again. Yet even with respect to these factors it is important to note that the cause-and-effect relations are closely intertwined. The government has made a major contribution to ensure adequate aggregate demand. The upsurge related thereto has stimulated population growth, which in turn has contributed to the upsurge. The war and the postwar upsurge have served to stimulate new techniques, and these in turn reinforce the upsurge. And finally, investment in new capital (together with corporate and individual savings to finance it) is a consequence, no less than a cause, of a high and growing national income.

Thus the American economic revolution of the last quarter-century constitutes a laboratory experiment in which the flow of events has tested on a broad front the Keynesian diagnosis and the Keynesian policies.

The problems of a highly developed economy are different, as we have seen, from those of an economy in the earlier stages of industrial development. The advanced industrial society, having attained a high level of technology together with entrepreneurial know-how and worker skills, has equipped itself with a vast accumulation of fixed capital. The underdeveloped economy is capital-poor; the advanced country is capital-rich.

No one will deny that the developed economies of Western Europe and North America have reached, after 150 years of technological progress and capital accumulation, a high level of productive capacity. These countries have,

[1]This is the highly important consideration which is overlooked by those who say that all that is needed is to cut government expenditures together with a *corresponding* cut in taxes.

moreover, within them the seeds of continued growth. Yet the output of the United Kingdom fell far below her potential throughout the two interwar decades, and in the United States the economy performed disastrously below her capacity for more than a decade before Pearl Harbor. How long must an economy fail notoriously to perform before it is generally admitted that something is seriously lacking?

Now it was Keynes' central thesis that the element that was woefully lacking was *adequate aggregate demand.* The classicals had argued that all that was needed was technology and capital, that the economy itself would automatically generate adequate demand. The interwar experience in the United Kingdom and the deep depression in the United States demonstrated, as conclusively as facts can, that the classical thesis, whatever may have been true of the early days of capitalism, was no longer valid.

But facts convinced no one. Facts alone can never destroy a theory. As President Conant has aptly put it, men strive desperately "to modify an old idea to make it accord with new experiments." An outworn theory will not be abandoned until it has been superseded by a better one. "It takes," says Conant, "a new conceptual scheme to cause the abandonment of an old one."[2]

In his *General Theory of Employment, Money and Interest,* Keynes challenged the view that the modern economic system can be *depended* upon to make automatically the adjustments needed to ensure full use of productive resources. The thing that private enterprise can certainly do efficiently and well is to *produce.* The thing that it cannot be *depended* upon to do well is to ensure adequate aggregate demand.

Just as the decade before the Second World War deepened the conviction that the classicals were wrong, so the last fifteen years have strengthened the conviction that Keynes was right with respect to his positive program. Governments throughout Western Europe, and in the United States, have on an unprecedented scale augmented aggregate demand beyond that generated by private enterprise. And all over the free world, but especially in the United States, we have witnessed what the economy can do when it is put under pressure. Government expenditures, government borrowing, government guarantees and lending operations, government policies in the area of social security, agriculture, public power, rural electrification, securities regulation, deposit insurance, and monetary, banking, and fiscal policies have provided much of the *fuel* needed for the full use of the productive capacity created by technology and capital accumulation.

[2]James B. Conant, *On Understanding Science,* Yale University Press, 1947, pp. 89, 90.

The Economic Steering Wheel or the Story of the People's New Clothes

ABBA LERNER

Currently Distinguished Professor of Economics at Florida State University, Abba Lerner is one of the most original and highly respected economists of our time. A student of Keynes, Lerner played a major role in "spreading the Keynesian revolution" to the United States and has since been instrumental in determining the direction that revolution has taken. Unlike many economists, Lerner is a wordsmith who creates images with his simple parables that forcefully and delightfully bring home his point. In the following selection, taken from his *Economics of Employment,* we see Lerner at work.

Our economic system is frequently put to shame in being displayed before an imaginary visitor from a strange planet. It is time to reverse the procedure. Imagine yourself instead in a Buck Rogers interplanetary adventure, looking at a highway in a City of Tomorrow. The highway is wide and straight, and its edges are turned up so that it is almost impossible for a car to run off the road. What appears to be a runaway car is speeding along the road and veering off to one side. As it approaches the rising edge of the highway, its front wheels are turned so that it gets back onto the road and goes off at an angle, making for the other side, where the wheels are turned again. This happens many times, the car zigzagging but keeping on the highway until it is out of sight. You are wondering how long it will take for it to crash, when another car appears which behaves in the same fashion. When it comes near you it stops with a jerk. A door is opened, and an occupant asks whether you would like a lift. You look into the car and before you can control yourself you cry out, "Why! There's no steering wheel!"

"Of course we have no steering wheel!" says one of the occupants rather crossly. "Just think how it would cramp the front seat. It is worse than an old-fashioned gear-shift lever and it is dangerous. Suppose we had a steering wheel and somebody held on to it when we reached a curb! He would prevent the automatic turning of the wheel, and the car would surely be overturned! And besides, we believe in democracy and cannot give anyone the extreme authority of life and death over all the occupants of the car. That would be dictatorship."

"Down with dictatorship!" chorus the other occupants of the car.

"If you are worried about the way the car goes from side to side," continues the first speaker, "forget it! We have wonderful brakes so that collisions are prevented nine times out of ten. On our better roads the curb is so effective that one can travel hundreds of miles without going off the road once. We have a very efficient system of carrying survivors of wrecks to nearby hospitals and for rapidly sweeping the remnants from the road to deposit them on nearby fields as a reminder to man of the inevitability of death."

You look around to see the piles of wrecks and burned-out automobiles as the man in the car continues. "Impressive, isn't it? But things are going to improve. See those men marking and photographing the tracks of the car that preceded us? They are going to take those pictures into their laboratories and pictures of our tracks, too, to analyze the cyclical characteristics of the curves, their degree of regularity, the average distance from turn to turn, the amplitude of the swings, and so on. When they have come to an agreement on their true nature we may know whether something can be done about it. At present they are disputing whether this cyclical movement is due to the type of road surface or to its shape or whether it is due to the length of the car or the kind of rubber in the tires or to the weather. Some of them think that it will be impossible to avoid having cycles unless we go back to the horse and buggy, but we can't do that because we believe in Progress. Well, want a ride?"

The dilemma between saving your skin and humoring the lunatics is resolved by your awakening from the nightmare, and you feel glad that the inhabitants of your own planet are a little more reasonable. But are they as reasonable about other things as they are about the desirability of steering their automobiles? Do they not behave exactly like the men in the nightmare when it comes to operating their economic system? Do they not allow their *economic* automobile to bounce from depression to inflation in wide and uncontrolled arcs? Through their failure to steer away from unemployment and idle factories are they not just as guilty of public injury and insecurity as the mad motorists of Mars?

DEPRESSION AND INFLATION CAN BE PREVENTED BY REGULATING THE RATE OF SPENDING

The outstanding problem of modern society is just this. All the other really important problems, such as wars and fascism, are either caused or aggravated by the failure to solve this one. What is needed more than anything else is a mechanism which will enable us to regulate our economy so as to maintain a reasonable degree of economic activity: on the one hand to prevent any considerable unemployment of resources and on the other hand to prevent the stresses of the overemployment of resources and the disorganization that we know as inflation. We need a regulator of employment—a mechanism for the maintenance of prosperity.

The instrument that can do this is as readily available as the steering wheel for automobiles, yet it has not been installed and put into operation. Instead, all our universities are engaged in studying and adding to the enormous literature about the path traveled by the economy when no steering wheel is used—the study of the business cycle.

In our present moderately competitive economy based on moderately free enterprise the level of economic activity is determined by how much money is being spent on the goods and services that can be produced. The immediate effect of a decrease in spending is that the goods accumulate on the shopkeeper's shelves. The shopkeeper may reduce the price in an attempt to move the goods, but this is not necessarily the case. He may prefer to let his stocks increase, especially if he believes that he will be able to sell them soon at the normal price. But whether he lowers the price or not, he will reduce his orders to the wholesalers and the manufacturers and there will result a reduction in output (and in the number of workers employed in making the goods). A reduction in the rate of spending is thus followed, after this adjustment, by a smaller supply of goods to be purchased, and if the price was lowered in the first place it will rise again to the normal level when the supply has been reduced in response to the reduction in demand.

The same thing happens in reverse when there is an increase in demand. The shopkeeper's stocks are reduced below normal and he may take advantage of the increase in demand to raise the price. But whether he raises the price or not he will increase his orders to the wholesalers and the manufacturers. There will then be an increase in the amount of goods produced (and in the number of people employed in making them). After this adjustment there will be a greater supply of goods corresponding to the greater demand for them, and if the price was raised when the demand first increased, it will fall again to the normal level when the supply has caught up with the demand. The important effect of an increase or of a decrease in spending is essentially, therefore, to increase or decrease the supply. The effect on prices is only temporary.

But if there are no unemployed resources available when spending increases, it is impossible for employment or output to increase. Prices then *must* be raised and they do not fall back again to normal. They stay higher. The increased spending cannot be absorbed by an increase in the supply of goods. It then shows itself in higher prices for the same supply of goods.

Nor is this the end of the story. Although the manufacturer cannot increase output where there are no unemployed resources available, the increased orders at higher prices induce manufacturers to *try* to increase their output to take advantage of the unusually high profits. In so doing they try to get men and materials away from each other by offering higher wages and prices (or merely agreeing to demands for higher wages and prices). This raises the money incomes of labor and of the owners of materials and results in a further increase in spending. Increased spending increases incomes, and increased incomes increase spending, and so the process becomes cumulative, with prices rising (and the value of money falling) faster and faster. If this process is permitted to continue by a monetary authority which provides the increasing amount of money that is needed as prices rise, we have an inflation. Inflation disorganizes the economy, works great hardship on persons whose money incomes are fixed or only slowly adjustable, and ruins persons whose savings are cautiously tied to the depreciating money.

The aim of any reasonable regulation of the level of economic activity (which we may call "employment" for short) must be to arrange for the rate of spending to be neither too small (which would cause unemployment) nor too great (which would cause inflation). A satisfactory level (or range) of employment must be chosen, and the total rate of spending must be raised when employment is too low and curtailed when employment rises too high.

Fiscal Policy

MILTON FRIEDMAN

Milton Friedman is perhaps the best known economist of our time. His television series, "Free to Choose," has spread his ideas far and wide, and recent inflation has vindicated to many his attacks on Keynesian economics. His books *Capitalism and Freedom* (1962) and *Monetary History of the U.S.* (1963) are regarded as classics in the literature. This selection, taken from *Capitalism and Freedom,* is a typical Friedman attack on Keynesian economics.

Ever since the New Deal, a primary excuse for the expansion of governmental activity at the federal level has been the supposed necessity for government spending to eliminate unemployment. The excuse has gone through several stages. At first, government spending was needed to "prime the pump." Temporary expenditures would set the economy going and the government could then step out of the picture.

When the initial expenditures failed to eliminate unemployment and were followed by a sharp economic contraction in 1937–38, the theory of "secular stagnation" developed to justify a permanently high level of government spending. The economy had become mature, it was argued. Opportunities for investment had been largely exploited and no substantial new opportunities were likely to arise. Yet individuals would still want to save. Hence, it was essential for government to spend and run a perpetual deficit. The securities issued to finance the deficit would provide individuals with a way to accumulate savings while the government expenditures provided employment. This view has been thoroughly discredited by theoretical analysis and even more by actual experience, including the emergence of wholly new lines for private investment not dreamed of by the secular stagnationists. Yet it has left its heritage. The idea may be accepted by none, but the government programs undertaken in its name, like some of those intended to prime the pump, are still with us and indeed account for ever-growing government expenditures.

More recently, the emphasis has been on government expenditures neither to prime the pump nor to hold in check the specter of secular stagnation but as a balance wheel. When private expenditures decline for any reason, it is said, governmental expenditures should rise to keep total expenditures stable; conversely, when private expenditures rise, governmental expenditures should decline. Unfortunatley, the balance wheel is unbalanced. Each recession, however minor, sends a shudder through politically sensitive legislators and administrators with their ever present fear that perhaps it is the harbinger of another 1929–33. They hasten to enact federal spending programs of one kind of another. Many of the programs do not in fact come into effect until after the recession has

Reprinted from *Capitalism and Freedom* by Milton Friedman by permission of The University of Chicago Press © 1962, pp. 75–79.

passed. Hence, insofar as they do affect total expenditures, on which I shall have more to say later, they tend to exacerbate the succeeding expansion rather than to mitigate the recession. The haste with which spending programs are approved is not matched by an equal haste to repeal them or to eliminate others when the recession is passed and expansion is under way. On the contrary, it is then argued that a "healthy" expansion must not be "jeopardized" by cuts in governmental expenditures. The chief harm done by the balance-wheel theory is therefore not that it has failed to offset recessions, which it has, and not that it has introduced an inflationary bias into governmental policy, which it has done too, but that it has continuously fostered an expansion in the range of governmental activities at the federal level and prevented a reduction in the burden of federal taxes.

In view of the emphasis on using the federal budget as a balance wheel, it is ironic that the most unstable component of national income in the postwar period is federal expenditure, and the instability has not at all been in a direction to offset movements of other expenditure components. Far from being a balance wheel offsetting other forces making for fluctuations, the federal budget has if anything been itself a major source of disturbance and instability.

Because its expenditures are now so large a part of the total for the economy as a whole, the federal government cannot avoid having significant effects on the economy. The first requisite is therefore that the government mend its own fences, that it adopt procedures that will lead to reasonable stability in its own flow of expenditures. If it would do that, it would make a clear contribution to reducing the adjustments required in the rest of the economy. Until it does that, it is farcical for government officials to adopt the self-righteous tones of the schoolmaster keeping unruly pupils in line. Of course, their doing so is not surprising. Passing the buck and blaming others for one's own deficiencies are not vices of which governmental officials have a monopoly.

Even if one were to accept the view that the federal budget should be and can be used as a balance wheel—a view I shall consider in more detail below—there is no necessity to use the expenditure side of the budget for this purpose. The tax side is equally available. A decline in national income automatically reduces the tax revenue of the federal government in greater proportion and thus shifts the budget in the direction of a deficit, and conversely during a boom. If it is desired to do more, taxes can be lowered during recessions and raised during expansions. Of course, politics might well enforce an asymmetry here too, making the declines politically more palatable than the rises.

If the balance-wheel theory has in practice been applied on the expenditure side, it has been because of the existence of other forces making for increased governmental expenditures; in particular, the widespread acceptance by intellectuals of the belief that government should play a larger role in economic and private affairs; the triumph, that is, of the philosophy of the welfare state. This philosophy has found a useful ally in the balance-wheel theory; it has enabled governmental intervention to proceed at a faster pace than would otherwise have been possible.

How different matters might now be if the balance-wheel theory had been applied on the tax side instead of the expenditure side. Suppose each recession had seen a cut in taxes and suppose the political unpopularity of raising taxes in the succeeding expansion had led to resistance to newly proposed governmental expenditure programs and to curtailment of existing ones. We might now be in a position where federal expenditures would be absorbing a good deal less of a national income that would be larger because of the reduction in the depressing and inhibiting effects of taxes.

I hasten to add that this dream is not intended to indicate support for the balance-wheel theory. In practice, even if the effects would be in the direction expected under the balance-wheel theory, they would be delayed in time and spread. To make them an effective offset to other forces making for fluctuations, we would have to be able to forecast those fluctuations a long time in advance. In fiscal policy as in monetary policy, all political considerations aside, we simply do not know enough to be able to use deliberate changes in taxation or expenditures as a sensitive stabilizing mechanism. In the process of trying to do so, we almost surely make matters worse. We make matters worse not by being consistently perverse—that would be easily cured by simply doing the opposite of what seemed at first the thing to do. We make matters worse by introducing a largely random disturbance that is simply added to other disturbances. That is what we seem in fact to have done in the past—in addition, of course to the major mistakes that have been seriously perverse. What I have written elsewhere in respect of monetary policy is equally applicable to fiscal policy: "What we need is not a skillful monetary driver of the economic vehicle continuously turning the steering wheel to adjust to the unexpected irregularities of the route, but some means of keeping the monetary passenger who is in the back seat as ballast from occasionally leaning over and giving the steering wheel a jerk that threatens to send the car off the road."

The Consequences of Mr. Keynes

JAMES M. BUCHANAN AND RICHARD E. WAGNER

James Buchanan is University Professor of Economics and Director of the Center for Public Choice at Virginia Polytechnic Institute. His work in public finance and public choice have made him highly respected as an original and dynamic economist.

Richard E. Wagner, Professor of Economics at Florida State University, is the author of numerous articles and books, including *The Fiscal Organization of American Federalism* and *The Public Economy.* He is one of the top political economists today.

Together, Buchanan and Wagner have mounted a major and cogent attack on Keynesian economics, as demonstrated in the following article.

VISIONS OF THE ECONOMIC ORDER: CLASSICAL AND KEYNESIAN

The Classical or pre-Keynesian notions of prudent fiscal conduct were reasonably summarised by drawing an analogy between the state and the family. It was another British intellectual 'export,' Adam Smith, who noted that 'What is prudence in the conduct of every private family, can scarce be folly in that of a great kingdom.' Prudent financial conduct by the state was conceived in basically the same image as that for the family. Frugality, not profligacy, was the cardinal virtue, and this norm assumed practical shape in the widely shared principle that public budgets should be in balance, if not in surplus, and that deficits were to be tolerated only in extraordinary circumstances. Substantial and continuing deficits were interpreted as the mark of fiscal folly. Principles of sound family and business practice were deemed equally relevant to the fiscal affairs of the state.

During this period, a free-enterprise economy was generally held as being characterised by 'Say's Equality'.[1] While fluctuations in economic activity would occur in such an economy, they would set in motion self-correcting forces that would operate to restore prosperity. Within this economic framework, the best action for government was simply to avoid injecting additional sources of instability into the economy. The profligacy of government was one latent source of disturbance, and it was considered important that this governmental proclivity should be restrained. Avoiding such sources of instability, along with keeping debt and taxes low so as to promote thrift and saving, was the way to achieve prosperity. A balanced or surplus budget was one of the practical rules that reflected such constraints and beliefs. Such siren songs as the 'paradox of thrift' were yet to come.[2]

---

[1] A recent re-statement of this perspective is in W. H. Hutt, *A Rehabilitation of Say's Law*, Ohio University Press, Athens, Ohio, 1974. 'Say's Equality' (after J. B. Say, the French 19th-century classical economist) is usually summarised as the proposition that 'supply creates its own demand', provided that markets operate in a competitive manner.

[2] The 'paradox of thrift' is the Keynesian proposition that a reduction in thriftiness (an increase in private or governmental spending propensities) will boost the economy.

Extracted from *The Consequences of Mr. Keynes* by James M. Buchanan and Richard E. Wagner (1978), pp. 13–17, 18, 23, 27. Reprinted by permission of The Institute of Economic Affairs.

From Classical Stability to Keynesian Instability

The idea that the spontaneous co-ordination of economic activities within a system or markets would generally produce economic stability was replaced in the Keynesian vision by the idea of an inherently unstable economy. Say's Equality was deemed inapplicable. The Keynesian paradigm was one of an economy alternately haunted by gluts and secular stagnation.[3] The prosperous co-ordination of economic activities was a razor's edge. The economic order is as likely to be saddled with substantial unemployment as it is to provide full employment. An important element in the Keynesian paradigm was the absence of an equilibrating process by which inconsistencies among the plans of the participants in the economic process became self-correcting. Prosperity, accordingly, could be assured only through deliberate efforts of government to help the economy avoid the buffeting forces of inflation and recession. 'Fine tuning' became the ideal of Keynesian economic policy.

The Keynesian message, in other words, contained two central features. One was the image of an inherently unstable economy, ungoverned by some 'natural law' of a generally smooth co-ordination of economic activities. The other was of government as having both the obligation and the ability to offset this instability so as to bring about a more smoothly functioning economic order. The notion of an unstable economy whose performance could be improved through the manipulation of public budgets produced a general principle that budgets *need not* be in balance: indeed, they *should not* be in balance, since that would mean government was failing in its duty. Some years of deficit and others of surplus were both necessary to, and evidence of, corrective macro-economic management. A stable relation between revenues and expenditures, say a relatively constant rate of surplus, would indicate a failure of government to carry out its managerial duties.

THE IDEALISED ENVIRONMENT FOR KEYNESIAN ECONOMIC POLICY

While Lord Keynes published his *General Theory* in 1936, his presuppositions did not infuse themselves into generally held understandings or beliefs for about a generation in America, though sooner in Britain, much as he anticipated in a famous passage on the time-lag between the articulation of an idea and its influence on policy.[4] While the Keynesian vision of the nature of our economic order and the proper pattern of budgetary policy gained dominance in academia in the 1940s and 1950s, it did not filter into the general climate of American opinion until the 1960s. With this conversion or shift in generally-held perspectives or beliefs, macro-economic engineering became the province of government.[5]

---

[3]A specific discussion of these two economic cosmologies is in Axel Leijonhufvud, 'Effective Demand Failures', *Swedish Journal of Economics*, 75, March 1973, pp. 31–33.

[4]'I am sure that the power of vested interests is vastly exaggerated compared with the gradual encroachment of ideas. Not, indeed, immediately, but after a certain interval; for in the field of economic and political philosophy there are not many who are influenced by new theories after they are twenty-five or thirty years of age, so that the ideas which civil servants and politicians and even agitators apply to current events are not likely to be the newest. But, soon or late, it is ideas, not vested interests, which are dangerous for good or evil.' (J. M. Keynes, *The General Theory of Employment, Interest and Money*, Macmillan, 1936, pp. 383–84.)

[5]A thorough survey of this shift in paradigm toward fiscal policy in the United States is in Herbert Stein, *The Fiscal Revolution in America*, University of Chicago Press, Chicago, 1969.

As developed by the economists who advocated macro-economic engineering, fiscal policy would be devoted to smoothing out cycles in private economic activity. Fiscal policy would be guided by the same principle during both recession and inflation. Deficits would be created during recession and surpluses during inflation, with the object of smoothing out peaks and troughs. The policy precepts of Keynesian economics were alleged to be wholly symmetrical. In depressed economic conditions, budget deficits would be required to restore full employment and prosperity. When inflation threatened, budget surpluses would be appropriate. The time-honoured norm of budget balance was thus jettisoned, but, in the pure logic Keynesian policy, there was no one-way departure. It might even be said that Keynesian economics did not destroy the principle of a balanced budget, but only lengthened the time-period over which it applied, from a calendar year to the period of a business cycle. In this way, rational public policy would operate to promote a more prosperous and stable economy during both recession and inflation.

While the idealised setting for the symmetrical application of Keynesian economic policy is familiar, the political setting within which the policy is to be formulated and implemented is much less familiar. We have now learned that mere exhortations to politicians to promote prosperity do not guarantee they will do so: they may lack the knowledge required to promote such an outcome, or the incentive to act in the required manner, or both. In other words, the actions of politicians on budgetary policy as well as on other types of policy depend upon both the knowledge politicians have and the incentives they confront.

Keynes's Defective Assumptions

Keynes largely begged questions pertaining to knowledge. Central to his approach was the presumption that economists could possess knowledge sufficient to enable them to give advice which, if acted upon, would facilitate the co-ordination of human activities within the economic order. This extremely questionable assumption about knowledge melded nicely with his normative assumptions about political conduct. Keynes was an élitist, and he operated under what his biographer called the 'presuppositions of Harvey Road'—that governmental policy, and economic policy in particular, would be made by a relatively small group of wise and enlightened people.[6] Keynes did not consider the application of his policy prescriptions in a contemporary democratic setting—in which government is tempted to yield to group pressures to retain or return to power. Rather, the small group of enlightened men who made economic policy would, he assumed, subconsciously—even if in defiance of historical experience—always tend to act in accordance with the 'public interest', even when this might run foul of constituency, sectional or other organised pressures.

In the unreal economic and political environment envisaged by Keynes, there could be little or no question raised about the application of the Keynesian policy instruments. To secure a stable, prosperous economy, expenditures would be

---

[6]'We have seen that he [Keynes] was strongly imbued with what I have called the presuppositions of Harvey Road. One of these presuppositions may perhaps be summarised in the idea that the government of Britain was and would continue to be in the hands of an intellectual aristocracy using the method of persuasion.' (The late Sir Roy Harrod, *The Life of John Maynard Keynes*, Macmillan, 1951, pp. 192–93.) Harvey Road was the location of the Keynes family residence in Cambridge.

expanded and contracted symmetrically. Budget deficits would be created during periods of sluggish economic activity, and surpluses as the pace of economic activity became too quick. There would be no political pressures, he implicitly supposed, operating to render the surpluses fictional and the deficits disproportionately large or ill-timed. The ruling élite would be guided by the presuppositions of Harvey Road; they would not act as competitors for electoral favour in a democratic political environment.

There was little awareness that the dictates of political survival might run contrary to the requirements of macro-economic engineering (assuming for now that the economic order is aptly described by the Keynesian paradigm). It was tacitly assumed either that the political survival of politicians was automatically strengthened as they came to follow more fully the appropriate fiscal policies, or that the ruling élite would act without regard to their political fortunes. But what happens when we make non-Keynesian assumptions about politics? What if we commence from the assumption that elected politicians respond to pressures emanating from constituents and the state bureaucracy? When this shift of perspective is made in the political setting for analysis, the possibilities that policy precepts may unleash political biases cannot be ignored.

KEYNESIAN PRESUPPOSITIONS, DEMOCRATIC POLITICS, AND ECONOMIC POLICY

Anyone, citizens no less than politicians, would typically like to live beyond his means. Individual citizens generally face a personal or household budget constraint which prevents them from acting on this desire, although some counterfeit and others go bankrupt. In the century before the shift in belief wrought by the Keynesian revolution, politicians acted as if they sensed a similar constraint when making the nation's budgetary choices.

Contemporary political institutions, however, are constrained differently because of the general belief in the Keynesian vision. This shift in constraints due to the shift in general beliefs alters the character of governmental budgetary policy. While there is little political resistance to budget deficits, there is substantial resistance to budget surpluses. Hence, fiscal policy will tend to be applied asymmetrically: deficits will be created frequently, but surpluses will materialise only rarely. This bias results from the shift in the general, public impression or understanding of the Western economic order, and of the related rules of thumb held generally by the citizenry as to what constitutes prudent, reasonable, or efficacious conduct by government in running its budget. Old-fashioned beliefs about the virtue of the balanced-budget rule and of redeeming public debt during periods of prosperity became undermined by Keynesian ideas, and lost their hold upon the public. In consequence, debt reduction lost its claim as a guiding rule. Budget surpluses lost their *raison d' être*. Deficits allow politicians to increase spending without having directly and openly to raise taxes. There is little obstacle to such a policy. Surpluses, on the other hand, require government to raise taxes without increasing spending—a programme far more capable of stimulating political opposition than budget deficits, especially once the constraining norm of debt retirement had receded from public consciousness.

Keynesian Economics in Political Democracy

The grafting of Keynesian economics onto the fabric of a political democracy has wrought a significant revision in the underlying fiscal constitution. The result has been a tendency toward budget deficits and, consequently, once the workings of democratic political institutions are taken into account, inflation. Democratic governments will generally respond more vigorously in correcting for unemployment than in correcting for inflation. Budgetary adjustments aimed at the prevention or control of inflation will rarely be observed as the result of deliberate policy. Budget deficits will come to be the general rule, even when inflation is severe. In slack years, when deficits might seem warranted by strict application of the Keynesian precepts, the size of these deficits will become disproportionately large. Moreover, the perceived cost of government will generally be lower than the real cost because of the deficit financing. As a consequence, there will also be a relative increase in the size of the government sector in the economy. Budget deficits, inflation, and the growth of government—all are intensified by the Keynesian destruction of former constitutional principles of sound finance.

CONCLUSION

Why does Camelot[7] lie in ruins? Intellectual error of monumental proportion has been made, and not exclusively by the politicians. Error also lies squarely with the economists. The 'academic scribbler' who must bear substantial responsibility is Lord Keynes, whose thinking was uncritically accepted by establishment economists in both America and Britain. The mounting historical evidence of the ill-effects of Keynes's ideas cannot continue to be ignored. Keynesian economics has turned the politicians loose; it has destroyed the effective constraint on politicians' ordinary appetites to spend and spend without the apparent necessity to tax.

Sober assessment suggests that, politically, Keynesianism represents a substantial disease that over the long run can prove fatal for the survival of democracy.

[7][Camelot was the capital of King Arthur's ideal society of chivalric literature from the 10th to the 13th centuries. It proved unfeasible because good intentions belied human nature.—ED.]

II/INFLATION AND UNEMPLOYMENT: THE DEATH OF THE PHILLIPS CURVE

Progress does not consist in replacing a theory that is wrong with one that is right. It consists of replacing a theory that is wrong with one that is more subtly wrong.

HAWKINS' THEORY OF PROGRESS

If Keynesian macroeconomics is dead, inflation killed it. Keynesian economics prescribed a deficit for unemployment and a surplus for inflation. When both inflation and unemployment exist simultaneously, macroeconomics has no answer.

To reconcile these two phenomena, economists initially fudged a bit and rounded the corners without any theoretical justification for doing so. Obviously, they argued, no sharp dividing line exists between too much and too little total spending. Instead, there is a smooth relationship between the two that leads to a smooth relationship between inflation and unemployment, as shown in the diagram below:

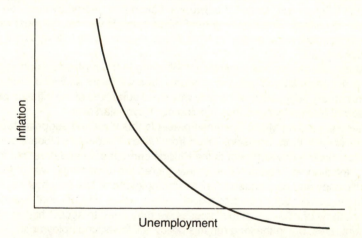

As unemployment decreases, we can expect tighter job markets and consequently more upward pressure on wages and prices—in other words, more inflation. Although its theoretical underpinnings were weak, the description sounded reasonable and fit the empirical evidence relatively well. It quickly became the basis of economic analysis dealing with inflation and unemployment, thus giving birth to the Phillips curve, which embodies an inverse relationship between inflation and unemployment.

As I reviewed the current literature on the Phillips curve, it was almost impossible to find any article strongly arguing that this curve is a reasonable description of the inflation/unemployment problem. Finally, I went back to the 1950s and found an early statement by two eminent economists, Robert Solow and Paul Samuelson, on the Phillips curve trade-off. Their article provides a good idea of how economists at the time saw this relationship. Notice, as you read, that even in 1959 economists were extremely careful about drawing policy conclusions from the Phillips curve. It was, they recognized, a short-run phenomenon, and an attempt to run a high-pressure economy might well change the relationship.

But policymakers do not always heed economists' admonitions and are instead influenced primarily by political considerations. Thus, they hear only what they want. Almost invariably an antagonism occurs between good economics and good politics. As government chose an easier high pressure policy, the trade-off worsened, the seemingly constant Phillips curve began shifting outward, the fears expressed by Solow and Samuelson were realized, and the Phillips curve was dead.

THE NATURAL-RATE HYPOTHESIS

There are two quite different explanations of the demise of the inflation/unemployment trade-off, representing quite different theories of the aggregate economy. The first of these is the most well known and is called the *natural-rate hypothesis.* Developed by Edmond Phelps and Milton Friedman, the natural-rate hypothesis differentiates between real and natural economic forces. The economy will always gravitate toward the natural rate of resource utilization. Differences between the actual and natural rates of unemployment are caused by unexpected changes in the real wage brought about by inflation. Such temporary deviations are possible because individuals' expectations only adapt slowly. However, once they adapt, the economy will gravitate back to the natural rate at a higher expected inflation level. Although a "short-run" trade-off between inflation and unemployment can occur, a long-run trade-off cannot. Since the long-run Phillips curve is vertical, the most we can hope from expansionary policy is a temporary high, which will quickly be followed by a crash and higher inflation rates.

This natural-rate theory has a significant following in the profession and suggests that the government can do little to help the economy, and we might as well accept our fate. Moreover, this theory suggests that the only way to rid ourselves of the inflation problem is to create temporary unemployment, thus purging our Keynesian sins.

In the second reading Milton Friedman presents this view and suggests that the need for atonement is even more pressing. Taken from Milton Friedman's Nobel Foundation Lecture, it recounts the development of the Phillips curve theory and presents a "modest elaboration." Inflation, in Friedman's new view, increases uncertainty, which decreases economic efficiency and consequently raises unemployment. Not only has Keynesian economics done poorly, but it has also made matters worse and will continue to do so until we rid the economy of inflation. In this process we may need to accept higher-than-desired unemployment rates, but in the long run this policy will lower unemployment.

Recently the monetarists' theory has been supplanted on the analytical circuit by a new development—rational expectations. Although the theory is tremendously complex and controversial, Walter Guzzardi, Jr., presents the central idea in an article describing it simply as an assumption that people are not so dumb. They will not form their expectations by using any ad hoc method assumed by the monetarists or Keynesians but by the best information at their disposal. In other words, they will form their expectations rationally. The available information includes economists' predictions, and if economists' models are correct, businessmen can use those models to make a profit. Thus, any model that incorporates expectations must rationally assume that individuals know as much as the modelers. But this assumption means that if the price level will eventually adjust, it will also adjust immediately. In other words, if there is no long-run trade-off, there will also be no short-run trade-off. Some interpret this assumption to mean that Keynesian stabilization policy is impossible.

The rational expectations story does, however, have a silver lining. The government can avoid the large unemployment necessary to reduce inflationary expectations in the monetarists' model if it preannounces the contractionary monetary policy and establishes a guarantee that it will be followed, regardless of the consequences. The Guzzardi article outlines the rational expectations theory while the following article, from the Federal Reserve Bank of Minneapolis, discusses its policy conclusions.

THE NONACCELERATING RATE HYPOTHESES

Neither the monetarists' nor the rational expectationalists' view goes unchallenged as a practical or theoretical matter. The theoretical challenge concerns the static nature of the monetarists' model. The monetarists' essentially static model assumes away the dynamic adjustment problems that cause inflation. In this anti-monetarist view, competition does not just exist but is a dynamic process of individuals attempting to monopolize. It is the process of continually achieving and breaking down monopolies.

Because of asymmetrical search costs these dynamic pressures of monopolization and competition cause a constant upward push on prices at full employment, which must be offset to avoid runaway inflation. To achieve this offset of dynamic asymmetry, the government must maintain sufficient unemployment to increase the downward competitive pressures on prices. If this argument is true, the monetary and real forces in the economy cannot be separated and the natural rate of unemployment is never reached. What the monetarists call the "natural rate" is really the "nonaccelerating rate" (NARU), which includes some unemployment that mainly tries to hold down the price level. In policy terms the NARU and the Natural Rate hypothesis differ primarily in their predictions about the effect of an incomes policy. In the NARU hypothesis, an effective incomes policy institutes direct downward pressure on the price level, allowing the economy to expand. In the natural rate hypothesis, no such expansion would be possible.

In the next article Michael Piore presents one version of the NARU hypothesis. He argues that external shocks cause inflation by violating wage contours and setting in motion a "catch-up" process. Piore supplements this "wage-contour" theory of inflation with a theory of dual labor markets. Although not fully developed, the theory emphasizes that there are two very different labor markets operating—a career and a secondary labor market. These two labor markets have little interconnection, and the secondary labor market, consisting primarily of the poor, experiences the most unemployment. As unemployment decreases, the aspirations of the poor exceed their opportunities, causing social strife and inflation.

The article by Robert Lekachman provides another nonmonetarist scenario in rather colorful language. In Lekachman's view, unemployment is used in the system for its effects on relative wages. Lekachman writes: "The fine Christian (and occasionally Jewish) men whom the good Lord has placed in the seats of authority and the halls of the mighty know that there are far worse phenomena than unemployment. One of them is full employment."

The views of Lekachman and Piore are quite different in form. Piore's is a version of an institutionalist paradigm while Lekachman's has Marxist overtones. Yet they come to similar conclusions about the inflation/unemployment trade-off, both agreeing that the monetarists' version is *wrong* and seriously misrepresents the nature of the economic system.

REBUTTING THE RATIONAL EXPECTATIONS CHALLENGE

While the two preceding articles challenged the monetarists' natural rate hypothesis, the final two articles in this section concern the rational expectations challenge of Keynesian stabilization policy. In the first of the two I draw a distinction between Lerner's balance wheel interpretation of Keynesianism and Hansen's secular stagnation theory, both of which were discussed above. Lerner's interpretation is unaffected by the rational expectations critique, and it is this interpretation that is relevant for the stabilization debate. In fact, I argue that Keynes proceeded far beyond rational expectations and that economic theory has no definitive answer to whether the government should or should not stabilize the economy. The answer to that question depends upon the government's cost of stabilization relative to the private sector's cost—it is an empirical not a theoretical conclusion.

The last article in this section, by Franco Modigliani, is a superb summary of the entire monetarist/antimonetarist debate. According to Modigliani, the rational expectations case against stabilization is incorrect, and rather than discard stabilization policy, "we should instead concentrate our efforts in an endeavour to make stabilization policies even more effective in the future than they have been in the past."

The debates touched on in the above articles are ongoing, and the arguments put forth here will help determine the future course of economic policy.

Policy Implications of the Phillips Curve

PAUL SAMUELSON AND ROBERT SOLOW

More than any other economist Paul Samuelson is responsible for the direction of theoretical economics over the last forty years. He was deservedly the winner of the first Nobel Prize in Economics—and he did it with his Ph.D. dissertation, *Foundations of Economic Analysis.*

Robert Solow ranks with Samuelson as one of the top theoretical economists in the United States. However, Solow has also taken an active policy role and has served as senior staff economist on the Council of Economic Advisers. Both Samuelson and Solow are professors of economics at the Massachusetts Institute of Technology. In this 1960 article these two top economists combine their skills in a discussion of the Phillips curve.

Consider . . . the question of the relation between money wage changes and the degree of unemployment. We have A. W. Phillips' interesting paper on the U.K. history since the Civil War (our Civil War, that is!). His findings are remarkable, even if one disagrees with his interpretations.

In the first place, the period 1861–1913, during which the trade-union movement was rather weak, shows a fairly close relationship between the per cent change in wage rates and the fraction of the labor force unemployed. Due allowance must be made for sharp import-price-induced changes in the cost of living, and for the normal expectation that wages will be rising faster when an unemployment rate of 5 per cent is reached on the upswing than when it is reached on the downswing. In the second place, with minor exceptions, the same relationship that fits for 1861–1913 also seems to fit about as well for 1913–48 and 1948–57. And finally Phillips concludes that the money wage level would stabilize with 5 per cent unemployment; and the rate of increase of money wages would be held down to the 2–3 per cent rate of productivity increase with about 2½ per cent of the labor force unemployed.

In spite of all its deficiencies, we think the accompanying scatter diagram in Figure 1 is useful. Where it does not provide answers, it at least asks interesting questions. We have plotted the yearly percentage changes of average hourly earnings in manufacturing, including supplements (Rees's data) against the annual average percentage of the labor force unemployed.

The first defect to note is the different coverages represented in the two axes. Duesenberry has argued that postwar wage increases in manufacturing on the one hand and in trade, services, etc., on the other, may have quite different explanations: union power in manufacturing and simple excess demand in the other sectors. It is probably true that if we had an unemployment rate for manufacturing alone, it would be somewhat higher during the postwar years than the aggregate figure shown. Even if a qualitative statement like this held

Extracted from "Problems of Achieving and Maintaining a Stable Price Level," *American Economic Review* (Dec. 1959), pp. 186, 189, 191–94.

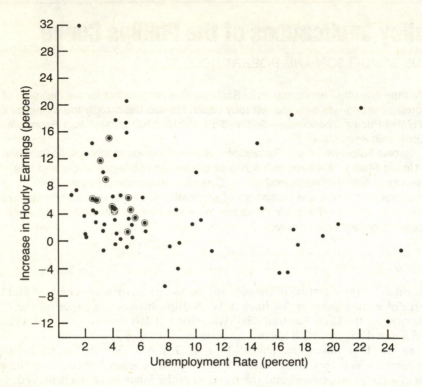

FIGURE 1
Phillips Scatter Diagram for U.S. (The circled points are for recent years.)

true over the whole period, the increasing weight of services in the total might still create a bias. Another defect is our use of annual increments and averages, when a full-scale study would have to look carefully into the nuances of timing.

A first look at the scatter is discouraging; there are points all over the place. But perhaps one can notice some systematic effects. In the first place, the years from 1933 to 1941 appear to be *sui generis:* money wages rose or failed to fall in the face of massive unemployment. One may attribute this to the workings of the New Deal (the 20 per cent wage increase of 1934 must represent the NRA codes); or alternatively one could argue that by 1933 much of the unemployment had become structural, insulated from the functioning labor market, so that in effect the vertical axis ought to be moved over to the right. This would leave something more like the normal pattern.

The early years of the first World War also behave atypically although not so much so as 1933–39. This may reflect cost-of-living increases, the rapidity of the increase in demand, a special tightness in manufacturing, or all three.

But the bulk of the observations—the period between the turn of the century and the first war, the decade between the end of that war and the Great Depression, and the most recent ten or twelve years—all show a rather consistent pattern. Wage rates do tend to rise when the labor market is tight, and the tighter the faster. What is most interesting is the strong suggestion that the relation, such as it is, has shifted upward slightly but noticeably in the forties and fifties. On the one hand, the first decade of the century and the twenties seem to fit the same pattern. Manufacturing wages seem to stabilize absolutely when 4 or 5 per cent of the labor force is unemployed; and wage increases equal to the productivity increase of 2 to 3 per cent per year is the normal pattern at about 3 per cent unemployment. This is not so terribly different from Phillips' results for the U.K., although the relation holds there with a greater consistency. When we translate the Phillips' diagram showing the American pattern of wage increase against degree of unemployment into a related diagram showing the different levels of unemployment that would be "needed" for each degree of price level change, we come out with guesses like the following:

1. In order to have wages increase at no more than the 2½ per cent per annum characteristic of our productivity growth, the American economy would seem on the basis of twentieth-century and postwar experience to have to undergo something like 5 to 6 per cent of the civilian labor force's being unemployed. That much unemployment would appear to be the cost of price stability in the years immediately ahead.

2. In order to achieve the nonperfectionist's goal of high enough output to give us no more than 3 per cent unemployment, the price idex might have to rise by as much as 4 to 5 per cent per year. That much price rise would seem to be the necessary cost of high employment and production in the years immediately ahead.

All this is shown in our price-level modification of the Phillips curve, Figure 2. The point A, corresponding to price stability, is seen to involve about 5½ per cent unemployment; whereas the point B, corresponding to 3 per cent unemployment, is seen to involve a price rise of about 4½ per cent per annum. We rather expect that the tug of war of politics will end us up in the next few years somewhere in between these selected points. We shall probably have some price rise and some excess unemployment.

Aside from the usual warning that these are simply our best guesses we must give another caution. All of our discussion has been phrased in short-run terms, dealing with what might happen in the next few years. It would be wrong, though, to think that our Figure 2 menu that relates obtainable price and unemployment behavior will maintain its same shape in the longer run. What we do in a policy way during the next few years might cause it to shift in a definite way.

Thus, it is conceivable that after they had produced a low-pressure economy, the believers in demand-pull might be disappointed in the short run; i.e., prices might continue to rise even though unemployment was considerable. Nevertheless, it might be that the low-pressure demand would so act upon wage and other expectations as to shift the curve downward in the longer run—so that over a decade, the economy might enjoy higher employment with price stability than our present-day estimate would indicate.

But also the opposite is conceivable. A low-pressure economy might build up within itself over the years larger and larger amounts of structural unem-

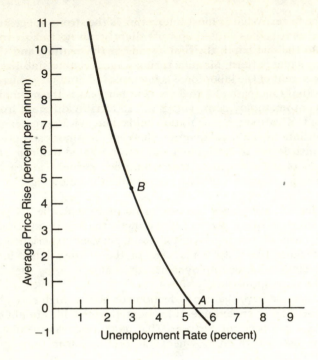

FIGURE 2
Modified Phillips Curve for U.S. (This shows the menu of choice between different degrees of unemployment and a price stability, as roughly estimated from last twenty-five years of American data.)

ployment (the reverse of what happened from 1941 to 1953 as a result of strong war and postwar demands). The result would be an upward shift of our menu of choice, with more and more unemployment being needed just to keep prices stable.

Since we have no conclusive or suggestive evidence on these conflicting issues, we shall not attempt to give judgment on them. Instead we venture the reminder that, in the years just ahead, the level of attained growth will be highly correlated with the degree of full employment and high-capacity output.

But what about the longer run? If the per annum rate of technical progress were about the same in a low- and high-pressure economy, then the initial loss in output in going to the low-pressure state would never be made up; however, in relative terms, the initial gap would not grow but would remain constant as time goes by. If a low-pressure economy could succeed in improving the efficiency of our productive factors, some of the loss of growth might be gradually made up and could in long enough time even be more than wiped out. On the other hand, if such an economy produced class warfare and social conflict and depressed the level of research and technical progress, the loss in growth would be compounded in the long run.

A final disclaimer is in order. We have not here entered upon the important question of what feasible institutional reforms might be introduced to lessen the degree of disharmony between full employment and price stability. These could of course involve such wide-ranging issues as direct price and wage controls, antiunion and antitrust legislation, and a host of other measures hopefully designed to move the American Phillips' curves downward and to the left.

The Stages of the Phillips Curve

MILTON FRIEDMAN

Milton Friedman is a delight for editors because regardless of how many of his selections one uses, there is always something new to write about him. He is currently senior research fellow at the Hoover Institution and has had a major impact on the economics profession with his views of the Phillips curve. The winner of the Nobel Prize in 1976, he is continually expanding his horizons and theory to account for new empiricial observations. In this selection from his Nobel Prize speech, he provides a new hypothesis about the Phillips curve.

STAGE 1: NEGATIVELY SLOPING PHILLIPS CURVE

Professional analysis of the relation between inflation and unemployment has gone through two stages since the end of World War II and is now entering a third. The first stage was the acceptance of a hypothesis associated with the name of A. W. Phillips that there is a stable negative relation between the level of unemployment and the rate of change of wages—high levels of unemployment being accompanied by falling wages, low levels of unemployment by rising wages. The wage change in turn was linked to price change by allowing for the secular increase in productivity and treating the excess of price over wage cost as given by a roughly constant markup factor.

Figure 1 illustrates this hypothesis, where I have followed the standard practice of relating unemployment directly to price change, short-circuiting the intermediate step through wages.

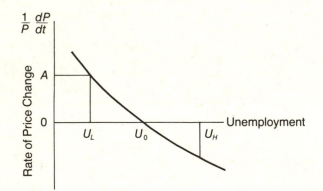

FIGURE 1
Simple Phillips Curve

Extracted from "Inflation and Unemployment," *Journal of Political Economy*, 85, No. 3 (1977), 454–60, 464–71. ©The Nobel Foundation.

Unfortunately for this hypothesis, additional evidence failed to conform with it. Empirical estimates of the Phillips curve relation were unsatisfactory. More important, the inflation rate that appeared to be consistent with a specified level of unemployment did not remain fixed: in the circumstances of the post–World War II period, when governments everywhere were seeking to promote "full employment," it tended in any one country to rise over time and to vary sharply among countries. Looked at the other way, rates of inflation that had earlier been associated with low levels of unemployment were experienced along with high levels of unemployment. The phenomenon of simultaneous high inflation and high unemployment increasingly forced itself on public and professional notice, receiving the unlovely label of "stagflation."

Some of us were skeptical from the outset about the validity of a stable Phillips curve, primarily on theoretical rather than empirical grounds. What mattered for employment, we argued, was not wages in dollars or pounds or kronor but real wages—what the wages would buy in goods and services. Low unemployment would, indeed, mean pressure for a higher real wage—but real wages could be higher even if nominal wages were lower, provided that prices were still lower. Similarly, high unemployment would, indeed, mean pressure for a lower real wage—but real wages could be lower, even if nominal wages were higher, provided prices were still higher.

There is no need to assume a stable Phillips curve in order to explain the apparent tendency for an acceleration of inflation to reduce unemployment. That can be explained by the impact of *unanticipated* changes in nominal demand on markets characterized by (implicit or explicit) long-term commitments with respect to both capital and labor. Long-term labor commitments can be explained by the cost of acquiring information by employers about employees and by employees about alternative employment opportunities plus the specific human capital that makes an employee's value to a particular employer grow over time and exceed his value to other potential employers.

Only surprises matter. If everyone anticipated that prices would rise at, say, 20 percent a year, then this anticipation would be embodied in future wage (and other) contrasts, real wages would then behave precisely as they would if everyone anticipated no price rise, and there would be no reason for the 20 percent rate of inflation to be associated with a different level of unemployment than a zero rate. An unanticipated change is very different, especially in the presence of long-term commitments—themselves partly a result of the imperfect knowledge whose effect they enhance and spread over time. Long-term commitments mean, first, that there is not instantaneous market clearing (as in markets for perishable foods) but only a lagged adjustment of both prices and quantity to changes in demand or supply (as in the house-rental market); second, that commitments entered into depend not only on current observable prices but also on the prices expected to prevail throughout the term of the commitment.

STAGE 2: NATURAL RATE HYPOTHESIS

Proceeding along these lines, we (in particular, E. S. Phelps and myself) developed an alternative hypothesis that distinguished between the short-run and long-run effects of unanticipated changes in aggregate nominal demand. Start from some initial stable position and let there be, for example, an unanticipated acceleration of aggregate nominal demand. This will come to each producer as an unexpectedly favorable demand for his product. In an environment in which changes are always occurring in the relative demand for different goods, he will not know whether this change is special to him or pervasive. It will be rational for him to interpret it as at least partly special and to react to it by seeking to produce more to sell at what he now perceives to be a higher than expected market price for future output. He will be willing to pay higher nominal wages than he had been willing to pay before in order to attract additional workers. The real wage that matters to him is the wage in terms of the price of his product, and he perceives that price as higher than before. A higher nominal wage can therefore mean a lower *real* wage as perceived by him.

To workers, the situation is different: what matters to them is the purchasing power of wages not over the particular good they produce but over all goods in general. Both they and their employers are likely to adjust more slowly their perception of prices in general—because it is more costly to acquire information about that—than their perception of the price of the particular good they produce. As a result, a rise in nominal wages may be perceived by workers as a rise in real wages and hence call forth an increased supply at the same time that it is perceived by employers as a fall in real wages and hence calls forth an increased offer of jobs. Expressed in terms of the average of perceived future prices, real wages are lower; in terms of the perceived future average price, real wages are higher.

But this situation is temporary: let the higher rate of growth of aggregate nominal demand and of prices continue, and perceptions will adjust to reality. When they do, the initial effect will disappear and then even be reversed for a time as workers and employers find themselves locked into inappropriate contracts. Ultimately, employment will be back at the level that prevailed before the assumed unanticipated acceleration in aggregate nominal demand.

This alternative hypothesis is depicted in Figure 2. Each negatively sloping curve is a Phillips curve like that in Figure 1 except that it is for a particular anticipated or perceived rate of inflation, defined as the perceived average rate

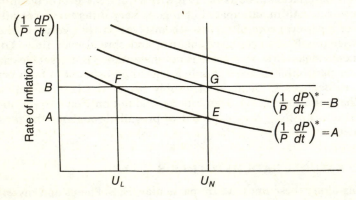

FIGURE 2
Expectations-adjusted Phillips Curve

of price change, *not* the average of perceived rates of individual price change (the order of the curves would be reversed for the second concept). Start from point E and let the rate of inflation for whatever reason move from A to B and stay there. Unemployment would initially decline to U_L at point F, moving along the curve defined for an anticipated rate of inflation $[(1/P)(dP/dt)]^*$ of A. As anticipations adjusted, the short-run curve would move upward, ultimately to the curve defined for an anticipated inflation rate of B. Concurrently unemployment would move gradually over from F to G.

This analysis is, of course, oversimplified. It supposes a single unanticipated change whereas, of course, there is a continuing stream of unanticipated changes; it does not deal explicitly with lags, or with overshooting, or with the process of formation of anticipations. But it does highlight the key points: what matters is not inflation per se but unanticipated inflation; there is no stable trade-off between inflation and unemployment; there is a "natural rate of unemployment" which is consistent with the real forces and with accurate perceptions; unemployment can be kept below that level only by an accelerating inflation; or above it only by accelerating deflation.

The "natural rate of unemployment," a term I introduced to parallel Knut Wicksell's "natural rate of interest," is not a numerical constant but depends on "real" as opposed to monetary factors—the effectiveness of the labor market, the extent of competition or monopoly, the barriers or encouragements to working in various occupations, and so on.

For example, the natural rate has clearly been rising in the United States for two major reasons. First, women, teenagers, and part-time workers have been constituting a growing fraction of the labor force. These groups are more mobile in employment than other workers, entering and leaving the labor market, shifting more frequently between jobs. As a result, they tend to experience higher average rates of unemployment. Second, unemployment insurance and other forms of assistance to unemployed persons have been made available to more categories of workers and have become more generous in duration and amount. Workers who lose their jobs are under less pressure to look for other work, will tend to wait longer in the hope, generally fulfilled, of being recalled to their former employment, and can be more selective in the alternatives they consider. Further, the availability of unemployment insurance makes it more attractive to enter the labor force in the first place, and so may itself have stimulated both the growth that has occurred in the labor force as a percentage of the population and its changing composition.

The determinants of the natural rate of unemployment deserve much fuller analysis for both the United States and other countries. So also do the meaning of the recorded unemployment figures and the relation between the recorded figures and the natural rate. These issues are all of the utmost importance for public policy. However, they are side issues for my present limited purpose.

The connection between the state of employment and the level of efficiency or productivity of an economy is another topic that is of fundamental importance for public policy but is a side issue for my present purpose. There is a tendency to take it for granted that a high level of recorded unemployment is evidence of inefficient use of resources, and conversely. This view is seriously in error. A low level of unemployment may be a sign of a forced-draft economy that is using its resources inefficiently and is inducing workers to sacrifice leisure for goods that they value less highly than the leisure under the mistaken belief that their real wages will be higher than they prove to be. Or a low natural rate of unemployment may reflect institutional arrangements that inhibit change. A highly static rigid economy may have a fixed place for everyone whereas a dynamic, highly progressive economy, which offers everchanging opportunities and fosters flexibility, may have a high natural rate of unemployment. To illustrate how the same rate may correspond to very different conditions: both Japan and the United Kingdom had low average rates of unemployment from, say, 1950 to 1970, but Japan experienced rapid growth, the United Kingdom, stagnation.

The "natural-rate" or "accelerationist" or "expectations-adjusted Phillips curve" hypothesis—as it has been variously designated—is by now widely accepted by economists, though by no means universally. A few still cling to the original Phillips curve; more recognize the difference between short-run and long-run curves but regard even the long-run curve as negatively sloped, though more steeply so than the short-run curves; some substitute a stable relation between the acceleration of inflation and unemployment for a stable relation between inflation and unemployment—aware of but not concerned about the possibility that the same logic that drove them to a second derivative will drive them to ever higher derivatives.

STAGE 3: A POSITIVELY SLOPED PHILLIPS CURVE?

Although the second stage is far from having been fully explored, let alone fully absorbed into the economic literature, the course of events is already producing a move to a third stage. In recent years higher inflation has often been accompanied by higher, not lower, unemployment, especially for periods of several years in length. A simple statistical Phillips curve for such periods seems to be positively sloped, not vertical. The third stage is directed at accommodating this apparent empirical phenomenon. To do so, I suspect that it will have to include in the analysis the interdependence of economic experience and political developments. It will have to treat at least some political phenomena not as independent variables—as exogenous variables in econometric jargon—but as themselves determined by economic events—as endogenous variables. The second stage was greatly influenced by two major developments in economic theory of the past few decades—one, the analysis of imperfect information and of the cost of acquiring information, pioneered by George Stigler; the other, the role of human capital in determining the form of labor contracts, pioneered by Gary Becker. The third stage will, I believe, be greatly influenced by a third major development—the application of economic analysis to political behavior, a field in which pioneering work has also been done by Stigler and Becker as well as by Kenneth Arrow, Duncan Black, Anthony Downs, James Buchanan, Gordon Tullock, and others.

A Tentative Hypothesis

I conjecture that a modest elaboration of the natural-rate hypothesis is all that is required to account for a positive relation between inflation and unemployment, though of course such a positive relation may also occur for other reasons. Just as the natural-rate hypothesis explains a negatively sloped Phillips curve over short periods as a temporary phenomenon that will disappear as economic agents adjust their expectations to reality, so a positively sloped Phillips curve over somewhat longer periods may occur as a transitional phenomenon that will disappear as economic agents adjust not only their expectations but their institutional and political arrangements to a new reality. When this is achieved, I believe that—as the natural-rate hypothesis suggests— the rate of unemployment will be largely independent of the average rate of inflation, though the efficiency of utilization of resources may not be. High inflation need not mean either abnormally high or abnormally low unemployment. However, the institutional and political arrangements that accompany it, either as relics of earlier history or as products of the inflation itself, are likely to prove antithetical to the most productive use of employed resources—a special case of the distinction between the state of employment and the productivity of an economy referred to earlier.

In the version of the natural-rate hypothesis summarized in Figure 2, the vertical curve is for alternative rates of fully anticipated inflation. Whatever that rate—be it negative, zero or positive—it can be built into every decision if it is fully anticipated. At an anticipated 20 percent per year inflation, for example, long-term wage contracts would provide for a wage in each year that would rise relative to the zero-inflation wage by just 20 percent per year; long-term loans would bear an interest rate 20 percent higher than the zero-inflation rate or a principal that would be raised by 20 percent a year; and so on—in short, the equivalent of a full indexing of all contracts. The high rate of inflation would have some real effects, by altering desired cash balances, for example, but it need not alter the efficiency of labor markets, or the length or terms of labor contracts, and hence it need not change the natural rate of unemployment.

This analysis implicitly supposes, first, that inflation is steady or at least no more variable at a high rate than at a low—otherwise, it is unlikely that inflation would be as fully anticipated at high as at low rates of inflation; second, that the inflation is, or can be, open, with all prices free to adjust to the higher rate, so that relative price adjustments are the same with a 20 percent inflation as with a zero inflation; third, really a variant of the second point, that there are no obstacles to indexing of contracts.

Ultimately, if inflation at an average rate of 20 percent per year were to prevail for many decades, these requirements could come fairly close to being met, which is why I am inclined to retain the long-long-run vertical Phillips curve. But when a country initially moves to higher rates of inflation, these requirements will be systematically departed from. And such a transitional period may well extend over decades.

Consider, in particular, the United States and the United Kingdom. For 2 centuries before World War II for the United Kingdom, and a century and a half for the United States, prices varied about a roughly constant level, showing substantial increases in time of war, then postwar declines to roughly prewar levels. The concept of a "normal" price level was deeply imbedded in the financial and other institutions of the two countries and in the habits and attitudes of their citizens.

In the immediate post–World War II period, prior experience was widely expected to recur. The fact was postwar inflation superimposed on wartime inflation; yet the expectation in both countries was deflation. It took a long time for the fear of postwar deflation to dissipate—if it still has—and still longer before expectations started to adjust to the fundamental change in the monetary system. That adjustment is still far from complete.

Indeed, we do not know what a complete adjustment will consist of. We cannot know now whether the industrialized countries will return to the pre–World War II pattern of a long-term stable price level, or will move toward the Latin American pattern of chronically high inflation rates—with every now and then an acute outbreak of super- or hyper-inflation, as occurred recently in Chile and Argentina—or will undergo more radical economic and political change leading to a still different resolution of the present ambiguous situation.

This uncertainty—or more precisely, the circumstances producing this uncertainty—leads to systematic departures from the conditions required for a vertical Phillips curve.

The most fundamental departure is that a high inflation rate is not likely to be steady during the transition decades. Rather, the higher the rate, the more variable it is likely to be. That has been empirically true of differences among countries in the past several decades. It is also highly plausible on theoretical grounds—both about actual inflation and, even more clearly, the anticipations of economic agents with respect to inflation. Governments have not produced high inflation as a deliberate announced policy but as a consequence of other policies—in particular, policies of full employment and welfare-state policies raising government spending. They all proclaim their adherence to the goal of stable prices. They do so in response to their constituents, who may welcome many of the side effects of inflation but are still wedded to the concept of stable money. A burst of inflation produces strong pressure to counter it. Policy goes from one direction to the other, encouraging wide variation in the actual and anticipated rate of inflation. And, of course, in such an environment, no one has single-valued anticipations. Everyone recognizes that there is great uncertainty about what actual inflation will turn out to be over any specific future interval.

The tendency for inflation that is high on the average to be highly variable is reinforced by the effect of inflation on the political cohesiveness of a country in which institutional arrangements and financial contracts have been adjusted to a long-term "normal" price level. Some groups gain (e.g., homeowners); others lose (e.g., owners of savings accounts and fixed-interest securities). "Prudent" behavior becomes in fact reckless, and "reckless" behavior in fact prudent. The society is polarized; one group is set against another. Political unrest increases. The capacity of any government to govern is reduced at the same time that the pressure for strong action grows.

An increased variability of actual or anticipated inflation may raise the natural rate of unemployment in two rather different ways.

First, increased volatility shortens the optimum length of unindexed commitments and renders indexing more advantageous. But it takes time for actual practice to adjust. In the meantime, prior arrangements introduce rigidities that reduce the effectiveness of markets. An additional element of uncertainty is, as it were, added to every market arrangement. In addition, indexing is, even at best, an imperfect substitute for stability of the inflation rate. Price indexes are imperfect; they are available only with a lag and generally are applied to contract terms only with a further lag.

These developments clearly lower economic efficiency. It is less clear what their effect is on recorded unemployment. High average inventories of all kinds are one way to meet increased rigidity and uncertainty. But that may mean labor hoarding by enterprises and low unemployment or a larger force of workers between jobs and so high unemployment. Shorter commitments may mean more rapid adjustment of employment to changed conditions and so low unemployment, or the delay in adjusting the length of commitments may lead to less satisfactory adjustment and so high unemployment. Clearly, much additional research is necessary in this area to clarify the relative importance of the various effects. About all one can say now is that the slow adjustment of commitments and the imperfections of indexing may contribute to the recorded increase in unemployment.

A second related effect of increased volatility of inflation is to render market prices a less efficient system for coordinating economic activity. A fundamental function of a price system, as Hayek emphasized so brilliantly, is to transmit compactly, efficiently, and at low cost the information that economic agents need in order to decide what to produce and how to produce it, or how to employ owned resources. The relevant information is about *relative* prices—of one product relative to another, of the services of one factor of production relative to another, of products relative to factor services, of prices now relative to prices in the future. But the information in practice is transmitted in the form of *absolute* prices—prices in dollars or pounds or kronor. If the price level is on the average stable or changing at a steady rate, it is relatively easy to extract the signal about relative prices from the observed absolute prices. The more volatile the rate of general inflation, the harder it becomes to extract the signal about relative prices from the absolute prices: the broadcast about relative prices is, as it were, being jammed by the noise coming from the inflation broadcast. At the extreme, the system of absolute prices becomes nearly useless, and economic agents resort either to an alternative currency or to barter, with disastrous effects on productivity.

Again, the effect on economic efficiency is clear, on unemployment less so. But, again, it seems plausible that the average level of unemployment would be raised by the increased amount of noise in market signals, at least during the period when institutional arrangements are not yet adapted to the new situation.

These effects of increased volatility of inflation would occur even if prices were legally free to adjust—if, in that sense, the inflation were open. In practice, the distorting effects of uncertainty, rigidity of voluntary long-term contracts, and the contamination of price signals will almost certainly be reinforced by legal restrictions on price change. In the modern world, governments are themselves producers of services sold on the market: from postal services to a wide range of other items. Other prices are regulated by government and require government approval for change: from air fares to taxicab fares to charges for electricity. In these cases, governments cannot avoid being involved in the price-fixing process. In addition, the social and political forces unleashed by volatile inflation rates will lead governments to try to repress inflation in still other areas: by explicit price and wage control, or by pressuring private businesses or unions "voluntarily" to exercise "restraint," or by speculating in foreign exchange in order to alter the exchange rate.

The details will vary from time to time and from country to country, but the general result is the same: reduction in the capacity of the price system to guide economic activity; distortions in relative prices because of the introduction of greater friction, as it were, in all markets; and, very likely, a higher recorded rate of unemployment.

The forces I have just described may render the political and economic system dynamically unstable and produce hyperinflation and radical political change—as in many defeated countries after World War I, or in Chile and Argentina more recently. At the other extreme, before any such catastrophe occurs, policies may be adopted that will achieve a relatively low and stable rate of inflation and lead to the dismantling of many of the interferences with the price system. That would reestablish the preconditions for the straight-forward natural-rate hypothesis and enable that hypothesis to be used to predict the course of the transition.

An intermediate possibility is that the system will reach stability at a fairly constant though high average rate of inflation. In that case, unemployment should also settle down to a fairly constant level decidedly lower than during the transtion. As the preceding discussion emphasizes, *increasing* volatility and *increasing* government intervention with the price system are the major factors that seem likely to raise unemployment, not *high* volatility or a *high* level of intervention.

Ways of coping with both volatility and intervention will develop: through indexing and similar arrangements for coping with volatility of inflation; through the development of indirect ways of altering prices and wages for avoiding government controls.

Under these circumstances, the long-run Phillips curve would again be vertical and we would be back at the natural-rate hypothesis, though perhaps for a different range of inflation rates than that for which it was first suggested.

Because the phenomenon to be explained is the coexistence of high inflation and high unemployment, I have stressed the effect of institutional changes produced by a transition from a monetary system in which there was a "normal" price level to a monetary system consistent with long periods of high, and possibly high variable, inflation. It should be noted that once these institutional changes were made, and economic agents had adjusted their practices and anticipations to them, a reversal to the earlier monetary framework or even the adoption in the new monetary framework of a successful policy of low inflation would in its turn require new adjustments, and these might have many of the same adverse transitional effects on the level of employment. There would appear to be an intermediate-run negatively sloped Phillips curve instead of the positively sloped one I have tried to rationalize.

CONCLUSION

One consequence of the Keynesian revolution of the 1930s was the acceptance of a rigid absolute wage level, and a nearly rigid absolute price level, as a starting point for analyzing short-term economic change. It came to be taken for granted that these were essentially institutional data and were so regarded by economic agents, so that changes in aggregate nominal demand would be reflected almost entirely in output and hardly at all in prices. The age-old confusion between absolute prices and relative prices gained a new lease on life.

In this intellectual atmosphere it was understandable that economists would analyze the relation between unemployment and *nominal* rather than *real* wages and would implicitly regard changes in anticipated *nominal* wages as equal to changes in anticipated *real* wages. Moreover, the empirical evidence that initially suggested a stable relation between the level of unemployment and the rate of change of nominal wages was drawn from a period when, despite sharp short-period fluctuations in prices, there was a relatively stable long-run price level and when the expectation of continued stability was widely shared. Hence these data flashed no warning signals about the special character of the assumptions.

The hypothesis that there is a stable relation between the level of unemployment and the rate of inflation was adopted by the economics profession with alacrity. It filled a gap in Keynes's theoretical structure. It seemed to be the "one equation" that Keynes himself had said "we are . . . short." In addition, it seemed to provide a reliable tool for economic policy, enabling the economist to inform the policymaker about the alternatives available to him.

As in any science, so long as experience seemed to be consistent with the reigning hypothesis it continued to be accepted, although, as always, a few dissenters questioned its validity.

But as the '50s turned into the '60s, and the '60s into the '70s, it became increasingly difficult to accept the hypothesis in its simple form. It seemed to take larger and larger doses of inflation to keep down the level of unemployment. Stagflation reared its ugly head.

Many attempts were made to patch up the hypothesis by allowing for special factors such as the strength of trade unions. But experience stubbornly refused to conform to the patched-up versions.

A more radical revision was required. It took the form of stressing the importance of surprises—of differences between actual and anticipated magnitudes. It restored the primacy of the distinction between real and nominal magnitudes. There is a natural rate of unemployment at any time determined by real factors. This natural rate will tend to be attained when expectations are on the average realized. The same real situation is consistent with any absolute level of prices or of price change, provided allowance is made for the effect of price change on the real cost of holding money balances. In this respect, money is neutral. On the other hand, unanticipated changes in aggregate nominal demand and in inflation will cause systematic errors of perception on the part of employers and employees alike that will initially lead unemployment to deviate in the opposite direction from its natural rate. In this respect, money is not neutral. However, such deviations are transitory, though it may take a long chronological time before they are reversed and finally eliminated as anticipations adjust.

The natural-rate hypothesis contains the original Phillips curve hypothesis as a special case and rationalizes a far broader range of experience, in particular the phenomenon of stagflation. It has by now been widely though not universally accepted.

However, the natural-rate hypothesis in its present form has not proved rich enough to explain a more recent development—a move from stagflation to slumpflation. In recent years, higher inflation has often been accompanied by higher unemployment—not lower unemployment, as the simple Phillips curve would suggest, nor the same unemployment, as the natural-rate hypothesis would suggest.

This recent association of higher inflation with higher unemployment may reflect the common impact of such events as the oil crisis, or independent forces that have imparted a common upward trend to inflation and unemployment.

However, a major factor in some countries and a contributing factor in others may be that they are in a transitional period—this time to be measured by quinquennia or decades not years. The public has not adapted its attitudes or its institutions to a new monetary environment. Inflation tends not only to be higher but also increasingly volatile and to be accompanied by widening government intervention into the setting of prices. The growing volatility of inflation and the growing departure of relative prices from the values that market forces alone would set combine to render the economic system less efficient, to introduce frictions in all markets, and, very likely, to raise the recorded rate of unemployment.

On this analysis, the present situation cannot last. It will either degenerate into hyperinflation and radical change, or institutions will adjust to a situation of chronic inflation, or governments will adopt policies that will produce a low rate of inflation and less government intervention into the fixing of prices.

I have told a perfectly standard story of how scientific theories are revised. Yet it is a story that has far-reaching importance.

Government policy about inflation and unemployment has been at the center of political controversy. Ideological war has raged over these matters. Yet the drastic change that has occurred in economic theory has not been a result of ideological warfare. It has not resulted from divergent political beliefs or aims. It has responded almost entirely to the force of events: brute experience proved far more potent than the strongest of political or ideological preferences.

The importance for humanity of a correct understanding of positive economic science is vividly brought out by a statement made nearly two hundred years ago by Pierre S. du Pont, a deputy from Nemours to the French National Assembly, speaking, appropriately enough, on a proposal to issue additional assignats—the fiat money of the French Revolution: "Gentlemen, it is a disagreeable custom to which one is too easily led by the harshness of the discussions, to assume evil intentions. It is necessary to be gracious as to intentions; one should believe them good, and apparently they are; but we do not have to be gracious at all to inconsistent logic or to absurd reasoning. Bad logicians have committed more involuntary crimes than bad men have done intentionally."

The New Down-to-Earth Economics

WALTER GUZZARDI, JR.

Mr. Guzzardi is a member of the Board of Editors of *Fortune* magazine and has written extensively on business matters, keeping the business community aware of recent developments in economic theory. He holds a master's degree in international affairs from Georgetown University and has been a vice president for Merrill, Lynch, Pierce, Fenner and Smith.

The recurrent recessions, high unemployment, and systemic inflation of recent years have effectively demolished the notion that the government could guarantee smoothly growing prosperity. Since the collapse of that great expectation, economists have been sifting through the wreckage, looking for explanations and clues to better designs. *What* went wrong—the failure of econometric models to forecast accurately, the disastrous swings that followed attempts at fine-tuning—now seems clear enough. But it's not so clear just *why* all that happened.

While the search through the wreckage will continue for a long time, a doctrine that is now attracting new attention offers some persuasive explanations. At the heart of the doctrine are two related propositions. First, people tend to respond rationally and intelligently in their own interest when they see change coming. Second, those sensible responses have an unforeseen collective effect: they forestall the very results that the government seeks when it tries to alter the economy's course by fiscal or monetary interventions. In the end, the interventions prove worse than useless.

That being the case, economists belonging to what is called the "rational expectations" school rationally propose that such interventions be ended. In place of economic guesswork, they would establish a national economic policy based on a few openly announced, well-understood rules. The rules would be consistently applied, and not altered in the futile pursuit of short-term benefits.

This conception of the way things work in the economy is being developed by a small but growing group of academic economists, mostly in their thirties. Their ideas are just now reaching college campuses and graduate schools. They are beginning to influence the ways in which economics is being taught. And they are adding to the skepticism that is growing in the academic world about just how much economists know and how much government can accomplish.

The intellectual leader of the rational-expectations school is Robert Lucas, forty-one, who is spoken of around the University of Chicago, where he teaches, as the likely successor to Milton Friedman. A dark and intense man, Lucas is given to delivering words in rapid bursts, with thoughtful pauses and a trip to the blackboard in between. He explains both the elegant simplicity and the

Walter Guzzardi Jr., "The New Down-to-Earth Economics," *Fortune*, 31 Dec. 1978, pp. 72–79. Reprinted by permission of *Fortune* magazine.

technical complexity of his ideas lucidly, at least for the brighter members of the class; but he is continually punctuating his explanations with "yeah" and "okay?" as though he were always doubting, just a bit, that he is really being understood.

Starting his explanation, Lucas postulates an economy ticking along with fairly stable prices, as ours was in the early 1960's. Then the Federal Reserve Board, to correct trouble that it thinks is coming, suddenly increases the money stock. People find themselves holding more dollars than they held before. That single fact, of course, doesn't make them any wealthier: an increase in the money supply doesn't by itself add goods or services. Still, the crinkle of those new bills in hand does induce a sense of prosperity. Businessmen may make new investments; consumers may spend more. As Lucas puts it, "Yeah, a real kick in output can result."

"But the stimulus is spurious, okay?" he adds grimly. In his view, what has really happened is that people have been fooled into acting as though their wealth had actually increased. Consumers have been deceived by the sense of "extra" money. Businessmen have been tricked because the sudden monetary increase has distorted price signals, and has led them to think that their industry was gaining relative to all the others. As Lucas sums it up, "Everybody thought he was gaining on everybody else. But everybody was wrong." When their true situation becomes clear, and real values reassert themselves, people find that they have overspent and overborrowed.

So when the government tries the same tactic again, the response is far different. "When expansionary monetary policy is used repeatedly over time," Lucas says, "it no longer accomplishes its purposes. The kick is lost. There is no stimulating effect on output. Expected expansions come out as inflation and nothing else." Thomas Sargent of the University of Minnesota, an important contributor to rational-expectations theory, carries the point a step further. "People recognize the truth and stop making the same mistakes," he says. "When they do, they eliminate the planned effects of the policy."

Tax reductions and deficit spending, the other favorite tools in the government's chest, are tainted with the same weaknesses. When taxes are cut for the first time, people may invest or spend as though they actually were richer. But then taxes start to creep up again. When new cuts come around, people have learned all about the inevitable secondary effects: the government will have to borrow more, and the expanded debt will have to be serviced. The implicit tax burden of the future increases. So people do not consume or invest in the same way that they did the first time. "Keynes's comment that in the long run we're all dead was among his stupider remarks," says Merton Miller, a colleague of Lucas's at Chicago. "In the long run, someone else is alive and will have to pay for today's policies."

In other words, a tax cut not balanced by a decrease in government spending signals higher taxes to come. There are differences of opinion among rational expectationists about whether such tax cuts will have to be repaid fully or only in part—it depends to some extent on future economic growth. But there's no question that expectations of future repayments erase a big part of the stimulus that the government's economic managers projected.

The nullifying effect of rational expectations might be avoided if the government had better information than everyone else, or were able always to do the unexpected, and catch people off guard. But as far as superior information is concerned, it seems impossible that, in a world full of analysts, the government could collect, keep secret, and then suddenly act on secretly collected economic data that no one else could get. The rewards for an outsider to dig out the same information would be just too great.

A continuing series of surprise moves is also impossible. As Lucas explains: "The government just can't increase the money supply at rates greater than expected forever, okay? It cannot perpetually surprise the private sector with actions related in a systematic way to the economy. To say that you can fool people with systematic inflation—that means nobody can be as smart as the modeler." To believe in such a notion is like believing that somebody could design a system to beat the house at roulette, or to clean up in the stock market. But, says Lucas, "the idea that somebody has worked out a system to make a bundle has a corollary—some smart bastard will catch on." And of course, once that happens, the vision of the bundle vanishes.

Not all economists share the democratic conviction that intelligence is spread out among the people, not concentrated in Washington. But Lucas does: "We think people are as smart as we are—we don't patronize them. They don't have to be brilliant or study the latest figures from the Fed. They do have to know about inflation and the effect of government spending—but you'd have to be living underground not to know about that by now. If you assume that people are stupid and can't see opportunities to act in their own interest, you're wrong. We say you must purge your model of such features and build in intelligence."

What's more, even if people were stupid, and even if the government could surprise them perpetually, Lucas would find that strategy reprehensible. "You can't run a democratic society by trickery," he says. Adds Robert Barro of the University of Rochester, another contributor to rational expectations theory: "It would be surprising if government deception had to be a part of an efficient economy."

Since people aren't stupid, mere declarations of government intentions are just about meaningless. Reductions in taxes, for example, might indeed have the desired result if they were accompanied by a corresponding and permanent decrease in government spending. But just to talk of such a decrease accomplishes nothing at all. People have heard that song before. They give to it the same credence speculators used to give to the declarations of central bankers that their currencies would never, never be devalued.

In the dissolvent light of the rational-expectations thesis, many of the old "scientific" theorems that supported the case for government activism melt away. For example, in Keynesian macroeconomic theory, when income goes up, consumption goes up, but in decreasing increments. That equation, however, does not allow for the way people really behave in an inflationary environment. Right now, people are very aware of rising rates of inflation. They plan ahead, worrying about rising interest rates and worsening tax bites. They consume and save and work differently as a result of what they think will happen to real dollar values. The old income-consumption ratio, which has been important in figuring the amount of stimulus government policies can give, does not adequately provide for this kind of inflation-induced behavior.

Systemic inflation also greatly limits the usefulness of other long-accepted correlations. Of basic importance to conventional macro modeling are two interconnected equations known as the IS and LM curves. They define the various combinations of interest rate and income at which investment equals saving (IS) and at which money demand equals money supply (LM). Lucas and the others belive that the curves, like many other Keynesian propositions, concentrate too much on demand and neglect the supply side of the economy, where important constraints often show up. Moreover, the curves are based on historical rates of inflation, which of course are far lower than current rates. When inflation is running high, and people are figuring out ways to protect themselves from price increases that they see coming, the curves seem to rational expectationists to be just about useless. Says Lucas: "It depends a bit on how clever a curve-bender you are. But it's very awkward to use these curves when there are inflationary expectations."

Perhaps partly in concession to the forceful arguments of Lucas & Co., latter-day Keynesian macromodelers have made increased efforts to take expectations into account. But they have done so by assuming that people would behave next time just as they did last time—for example, that people might respond in the same way every time a 5 percent tax cut comes along. The trouble with such assumptions, of course, is that they overlook the perplexing element of intelligence—in this case, the capacity of people to learn from experience.

While lots of scientific work is going forward in the field, there are great difficulties with efforts to crank expectations into a model and get results useful for forecasting. Jack Gould, an economics professor at Chicago, points out the complicated interactions that such efforts must deal with. "A household's inflationary expectations affect the demand for money," he says. "That affects the supply, and that affects the rate of inflation—and *that* changes the expectations." And the complications of modeling are made worse by the fact that nobody can repeatedly break the bank at Monte Carlo. "You can't make a prediction of how the world is going to be, or thousands of people would exploit it," Gould observes. "And if thousands exploit it, it will fail—participants in the market will by their participation invalidate the pattern." The main application of rational expectations to modeling, therefore, takes a different turn: it concentrates on revealing the reasons for the government's past mistakes, and leads to recommendations for an entirely different national economic policy.

All the theoretical deficiencies of conventional macro-economics have led to the dramatic real-life failures of the past ten years. Summing them up, Lucas says: "If in the early Sixties we had asked a designer of macro models what the result would be of a doubling of the money stock and a $60-billion deficit, the answer would have been 1 percent unemployment. Such predictions were wildly inaccurate—the inflation of the Seventies produced the highest unemployment since the Thirties. This is econometric failure on a grand scale. From the point of view of annual diagnoses and consequent government-initiated economic action, macro models are useless."

So tough a judgment naturally calls forth loud protests, some from economists whose own expectations would be very much reduced if the profitable business of economic diagnosis and prescription were to end. No one denies the forecasting errors, since the evidence is too strong for that. But some take the tack that the failures are explained by neglect of a few factors. When the models are corrected for those oversights, the results look great. Lucas determinedly resists this line of argument. To crank "add factors" into models when they drift too far from reality, he thinks, is not an admissible scientific procedure. So he sticks with his conclusion: "The flaws are fatal. This condition cannot be remedied by modifications."

Robert Solow, a leading liberal economist from M.I.T., makes a different kind of assault on the rational-expectations school. He admires the technical skill that some of its members possess. "If you ask me, 'Are they clever fellows?' I'd have to say, 'Yes, they are clever fellows, virtuoso performers,'" Solow says. "But they believe people make efficient use of the information they have. Some people do. But homeowners and small businessmen—no, I don't think they make efficient use of the information that's around." Then Solow, a man whose wit and charm make him very popular with students, takes off on a typical flight: "These guys—they see the world as altogether different than it appears to me. I can't talk to them. They're like little green men who just tripped out of a spaceship."

Responds Lucas, who is neither physically nor intellectually green: "Everybody doesn't use information efficiently, of course. But on the average, people do. That's the assumption throughout economic theory. Rational expectations give us some damn good approximations, which is all that economics can do anyway. We're not talking about astronomy. Our ideas are not theoretically elegant. But a rough theory that's refinable can catch more truth than an elegant model that doesn't fit the world."

Lucas is also jabbed at by other critics who insist that people are not rational—that they act idiosyncratically, and for other than economic motives. Answers he: "Irrational behavior can't be predicted. You can't model it, just because it *is* irrational. But good models have to assume that people act rationally. We believe, for example, that if there is a big increase in the excise tax on cigarettes, people will smoke less. Some may smoke more—who knows? But on the average people do smoke less when that happens." Adds Tom Sargent of Minnesota: "The economist always has to hope that neurotic or irrational behavior won't dominate markets. If it does, there's nothing he can do about it. But remember that in competitive markets, irrational people go out of business."

As an explicit theory, rational expectations is not yet taught in economics at the college level: formal incorporation of new theories into the curriculum is always slow. But the intellectual moods and attitudes that the thesis engenders—its skeptical posture, its insistence on real-world testing, its suggestion that both economists and government have overreached themselves to society's detriment—all these have penetrated the minds of many teachers. They also show up in incipient form in some of the new economics textbooks. The rational-expectations doctrine is by no means the sole determinant of all these changes, of course, but it is increasingly influential in many of them.

One major principle of the rational-expectations school is that if the economy were not subjected to the shocks repeatedly administered by government, it would be basically stable. This respect for what an untrammeled economy could do has led teachers to encourage students to think about why government should interfere in the first place. At the University of Virginia, Kenneth Elzinga asks students to consider: "What will be the costs of a government program? If it is inaugurated, will the incentives that work against it end by destroying the purposes that the program was intended to accomplish?"

W. Robert Brazelton, a professor at the University of Missouri, points out to students that "the government's expansionary stance leads unions to push for higher wages. Then we blame the unions for causing inflation. Maybe we should blame the government instead."

Academic thought, in fact, has shown a surprising willingness to adapt itself to the lessons of recent experience. To find out what teachers are thinking today, FORTUNE conducted a survey of professors of economics at fifty-five American universities. These were for the most part big state institutions—in the Southeast, Midwest, and Southwest. The professors were chosen at random. Most turned out to be under forty years old, and all were teaching undergraduate economics. The results showed a profession in flux, losing confidence in its ability to make forecasts, and doubtful about the usefulness of the government's presence in the economy. A summary (the percentages are based on the number who answered each question):

	Yes
• Is there a sense of lost moorings in economics?	66%
• Increasing doubt about the accuracy of macroeconomic models?	75%
• Less confidence in the ability of the government to fine-tune the economy?	82%
• Less confidence in government programs as solutions to economic problems?	87%
• Are you teaching economics differently than you did five years ago?	98%

Another basic shift in the character of teaching and learning about economics comes with a new emphasis on and interest in microeconomics—the way in which markets, companies, consumers, and wage earners actually behave in economic terms. Awareness of the weakness of conventional macroeconomics, which has been heightened by the rational-expectations school, is moving students to study the economy's roots. In micro work, says Sam Peltzman, a professor of economics at Chicago, "we can teach students to understand consequences. They can learn how to figure that if you do this, and nothing else happens, you get this result. Micro can tell us, for example, that if the airlines are deregulated, tickets will cost, say, 50 percent less than they otherwise would. Notice that I don't say that the price of tickets *will* be 50 percent lower. That depends on the possibility of war, on OPEC, and a lot of other things that I don't know anything about."

The appeal of microeconomics is also growing because so many new discoveries and changes are taking place in the field. The work of Martin Feldstein, a Harvard professor who is president of the National Bureau of Economic Research, has revealed a great deal about the effects of the government's presence in a whole series of individual markets. Generally, Feldstein has found that, as he says, "the market is cleverer than any models."

Courses in labor economics, a micro field full of importance for the future, have been totally transformed. Many courses once concentrated on the history of labor unions and collective bargaining—"descriptive, institutional, and dead" is the way one economist describes them. Now labor economics talks more about how costs affect the number of years young people spend in school, about what induces people to enter the labor force when they do, what the job market is really like, why people marry, and why they migrate. The subject concerns itself with the marketplace, and people's critical choices about it. It has turned out to be detailed, interesting, alive, and well.

The new microeconomists and the rational-expectations economists tend to find themselves on the same side of policy issues. The two approaches, as Lucas says, "come from different intellectual roots," but both also represent the latest and the best in academic thinking. And both are delivering the same judgment that less government means better performance.

Generalized, this seems to be the central lesson that younger economists are teaching students today. For his part, the career-oriented student, thinking of his own financial future, interested in making society's organizations work for him rather than in changing them, seems receptive to the message. In any case, there's no doubt about the size of the audience—economics courses all over the country are jammed with students.

These new voices may be giving the government quite a different sort of economic advice in ten years or so, but for the present, dial-diddling remains embedded in American political institutions. Addressing the long-resident economic advisers and manipulators in government, Lucas was probably like to utter a cry similar to Oliver Cromwell's defiant appeal to the Long Parliament: "You have sat here too long for any good you have been doing. Depart, I say, and let us have done with you. In the name of God, go!" But Lucas is too polite—and anyway, it's far less likely that a crowd would disperse. The role of economic expects in government has been expanding ever since the New Deal, and academic macroeconomists have been perpetually fed by the experts with ideas. Many have turned out badly, such as rapid monetary growth to keep interest rates down and massive deficits to correct projected short-range trends in the economy. Now there is a flood of untested new proposals, such as the recent suggestions by Arthur Okun and Henry Wallich that the government should use tax incentives to curb inflation. Lucas deplores such notions as examples of faith in new solutions defended by promises rather than scientific justifications.

All these institutionalized functions of economics have been built in by legislation. But there are good reasons why the legislation should now be changed. One is public opinion: Lucas thinks that the Proposition 13 discontent showed the public's eagerness to break into an established dialogue between economic modelers and government officials. And he hopes that will happen soon. "Not only have we been doing badly following economic advice, but the prospects are that we will do still worse," he says. "As an advice-giving profession, we're in way over our heads."

While explaining how ambitious policies have damaged us, the doctrine of rational expectations also points toward modest policies that might help. Lucas declares that the profession cannot really assess the consequences of policies unless they are free of surprises, and innocent of all efforts to make those short-term adjustments that people defeat by their intelligent anticipations. Therefore Lucas prefers the establishment of declared and permanent rules. He says that we should, for example, fix an annual rate of growth for the money supply and stick with it. And we should set tax rates that would on average balance the budget. These are old ideas of conservative economists such as Milton Friedman, but they have been whetted by recent experience and by the work of the rational-expectations school.

Lucas fears that these ideas may appear "discouragingly modest." But by recommending them, economists would be making clear to government and citizenry that they recognize the limitations of their profession. They would also be recognizing, as Lucas remarks, that "the main task of monetary and fiscal policy is to provide a stable, predictable environment for the private sector, okay?"

Eliminating Policy Surprises: An Inexpensive Way to Beat Inflation

FEDERAL RESERVE BANK OF MINNEAPOLIS

The Federal Reserve System is composed of twelve districts, each with its own staff economists. These economists are generally top rate, and their reports are a major source of discussion concerning theoretical and practical monetary policy issues. Often a branch develops a particular line of thought, as is the case with the Federal Reserve Bank of Minneapolis, which is known as the home of rational expectations. In the following article, taken from the 1978 Annual Report, we see a statement of the rational expectations theory.

Most economic analysts believe that inflation could be fought by lowering the rate of growth of money and cutting the federal budget deficit. They feel that this would slow real economic growth and, in turn, ease inflation by lowering capacity utilization rates in plants and factories and by causing higher—perhaps significantly higher—unemployment.

Some analysts argue in favor of such an anti-inflation plan because they feel it's necessary even if it causes more unemployment. Others think that higher unemployment is so undesirable that the government should fight inflation by imposing economic controls on wages, prices, or credit.

In the last two decades, inflation in the United States has been fought with abrupt cuts in money and debt growth that reduced real economic activity. Inflation slowed in response to these policies, but because unemployment rose substantially these policies were soon abandoned. In order to achieve a permanent reduction in inflation, policymakers must avoid politically intolerable rises in unemployment. To do this in today's political and economic environment, cuts in money and debt growth must be gradual and announced well in advance.

What policymakers must do to fight inflation effectively, in other words, is to eliminate, whenever possible, surprises in monetary and fiscal policies. They must build a set of policies that the public has faith in and will take into account when forming expectations of future inflation and spending. In short, policy must be credible. And the only way to make policy credible is to announce it, implement it faithfully, and avoid shifting it abruptly.

WHY POLICY SURPRISES ARE COSTLY

The concept of a policy surprise is important because policies affect real economic activity principally through surprises. This point can be illustrated

"Eliminating Policy Surprises: An Inexpensive Way to Beat Inflation," *Annual Report of Federal Reserve Bank of Minneapolis* (1978), pp. 1–7. Reprinted by permission of the Federal Reserve Bank of Minneapolis.

most easily with an example that ignores some of the complexities of the world we live in. Although this example is simplified, making it more complex or more like the real world would not change the conclusions. Suppose that existing wages and their rate of growth were established in contract negotiations between firms and workers, negotiations that were undertaken in the belief that the inflation rate would remain constant because the monetary authority would keep the growth of money unchanged. Putting aside uncertainties from sources other than the government, labor contracts would allow wages to grow at a rate equal to the rate of productivity growth plus the expected rate of inflation.

Now suppose that the monetary authority considers the inflation rate too high and unexpectedly decides to reduce the growth of money. This lowers the growth rate of aggregate demand, and businesses, in order to maximize profits, must raise prices more slowly than they had expected. They soon find it in their best interests to lay off some workers, because each worker produces the expected amount of goods, but the goods now have lower market value than expected and bring in less revenue than was expected when wage rates were established. In effect, marginal workers are priced out of their jobs.

As a result of the surprise policy change, the economy has achieved a lower inflation rate. But production employment, personal income, and profits are also lower. (See boxed material opposite for a more formal discussion of the effect of policy surprises on output and prices.)

Once the policy change is recognized, an adjustment process begins. Since there are workers without jobs and since the inflation rate is lower than previously expected, newly negotiated labor contracts specify slower wage growth. Marginal workers, who had been laid off, return to their jobs as their wages no longer outstrip the value of their output. Aggregate output then returns to its original level. That is, after the policy change is recognized, the system adjusts. It regains its initial level of economic activity and real income, but price and wage increases become smaller.

If firms and laborers were able to anticipate the monetary authority's decision to reduce the rate of money growth, inflation would slow without higher unemployment or lower output. The temporary rise in unemployment and shortfall in output could be avoided if the monetary authority announced well in advance that money growth was going to be reduced and if people believed this announcement. Firms and workers could then negotiate appropriate wage contracts. They could agree to clauses that permit money wages to be adjusted in order to keep real wages constant. Or they could negotiate the growth in their money wages, taking into acocunt the new and lower money supply growth and the new rate of inflation. It is in their own best interests to do this. If they don't, they make their labor too expensive and encourage firms to lay them off.

FIGHTING INFLATION WITH SURPRISE POLICY CHANGES:
THE LAST 15 YEARS

The theory that surprise policy changes affect the economy quite differently than well announced, well understood policy changes does much to explain the accelerating inflation in the United States during the last 15 years. During this period there have been three times when inflation was considered rapid enough to call for restrictive monetary and fiscal policies. The first was in 1966, the

HOW POLICY SURPRISES AFFECT OUTPUT AND PRICES

Adjustment to a policy surprise is illustrated in the chart below. The curve D_0, the aggregate demand curve, represents the output demanded by consumers, investors, and government at each price level before the surprise policy change. The curve S_0, the aggregate supply curve, represents the output supplied by all producers at each price level before the surprise policy change. The price level is P_0 and output is equal to Q_0.

Before the surprise policy change, private decision makers were expecting aggregate demand to rise to D_1. Wage contracts were settled that called for wage increases just sufficient to maintain real purchasing power, that is to push the aggregate supply curve—or what is the same thing, the economy's cost curve—to S_1. If the surprise policy change did not occur, prices would rise to P_1 and output would remain at Q_0.

But when the surprise policy comes and the slower growth of money takes effect, aggregate demand rises less than expected, to D_1. Prices, as a result, rise more slowly than expected, reaching P_1 instead of P_1^e. This slower growth in prices, however, lowers the value of the output of workers. In fact, for all workers the value of output is less than expected when wage contract settlements were reached. And for many marginal workers, this value is below their wage costs. Some workers are laid off and output falls to Q_1.

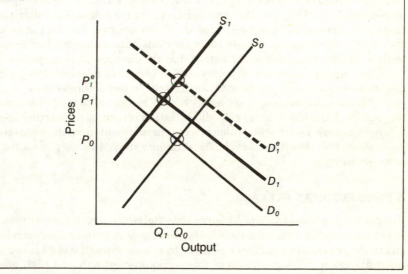

second in 1968–69, and the third in 1973–74.[1] But these actions were abruptly initiated and abruptly discontinued.

[1]The behavior of prices was, of course, a concern at other times, including 1971 when mandatory price and wage controls were set in place. However, it was only in these periods that government policies were attempting purposively to curb aggregate demand in order to slow the rise in prices. All three periods were preceded by years in which policy had been expansionary. And in 1973–74, the inflation stemming from past expansionary policy was aggravated by the release of mandatory controls, permitting increases in previously suppressed wages and prices, and by the quadrupling of oil prices by OPEC.

Perhaps because they were so abrupt, these actions seemed to be surprises. In the spring of 1969, for instance, a leading forecasting service commented that the restraints considered by government policymakers (retention of the 1968 tax surcharge, strict monetary policy, repeal of the investment tax credit, increases in Social Security taxes, and cuts in expenditures) were "highly unlikely." But what was judged unlikely turned out to be what happened. Again, at the beginning of 1974, a time when the economy was at a standstill as the result of past restrictive policies and the OPEC oil shock, many forecasters expected the Fed to permit faster growth of money, which in turn would allow short-term interest rates to edge down. As before, this assessment of how policymakers would behave was off the mark—money growth was further slowed and interest rates rose to record highs at midyear. If these policy changes were surprises, as seems likely, then they contributed to the losses in employment and production that subsequently developed.

The attempts of 1968–69 and 1973–74 to abruptly check the growth of aggregate spending and thereby lower inflation were partially successful. Rates of inflation, responding after a lag to the restrictive policies, declined as desired. Almost simultaneously, however, production slipped lower and unemployment rose. These effects were sufficiently prolonged and extensive for the periods December 1969 through November 1970 and November 1973 through March 1975 to be designated recessions.

Reacting to the high unemployment that preceded these recessions, policymakers changed direction again. They tried to stimulate spending with expansive policies. They did this just before or, at the latest, just after the recessions. The changes in policy reflected their concern over declines in production and employment, but ironically their previous policy changes had contributed to these declines, at least to the extent that the changes were surprises.

The surprise reversals of policy—from checking to stimulating aggregate demand—helped to revive production and make the economy grow. Each time policy became expansive, however, it did so before inflation could drop to its preceding cyclical low. In no case did inflation return to its starting level, even when monetary and fiscal policies were supplemented with wage and price controls in 1971. With each cycle the economy moved further from the goal of price stability.

A FUNDAMENTAL FALLACY

Virtually all economists would agree that tighter macroeconomic policies can lower inflation. But based on past experience, many believe that even a modest cut in the government budget deficit or in money growth would cause massive unemployment or long periods of slow economic growth and high unemployment. Such beliefs are based on a confusion. Because labor markets often have not adjusted immediately to surprise policy actions, some observers believe that any policy action aimed at cutting money growth and the federal budget deficit will produce high unemployment, no matter how it is implemented. They seem to assume that labor markets adjust very slowly, if at all, to changes in policy.

If restrictive policies were pursued and were somehow kept as surprises, it would take many years of high unemployment to bring the inflation rate down to zero. But this is not very plausible. A new permanent policy can be a surprise year after year only if people can be fooled for very long periods of time and if

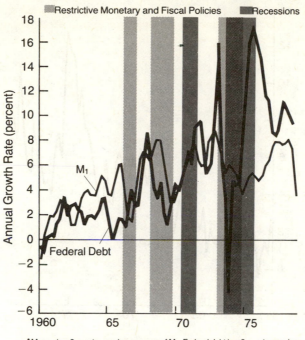

FIGURE 1
Growth of Money and Federal Debt* 1960–1978

their expectations of future inflation are based exclusively on the policies and economic circumstances of an earlier period.[2]

In reality, when policy changes, decision makers' expectations change. Their expectations are based not just on past inflation rates but on all available information, including information on new policies or new anti-inflation programs. Their expectations must change when policy changes if people do indeed behave as economists for the last 200 years have said they behave—in their own best interests. When people believe that money growth or inflation rates have changed, they will not be acting in their own best interests to ignore this when negotiating wage contracts. A firm could lose money if it ignored a new economic policy, because the policy affects the wages it must pay its workers and the prices it can charge for its products. Workers could price themselves out of their jobs if they assume that inflation is going to be higher than it turns out to be and bargain for high wage settlements. On the other hand, if workers

[2]For example, Paul A. Anderson of the Federal Reserve Bank of Minneapolis used a prominent econometric model to simulate what would happen if the money growth rate doubled permanently. He then asked the model to compare price expectations used in the model over a three-year period with the actual performance of prices over that same period. In the model, expectations were way off. For the three-year period, according to the model, people would not even begin to respond accurately to the increased inflation. Their estimates of inflation would stray further and further from the actual performance of prices and would begin to improve only in the fourth year. See "Rational Expectations: How Important for Econometric Policy Analysis?" *Quarterly Review*, Federal Reserve Bank of Minneapolis (Fall 1978).

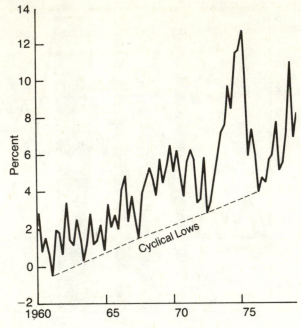

FIGURE 2
Rate of Inflation (GNP Deflator 1960–1978)

assume that inflation is going to be lower than it turns out to be and bargain for low wage settlements, they could find that their incomes, when adjusted for inflation, are falling.

The data suggest that people are not naive about permanent policy changes. In the United States from 1960 to 1978, there appears to be no trade-off between inflation and unemployment. This is consistent with the theory that people are not fooled for long periods by changes in policy. Indeed, the relationship between inflation and unemployment appears to be the opposite of what many people have claimed. Higher inflation tends to be associated with higher, not lower, unemployment. Apparent trade-offs have existed only for short periods of time, as might be expected if people temporarily failed to perceive a shift in the course of macroeconomic policy.

Increases in inflation were generally associated with a decline in unemployment during the first half of 1960. During the 1960s money growth accelerated and a sizable budget deficit began to emerge. After the many years of virtual price stability in the 1950s, this shift in policy probably came as a surprise to most market participants and helped to boost output and lower unemployment. But after a short while, when the basic policy change was presumably recognized, wage demands began to adjust. Thus, in the late 1960s and early 1970s when inflation rose, unemployment generally rose.[3]

[3]Part of the reason for this relationship is that average unemployment rates have risen during the last two decades as the labor participation rates of women and teenagers, who have traditionally experienced higher than average unemployment rates, have risen. Also, the liberalization of income maintenance programs has tended to raise average unemployment rates. The 1974–75 points are especially high because they were influenced by the OPEC price hike and the dismantling of price controls.

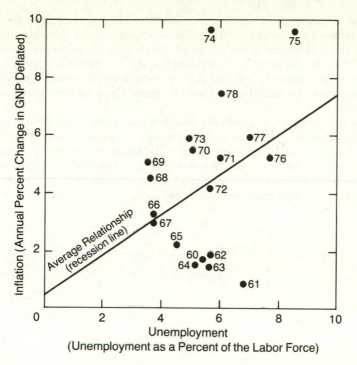

FIGURE 3
Inflation and Unemployment 1960–1978

The correlation of inflation and unemployment over the last two decades suggests that labor markets do, in fact, react to basic changes in macroeconomic policies. Once a change in policy and the resulting inflationary consequences are understood, labor markets adjust. If history is any guide, this means that if more stimulative policies are expected, then we should get more inflation and more unemployment. Conversely, if tighter policies are expected, we should get less of each. Gains can thus be made against inflation without incurring the high costs of increased unemployment.

NEEDED: A CREDIBLE MACROECONOMIC POLICY

A policy of gradually slowing money growth and reducing the federal budget deficit can lower and, ultimately, eliminate inflation in the United States. There are compelling political or psychological reasons that the steps should be gradual. In the years since World War II, macroeconomic policy has been characterized by stop-and-go actions and by many surprises. On the basis of this experience, many observers doubt that government has the will to change and to persist patiently in a sequence of announced, gradual steps to achieve price stability. To these skeptics, as well as others who may not fully understand the new policy approach and its implications, the change in approach will come as a surprise.

If it does surprise some people, then real costs will arise, at least during the early steps of the new approach. In fact, large changes could shock the economy and cause a recession. A serious recession could lead, as in the past, to the abandonment of attempts to bring inflation under control. For this reason, it is essential that the initial steps be small. Of course, if people for some reason believed that the government was going to take the monetary and fiscal steps necessary to control inflation and if they were not restricted by previous contracts, then even the initial steps could be made large without causing a shock or a recession.

Once the program of gradually slowing growth in aggregate demand has begun and the government has unambiguously demonstrated its determination to carry it out, the costs of the program will decline. When the new approach is well known and understood, then even large steps will not lead to higher unemployment. As surprises gradually disappear, so will the high costs of fighting inflation with macroeconomic policies.

Unemployment and Inflation: An Alternative View

MICHAEL J. PIORE

Described as a successor to Galbraith on the left, Michael Piore is one of the brightest young economists around. His views are somewhere between neoclassical theory on the one side and radical economics on the other, but they are almost always original and difficult to classify. As one of the creators of the *dual labor market hypothesis*, he has entered the group of economists whose ideas will be known to almost all economists. He is currently professor of economics at the Massachusetts Institute of Technology.

An overwhelming majority of academic economists holds that there is a functional relationship between the rate of wage (and price) inflation and the level of unemployment. That relationship is known as the Phillips curve. It implies in the simplest, most straightforward, and most brutal terms that full employment *causes* inflation. Thus, the fundamental conflict between the two basic goals— price stability and low unemployment—has become the central dilemma of American economic policy.

But there is an alternative view of inflation and unemployment that grows out of two bodies of thought and research. One of these is the tradition of institutional labor economics, particularly the theories of wage determination which emerged from that school in the 1940s and 1950s. The leading representative of that way of thinking today is John T. Dunlop, and the kind of policy it suggests to cope with inflation is very close to that which Dunlop advocated and tried to pursue within the Nixon administration. The other important school of thought is that of labor market stratification, which developed in the context of the civil rights experience, the black revolt, and the war on poverty in the 1960s. Many—although not all—of the proponents of the stratification theories are political radicals. The conflict between their political views and those of older institutional economists like Dunlop has served to obscure a shared intellectual perspective and is undoubtedly one of the factors underlying the complete domination of the debates about economic policy by other views of economic processes.

The conventional view that there is a functional relationship between unemployment and inflation is based, at root, on the notion that the wage is set by supply and demand in a market process. Inflation is generated when demand exceeds supply, and the demanders drive up wages, competing with each other to attract labor that isn't there. Unemployment, in this view, is supposed to measure the gap between supply and demand. When it is very high, supply exceeds demand and wages are stable or falling. Were the term "unemploy-

Michael J. Piore, "Unemployment and Inflation: An Alternative View," *Challenge*, May/June © 1978, pp. 24–32. Reprinted by permission of M. E. Sharpe, Inc., White Plains, New York 10603.

ment" taken literally, the unemployed would always represent unutilized resources, and wage inflation would begin only at zero unemployment. In fact, however—the argument runs—unemployment is an imperfect measure of the gap between demand and supply. There are always some people between jobs; not all people who want work are qualified for the jobs available; not all people who claim to be unemployed really want to work. At some level of unemployment greater than zero, demand actually begins to exceed supply, and it is at this point that wage inflation begins. As unemployment is driven further below that level, the inflation accelerates.

Those who hold the alternative view challenge this basic notion. They assert that wage determination and unemployment are two essentially distinct processes which must be understood independently of each other, and can be attacked through separate policies.

THE WAGE DETERMINATION PROCESS

The distinction between wage determination and unemployment arises because in most contexts the wage does not, and cannot, function to equate supply and demand. Instead, wage rates perform certain basic social and institutional functions. They define relationships between labor and management, between one group of workers and another, among various institutional entities (the locals in a national union, the various branch plants of a national company, the major employers in a local labor market, the major international unions which compose the American labor movement), and last, the place of individuals relative to one another in the work community, in the neighborhood, and in the family.

The role of wages in this respect results in a series of fixed relationships among the wage rates of certain groups of jobs and workers; these relationships are known as wage contours. The economy is composed of a series of these more or less self-contained contours. The boundaries of the contours evolve over time, as do the relationships within them. But at any given moment of time, the boundaries and the internal wage relationships are fixed. When a wage breaks out of line, distorting one of these fixed relationships, immense pressure is generated to restore it. The pressures emanate directly from rank-and-file workers and take the form of job action and strikes. They also generate political and organizational conflicts among various branches and divisions of such bodies as trade unions and corporations.

The most prominent example of the operation of these forces at present is New York City. There, as in most cities, the various municipal employee wage rates form a single contour. In 1976, the police attempted to distort the traditional relationships among these different groups of workers, demanding a special accommodation in the city's budgetary crisis. The city's resistance resulted from the fear that any special settlement with the police would lead to pressures from the other workers to restore the traditional wage pattern by granting equivalent wage increases, and the resulting wage adjustments would undermine the city's fiscal stabilization program. This year, conflict has centered around the negotiating structure. The city has sought to bargain with the unions as a group, but the police and firefighters have insisted upon separate negotiations. These disputes have national implications, because New York is loosely linked to a national wage contour comprising the major American cities.

In the last round of major negotiations, there were several other prominent examples of the same process. The rubber workers had fallen behind industrial wage patterns in steel and automobiles, to whose wage contour they belonged, and their long strike with its high ultimate settlement was an attempt to restore the traditional pattern. The teamsters, too, have had a relatively self-contained wage contour; in that case, disruption emanating from the Chicago local has been the focal point of wage determination. In the construction industry, a national contour is formed out of a patchwork of settlements in which there are traditional relationships both among different crafts within a given city and among the same crafts across cities. Thus, one out-of-line local settlement will generate ripples through these interlocking wage relationships that spread out across the national economy.

THE INFLATIONARY PROCESS

This view of wage determination suggests that inflation is a two-part process. It is triggered by external shocks which drive a wage within a stable contour out of line. Individuals and institutions then react to restore the original differentials. The process of restoration generates the bulk of the actual inflation. But the initial shocks are the strategic factors.

These shocks appear to come from any number of sources, and it is probably not possible to formulate a single theory about how they are generated. In the examples cited above, many of the disruptive elements are, in fact, accidental. The New York police won a fortuitous court victory which gave them negotiating leverage; the rubber workers' old contract had no escalator clause, other settlements in the contour did, and an unprecedented inflation made such a clause the central determinant of the wage. Other disruptions are more systematically related to social and economic events: for example, the opening of a new plant in a community with a well-defined wage hierarchy; the organization of a new trade union (in recent years, very important in the public sector); political contests among union leaders (important in trucking, in construction, and also in the New York City police case); labor supply problems; product market bottlenecks. Inflation, on the national level, appears particularly responsive to shocks which hit a number of contours simultaneously. To the extent that there is a relationship between full employment and wage inflation, it is because full employment, or the levels of economic activity which produce it, have a tendency to produce shocks of this kind. But the shocks that produced inflation earlier in the 1970s appear to have been connected with the oil crisis and with food costs. Such shocks are virtually impossible to predict. I would guess that if there is a single set of national pressures in the next few years, it is likely to be connected with the retirement of George Meany, the emergence of younger, more militant labor leaders, and the effect of insurgent challenges to established union leaders over wage demands.

ANTI-INFLATIONARY POLICY

This view of the inflationary process suggests that, in the short run, wage policy must be directed at controlling the initial shocks and the process through which the shocks spread within fixed wage contours. Over the long term, the policy might also be concerned with changing either the composition of the contours themselves, or the relationship among wage rates within them.

To develop such a policy in detail would require an extensive analysis of each of the component elements. It is not possible to present that analysis here. The important conclusions and the incomes policy which follows from them may be summarized in the following brief points:

1. It appears possible to forestall most, if not all, of the shocks that generate the initial distortions through persuasion, pressure, and control directed by a national wage board. The basic leverage for this policy comes from the recognition by rank-and-file workers that the distortions are unjust and inequitable, however advantageous they may be from a personal point of view. Employers and trade union leaders also consider the distortions troublesome, because they know the countervailing pressure which will follow. Hence, there is a predisposition to accept government intervention, so long as it is confined to forestalling disruptive shocks.

2. It is not possible to forestall attempts to restore traditional relationships once they have been distorted. The pressures for restoration tend to be commanding. Attempts to stop them are likely to produce resistance in the form of wildcat strikes and a black market for labor. These attempts also undermine the political support for wage policy. Most of the current political opposition to incomes policy is generated by the failure of public policy-makers in the past to distinguish between initial distortions and efforts at restoration.

3. The necessity of making the distinction between disruptive shocks and the restoration of traditional relationships means that labor and management must participate extensively in the policy machinery; it cannot be run by "neutrals" or by government officials alone. Only people intimately involved in labor-management relations are capable of supplying the detailed information which will distinguish the boundaries of the various wage contours of which the economy is composed, and will separate the two types of wage changes. Incidentally, the participation of labor and management may also be required for the political success of the program.

4. This type of wage policy implies that there cannot be a single national wage guideline or even a technically determined set of wage standards. Instead, wage policy must be tailored individually to each wage contour. The institutional structure through which policy is implemented should probably reflect this as well. Thus, a national wage board would have to operate through a series of subsidiary bodies which specialized in the control of particular wage contours.

5. The machinery described above can be distinguished from a long-term strategy designed to eliminate systematic sources of wage distortion and to change the dimensions of existing wage contours or the relationships within them so as to make them more consistent with the surrounding economic and social environment. Again, the precise content of such a policy would depend upon the peculiarities of each sector, the nature of its individual problems, and the actual leverage which government can bring to bear upon a solution. In construction, in trucking, and among municipal unions, for example, it can be argued that union mergers and centralization of power within national unions would operate over the long run to foster wage stability. In the medical care sector, it appears that adjustments in job structure and manpower policies are required. The most troublesome wage problem in the immediate future is undoubtedly the adjustments that must be made in the public sectors due to the conflict between the pressures of unionization, and the financial crises of state and local governments. Here the role of the federal government is extremely varied and complex and ought, at the very least, to be coordinated in a more studied and deliberate fashion.

UNEMPLOYMENT

The view of unemployment which complements the foregoing view of wage determination is less fully developed, and its specific public policy implications are less clear. Though this makes it somewhat more difficult to present concisely, it does nonetheless constitute a coherent alternative perspective.

First, a sharp distinction must be made between the level of unemployment and its distribution among various demographic groups. The level of unemployment is determined by the aggregate demand. Demand, in turn, can be regulated by the government through monetary and fiscal policy. The techniques for doing so have been clear since the publication of Keynes' *General Theory* in the 1930s. The chief constraint upon reductions in the level of unemployment in the postwar period has thus been the unwillingness of the federal government to pursue more expansionary policies. Since the 1960s, the ostensible reason for the government's reluctance has been that this course was alleged to generate inflation. As we have just seen, this supposed relationship between inflation and unemployment is questionable, which leads one to wonder if there is not some other, more fundamental constraint upon economic expansion. These are matters which will be discussed further below. In the present context, the basic point is simply that the level of unemployment is directly controllable by the government through known and generally accepted techniques.

This brings us to a second related point: the conventional interpretation of unemployment seems to imply that labor supply constitutes an absolute barrier to expansion; the barrier is indicated by some level of measured unemployment greater than zero. Those who hold this view argue that the intuitive idea of unemployment as unutilized resources which can be brought into production is wrong because the measured figure is "contaminated." Presumably, there is an irreducible residual level of unemployment composed of people who don't want to work, who are moving between jobs, or who are unqualified. If there is in fact some such residual level of unemployment, it is not one we have encountered in the United States. *Never in the postwar period has the government been unsuccessful when it has made a sustained effort to reduce unemployment.* On several occasions, unemployment has even fallen below the government target.

Third, the above interpretation of the level of unemployment does not explain why, at virtually any level, it is concentrated among certain demographic groups. In the United States in the postwar period, those groups have been youth, women, and black workers. There have been two basic ways of explaining this concentration. The usual approach has been in terms of the characteristics of the groups themselves. This had led to policies which are targeted at the specific groups, attempting to change their characteristics. The alternative approach is to account for the distribution of unemployment in terms of the functions which the groups perform in the economy. The result for policy would be a concern with two contingencies for which the conventional view does not allow: the possibility of changing the economic structure so that the functions of these groups would be eliminated; and the likelihood that if the functions are not eliminated, any success in dealing with the problems of one particular group will simply lead to the creation or discovery of some other group to take its place. The most graphic example of this latter contingency is the phenomenal growth of the illegal alien population since the late 1960s, which seems to be a response to the reluctance of black workers to play their traditional economic role and the resulting search by employers for alternative sources of labor.

What are these economic functions and why do they lead to high relative unemployment rates among those who perform them? The perspective I am developing here provides responses to these questions, but it is deficient in transforming those responses into operational policy proposals. It appears that the basic characteristics of the jobs held by the high unemployment groups are that they pay low wages, are often menial, and require little skill. In addition, many are also subject to seasonal variations, are sensitive to sudden shifts in taste and fashion, are in declining industries or marginal firms, and offer little prospect for continuous employment, let alone meaningful career opportunities.

It might be possible to reduce the number of such jobs but it is apparently not possible to eliminate them entirely without radical adjustments in the patterns of consumption and production of the rest of the society—perhaps without a fundamental change in the nature of the economic system. There are a number of examples of how these kinds of jobs are related to the broader economic structure. Here is one: the job security arrangements in many industries are predicated upon the ability of employers to transfer peaks in demand to other firms, or to sectors of the economy where firms are freer to hire and fire at will. Major nonunion employers who have "full employment" or guaranteed employment apparently fulfill their commitment in this way. Unionized firms in industries ranging from automobiles to blue jeans use subcontractors in a similar manner. But if the firms with freer hiring and firing patterns, and the sectors of the market from which they draw their labor, were eliminated, all employers would be forced to absorb the flux and uncertainty of economic activity themselves, and could not afford to provide the kind of employment security which most white males enjoy at prime age. Another example: without a low-wage labor force willing to bear economic flux and uncertainty, most of our declining industries such as textiles, shoes, and garments would be forced to move abroad much more rapidly. This would, in turn, threaten the employment of higher-paid, more secure workers who service these industries. It would also force adjustments in our balance of payments which would lead to a decline in our standard of living. A third example involves the direct effects of the elimination of low-wage menial labor upon the standard of living. The most dramatic effects would undoubtedly be to intensify the inflationary pressures and organizational problems in medical care, an industry which is already a focal point of social concern.

Why do such jobs generate high relative levels of unemployment? A partial reason is the characteristics of the jobs themselves. Obviously, jobs which are especially sensitive to economic flux and uncertainty are going to be most likely to end in people being thrown out of work. This cultivates a high voluntary turnover among the labor force: if the job offers no career prospects and is likely to disappear pretty soon anyway, there is obviously no incentive to make special sacrifices to hold it. But probably more fundamental is the fact that where there is a set of jobs so clearly inferior to other employment opportunities, social stability is possible only if the groups holding the poor jobs have special reasons for doing so. With the possible exception of blacks, groups which hold the inferior jobs have all had other, more basic social commitments. Work is often secondary or tangential; as a consequence, these groups frequently move in and out of the labor force. It is that movement which produces most of the unemployment. Thus, women have been committed to the home and children; youth to school and to adolescent pursuits before they settle down to regular employment; migrants from abroad and often from rural areas in the United States to a life in their home communities to which they return frequently. Blacks constitute an exception in the South where they were forced into their roles by a racial caste system. In the North, however, their acceptance of low-wage jobs and their high unemployment was more attributable to the fact that they were a migrant poplulation, attached to the South and viewing their northern experience as temporary. When the black population in northern cities began to be dominated by second-generation, permanent residents who had grown up there, it rebelled against its assigned role in the labor market.

It has been argued that the social structure *creates* these groups in order to have people who will play these economic roles. But, again with the exception of the black workers in the South, it seems more plausible to argue that the society "finds" groups within an already existing social structure who are willing to play these roles. American society did not invent adolescents, or migrants, or housewives. But it has used them and, in the process, become dependent upon them. The difficulty is that precisely because it did not invent them, it has a very limited capacity to control their aspirations and self-conceptions. These are subject to an independent evolution, and, as they evolve, they create pressures for change. This happened with blacks and, to a lesser extent perhaps, youth in the 1960s. It is happening today with women. This is the policy problem—not the unemployment of the groups, but rather, the place of these groups within the economic system and their growing disenchantment with the roles and social organization which once made that place acceptable. This implies that relatively high unemployment among certain groups is a problem, first, of upward mobility for these groups in the labor market and, second, of the economic functions which these groups currently perform.

In sum, then, the basic explanation of the high relative unemployment of certain groups is that the jobs which they hold have relatively high rates of discharge and layoff, and the workers who hold these jobs have relatively high rates of entrance into and exit from the labor force. The two factors are related: in order to get people who are willing to accept the menial, low-wage jobs involved, one has to call upon groups with a marginal attachment to the labor market and these groups tend to have high rates of movement into and out of the labor force. The nature of these groups explains why their high relative rate does not impair our ability to reduce the *level* of unemployment: the groups are such that, with relatively little effort on the part of employers, it is possible to induce a large increase in the amount of labor they supply. At the same time, because of the character of the jobs to which they are confined, those members of groups who are already working constitute a reserve of people ready to move up to higher-level jobs. Thus, for practical purposes, there is an infinite supply of labor both for menial and for better-paying jobs. This also explains why institutional and social factors are so important in wage setting. Supply is not a constraining factor, and in terms of conventional theory, which relies on the forces of supply and demand to set wage rates, these rates are indeterminate. This way of looking at the problem leads to the conclusion that the fundamental economic problem is neither unemployment nor inflation, but economic opportunity and social mobility.

PUBLIC POLICY FOR UPWARD MOBILITY

The problem of upward mobility must in turn be considered not simply in terms of the workers holding the jobs, but also of the social function which these workers now perform; if they are to be upwardly mobile, their current jobs must either be eliminated or filled by others. How are policy-makers dealing with this problem?

1. *Administration.* The United States already has a substantial number of public policies designed to promote the upward mobility of minorities and women. These include equal employment policies to insure that opportunities are open to qualified workers, and education and training policies to equip workers to fill newly opened jobs. The major difficulties with this range of policies appear to have been internal administration and coordination. Of particular concern was the administration of the Equal Employment Opportunities Commission (EEOC). Until now, no president has ever given top priority to staffing the agency with good administrators; the appointments were always dominated by short-run political considerations. Hence, the new administrators will be faced with a history of poor practice, and of failure on the part of the agency to act as the key instrument of economic policy which it ought to have been. As for coordination, at least three distinct aspects of the problem may be distinguished: coordination between the EEOC and other agencies promoting equal opportunity, for example, the Labor Department, HEW, the Civil Service Commission; coordination between agencies providing education and those providing training (HEW and Labor); and coordination between equal opportunity policy and education and training policy.

2. *Planning.* The policies for both equal employment and education and training need to be conceived in terms of a broader framework which takes account of available job opportunities. Few have ever asked the elementary question whether there are going to be enough "good" jobs to promote the upward mobility of women and blacks without displacing white workers and if not, what can be done about it. There are a number of policies which would reduce conflicts if there did indeed turn out to be a scarcity of "good" jobs. We could delay the entrance of white males into the labor force by expanded education and training, for example, or promote early retirement in certain sectors by adjustments in the social security system.

3. *The vacuum.* Conversely, there is the question who will perform the jobs vacated by upwardly mobile workers. As noted earlier, what appears to be happening now is that undocumented alien workers are filling these jobs by default. This raises issues which should be the subject of study and ultimately of policy. First, are the aliens subject to special exploitation because they are illegal? Are minimum labor standards being violated? Second, will the children of alien workers want upward mobility, and is the society capable of providing them with job opportunities?

4. *Elimination of low-wage jobs.* This area is one which needs special study, planning, and experimentation. There is now no policy, and virtually no base of knowledge upon which policy could be built.

THE PHILLIPS CURVE, THE EVIDENCE, AND THE DETERMINANTS OF ECONOMIC POLICY

The foregoing suggests that the central issue of economic policy is the upward mobility of discontented low-wage workers. In fact, the problem of discontent and frustrated aspirations is a good deal more widespread, and the policy problem more complicated, than we have indicated here.

In light of this alternative view of inflation and unemployment, the total acceptance of the Phillips curve in recent debates about economic policy becomes astonishing—so astonishing that an explanation is called for. In fact, the evidence for the existence of such a relationship is very weak. There are virtually no grounds for assuming a simple functional relationship between the level of unemployment and the rate of wage (or price) inflation in the last ten years. A simple plot of unemployment and inflation would show that the points lie all over the map; in no way would they trace out the regular relationship which the theory postulates.

The notion of such a relationship has been rescued in academic debate by introducing two principal refinements into the theory. First, it was argued that measured unemployment did not represent true unemployment, and the unemployment rate was therefore adjusted in various ways. When these adjustments proved insufficient, a second refinement was introduced—the notion that inflation gets built into expectations. To account for this effect, past rates of wage inflation were used along with unemployment in the estimating equations. Both these refinements have been handled in such a way that one is unsure whether the theory is being used to explain the data or the data reworked to fit the theory. Indeed, in the case of the expectations variable, there is almost certainly a good deal of the latter effect: the estimation techniques have allowed the researcher to pick out from a range of possible data precisely those which best fit the theory. What is surprising in all of this is not that it occurred, but that there has been so little discussion of it among economists and econometricians, who are normally so careful to avoid such procedures and so quick to point out their dangers when others use them. It is also surprising that there have been no independent attempts to define and test the theories of either "true" unemployment or of expectations. All of this leads one to suspect that the Phillips curve is really a rationalization of something else. But of what? One must suspect that for economists, the use of the curve is designed, consciously or unconsciously, to rescue the notions of supply and demand, which constitute the central ideas of the discipline. But what about the rest of society? Is it simply being "taken in" by the economists?

The intellectual history of economic debate in the postwar period indicates that just the opposite is the case. The Phillips curve and the lessons it teaches won widespread public acceptance only in the middle sixties. Before that time, the intellectual obstacle to full employment was a completely different but equally effective notion: that of the need for a balanced federal budget. That idea had very little support among professional economists, but it was almost universally accepted by politicians and by the public at large. The push for a balanced budget was abandoned early in the 1960s by President Kennedy, and its intellectual respectability in informed political debate declined very rapidly thereafter. It is at that point in history that the concept of the Phillips curve, which until then had been largely confined to professional discourse among economists, became prominent in public discussions of economic policy. The coincidence of the growing acceptance of the curve and the declining commitment to a balanced budget can hardly be accidental. It seems to suggest that Americans have always had some intellectual construct which served as an obstacle to an economic policy for full employment. This leads one to suspect that the arguments which justify the dampening of employment are actually rationalizations of policies decided on other grounds.

Economic policy is the outcome of a political process. The important actors in the process are, on one side, the trade union movement and organized minority groups pushing for expansion and a low rate of unemployment and, on the other side, the business and banking communities which have been infinitely more cautious and conservative. Actual policy is the outcome of the balance of pressures exerted by these two groups and one can almost say that the target rate of unemployment, indeed even the rate of unemployment itself, shifts continually as that balance is adjusted. The debate is conducted in a vocabulary supplied by economists and through professional economic spokesmen, but the result is the outcome of direct political pressure. The change in economic policy from aggressive expansion in the 1960s to the recessionary conditions of the 1970s was produced by a large shift in the balance of these political forces. And an analysis of that shift is critical to an understanding of the factors which really act to undermine full employment in the United States.

What I find most impressive in the climate of the period in which this shift occurred is not so much the gain in the power of the business and banking communities—although after the Republican election victory there certainly was such a gain—but the weakening of will and conviction among trade union leaders on the full employment issue. The trade unions did not actually abandon their commitment to full employment but they certainly expressed themselves with a lot less fervor. Their changing attitudes were, in turn, attributable to incipient problems with the rank-and-file. In the late 1960s, trade union officials and lower level management shared a general feeling that rank-and-file workers were becoming increasingly aggressive, difficult to manage, and restive about existing organizational structures, and that these attitudes were the direct result of a prolonged period of low unemployment which taught workers, especially the younger ones, to "undervalue" what they had already achieved and to aspire to "unrealistic" improvements in employment and working conditions. If prolonged full employment was spurring these feelings, a taste of unemployment and recession, it was felt, would help cure them.

It would seem that full employment generated among the favored members of the American labor force a set of discontents and desires not unlike those expressed by disfavored groups like minorities and women: discontent with existing employment opportunities and desires for improvement and upward mobility. If this is true, it implies in turn that there is a systematic tendency in the United States at full employment for aspirations to outrun opportunity. In a country such as ours, whose national ideology is built around its self-conception as the land of opportunity, this is bound to be a very difficult thing to face. And it is easy enough to understand why we would prefer theories which located the limitations upon full employment elsewhere, in events and processes such as inflation or the need for a balanced budget, which have nothing fundamentally to do with the national ideology. By the same token, however, so long as we conceive the problem in these terms, we will never be able to achieve full employment. More important, we will never be able to meet the ideological commitments upon which the country was founded and upon which our identity as a nation rests. To meet the goals we have defined for ourselves as a people, we must make the issue of the quality of economic opportunity central to our thinking about economic problems and the direct focus of our economic policies.

In what direction should we move? Unfortunately, because our mode of economic discourse has served more than anything else to obscure and suppress these issues, it is very difficult to move directly to operational policy. The immediate steps are rather to encourage a new mode of thinking, an alternative line of research, and a different political rhetoric.

The Specter of Full Employment

ROBERT LEKACHMAN

Robert Lekachman is a professor of economics at Lehman College, City University of New York and is a well-known critic of mainstream economic thinking. He is the author of numerous books—including *The Age of Keynes* (1966), *The Permanent Problem of Boom and Bust* (1973) and *Economist at Bay* (1976)—and is also a columnist for *Dissent*.

As we embark on Year One of the Carter Era, it is perhaps permissible to wistfully recall that its chronological predecessor was the 200th anniversary of the Declaration of Independence, Adam Smith's *Wealth of Nations*, and Edward Gibbon's *Decline and Fall of the Roman Empire*. To postpone anticlimax no further, 1976 was also the thirtieth birthday of the Employment Act of 1946.

Antiquarians can testify that the new statute was the emasculated survivor of the Full Employment Bill of 1945, which threatened concrete action against unemployment. All that the Employment Act specifically did was create the Council of Economic Advisers and the Joint Economic Committee of Congress, two of Washington's more talkative and less influential groups. The act's wordy preamble did, it is true, promise something called "maximum employment," but it never paused to explain what that might be and how it was to be attained.

Since 1946 we have staggered through a couple of recessions courtesy of Harry Truman, three sponsored by Dwight Eisenhower, and two conferred upon their country-persons by Richard Nixon and Gerald Ford. During the 1950s, which those of hazy recollection now glorify as a veritable Gold Age, unemployment averaged around 5 percent and general economic growth lagged enough to provide a winning issue for John Kennedy in 1960. A combination of Kennedy-Johnson tax cuts, subsidies to the Pentagon, the war on poverty, and, not least, the Vietnam public works program, turned the 1960s into a better than average decade for jobs. In the 1970s things are back to normal or worse.

This abbreviated business history does call attention to a puzzle, at least for the naive. For thirty years it has been declared national policy to run the economy rapidly enough to give every American willing and able to work at a job roughly commensurate with his or her skills if not expectations. All political candidates extol the work ethic and dutifully recall hard boyhoods spent jerking sodas, shining shoes, delivering newspapers, or digging up peanuts. In the course of the late, unlamented Presidential campaign, Carter was no less eager than Ford to get people off welfare rolls onto payrolls, to recall the felicitous language of the departed Nixon. Certainly no shortage looms of things to be done and goods and services to be supplied. A community whose median income hovers around $14,000 and in which average families are noticeably worse off than they were two or three years ago, has not lost interest in getting more income to buy cars, houses, and vacations in the sunny South or the snowy North.

THE USES OF UNEMPLOYMENT

Men and women want to work. Work, private and public, is there to be done. How come, a wandering rationalist might ask, the work and the workers are not happily married? Well, as the radicals of my youth were wont to intone, it is no accident that we tolerate as a nation years of 7, 8, even 9 percent general unemployment and horrifying rates of teen-age joblessness which among urban blacks exceed, by some estimates, 50 percent.

The brutal fact is that unemployment at "moderate" rates confers a good many benefits upon the prosperous and the truly affluent. If everyone could be employed, extraordinarily high wages would have to be paid to toilers in restaurant kitchens, laundries, filling stations, and other humble positions. Whenever decent jobs at living wages are plentiful, it is exceedingly difficult to coax young men and women into our volunteer army. Without a volunteer army, how can the children of the middle and upper classes be spared the rigors of the draft?

Unemployment calms the unions and moderates their wage demands. Business periodicals have been noting with unconcealed gratification that last year's contract settlements between major unions and large corporations were considerably less expensive for employers than those of 1975, even though union members were steadily losing ground to inflation. When people are scared about losing their jobs, they work harder and gripe less. In more dignified language, absenteeism declines and productivity ascends.

Better still, factory and office workers, alert to potential layoffs and plant shutdowns, are unlikely to nag unions and employers to make work more interesting, and less menacing to health and personal safety. It cannot be mere coincidence that in Sweden, where job enrichment and plant democracy have had their greatest success, unemployment is practically zero and astute management of their economy protected Swedes even from the worldwide economic crisis of 1973–75. The new government, elected on the fortuitous issue of nuclear safety, has promised to extend even further the social benefits for which Sweden has become celebrated. American employers preserve themselves from Swedish experiments in good part by keeping the industrial reserve army plentifully manned.

Nor is this quite the end of the tale. The hunger of communities and regions for jobs and tax revenues has allowed large corporations to extort an endless assortment of valuable concessions from local and state governments, either as blackmail to keep existing installations or bribes to lure new ones. Few major corporations pay their fair share of property taxes. Propaganda by oil, steel, chemical, and paper industries has noticeably slowed the pace of regulation to protect the environment. Leonard Woodcock, who knows better has allied himself with the major auto companies in seeking to postpone the application of the next wave of auto standards, entirely out of concern for the jobs of his UAW constituents.

By contrast, full employment on a sustained and assured basis (the system can stand a spell of full employment so long as all parties understand that it is temporary) presents an embarrassment to the movers and shapers of American plutocracy. To begin with, full employment is the most efficient agent of equitable income redistribution which is at all politically feasible in the United States. Full employment sucks into the labor force men and women who now struggle on welfare, food stamps, Social Security, and unemployment compensation. It pushes up the wages of low-paid people whose position is scarcely less precarious than that of the unemployed. It is an especial boon to blacks, Hispanics, teen-agers, and women—last hired and first fired in expansion and recession alike. A long spell of full employment would substantially narrow existing wide differentials between the earnings of these groups and those of white males. In a time of layoff and business contraction, affirmative action is a mockery, but when there is full employment the cry for justice is heard more sympathetically by members of a majority whose own security is not threatened.

These repercussions are severe enough to alarm gentlemen in their clubs and boardrooms. The threat, I suspect, is still more grave. For men of property the charm of the 1970s lies in the way economic adversity has cooled the campuses and shoved American politics, already the most conservative in the developed world, still further right; one only has to look at Gerald Ford of all people, after Watergate and the Nixon pardon, and in the middle of a messed-up economy, very nearly winning the Presidential election. This could not have happened without general apprehension and dampened expectations of the efficacy of action by any national administration. As one comedian commented upon the stock-market decline which preceded the election, investors were selling out of deadly fear that one of the candidates would win. Lift the burdens of apprehension and apathy from the pysches of ordinary folk and—who knows?—they might entertain radical thoughts of inviting the rich to share rather more of their capital gains and inheritances.

It goes without saying that it is scarcely respectable for the rich and their mercenaries, lawyers, economists, politicians, public-relations types, and so on, to openly proclaim their affection for unemployment, although among friends they tend to be more candid. One requires a respectable rationale, a convenient theory that combines apparent concern about the sufferings of the unemployed with actual capacity to avoid any action realistically calculated to alter their status.

My colleagues (I am an economist, but I am confessing, not boasting) have risen to the challenge. As their apologetic runs, we can't proceed sensibly toward universal job guarantees, even in the cautious, timid shape of the Humphrey-Hawkins Full Employment Bill, a revival of the 1945 original effort to write a serious job guarantee into law, because of the horrifying menace of more inflation. That menace is among economists embodied in a marvelous constriction interred in the textbooks under the rubric of the Phillips curve.

The provenance of this notion that democratic societies must choose between inflation and unemployment deserves a paragraph. The late A. W. Phillips, a British economist who taught for much of his career in Australia, published in 1958 an article catchily entitled "The Relationship between Unemployment and the Rate of Change in Money Wage Rates in the United Kingdom, 1862–1957." Phillips's data appeared to demonstrate that, as unemployment rose, wages increased less and less rapidly. The man said nothing at all about prices, price inflation, or the manner in which rising wages might or might not be translated into commensurate increases in the cost of living. Nevertheless, his findings were rapidly extended in statements like this typical textbook pronouncement: "Low rates of unemployment tend to be associated with high rates of inflation and, conversely, price stability or low rates of inflation tend to be associated with high rates of unemployment." Triumphant conclusion: "There seems to be a trade-off between employment and the price level."

Economists shifted from Phillips's cautious conclusions about unemployment and wage rates to the words just cited very simply. After all, wages and salaries, including those of executives and other overpriced folk, amount to about 70 percent of business costs. Wherever competition reigns, employers have no choice except to pass along plumper labor costs to their customers in the shape of higher prices. The line of causation is direct: low unemployment stimulates wage demands, higher wages enlarge business costs, and these in turn lead to higher prices. It's an indisputable pity, but if we are to restrain demand inflation, we simply must operate the economy at what an MIT economist, Robert Hall, has recently labeled the "natural" rate of unemployment. A bit hard on those selected to serve their country by losing their jobs, but their patriotic sacrifice is nothing less than a valuable public service.

Let us absolve A. W. Phillips of blame for the intellectual sins committed in his name and look calmly, on its merits, at the Phillips curve in its modern guise. It is to start with an embarrassingly inaccurate explanation of recent stagflation—the malignant combination of persistent inflation and high unemployment. To those untutored in economics, the causes of a good part of current inflation have nothing at all to do with the Phillips curve. Out there in a world mostly beyond American control, OPEC has been busy quintupling petroleum prices, the Russians have been bidding up the cost of food in American supermarkets by vast grain purchases, and the world market for American farm products, temporary fluctuations aside, has been exerting steady upward pressure upon domestic food supplies.

These external shocks initiated an inflationary surge in 1973 and 1974. In spite of the sharpest recession (1974–75) since the 1930s, that inflation continued, somewhat abated in 1976, and gave ominous signs of spurting once more by the end of that year. Here is the real embarrassment for Phillips curve groupies. Their mechanism has simply failed to work. Unemployment has escalated and stuck at the highest recorded levels since the Great Depression. Wages have risen more slowly than the cost of living. Productivity is improving. Nevertheless, prices continue to rise. It has proved perfectly possible to suffer simultaneously from severe inflation and still more severe unemployment and factory underutilization.

As it happens, there is a reasonable explanation at hand for events so baffling to partisans of inflation-unemployment trade-offs. Clearly, inflation is not a simple matter of translation of higher wages into higher prices. Rather, it is an aspect of the distribution and concentration of market power among suppliers and sellers, abroad and here at home, who are in a position, within generous limits, to set their own prices for the goods and services that they sell. In both recession and expansion, sellers with market power have chosen to charge more, even if, as a result, they sell less. Businessmen and respectable mainstream economists who judge full employment to be inflationary are utterly correct. It is only their reasons that are wrong.

Prices rise during both phases of the business cycle because in recession businessmen who enjoy monopoly or quasimonopoly power over their markets push prices upward in order to maintain their profit margins. When better times come, businessmen seize the opportunity to improve their profit margins. As fair example, recall that during 1974 and 1975, two of the auto industry's worst years since the 1950s, General Motors and its amiable rivals marked up auto sticker charges an average of $1,000 per car, even though the customers were reluctant to buy. The rarer the customers, the larger the profit that needed to be attached to the selling price of each unit. Now that sales are behaving more wholesomely, prices continue to rise. Why not get more when the customers are willing to pay more? As in autos, so in steel, aluminum, and a long list of other industries in which one, two, three, or four dominant corporations set prices and conduct orderly markets unblemished by unseemly price rivalry. The manufacturers have company. In the delivery of health services, a pleasant cartel of health insurers, hospitals, medical societies, and complaisant federal authorities has propelled medical costs higher at twice the pace of general inflation. The television monopolies have raised the charges for network time, and the university professors who lecture and consult have done rather better than the inflation rate. Lawyers have long judged advertising and price competition two serious breaches of legal ethics. Food prices rise partly because of the widening profit margins of food processors.

WORSE THAN THE DISEASE

The diagnosis dictates the choice of remedies. One is as old as the 1890 Sherman Antitrust Act: break up the monopolies and end price-fixing in restraint of trade. The remaining true believers in antitrust would cheerfully fragment the large corporations, which, either by themselves or in combination with one or two peers, dominate many markets. Alas, the nonprogress of former Sen. Philip Hart's oil divestiture bill in the last Congress and its dim prospects in the new one are the latest evidence of the political futility of this tactic. Although no technical reasons justify the size of Exxon or General Motors, the public is yet to be persuaded that small is beautiful.

The only feasible alternative is control of key prices and profit margins in the very large proportion of the economy where old-fashioned competition is celebrated only by banquet speeches. Such controls were imposed during World War II and the Korean War. It is a historical curiosity that John Kenneth Galbraith, who was a price administrator, and Richard Nixon, who briefly served as a compliance attorney, drew diametrically opposite conclusions from their respective experience. Galbraith continues to believe that price control is both necessary and feasible. Nixon preached the wickedness of interference with private markets, but nevertheless suddenly froze prices August 15, 1971, and followed the ninety-day freeze with a year or so of more flexible but astonishingly successful wage- and price-hike limitations. As the Nixon experience suggests, wage controls generally accompany price controls. There recently has been the rub. The wage controls in 1972 and 1973 were considerably more effective than the price controls, for two excellent reasons. The Nixon controllers, probusiness to a man, were far more eager to check union demands than to interfere with business earnings, and employers gladly cooperated with Washington to police the wage-rise limits. Seldom did patriotism pay better.

The fact is that in the United States (England is, of course, quite a different matter) mandatory price controls over concentrated industries and the health sector, together with voluntary wage guidelines, would probably work very well for a time. American unions are, after all, both weak and conservative. The path to full employment without inflation is impassible without a firm incomes policy and the statutory authorization of price controls administered by individuals who believe in what they are doing.

Does the political will to shape a national full employment policy exist? It is difficult to answer yes to that question. Last year full employment struck a Democratic Congress as sufficiently radical to bury Humphrey-Hawkins. For, as has been noted, full employment means diminishing long-standing inequalities of income, wealth, and power; inviting the black, brown, young, and female to the American celebration; and controlling the rapacity of doctors, lawyers, giant corporations, and other reputable extortionists. After full employment who will iron Russell Long's shirts, clean up after the Lutèce diners, and do the world's dirty work? Settle the job issue once and for all, and even American unions will begin to entertain dangerous thoughts about job redesign, codetermination, and similarly radical Swedish and German nonsense.

The fine Christian (and occasionally Jewish) men whom the good Lord has placed in the seats of authority and the halls of the mighty know that there are far worse phenomena than unemployment. One of them is full employment.

Jobs were the most frequently reiterated of Carter's campaign themes and the President's squeak to victory required essential aid from blacks, Chicanos in Texas, the AFL-CIO, and aggrieved New Yorkers persuaded that Ford, not the *Daily News* headline writer (a great man), had actually told their city to drop dead. The ingratitude of Presidents is as notorious as that of princes, so there is no certainty that the new Chief Executive will automatically move toward genuine full employment, as distinguished from the moderate stimulation of a quick tax cut. Carter cautiously, reluctantly, and belatedly endorsed Humphrey-Hawkins, in the wake of his ethnic-purity blunder. He repeatedly emphasized his preference for job creation in the private sector and his desire to avoid expanding the weight of federal activity. At that famous luncheon at 21 for Henry Ford II and other corporate heavyweights, Carter promised that he would study the tax code a year or so before making recommendations for revision to Congress—the same tax code that he had described before less affluent audiences as a disgrace to civilization.

Nevertheless, there is some reason to believe that Carter will pursue more expansionary tax and spending policies than did his predecessor. Even businessmen who mostly voted for Ford are concerned about the continued sluggishness of the economy. When retail sales falter, profits are threatened and the long-awaited boom in investment never occurs. It appears that the "pause," "lull," or just plain old recession has gone further and lasted longer than is needed to serve the laudable purposes which unemployment serves.

A genuine commitment to sustained full employment demands a good deal more than a temporary tax cut or a brief loosening of the federal purse strings. The United States will move toward a coherent high-employment economy at the same time as it becomes politically feasible to diminish the power of great wealth and reduce inequalities of income and wealth.

The fate of George McGovern in 1972 and Fred Harris in 1976, two brave souls who rose to the perils of open discussion of such political dynamite, makes it depressingly plain that Americans continue to admire the people and institutions that make life harder for them than it need be. As Prof. Walter Burnham of MIT pointed out last year, the missing 45 percent of the American electorate who don't turn up on Election Day in Europe vote Labor, Socialist, or Communist.

All my life my country has suffered from the absence of a significant political Left. As I trudge through middle age toward the golden years of senior citizenship, I glimpse even less hope of the emergence of a democratic socialist party than I did during the late 1930s and early 1940s when, at least in Manhattan, revolution was in the air.

Until a credible left rises in the United States, unemployment will be a little higher when the Republicans are in the White House, a little lower when the Democrats take their turn. Genuine full employment, decent jobs at decent wages for every man, woman, and youth interested in working, has been a myth, is a myth, and will stay a myth so long as every four years voters choose between one party minimally to the right of dead center and a second minimally to the left.

Rationality, Expectations and Functional Finance

DAVID C. COLANDER

David Colander is a professor of economics at the University of Miami. Together with
Abba Lerner, he has consistently argued that Keynesian economics follows directly
from microeconomic analysis. This microeconomic view of Keynesian economics
has led the two of them to propose a market anti-inflation plan and to Colander's
alternative interpretation of Keynesian economic theory in a rational expectations
framework.

Imagine yourself in a Buck Rogers interplanetary adventure, looking at a highway in a City of Tomorrow. The highway is wide and straight, and its edges are
turned up so that it is almost impossible for a car to run off the road. What
appears to be a runaway car is speeding along the road and veering off to one
side. As it approaches the rising edge of the highway, its front wheels are turned
so that it gets back onto the road and goes off at an angle, making for the other
side, where the wheels are turned again. This happens many times, the car
zigzagging but keeping on the highway until it is out of sight. You are wondering
how long it will take for it to crash when another car appears which behaves in
the same fashion. When it comes near you it stops with a jerk. A door is opened,
and an occupant asks whether you would like a lift. You look into the car,
and before you can control yourself, you cry out, "Why there's no steering
wheel. . . ."

A CHALLENGE TO KEYNESIANISM

When Abba Lerner first wrote this parable in 1951, he ended it with the question, "Well, want a ride?" His rational expectations were that everyone would
answer, emphatically, "No!" In the 1950s and 1960s, his expectations were
fulfilled, albeit belatedly, as economists accepted Keynesian economics, and
almost everyone realized the need for government stabilization. The 1960s style
monetarist theory modified, but did not fundamentally alter, Lerner's parable;
within the Keynesian-monetarist reconciliation, there remained a role for active
government stabilization policy, limited mainly by our lack of knowledge.

Today, however, more and more economists are changing their views, and
answering "Yes." to Lerner's question: A car without a steering wheel may not
be ideal, but it may be better than one with a steering wheel when the driver is
either blind or myopic. And with these views gaining more credibility and
acceptance, Lerner's three rules of functional finance are being questioned and
criticized:

Reprinted with permission from *Essays in Post-Keynesian Inflation*, eds. James Gapinski and Charles
Rockwood, Copyright 1979, Ballinger Publishing Company, pp. 197–98, 203–207, 209–11.

1. Rather than a rule for the government to maintain a reasonable level of spending, the call is for a balanced budget.

2. Rather than maintaining a rate of interest which induces an optimal amount of investment, the government is now being advised to avoid affecting the rate of interest.

3. Rather than printing money which is needed to carry out the first two rules, the government is now advised to set a rule for money supply growth which would take precedent over them.

These new policy recommendations are definitely not Keynesian, or even modifications of Keynesian policies; in fact, the new "rules" are distinctly classical, which means that we have come full circle in our thinking. The long run has arrived.

The reason for the changing views is inflation's persistence in the past five years. Keynesian theory has been unable to cope with the problem, and government authorities have been forced to reexamine their policies. The new challenge to Keynesian policies has its origins in the monetarists' position, but has far stronger implications. It is not only argued that Keynesian theory cannot handle inflation, but also that Keynesian policies are themselves the cause of inflation; only by discarding Keynesian policies will we be able to control inflation. This influential challenge is made in the name of "rational expectations," and is directed at the heart of Lerner's principles of functional finance.

POLICY IMPLICATIONS OF THE RATIONAL EXPECTATIONS HYPOTHESIS (REH)

Significant interest in the REH only developed with its application to macroeconomic policy, and with the suggestion that it greatly modified or eliminated government's role in the stablization process. Two quite distinct hypotheses have been advanced. William Fellner produced a dramatic reconstruction of macroeconomics organized around a game theoretic rational expectations argument. He argued that wages and prices no longer respond to restrictions in demand because individuals have been conditioned to believe—through thirty years of commitment to full employment—that the government will not maintain its resolve in restricting demand to control inflation. In Fellner's view, the government's full employment guarantee has undermined its ability to control the price level. Consequently, the government is faced today with an almost intractable problem: How to convince individuals that it is committed to price stability. This component of the REH argument is, in my opinion, extremely powerful, and demonstrates the insufficiency of functional finance to cope with inflation.

However, a second group of REH supporters has made much broader claims. In their view, the REH not only makes price stability maintenance impossible, but it also makes functional finance ineffective as a short-run stabilization tool. These stronger claims fall into three categories:

1. REH negates monetary policy's role in the short run.

2. REH implies that a fixed monetary rule is preferable to discretionary policy.

3. REH implies that fiscal policy will have no effect and therefore the government should balance the budget.

While the claims are often not put so directly, these underlying themes are discernible in the literature.

The initial focus of the debate concerned Category 1, and considered the question of whether monetary policy can have any short run effect in an economy characterized by rational expectations and a natural rate of unemployment as depicted by Edmund Phelps and Milton Friedman. Such an economy would have a short-run Phillips curve tradeoff, but the long-run or steady state Phillips curve would be vertical. In a major contribution to the debate, Sargent and Wallace demonstrated that an adaptive expectations hypothesis led to a short-run role for monetary policy, while a rational expectations hypothesis led to no short-run role. In developing this model, similar to many others in the literature, they used an aggregate supply specification suggested by Lucas which required any effect on real output to be achieved through an unexpected movement in the price level. This assumption was crucial to their conclusions because, from this assumption, it followed that in order for the monetary authority to affect real output, it must induce an unexpected movement in the price level. Rational expectations eliminated that possibility by assumption and thus removed the potential role for monetary policy.

In evaluating the relevance of their conclusion to functional finance, it is useful to reinterpret the question they posed in the following manner: Can the government cause an economy to deviate from the natural rate, which by assumption is given exogenously? I think all would agree that the answer to that question is no. However, that question is fundamentally different from the one implicitly posed by Lerner's parable in which the "natural rate" or the "equilibrium rate of unemployment" in any particular short run fluctuated. Cast into a modern framework, Lerner's question could be rephrased in the following manner: Is it possible for the government to reduce the loss function associated with the variance in the short run natural rate?

Notice that the difference in the two stories is in their interpretation of the short run. For Sargent and Wallace, the short run is a transition phase to a long-run steady-state equilibrium; the short run in which monetary policy can be effective, and which I argue Keynesian economics meant (or should have meant) is in a specific subperiod of a steady-state equilibrium in which random disturbances occur. In the first case the road is straight and the policymakers are trying to steer off the road—deviate from the natural rate—whereas in the second, the road is curved and the policymakers are attempting to stay on the road—optimally adjusting to the temporary random shocks.

In both cases, the policy prescriptions follow from the specification of supply conditions and not from the assumption of REH. In the Sargent and Wallace world, even if monetary policies could have a short-run effect, it would do little good because expectations would finally adapt. In my suggested example, supply was constantly shifting and the relevant question was how best to adjust to the temporary shocks that hit the system—through government action or through private action. If the strong REH claim is to hold, REH must imply that it is not optimal for the government to adjust; the private sector would eliminate all possible gains. This, I suggest, does not follow because of the central difference between possibilities for rents and possibilities for profits within the REH. Government cannot make a profit, but since there is no market for government services, there is no way of knowing whether the government can make a potential rent in equilibrium. Whether or not it can depends on the government's cost of stabilization relative to the private sector's cost of stabilization. If the adjustment can best be achieved through government action, then government action is optimal even in a strong REH Model.

The following example from the *General Theory* provides a reason why the government might be able to achieve stabilization in a less costly manner through flexible monetary policy than the private sector could through relative price and wage adjustment:

> . . . while a flexible wage policy and a flexible money policy come, analytically, to the same thing, in as much as they are alternative means of changing the quantity of money in terms of wage-units, in other respects there is, of course, a world of difference between them. Let me briefly recall to the reader's mind (an) outstanding consideration.
>
> Except in a socialized community where wage policy is settled by decree, there is no means of securing uniform wage reduction for every class of labour. The result can only be brought about by a series of gradual, irregular changes, justifiable on no criterion of social justice or economic expediency. . . . A change in the quantity of money, on the other hand, is already within the power of most governments by open-market policy or analogous measures. Having regard to human nature and our institutions, it can only be a foolish person who would prefer a flexible wage policy to a flexible money policy, unless he can point to advantages from the former which are not obtainable from the latter.

Thus, within the Keynesian paradigm, an activist monetary policy of the government may be totally consistent with rational expectations, because it is rationally expected that the government is the correct agent to undertake the stabilizing role, and it is merely accomplishing a result which the free market would have achieved in a more costly fashion.

Keynes's discussion of both money wages and prices has a very modern flavor to it, and is suggestive of the implicit contract literature that has developed to explain wage and price rigidity. Interpreted in modern terminology, Keynes's suggestion is that the nature of the optimal contingency contract is such that when uniform changes in real wages and real prices are needed, it is less costly to achieve that desired result through government action than by initially writing it into the contingency contract or by renegotiating their contract. Changing the money supply is not meant to fool anyone.

Individuals will rationally expect that numerous contingencies might occur and will include them in their contract; however, negotiating involved contingent contracts for events that will most likely never occur is a costly prospect. Thus individuals negotiate the contract in money terms with the implicit understanding that the monetary authorities will react optimally to contingencies, pushing the price level up or down as the need arises. Thus an activist monetary policy is a necessary part of the contract, and is merely a public good supplied for private individuals by the government.

As an example, consider a sudden exogenous foreign supply shock which has the real effect of lowering domestic income by two percent on the average. Since contracts did not specify this contingency, the optimal monetary policy is to accommodate this higher price, reducing everyone's income by inflation, and allowing individual adjustments to this general change to take place by private recontracting.

If the above argument is accepted, the answer to whether there is a short-run role for monetary stabilization within a strong REH depends on two conditions: (1) Does the short-run equilibrium rate of unemployment and short-run price level shift from period to period? (2) If it does, do the monetary authorities have a comparative advantage in achieving the desired result.

A similar argument can be made concerning the possibility of short run fiscal policy. The question is again one of comparative costs. If government can adjust its revenues and expenditures with a lower cost of adjustment than can the private sector, then optimally they should stabilize in this manner; if they cannot, then they should not.

REDESIGNING THE WHEEL

Despite the above arguments, Lerner's rules of functional finance do not escape the REH critique; the parable of the steering wheel misses an important point. The steering wheel gives the economy horizontal (employment) control but does not provide vertical (price stability) control. Under functional finance, full employment and a stable price level seem to be incompatible, and as the REH suggests, a likely reason is structural changes induced by functional finance. In today's world, expectations of government accommodation of specific price and wage setting policies have become built into expectations so that the threat of long-term unemployment consequences of any particular decision is lessened. Therefore the fear of unemployment no longer has a significant dampening effect on prices or wages.

The policy question is: What to do? The rational expectationalists propose that the government should abandon all functional finance rules; above I argued that this conclusion does not follow. Instead of retreating to classical economics, forgetting the experience of the last thirty years, we should recognize both the insights and the flaws of the old rules and modify, but not discard, them. This entails supplementing the three rules of functional finance with a fourth rule:

4. The government must establish policies which stabilize the price level and coordinate both the money supply rule and the aggregate total spending rule with this stable price level.

With this additional rule the structural effects of functional finance on price stability will be incorporated into the policy, and the new policies will be stablizing for both employment and the price level. To many this fourth rule raises the specter of price control, much as functional finance first raised fears of impending socialism. My fears are of a different kind. I fear that unless economists find a way to implement Rule 4, the market economy is endangered. Thus the issue is not controls versus the market. The issue is how to design controls so that they are compatible with the market.

There are two potential economic methods by which this price stability control can be implemented. One method is to incorporate price stability control directly into the existing stabilization tools. To suggest how this might be accomplished, consider the unemployment insurance program. Initially the program was designed to achieve both humanitarian and functional finance goals. However, its design made the price and wage level more rigid and also increased the average level of unemployment in the long-run, shifting the short-run Phillips curve upward. The reasons is as follows: Unemployment insurance acts as a subsidy for individuals who are fully unemployed. In designing long run contracts, the firm and workers will take that subsidy into account, choosing a contract with a higher probability of layoff and less wage flexibility than it would otherwise have. Thus a group of workers who met a downturn in demand by reducing wages by 5 percent, or by reducing everyone's hours of work by 5 percent, would receive no subsidy, whereas workers who had a contract which included potential layoffs would receive a higher expected income inclusive of the insurance program.

Suppose that instead of our present system, a similar program of wage rate insurance were instituted, under which workers who accepted a lower wage rate in response to a decrease in aggregate demand would be subsidized. Such a wage rate insurance plan would accomplish the identical stabilization effect as would unemployment insurance, but it would decrease wage rates paid by the firm, encouraging the employment of additional workers along with holding wage rate insurance plan would accomplish the identical stabilization effect as impractical, but there are other methods of accomplishing the desired result. The concept is what is important. Functional finance policies must be designed with their effects on price stabilization in mind.

However, even if the tools were not redesigned, there is an alternative method of implementing Rule 4. It would be done directly under the Market Anti-inflation Plan.* Under MAP, the price level is determined by law, and the money supply aggregate demand, and expectations of inflation are adjusted to that price level. Individuals do not have to worry about how to rationally predict the price level; the government has set it by a direct rule.

Theoretically, implementing Rule 4 is possible. The real problems are technical and practical difficulties, and I can think of no better statement about those problems than the one Abba Lerner wrote in 1951 when he was commenting on the difficulties of implementing the first three rules of functional finance:

> . . . these problems . . . will make life difficult for the administrators of the economy. . . . But there is no reason for supposing that life will be any more difficult than in any other financial system which does not give the society the benefits of Functional Finance. . . . Functional Finance will not inaugurate a problemless world. Life will not be effortless. There will still be struggles and conflicts and difficulties and defeats. . . . But it is an important step forward.

---

*EDITOR'S NOTE: MAP is fully explained in Abba Lerner and David C. Colander, *MAP: A Market Anti-Inflation Plan* (New York: Harcourt Brace Jovanovich, Inc., 1980). See also *Solutions to Inflation*, ed. David C. Colander (New York: Harcourt Brace Jovanovich, Inc., 1979).

The Monetarist Controversy, or Should We Forsake Stabilization Policies?

FRANCO MODIGLIANI

Franco Modigliani is a professor of economics at the Massachusetts Institute of Technology and is one of the foremost macroeconomists today. He and his many former students are an influential force in both modern macroeconomic theory and macroeconomic modeling. He was elected president of the American Economic Association in 1977 and the following is excerpted from his presidential address.

In recent years and especially since the onset of the current depression, the economics profession and the lay public have heard a great deal about the sharp conflict between "monetarists and Keynesians" or between "monetarists and fiscalists." The difference between the two "schools" is generally held to center on whether the money supply or fiscal variables are the major determinants of aggregate economic activity, and hence the most appropriate tool of stabilization policies.

My central theme is that this view is quite far from the truth, and that the issues involved are of far greater practical import. There are in reality no serious analytical disagreements between leading monetarists and leading non-monetarists. Milton Friedman was once quoted as saying, "We are all Keynesians, now,", and I am quite prepared to reciprocate that "we are all monetarists"—if by monetarism is meant assigning to the stock of money a major role in determining output and prices. Indeed, the list of those who have long been monetarists in this sense is quite extensive, including among others John Maynard Keynes as well as myself, as is attested by my 1944 and 1963 articles.

In reality the distinguishing feature of the monetarist school and the real issues of disagreement with nonmonetarists is not monetarism, but rather the role that should probably be assigned to stabilization policies. Nonmonetarists accept what I regard to be the fundamental practical message of *The General Theory:* that a private enterprise economy using an intangible money *needs* to be stabilized, *can* be stabilized, and therefore *should* be stabilized by appropriate monetary and fiscal policies. Monetarists by contrast take the view that there is no serious need to stabilize the economy; that even if there were a need, it could not be done, for stabilization policies would be more likely to increase than to decrease instability; and, at least some monetarists would, I believe, go so far as to hold that, even in the unlikely event that stabilization policies could on balance prove beneficial, the government should not be trusted with the necessary power.

I propose first to review the main arguments bearing on the *need* for

Extracted from Franco Modigliani, "The Monetarist Controversy, or Should We Forsake Stabilization Policies?" *American Economic Review*, 69 (March 1977), 1–8, 12, 14, 15, 17, 18.

stabilization policies, that is, on the likely extent of instability in the absence of such policies, and then to examine the issue of the supposed destabilizing effect of pursuing stabilization policies.

THE KEYNESIAN CASE FOR STABILIZATION POLICIES

The General Theory

Keynes' novel conclusion about the need for stabilization policies, as was brought out by the early interpreters of *The General Theory* (for example, John Hicks, the author, 1944), resulted from the interaction of a basic contribution to traditional monetary theory—liquidity preference—and an unorthodox hypothesis about the working of the labor market—complete downward rigidity of wages.

Because of liquidity preference, a change in aggregate demand, which may be broadly defined as any event that results in a change in the market clearing or equilibrium rate of interest, will produce a corresponding change in the real demand for money or velocity of circulation, and hence in the real stock of money needed at full employment. As long as wages are perfectly flexible, even with a constant nominal supply, full employment could and would be maintained by a change of wages and prices as needed to produce the required change in the real money supply—though even in this case, stability of the price level would require a countercyclical monetary policy. But, under the Keynesian wage assumption the classical adjustment through prices can occur only in the case of an increased demand. In the case of a decline, instead, wage rigidity prevents the necessary increase in the real money supply and the concomitant required fall in interest rates. Hence, if the nominal money supply is constant, the initial equilibrium must give way to a new stable one, characterized by lower output and by an involuntary reduction in employment, so labeled because it does not result from a shift in notional demand and supply schedules in terms of real wages, but only from an insufficient real money supply. The nature of this equilibrium is elegantly captured by the Hicksian *IS-LM* paradigm, which to our generation of economists has become almost as familiar as the demand-supply pardigm was to earlier ones.

This analysis implied that a fixed money supply far from insuring approximate stability of prices and output, as held by the traditional view, would result in a rather unstable economy, alternating between periods of protracted unemployment and stagnation, and bursts of inflation. The extent of downward instability would depend in part on the size of the exogenous shocks to demand and in part on the strength of what may be called the Hicksian mechanism. By this I mean the extent to which a shift in *IS*, through its interaction with *LM*, results in some decline in interest rates and thus in a change in income which is smaller than the original shift. The stabilizng power of this mechanism is controlled by various parameters of the system. In particular, the economy will be more unstable the greater the interest elasticity of demand for money, and the smaller the interest responsiveness of aggregate demand. Finally, a large multiplier is also destabilizing in that it implies a larger shift in *IS* for a given shock.

However, the instability could be readily counteracted by appropriate stabilization policies. Monetary policy could change the nominal supply of money so as to *accommodate* the change in real demand resulting from shocks in aggregate demand. Fiscal policy, through expenditure and taxes, could *offset* these shocks, making full employment consistent with the initial nominal money stock. In general, both monetary and fiscal policies could be used in combination. But because of a perceived uncertainty in the response of demand to changes' in interest rates, and because changes in interest rates through monetary policy could meet difficulties and substantial delays related to expectations (so-called liquidity traps), fiscal policy was regarded as having some advantages.

The Early Keynesians

The early disciples of the new Keynesian gospel, still haunted by memories of the Great Depression, frequently tended to outdo Keynes' pessimism about potential instability. Concern with liquidity traps fostered the view that the demand for money was highly interest elastic; failure to distinguish between the short- and long-run marginal propensity to save led to overestimating the long-run saving rate, thereby fostering concern with stagnation, and to underestimating the short-run propensity, thereby exaggerating the short-run multiplier. Interest rates were supposed to affect, at best, the demand for long-lived fixed investments, and the interest elasticity was deemed to be low. Thus, shocks were believed to produce a large response. Finally, investment demand was seen as capriciously controlled by "animal spirits," thus providing an important source of shocks. All this justified calling for very active stabilization policies. Furthermore, since the very circumstances which produce a large response to demand shocks also produce a large response to *fiscal* and a small response to *monetary* actions, there was a tendency to focus on fiscal policy as the main tool to keep the economy at near full employment.

The Phillips Curve

In the two decades following *The General Theory*, there were a number of developments of the Keynesian system including dynamization of the model, the stress on taxes versus expenditures and the balanced budget multiplier, and the first attempts at estimating the critical parameters through econometric techniques and models. But for present purposes, the most important one was the uncovering of a "stable" statistical relation between the rate of change of wages and the rate of unemployment, which has since come to be known as the Phillips curve. This relation, and its generalization by Richard Lipsey to allow for the effect of recent inflation, won wide acceptance even before an analytical underpinning could be provided for it, in part because it could account for the "puzzling" experience of 1954 and 1958, when wages kept rising despite the substantial rise in unemployment. It also served to dispose of the rather sterile "cost push"—"demand pull" controversy.

In the following years, a good deal of attention went into developing theoretical foundations for the Phillips curve, in particular along the lines of search models (for example, Edmund Phelps et al.). This approach served to shed a new light on the nature of unemployment by tracing it in the first place to labor turnover and search time rather than to lack of jobs as such: in a sense unemployment is all frictional—at least in developed countries. At the same time it clarified how the availability of more jobs tends to reduce unemployment by increasing vacancies and thus reducing search time.

Acceptance of the Phillips curve relation implied some significant changes in the Keynesian framework which partly escaped notice until the subsequent monetarists' attacks. Since the rate of change of wages decreased smoothly with the rate of unemployment, there was no longer a unique Full Employment but rather a whole family of possible equilibrium rates, each associated with a different rate of inflation (and requiring, presumably, a different long-run growth of money). It also impaired the notion of a stable underemployment equilibrium. A fall in demand could still cause an initial rise in unemployment but this rise, by reducing the growth of wages, would eventually raise the real money supply, tending to return unemployment to the equilibrium rate consistent with the given long-run growth of money.

But at the practical level it did not lessen the case for counteracting lasting demand disturbances through stabilization policies rather than by relying on the slow process of wage adjustment to do the job, at the cost of protracted unemployment and instability of prices. Indeed, the realm of stabilization policies appeared to expand in the sense that the stabilization authority had the power of choosing the unemployment rate around which employment was to be stabilized, though it then had to accept the associated inflation. Finally, the dependence of wage changes also on past inflation forced recognition of a distinction between the short- and the long-run Phillips curve, the latter exhibiting the long-run equilibrium rate of inflation implied by a *maintained* unemployment rate. The fact that the long-run tradeoff between unemployment and inflation was necessarily less favorable than the short-run one, opened up new vistas of "enjoy-it-now, pay-later" policies, and even resulted in an entertaining literature on the political business cycle and how to stay in the saddle by riding the Phillips curve (see for example, Ray Fair, William Nordhaus).

THE MONETARISTS' ATTACK

The Stabilizing Power of the Hicksian Mechanism

The monetarists' attack on Keynesianism was directed from the very beginning not at the Keynesian framework as such, but at whether it really implied a need for stabilization. It rested on a radically different empirical assessment of the value of the parameters controlling the stabilizing power of the Hicksian mechanism and of the magnitude and duration of response to shocks, given a stable money supply. And this different assessment in turn was felt to justify a radical downgrading of the *practical relevance* of the Keynesian framework as distinguished from its *analytical validity*.

Liquidity preference was a fine contribution to monetary theory but in practice the responsiveness of the demand for money, and hence of velocity, to interest rates, far from being unmanageably large, was so small that according to a well-known paper by Milton Friedman (1969), it could not even be detected empirically. On the other hand, the effect of interest rates on aggregate demand was large and by no means limited to the traditional fixed investments but quite pervasive. The difficulty of detecting it empirically resulted from focusing on a narrow range of measured market rates and from the fact that while the aggregate could be counted on to respond, the response of individual components might not be stable. Finally, Friedman's celebrated contribution to the theory of the consumption function (1957) (and my own work on the life cycle hypothesis with Richard Brumberg and others, reviewd by the author, 1975) implied a very high short-run marginal propensity to save in response to transient disturbances to income and hence a small short-run multiplier.

All this justified the conclusion that (i) though demand shocks might qualitatively work along the lines described by Keynes, quantitatively the Hicks mechanism is so strong that their impact would be *small* and *transient*, provided the stock of money was kept on a steady growth path; (ii) fiscal policy actions, like other demand shocks, would have *minor* and *transitory* effects on demand, while changes in money would produce *large* and *permanent* effects on money income; and, therefore, (iii) the observed instability of the economy, which was anyway proving moderate as the postwar period unfolded, was most likely the result of the unstable growth of money, be it due to misguided endeavors to stabilize income or to the pursuit of other targets, which were either irrelevant or, in the case of balance of payments goals, should have been made irrelevant by abandoning fixed exchanges.

The Demise of Wage Rigidity and the Vertical Phillips Curve

But the most serious challenge came in Friedman's 1968 Presidential Address, building on ideas independently put forth also by Phelps (1968). Its basic message was that, despite appearances, wages were in reality perfectly flexible and there was accordingly *no* involuntary unemployment. The evidence to the contrary, including the Phillips curve, was but a statistical illusion resulting from failure to differentiate between price changes and *unexpected* price changes.

Friedman starts out by reviving the Keynesian notion that, at any point of time, there exists a unique full-employment rate which he labels the "natural rate." An unanticipated fall in demand in Friedman's competitive world leads firms to reduce prices and also output and employment along the short-run marginal cost curve—unless the nominal wage declines together with prices. But workers, failing to judge correctly the current and prospective fall in prices, misinterpret the reduction of nominal wages as a cut in *real* wages. Hence, assuming a positively sloped supply function, they reduce the supply of labor. As a result, the effective real wage rises to the point where the resulting decline in the demand for labor matches the reduced supply. Thus, output falls not because of the decline in demand, but because of the entirely voluntary reduction in the supply of labor, in response to erroneous perceptions. Furthermore, the fall in employment can only be temporary, as expectations must soon catch up with the facts, at least in the absence of new shocks. The very same mechanism works in the case of an increase in demand, so that the responsiveness of wages and prices is the same on either side of the natural rate.

The upshot is that Friedman's model also implies a Phillips-type relation between inflation, employment or unemployment, and past inflation—provided the latter variable is interpreted as a reasonable proxy for expected inflation. But it turns the standard explanation on its head: instead of (excess) employment causing inflation, it is (the unexpected component of) the rate of inflation that causes excess employment.

One very basic implication of Friedman's model is that the coefficient of price expectations should be precisely unity. This specification implies that whatever the shape of the short-run Phillips curve—a shape determined by the relation between expected and actual price changes, and by the elasticity of labor supply with respect to the perceived real wage—the long-run curve *must be vertical*.

Friedman's novel twist provided a fresh prop for the claim that stabilization policies are not really needed, for, with wages flexible, except possibly for transient distortions, the Hicksian mechanism receives powerful reinforcement from changes in the real money supply. Similarly, the fact that full employment was a razor edge provided new support for the claim that stabilization policies were bound to prove destabilizing.

The Macro Rational Expectations Revolution

But the death blow to the already badly battered Keynesian position was to come only shortly thereafter by incorporating into Friedman's model the so-called rational expectation hypothesis, or *REH*. Put very roughly, this hypothesis, originally due to John Muth, states that rational economic agents will endeavor to form expectations of relevant future variables by making the most efficient use of all information provided by past history. It is a fundamental and fruitful contribution that has already found many important applications, for example, in connection with speculative markets, and as a basis for some thoughtful criticism by Robert Lucas (1976) of certain features of econometric models. What I am concerned with here is only its application to macro-economics, or *MREH*, associated with such authors as Lucas (1972), Thomas Sargent (1976), and Sargent and Neil Wallace (1976).

The basic ingredient of *MREH* is the postulate that the workers of Friedman's model hold rational expectations, which turns out to have a number of remarkable implications: (i) errors of price expectations, which are the only source of departure from the natural state, cannot be avoided but they can only be short-lived and random. In particular, there cannot be persistent unemployment above the natural rate for this would imply high serial correlation between the successive errors of expectation, which is inconsistent with rational expectations; (ii) any attempts to stabilize the economy by mans of stated monetary or fiscal rules are bound to be totally ineffective because their effect will be fully discounted in rational expectations; (iii) nor can the government successfully pursue *ad hoc* measures to offset shocks. The private sector is already taking care of any anticipated shock; therefore government policy could conceivably help only if the government information was better than that of the public, which is impossible, by the very definition of rational expectations. Under these conditons, *ad hoc* stabilization policies are most likely to produce instead further destabilizing shocks.

These are clearly remarkable conclusions, and a major *re*discovery—for it had all been said 40 years ago by Keynes in a well-known passage of *The General Theory:*

> If, indeed, labour were always in a position to take action (and were to do so), whenever there was less than full employment, to reduce its money demands by concerted action to whatever point was required to make money so abundant relatively to the wage-unit that the rate of interest would fall to a level compatible with full employment, we should, in effect, have monetary management by the Trade Unions, aimed at full employment, instead of by the banking systems.
>
> [p. 267]

The only novelty is that *MREH* replaces Keynes' opening "if" with a "since."

If one accepts this little amendment, the case against stabilization policies is complete. The economy is inherently pretty stable—except possibly for the effect of government messing around. And to the extent that there is a small residual instability, it is beyond the power of human beings, let alone the government, to alleviate it.

HOW VALID IS THE MONETARIST CASE?

The Monetarist Model of Wage Price Behavior

In setting out the counterattack it is convenient to start with the monetarists' model of price and wage behavior. Here one must distinguish between the model as such and a specific implication of that model, namely that the long-run Phillips curve is vertical, or, in substance, that, in the long run, money is neutral. That conclusion, by now, does not meet serious objection from nonmonetarists, at least as a first approximation.

But the proposition that other things equal, and given time enough, the economy will eventually adjust to any indefinitely maintained stock of money, or *n*th derivative thereof, can be derived from a variety of models and, in any event, is of very little practical relevance, as I will argue below. What is unacceptable, because inconsistent with both micro and macro evidence, is the specific monetarist model set out above and its implication that all unemployment is a voluntary, fleeting response to transitory misperceptions.

One may usefully begin with a criticism of the Macro Rational Expectations model and why Keynes' "if" should not be replaced by "since." At the logical level, Benjamin Friedman has called attention to the omission from *MREH* of an explicit learning model, and has suggested that, as a result, it can only be interpreted as a description not of short-run but of long-run equilibrium in which no agent would wish to recontract. But then the implications of *MREH* are clearly far from startling, and their policy relevance is almost nil. At the institutional level, Stanely Fischer has shown that the mere recognition of long-term contracts is sufficient to generate wage rigidity and a substantial scope for stabilization policies. But the most glaring flaw of *MREH* is its inconsistency with the evidence: if it were valid, deviations of unemployment from the natural rate would be small and transitory—in which case *The General Theory* would not have been written and neither would this paper. Sargent (1976) has attempted to remedy this fatal flaw by hypothesizing that the persistent and large fluctuations in unemployment reflect merely corresponding swings in the natural rate itself. In other words, what happened to the United

States in the 1930's was a severe attack of contagious laziness! I can only say that, despite Sargent's ingenuity, neither I nor, I expect, most others at least of the nonmonetarists' persuasion are quite ready yet to turn over the field of economic fluctuations to the social psychologist!

Equally serious objections apply to Friedman's modeling of the commodity market as a perfectly competitive one—so that the real wage rate is continuously equated to the *short-run* marginal product of labor—and to his treatment of labor as a homogenous commodity traded in an auction market, so that, at the going wage, there never is any excess demand by firms or excess supply by workers. The inadequacies of this model as a useful formalization of present day Western economies are so numerous that only a few of the major ones can be mentioned here.

Friedman's view of unemployment as a voluntary reduction in labor supply could at best provide an explanation of variations in labor force—and then only under the questionable assumption that the supply function has a significantly positive slope—but cannot readily account for changes in unemployment. Furthermore, it cannot be reconciled with the well-known fact that *rising* unemployment is accompanied by a fall, not by a *rise* in quits, nor with the role played by temporary layoffs to which Martin Feldstein has recently called attention. Again, his competitive model of the commodity market, accepted also in *The General Theory*, implies that changes in real wages, adjusted for long-run productivity trend, should be significantly negatively correlated with cyclical changes in employment and output and with changes in money wages. But as early as 1938, John Dunlop showed that this conclusion was rejected by some eighty years of British experience and his results have received some support in more recent tests of Ronald Bodkin for the United States and Canada. Similar tests of my own, using quarterly data, provide striking confirmation that for the last two decades from the end of the Korean War until 1973, the association of trend adjusted real compensation of the private nonfarm sector with either employment or the change in nominal compensation is prevailingly positive and very significantly so.

This evidence can, instead, be accounted for by the oligopolistic pricing model—according to which price is determined by *long-run* minimum average cost up to a mark-up reflecting entry-preventing considerations (see the author, 1958)—coupled with some lags in the adjustment of prices to costs. This model implies that firms respond to a change in demand by endeavoring to adjust output and employment, without significant changes in prices relative to wages; and the resulting changes in available jobs have their initial impact not on wages but rather on unemployment by way of layoffs and recalls and through changes in the level of vacancies, and hence on the length of average search time.

If, in the process, vacancies rise above a critical level, or "natural rate," firms will endeavor to reduce them by outbidding each other, thereby raising the rate of change of wages. Thus, as long as jobs and vacancies remain above, and unemployment remains below, some critical level which might be labeled the "noninflationary rate" (see the author and Lucas Papademos, 1975), wages and prices will tend to accelerate. If, on the other hand, jobs fall below, and unemployment rises above, the noninflationary rate, firms finding that vacancies are less than optimal—in the limit the unemployed queuing outside the gate will fill them instantly—will have an incentive to reduce their relative wage offer. But in this case, in which too much labor is looking for too few jobs, the trend toward a sustained decline in the rate of growth of wages is likely to be even weaker than the corresponding acceleration when too many jobs are bidding for too few people. The main reason is the nonhomogeneity of labor. By far the largest and more valuable source of labor supply to a firm consists of those already employed who are not readily interchangeable with the unemployed and, in contrast with them, are concerned with protecting their earnings and not with reestablishing full employment. For these reasons, and because the first to quit are likely to be the best workers, a reduction of the labor force can, within limits, be accomplished more economically, not by reducing wages to generate enough quits, but by firing or, when possible, by layoffs which insure access to a trained labor force when demand recovers. More generally, the inducement to reduce relative wages to eliminate the excess supply is moderated by the effect that such a reduction would have on quits and costly turnover, even when the resulting vacancies can be readily filled from the ranks of the unemployed. Equally relevant are the consequences in terms of loss of morale and good will, in part for reasons which have been elaborated by the literature on implicit contracts (see Robert Gordon). Thus, while there will be some tendency for the rate of change of wages to fall, the more so the larger the unemployment—at least in an economy like the United States where there are no overpowering centralized unions—that tendency is severely damped.

And whether, given an unemployment rate significantly and persistently above the noninflationary level, the rate of change of wages would, eventually, tend to turn negative and decline without bound or whether it would tend to an asymptote is a question that I doubt the empirical evidence will ever answer. The one experiment we have had—the Great Depression—suggests the answer is negative, and while I admit that, for a variety of reasons, that evidence is muddled, I hope that we will never have the opportunity for a second, clean experiment.

In any event, what is really important for practical purposes is not the long-run equilibrium relation as such, but the speed with which it is approached. Both the model sketched out and the empirical evidence suggest that the process of acceleration or deceleration of wages when unemployment differs from the noninflationary rate will have more nearly the character of a crawl than of a gallop. It will suffice to recall in this connection that there was excess demand pressure in the United States at least from 1965 to mid-1970, and during that period the growth of inflation was from some 1.5 to only about 5.5 percent per year. And the response to the excess supply pressure from mid-1970 to early 1973, and from late 1974 to date was equally sluggish.

THE OVERALL EFFECTIVENESS OF POSTWAR STABILIZATION POLICIES

Even granted that a smooth money supply will not produce a very stable world and that there is therefore room for stabilization policies, monetarists will still argue that we should nonetheless eschew such policies. They claim, first, that allowing for unpredictably variable lags and unforseeable future shocks, we do not know enough to successfully design stabilization policies, and second, that the government would surely be incapable of choosing the appropriate policies or be politically willing to provide timely enforcement. Thus, in practice, stabilization polices will result in destabilizing the economy much of the time.

This view is supported by two arguments, one logical and one empirical. The logical argument is the one developed in Friedman's Presidential Address (1968). An attempt at stabilizing the economy at full employment is bound to be destabilizing because the full employment or natural rate is not known with certainty and is subject to shifts in time; and if we aim for the incorrect rate, the result must perforce be explosive inflation or deflation. By contrast, with a constant money supply policy, the economy will automatically hunt for, and eventually discover, that shifty natural rate, wherever it may be hiding.

This argument, I submit, is nothing but a debating ploy. It rests on the preposterous assumption that the only alternative to a constant money growth is the pursuit of a very precise unemployment target which will be adhered to indefinitely no matter what, and that if the target is off in the second decimal place, galloping inflation is around the corner. In reality, all that is necessary to pursue stabilization policies is a rough target range that includes the warranted rate, itself a range and not a razor edge; and, of course, responsible supporters of stabilization policies have long been aware of the fact that the target range needs to be adjusted in time on the basis of foreseeable shift in the warranted range, as well as in the light of emerging evidence that the current target is not consistent with price stability. It is precisely for this reason that I, as well as many other nonmonetarists, would side with monetarists in strenuous opposition to recent proposals for a target unemployment rate rigidly fixed by statute (although there is nothing wrong with Congress committing itself and the country to work toward the eventual achievement of some target unemployment rate through *structural* changes rather than aggregate demand policies).

Clearly, even the continuous updating of targets cannot guarantee that errors can be avoided altogether or even that they will be promptly recognized; and while errors persist, they will result in some inflationary (or deflationary) pressures. But the growing inflation to which Friedman refers is, to repeat, a crawl not a gallop. One may usefully recall in this connection the experience of 1965–70 referred to earlier, with the further remark that the existence of excess employment was quite generally recognized at the time, and failure to eliminate it resulted overwhelmingly from political considerations and not from a wrong diagnosis.

There remains then only the empirical issue: have stabilization policies worked in the past and will they work in the future? Monetarists think the answer is negative and suggest, as we have seen, the misguided attempts at stabilization, especially through monetary policies, are responsible for much of the observed instability. The main piece of evidence in support of this contention is the Great Depression, an episode well documented through the painstaking work of Friedman and Anna Schwartz, although still the object of dispute (see, for example, Peter Temin). But in any event, that episode while it may attest to the power of money, is irrelevant for present purposes since the contraction of the money supply was certainly not part of a comprehensive stabilization program in the post-Keynesian sense.

When we come to the relevant postwar period, the problem of establishing the success or failure of stabilization policies is an extremely taxing one. Many attempts have been made at developing precise objective tests, but in my view, none of these is of much value, even though I am guilty of having contributed to them in one of my worst papers (1964). Even the most ingenious test, that suggested by Victor Argy, and relying on a comparison of the variability of income with that of the velocity of circulation, turns out to be valid only under highly unrealistic restrictive assumptions.

Dennis Starleaf and Richard Floyd have proposed testing the effectiveness of stabilization by comparing the stability of money growth with that of income growth, much as I have done above for the United States, except that they apply their test to a cross section of industrialized countries. They found that for a sample of 13 countries, the association was distinctly positive. But this test is again of little value. For while a negative association for a given country, such as suggested by my U.S. test, does provide some weak indication that monetary activism helped rather than hindered, the finding of a positive association across countries proves absolutely nothing. It can be readily shown, in fact, that, to the extent that differential variability of income reflects differences in the character of the shocks a most likely circumstance for their sample—successful stabilization also implies a positive correlation between the variability of income and that of money.

But though the search for unambiguous quantitative tests has so far yielded a meager crop, there exists a different kind of evidence in favor of Keynesian stabilization policies which is impressive, even if hard to quantify. To quote one of the founding fathers of business cycle analysis, Arthur Burns, writing in 1959, "Since 1937 we have had five recessions, the longest of which lasted only 13 months. There is no parallel for such a sequence of mild—or such a sequence of brief—contractions, at least during the past hundred years in our country" (p. 2). By now we can add to that list the recessions of 1961 and 1970.

There is, furthermore, evidence that very similar conclusions hold for other industrialized countries which have made use of stabilization polices: at any rate that was the prevailing view among participants to an international conference held in 1967 on the subject, "Is the business cycle obsolete?" (see Martin Bronfenbrenner, editor). No one seemed to question the greater postwar stability of all Western economies—nor is this surprising when one recalls that around that time business cycle specialists felt so threatened by the new-found stability that they were arguing for redefining business cycles as fluctuations in the *rate of growth* rather than in the *level* of output.

It was recognized that the reduced severity of fluctuations might in part reflect structural changes in the economy and the effect of stronger built-in stabilizers, inspired, of course, by the Keynesian analysis. Furthermore, the greater stability in the United States, and in other industrialized countries, are obviously not independent events. Still, at least as of the time of that conference, there seemed to be little question and some evidence that part of the credit for the greater stability should go to the conscious and on balance, successful endeavor at stabilizing the economy.

WHAT MACRO STABILIZATION POLICIES CAN ACCOMPLISH, AND HOW

[Arguing] that the adherence to a stable money growth path through much of 1974 bears a major responsibility for the sharp contraction does not per se establish that the policy was mistaken. The reason is that the shock that hit the system in 1973–74 was not the usual type of demand shock which we gradually learned to cope with, more or less adequately. It was, instead, a supply or price shock, coming from a cumulation of causes, largely external. This poses an altogether different stabilization problem. In particular, in the case of demand shocks, there exists in principle an ideal policy which avoids all social costs, namely to offset completely the shock thus, at the same time, stabilizing employment and the price level. There may be disagreement as to whether this target can be achieved and how, but not about the target itself.

But in the case of supply shocks, there is no miracle cure—there is no macro policy which can both maintain a stable price level and keep employment at its natural rate. To maintain stable prices in the face of the exogenous price shock, say a rise in import prices, would require a fall in all domestic output prices; but we know of no macro policy by which domestic prices can be made to fall except by creating enough slack, thus putting downward pressure on wages. And the amount of slack would have to be substantial in view of the sluggishness of wages in the face of unemployment. If we do not offset the exogenous shock completely, then the initial burst, even if activated by an entirely transient rise in some prices, such as a once and for all deterioration in the terms of trade, will give rise to further increases, as nominal wages rise in a vain attempt at preserving real wages; this secondary reaction too can only be cut short by creating slack. In short, once a price shock hits, there is no way of returning to the initial equilibrium except after a painful period of both above equilibrium unemployment and inflation.

There are, of course, in principle, policies other than aggregate demand management to which we might turn, and which are enticing in view of the unpleasant alternatives offered by demand management. But so far such policies, at least those of the wage-price control variety, have proved disappointing. The design of better alternatives is probably the greatest challenge presently confronting those interested in stabilization. However, these policies fall outside my present concern. Within the realm of aggregate demand management, the only choice open to society is the cruel one between alternative feasible paths of inflation and associated paths of unemployment, and the best the macroeconomist can offer is policies designed to approximate the chosen path.

CONCLUSION

To summarize, the monetarists have made a valid and most valuable contribution in establishing that our economy is far less unstable than the early Keynesians pictured it and in rehabilitating the role of money as a determinant of aggregate demand. They are wrong, however, in going as far as asserting that the economy is sufficiently shockproof that stabilization policies are not needed. They have also made an important contribution in pointing out that such policies are not needed. They have also made an important contribution in pointing out that such policies might in fact prove destabilizing. This criticism has had a salutary effect on reassessing what stabilization policies can and should do, and on trimming down fine-tuning ambitions. But their contention that postwar fluctuations resulted from an unstable money growth or that stabilization policies decreased rather than increased stability just does not stand up to an impartial examination of the postwar record of the United States and other industrialized countries. Up to 1974, these policies have helped to keep the economy reasonably stable by historical standards, even though one can certainly point to some occasional failures.

The serious deterioration in economic stability since 1973 must be attributed in the first place to the novel nature of the shocks that hit us, namely, supply shocks. Even the best possible aggregate demand management cannot offset such shocks without a lot of unemployment together with a lot of inflation. But, in addition, demand management was far from the best. This failure must be attributed in good measure to the fact that we had little experience or even an adequate conceptual framework to deal with such shocks; but at least from my reading of the record, it was also the result of failure to use stabilization policies, including too slavish adherence to the monetarists' constant money growth prescription.

We must therefore, categorically reject the monetarist appeal to turn back the clock forty years by discarding the basic message of *The General Theory*. We should instead concentrate our efforts in an endeavor to make stabilization policies even more effective in the future than they have been in the past.

III/THE REAL DEBATE ABOUT UNEMPLOYMENT

When more and more people are thrown out of work, unemployment results.

CALVIN COOLIDGE

The debate about unemployment policy and the debate over the validity of Keynesian economics are separable issues, tied together by the vagaries of history rather than logic. With the death of Keynesian economics, it is only natural that the two issues are again separated. Unemployment is a major problem independent of whether Keynesian economics is true or not. If macroeconomic policy cannot solve unemployment, we need to consider other policies that will.

One of the biggest problems in coming to grips with the issues of the unemployment debate is the schizophrenic attitude our society takes toward work. On the one hand, it is a rewarding experience necessary for self-fulfillment; on the other hand, it is the drudgery we must do in order to bring in sufficient income to prevent starvation. As individuals' views of work differ, so too do people's views of unemployment. On the one hand, it is seen as a loss of one's place in society and of the self-respect that goes with it; on the other, it is considered an opportunity for a vacation, which, if unemployment benefits are high enough, is preferable to being employed.

The first reading, a Letter to the Editor of *The New York Times,* provides a sense of the despair that can accompany unemployment. As you read it, consider the following questions: Is the writer's plight a legitimate concern of government? Must there be such unemployment? If so, what can be done to relieve it? The writer was an executive. How does his plight compare with that of a blue-collar worker? Do the same considerations apply?

In the next reading Milton Friedman presents a different view of unemployment, elegantly stating some of the problems with our present measures of the unemployment rate. He suggests that the quickest way to reduce unemployment is to tighten unemployment benefits. Implied in this suggestion is the view that much of our present unemployment is really a type of vacation that should not be a specific policy concern of government. As you read it, consider how Friedman might respond to the first article.

Geoffrey Moore carries Friedman's argument further in the next article, suggesting that the employment ratio may provide a more accurate measure of the tightness in the labor market than does the unemployment rate. The next article by Bertram Gross and Stanley Moss provides a rather different view of the unemployment rate. Although it is again under attack, this time it is because it underestimates, not overestimates, the unemployment problem.

Each of the above characterizations of unemployment embodies part of the truth. Unemployment is not one dimensional; it is merely a catch-word we use to describe numerous situations. No precise welfare judgment can be made about unemployment without knowing much more about its precise nature and cause—who is unemployed and what alternatives they have. A 2 percent unemployment rate might be horrendous while an 8 percent unemployment rate might not be so bad. Similarly, if individuals are sitting around at work with nothing to do, they are, in a way, as much unemployed as someone laid-off; the only difference is that the former are being paid by the firm. Moreover, individuals who are so discouraged that they are no longer looking for a job are probably much more worthy of social concern than many of the people collecting unemployment insurance.

Because of these and similar considerations, we must go beyond any simple characterizations of the employment and unemployment rates to truly understand the unemployment problem. Russell Nixon does this in the next reading, providing a history of the full employment concept from its World War II apex as a primary goal of social policy to its present nadir. As you read the article, carefully notice the four alternative definitions of full employment he presents and how they interrelate (and do not interrelate) with Keynesian macroeconomics and our present measures of unemployment.

Nixon argues that macroeconomic theory was not a full employment theory but one that achieved and even justified "a stabilizied level of 'acceptable unemployment.' " Implicit in such a view is a belief that Keynesian economics did not nearly go far enough in eliminating unemployment. This view and the contrasting views implicit in the earlier Buchanan and Wagner article (Part I) provide the basis of the new policy debate. The issue is not one of Keynesian versus non-Keynesian economics; rather it is one between activists or interventionists, who favor more specific government action in eliminating unemployment, and *nonactivists,* who fear such government involvement as an infringement on the rights of the individuals.

The two positions result in part from the two underlying views of how the economy functions: one side, the noninterventionists, sees the economy as a large marketplace where individuals come together, driving the best bargain they possibly can. The market outcome reflects the underlying power and ability of individuals and is essentially the fairest outcome that can be arrived at without violating liberty and freedom of individuals. The other side, the activists, sees the economy as a street brawl where some big bullies take everything for themselves and leave, at best, scraps for the others. The market process is fundamentally unfair and so government must step in and see that at least the fight remains fair.

This blunt statement of views, while partially correct, is unfair to both sides. The noninterventionists agree that sometimes "bullies" take advantage of the weak, leaving them with no jobs; but they argue that if the government steps in the weak will never learn to fend for themselves. Thus, helping them now will hurt them in the long run, destroy their self-respect, and leave them always susceptible to bullying. The activists admit the potential truth in this argument but defend their position by claiming that there are ways of helping the weak—such as placing constraints on the powerful and developing training programs—that will actually improve, rather than destroy, the self-image of the less powerful.

There is no easy or right answer to the above argument; reasonable individuals may differ. It is a debate not only of underlying philosophies of what constitutes fairness, but also of the relative importance of long- and short-run considerations. How fast and how far can we and must we change within the political framework? Activists would argue that if we don't change, the system will self-destruct; thus, change is a necessary part of the system. Nonactivists argue that little or no change is necessary. (Radicals argue that the system will self-destruct regardless of what is done.)

Although this activist/nonactivist debate has often been called a conservative/liberal debate, I am hesitant to do so. Over time, the meanings of the words liberal and conservative have been reversed. Classical liberalism stemming from John Stuart Mill was founded on a belief in individual rights and generally counseled against state intervention. The conservative philosophy, stemming from the writings of Edmund Burke, meant precisely the opposite—that the state had to perform certain tasks and that individual rights must be subordinated to those needs of the state. Somehow over the years the intuitive concept associated with each of these positions has been reversed so that the conservative position has become the classical liberal position and vice versa. For this reason many individuals who are classified by the press as conservatives actually call themselves liberals. Milton Friedman is a well-known example.

A second reason for not using the conservative/liberal distinction is that it is often associated with our already formed prejudices. Once we have categorized ourselves, we automatically disregard any argument associated with opposing viewpoints. Ideally, we would follow precisely the opposite strategy and listen primarily to the opposing positions; after all, we already know our own views. But to reach this ideal we would need the dispassion of a Mr. Spock. Unfortunately, it is hard to be dispassionate about unemployment, to consider it rationally from all relevant points of view. However, it is precisely the questions about which it is so hard to be dispassionate that require it the most.

The last article in this section, by Robert Lucas, provides just such a dispassionate look at the unemployment problem, arguing that full employment cannot be defined and that the often-used voluntary/involuntary distinction is not a useful characterization of the issue.

The problem is that the same unemployment can be both voluntary and involuntary. Say an individual takes a job in the construction industry at twice the pay he would receive in a factory, but that because of the cyclical nature of demand in the construction industry, he faces a higher chance of being laid-off. If he is laid-off for one month a year, he is, in one sense, voluntarily unemployed for that month, since he chose the job that had the cyclical demand. In another sense, however, he is involuntarily unemployed since he would be willing to work at the going wage in the construction industry. Therefore, depending on our value judgments, we arrive at different conclusions.

Rather than using a casual voluntary/involuntary distinction, Lucas' article suggests that we should extend beyond macroeconomics and specify the characteristics of unemployment that we find objectionable and that can be affected by a given policy. Having done that, we must design policies to directly affect those aspects.

As you ponder Lucas' article, think about the following job characteristics:

1. status
2. wage rate
3. degree of special training needed
4. degree of special ability needed
5. amount of effort required
6. job security
7. location
8. flexibility and hours worked
9. fringe benefits and "perks"

What level of job characteristics must an individual be unwilling to accept before you would classify him as unemployed? For example, should an individual looking only for a job as a major league baseball player be considered unemployed? Should his qualifications matter? Should his independent income matter? Should an individual who refuses to accept a job at the same pay as his last be considered unemployed? Should an individual who happens to find a good job initially be allowed to wait until another similar one comes along? These are difficult questions, but they must be answered before the real unemployment problem can be faced.

The Fear, the Numbing Fear

EDWARD B. FUREY

When this article was written in 1975, Edward Furey was unemployed and had nine children.

Let me tell you what it's like for one guy to be 52 years old and jobless in America.

As a recently fired middle management executive of a divison of one of America's top 500 companies, I have sent out over 150 resumés. Less than ten percent have drawn a response of any kind. Five percent drew requests for additional information, while less than four percent resulted in a personal interview. Not one resulted in a job.

As an infantry veteran of World War II in the South Pacific, I've had some experience with fear, and how men deal with it. I like to feel that I don't scare any easier than the next guy, but to be 52 years old and jobless is to be frightened—frightened to the marrow of your bones. Your days start with it, and end with it. It's all pervasive. It's numbing. It's mind-boggling.

Things you've always taken for granted fall apart. You can no longer maintain your hospitalization insurance, and for the first time in twenty-eight years you and your family are unprotected against a medical emergency. You are unable to meet the payments on your life insurance. The bank holding your mortgage warns that foreclosure is being considered. Bills to the utilities are overdue and you're keeping vital services only through partial payments, aware of the fact that time is running out. It's to tell a fine fourteen-year-old son that you haven't got the five bucks you owe him for the great report card he brought home. It's to pass local merchants on the street and feel embarrassment, wondering when you'll be able to pay them what you owe them. To feel the disintegration of your confidence as a man, and your ability to protect your famliy from economic disaster. It's to envy just about everybody who has a job, any job.

It's to see the doubt on the faces of your children about what's going on in their house, when so many of their friends are unaffected. It's to add a crushing dimension to the natural self-doubts that are part of the process of growing older. It's to stand silently on unemployment lines with other surplus members of America's work force, waiting to sign for your unemployment check. It's to see what the neighborhood looks like at 10:30 on a Tuesday morning. It's to feel embarrassed to answer the ring of the telephone at the same hour. It's to watch assorted politicians in dialogues with fat-cat television interviewers in an atmosphere replete with camaraderie, purporting to discuss America's problems, where the right questions are not asked, and the unchallenged responses consist mostly of noncommittal and vacuous banalities.

It's to realize the simple stunning fact that you are without meaningful representation in this society.

And in the late evening when your household is quiet and you switch off the bedroom light it's to be alone, alone like you've never been before. To lie there looking at the darkness and wonder if you're going to lose the home that you've worked all your life for, the home that represents the only equity you've been able to accumulate in thirty years of working and raising a family.

It's to realize that for many Americans the problem you are facing for the first time has become a way of life. The carnage is strewn about America for anyone with eyes to see. In our mental hospitals, in our drug-abuse centers, in the alcoholic wards of our hospitals, in our juvenile shelters, in our prisons, and on the streets of our cities.

And finally, it's to lie sleepless in bed waiting for the dawn of a new day and realize that something is terribly wrong in America.

Behind the Unemployment Numbers

MILTON FRIEDMAN

Besides his many other activities, Milton Friedman writes a column for *Newsweek* in which he condenses complex theoretical ideas into simple arguments. His superb ability to do this, as evidenced in the following short piece, accounts for some of his fame.

We are spending more than $15 billion a year on unemployment-insurance payments because unemployment has stubbornly remained in the neighborhood of 8 per cent. *OR:* Unemployment has stubbornly remained in the neighborhood of 8 per cent because we are spending more than $15 billion a year on unemployment-insurance payments. Which is the cause, and which the effect?

SOMETIMES IT PAYS . . .

In a recent column (Boston Herald American, Dec. 29), Warren T. Brookes reports that unemployment in Massachusetts went from 7.5 per cent of the labor force in October 1974 to 11.1 per cent in October 1975, to 7.1 per cent in October 1976—yet *employment* changed hardly at all. The drastic changes in unemployment were produced by an initial increase and subsequent decrease in the number of persons recorded as in the labor force.

What produced those changes? According to Brookes, the extension of benefits effective January 1975 "brought 100,000 people out of the woodwork and on to the unemployment rolls—not because they had lost their jobs, but because the state and the Federal government were offering a good deal."

"About a year ago, the governor and the legislature tightened up the state's unemployment-compensation program—making it impossible for people who quit their jobs voluntarily to collect benefits."

The result? "The work force declined by 120,000 . . . while jobs went up about 19,000 . . . Unemployment plummeted—not because our economy was booming, but because the benefits were no longer available."

On the national level, the same phenomenon is shown dramatically in the accompanying charts.

The left-hand chart plots *employment*, expressed as a percentage of the working-age population (i.e., 16 to 64 years old). The solid line is for the current expansion. The dotted line is for the corresponding period of the 1961-1966 expansion. The employment percentage has not only been consistently higher during the current expansion, it has risen more rapidly and is at or near an all-time high. By this standard, the current expansion has been exceptionally vigorous.

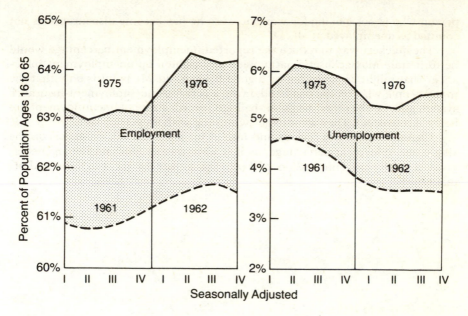

Seasonally Adjusted

The right-hand chart provides a sharp contrast. Unemployment—expressed also as a percentage of the working-age population rather than (as it usually is) as a percentage of the labor force—has not only been systematically higher during this expansion than during the earlier expansion, but has declined much less. By this standard, the current expansion has been exceptionally slow.

...TO BE UNEMPLOYED

The number of people unemployed is not a hard number. It depends on the answer, in a sample survey, to the questions: "Has [member of the household] been looking for work during the past four weeks?" The answer may well depend on the availability of the unemployment benefits. If they are not available, people who do not really want a job have no incentive to look for work or say that they are looking for work; but if eligibility for benefits depends on being available for employment, such people do have a strong incentive to go through the motions of looking for work (to cite a dramatic example, pro baseball players during the off season). Moreover, the availability of unemployment insurance establishes an incentive for people who might otherwise not be in the labor market at all to take a job in order to qualify.

As evidence, note that the sharp rise in the unemployment percentage from the first to the second quarter of 1975 followed the extension and liberalization of unemployment benefits; the milder rise since the second quarter of 1976 followed a further extension.

The reports of unemployment percentages are misleading also since they mix soft cases with hard: the college youngster seeking a part-time job is one unemployed person; the head of a household seeking a full-time job to support a family is one unemployed person. On the other hand, the hard-core unemployed person who is not looking for work because he has become discouraged is not counted as unemployed at all.

The quickest way to reduce the reported unemployment percentage would be to imitate Massachusetts nationwide and tighten up unemployment insurance. That might or might not be a good thing to do. My point is only that the many people who, on the one hand, favor a generous unemployment-insurance system and, on the other, bemoan the high recorded rate of unemployment are being inconsistent. They want to go swimming without getting wet.

Unemployment is a serious and important problem. But emphasis on the single unemployment percentage, as if it were meaningful and homogeneous, gives a misleading impression of both the nature of the problem and its magnitude.

A Measuring Stick for Employment

GEOFFREY MOORE

Geoffrey H. Moore is director of Business Cycle Research at the National Bureau of Economic Research, Inc., and was previously a senior research fellow at the Hoover Institute. He is highly regarded as an economist and statistician, and as former U.S. commissioner of Labor Statistics is acutely aware of the limitations of aggregate measures of the economy's performance.

During 1974 the unemployment rate averaged 5.6%, a relatively high figure by historical standards. At the same time, the percentage of the population of working age that had jobs averaged 57%, exceeding any preceding year since World War II and probably before that. According to the unemployment rate, the economy was a considerable distance away from full employment. According to the employment ratio, it was more fully employed than ever before. Which is the more appropriate guide to the hypothetical condition of full employment?

Although no categorical answer can be given, a substantial case can be made for the employment ratio on the grounds of its objectivity, its statistical reliability, and its close relation to wage and price inflation. While the economy currently is far short of full employment as a result of the recession, and inflation also is receding for the same reason, it is a good time to take a look at this issue, well before it confronts us once again.

With respect to objectivity, the concept of employment is firmer than the concept of unemployment. Having a job and being paid for it is, for the most part, an observable experience. True, there are some fuzzy situations—as when a person is on strike, or has accepted a job but hasn't yet started to work, or is on vacation without pay, or is working only a few hours a week. But most of these situations can be objectively identified and don't affect the great bulk of those who are employed.

The concept of unemployment is quite different. For those who have had a job and have just been laid off, the situation may be obvious. Nevertheless, unless the worker is doing something to seek work, he will not be counted as unemployed according to the definition used for many years in the United States. Moreover, those who are unemployed because they have been laid off usually constitute less than half of the unemployed. The rest have either quit their jobs voluntarily or have not recently (or ever) had a job. Now they are seeking one.

SEEKING A JOB

Seeking a job is not as clear-cut a condition as having a job. One can seek work now and then, or systematically. One can seek a job, yet turn down one or more offers. One can set realistic or unrealistic standards for pay, hours, type of work or location. Or one can give up seeking a job because none is to be found, yet be quite ready to take one if the opportunity comes along. Indeed, not a few persons become employed without having been unemployed in the strict sense of the term.

In short, for a sizable number of the jobless, whether one is unemployed or not is to some degree a matter of opinion. In the monthly household survey conducted by the U.S. Census Bureau from which estimates of total employment and unemployment are derived, questions are answered by the respondent—often the housewife who happens to be at home and who answers for the entire family. Hence there is bound to be some variability in opinion from one household to another, or from the same household at different times. A serious effort is made to reduce this variability, but much of it is inherent in the concept itself.

This is one reason for paying close attention to unemployment rates for those whose unemployed status is not likely to be in doubt—married men or heads of household, those who have lost their jobs or those who are seeking full-time work. It is also a reason for focusing on the employment figures, since variability of opinion is likely to be much less important regarding whether the individual is employed.

With respect to statistical reliability, the employment figures also have an edge. Because the number of unemployed is much smaller than the number who are employed, the former is subject to a much larger sampling error than the latter. The sampling variability of the unemployment count is somewhat less than 2%; for the employment count it is about one-fourth of 1%. Moreover, seasonal variations are easier to eliminate in employment than in unemployment so the results are less subject to revision.

When the comparison pertains to the unemployment rate, which is the number of unemployed divided by the civilian labor force (employed plus unemployed), and the employment ratio, which is the number employed divided by the noninstitutional population 16 years old and over, the conceptual and statistical differences also favor the employment ratio. The labor force, since it includes the unemployed, is subject to many of the same problems that pertain to the identification of who is unemployed. The population figure, of course, is free of these definitional difficulties. Similarly, the labor force figure is subject to sampling error while the population figure is not. Other types of estimating errors, which do affect the population figure, equally affect the labor force figure, because the latter is estimated on the basis of proportions derived from the sample and applied to the population estimate.

These considerations point to the desirability of giving careful attention to the employment figures as well as the unemployment figures in assessing the economic situation. This would not be true if employment and unemployment were simply reverse sides of the same coin. But unemployment does not always rise when employment declines, or vice versa. Job loss is not the only source of unemployment. Decisions to enter the labor market, i.e., to seek work and therefore become unemployed, can be made quite independently of changes in employment, for example, by those who have never had a job before. Moreover, increases in the number of persons with jobs can induce others to seek work because they view the opportunities more favorably. Hence an increase in employment can add to unemployment, and a reduction in employment can eliminate some unemployment.

For all these reasons, therefore, it is important to determine whether the percentage of the population employed is useful as a measure of the degree to which the economy is fully employed and in particular to see how closely related it is to the rate of inflation. As it turns out, the employment ratio is quite closely related to the rate of change in the consumer price index during the same year. High employment ratios have been associated with high rates of inflation. The relationship seems to be somewhat curvilinear. There has been relatively little inflation when the percentage employed has been in the range of 53.5% to 55.5%, but higher employment ratios have been associated with increasingly sharp advances in the rate of inflation.

Moreover, the relation is reversible. Peak years in the business cycle bring forth higher employment ratios and higher inflation rates while tough years do the opposite. However, a reduction in the employment ratio during a recession is associated with a smaller reduction in inflation than an equal increase in the employment ratio during an expansion phase of the cycle. Perhaps this is an additional bit of evidence that it is harder to get rid of inflation than to generate it.

THE HISTORICAL RELATIONS

During the current recession the employment ratio declined from its all-time high, 57.5%, in October 1973 to 54.9% in March 1975. The April figure was up a bit, to 55%. Although the reduction in employment has been sharp, the percentage employed in March and April was higher than in any previous recession year, save 1970. As the historical relation would lead one to expect, the rate of increase in consumer prices has declined also. The latest figure, for March, showed an increase at an annual rate of less than 4%, down sharply from the double digit rates of last year.

In general, rates of wage and price inflation have been far more closely correlated with the employment ratio than with the unemployment rate. The relation between inflation and unemployment is a very loose one, despite all the discussion about the trade-off. In particular, 1974 was off in a class by itself, with considerable unemployment and a gret deal of inflation. What was largely overlooked was the record high employment ratio.

How is it possible, as in 1974, that a large percentage of the working age population is employed and at the same time a large percentage is unemployed? A high employment percentage demonstrates that opportunities to find work exist and that efforts to find work are likely to be successful. It is not surprising then, that more people are induced to look for work. By definition, they become unemployed. Under such circumstances a high unemployment rate is not an indication of difficulty in finding work, but rather the opposite. Nor is it an indication of softness in the labor market and that smaller wage increases would be acceptable—quite the opposite.

Of course it is true that much of the time a high employment ratio and a low unemployment rate go together, and vice versa. During the current recession the employment ratio has declined and the unemployment rate has risen. But here again it is well to keep both measures in mind. The unemployment rate is high now partly *because* the employment ratio was extraordinarily high in 1973 and 1974. Many of those who were employed then but not employed now are naturally seeking to be reemployed; if they had not been employed in 1973–74 some of them might not be seeking employment now.

Moreover, when a recovery develops and the employment ratio rises again to a higher level, the overhang of unemployment created by the unusual employment experience of 1973–74 may still remain for some time. A condition of "full employment" in terms of the employment ratio (and in terms at the rate of inflation) may again be accompanied by less than "full employment" in terms of the unemployment rate. Alternatively, a recovery, at least initially, might reduce unemployment as some drop out of the labor force but be insufficiently vigorous to raise the employment ratio, which is what happened during the first two years of recovery after the 1961 recession. Would such a recovery, with a lower unemployment rate but a stable employment ratio, be moving the economy closer to full employment, or not?

REVISING A '20s THEORY

It should not be supposed that the close relation between price and wage changes and the employment ratio reflects only the effect of high employment on wages and therefore on prices. It may also reflect the effect of rapid price increases on incentives to hire and the effect of rapid wage increases on incentives to become employed. Indeed, when Irving Fisher wrote about this relationship in the 1920s he thought the influence of price inflation on employment was dominant. Nowadays, as a result of the attention given to the "Phillips curve," the casual relation, if any, is thought to run mainly the other way. Probably it runs in both directions. Moreover, employment, prices and wages are also affected jointly by other factors.

At this point it seems reasonable to conclude only that the employment ratio should not be ignored in measuring the tightness of the labor market and the position of the economy with respect to the goal of full employment without inflation.

How Many Jobs for Whom

BERTRAM GROSS AND STANLEY MOSS

Bertram M. Gross is a professor at both Hunter College and the City University of New York and served as chief draftsman of the Employment Act of 1946.

Stanley Moss was a colleague of Professor Gross' at Hunter College and was previously associated with Syracuse University. Both have been important critics of United States employment policy.

As reported "officially" by the Department of Labor, the annual average rate of unemployment during the year of 1971 was 5.9 percent. Based on the "official" civilian labor force, which was reported as being 84.1 million, this percentage represented a total of 4.99 million persons who were unemployed. As a result of the assiduous activity of the Department of Labor, the Bureau of the Census, and various other agencies of government, we possess a great deal of information about the numbers and characteristics of the employed and unemployed. They have been studied and restudied and researched and analyzed according to the various sorts of attributes that distinguish people—sex, age, color, industry, occupation, and income, among others—and presented to us in an impressive array of data and information. The most critical of all these indicators in terms of political interest and concern is the unemployment rate. Its rise or fall is taken as the major indicator of the extent to which society is succeeding in meeting the needs and aspirations of people regarding work. Indeed the official rate is an important indicator of economic trends and developments regarding the economy, people, and jobs.

The official rate, though, is far from being a complete and accurate picture of the "real" dimensions of unemployment in the United States. The official figures are calculated in relation to the official labor force. To be considered a part of the labor force a person must be willing and able to work, and in addition must have actively sought a job during the last four weeks immediately proceeding the monthly Current Population Survey. It is the combination of willingness and ability with the active pursuit of work that constitutes the criteria for defining a person as being in the labor force and consequently eligible for inclusion in the ranks of the unemployed. But, and here is the rub, what about the many people of different sexes, ages, and colors who are willing and able to work but who are not seeking employment because they have concluded, quite rightly, that suitable opportunities do not exist. It is these millions of persons who are the major focus of this [article] and of our investigation into the dimensions of real employment in the United States. . . .

Our estimates reveal a "real," as contrasted with "official," unemployment rate of 24.6 percent for the nation. This results in 25.6 million being unemployed nationally. Are these incredible statements? Yes they are, if one accepts official labor force concepts as being a true definition of the ability and willingness that people have for jobs. No they are not, if one examines carefully the nature of the labor force definition, and the way it has been constructed so as to exclude millions of people in order to understate the dimensions of unemployment, together with the extent to which the economic system has failed to generate adequate and suitable job opportunities for millions of people who consequently have been discouraged and have dropped out, or often been pushed out, of the labor market into various other activities, where they do not disturb official data reporting.

These people must be considered at the forefront of any attempts to restructure the economic system in order to provide meaningful and socially desirable work for the millions who currently do not have jobs but would be able and willing to work if suitable opportunities were presented. What is involved is a redefinition of what we mean by full employment and a return to some of the original intent of the proposed Full Employment Bill of 1946, before it was transmitted into the Full Employment Act of 1946, calling upon the federal government to create and maintain conditions under which "there will be afforded useful employment opportunities, including self-employment, for those able, willing, and seeking to work, and to promote maximum employment, production and purchasing power." The turning away from real full employment as a goal of national policy .... is reflected in the development of a labor force concept that applies restrictive and exclusive criteria so as to understate the real number of people who want jobs and whose desires are not being met.

To break out of these narrow confines and restate a full employment guarantee in terms appropriate to the last third of the twentieth century is an exciting task. Above all it requires breaking loose from many tortuous establishment concepts bearing on the questions of "how many additional jobs?" and "what kind of jobs?"

The original Full Employment Bill used the words "regular," "remunerative," and "useful." The first of these is still good. The second must now be interpreted in terms of decent wages with opportunities for advancement. The third needs substantial redefinition. Far too many jobs—including many in the human services sector—are "useful" only in the sense that they serve to augment profits, bureaucratic power, or careerist rat races. Many of us used to think that the major task of readjustment was to replace war work with civilian work. It is now becoming increasingly clear that merely adding budgets and job slots will by itself do nothing to humanize a brutalizing public service bureaucracy.

To these there must now be added another five words: suitable, fair, fulfilling, nonexploitative, and peaceful. *Suitable* covers far more matters than we have time to touch on at this point. But one aspect is essential: part-time employment opportunities with fringe benefits for those not willing or able to work full-time. True full employment must also be *fair*—not only for blacks and other minority groups but also for women, who comprise the majority of the country's labor potential. It should also be *fulfilling*, rather than humiliating or dehumanizing. It should be *nonexploitative*—in the double sense of neither taking the resources of developing nations on unfair terms of trade nor of degrading our own physical environment through excessive increases in energy conversion and materials processing. And above all it should be *peaceful* in the double sense of getting along without the stimulus of either military expenditures or "beggar thy neighbor" policies of trade with other countries. Casual reflection on these various points suggests that any new-style full employment program for techno-industrial America requires fundamental changes in America's political-economic structure. This is why it is important not to let the struggle over jobs for the poor continue to play its historic function of distracting attention from more fundamental forms of social change.

Most recent debates on the number of additional jobs needed have revolved around a numbers game in which percentages of the so-called "labor force" are juggled around by so-called "experts." The more liberal economists have tended to set a goal of reducing official unemployment to 4, 3, or even 2 percent. This would bring current official unemployment down from 5 million to, respectively, 3.4 million, 2.6 million, or 1.7 million. Others say that Nixonian full employment will exist when the number is reduced to 5 percent—or about 4.3 million. Some of the Nixon Administration officials are even maintaining that *real* unemployment is just a little over 2 million—since about 3 million of the reported unemployed are women and teenagers, and *women and teenagers don't really count.* Beyond these areas of dispute, official recognition is now given grudgingly to a *poverty undercount*—that is, about 2 million additional people who do not appear in the official statistics because of the census undercount in poverty areas, because they had given up looking for jobs that are not there, or because they had a part-time job at babysitting or minding a store.

The genuine undercount, however, is far more substantial. It stems from the very concept of officially defined unemployment, which includes only those who have been actively seeking work. The more logical—and human—definition of unemployment, in contrast, would be *all those who are not working and are able and willing to work for pay.* Whether or not someone is actively seeking a paid job would no longer be the important point. The question, rather, would be whether or not he or she *wanted* full or part-time work and was able to do something that might be truly useful. Under this concept we would certainly find many millions of additional people now stamped "unemployable" or pushed out of the official labor force by one or another device. . . .

The concepts of real labor force and labor potential refer to those who would be potentially employable in conditions of peacetime full employment. We are not talking about the potential labor force that may exist during conditions of national mobilization, when all people who are capable of accomplishing any sort of work would be encouraged or compelled to take jobs. The real labor force differs from the national mobilization potential in that it considers only the official labor force plus the millions of others who have tried to get work and are no longer seeking it because they have become discouraged, and also those who could be encouraged to become available if suitable opportunities were presented.

We have been deliberately somewhat conservative in many of our estimates. Both in the literature of labor economics and in the survey and reporting work of the Department of Labor there has always been a recognition and admission of the limitations of the labor force concept and the fact that it understates the dimensions of real unemployment. In fact considerable work has been done to

TABLE 3.1
Summary of Real Unemployment in the United States, 1971
(Preliminary Estimates)

Category	Number (in millions)
Official labor force (incl. armed forces)	85.8
Gainfully employed (incl. armed forces)	81.1
Official unemployment	
Number	4.7
(As percent of civilian labor force)	(5.7%)
Unofficial unemployment	
Disclosed but set aside	7.1
Hidden and ignored	13.8
Real labor force*	104
Real unemployment	
Number	25.6
(As percent of real labor force)	(24.6%)

*Official labor force plus unofficial unemployed, excluding underemployed.

clarify some of the gray areas of understatement—especially as regards to the concept of underemployment and discouraged workers. We have built upon the research done in both of these areas and have considered them as an example of unemployment that is "officially disclosed but set aside." To this group of 7.1 million we have added our estimates of what percentage of the millions of other persons not in the labor force would desire jobs if suitable opportunities were available. We have divided this group of "hidden and ignored" employables into six major groups—unemployables, housewives, men (25–54), older people (55 and over), students, and enrollees in manpower programs.

The Historical Development of the Conception and Implementation of Full Employment as Economic Policy

RUSSELL A. NIXON

Russell A. Nixon is a professor at Columbia University who specializes in manpower and labor economics. He has been active in both the political and theoretical development of U.S. employment policy and served as co-chairman of the National Conference on Public Service Employment.

THE TAXONOMY OF FULL EMPLOYMENT

There has been an almost incredible lack of precision in the definition of "full employment." This fuzziness has persisted even though the issue of unemployment/full employment has long been of central importance in economic theory and economic policy. "Full employment," "high employment," "maximum employment," and "full employment" (meaning "acceptable" 4 or 5 percent of officially reported unemployment) have all been used indiscriminately and often interchangeably. But the differences, and particularly the different policy implications, between the economic goal of achieving high employment/low unemployment and the goal of guaranteeing full employment (a good job for everyone able and willing to work) are profound.

The High Employment Goal

The aim of minimizing unemployment and maximizing employment has always been a major avowed objective of capitalist economic policy. Within this general agreement, however, there have been and are wide variations. In practical terms powerful economic influences have welcomed a degree of unemployment as essential to dampen wage demands and assure a flexible and cooperative labor force. For example, in 1952 when the official unemployment rate was 3 percent, *Business Week* commented:

> Unemployment remains too low for the work force to have flexibility. Anytime the jobless total is less than 2 million, even common labor is scarce. Many employers must tend to hoard skills. And certainly, the labor unions are in the drivers seat in wage negotiations. More workers can be had, to be sure. But only at considerable cost. And they probably wouldn't be of the skills most desired. There's no assurance against inflation like a pool of genuine unemployment. That is a blunt, hard-headed statement, but a fact.

In a similar vein others have objected to the high employment goal as an absolute priority, and have urged other modifying considerations, such as avoidance of inflation and economic planning, wage and price controls. Thus Friedrich von Hayek, in *The Road To Serfdom*, objects that "the fascination of vague but popular phrases like 'full employment' may well lead to extremely shortsighted measures, and where the categorical and irresponsible 'it must be done at all cost' of the single minded idealist is likely to do the greatest harm."

In contrast others pursue the goal of maximum employment with much more urgency and demanding standards, aiming at the elimination of all but frictional unemployment by far-reaching government intervention. But in spite of these differences, all of these approaches accept the fact of unemployment in the unplanned capitalist system and seek through varied means to minimize it. They stand in very stark contrast with the approach that accepts as a basic first premise the guarantee of meaningful work for all.

Those who seek the goal of high employment/low unemployment divide on methods of achievement. The classical Walras-Marshall economic school of free competition equilibrium relied on laissez-faire to achieve the full optimum use of all resources, labor included. Give or take some minor but self-correcting imperfections and deviations, Say's law equating supply and demand could be relied upon to avoid serious and lasting unemployment. In its essentials this approach dominated capitalist economic policy until the Great Depression of the 1930s.

The laissez-faire approach contrasts with that of interventionists, most notably coalesced around the analysis of John Maynard Keynes. This school of thought and policy envisaged government intervention as a means of achieving equilibrium with unemployment, and as a means of maximizing employment and reducing—and keeping low—the volume of unemployment. The major strategy of intervention would stimulate the private economy through a combination of monetary and fiscal policies, including direct subsidies for the economic growth of private companies and industries. The pattern of intervention also includes the public sector as a manipulable factor for job creation either on a short-term cyclical basis or on a long-term scale. Public works, of which military spending has been the most important, augment the labor demand of the private sector. Direct job creation through planned public service employment is a means of intervention aimed at lessening the gap between high employment and private labor demand. A more active manpower policy, usually of widely eclectic dimensions, aims intervention at structural unemployment and labor market imperfections so as to reduce the roadblocks to fuller employment.

Obviously there are almost endless and not unimportant differences between the alternative strategies of intervention, in the priorities affecting unemployment, and in the closeness to full employment accepted as a guiding premise. But all the interventionists, liberal and conservative alike, eschew the absolute guarantee of genuinely full employment and instead pursue systemic interventions toward a high level of use of human resources and the diminution/minimization of unemployment.

The Guaranteed Full Employment Goal

The *guarantee* by a government of full employment, of guaranteed employment for everyone able and willing to work, represents a social, political, and economic policy fundamentally different from even the most eager and progressive interventionist approach to minimizing unemployment. It posits full employment as a first and irreducible commitment. It is founded on a definition of "full employment" that reduces involuntary lack of work to temporary and frictional factors.

In his June 1944 report, *Full Employment in a Free Society*, Sir William Beveridge defined full employment as meaning "having always more vacant jobs than unemployed men [sic], not slightly fewer jobs. It means that the jobs are at fair wages, of such a kind, and so located that the unemployed men [sic] can reasonably be expected to take them; it means, by consequence, that the normal lag between losing one job and finding another will be very short. . . . Those who lose jobs must be able to find new jobs at fair wages within their capacity, without delay."

In the epochal 1949 United Nations report by "A Group of Experts" on *National and International Measures For Full Employment*, "the practical meaning of Full Employment" is defined as "a situation in which there are no unemployed persons . . . a situation in which unemployment does not exceed the minimum allowances that must be made for the effects of frictional and seasonal factors."

In practical terms two concrete situations of full employment are illustrative. In the United States during the five years of World War II the equivalent of 25 million full-time workers moved into employment (military or civilian), raising the labor force from 45 million to 70 million. The anticipated labor force growth during 1940–45 was exceeded in actuality by almost 8 million. The overall labor force participation rate rose from 56 percent of the noninstitutional population to over 63 percent in 1944. Unemployment was officially reported as 1.2 percent for 1944. For the short-term at least, there was full employment.

The Soviet Union represents a second concrete example of full employment. As reported in a paper prepared by the U.S. Department of Commerce for the Economic Committee of NATO in June 1971 on "Manpower Trends in the USSR: 1950 to 1980": "During the 1960's a steadily increasing number of newspaper articles, scholarly papers, and official documents published in the Soviet Union noted the existence of a labor shortage throughout the Soviet Economy. Many of these publications contained warnings that the shortage would continue throughout the 1970's and have serious effects on the growth of the economy, and there is ample evidence to support this thesis. . . ."

Obviously there are basically different routes to full employment in a socialist planned economy and in a capitalist free enterprise system. The UN experts emphasized in their 1949 report to the secretary general the point of view that there is a "compatibility of full employment with the essential principles of any economic system. . . . The full employment pledge does not impose upon any country the obligation of altering the basic features of its economic system. . . ." The experts noted that:

> In countries in which there is a considerable degree of central direction of the economic system, the mechanism of planning and control can be used to ensure that all available labour is in fact employed. In countries which rely primarily on the system of private enterprise, concern is sometimes

expressed lest a policy of full employment may entail the introduction of controls of a type considered foreign to their economic institutions. In our view, however, the steps required to promote full employment in free enterprise economies are fully consistent with the institutions of such countries.

Without pursuing the matter at length, there is a presumption that the planned economy can maintain full employment easily, even that it is a condition inherent in a fully planned system. In a basically unplanned economy, of which the United States is a major example, full employment would seem to involve a combination of strategies such as those outlined earlier as relevant to seeking high employment. The distinguishing feature between the high and full employment strategies may well include different degrees of fiscal and monetary intervention. But most particularly job creation shifts from minimization of unemployment to an open-ended program whose size is determined simply by the size of the job gap unfilled by the stimulated private economy. In a sense, and even though there are good grounds for opposing the reference as demeaning to public employment, job creation through planned public works and public service employment becomes a "last resort" strategy aimed at meeting the residual employment need that remains after the private sector has "done its best."

There are important and expanding varied conceptions of full employment going beyond the definitions cited and having major policy implications. They represent increased sophistication and higher standards, which reflect advanced social and economic perceptions and enhance and extend the full employment goal, making it more and more difficult to achieve. They also reflect different time and structural change dimensions. The phases of this progressing conception of full employment are more or less as follows.

Jobs for All—Everybody Has an Opportunity to Work The central point of this conception is that no person able and willing to work lacks a job. Jobs may be make-work jobs, and a type of sheltered workshop approach may assure that no one need be idle. At one extreme this situation can be represented statistically in much the same terms as our current official estimates of unemployment—that is, everyone actively seeking work who works even one hour in the survey week is classified as employed, and everyone who does not find at least one hour's work is deemed unemployed; considerations of pay, conditions, and duration of work are not taken into account. The quantitative measure may expand to include involuntary part-time work, but this concept is essentially quantitative without regard to the quality of employment.

A Good Job at a Living Wage for All In this concept the ante is raised—full employment is seen as requiring a certain quality in the jobs provided, which eliminates involuntary part-time work and pays a living wage with good working conditions. This conforms with the Universal Declaration of Human Rights adopted by the United Nations General Assembly on December 10, 1948, which provides as "the common standard of achievement for all peoples and all nations . . . the right to work, to free choice of employment, to just and favorable conditions of work and protection against unemployment" and a living wage.

This standard is reflected in the special U.S. Labor Department subemployment index based on a survey in 13 slum areas in 1966, which included involuntary part-time employment, subpoverty level wages, and the "discouraged workers" not counted in the labor force.

Jobs for All with Decent Pay and Conditions and Realistic Opportunities for Upward Mobility and Work at Full Capacity A very major dimension is added to the concept of unemployment and full employment when underutilization of the current actual and the potential capacity of the labor force is considered. The quantity of human resources unused due to lack of opportunity is not quantifiable, but it is undoubtedly a unemployment factor of great importance. It has been emphasized by the impact of the civil rights, manpower, and antipoverty movements in the 1960s, with their attention to upward mobility, upgrading, and career advancement. The new work opportunities for the disadvantaged, the New Careers programs with job restructuring and the reduction of artificial credentials barriers, and the provision of new support and remedial services are all directed toward this aspect of unemployment.

Full Employment That Means Full Development and Full Utilization of the Total Voluntary Potential of Human Resources over Time The ultimate in full employment is achieved when adequate training, rehabilitation, and labor market structural adjustments are combined with overall demand for labor, which provide jobs and careers for all able and desiring to work. This is a full employment dimension rarely achieved, and it is enhanced as more time is allotted to the process. This conception involves time to overcome handicaps of all sorts of disabilities—physical, mental, and social. It includes adjustments in work schedules, such as increased part-time and flexible work hour arrangements, as well as facilitating transportation, location, etc. As the ultimate full employment dimension, anyone not working in this model has essentially chosen leisure over increased income.

Clearly the differences and the different policy implications of varying full employment models are very important. Essentially what is required is unlimited demand pressing on limited labor resources, with the magnet of opportunity constantly pulling on each person as he chooses to work and to expend the efforts necessary to advance occupationally in return for differential rewards. The assumption is that each individual has free choice whether to work and to advance.

The development of the conception and the realization of full employment over time and in varied situations reflect these different perceptions of what full employment means.

THE CONCEPT OF FULL EMPLOYMENT—BEFORE WORLD WAR II

Unemployment has been the subject of economic and social concern since the earliest days of mercantilism in the fifteenth century. Until the twentieth century, relief of the unemployed poor consisted of either direct "outdoor relief" or the workhouse, with encouragement of the economic growth of the factory system as the ultimate solution. While the general antagonism to idleness may have represented a back-handed concept of full employment, there was no such general concept in effect.

The idea of assuring jobs for all was an idea, as Michael Harrington has commented, "that has been loitering in the corridors of socialist thought for at least 145 years. Louis Blanc, a French historian and, briefly, a government official, first formulated the concept of governmentally guaranteed work in 1836. It was tried in Paris during the Revolution of 1848 and, until the philosophical ascendance of Marxism in the last quarter of the 19th Century, it was what most Europeans understood to be socialism."

Full employment was assumed to be an inherent feature of Utopian socialist plans. For example, in Edward Bellamy's *Looking Backward—2000–1887*, Dr. Leete told Julian West that in the old system "It eventually happened then (1887) that vast numbers who desired to labor could find no opportunity" but that now "the principle of universal military service, as it was understood in (1887) . . . is simply applied to the labor question."

> This, Dr. Leete explained in the Bellamy fantasy, was something which followed as a matter of course as soon as the nation had become the sole capitalist. The people were already accustomed to the idea that the obligation of every citizen, not physically disabled, to contribute his military services to the defense of the nation was equal and absolute. That it was equally the duty of every citizen to contribute his quota of industrial or intellectual services to the maintenance of the nation was equally evident, though it was not until the nation became the employer of labor that citizens were able to render this sort of service with any pretense either of universality or equity.

In his analysis of capitalism, Marx developed the thesis that the system has a chronic incapacity to achieve full employment and that the creation of "a reserve army of the unemployed" was an inherent feature of the system. On the other extreme the classical economists denied the possibility of serious continuing unemployment in the competitive free enterprise system. Thus in Alfred Marshall's *Principles of Economics*, the classic statement in 1890, unemployment or "inconstancy of employment" is mentioned in less than 10 of the book's 858 pages. Unemployment was only an accidental aberration, as the system maintained the essentially optimal level of employment on almost an automatic basis. Later, in 1909, the eminent economist H. Stanley Jevons wrote on "The Causes of Unemployment" and made the point that the "unemployable" and the unemployed are really identical. The causes of unemployment were (1) the inefficiency of the education system which produced unemployable children, (2) the trade unions that pushed wages too high, and (3) trade fluctuations related to "Solar Activity" affecting the sun's heat.

Gradually economists began to recognize that all unemployment was not simply frictional, and they gave their attention to technological, tradecycle, and monetarily caused unemployment. But these were almost "by the way" observations that persisted until the Great Depression. As Schumpeter suggests, the "indictment stands against the vast majority of the economists of that period . . . with few exceptions, of which Marx was the most influential one, they treated cycles [read unemployment] as a phenomenon that is superimposed upon the normal course of capitalist life and mostly as a pathological one; it never occurred to the majority to look to business cycles for material with which to build the fundamental theory of capitalist reality."

The Great Depression forced a revolution in the way of thinking and acting about unemployment. That story has been told many times and need not be repeated here. Pragmatic considerations led to large-scale job creations, with relief and preservation of the system as the primary objectives. In his first inaugural address, on March 4, 1933, President Franklin D. Roosevelt said "Our greatest primary task is to put people to work." In his second "Fireside Chat," on September 30, 1934, Roosevelt said, "I stand or fall by my refusal to accept as a necessary condition of our future a permanent army of unemployed. On the contrary, we must make it a national principle that we will not tolerate a large army of unemployed. . . ." This obvious emphasis had no need for any sophisticated or well-developed concept of full employment: the totally unemployed are estimated officially to have been 25 percent of the labor force in 1933, and the official National Resources Committee (NRC) estimated that on the basis of "full time equivalents" unemployment averaged 45 percent of the total available labor supply for 1932, 1933, and 1934. It should be noted that the NRC data prepared by David Weintraub, then director of the WPA National Research Project on Reemployment Opportunities and Recent Changes in Industrial Techniques, approximately doubled the unemployed labor force estimates indicated by the official Census Bureau data.

The conceptual approach to unemployment was revolutionized in 1936 by the appearance of John Maynard Keynes' seminal volume, *The General Theory of Employment, Interest and Money*. Keynes destroyed the Walras-Marshall laissez-faire equilibrium approach to full employment and built the theoretical and analytical case for government intervention to affect the levels of employment/unemployment. Economists and public officials of the New Deal eagerly grasped Keynes' General Theory as the bible guiding activist interventions to reduce unemployment. With unemployment in the 15–30 percent range, liberals and even radicals marked themselves in "Keynes clothing" as they advocated strong government actions for "full employment," both to meet the continuing Depression crisis and then to prepare for defense and wartime production.

Although the left was attracted to Keynes' advocacy of government intervention against unemployment, the Keynes theory was not a full employment theory. It essentially gave a theoretical foundation to and even justified a stabilized level of "acceptable unemployment." Although originally embraced primarily by liberals, Keynesism is essentially a conservative "state capitalist" approach to the economy and to unemployed resources. This is exemplified by a statement of President Richard M. Nixon's: "I am a Keynesian." Given the real political economy of capitalism that is the fame of Keynes' analysis, conservative Keynesism is the real Keynesism. Keynes has given us a theory of unemployment, not a theory of full employment. Keynes sets the stage for, and makes viable in a managed way, a concept of spurious full employment. Lacking a rigorous conceptualization of what full use of labor resources means, the way is open for the game of debating whether an official unemployment rate of 2, 3, 4, or 5 percent is "full employment." Moreover the long and devious process of statistically manipulating official unemployment data so as to minimize the publicly acknowledged gap between actual and potential labor power utilization is perfectly compatible with the spurious full employment concept.

Various expressions of full employment did begin to appear after Keynes' General Theory. The often cited *An Economic Program for American Democracy* published by seven young Harvard and Tufts Keynesian economists in 1938 spoke vaguely of "eradicating unemployment." In 1939 one of the leading liberal New Deal economists, Mordecai Ezekiel, wrote a polemic for democratic economic planning that he titled *Jobs For All: Through Industrial Expansion*. The author warned:

> Democracy is doubly challenged. Communism on the one side, and Fascism on the other, both proclaim that they are the way to full employment and opportunity for the common man . . . we must solve our own problem of unemployment. We must reopen the doors of opportunity for all our growing youth and our displaced middle-aged. . . . There should be a stirring call to press forward *now* for a full bodied War on Poverty. We should center our national effort *now* on expanding production and doing away with unemployment and poverty. . . .

A pioneering and more precise conception of "practical full employment" was developed by the National Resources Committee in its efforts to quantify the "Loss in Potential Real National Income Due To Depression Unemployment of Men and Machines, 1930–37." Using WPA labor force estimates it was assumed that a "residual unemployment" of about 3.7 percent of the total labor force actually represented "practical full employment" in 1938. As the beginning of World War II drew near, the vague approach to full employment began to merge from concern about economic recovery to potential war mobilization. Even conservative sources sought to debunk the size of the published estimates of unemployment needing public attention, New Deal economists were being called upon to estimate how much unused labor might be realized for the very practical "full employment" of war. Even the most expansive estimates were soon to be surpassed by reality, as World War II moved the country from massive unemployment in 1939 to at least full and perhaps "over-full" employment in 1944.

BEFORE WORLD WAR II:
JOB CREATION TOWARDS FULL EMPLOYMENT?

Precise data about the labor force, employment, and unemployment during World War I are not available. Although U.S. involvement actively covered only 20 months of the war, from April 6, 1917 to November 11, 1918, military personnel on active duty rose from just under 180,000 in 1916 to almost 2,900,000 in 1918. There was considerable expansion of war work, and the inflow of the anticipated 500,000 immigrants was suddenly ended. Together these factors created a tight labor market, with the reported result that "the actual shortage in man power was in effect the most significant economic shortage in the war." But the problem was satisfactorily met by a system of labor exchanges, some special training efforts, the beginnings of "dilution of skilled labor," and a system of labor priorities that "guided the flow of labor from less essential to more essential industries and to prevent the very wasteful rapid turnover which war conditions engendered. . . ." But the chairman of the War Industries Board, Bernard M. Baruch, was able to successfully oppose the drafting of labor as unnecessary "given the country's large reservoir of labor." Full employment was not achieved, and a serious *general* labor shortage was not a problem in World War I.

In practical terms full employment was never an issue during the Great Depression and the New Deal. The economic breakdown was so massive that all concrete programs were aimed simply—and totally inadequately—at reducing the 15–25 percent overall jobless level. Even limited goals of "acceptable unemployment" and "high employment" were never really within reach, let alone aiming at the prospect of any of the four "full employment" models mentioned earlier. As late as 1940 the official unemployment rate was about 15 percent. As summarized by Arthur E. Burns and Edward A. Williams, "Since 1935 the total number given employment on various public work programs has ranged from a low of 2.3 million to a high of 4.6 million. Large as these figures are, at the peak they represented less than half of the number estimated as unemployed. Indeed, thoughout this period these programs have averaged only between one-quarter and one-third of the estimated unemployed."

The relevance of the New Deal experience was practical, not conceptual, insofar as full employment was concerned. It was demonstrated that large-scale government intervention through both public works and direct public employment is a viable and effective way to create jobs and reduce the volume of unused human resources.

As the Great Depression led to large-scale unemployment and attendant destitution, "emergency" became the prime factor in the development of public programs. In the initial stage of the Depression, 1930–32, the central issue was transfer of traditional state and local relief responsibility to the federal government. For a while in this period contradictory programs developed as many states and localities cut down on such usual public services as schools, hospitals, sanitation, and police in order to divert funds to relief.

The history of the development of work-relief programs from 1930 to 1940 is one of experimentation and improvisation. One program led to another revised program reflecting the previous experience. The sequence moves from the early state and local relief efforts to the assumption of federal responsibility in the Federal Emergency Relief Program of 1933, to the transitional Civil Works Program in 1934, to a revised Federal Emergency Work Relief Program from mid-1934 through 1935, and finally to the Works Progress Administration (WPA) that dominated the scene from 1935 to 1940. Special programs for special groups of employables paralleled the above sequence: the National Youth Administration and the Civilian Conservation Corps provided work and income to youth, while the Public Works Administration stimulated employment by financing public construction projects.

From the standpoint of current interests and issues, the experience of the 1930s with job creation suggests four major conclusions:

1. It is feasible for the government, through direct job creating intervention, to create large-scale employment and to cut unemployment extensively.

2. The productive results of direct government job creation are impressive and socially are dramatically useful.

3. The job programs of the 1930s were primitive by today's standards. They did not include systematic or significant on-the-job or off-the-job training, had no program of employability creating remedial or support services, and included nothing at all in the direction of career development, upgrading, or upward mobility.

4. Expansion of the job creation programs was successfully opposed by established political powers at all stages so that those programs fell "far short of utilizing as fully as possible the idle economic resources at hand."

The job creation activities of the New Deal did not approach the goal of high employment or of acceptable unemployment. That achievement was to require the spur provided by Hitler.

FULL EMPLOYMENT IN WORLD WAR II

As has already been noted, World War II led to an unprecedented and spectacular increase in the U.S. labor force, to the virtual extinction of unemployment, to full employment. The gross national product more than doubled from less than $100 billion in 1940 to $212 billion in 1945. Besides this growth some 12 million men and women were added to the armed services. Almost 8 million persons entered the labor force as a result of the aggregate demands of World War II, *beyond* the normally expected growth of the labor force due to population and secular change.

The major work force growth came from youth under twenty. Between April 1940 to April 1945 the labor force participation rate for boys was 57.1 percent instead of the projected 31.8 percent; for girls it was 33.9 percent instead of 16.8 percent. The second major source of labor was the adult female population: instead of an anticipated participtation rate, for example, of 30.4 percent for women aged thirty-five to forty-four, the actual rate was 38.4 percent. A further sharp increase in labor force came from men over fifty-five. And as Durand notes, "Data on patients in mental institutions and on prisoners in state and federal penal institutions indicate that the institutional population grew more slowly during the war than would normally have been expected; if it did not actually decrease. A considerable contribution to the labor force probably came from this source." There was a job for everyone.

The full employment of World War II resulted from three major factors:

1. Aggregate demand, in the Keynesian sense, grew as the gross national product (GNP) doubled and as the federal budget deficit averaged $50 billion ($250 billion in comparable 1972 GNP terms) for each of the years 1943, 1944, and 1945.

2. There was massive direct government "public service employment" created, both for 12 million in the armed forces and for millions more in the related supply services. National security expenditures equaled about 42 percent of GNP in 1943 and 1944.

3. Federal economic controls and planning took over the economy. The War Production Board planned output, allocated material and production quotas, assigned priorities, and administered rationing of essential commodities. The Office of Price Administration and the War Labor Board set prices, rents, and wages. In the labor supply area the War Manpower Commission, the Selective Service System, a federalized employment service and fair employment practices system controlled and guided—short of a general labor draft—the preparation, allocation, and utilization of all manpower.

It is easy but very unimaginative to ask, "If for war, why not for peace?" But the question does persist. And the conditions and procedures that led to our one clear experience with full employment remain as powerful and revealing guides for the future.

WORLD WAR II AND THE FULL EMPLOYMENT GOAL

The complex juxtaposition of the quick shift from depression to wartime full employment, the constructive and hopeful political and economic élan flowing from the defeat of the Axis in unity with the USSR, the possibly subtle challenge of the revolutionary and socialist alternatives—all combined to put full employment in the center of the contemplated postwar economic agenda. As Herbert Stein put it in an excellent discussion of this period:

> Full employment became the flag around which every one could rally. . . . Political leaders, government officials, and all private parties directly concerned with influencing economic policy came to give much higher priority to full employment in their own scale of national objectives for peacetime. They also came to believe that the "people" gave it such high priority that no political party or person could hope to be successful unless identified with the achievement of this goal. No party in office could remain in office without delivering full employment.

But even as the rhetoric of full employment soared, political realities were at work to undermine and divert the integrity of the goal. As Stein remarks, there was uncertainty about "the degree of fullness," and the significant semantics began to mix the terms "high employment" and "full employment." The way began to be opened to supplant genuine full employment by spurious full employment so as to conform to the realities of economic-political power in the country.

Inextricably and perhaps fatally in the context of the growing opposition to planning, the full employment goal was seen as connected with the concept of planning of the nation's economy. Throughout the New Deal, the National Resources Planning Board (NRPB) created by President Roosevelt in 1934 had studied, researched, and reported on the theme of rational, planned use of all national resources. It reflected the mild "socialistic" inclinations of New Deal liberals such as Rexford G. Tugwell, Mordecai Ezekiel, Leon Keyserling, and an impressive group of liberal economists championing Keynesian economic intervention as essential to economic planning. In wartime this agency was instructed to address the problem of conversion and the postwar economy. Early in 1943 the NRPD submitted a lengthy program based on a "New Bill of Rights" and entitled *Security, Work, and Relief Policies*. Submitted to Congress by President Roosevelt, the first item in the "New Bill of Rights" was the "Right to work, usefully and creatively through the productive years," and the second item was "The right to fair pay, adequate to command the necessities and amenities of life. . . ." The implications of this report were for strong, central government planning and for drastic redistributive social and economic policies. Three months after the submission of this report, Congress killed the National Resources Planning Board. This was a harbinger of the fact that, after lengthy and involved attention to the problems of postwar conversion, the aims of liberals for "comprehensive planning for jobs" were to be effectively put aside by the conservative force of Congress led by Senator George of Georgia, who headed the Senate Finance Committee, and Republican leaders such as Senator Robert Taft of Ohio. While the liberal-conservative battle was to be resumed in the debate over the proposed Full Employment Bill in 1945, the results were not to be changed. The political-economic establishment as reflected in Congress was not ready to commit the country to full employment or to authorize the programs necessary for that objective, whether the issue rose around postwar reconversion policy or legislation to guarantee jobs for everyone.

A wide range of authorities and political and economic leadership had defined the full employment goal during World War II. In his 1944 annual address to Congress, Franklin D. Roosevelt formulated a "Second Bill of Rights" with the first right being that of the "right for all [to] . . . a useful and remunerative job in the industries or shops or farms or mines of the nation. . . ." He asked Congress to support government and planning agencies to provide the 60 million jobs this goal required. On October 28, 1944, at Soldier's Field in Chicago, while campaigning for reelection, the President restated the goal of postwar full employment as "sixty million jobs." Henry A. Wallace, then Vice President, put this into the title of his book, saying "I use the total of sixty million jobs as synonymous with the peacetime requirements of full employment . . . work for everyone who wants or needs it."

Parallel to this liberal projection of full employment, business and conservative spokesmen began to endorse the aim of "full" or "high" employment, to be assured by government fiscal interventions if necessary. Thus, in 1942, *Fortune* magazine called upon government to guarantee full employment after the war. The Republican candidate for President in 1944, Thomas Dewey, said in his nomination acceptance speech: "This must be a land where every man and woman has a fair chance to work and get ahead. Never again must free Americans face the specter of long-continued mass unemployment. We Republicans are agreed that full employment shall be a first objective of national policy. And by full employment, I mean a real chance for every man and woman to earn a decent living."

Liberal businessmen in 1942 set up the Committee for Economic Development (CED), which aimed at "high employment" through Keynesian-type economic interventions. The limits of the CED insofar as full employment was concerned are suggested in the language employed by their then-leading spokesman, Beardsley Ruml of Macy's Department Store. Speaking in 1943, Ruml made reference to "high employment—as many jobs as we can—plenty of jobs—satisfactory high level of employment—the jobs we want." This language represented more than simple semantic caution. Reflecting dominant enlightened business influence, it represented the diminution of the full employment goal that was really to control public policy after World War II. It certainly meant rejection of a return to Depression unemployment levels and a liberal acceptance of government Keynesian intervention for that objective. But it also meant that the establishment was not accepting a government commitment to guarantee any model of full employment. It was a "kiss of death."

Unemployment Policy

ROBERT E. LUCAS, JR.

Robert Lucas, Jr., has inherited the Chicago mantle of monetarism from Milton Friedman. A superb theoretician, most of his work is highly technical and extremely complicated. His theoretical work on the foundation of the Phillips curve with Leonard Rapping was instrumental in converting economists from Keynesian economics to the new supply side economics, and he is probably the foremost rational expectation theorist today. This article demonstrates his ability to derive meaningful implications from his theoretical work.

The *U.S.* unemployment rate was certainly too high in 1975, and most economists would agree that it is too high today. It will also be agreed that this observation poses a problem for public policy (in a sense that the observation that winters in Chicago are "too cold" does not). But what exactly is meant by the statement that unemployment is "too high," and what is the nature of the policy problem it poses? This question can be answered in more than one way, and the answer one chooses matters a great deal.

One common answer to this question is that there exists a rate of unemployment—call it "full employment"—which can and should serve as a "target" for economic policy. Unemployment above this rate is regarded as being of a different character from the "frictional" unemployment required to match workers and jobs efficiently, and is treated from a welfare point of view as waste, or deadweight loss. Elimination of this waste is an objective of monetary, fiscal, and perhaps other policies. In the first part of this [article] I will argue that this way of posing the issue does not lead to an operational basis for unemployment policy, mainly on the ground that economists have no coherent idea as to what full employment means or how it can be measured.

An alternative view, prevalent prior to the Great Depression and enjoying something of a revival today, treats *fluctuations* in unemployment and other variables as posing a policy problem. On this view, the average (or natural, or equilibrium) rate of unemployment is viewed as raising policy issues only insofar as it can be shown to be "distorted" in an undesirable way by taxes, external effects, and so on. Nine percent unemployment is then viewed as too high in the same sense that 2 percent is viewed as "too low": both are symptoms of costly and preventable instability in general economic activity. In the concluding part of this [article] I will sketch the approaches to unemployment policy which are suggested by this alternative view and some which are not.

I. FULL EMPLOYMENT: DEFINITION AND MEASUREMENT

The idea that policy can and should be directed at the attainment of a particular, specifiable *level* of the measured rate of unemployment (as opposed to

Robert E. Lucas, Jr., "Unemployment Policy," *American Economic Review*, 68 (May 1978), pp. 353–57.

mitigating *fluctuations* in unemployment) owes its wide acceptance to John Maynard Keynes' *General Theory*. It is there derived from the prior hypothesis that measured unemployment can be decomposed into two distinct components: "voluntary" (or frictional) and "involuntary," with full employment then identified as the level prevailing when involuntary unemployment equals zero. It seems appropriate, then, to begin by reviewing Keynes' reasons for introducing this distinction in the first place.

Keynes (ch. 2, p. 7) classifies the factors affecting equilibrium employment in a real general equilibrium theory: the mechanics of matching workers to jobs, household labor-leisure preferences, technology, and the composition of product demand. Is it the case, he asks, that spontaneous shifts in any of these four real factors can account for employment fluctuations of the magnitude we observe? Evidently, the answer is negative. It follows that two kinds of theory must be needed to account for observed unemployment movements: granted that real general equilibrium theory may account for a relatively constant, positive component, *some other theory* is needed for the rest.

Accepting the necessity of a distinction between explanations for normal and cyclical unemployment does not, however, compel one to identify the first as voluntary and the second as involuntary, as Keynes goes on to do. This terminology suggests that the key to the distinction lies in some difference in the way two different types of unemployment are *perceived by workers*. Now in the first place, the distinction we are after concerns *sources* of unemployment, not differentiated types. One may, for example, seek very different theoretical explanations for the average price of a commodity and for its day-to-day fluctuations, without postulating two types of price for the same good. Similarly, one may classify motives for holding money without imagining that anyone can subdivide his own cash holdings into "transactions balances," "precautionary balances," and so forth. The recognition that one needs to distinguish among sources of unemployment does not in any way imply that one needs to distinguish among types.

Nor is there any evident reason why one would *want* to draw this distinction. Certainly the more one thinks about the decision problem facing individual workers and firms the less sense this distinction makes. The worker who loses a good job in prosperous times does not *volunteer* to be in this situation: he has suffered a capital loss. Similarly, the firm which loses an experienced employee in depressed times suffers an undesired capital loss. Nevertheless the unemployed worker at any time can always find *some* job at once, and a firm can always fill a vacancy instantaneously. That neither typically does so *by choice* is not difficult to understand given the quality of the jobs and the employees which are easiest to find. Thus there is an involuntary element in *all* unemployment, in the sense that no one chooses bad luck over good; there is also a voluntary element in all unemployment, in the sense that however miserable one's current work options, one can always choose to accept them.

Keynes, in chapter 2, deals with the situation facing an *individual* unemployed worker by evasion and wordplay only. Sentences like "more labor would, as a rule, be forthcoming at the existing money wage if it were demanded" are used again and again as though, from the point of view of a jobless worker, it is unambiguous what is meant by "*the* existing money wage." Unless we define an individual's wage rate as the price someone else is willing to pay him for his labor (in which case Keynes' assertion above is *defined* to be false), what *is* it? The wage at which he would *like* to work more hours? Then it is *true* by definition and equally empty. The fact is, I think, that Keynes wanted to get labor markets out of the way in chapter 2 so that he could get on to the demand theory which really interested him. This is surely understandable, but what is the excuse for letting his carelessly drawn distinction between voluntary and involuntary unemployment dominate aggregative thinking on labor markets for the forty years following?

It is, to be sure, possible to write down theoretical models in which households are faced with an "hours constraint" limiting the hours they can supply at "the" prevailing wage, and in which, therefore, there is a clear distinction between the hours one can supply and the hours one would like to supply. Such an exercise is frequently motivated as an attempt to "explain involuntary (or Keynesian) unemployment." This misses the point: involuntary unemployment is not a fact or a phenomenon which it is the task of theorists to explain. It is, on the contrary, a theoretical construct which Keynes introduced in the hope that it would be helpful in discovering a correct explanation for a genuine phenomenon: large-scale fluctuations in measured, total unemployment. Is it the task of modern theoretical economics to "explain" the theoretical constructs of our predecessors, whether or not they have proved fruitful? I hope not, for a surer route to sterility could scarcely be imagined.

In summary, it does not appear possible, even in principle, to classify individual unemployed people as either voluntarily or involuntarily unemployed depending on the characteristics of the decision problems they face. One cannot, even conceptually, arrive at a usable definition of full employment as a state in which no involuntary unemployment exists.

In practice, I think this fact has been recognized for some time. Estimates of full employment actually in use have been obtained using aggregate information rather than data on individuals. As recently as the 1960's it was widely believed that there was some level of aggregate unemployment with the property that when unemployment exceeded this rate, expansionary monetary and fiscal measures would be noninflationary, while at rates below this critical level they would lead to inflation. One could then identify unemployment rates at or below this full-employment level as frictional or voluntary, and unemployment in excess of this level as involuntary. It was understood that only unemployment of the latter type posed a problem curable by monetary or fiscal policy. As Walter Heller wrote, "Gone is the countercyclical syndrome of the 1950's. Policy now centers on gap closing and growth, on realizing and enlarging the economy's non-inflationary potential" (Preface). Later, Heller refers to "the operational concepts of the 'production gap,' 'full-employment surplus,' the 'fiscal drag,' and 'fiscal dividends'" (p. 18).

For the purpose of calculating the production gap to which Heller referred, it makes little difference whether the voluntary-involuntary terminology accurately reflects differences in the way unemployed people view their situations. The issue here is rather whether there exists an aggregate rate of unemployment (on the order of 4 or 5 percent) which is of use in measuring an economy's noninflationary potential. If there were, then objections of the sort I have raised above could be dismissed as merely terminological: if one objected to calling unemployment above the designated full-employment level involuntary, one could call it something else, perhaps wasteful or unnecessary.

The last ten years have taught us a great deal about this operational concept of a production gap. In 1975, the *U.S.* economy attained the combination of 9 percent inflation and an unemployment rate of 9 percent. Applying the concept of a production gap to these numbers, does one conclude that the noninflationary potential of the *U.S.* economy is associated with unemployment rates in excess of 9 percent? Does one redefine 9 percent inflation to be noninflationary? Or can the entire episode be somehow pinned on oil prices?

I have reviewed two possible routes by which one might hope to give the term full employment some operational significance. One was to begin at the individual worker level, classifying unemployment into two types, voluntary and involuntary, count up the number classed as voluntary, and define the total to be the unemployment level associated with full employment. A second was to determine the operating characteristics of the economy at different rates of unemployment, and then to define full employment to be the rate at which inflation rates are acceptable. Neither of these approaches leads to an operational definition of full employment. Neither yields a coherent view as to why unemployment is a problem, or as to the costs and benefits involved in economic policies which affect unemployment rates. The difficulties are not the measurement error problems which necessarily arise in applied economics. They arise because the "thing" to be measured does not exist.

II. BEYOND FULL-EMPLOYMENT POLICY

Abandoning the constraint that any discussion of unemployment must begin first by drawing the voluntary-involuntary distinction and then thinking in separate ways about these two types of unemployment will, I think, benefit both positive and normative analysis. Practicing social science is hard enough without crippling oneself with dogmatic constraints. A terminology which precludes asking the question: "Why do people choose to take the actions we see them taking, instead of other actions they might take instead?" precludes any serious thinking about behavior at all.

Whether or not the body of work stemming from the Edmund Phelps volume, and earlier work of George Stigler, John McCall and others, has produced all the right answers about the determinants of employment and unemployment, it has at least begun to pose some of the right questions. By treating all unemployment as voluntary, this work has led to the examination of alternative arrangements which firms and employees might choose to adopt for dealing with fluctuations in product demand, and their reasons for choosing to react to such fluctuations in the way we observe them doing. Pursuit of this question has indicated both how very difficult it is, and even more so how much economics was swept under the rug by "explaining involuntary unemployment" by incompetent auctioneers or purely mechanical wage and price equations.

Practicing normative macroeconomics without the construct of full employment does take some getting used to. One finds oneself slipping into such sentences as: "There is no such thing as full employment, but I can tell you how it can be attained." But there are some immediate benefits. First, one dispenses with that entire meaningless vocabulary associated with full employment, phrases like potential output, full capacity, slack, and so on, which suggested that there was some *technical* reason why we couldn't all return to the 1890 workweek and produce half again the *GNP* we now produce. Second, one finds to one's relief that creating unemployment as a voluntary response to an unwelcome situation does not commit oneself to normative nonsense like blaming depressions on lazy workers.

The effect it does have on normative discussion is twofold. First, it focuses discussion of monetary and fiscal policy on *stabilization*, on the pursuit of price stability and on minimizing the disruptive effects of erratic policy changes. Some average unemployment rate would, of course, emerge from such a policy but as a by-product, not as a preselected target. Second, by thinking of this natural rate as an equilibrium emerging from voluntary exchange in the usual sense, one can subject it to the scrutiny of modern methods of public finance.

To take one example, as the level of unemployment compensation is varied, an entire range of average unemployment rates, all equally "natural," is available to society. At one extreme, severe penalties to declaring oneself unemployed could reduce unemployment rates to any desired level. Such a policy would result in serious real output losses, as workers retain poor jobs too long and accept poor jobs too readily. An output-maximizing unemployment compensation scheme would, with risk-averse workers, involve a subsidy to being unemployed, else workers retain a poor but relatively sure current wage in preference to the riskier but, on average, more productive return to seeking a new job. In view of the private market's inability to provide sufficient insurance against unemployment risk, still further gains in expected utility could be expected by still higher unemployment compensation, resulting in a deliberate sacrifice in real output in exchange for a preferred arrangement for allocating risk. Notice that as one traces out tradeoffs of this sort, the issue of slack or waste does not arise. Different policies result in different levels of real output, but output increases are necessarily obtained at the expense of something else. Whether any particular level of unemployment compensation is too high or too low is a difficult issue in practice, but it is one that cannot be resolved simply by observing that other, unemployment reducing, compensation levels are *feasible*.

The policy problem of reducing business cycle risk is a very real and important one, and one which I believe monetary and fiscal policies directed at price stability would go a long way toward achieving. The problem of finding arrangements for allocating unemployment risks over individuals in a satisfactory way is also important, and can be analyzed by the methods of modern welfare economics. The pursuit of a full-employment target which no one can measure or even define conceptually cannot be expected to contribute to the solution of either problem.

IV/BEYOND MACROECONOMICS: SUPPLY SIDE SOLUTIONS TO UNEMPLOYMENT

Both of the two opposed errors of pessimism which now make so much noise in the world will be proved wrong in our time—the pessimism of the revolutionaries who think that things are so bad that nothing can save them but violent change, and the pessimism of our reactionaries who consider the balance of our economic and social life so precarious that we must risk no experiments.

J. M. KEYNES

The unemployment problem can be solved. As we shall see, there are a variety of proposals that directly eliminate unemployment without using macroeconomic demand policies. These are the supply side solutions to unemployment.

But the fact that these solutions exist does not mean that they should necessarily be used. Once one leaves the world of macroeconomics, where unemployment is considered bad almost by definition, and enters the world of microeconomics, the imperative to eliminate unemployment is lost. In microeconomics unemployment serves useful functions. Too little unemployment is as bad as too much unemployment, and policy must be directed toward achieving the *optimal level* of unemployment. In any microeconomic discussion of unemployment, one must be much more explicit about types of unemployment and about the desired relationship between the individual and the state. Consequently such "solutions" must build upon the foundation established in the earlier sections, necessarily embodying philosophical, political, and practical judgments.

In those earlier sections, two opposing views of the economy were explored—the natural rate theory and the nonaccelerating rate (NARU) theory. In the natural rate theory, we saw that aggregate demand policies cannot be used to solve unemployment and that an alternative direct approach must be used. In the NARU theory, we learned that an effective incomes policy makes it possible to expand output and employment, and therefore an incomes policy is a solution to unemployment in that it allows the government to let the economy expand. However, even in the NARU view, there are limits to aggregate demand policy, since too much demand pressure would cause the incomes policies to break down. Thus, there is a need to search for direct ways to attack unemployment, regardless of which theory one holds.

The proposals presented in this section are not directly tied to either side of the monetarist/antimonetarist argument. They circumvent the aggregate demand issue by directly affecting individual incentives. Thus, they are microeconomic, not macroeconomic, solutions to unemployment in that they rely on individuals' responses to microeconomic incentives.

141

FOUR MICROECONOMIC APPROACHES TO ANY PROBLEM

Because the microeconomic approach to macroeconomic problems is new, it is useful to review potential microeconomic, or incentive, approaches to a problem. There are four general incentive approaches one might try:

1. Modify the existing set of incentives; for example, change the unemployment insurance system.

2. Establish property rights and allow the market to solve the problem; for example, create contracts in employment guarantees that sell on an open market and require the holder to hire an individual.

3. Analog the "market solution" with tax and subsidy incentives; for example, employment tax credits.

4. Eliminate the problem by direct regulation; for example, mandate that all individuals must work and supply jobs to those who cannot find one.

None of these policies is a priori preferable; the preferable policy depends upon a comparison of relative costs and benefits of each. Although each method can "solve" the unemployment problem, each is costly and will create problems of its own. Reasonable people are likely to differ over the relative costs and benefits of the various approaches; therefore, significant debate is likely to continue.

The following articles provide examples of each proposed approach listed above. The choice among them (along with the decision as to whether to use *any* "solution") is up to you.

SUPPLY SIDE ECONOMICS

The least drastic of the variety of microeconomic approaches is to modify the incentives embodied in our existing set of institutions rather than to create a new set of institutions. Thus, it is not surprising that this supply side approach has been given the most press coverage and explored in the greatest depth. At times the press is guilty of writing as if the specific set of proposals modifying the existing system is the entirety of supply side economics. It is not. More properly, "supply side" should be used for all the proposals that emphasize microeconomic incentives rather than the aggregate demand of macroeconomics.

The organizing idea of all supply side proposals is the proposition that all aggregate results—such as the amount of unemployment—stem from individual decisions. Thus, if there is unemployment, it is because incentives embodied in the system cause that unemployment. In this sense, as Lucas argued in the preceding section, all unemployment is "voluntary." This approach contrasts significantly with the normal macroeconomics approach that views unemployment as primarily *involuntary.* This "all unemployment is voluntary" approach is preferable in that it channels the analysis in a useful direction—toward the question, How can the incentive structure be changed?

But avoiding the Charybdis on the left, we must also avoid the Scylla on the right.* In microeconomics it is easy to fall into the "market is optimal" trap. The problem is that the market depends upon property rights and the institutional structure that supports those

---

*In Greek mythology there was an extremely dangerous passage off the coast of Italy with jagged rocks and whirlpools on both sides. They characterized these rocks as female sirens, Scylla and Charybdis, who would lure unsuspecting sailors to them, and death, in the treacherous rocks. Only the sailor who kept to the middle of the passage could survive.

property rights. Change the property rights and you change the market solution. The market leads to an optimal solution only if one begins from an optimal set of property rights. Views on what set of property rights is optimal differ drastically and, thus, so do views on the need for institutional change. Good microeconomics remains neutral among results using alternative sets of property rights. It only provides an answer to the question, *Given* a set of property rights, what are the expected consequences? What one believes is "optimal" depends upon the value judgments one uses. These must be made clear in the analysis.

Although many of the new "incentive" school or supply side economists are associated with an antigovernment ideology, there is nothing inherently contradictory between an "incentive" approach and the belief in either an active government sector or substantial redistribution. Indeed, a less publicized, but substantial, group of pro-government action economists should also be included in the incentive school. These include well-known economicsts such as Abba Lerner, Art Okun, and Charles Schultze. It might even be said that all economists who have studied and believed in microeconomics (and breathes there an economist who has not even slightly believed?) have incentive school tendencies and are, at a minimum, fellow travelers. It follows that there is nothing necessarily contradictory in being both a Keynesian macroeconomist and an "incentive" school or "supply side" economist.

PROPOSALS TO SOLVE UNEMPLOYMENT
As stated above, modifying the existing institutions is the least drastic change. It has therefore been the most widely discussed in the press as is evidenced by the first article of this section, "To Set the Economy Right." This article from a *Time* magazine cover story reviews the popular view of supply side economics and its policy implication. Notice as you read it the tendency of associating "supply side" economics with conservative economic policies and the tendency to regard it as a substitute for, rather than a complement to, Keynesian macroeconomics. This tendency should be avoided.

Modifying Existing Incentives
The next two readings, "How to Deal with the 'New Unemployment' " and "The Private and Social Costs of Unemployment," provide a more in-depth analysis of the proposals—especially those of Martin Feldstein who coined the phrase "the new unemployment." Feldstein argues that we can, and should, institute policies to lower the average level of unemployment. Since aggregate demand management cannot be relied upon to achieve the goal, we must institute new types of policies. In developing this theme, he considers the composition of unemployment and argues that most unemployment in the American economy is not hard core unemployment but lay-off unemployment of short duration.

To cope with this "new unemployment," Feldstein has suggested in previous works a range of programs targeted for specific groups. These include youth employment scholarships, modification of the minimum wage standards, improved manpower programs, and a re-examination and redesign of the current adverse incentives embodied in unemployment insurance. Of these, unemployment insurance reform is given the most prominence. The important question is whether such a redesign can be accomplished while retaining the positive attributes of unemployment insurance. One must hope that the answer is yes, because, as the next two readings demonstrate, the existing system is already strained and in need of reform. The first compares unemployment during the Depression with unemployment today while the second provides insight into the financial plight that the unemployment benefit fund is in.

Tax and Subsidy Incentives

An alternative to improving the incentives in the existing system is to introduce direct tax and subsidy incentives for employment. The next two selections outline proposals for implementing this approach. In the first, Robert Eisner suggests a specific tax credit for employers who hire individuals without jobs, while in the next, Layard and Nickell examine the arguments in favor of subsidizing extra jobs.

The proposals discussed in these articles are actually subsidy incentives, which would give a firm tax credits or subsidies for any contribution it makes toward a reduction in unemployment, but they would not impose taxes for any contribution it makes toward a increase in unemployment. Thus, the proposals embody a positive aggregate demand stimulus in addition to the incentive, because they increase government expenditures without increasing revenues. A true supply side solution would rely only on incentive effects, taxing firms that do not increase their employment by X percent and subsidizing firms that increase employment by more than X percent. The true supply side plan would thus finance itself. But such a neutral plan would likely raise serious political questions; taxes are much more difficult to impose than are subsidies. Consider as you read the articles (1) whether the proposals would reduce the overall unemployment or merely affect its variability, (2) how high a tax and/or subsidy rate would be needed to achieve full employment, and (3) whether such a rate would be politically feasible.

Market Incentives

The third incentive approach to the unemployment problem is the "market solution." The next article provides an example of this alternative, although it, too, is biased in that it offers only a subsidy. This "market solution" may at first appear rather unusual, provoking the question, Don't we already rely upon the market to "solve" unemployment? The answer is yes and no. Yes, we rely upon the market to establish relative wages and hence to establish the *division* of the total amount of employment; but the market does not *directly* determine the total amount of employment. At present it only indirectly determines it. The reason is that each person or firm does not consider the effect of a decision about employment on the overall employment rate. The net result of all individuals' decisions may lead to *any* level of employment, although significant deviations from the desired employment level will likely set forces in motion that will eventually achieve the desired employment levels. Keynesian macroeconomics suggests that these indirect market forces are too slow and that the government should institute policies that speed up the adjustment. Establishing a new market in employment rights is one method to achieve this end.

If the society cares what the employment level is and that level is not considered in private decisions, the employment level is an externality—a result of a decision not taken into account by the decision maker. If a program can be found that achieves a "preferable" employment level, it can "internalize" that externality. One's beliefs about a preferable employment level and whether it is an externality necessarily depend on welfare judgments and on the expected administrative costs of alternative policies. These you must judge for yourself.

An example of a "market" solution to unemployment that internalizes the employment externality is presented in the Hazelett article on "money pumps." Here, firms guarantee that they will hire a certain number of employees for whom they have contracted. In this manner, the government can control the amount of employment through the control of these contracts, or "money pumps." An alternative "market" solution embodying a different set of property rights would be to require firms to pay other firms to hire an individual for every one that they fire. Alternatively, firms could be required to hire X percent more workers and could buy contracts only if they hired more than X percent. Each is a potential market solution embodying alternative property rights. All the above will likely seem a bit confusing; the concepts are not easy. The following reading by Albert Hart helps clear up the confusion by placing the Hazelett proposal in perspective relative to a variety of market control systems, providing insight into the general use of market control instruments.

The administrative burdens of any market solution are great, but the proposals serve as a benchmark by which to judge other proposals. The important point to remember is that markets have meaning only in reference to a set of property rights, and an analysis of the development, administrative costs, and equity of property rights is fundamental to the study of markets and market solutions to problems.

Guaranteed Jobs

The final group of articles represents the administrative or regulatory approach. In these proposals the government directly "solves" the unemployment problem by guaranteeing jobs for all individuals. As with the other proposals, a variety of administrative approaches exists within the general framework, ranging from "conservative" to "liberal." The first reading suggesting this approach discusses the Soviet solution to unemployment. Not only are graduates of Soviet colleges guaranteed jobs, but they are also forced to take whatever is assigned, and the Day of Distribution is one of the most important days in any college student's life. As you read it, consider whether you would prefer such a system to our present one. How much chance of being unemployed would you be willing to face before you would favor such a system? Are all the problems discussed in the article endemic to any job assignment system—including the market—or are they specific to the Soviet approach?

The Soviet system of solving unemployment has never been seriously considered for the United States, but other "guaranteed jobs" proposals—embodying more freedom of choice—have been. The next reading provides a rather far-out approach. Instead of modifying the existing incentives in the unemployment insurance system, it suggests replacing it with a "guaranteed jobs" system where the "work" provided is merely calisthenics and self-improvement. As you read it, compare its effects with those of the less dramatic revisions in the unemployment insurance system suggested by Feldstein. Which would you describe as the most "conservative"?

The next reading, by Michael Harrington, provides a rather different guaranteed jobs approach. In his view the government is responsible for more than merely providing an able-bodied individual with a means of translating his time into money. Attacking the "workfare" program, Harrington argues that the government is responsible for supplying "meaningful employment" for all Americans. Notice as you read it that the "workfare" program he attacks was designed for welfare recipients and not for individuals already in the work force. Notice also the direct opposition of values about the role of the state in the Harrington proposal and the preceding Colander proposal.

The last two articles, about the Humphrey-Hawkins Act, tell a story of dreams versus reality. Initially designed to be the fulfillment of the guaranteed jobs dream that dates back to the Employment Act of 1946, it, in fact, developed into a guarantee of nothing. The first selection, "Full Employment and Balanced Growth Act of 1976," is an early version of the act and includes a summary of Leon Keyserling's statement to the committee about the act. The final reading is Keyserling's 1980 reflection about the act.

CONCLUSION

It seems obvious that no one is especially happy with where we are. It is also obvious that there is no clear-cut consensus of where to go. Can such a consensus be found? Is compromise possible among the various positions? And even if a theoretical "solution" can be agreed upon, can it be translated into practice?

Most of us might agree that the ideal system would help those who "need" it; but those "needy" groups are precisely the ones without political muscle. Given the distribution of power in society, it is likely that in order to get something for the least powerful, slices of the pie must be given to the large number of other groups who are more powerful, with the net result being that any program will be far more costly than any that was originally proposed.

For any progressive action this represents a fundamental dilemma. The distribution of income and wealth in our society already represents the distribution of power in the society. Large changes are unlikely to occur, since any attempt to change that distribution will run counter to the actual distribution of power. Thus, there will be no easy answer.

To Set the Economy Right

TIME MAGAZINE

Time magazine is the news magazine that created news magazines. Its articles are generally witty, readable, and informative, and its coverage of economics is no exception. The following article on the new "supply side" economics provides a good example.

Nobody is apt to look back on the 1970s as the good old days. The economy's most disruptive decade since the Great Depression has borne the stagflation contradiction of no growth amid rampaging inflation, the can't do trauma of receding productivity in the nation that was long the world's cornucopia, the reality of an energy shortage in the land of supposedly boundless resources, and the debauch of a dollar that once was "as good as gold."

Economists, proud and powerful in the 1960s, now look like Napoleon's generals decamping from Moscow. Their past prescriptions—tax tinkering and Government deficit spending to prop up demand, wage and price guidelines to hold down inflation—have been as helpful as snake oil. "Things just do not work now as they used to," says former Federal Reserve Chairman Arthur Burns, and who can contradict him? The U.S. economy, bloated and immobilized, has been turned topsy-turvy.

Yet a revisionist group of economists, eclectic and unorthodox, is on the rise, and they have provocative views about what has mucked up the economy and how to start fixing it. These academics, still in their 30s or early 40s, admit to many more questions than answers and are sometimes unfairly dismissed by their more traditionalist colleagues as "N.C.s" (Neanderthal Conservatives). Hardly Neanderthal, they are instead moderate, pragmatic economists of the late 1970s who are bringing fresh air, and fresh hope, to the dismal science. Says Rudolph Penner, head of tax-policy studies at the American Enterprise Institute: "The exciting ideas are now coming from the under-40 crowd, and they are saying that Government is not efficient."

That heresy shakes the almost reverential respect accorded by the profession to Britain's late John Maynard Keynes, the century's most influential economist. The belief of Keynes's disciples that governments often could manage economic affairs as efficiently and effectively as free markets themselves has been rejected by the accumulating research of the new economists.

Still undergraduates when Keynesianism was flourishing in the late 1950s and the 1960s, the new economists are now professors in their own right at universities around the country. Among them: Martin Feldstein, 39, of Harvard, who is the leading thinker in the group; Robert Lucas, 41, of the University of Chicago; Michael Boskin, 33, of Stanford; Rudiger Dornbusch, 37, and Stanley Fischer, 35, both of M.I.T.; as well as many, many others.

"To Set the Economy Right," *Time*, 27 Aug. 1979, pp. 24–35. Reprinted by permission from *Time*, The Weekly Newsmagazine; Copyright Time Inc. 1979.

147

The new group represents what might be termed the rubber band school of economics—what the profession itself calls "elasticity." The sensible notion is that people respond to the specific incentives of price and supply and that, given the right incentives, the market itself is better equipped than the Government to bring about lower prices and more supplies of what people want and need.

The economists argue that instead of providing the right incentives, government policy has been coming up with all the wrong ones. They assert that Government has motivated Americans to spend too much and save too little. They charge that federal tax, budget and monetary policies have promoted immediate consumption instead of investment for the future. Their fundamental warning: America has been living off, and eating into, its capital stock. Many of its factories and machines have become outmoded; its old industrial cities have become rundown; its work force has become less productive; real growth has swung low while demand has remained high. The nation is, in short, losing its economic edge in the world, and the hour is late—very late.

The price that every American pays for these failures is a decade-long inflation that is the most pernicious price spiral since the Korean War, and certainly the most alarming one in the nation's history. Because competitiveness and efficiency have declined, and productivity growth, that most basic yardstick for measuring a nation's economic vitality, has slowed, the real cost of producing goods has jumped. Meanwhile, to keep demand up, the Government has created money and credit at far faster rates than businessmen can turn out products and services. The result: too much money chasing too few goods, which is a classic inflation. Largely because of the rapid expansion of money, the average household income is more than twice as much as it was ten years ago, or $16,100. Yet because of inflation, real purchasing power is up only 11%, and for millions of Americans it is now only the second income from a working wife that enables families to make ends meet.

Inflation has spread a financial virus of unwanted dollars to the economies of the nation's trading partners, turning the once mighty greenback into the sick man of international finance. Since 1970, some $650 billion has piled up in so-called Eurodollar accounts in banks overseas, and the threat is ever present that holders might stampede to sell their dollars. Since 1971, minipanics have led to the collapse of worldwide fixed exchange rates against the dollar, the slide of the dollar against gold and other precious metals, and the progressive disintegration of global confidence in the dollar itself.

The Federal Reserve Board over the years has jumped back and forth capriciously from tightening the nation's money supply in an effort to slow inflation, to running the printing presses full blast when the economy seemed in need of a lift. But its new chairman, Paul Volcker, seems committed to a more consistent and tougher policy. Last week the Fed lifted its discount rate, the amount that it charges for loans to commercial banks, from 10% to a record 10½%, suggesting that even in the face of a business slowdown the board is at last determined to halt the excessive expansion of money and credit.

That would be a welcome development because it is reasonable to wonder just how much more inflation the U.S. can safely absorb. A nation that hardly noticed when prices inched up, on average, little more than 1% a year during the 1950s and early 1960s, now endures such rises every month. The jarring discovery that the prudent no longer save for tomorrow but spend their dollars as soon as they get them has shaken not only the American economy but also the American psyche. Since 1970, the U.S. has become a nation of spendthrifts, and the personal-saving rate has slipped from 7.4% to 5.2% of aftertax income, the lowest among all industrial nations. The saving slump, which starves investment and feeds consumption, reflects the inflationary attitude of "buy it now" or, worse, "borrow to buy it now." Whatever "it" is will probably cost more tomorrow.

The new economists have no monopoly on accurate diagnoses of the inflation malady. Economists everywhere agree that excessive federal spending, too rapid expansion of money, too much costly regulation by Government have been among the primary causes. But many of the experts admit to being puzzled about possible cures. This bafflement is not shared by the new economists. Observes former Treasury Secretary W. Michael Blumenthal: "Economists from the 1940s and 1950s just did not have a decent theory for productivity or inflation. It is only the new generation of Ph.D.s from the end of the 1960s onward who are asking these questions." On the other hand, the solutions they propose will hardly be easy. Among the recommendations:

• Adopt consistent, year-after-year policies of moderate monetary growth so that inflation will be held back and people can plan ahead intelligently.

• Give long-term tax incentives to encourage saving and investment by individuals, entrepreneurs and companies.

• Avoid quickie tax cuts or fiddling with the federal deficit to stimulate consumer spending, and work instead to balance the budget.

• Reduce Government spending, in particular so-called uncontrollables such as social and pension programs that are committed by previous acts of Congress to rise and rise; by cutting spending, more money, more of the nation's capital will be made available to job-creating private businesses.

• Soften or scrap wasteful and production-retarding Government regulations that devour capital but produce no wealth.

• Restrict Government's overall role in the economy in order to enhance personal incentive.

• Above all, stimulate increased supply and production instead of increased demand and consumption.

The case for more consistency and less short-term meddling reflects the spreading awareness that efforts to manage effectively a complex $2.3 trillion economy is hopelessly beyond any government's power. Admits one of the new economists, Thomas Sargent, 36, of the University of Minnesota: "We just don't have the kinds of detailed knowledge to fine-tune the economy. We are further from that goal than we were ten years ago."

Just as forcefully, the new economists argue that the Government can and should come up with specific programs to bring more goods and services to market, letting competition curb the price spiral. Economist Jerry Jasinowski, 40, Assistant Commerce Secretary for Policy, is one of many who believe that boosting supply is the only long-term antidote to rising prices. Says he: "We must admit openly that manipulation of demand via public expenditure, taxes and control over credit does not get to the heart of the problems of the 1970s and 1980s. The source of these problems lies not with the ability to consume but with the capacity to produce."

The unsettling ideas of the incentive economists are becoming a new orthodoxy in much of Government. Last week the congressional bipartisan Joint Economic Committee issued a grave warning in its midyear report: unless major improvements are made in expanding the "supply side" of the economy by boosting saving and investment in order to lift productivity, the nation will face a drastically declining standard of living in the 1980s. Inflation will push prices up to almost incredible levels—$5.80 for a gallon of gasoline, $2.06 for a loaf of bread—even as unemployment itself stays high. But, wrote Chairman Lloyd Bentsen, the Democratic Senator from Texas, "this committee believes we can and we must produce our way out of our economic problems."

Legislative and Administration leaders are pressing new policies to enhance production and supply. New Treasury Secretary G. William Miller, among many others, urges faster write-offs for business spending on factories and tools—to spur capital investment in expansion, modernization and automation. Last year's passage of a version of the Steiger Amendment to reduce capital-gains taxes and stimulate investment has boosted venture capital (the money that investors risk on new businesses) by 1,000%. To shift still more money into investments, Senate Finance Chairman Russell Long and House Ways and Means Chairman Al Ullman champion lower taxes on capital, profits and personal income, and correspondingly higher sales taxes.

Support is also building for proposals by Long and many other legislators to reduce income taxes on interest from bank accounts to encourage people to save instead of spend. Dollars put into saving are reinvested by banks in wealth-creating projects, such as home construction and factory expansion. That not only provides jobs but also slows rising prices by stimulating production. On the other hand, money spent on end-use consumer items, such as a car or TV, buys just one thing.

The incentive economists, and even many of their older, more traditional peers urge the scrapping of outmoded and costly Government regulations and programs that amount to little more than self-inflicted wounds on the economy. Not only do they often aggravate inflation and reduce productivity, but they frequently produce results that their well-intentioned authors never envisioned. Some of the programs have been around since the New Deal and have become patent sops for special interest groups. The nation needs more food, and at lower prices, but federal price-propping subsidies last year paid farmers some $2.2 billion in supports; and almost one-third of that was payments not to plant crops at all. The nation desperately requires all the domestic oil and gas it can find, but the Government's five-year-old mishmash of domestic price controls encourages Americans to burn more oil and U.S. oil companies to do their exploring in other countries.

Some of the more recent regulations make the Government look like a neurotic nanny. Just one example: federal health rules require hospitals to use plastic liners for wastebaskets, but Government safety rules ban their use as fire hazards. Says Charles Schultze, chief White House economic adviser: "We have to regulate with more rationality and sensitivity. The major problem of Government management over the next 20 years will be management of the regulatory process."

Making economic sense out of Government's tax policies is a paramount concern of the incentive economists. One of the best known, and certainly most flamboyant, of them is the University of Southern California's Arthur Laffer, 39, creator of the "Laffer Curve," which he sketched on a napkin after dinner at the Two Continents restaurant in Washington, D.C. The curve illustrates that after a certain level is reached, tax increases do not raise Government revenues but actually lower them. Reason: higher taxes discourage people from working or investing to earn more money since the Government simply takes it away. Conversely, lower taxes encourage people to work harder and earn more, leading to higher revenues. Thus the best way to increase Government income—as well as productivity, investment and general wealth—is to hold taxes low.

The incentive economists also urge predictability and stability in Government monetary policy. The University of Minnesota, home of Liberal Walter Heller, and the University of Chicago, where Milton Friedman did pioneering work in monetarist theory, have lately produced one money-oriented branch of the new economists, the "rational expectations" group. Their thesis: if politicians promise to cut inflation but pursue policies that just make prices rise faster, the people eventually will get the message and act on the rational assumption that inflation will keep increasing. Recognizing that savers are suckers, citizens will just spend their money as soon as they get it. Thus, in order to increase savings, the Government's wisest course would be to keep the growth of money consistently low. People then would rationally expect inflation to diminish and, acting on that belief, would save and invest.

The intellectual leader of the young economists is Harvard's Feldstein, a soft-spoken family man from The Bronx, whose looks and middle-class background and mannerisms call to mind a benign dentist. While most of his peers remain academically cloistered, concentrating on the higher mathematics and econometric concepts of modern research, Feldstein is at home in both academe and Government. He is equally comfortable pondering a regression equation for a computer program or testifying to a congressional committee, which he often does. Both political parties eagerly seek his counsel. He was an adviser to Jimmy Carter's '76 campaign, turned down a bid to join Gerald Ford's Council of Economic Advisers, and is often spoken of as a future CEA chairman, probably in a Republican Administration.

Along with the other incentive economists, Feldstein argues that the Government is trying to do too many things that it either cannot do efficiently or that people can do better for themselves. That, of course, is a direct affront to Keynesian doctrine. Beginning in the mid-1930s, Establishment pillars of the dismal science have propagated Keynes' captivating notion that governments could tame beastly economies, making them stand up and jump through hoops. His prescription succeeded in lifting Western countries out of the 1930s Depression that had been triggered by an almost complete collapse in demand both in the U.S. and in Europe. Keynes' idea was simple enough: if people were so fearful of the future that they simply would not spend, government would have to prime the pump by doing much of the spending itself.

For almost 40 years the formula worked. Increased Government spending stimulated demand; companies hired more workers to meet the demand; then employees spent, bringing forth more demand and more production, and the virtuous cycle continued. But, says Economist Arthur Okun, long a Keynesian Counsellor to Democratic Presidents: "We were victims of our own success and a good press."

There were shortcomings and pitfalls, little recognized when Keynesianism was flourishing a decade and more ago. One shortcoming was the Keynesian assumption that supply would simply take care of itself once demand was stimulated. So long as inflation stayed low, that is in fact what happened. Even modest increases in consumer demand would bring quick jumps in output. So productive were U.S. plants and factories that they not only filled the needs of the nation's domestic market but also deluged the world with material abundance.

Between 1889 and 1970, the nation ran a trade deficit only once, in the midst of the Depression, in 1935. Yet since 1971, the combination of low productivity and high inflation has reduced both the supply and the competitiveness of U.S. products. Consequently, export growth has been sluggish, and foreign goods have poured into the U.S. at an ever increasing rate. Coupled with the nation's increasing dependence on foreign oil, this has meant that the U.S. has managed to eke out a trade surplus only twice since 1971, running up a cumulative deficit of $59 billion in those years.

Meanwhile, shortages have begun turning up everywhere. Aluminum is in short supply, and such companies as Boeing and McDonnell Douglas must place their orders far in advance to have enough on hand to meet aircraft delivery schedules. Metalworking machinery is also scarce, as are the steel forgings needed by automakers. That, in turn, has helped create shortages of small, fuel-efficient cars, and boosts imports of competing foreign models. There is even a squeeze on fans for people who want to save money by turning off air conditioners, and shortages of insulation for homeowners who are eager to cut winter fuel bills.

True, Keynes argued that excessive demand and price rises could be countered by reversing the cycle—that is, by reducing government spending. But that required a degree of wisdom seldom seen in the spend-and-spend, elect-and-elect politicians of a democracy. Apostles of Keynes contended that to maintain the proper level of demand, the Government regularly had to "fine-tune" the economy with just the right amount of stimulus, either tax cuts or spending increases, or maybe both at once. As Feldstein puts it, the nonstop jiggling and juggling amounted to "an embellishment of Keynes beyond anything that he had claimed."

The reckoning came with Viet Nam. Lyndon Johnson's Keynesian economic advisers warned him not to finance both the war and his cherished Great Society programs without asking for a tax increase, but he refused to take the unpopular step until much too late. From 1965 to 1969, more than $42.5 billion in Government deficit spending flooded into the economy, which was already surging ahead at nearly full capacity. Result: inflation leaped from 2.1% in 1965 to 6% in 1969.

No quick fixes have lastingly slowed the spiral. Temporary cuts in Government spending, coupled with a tight rein on monetary growth, as Richard Nixon tried in 1969, brought on recession and aggravated unemployment, but inflation stayed strong. Freezing wages and prices, as Nixon did in 1971, merely built up pressure for huge price increases later on.

The period from 1975 to the spring of 1979, when the third recession of the decade probably began, is often called "the longest peacetime expansion in U.S. history." Some expansion! Unemployment stands at almost 6%, and to keep the rate from climbing even higher than its 1975 recession peak of nearly 9%, both the Ford and Carter Administrations have had to stuff the people's pockets with almost as much inflationary funny-money, in the form of Government deficit spending, as was generated in all of World War II.

Inflation has, of course, been seriously aggravated by a host of outside or "exogenous" factors that lie beyond the power of economists to control. They cannot be held accountable for poor grain harvests, such as occurred in 1972, for the harsh winters of 1977 and 1978, or for the weather of last year that cut into harvests in the citrus belt. Government economists also argue that price gouging by foreign oil producers is exogenous. True, but only partly so. Not only did inflation in the industrial countries encourage the 13-nation OPEC cartel to quintuple its prices in 1973–74, but the accelerating U.S. price spiral provides the cartel with its only excuse for raising its prices still higher.

When demand turns slack and unemployment shoots up, Keynesianism can still play an important role. But now the economic pendulum has swung from underutilization of capacity to overstraining of productive resources, and policies aimed at further firing consumer demand without simultaneously increasing investment and supply have become about as useful as Gerald Ford WIN buttons. Says Feldstein: "It is a much more complex world than Keynes or anyone else admits, and it is constantly changing. We know enough to move the economy out of a trough but not to control the business cycle."

Observes Bruce MacLaury, president of the Brookings Institution, which is no longer quite the hotbed of Keynesianism that it once was: "It has been hard for the Keynesians to contend that their prescriptions are the way out of stagflation. Ultimately, they are forced to admit that Keynesian techniques just bring forth inflation and not real growth. They answer that the solution is wage price guidelines or another form of an incomes policy, but that is a very weak reed to lean on."

Not only in the U.S., but in countries as disparate as Sri Lanka, Canada and Algeria, there is an attraction to the new, incentive economics. Among developing nations, those that have prospered most have had the freest, most market-oriented economies: Singapore, Taiwan and South Korea, among others. In industrial Europe, incentive economics is making particularly rapid progress:

• In France, Premier Raymond Barre is scrapping much of the policy, which dates back to Louis XIV, that the government should determine the amount of investment and fix prices. Controls on goods from bread to books, from steel to cars, have been freed. State-owned companies, which control more than 25% of France's economy, have been instructed to operate as if they were private enterprises by relying less on subsidies and making a determined effort to turn a profit.

• In Britain, Margaret Thatcher's Tory government was swept into office in May on a tide of popular fury at the dismal results of Labor rule and is now rapidly unwinding much of the high-tax, nationalized welfare state. Income tax rates have been reduced from a top of 83% to 60%; a third of Britain's nationalized North Sea oil industry has been put up for private sale; and the government now has plans to sell off its shares of other state industries, including British Airways.

• In West Germany, Chancellor Helmut Schmidt's Social Democratic government, supported by powerful but reasonable trade unions, has largely held a noninterventionist course and ignored demands that the government cut taxes or raise spending every time a troubling economic forecast is issued. Result: West Germany's inflation rate is one-third as steep as the U.S.'s, its unemployment rate is only slightly over half as high, and the country's living standards are rising.

The economies of Europe and Japan already benefit from government programs that encourage saving. While Americans save little more than a nickel of every dollar of take-home pay, the Japanese save 20% or more, in part because they have no well-developed system of social welfare and must provide for their old age themselves. Citizens of major Western European countries, which have more substantial social welfare programs, save from 13% to 17% of their disposable income anyway.

A big stimulus to saving in Europe and in Japan is government tax policy, which exempts at least some interest income from taxation or offers premiums to savers. In the U.S., interest is sometimes considered "unearned" and taxed at higher than normal rates. Yet in France, savers can deposit up to $9,600 and receive the maximum 6.5% interest tax-free. In West Germany, couples earning up to $26,300 can put up to $900 in a six-year term account and earn not only 4.5% but also receive a tax-free government bonus payment amounting to 14% of the deposit. In Japan, savers do not have to pay taxes on interest from deposits of up to $65,000.

More than 50 bills have already been introduced in Congress to give Americans similar inducements. Most proposals focus on exempting income in varying amounts up to $4,000, though the greatest support seems to be building behind a Republican-backed bill by Missouri Senator John Danforth to exempt up to a more modest $400 in interest income if the money is reinvested in either stocks or saving.

In the U.S., it will take years to reduce inflation's bloat, revive productivity and restore real growth. More and more evidence is accumulating that a slow and persistent effort is the best hope for turning the economy around.

It would be tempting to try to fight unemployment by temporarily increasing federal deficit spending and hoping that merely shoveling more money out to consumers would encourage companies to hire workers and expand production. But the 1970s proved that such erratic pumping-up policies only inflate the economy without significantly reducing unemployment.

A basic reason, say Feldstein and other incentive economists, is that much of the unemployment problem has become structural, that is, deeply imbedded and immune to quick fixes. More than half of the nation's 6 million unemployed—many of them blacks, Hispanics, teen-agers or poorly educated rural people—are out of work not because of a lack of jobs but because they need marketable skills. Warns Feldstein: "If we do not attack the structural causes of our high unemployment, we will face growing pressure to deny firms the right to lay off workers without Government approval, and deny those workers who lose their jobs the right to decide where and when they will return to work."

Feldstein's solution is to train these work seekers, with the help of private companies, for particular jobs without inflating the whole economy. Initially, Feldstein concedes, unemployment might rise from the present 5.7% to about 8% and stay there for perhaps as long as five years. But society in general would benefit because this period of slack would reduce pressure on prices. Meanwhile, the unemployed would be taken care of through existing unemployment programs.

High unemployment, of course, would complicate the Government's budget problem by retarding tax revenues and raising outlays for unemployment compensation and other social programs. The new economists would counter this by reducing spending, or at least the growth of spending, in other areas. Their targets are notably the large number of subsidies to the employed middle class and prosperous industry, handouts as varied as farm price props, generous Civil Service retirement benefits, and subsidies for shipping lines.

In the view of the incentive economists, and an increasing number of Keynesians, long-term progress against inflation can be achieved only at the cost of short-term pain. Gains will require a long period of slow but steady growth of the money supply and a shrinking of total Government spending as a share of the nation's output of goods and services. Economist Robert Lucas, for example, calls for limiting the growth of money to around 4% a year, less than half the average of the 1970s, for at least three to four uninterrupted years and preferably for as long as seven. That would purge the public of its assumption that the Government has no stomach for holding to a steady anti-inflationary course that would encourage saving instead of spending. But keeping money tight would push up interest rates and aggravate the economic slowdown that politicians instinctively fear.

Fitfully, the Government appears to be moving toward the incentive prescription. Asserts Treasury Secretary G. William Miller: "For too long we have focused on consumption and have not invested enough in productive capacity." Not only is the Federal Reserve now tightening money but federal spending as a share of gross national product has declined from 22.6% in 1976 to 21.1% currently, and President Carter aims to get it even lower in fiscal 1981.

Feldstein foresees that these developments, if they continue, would enable growth to be spurred on not by inflationary Government spending but by productive private investment. While consumer buying would slow, saving and business investment would rise. In brief, the total demand in the economy would be no lower, but the mix would be different.

Ultimately, the challenge is whether the nation has the will and the determination to take the necessary hard steps. Observes a humbled Lester Thurow, one-time economic adviser to George McGovern during his 1972 presidential campaign: "When there are economic gains to be allocated, our political process can allocate them. But when there are large economic losses to be divided up, the process is paralyzed. Unfortunately, with political paralysis comes economic paralysis."

The U.S. is by no means paralyzed, but it is at a significant turning point. From Congress to the statehouses, the tax-reforming, investment-boosting, regulation-cutting, supply-expanding recommendations of incentive economics are gaining more support every day and are being increasingly translated into policies. If those beneficial trends continue, the 1980s may yet become the beginning of the good new days.

How to Deal with the "New Unemployment"

WALTER GUZZARDI, JR.

After graduating from Princeton and Georgetown universities, Walter Guzzardi worked with the State Department and then with Time-Life where he was chief of the Time-Life News Service in Rome. He joined *Fortune* magazine in 1960 and headed *Fortune's* first overseas bureau.

Old imagery inhibits new ways of thought—a truth with special relevance when the issue is unemployment. Listening to the politicians describing and decrying unemployment, one would think it to be the same phenomenon that it was forty years ago: the sorrowful people in line, the long hopeless wait, the eagerness for work. And in current legislative proposals, too, one sees the fondness for the old familiar cures: stimulating the economy and creating government jobs.

Thus to summon up the ghost of unemployment past, and then to legislate to exorcise the ghost, weakens our ability to deal sensibly with the realities of unemployment present. The unemployment rate today—the most frequently cited and politically potent statistic in the land—stands at 7.9 percent, the highest since World War II except for last year. Those post-recession levels, however, will come down as the economic recovery continues.

Before the rates drop very much further, the popular understanding of what unemployment is had better correspond more closely to reality than it does today. And the proposed correctives had better be much less grandiosely governmental. Otherwise, we shall have profited very little from the lessons of the early 1970's, and we shall be faced with another onset of inflation even more punishing than the last.

Unemployment, American style, has several arresting qualities. Perhaps most striking is the fact that it does not arise from a scarcity of jobs, the stark enemy in Depression days. Out there in the marketplace, there may be an unfilled job for every one of the 7.5 million unemployed; if not, there are surely enough jobs to reduce the number drastically. But the new composition of our labor force, the new attitudes toward the institution of work, the buffers that shield the jobless from attendant hardships—all these are blocking the flow of people to jobs.

To point out these realities is not to suggest that unemployment is not serious, or that nothing should be done about it, or that the only solution is to remove the buffers, leaving those out of work unprotected from misery. But what is done must be consonant with actuality, and not tied to the fearful imagery of the 1930's. Some provocative new ideas about what to do are now in the air. They deserve a public hearing because they show an understanding of the true nature of unemployment.

Walter Guzzardi, Jr., "How to Deal with the 'New Unemployment,'" *Fortune*, Oct. 1976, pp. 132–35, 208, 210, 212, 214.

MILLIONS ON A SHUTTLE

People hopelessly waiting, destitute, asking only for a job—these emotion-fraught phrases tell very little about most of the unemployment in the 1970's. In fact the unemployed are an ever-changing mass, on a kind of shuttle, moving between working and waiting, never fitting comfortably into any job, yet usually able soon to find another. Testimony to their restlessness is found in a startling statistic: only about half of the 7.5 million left jobs involuntarily. The other half is made up of people who quit, or who have just entered or reentered the labor force. The average duration of unemployment is not very long, and the individuals involved keep changing. Although the number of unemployed in 1975 never exceeded 8,540,000, the number who experienced unemployment was much higher: about 21 million people knew some unemployment last year.

This turbulence tracks back to shifts in the composition of the civilian labor force, which now numbers 95 million. The number of adult white men, who have a low rate of unemployment, has been dwindling in relation to the total force. But teenagers, blacks, and women, who have high rates, have been joining in record numbers; surprisingly, they now make up half its total. Last year's increases illustrate the trend: the labor force expanded by 1.6 million, of whom 1.2 million were women or teenagers.

WHEN TEENAGE UNEMPLOYMENT MATTERS

These rapidly growing segments of the labor force are precisely the ones that have trouble finding jobs with stability and promise. For many of the young, of course, unemployment is not really a very serious condition. One-fourth of the members of the labor force between sixteen and twenty-one, and one-half of those between sixteen and nineteen, are students. Mostly they are looking for only part-time work. When they can't find it, in a kind of definitional anomaly they are counted among those who are unemployed.

For young people who are not students, however, the inability to find jobs that they want to keep is much more important. A special survey for the Department of Labor showed that unemployment among recent high-school graduates ranged up to 20 percent last year. Among high-school dropouts—all those in the labor force between the ages of sixteen and twenty-four who neither finished school nor are now enrolled—the rate was a horrendous 34 percent. And even more ominous social implications can be found in the rates for young blacks: 37 percent for all black teenagers, 61 percent for black high-school dropouts, 38 percent for those triply disadvantaged black teenage girls.

For blacks as a whole, instability is the dominant trait of working life. For years their unemployment rate has averaged twice that of whites. In former recessions the differential narrowed somewhat, but there was no such improvement in the 1974–75 downturn. A study by Stephen Marston for the Brookings Institution shows that among the currently unemployed a higher percentage of blacks than of whites were laid off from their last job. The earnings of blacks who stay on the job do not rise much with seniority, even where their education matches that of their white peers. Lacking incentives to stay on the job, blacks are of course more willing to leave it.

Women share some of those troubles. Most employed women are working in the same old occupations with low pay and little future: they are secretaries, retail clerks, and waitresses. Such jobs are easy to get, and easy to leave. Moving in and out of the labor force, women have higher unemployment rates than men—typically 1.5 percentage points higher.

It is the clear judgment of our society that people who are unemployed must be shielded, at least in part, from unemployment's hardships. Toward the end of 1974, with unemployment on the rise, Congress extended unemployment benefits from thirty-nine to sixty-five weeks, and made the benefits available to some workers, such as farm workers, who were not previously covered. Some states raised supplementary payments for dependents as well. Other forms of public assistance, such as food stamps and aid to families with dependent children, are also sometimes available to the unemployed. These are humanitarian provisions, but they have the undesirable effect of keeping the unemployment rate high.

FUEL HERE, COOL THERE

Given the anatomy of today's unemployment, new public attitudes and policies are clearly called for. It would be well to start by recognizing that some unemployment reflects the strength of our system: the mobility of the labor force, the willingness of people to shift around to increase their earnings, and the insistence of young people on keeping their options open. Jack Gould, an economist at the University of Chicago's Graduate School of Business, believes that some unemployment helps to make the system efficient. "To try to run the economy at zero unemployment would be like an automobile dealer trying to run his operation with zero inventory," Gould says.

The new policies must be based on an understanding of this new kind of unemployment. They should therefore avoid the deceptive appeal of employment-by-government as a serious alternative to our kind of unemployment. Instead, they should be aimed at stoking up positive incentives in the private sector—the kind that add to the attractions of work and motivate people to stay on the job. They must also dampen down the negative incentives—the kind that add to the attractions of not working. And they must not rekindle inflation: in the postwar years, we have entered every new recession with higher inflation than we had when we entered the preceding one.

A WAY AROUND THE MINIMUM WAGE?

Economists specializing in manpower policies believe that the way to begin this undertaking is to raise the level of skills among the sectors of the population now most prone to unemployment. According to Lloyd Ulman, professor of economics and director of the Institute of Industrial Relations at the University of California, the result of raising skills would be to increase the supply of better-trained workers relative to the untrained. Then, Ulman says, the wages of the untrained would go up, because they would be scarcer. The wages of the skilled would be held somewhat in check, because they would be more abundant. Since there is usually an unsatisfied demand for skilled labor, total employment would be increased, without additions to aggregate demand. That logic seeming to be impeccable, the question becomes this: how do we create a more highly skilled labor force?

In an economic downturn, low-skilled young workers bear a disproportionate share of transitional unemployment. Some economists have long blamed the minimum-wage laws for this state of affairs: the trade unions have violently disagreed; ponderous studies of numbing tedium have not persuaded either side that it is wrong. Without taking sides in this debate, Martin Feldstein, a thirty-six-year-old economist at Harvard and an expert in unemployment, thinks he can show how the minimum-wage law operates to the detriment of one particular group: the needy teenage worker. And Feldstein, who is also a member of Jimmy Carter's economic advisory group, thinks he has hit on a proposal for modifying the minimum wage that ought to be acceptable to both liberals and conservatives.

Feldstein's thesis is that the poor, working teenagers do not possess the skills necessary to produce value in excess of the minimum wage, which is now $2.30 an hour. They can barely earn their wages with their output. With no margin, the employer cannot afford to make an investment in training them. As Feldstein says, "These young people bring little to their employer, and they get little in return." Without training, in an economic sense they are never worth more than dead-end, low-level jobs pay them—so those are the kinds of jobs they get, and they are frequently unemployed. Even if they wanted to or could afford to do so, the law would not allow them to work for less in return for training. "We subsidize formal education for the more affluent, but we refuse to allow the poor to buy on-the-job training," says Feldstein.

What he proposes is that the government subsidize just that special kind of purchase, in the following way. The government would issue vouchers to young people looking for jobs. Those who find jobs at the minimum wage would give the voucher to their employer. He would redeem the voucher at the government window for perhaps 30 to 40 percent of the minimum wage. The employer then would be obliged to spend the sum he collects to train the young. Some kind of surveillance by the Department of Labor might be required to make sure that the training actually took place.

The scheme differs importantly from the proposal that the minimum wage simply be lowered for the young. If that were to happen, Feldstein says, "It's the young who would bear the burden." This way, the young person still makes the minimum wage, but he gets trained as well. Presumably, the training leads to a higher-paying job, stronger job attachment, and less unemployment. The choice of work would be up to the young person: as Feldstein says, "the idea is to put the initiative at the kid's level." An associated service might extend employment counseling—a proposal also advanced by Charles Holt, an expert on manpower at the Urban Institute—to advise young people where they could find the work they want.

Thoughtful ideas attract critics. Many economists like Feldstein's plan because it amounts to a long-overdue revision of the antiquated minimum-wage law. Jack Gould of the University of Chicago calls the idea "correct economics" in that respect. And Mark C. Kendall, an economist at the National Planning Association, sees "a lot of enticement" in the scheme. But he fears that if a voucher were given to every young person, money would be spent on affluent as well as needy youths. To prevent that overlapping, a means test, with all its complicated individual judgments about skills and poverty levels, would be necessary—but such tests are rarely successful.

A WORRY ABOUT DISPLACEMENT

Feldstein sees that difficulty, too. But he is inclined to think that even if the vouchers were available to all young people, they would probably only be used by those in need, since the others go on to college or good jobs. If some were helped who didn't need it, Feldstein would accept that waste in order to help those otherwise headed for the bad-job—unemployment—bad-job sequence.

The trade unions tend to look on Feldstein's proposal as simply one more camouflaged attack on the sacrosanct minimum-wage laws. To begin with, John Zalusky and Clara Schloss, two economists at the AFL-CIO, insist that "good" employers don't hire at the minimum wage anyway. Only marginal employers and a few big retail chains do that, and they neither deserve nor can be trusted with any government subsidy. Zalusky singles out McDonalds, a big employer of the young, for particularly bitter attack, saying that "training for the job takes only a few days. But they're the ones who would so frequently be running to the government for their training allowance. This 'Hamburger College' is a great facade." (McDonald's is reluctant to discuss its hiring practices.)

As the foregoing suggests, Zalusky and Mrs. Schloss are doubtful that employers would really use the government rebate for training. Some employers, they believe would simply pocket the money—leading to what they call "the displacement effect." Employers having before them a choice between experienced older workers and inexperienced young ones would now find that the young ones were cheaper than ever. The result would be that unemployment would shift to a different group, but the overall rate would not be lowered, Zalusky and Mrs. Schloss say. Feldstein, however, sees a kind of endless upgrading taking place to the benefit of all.

And Mrs. Schloss has a parting shot. She notes that some high unemployment among teenagers is caused by their great numbers. But that demographic bulge will soon recede, and the most numerous members of the labor force will be those in their early twenties. Asks Mrs. Schloss: "What do you do then—tinker with the minimum wage for the older group?"

IF IT'S GOVERNMENT, THEY'RE AGAINST IT

Before Feldstein's plan could be tested on a national level, a good deal of missionary work would have to be done among big corporations. They have experienced so many government interventions in recent years that the thought of yet another stirs immediate resistance and resentment. Banks and insurance companies in New York recall what happened a few years ago with a government project that entitled them to rebates if they hired disadvantaged members of a particular minority group. Describing the consequent confusion, Frank McMullin, director of the American Institute of Banking in New York, says: "First a government agency had to certify that the person was disadvantaged. Then each employer had to keep track of all the certifications. If he couldn't produce the certificates, he couldn't get the rebate. If he could, he found that the government would only pay for certain things, and not for other things. There was no set percentage." Says Ronald Woods, vice president of personnel for Manufacturers Hanover: "We preferred to fund the training ourselves."

Also, many big corporations neither hire at the minimum wage nor seem very interested in having the government help them with training. The Gillette Co. in Boston, for example, does no hiring at minimum-wage rates. Pete Cruikshank, Gillette's domestic personnel director, says that "if training is worth doing, we'll do it, with or without the government."

Some big employers also disagree with Feldstein's assumption that teenagers can barely produce their value when they work at the minimum wage, and so are not worth training. Many companies don't know exactly what young people are worth, but they seem prepared to make an investment in those new employees nonetheless. Says Woods of Manufacturers Hanover: "Do we lose money in the beginning on newly employed persons? If we pay them $3 an hour, are we losing $2 the first hour? Nobody knows. We do have product standards, and we know what's expected over a period. I'm sure we are paying for the potential vis-a-vis the value of the immediate. But the real question is—what's the return on investment?"

In view of all these practical difficulties, one way to prove the validity of Feldstein's thesis might be to start by trying it out with smaller employers first. They are the ones who feel the cost pressures the most. They do most of the minimum-wage hiring. And their environment lends itself naturally to the kind of on-the-job training that Feldstein is talking about. If the plan were worked out carefully on that limited scale, confrontation with the unions might be avoided, too.

Martin Feldstein has also given some thought to another issue that bears on the unemployment ratios. He calls attention to a paradox: that programs designed to reduce unemployment work to cancel out the effect of those designed to help the unemployed. This paradox shows nowhere more clearly than in the application of the unemployment-compensation laws, originally passed in 1935 and, except for extensions of coverage, not substantially altered since.

It is often said that unemployment compensation comes to around one-third of the unemployed person's former earnings, with a ceiling on the total amount. But studies by Feldstein show some startlingly different ratios. He postulates a married couple with two children, living in Massachusetts, where the husband makes $120 a week and the wife $80.

If the husband is out of work for ten weeks, he loses $1,200 in gross income. But his net loss—gross earnings less federal and state taxes and Social Security payments—comes to only $875. After one week, he can start to collect benefits of $72 (50 percent of his wage, plus $6 a week for each child). The benefits are tax free. Ten weeks after he has lost his job, the man has received benefits totaling $648, or 74 percent of his take-home pay. After compensation begins, Feldstein figures, the man's reward for returning to work would be less than 50 cents an hour; had it been his wife who was unemployed, the figure would be less than 30 cents an hour.

Nor is this an extreme example. The combination of forgone taxes and tax-free compensation sometimes adds up to 90 percent or more of income earned by work. Instances can be found in which annual family income is actually higher when the husband is unemployed for three months than when he goes on working the whole year.

The extent to which the generous benefits for not working prolong unemployment is not precisely calculable. But the benefits could encourage job searches that may go on for a year, at little cost to the unemployed person. Stretched-out searches, Feldstein says, "are economically rational from the individual's point of view, but damaging to the economy as a whole." On that point, Feldstein gets some high-powered support: Arthur Burns, chairman of the Federal Reserve Board, thinks that Congress made a mistake by extending benefits to sixty-five weeks. He suggests that coverage not run past thirteen weeks.

Feldstein's ideas for reform, like his ideas about the minimum wage, are novel and realistic. He makes the simple and logically compelling proposition that the payments be treated for what they are—income—and be taxed. That would impose no burden on the poor. But it would encourage others to return to work more quickly. It would also end the drama of the absurd, in which a family's annual income can be higher if some working member of it spends part of the year unemployed.

WHY SOME EMPLOYERS SUBSIDIZE OTHERS

Besides increasing the duration of unemployment, the compensation system subsidizes employers and employees in cyclical industries, and insulates both from the free-market forces that should operate—at least, that is Feldstein's contention. Understanding the contention requires some grasp of how the system works. Until recently, the unemployment-compensation mechanism has interested only a few experts with a taste for the exotic (including Joseph Becker, a Jesuit at Georgetown University, who has written six volumes on the subject). But all the recent and coming cost increases to employers may stimulate wider interest.

In practically every state, unemployment compensation is paid for entirely by taxes on employers. The tax rates are determined by a system of "experience rating," meaning that the rate depends on the ratio between benefits paid to a company's former employees and its average annual taxable payroll. Since the states run the programs, there are lots of variables; however, the taxable base, comparable to Social Security's, is usually $4,200 multiplied by the number of employees.

As a general proposition the tax rates run between 1 percent and 5 percent of the taxable base. Generally speaking, every employer pays something, probably at least 1 percent, even if he never fires anybody. And none pays more than 5 percent, no matter how many people he lays off. Should a company's annual tax exceed the benefits paid to its erstwhile employees, it gets a lower rate for the next year, and a reserve builds up. (No matter how big the reserve grows, however, the employer never gets a refund. "The balance favorable to you can get quite large," says Tim Horan, compensation manager at Gillette. "After it gets to a certain size, they just scoop it in.") Should the benefits paid to its former employees exceed the amount it has paid into the fund, the company's tax goes up the next year—but never surpasses the 5 percent limit. After that, an employer pays no penalty no matter how many people he lays off. Additional money required to pay benefits to his account comes from premiums paid by other employers.

All these complications lead Feldstein to some perfectly simple conclusions. Employers who do not lay off many people are subsidizing those who lay off a lot. Since an employer with heavy layoffs does not pay his own way—indeed, the more he lays off, the less of his own way he pays—he has no incentive, at least so far as payroll costs are concerned, to stabilize production and smooth out cyclical operations.

For his part, the cyclical employee, who gets unemployment compensation during layoff periods (coming in part from employers other than his own), is not motivated to press for the higher pay that cyclical work should get. In many cases the employee has agreed through his collective-bargaining agents to accept layoffs for specified periods, knowing that unemployment compensation will be coming in. (The arrangement can be so attractive that some contracts, adapting admirably to lunatic circumstances, call for employees with the *most* seniority to be laid off first.) One further effect, Feldstein believes, is that the cost of certain products of cyclical industries is kept artificially low, and "the economy consumes too much of the goods produced in this way."

LET'S TRY DUTCH TREAT

The way to regularize all that, Feldstein thinks, is to remove the floors and ceilings on the tax, and go to a true experience rating—to a system in which each employer paid his own way. Every employer should be taxed enough to cover all the benefits paid out to his former workers, so that no employer would be subsidizing another's employees. There would be more incentive to stabilize payrolls. Prices would reflect real costs, and consumption would adjust accordingly.

Like all of Feldstein's ideas, this has the direct appeal of simplicity and, apparently, of equity. But, also like all of them, it has elicited arguments.

One that sounds cogent comes from Sidney Korzenik, lawyer for the Apparel Industries Inter-Association Committee in New York and a spokesman for small employers in the clothing industry. Korzenik says that the present system is rigged against the small employer as it is, and to go to full experience rating would only make matters worse. A firm that is already having a hard time surviving would be unable to pay the costs of letting a few people go. So the firm would go bankrupt—after which other employers would be paying for the compensation of the bankrupt firm's employees.

Korzenik also opposes experience rating because, he says, the employer doing the firing isn't necessarily the one responsible for throwing his former employee out of work. "Take a swimsuit manufacturer who hires a few people," urges Korzenik genially. "His business is dictated by the big retail chains. They are so afraid that they won't sell all their swimsuits that they don't buy any after July 1—you don't believe it, try to find one. You want to go on vacation, there's nothing but picked-over merchandise. The manufacturing season for swimsuits is not determined by the manufacturer at all. Factors that cause unemployment are so diffused throughout the system that all employers must be involved in this kind of social responsibility. It isn't a question of good guys who don't lay off and bad guys who do."

That leaves the possibility, of course, that big companies may pay out more in premiums than their employees get in benefits. But to Korzenik, that seems perfectly fair—unemployment is a national problem, not confined to small firms in the garment district. Besides, it's the first principle of insurance that premiums should be geared to risk. And the big companies are the ones with all those risks—all those thousands of employees who might be laid off some day. . . .

The new ideas no doubt have their flaws. But they surely have the great merit of recognizing the true nature of the condition that we are setting out to correct.

The Private and Social Costs of Unemployment

MARTIN FELDSTEIN

Martin Feldstein is one of the most dynamic economists of our time. His Joint Economic Committee Study on how to lower the permanent rate of unemployment outlined a variety of proposals that have been widely discussed and that formed the basis of many of the new supply side proposals for attacking unemployment. A professor of economics at Harvard University, he recently won the John Bates Clark Award as the nation's most distinguished economist under forty.

We do not need a careful quantitative analysis to establish that the unemployment of seven million workers involves very substantial private and social costs. Why then should we bother to think about measuring the cost of unemployment? There are two quite different reasons. First, by measuring the private costs of unemployment that are borne by the unemployed themselves, we can better understand why our unemployment rate is so high. Second, by examining the social costs of unemployment (i.e., the costs of unemployment to the nation as a whole regardless of how they are distributed), we can better decide when the benefits of a reduction in unemployment outweigh the costs of achieving it. The present paper considers both of these problems, emphasizing the conceptual issues rather than presenting specific estimates.

Since unemployment is so often thought of in aggregate terms, it is worth emphasizing at the outset that a proper analysis of the costs of unemployment must begin by disaggregation. The private cost of unemployment is very large for some of the unemployed, but is quite small for many others. The average private cost of unemployment is therefore much less relevant than the distribution of such costs. Similarly in considering the social costs of unemployment, it is important to distinguish several kinds of unemployment since the cost of each type of unemployment and the costs of reducing that unemployment differ significantly.

PRIVATE COSTS

The cost of unemployment that is borne by the unemployed person himself varies from the overwhelming to the trivial. At one extreme is the very substantial loss by those who experience a long period of unemployment with little or no help from transfer payments. At the other extreme is the minimal loss of those who are out of work very briefly and whose lost net income is fully replaced by unemployment compensation. Although there is a wide range of experience, the typical spell of unemployment is closer to the low cost extreme

Martin Feldstein, "The Private and Social Costs of Unemployment," *American Economic Review* (May 1978), pp. 155–58.

than to the high cost extreme. Even now, more than half of the unemployment spells last four weeks or less. Moreover, more than half of the unemployed received unemployment compensation. I believe that the relatively low cost of unemployment in these circumstances is a substantial cause of our high permanent rate of unemployment.

The principal reason for low private cost of unemployment is the interaction of our tax and unemployment compensation systems. It is particularly important to consider these two together. Income and social security taxes now imply a marginal tax rate in the neighborhood of 30 percent for a worker in a median income family. It is therefore very significant that unemployment compensation is not subject to tax. The combination of a relatively high marginal tax on earnings and no tax on unemployment compensation implies that unemployment benefits replace a very high fraction of lost net income, typically about two-thirds.

An example will illustrate how this occurs. Consider a worker in Massachusetts in 1977 with a wife and two children. His gross earnings are $140 per week while hers are $100 per week. If he is unemployed for ten weeks, he loses $1400 in gross earnings but only $279 in net income. Why does this occur? A fall in gross earnings of $1400 reduces his federal income tax by $226, his social security tax by $82, and his Massachusetts income tax by $75. Thus, total taxes fall by $383, implying that net wages are reduced by $1017.

Unemployment benefits are 50 percent of his wage plus a dependents' allowance of $6 per child per week. The benefit is thus $82 a week. Since there is an annual one week "waiting period" before benefits begin, nine weeks of benefits are paid for the ten week unemployment spell. Total benefits are thus $738. The loss in net income is only the $279 difference between these benefits and the fall in after-tax wages. The $279 private net income loss is less than 20 percent of the loss in output as measured by the gross wage.

Because of the one week waiting period, the private cost of unemployment is even lower for an additional week of unemployment. If he stays unemployed for eleven weeks instead of ten, he loses an additional $140 in gross earnings but only $16 in net income. The private net income loss is less than 12 percent of the loss in output as measured by the gross wage. If the individual values his leisure and nonmarket work activities at even 50 cents an hour, there is no net private cost of unemployment!

The great reduction in the private cost of unemployment that results from this interaction of high taxes on earnings and the untaxed unemployment benefits produce substantial adverse incentives that magnify the cyclical volatility of unemployment and raise the noncyclical "baseline level" of unemployment. The most obvious effect is to increase the average duration of unemployment spells. With little or no personal cost of a longer period of unemployment, it is rational for the individual to look for a new job until the potential gain from additional serach is extremely small or to use the low cost time to do chores at home or just to enjoy a period of vacation. In addition to increasing the average duration of existing unemployment spells, the low private cost of unemployment also causes an increase in the number of unemployment spells. Since workers who quit their jobs are eligible for benefits in a number of states, the low private cost of unemployment is responsible for many of the one million unemployed who quit their last job.

More significant, however, is the incentive for temporary layoffs. Approximately half of the unemployment spells that are officially classified as "job losses" are actually temporary layoffs in which the unemployed worker expects to return to his original job. In manufacturing, approximately 80 percent of those who are laid off return to their original jobs. Our system of unemployment compensation lowers the cost of such temporary layoffs to both firms and workers, making unemployment more attractive than accumulating inventories or cutting prices.

I have concentrated these comments on unemployment compensation because this is the most significant program for reducing the private costs of unemployment. Those who are not eligible for unemployment compensation often receive other forms of income replacement such as food stamps, social security, and welfare. It is also important to remember that a very large fraction of the unemployed who do not receive unemployment compensation are young people who are supported by their families.

It is easy to see how our system of taxes and transfers drastically lowers the relative private cost of unemployment and thereby induces a higher unemployment rate. The real puzzle is why the low private cost of unemployment does not result in a higher rate of unemployment. What are the forces of self-restraint that limit the public's willingness to exploit the full opportunities for subsidized unemployment? And will they continue to be effective in the future? Public attitudes about accepting transfer payments appear to have been changing rapidly during the past decade, resulting in the rapid growth of such things as disability insurance benefits, food stamps, and health insurance payments. The contagiousness of social attitudes suggests that this trend may accelerate in the future. It carries with it an ominous prospect for unemployment.

SOCIAL COSTS

The social cost of an unemployment spell depends on the social opportunity cost of the unemployed person's time. In measuring the social cost of unemployment, it is therefore crucial to ask "Unemployment as compared to what?" As economists, we tend to define the opportunity cost of any resource as its value in the best possible use to which it might be put. But the relevant opportunity cost in the current context is not this "best allocation" of full employment general equilibrium theory. We are interested in the social costs of unemployment in order to assess the desirability of particular unemployment policies. Different policies imply different opportunity costs for the unemployed workers. In each case, we should compare the particular net social cost of unemployment—that is, the potential benefit of returning the unemployed person to work—with the cost of the policy itself.

The format of this session suggests that all policies to reduce unemployment entail increasing inflation, implying that the relevant comparison is between the social costs of unemployment and the social costs of inflation. If this were true, the implication would be quite dismal since most economists now agree that a permanent increase in inflation cannot achieve more than a temporary reduction in unemployment.[1] Fortunately, there are policies for reducing

---

[1] In a growing economy, the present value of the social cost of a permanent increase in inflation can be extremely large relative to the gain from a temporary reduction in unemployment.

unemployment permanently that do not involve increases in inflation. These policies may involve such costs as a reallocation of some workers from more productive to less productive activities, a reduction in unemployment insurance protection, or a redistribution of income with losses by some groups and gains by others. A proper evaluation of available policies requires quantifying the costs and benefits of each.

Before looking at some examples of the social costs associated with different types of unemployment, it is useful to comment on two extreme but common views of the social cost of unemployment. According to one view, unemployment has no social or private cost. The individual's loss of wage income is at least offset by the value of his leisure and of the information that he acquires by his job search activity. This conclusion is false even if we accept its premise that all unemployment is voluntary. The taxes and unemployment insurance described above imply a substantial gap between the individual's gross wage and the value of his time when unemployed. The existence of the rigidities that cause involuntary unemployment only strengthens the reason to reject this view.

At the other extreme is the view that the loss in wage income is equal to the social cost of unemployment. This ignores the value of the individual's leisure and of the information gained by searching for a new job. Moreover, even if both of these were zero, it would be wrong to regard the individual's normal or potential wage as a measure of the gain that would result from his reemployment without specifying the policy that would be used to achieve his reemployment.

Consider, for example, the case of workers on temporary layoff. As I noted above, some 80 percent of workers who are laid off by manufacturing firms soon return to their original jobs at those firms. Such temporary layoffs are almost completely unknown in Europe and Japan. This important source of unemployment could be significantly reduced if the employer tax that is used to finance unemployment compensation were changed to eliminate the current subsidy of excessive layoffs by some firms. While I believe that this would be a worthwhile reform, the benefit of such a change should not be overstated. The social cost of the unemployment that would thereby be eliminated is not the normal wage of these workers or even that wage reduced by the value of their leisure. A reduction in temporary layoffs would mean more production for inventory and more spells of below average productivity.

This example also illustrates the familiar principle of welfare economics that it may be possible to identify a good policy in terms of the marginal conditions without explicitly evaluating the gains from the policy. In this case, it seems clear that eliminating the subsidy that increases temporary layoff unemployment would be a move in the right direction even though the value of the gain is unknown. Although the theory of the second best cautions against this general line of reasoning, an explicit partial equilibrium calculation of the gain from reducing unemployment is unlikely to be an improvement in this regard. An explicit calculation of the social cost of temporary layoff unemployment would be of value primarily in deciding whether the economic gains of the reform outweighed the political costs of achieving it.

Although the potential wage will generally overstate the social cost of unemployment, there is an important case in which it is an understatement. For young workers, unemployment means not only the loss of output and earnings but, more important, the missed opportunity for on-the-job training and experience. The very high unemployment rate among low-skilled youth is symptomatic of the more serious problem that the jobs available to them generally offer little opportunity for training or advancement. The social cost of youth unemployment thus depends very much on the contemplated alternative. If we judge the social cost of youth unemployment by the type of no-training jobs that are currently available, the cost is relatively low. But if employment with useful on-the-job training is a feasible alternative, the social cost of youth unemployment is substantially greater than the immediate loss of output.

CONCLUSION

In this short paper, I have emphasized two basic points. First, the private cost of unemployment varies substantially and is often extremely low. This low private cost is an important cause of the permanently high unemployment rate in the United States. Second, the social costs of unemployment must be judged by considering the specific policy by which a worker would be reemployed.

In selecting these points for emphasis, I have ignored many of the issues generally associated with measuring the costs of unemployment. In conclusion, however, I want to call attention to two further costs of a chronically high unemployment rate that are likely to be of great long-run importance.

If we do not change the structural causes of our high unemployment rate, we will face growing pressure to adopt the strategy of some European countries that supress unemployment by denying firms the right to lay off workers without government approval and by denying those workers who lose their jobs the right to decide where and when they will return to work. In addition, a chronically high unemployment rate will create strong pressures for expansionary macroeconomic policies that will serve only to exacerbate inflation. The loss of freedom in labor markets and the increase in inflation throughout the economy would be an extremely high cost to bear for our failure to reform the incentives and eliminate the barriers that create our unemployment problems.

Union Compensations Help to Loosen Financial Pinch on Laid-Off Workers

MONROE W. KARMIN

Mr. Monroe W. Karmin is currently the national economics correspondent for the Knight-Ridder Newspaper Group. A Pulitzer Prize winner, he has covered Washington for twenty-five years and has received a series of awards for distinguished reporting.

BLOOMFIELD, N.J.—Gray-haired Tony Genuario, a local painters union official, closed his eyes for a moment as he recalled the Great Depression.

"In those days when a man was unemployed, he was a desperate man. Today he gets at least half a loaf."

Genuario knows from whence he speaks. As a young man, he lived through the bitter experience of unemployment during the 1930s when there was very little "relief" available to help families endure.

Today Genuario is business manager and secretary-treasurer of the Painters District Council No. 10, based in Bloomfield, N.J., a suburb of Newark.

"I'm thankful, every working man is thankful, that we don't have to live like we did in the 1930s," Genuario said, "that we have these benefits today."

With unemployment now at 7.8 per cent, the highest level of the Carter presidency, and expected to go even higher, the comparison with the 1930s is natural for workers and voters.

As Genuario said, being out of work today, painful as it is, is nowhere near the disaster it was during the Great Depression, especially for unionized workers.

"In the 1930s when a man was out of work, he had no other choice but to go on welfare," the painter said. "Today he can collect unemployment compensation and other benefits."

People thrown out of work in New Jersey are eligible for 39 weeks of unemployment compensation at $123 a week. (In Florida, the Legislature this year raised weekly compensation from $95 to $105. A Floridian can draw the jobless benefits for 26 weeks.)

For painters in Genuario's union, the $123 compares with a normal wage of $468 a week, before deductions.

Theoretically, according to an AFL-CIO spokesman in Washington, unemployment compensation in most states is supposed to replace from 50 per cent to 60 per cent of a jobless worker's lost gross earnings.

In reality, because of legal ceilings placed on payments, the AFL-CIO said that many high-wage workers, such as those in autos and steel, get only 20 to 33 per cent of their pay when they're laid off.

Monroe W. Karmin, "Union Compensations Help to Loosen Financial Pinch on Laid-off Workers," *Miami Herald*, 15 June 1980, p. 1. Reprinted by permission of Miami Herald Publishing Company.

Some unions, of course, have better benefits than others.

The painters, for instance, are not as well protected as members of the auto, steel or rubber unions.

"We don't have 'SUB' benefits," Genuario said, "because at our income level we must concentrate our bargaining on wages."

SUB is the acronym of Supplemental Unemployment Benefit funds that pay laid-off workers during times of prolonged unemployment. SUB monies come from employer contributions, negotiated in collective-bargaining contracts.

The SUB funds afford major protection to workers in auto, steel and rubber. Workers in the glass, garment and aerospace industries have similar, but lesser plans.

In the auto industry, for example, the SUB plan, when combined with state unemployment benefits, pays about 95 per cent of take-home pay.

The laid-off auto worker also is eligible for special federal unemployment payments because President Carter has decreed that the industry has been hurt by foreign imports.

What this means to the unemployed autoworker is illustrated at the Ford Motor Co. plant in Mahwah, N.J., where a shutdown next Friday will lay off 3,800 workers.

The take-home pay of the average autoworker there is about $300 a week. When laid off, the worker will be eligible for a maximum of $269 a week for up to 36 weeks through a combination of federal assistance and unemployment compensation.

After that, when the federal aid runs out, the laid-off worker can get a SUB payment amounting to 95 per cent of his take-home pay for another 52 weeks.

In Mahwah, therefore, laid-off autoworkers will be paid a minimum of 89 per cent and a maximum of 95 per cent of their normal pay for more than a year and a half.

This assumes that Ford's SUB fund remains solvent. In May, the fund was down to $63 million from $97 million in March.

If Congress approves the $1.5 billion that Carter has sought for payments to industries hurt by imports, it is estimated that the Ford fund will be able to finance a year's worth of SUB payments.

If not, it is feared the fund could run out of money this summer because of the company's mounting layoffs.

At ailing Chrysler, the SUB fund went broke last fall. Now the fund is slowly building up as the company recovers with the help of loan guarantees from the federal government.

With about one-third of the auto work force on indefinite layoff, all of the industry's SUB funds are being squeezed.

In the rubber industry, about 20 per cent of the employes at the four major tire manufacturers have been laid off. The total is expected to double when more plants are closed this summer.

Rubber industry SUB plans pay 80 per cent of straight-time pay, minus unemployment compensation.

Steel industry layoffs have been minor compared with those in auto and rubber, but more plant shutdowns are due later this year.

Steel's plans pay a maximum of $131 a week when a worker is receiving unemployment compensation and up to $176 a week when he is not. Those maximums will increase to $166 and $206 on Aug. 1 under the terms of the new basic steel industry settlement.

When a jobless worker exhausts all his benefits and still hasn't found employment, he becomes eligible for a variety of federal social-welfare assistance.

This ranges from welfare to food stamps to Medicaid benefits. He also retains the Social Security retirement benefits he earned while working.

Although this will not finance a worker's current lifestyle, as Anthony Genuario pointed out, it doesn't leave him quite as "desperate" as unemployment did in the 1930s.

A Recession Could Strain Jobless Funds, Widen Federal Role in Insurance Program

URBAN C. LEHNER

Urban C. Lehner is Tokyo bureau chief of *The Wall Street Journal.* He covered economics and labor for the *Journal* in Washington for almost five years and has also worked in the *Journal's* New York, Chicago, and Philadelphia bureaus. In addition to his eight years as a *Journal* reporter, Mr. Lehner, age thirty-three, spent two years as a minesweeping officer in the U.S. Navy.

WASHINGTON—During the last recession, Pennsylvania handed out so many unemployment-benefit checks to jobless workers that the state exhausted its unemployment-insurance "trust fund" and had to borrow $1.2 billion from the U.S. Treasury to keep the checks from bouncing.

Today, with another recession threatening, Pennsylvania still hasn't repaid the $1.2 billion. Nor have 11 other states repaid a total of $2.5 billion they owe the Treasury from the 1973–75 downturn. And on top of the states' $3.7 billion in debts, the federal government, in effect, owes itself $7.9 billion—the sum that a federal trust fund borrowed from general Treasury revenues to finance additional weeks of benefits during the recession.

In short, the nation's much-used but little-understood unemployment-insurance machinery, which ran smoothly from its creation during the Depression through the early 1970s, has had a financial monkey wrench thrown into its works. With $11.6 billion in debt overhanging, there is, a national study commission has declared, "good reason to think that the financial integrity of the unemployment-compensation system as it has functioned for 41 years now is in question."

Congress so far has moved cautiously on the question of whether the system needs an overhaul. But the matter may become more urgent later this year, after the study commission issues it final report, if a recession has begun by then and jobless payments are rising.

LAST STRAW?

"Going into a recession could be the straw that breaks the camel's back and forces Congress to restructure the system," says Democratic Rep. William Brodhead of Michigan, a member of the House Ways and Means Committee, which would review any legislation.

The main issue is whether the federal government should permanently shoulder part of the cost of financing jobless payments. Currently, benefits are financed wholly by employers, who pay unemployment-insurance taxes that go into state and federal trust funds. If the trust funds run out of money, they can borrow from the U.S. Treasury. Critics of permanent federal financing, including some business groups and states with solvent trust funds, argue that a wider federal role would turn what is an unemployment-insurance system into a welfare system.

If a recession begins and Congress doesn't act, there is little question where a lot of the money to pay jobless benefits will come from: more loans from Uncle Sam. The borrowings will be needed because "in a recession period such as we are facing, massive job layoffs will deplete the unemployment coffers of many states," says Wilbur Cohen, former Health, Education and Welfare Secretary and chairman of the national study group.

But while the ability to borrow guarantees that a state's unemployed will be taken care of in hard times, it raises the specter of serious, long-term economic troubles for states that do borrow—often states that already have deep problems. That's because repaying the Treasury loans sooner or later drives up the unemployment taxes of the borrowing state's employers.

Specifically, either such states must raise their unemployment taxes on employers or, after two years without repayment, federal unemployment taxes on the state's employers automatically go up. This year, for example, the maximum federal tax on Pennsylvania employers will rise to $60 a year per employee from last year's $42 maximum, the amount that employers in most other states will continue to pay this year. Next year, if Pennsylvania still hasn't repaid the debt out of state taxes, the federal tax on its employers will rise to a maximum of $78 per employee a year. The $18-a-year rises in the maximum tax continue until the debt is repaid.

To the big Northeastern and Midwestern states that suffer the most unemployment during recessions (and thus do most of the borrowing), these higher taxes become part of a vicious circle. Higher unemployment leads to higher taxes, which encourage employers to leave the state, which leads to still-higher unemployment and still-higher taxes.

The debtor states thus favor putting part of the burden of financing the system permanently on federal taxpayers, on the theory that most unemployment is really a "national problem." These states would like outstanding state debts to be forgiven, at least in part. They also want to avoid most future debts by providing that after unemployment in a state rises above a certain level, the federal Treasury will share the cost of unemployment benefits there.

UNIONS' PROGRAM

Organized labor would move even further toward federalizing the system. Union leaders would like to take away the states' current freedom to decide for themselves, within certain broad guidelines, who is eligible for jobless benefits and how high benefits will be. Labor also would abolish federal laws encouraging states to set higher state unemployment-tax rates for employers whose former workers have collected the most from the state's unemployment fund.

All this leeway "serves only to foster unhealthy competition between states, hinder the development of more-adequate benefits for workers and create entirely unnecessary confusion," argues Sol Chaikin, president of the International Ladies' Garment Workers' Union.

Most Capitol Hill observers consider organized labor's proposals a pipe dream. Even the mildest cost-sharing proposals appall some debt-free states, along with many employers. They say the debtor states are simply reaping what they sowed during too many years when they paid too much a week to too many recipients while collecting too little in taxes. Cost sharing would reward the debtor states' profligacy, the opponents say.

Generosity to the unemployed certainly does vary. The average weekly benefit payments made in 1978 ranged from $59.57 in Mississippi to $103.59 in the District of Columbia. Of the five states or districts tht paid the highest average weekly benefits, three (the District of Columbia, Pennsylvania and Illinois) are among the dozen that still have debts to the Treasury from the last recession. Moreover, while most states allow recipients to collect benefits for 26 weeks, Pennsylvania provides aid for 30 weeks.

THE PEOPLE IN THE LINES

Ironically, few of the people most directly affected by the system—jobless workers themselves—know of its financial straits or the debate over restructuring it. Standing in lines for a few hours in an unemployment-insurance office in Philadelphia, an observer hears talk of many things: of the length of the lines, of the rudeness of the clerks, of the meagerness of the benefits (although some receive as much as $157 a week, tax-free).

But no one in the lines knows or much cares where the money comes from. What the jobless workers do know is that the system that provides their checks is insurance, not welfare. Says Wilson Rodgers, a 47-year-old laid-off Philadelphia cement finisher: "You don't get this unless you've worked a job. You don't get anything that isn't yours by right."

In Washington, a $40,000-a-year congressional aide who quit his job in a dispute with his boss puts it this way: "If I were sick, I'd collect my health insurance. Well, I'm unemployed; why shouldn't I collect my unemployment insurance?"

MOVING TOWARD WELFARE

But even some defenders of the system worry that it is becoming less like insurance and more like welfare. They cite the heavy borrowing from the Treasury as one symptom of the metamorphosis. As another sign, they note that until recently, high-income workers who lost their jobs midway through a year weren't penalized, it being irrelevant to an insurance system how badly recipients needed benefits. But since 1978, the normally nontaxable jobless benefits have been taxable for recipients who have substantial earned income in the same year.

A congressional watchdog agency, the General Accounting Office, applauded that 1978 change. It said the change would help to make the system fairer and to provide recipients with an incentive to work, and it urged that all unemployment benefits be made taxable.

But the system's defenders say such critics confuse welfare with insurance. As one congressional staffer puts it, "The system is trying to maintain the skills of the work force. If a worker is forced to take another job right away, he may have to take one that doesn't use all the skills he has acquired." Worries about transforming unemployment insurance into a welfare system, to the detriment of its public image, are part of the reason Congress has been cautious about restructuring it.

A Direct Attack on Unemployment and Inflation

ROBERT EISNER

Robert Eisner is currently a professor at Northwestern University and is well known among economists for his knowledge of alternatives to fiscal policy. Eisner has served on the editorial boards of numerous academic journals, and in this capacity, he has played an important role in the development of macroeconomics.

With unemployment still reported at six million the administration urges tax cuts to stimulate the economy. Critics object that further stimulus will fuel a stubborn continuing inflation. I propose a tax program focused directly on reducing unemployment *and* inflation.

We have an income tax credit of 10 percent for business purchase of machinery—a credit that the administration proposes to extend and increase. We have payroll taxes of 12 to 16 percent against employment. Let us redress the balance. Eliminate the investment credit and substitute a judicious mixture of lower payroll taxes and an expanded system of tax credits for the creation of new jobs for the unemployed.

Employment subsidies or tax credits are not new. Nicholas Kaldor urged them in 1936. A number of economists have explored them over the years in various contexts. Most recently, Gary Fethke and Samuel Williamson, and John Bishop and Robert Lerman have examined them sympathetically. They have been applied in other countries and have already been introduced in limited fashion in the United States.

Adequate aggregate demand is vital to combat unemployment. But the glory of payroll tax reductions and employment credits is that they can do everything general demand stimulus can do while reducing critical marginal labor costs. What is more, they can be pointed and guided precisely to our unemployment targets.

I propose two measures:

1. Elimination of all payroll taxes for workers under the age of 20.

2. Institution of a new 50 percent tax credit (or subsidy), subject to certain key restrictions, to employers who hire those without jobs.

The payroll tax elimination for youths, which I have urged before, has various merits. First, to the extent minimum wage provisions may particularly restrict hiring of generally low-paid teenagers, employers are given an extra cushion of 6.05 percent (or up to 10 percent, when unemployment insurance charges are added to contributions for social security). Second, some teenagers

Robert Eisner, "A Direct Attack on Unemployment and Inflation," *Challenge*, July/August 1978, pp. 49–51, ©1978. Reprinted by permission of M. E. Sharpe, Inc., White Plains, New York 10603.

will be more attracted to low-paying jobs since their take-home pay will now be higher. Third, employers conscious of experience-rating charges for unemployment insurance contributions will be less loath to hire teenagers, whose unemployment rates can generally be expected to be high, if they are excluded from the calculations. Fourth, in all equity, teenagers should be relieved of the burden of contributions for which the expected present value of benefits must inevitably be extremely low. For those who begin work in their teens have a long way to go before retirement, and disproportionately, many never live long enough to get there.

My major measure, the new expanded jobs credit, would be available only for hiring those without jobs. Employers could not benefit by bidding away workers already employed. I would suggest that a sufficient condition for eligibility would be unemployment for five weeks or more, which currently would cover 3.2 million of 6 million officially counted as unemployed.

But what about youths looking for their first job, and child-rearers and veterans returning to the civilian labor force? Would they necessarily have to endure five weeks of unemployment before prospective employers would find them eligible for the credit? To avoid this, I would make them eligible without such delay. We might, however, restrict that special eligibility for youths to those who have not already had six months of employment.

HOW TO COPE WITH PROBLEMS OF COMPLIANCE

How could we avoid having employers discharge current employees in order to gain the credit on new workers? This can be readily accomplished by making the credit explicitly incremental or marginal. Employers could enjoy it for eligible new workers only to the extent that their total employment in the tax year was more than some base figure, say 98 percent of that of the average of the three previous years. This provision would mean also that, unlike the situation with the current investment tax credit, employers would receive relatively little advantage for what they would be doing anyway without the credit. It would also permit a relatively large credit with a major impact on incentives, yet small sacrifice in Treasury revenues.

How about the danger that the jobs credit would encourage employers, with a 50 percent government subsidy, to bid up already high salaries unconscionably? This can be prevented largely by setting an upper bound to the amount of the credit per employee. I would suggest a cap at $80 per week, which is approximately the average unemployment insurance benefit. This would dramatize the fact that at worst the credit would be costing the Treasury no more than would be paid to an unemployed worker receiving benefits. Society would be better off, if he were employed, by the value of his output. And this would be equal at least to the half of wages or salaries for which the employer would *not* be compensated.

Would some workers not subject to the credit suffer to the extent those in the various eligible categories are aided? For example, would an adult worker trying to change jobs find no new employer willing to hire him until he had been unemployed for five weeks and hence could carry with him his certificate of credit eligiblity? Much of whatever difficulty might occur on this account could be mitigated by the simple expedient of extending the temporary jobs credit enacted by Congress in 1977 but due to expire at the end of 1978. That credit did not have restrictions on eligibility of workers but was limited to a maximum of only $2,100 per year per worker, $100,000 per firm and, most important, employment in excess of 102 percent of that of the previous year. It should be extended with the amounts raised to the $80 per week I have suggested, with the $100,000 limitation eliminated, but with benefits for employment above the 102 percent benchmark (preferably again related to *average* previous employment) still applied to all new employees. Thus, for employment between 98 percent and 102 percent of their base, employers would find the credit available to them only for the designated jobless categories: those unemployed five weeks or more, youths child-rearers and veterans. Beyond 102 percent of their base employment, however, they could gain the credit on anyone they hired.

Would there be a possibility of layoffs of higher-priced employees in order to take maximum advantage of the credits of $80 per week, or at most $4,160 per year applicable thus to only the first $8,320 of compensation? This could be avoided by a further restriction, akin to that in the current jobs credit, limiting benefits to 50 percent of the excess of total wages over 105 percent of those of the previous year (the extra five percent allowing for modest wage inflation).

The credit I suggest should be tied not to business income taxes but to payroll taxes. A major advantage of this is that it would entail a direct reduction in labor costs, and in marginal labor costs at that. These could be lowered as much as fifty percent, and more for youths no longer subject to payroll taxes at all. The removal of upward pressure on prices and indeed the pressure of competition to drive product prices down with costs could be dramatic.

By tying the credit to payroll taxes we also could readily include nonprofit institutions and nonfederal governmental bodies, both of which could prove important sources of increased employment. Little additional bookkeeping would be necessary for any employers, as FICA records (for social security contributions) could be readily adapted to calculation of the credit. If we are concerned with loss of revenues to social insurance trust funds, we can earmark, say, the first nine percent on all individual and corporate income tax returns for compensating contributions to those funds.

COSTS AND GAINS

How much would all this cost and what would it gain us? Estimates will vary with the distribution of employment possibilities for firms and elusive elasticities of substitution and demand. Simultations reported by Bishop and Lerman yield remarkably large potential effects from even the much smaller and more limited credit enacted by Congress last year, employment demand rising by 4.6 percent and prices declining by 1.78 percent. With back-of-the-envelope-type calculations, I suggest much more conservatively that we might achieve with my proposals, multiplier effects aside, a net increase in employment of two million with credits for some five million man-years of employment involving a gross tax credit subsidy of $20 billion. Adjusting for savings on unemployment benefits and other income maintenance, as well as increased payroll and income tax receipts from the increased employment and a loss of $5 billion on payroll taxes for teenagers, leaves a net cost to the Treasury of perhaps $10 billion.

This amount is of course considerably less than the $19.4 billion net tax reduction now proposed by the administration. And whatever the imagined or real dangers of a general tax cut aggravating inflation, the measures here proposed would contribute directly to lower marginal labor costs and prices. If we wish a general tax reduction as well, and some temporary stimulus to lagging business investment, I have the accompanying tool for that. Legislate now not the extension and expansion of the investment tax credit, as the administration proposed, but its abolition effective in 1980. We could couple that with a corresponding reduction in corporate and other business income taxes. Then firms would have every incentive to acquire equipment now while the credit is still available and the higher current business income tax rates make associated depreciation and other tax-deductible charges more valuable.

ADVANTAGES OF JOB CREDITS

A great appeal of the job credit core of my proposal should be its potential to find and strike directly at its target. Employers will receive benefits only to the extent that they hire the jobless without laying off those with jobs. If, as is the case, unemployment is high among blacks, firms will find themselves drawn to hiring blacks in order to receive their benefits. If, as is the case, unemployment is higher among women, firms will be drawn to hiring women to receive their benefits. If, as is the case, unemployment is much higher among teenagers, and particularly among black teenagers, employers will be drawn to hiring teenagers and black teenagers in order to receive their benefits. Like a heat-seeking missile, a jobs credit tied to nonemployment will lead employers to seek out exactly those who need jobs.

Leaders of organized labor or others concerned with tax breaks for business should think again before criticizing this. The investment tax credit, for example, will cost the Treasury, even in its present form without extension to structures as proposed by the Carter administration, about $13 billion in calendar 1978. Whatever impact this may have on business investment, the bulk of the credit surely goes to firms for buying machinery and equipment that they would have purchased without the tax break. To the extent that more machinery is installed, the substitution of machines for workers is likely to take away more jobs than any initially created to produce the machines. But an employment tax credit will increase the demand for labor. It will do far more than a minimum wage law for wages of low-paid workers, let alone their employment. And even with all of its focus on those without jobs, it cannot help but increase the general tightness of labor markets and hence the wages and bargaining positions of all of labor.

So, if we are contemplating general tax reductions of some 20 billion dollars for general stimulus to the economy, how about this modest investment for a direct attack on unemployment? If it doesn't work, because employers find even a 50 percent tax credit insufficient to get them to hire the unemployed and increase employment, it will hardly cost much. And if it does work, we will have a big bang for our bucks and peace and prosperity without inflation.

The Case for Subsidizing Extra Jobs

RICHARD LAYARD AND STEPHEN NICKELL

Stephen Nickell is professor of Economics at the London School of Economics. He has written extensively on investment and labor economics. Among his many publications is *The Investment Decisions of Firms*.

Richard Layard is professor of Economics at the London School of Economics and Head of the Centre for Labour Economics. Books that he has authored include *Cost Benefit Analysis*, *Microeconomic Theory*, and *The Causes of Poverty*.

The unemployment situation is serious. But what can be done? General reflation would lead to unacceptable inflation and balance of payments difficulties. But suppose unemployment could be reduced with less unfavourable effects by some other scheme. Then this method should be applied, and applied fast. If it takes a hammer to crack a nut, the nut may not be worth cracking. But if a nutcracker will do the job, it should be used. We believe a nutcracker is available.

The idea is that any firm which expands its employment should be paid a subsidy of $50 a week for each additional job it provides above its average level of jobs in 1975. Thus if a firm employed 1,000 workers in 1975 and now employs 1,050, it will at once get a subsidy of $2,500 a week. But the subsidy will also encourage it to expand further, and if it takes on another 50 workers its subsidy will rise to $5,000 a week.

The scheme should be guaranteed to last in this form for 20 months. However, the subsidy per worker should fall progressively from $50 to zero over, say, four years. The reason for a six year guarantee is that this will induce employers to act more strongly in taking on workers earlier, while the gradual reduction in the subsidy should discourage them from any precipitate layoffs as the subsidy is dismantled. If, of course, the gloomier forecasts of unemployment prove right, then the subsidy could be extended later.

The scheme is not pie in the sky. As we shall show, it was used successfully in Germany in 1932 and, in a limited way, more recently.

A MARGINAL JOB SUBSIDY

Unemployment arises because the money wage cost of employing labour is too high relative to the level of monetary demand in the economy, given the level of indirect taxes. At this cost firms are not willing to employ the whole labour force. So two types of option exist: to inflate monetary demand or to reduce costs or indirect taxes. Any general expansion of monetary demand ought to be resisted. Apart from the income tax cuts and benefit increases needed to protect

Richard Layard and Stephen Nickell, "The Case for Subsidizing Extra Jobs," *The Guardian*, 2 April 1976. Reprinted by permission.

low-income families from the effects of past inflation, the emphasis should obviously be on measures that reduce costs and prices. Here again there are two broad options. There could be a *general* employment subsidy, such as a cut in employers' social security contributions (or a general indirect tax cut, which would have similar effects). Or there could be an employment subsidy *confined to the extra jobs provided as a result of the subsidy.*

Such a "marginal" job subsidy has enormous advantages over a general one. To generate a given number of extra jobs within a reasonable space of time, it would obviously require larger total subsidy payments if payments were general than if they were concentrated on marginal workers only. This difference would be strengthened if the marginal subsidy were only paid out for additional workers employed *within the next two years.* Such a device would encourage firms to bring forward their expansion plans so as to qualify for the subsidy, and quite substantial employment effects might be secured by relatively small epxenditures of public money.

Moreover, while a general subsidy would increase the budget deficit, an ideal marginal job subsidy would be self-financing. For suppose a subsidy of $50 a week induces an extra man to be employed. If he gets average wages and has one child he will pay about $35 in taxes which would not have been paid before. The government will also save, say, $60 on unemployment relief; so the net saving is $35. Such savings will help the fight against inflation, and the subsidy itself will directly reduce the level of costs. Furthermore, if the subsidy is at a *flat rate* for each extra worker it will encourage firms to produce extra output by employing extra men rather than by lengthening the hours of those already employed. So a given level of employment will be achieved at a lower level of capacity utilisation and hence at a lower level of inflationary pressure.

One needs of course to check that there will be sufficient demand to absorb the additional output generated. We shall come to this again later. For now, there are two points to be made. First, a subsidy to marginal employment will raise exports, so that a given level of employment will be accompanied by a more favourable balance of payments than if that level of employment resulted from general reflation. Second, if output grows slightly faster than demand for a while, the resulting increase in stockbuilding would do no harm, since the higher level of stocks would help to offset the inflationary pressures of higher demand when it arrives in the boom.

WHAT IS PRACTICABLE?

However, is a marginal wage subsidy administratively possible? The answer is that it is not. For a marginal wage subsidy involves a dialogue between government and firm going roughly as follows.

Government: How many men would you employ if we paid no subsidy for any of them?
Firm: N.
Government: Thank you. We will now pay you $50 a week for any workers you employ in excess of N.

It is difficult to see how firms could be made to give a truthful estimate of N.

Yet in effect this is what they are meant to do to obtain the Temporary Employment Subsidy. To get this a firm has to prove that it would have made redundant 10 or more workers in the absence of the subsidy. Having proved this, it qualifies for $25 per week for a year for each job preserved. The government expects that 55,000 jobs will be preserved as a result of the scheme. Though this achievement is well worth while, it is not large relative to the 1,250,000 unemployed. It reflects in part the difficulty of operating a criterion relating to hypothetical behaviour.

This difficulty is even more acute when it comes to proving that you would not have *expanded* your labour force but for the subsidy. And yet *it is at least as important to induce expanding firms to expand more, as it is to induce contracting firms to contract less.*

The main reason why unemployment has risen is not that more people have *become* unemployed, but that those who are unemployed have remained unemployed longer. So it is crucially important to complement the Temporary Employment Subsidy with a scheme that subsidises newly-created jobs. Perhaps we should stress that this does not mean subsidising all newly recruited workers. This would be totally impracticable, since millions of job changes occur each year; and it would be quite undesirable, since it would encourage excessive turnover.

A JOB-EXPANSION SUBSIDY

What is wanted is a subsidy confined to extra jobs created as a result of the subsidy. However, as we have said, this is not practical. The administrative effort involved in checking that the job is due to the subsidy would be quite intolerable. So we are proposing a perfectly general subsidy to *all* new jobs created, whether due to the subsidy or not. The subsidy would have to relate to changes in employment at the level of the firm not the workplace (i.e. establishment). For, if it related to the latter, this would encourage firms to transfer jobs from one workplace to another and so obtain the subsidy without providing extra jobs. If two firms merged, the original calculated level of those employed in the base year should include both the constituent firms. The subsidy would be paid at $25 a week for part-time workers, and $50 for full-timers. The flat rate nature of the subsidy means, of course, that it raises the relative demand for unskilled workers. But its supreme virtue is its administrative simplicity. The firm would supply an easily-checked record of its employment and be paid the relevant sum.

EFFECTS OF THE SCHEME

It is time now that we looked more carefully at its probable effects. The key questions are: What will it do to prices, employment and the balance of payments? These can be looked at in a short-term or a longer-term perspective. We have already referred to the very short-term during which some extra stock-building may occur. Now we shall mainly consider a medium time period of, say, two years. We shall also point to the effects on the budget deficit, which, both for Keynesians and monetarists, has a bearing on the longer-term prospects for inflation.

Putting down numbers is giving hostages to fortune, but it is shirking not to do so. Those that follow are the best we can manage, using a very simple model. But they involve much guesswork and are mainly given to illustrate the mechanisms at work.

Let us start with prices. Domestically sold output is, primarily, priced at a proportional mark-up over its average direct cost. Thus the subsidy will tend to lower domestic prices by lowering costs. The size of this price effect depends, of course, on the number of workers covered by the subsidy. These will include not only workers whose jobs were created as a result of the subsidy, but also the spontaneous growth that would have happened in expanding firms. The available evidence suggests that over a two year period this spontaneous growth might be around 3 per cent of the labour force. After allowing for the share of imports in costs, this implies that a one-third subsidy to the wage of subsidised workers would reduce domestic prices by about ¾ of a per cent.

This in itself would have a fairly small effect in stimulating employment, by encouraging consumption and import substitution. The big effect on employment would come through exports. Here the fall in the costs of additional production would have two effects. Firms that are operating in competitive markets would have strong incentives to increase output, while firms in monopolistic markets would be led to drop their prices and thus expand their demand. There is good evidence to suggest that a substantial proportion of large exporters base their export decisions on marginal criteria. A crude way of illustrating these effects is to suppose that the elasticity of exports with respect to domestic "costs" is 1.3 and that in these "costs" marginal costs get a weight of ⅓ and average costs ⅔. A *marginal* wage subsidy of ⅓ will thus reduce wage "costs" by about 1/9 and all costs by about 1/27, assuming wages are a third of costs in export industries. This will raise exports significantly and simultaneously improve the balance of payments.

The change in the budget deficit is a more close run thing. As we have emphasised, when one extra job is created there is a direct saving to the Treasury of about $40. There is also an indirect saving. For output normally expands twice as fast as employment, so if there is "normal" average cost pricing, profits increase by about $150 when an extra man is employed. Of this, $75 goes to the Treasury. This gives a $115 a week saving per job created, and there are ¼ million new jobs—making a saving of $30 million a week. This looks good. However, against it must be set the subsidy to the spontaneous growth in expanding firms, which of course generates no corresponding saving. If this spontaneous growth is 3 per cent of the workforce, this means that 750,000 workers are being paid for a $50 a week—$40 million a week. So we do not claim that the budget deficit will improve, but we do claim that it will not worsen anything like as much as it would as a result of general reflation.

OBJECTIONS

The preceding analysis is essentially Keynesian. We have also analysed the subsidy in a monetarist framework, and this gives very similar results. But we ought now to tackle some of the specific objections that have been made to the scheme. First, some people have argued that it would not generate extra total employment because the extra jobs created in expanding firms would displace an equal number of jobs in contracting firms. This argument assumes that real demand remains unaffected by the subsidy. But we have just shown how it increases, so the "displacement" effects have already been allowed for.

Second, the scheme has been criticised as being a charter for overmanning. But, it is difficult to see why firms should create jobs where nothing is produced if it costs them $100 a week to do so. Over-manning may be a problem in many existing jobs, but it is hardly encouraged by steps to bring forward the creation of new jobs.

Third, we have not so far considered the likely effects of this policy on future wage increases. Any policy which reduces unemployment runs the risk of increasing the pressure on wages. But this pressure will certainly be less if prices are less than they would otherwise have been.

CONCLUSION

Unemployment, at its present level, is a manifest evil; and so is inflation. A job-expansion subsidy offers a way of reducing the former at a lower cost in terms of the latter than any other proposal we know. By subsidising marginal workers it encourages firms to expand, particularly into exports. Unlike other expansionary policies it thus offers a prospect of actually improving the balance of payments. But the time to introduce it is now.

Public Management of Private Employment Volume—A Proposal

RICHARD HAZELETT

Richard Hazelett is an engineer who was vice president of Hazelett Strip Castings Corporation. He is one of the few noneconomists who has had an article published in the *American Economic Review*.

Economics rivals philosophy in the ease with which the rash innovator can become entangled in subtle pitfalls. But the author of proposals that diverge sharply from currently accepted thought has one advantage if he is a nonprofessional, for if his schemes fall through, the danger to his personal way of life is less. I have been warned that simple answers to the problem of economic stability in a free society are not likely to be found. Quite possibly this is true. Yet it will be plain that my hopes are not small ones.

No analysis of how slumps come about will be found herein. The omission is deliberate. Rather we will seek methods of economic management having firmness enough to override ordinary causes of instability. But the firmness we seek must not notably impair flexibility or freedom in economic life.

Although the approach here is reminiscent of the Papen Plan tried in Germany in 1932 and '33, under which subsidies and concessions were granted to those employers who hired more help, the present scheme is more similar to a wage subsidy. Yet such a classification of the present proposal is inadequate, as will be seen.

THE MONEY-PUMP PLAN

Let us imagine ourselves in a country where the plan is put into operation during prosperous times. The government announces that it will pay a lump sum to any employer who will contract with the government to spend at a certain minimum rate for employing people during, let us say, a year. For example, an employer of one man might agree to pay out for employment at a minimum rate of, say, $500 per quarter, which would come to $2,000 for the year. It will prove convenient to describe this employer as having acquired one "money-pump contract" or one "money pump." If he contracts to spend for employment at the rate of $1,000 per quarter, we may say that he has acquired two "money pumps." An employer of 100 men planning to pay them a total of $100,000 for steady employment during the year might acquire 200 money pumps. Thus a "money pump" or "money-pump contract" is a unit share of contracted employment responsibility—a unit-contract to spend, say, $500 per quarter for employment, but not for the benefit of specific employees. Most

Richard Hazelett, "Public Management of Private Employment Volume—A Proposal," *American Economic Review*, 47 (1957), 136–44, 146–48.

money pumps would be held in groups of more than one and would be separable in case of subcontracting or, to put it simply, in case of sale.

A lump-sum negative-price payment accompanies each money-pump contract when originally made or when transferred, whether paid by the government at original issue, or paid by an employer when selling his money pumps. Except for this compensation, no new rights are granted to the holder. Stated bluntly, all that money pumps themselves do is to pump money out of the employers' pockets and into the pockets of employees. Thus their value in a free market is always negative. If the plans of our employer were curtailed unexpectedly during the year, he could subcontract some of his money-pump contracts to others, for a price; that is to say, he could sell his money pumps at the prevailing negative price, and the recipients would assume his employment responsibilities.

Since it doesn't matter who holds the money pumps so long as someone does, the government permits them to be traded at will. The market value of money pumps being negative, no certificates evidencing ownership are issued; they would be quite pointless and would be thrust down the nearest open manhole. Rather, entries in government files are the evidence of the existence of money pumps. Free private markets for transferring them spring up around regional government offices where such records are maintained.

Unlike most government contracts, the responsibility incurred would not be primarily that of the contractor to government, but rather of the contractor to a third party—the employee. Such a characteristic in a contract is somewhat unusual, but not unknown; for instance, I am told that it is not very rare for A to insure the life of B with Company C for the benefit of D. The employer might be regarded as insuring employees' jobs; the remarketing of contracts would be analogous to reinsurance.

The objective is to float a quantity of money-pump contracts sufficient to cover nearly the entire employed private labor force, thus maintaining a high level of employment and a guaranteed national annual wage. As the money-pump contracts are for definite terms, they are perpetually reissued as they expire. The expiration dates are arranged to be smoothly staggered so that the reissuing will be a continual operation.

The Negative Price

The negative price of money-pump contracts depends on the amount outstanding and on the state of business confidence. The negative price is preferably low, in order to ease the financial burden both on government in issuing them and on businessmen in subcontracting or selling them. As an educational plan to familiarize business with these new instruments, it would be possible to market short-term money-pump contracts adding up to only a fraction of actual employment. Since this operation would entail only finding *some* employers who would accept a fee for contracting to do what they aimed to do anyhow, the market would soon shake down to a token price. However, pushing up the outstanding volume of money-pump contracts to the point where they would offer a serious guarantee against mass unemployment would impose some risk on the contracting employers. Even though the risk were limited by holding down the maximum length of contract to a year from date of issue, the negative price would no doubt be appreciable. In case there were a fall in the public's propensity to spend, creating a real incentive to reduce employment below the contracted volume, the negative price would grow stiffer. This would of course mean that society (by paying more to get money pumps into circulation) would be translating the avoidance of unemployment into a financial cost of government. If the scheme was fully successful, the forces tending to produce fluctuations in employment would instead only produce fluctuations in the price of money-pump contracts and in the corresponding stream of transfer payments.[1]

The demand for money-pump contracts—the desire to possess them—is always a minus quantity except at a negative price. In order to make this fact continually obvious, the horizontal axis in Figure 1 is placed at the top, even though this makes it somewhat inconvenient to speak of "rises" or "falls" in negative prices, or of "ceilings."

FIGURE 1

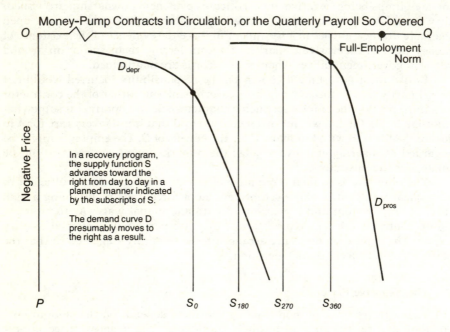

In Figure 1 the demand curves D for money-pump contracts are affected by such things as the supply of labor available to be covered. But the shifts in which we are mainly interested are those associated with business cycles. Curve D_{depr} is assumed to correspond to a condition of unemployment and low economic confidence. Curve D_{pros} corresponds to full employment and high confidence. Government's objective is to issue and keep issued a supply of money pumps that will insure achievement of the full-employment norm.

[1]Two main elements of the scheme arose from consultation with A. G. Hart. The first is that of term obligations as opposed to my previous perpetual obligations. The second is that of a market mechanism for original issue, as opposed to coercive assignment of perpetual obligations. A number of observations, including the ones just made in the text, arose similarly.

The Method of Marketing

A money-pump program might be readily initiated during prosperity as a precaution against emergencies. But if a plan were put into effect during an emergency, buyers of money pumps would wish to protect themselves from capricious government action by assurance of, or even guarantee of, a vigorous government program for pushing money pumps onto the market during the term of the pumps being bought. For the purpose of recovery several types of marketing procedures may be distinguished. However, only one will be presented—the preferred form.

In Figure 1, predetermined rates of sale of money-pump contracts are rigorously maintained, the method of sale being essentially an auction. This method assumes that it is possible practically to coerce recovery, or rather to offer irresistible enticement, by allowing the negative price to reach perhaps a relatively high level at first for a short period. The supply function S for money-pump contracts at any one time is simply a rigid vertical line, indefinite in length. It is made to progress across the figure from left to right during the course of a year, more or less, come what may—slowly at first and faster later. Thus the government says to employers, in effect: "You'll buy these things at a certain speed, no matter what we have to pay you to take them." There is a special psychological value in such a program. The government can point to a graph of future employment and say, "That's the way we aim to make it happen." With a goal thus clearly defined and a plausible way to bring it about, confidence will be engendered perhaps to a high degree, helping to make the employment program a reality and preventing too severe or prolonged up-swings in the negative price; or, what is the same thing, by dispelling that fear which would manifest itself by a sticky or capricious demand function.

It is unnecessary and no doubt undesirable to try to reach the full-employment goal until the plan is several months old. For instance, in fields such as custom construction and fashionable clothing, orders must precede increases in payroll. Recovery in such fields would have to lag somewhat.

An actual auction might be conducted by the government once a week in the principal financial city, during which all the week's supply of new money pumps would be sold to the low-bidding brokers and dealers present. But much the same result may be achieved by the use of written bids submitted daily. These bids would be opened every afternoon and the day's supply of money pumps would be sold accordingly. If by chance there were insufficient bids, the residue would be offered the next day. The weekly auction of Treasury bills is an analogous procedure.

For the accommodation of dealers, new money pumps would have a dormant period of, say, two weeks; that is to say, their effective period would be postdated. This interval would also serve for the formal binding of employers to their money-pump contracts.

The Quantity of Money Pumps

A legal norm for frictional unemployment has to be determined and taken into account so as to avoid the difficulties of overemployment as well as those of unemployment. A politically palatable expression of this norm might be in terms of the average number of days out of work between jobs. The percentage of unemployment to be steered for could thus be derived.

But the fates of individual firms and of small economic sectors and geographical areas can hardly be anticipated adequately, nor can nationwide money pumps be of much help in such problems in the short run. The residue of unpredictable and uncontrollable change is allowed for by routinely failing to issue quite enough money pumps to match the full-employment norm. In Figure 1 this gap appears as the distance between the final vertical supply function S_{360} and the star representing the full-employment norm steered for. The vertical supply function provides a "wall" against depression. But employment may of course go higher, even higher than the norm, for an employer is not compelled to hold money-pump contracts in order to employ. The vertical supply function is set at a level at which the actual employment over a period of time should average out fairly close to the full employment norm. Some experience will of course be required to accomplish this. Thus the economic ship is allowed to deviate from its course a bit with each swell, so to speak, but the average course is presumably maintained if tides and currents are compensated for.

Financing

If a money-pump program is to have the power it needs, a considerable supply of money must be on tap. If the negative price were to bump into a "ceiling," confidence in the plan would be sapped. If funds ran out, the results would be worse. Even a reasonable possibility of either of these occurrences would sap confidence in the plan and make necessary higher expenditure rates than would be required if plenty of money were known to be ready to use.

On the other hand, the receipt of much money in this way by business would hardly be politically acceptable unless the business community as a whole were ultimately to pay it back. The closer the tie-in between what business was paid and what business would later pay back, the more money could be made available to implement the money-pump program. Although I am not one to whom the corporation income tax is very attractive, business income does seem to be the only base which could furnish the potential which a money-pump program ought to have behind it. To complete the tie-in, part of the present corporation income tax might be declared an adjustable surtax, continually adjusted by a formula which would smooth the repayments over a period of several years so that they would tend to offset the sums paid out in the long run. The negative-price payments would be received largely by the same parties who would reimburse the government out of profits later—received, that is, provided they cooperated in the money-pump program.

Under this financing arrangement, the national business community as a whole would be levying future taxes on itself according to its current acceptance of negative-price payments. But it will be clear that the acquiring of money pumps by a business would not appreciably affect national taxes on that one business, unless that business constituted a large fraction of the business community. Even in the latter case the incentive for small businesses to expand and to accept money pumps would remain in nearly full force, since each of these smaller firms would later pay but little of the tax revenue collectible as a result of their own accepting.

The fiscal aspect of money-pump contracts is countercyclical, since payments from government would be large only at a time of stress. Fiscal policy is a main reason for delaying the reimbursement of government by the business community. Business taxes earmarked for this purpose should be adjusted to reimburse the government over a period of up to, say, ten years. To try to square accounts between the business community and government every year or two would spoil this merit of the scheme.

Life-Span

So far we have mostly ignored the question of varying terms or life-spans of money-pump contracts. But the negative price of a contract would no doubt tend to be proportional to the term of the contract. Similarly, in cases of sale by employers the negative price would be prorated according to the unexpired term.

What is the optimum life-span for money-pump contracts? Suppose for a moment that they were all of two years' life-span. The general knowledge that the business community had contracted for an average of one year of future employment would be a powerful builder of confidence. This factor would tend to hold the negative price down. On the other hand, some employers with uncertain prospects (or with seasonal business) would hesitate to assume money-pump contracts for so long as two years, even though transferable. For a given quantity of money pumps issued, this factor would tend to raise the negative price.

Now suppose instead that an assortment of money-pump life-spans are available, all the way from three-month "bills" through one-year "certificates" up to five-year "notes." Thus the best balance of the above considerations may be obtained. One particular combination of life-spans offered for sale would presumably result in the lowest cost to the government over a long period. This combination is presumably the right one and could be approximated by the experience of the issuing agency.

For analytical purposes another quantity besides that of the negative price will prove useful. If the negative price of a money pump is divided by the total amount of the payroll disbursements contracted for by the buyer in buying it, then the quotient is a ratio (or percentage) which may be termed the "employment cost ratio." This is the cost of issuing money pumps relative to the results produced. From the employer's point of view it is the compensation received relative to the employment burden assumed during a term. The form of Figure 1 would remain unchanged if the employment cost ratio were substituted for the negative price therein. The reciprocal of the employment cost ratio may be termed the "money-pump multiplier," for this indicates the relative efficiency of negative-price payments in maintaining employment.

PROBLEMS OF ADMINISTRATION

Compliance

The money-pump records are kept on punched accounting cards in the regional offices of the appropriate government agency. A penalty of 30 per cent of any unfulfilled employment obligations during a quarter is suggested. This is intended to be prohibitive under any conceivable condition. Because money pumps are acquired voluntarily and can be remarketed, they can and should be made to pump inexorably. On the other hand, hardship need not be imposed as a consequence of sudden resignation of employees or of some negligence in carrying too many money-pump contracts. Carry-over privileges may be permitted, by which small deficiencies may be made up in the next quarter. In addition, the penalty for small residual deficiencies might be set as low as 5 per cent.

What if an occasional family firm were to grant themselves high salaries in order to hold more money pumps than they were really entitled to? This loophole may be closed by denying money-pump credit to that portion of compensation in excess of, say, $2,000 paid to a person during a quarter (or $8,000 a year).

Self-Employed Persons

Should a lone proprietor or an "own-account" worker have the privilege of buying money pumps just because he employs himself? For this purpose, his earnings might be construed as a salary from himself as owner to himself as employee and thus eligible for money-pump coverage. Should not such individuals be on the same footing with enterprises of more than one man, which would be receiving negative-price payments?

The most workable approach appears to be to exclude proprietors and self-employed individuals, partners, and corporation officers both from money-pump coverage and from the labor force as calculated for present purposes. This is within the general spirit of the scheme, which is to protect those who can hardly choose, under modern conditions, to become self-employed.

Strikes

At first thought it might be supposed that employers experiencing strikes should be permitted to sell their money-pump contracts back to the government for the duration of the strike. But this would set up the perverse incentive for some employers to incite strikes by imposing ridiculous terms on workers whom they wished to discharge during times of incipient contraction. Perhaps the most that can be done for employers directly is to allow a period of grace for negotiating sale of their money-pump contracts to other private parties. (Such lenience might be applicable to certain other emergency situations.)

The government can assure that there will be a market somewhere in the economy for such "jammed" money pumps by excluding strikers from the labor force as computed for present purposes, when they are not actively seeking other employment. This arrangement would protect employers from the otherwise crushing money-pump obligations of widespread strikes, while at the same time assuring employees that competition to employ them will remain prevalent.

Inflation

It will be clear that the general effect of the money-pump plan would hardly be deflationary. Rather it might be argued that wages would be bid up during a condition of assured full employment. Or it might happen that people would become so confident of the economic future that they would fail to save money. Would money pumps swamp us in an inflationary deluge, in the manner of the multiplied buckets of The Sorcerer's Apprentice?

We may presume that money pumps would be secure enough in their function to withstand inflation-arresting measures that would at present seem risky. Restrictive monetary measures could be applied without fear of causing another 1937. The government could show an occasional surplus as in days of yore without fear of consequences. In short, price-level policies could be pursued without at the same time threatening employment stability.

The graduated expenditure tax (or spendings tax), as analyzed most thoroughly by Nicholas Kaldor,[2] would deserve the fullest of consideration, since any deflationary tendencies of such a tax would be readily overcome. With such a tax, high rates may be levied when necessary without impairing the ability to save and invest. Such a tax can largely sterilize the inflationary effects of liquid accumulations in the hands of individuals, something the income tax cannot do. Heavy evasion might be less of a problem than with the income tax, since high spending is likely to be readily visible to all, and since the expenditure tax seems more just in that it makes important distinctions in favor of socially desirable private uses of money.

But measures involving as much change as the spendings tax probably are not essential to the reasonably smooth working of the plan. More familiar fiscal measures will no doubt suffice, and the money-pump plan renders all the conventional brakes on the economy safer to use vigorously. Yet in all this it should be remembered that money pumps exert no special stimulus on the economy in good times, aside from the confidence engendered.

ADVANTAGES OVER SIMILAR PLANS

Wage Subsidies

Money-pump contracts might be described, in part, as a wage subsidy paid to business according to total employment provided. But if reimbursement is to be made by the buisness community in the long run, the name of subsidy seems inappropriate, except when speaking of individual businesses. Perhaps the term "incentive loan" is better for describing what the business community as a whole receives.[3]

There are other differences between wage subsidies as usually understood and the present scheme. A wage-subsidy scheme lacking the marketable-contract feature would have to disburse money *after* performance by employers. These disbursements would not be directly related to future employment. If an increase in the rate of subsidy were offered for the following quarter, its effect could not be measured until fresh employment statistics were accumulated. Meanwhile, the administrators could not know whether they had made the subsidy high enough or not. If they were to find that they had not, they might

---

[2]*An Expenditure Tax* (London, 1955).

[3]However, see Kaldor, *loc. cit.* Much of the analysis in that paper will apply to the present scheme. *Cf.* William Vickrey, "Wage Subsidies and Unemployment," unpublished Master's thesis, Columbia University, 1937.

promise a higher subsidy rate for the remainder of the quarter, but that would complicate the administration of the subsidy. The result might be never-ceasing political demands for an increased subsidy, in order to feel sure that it was high enough.[4]

In contrast, the negative price of money-pump contracts changes itself from day to day. Thus the demand for money pumps is continuously measured and met. The rate of disbursement by government is impersonally determined by the market.

The Papen Plan

In Germany between September 1932 and April 1933, producers were paid 400 reichsmarks for each new employee hired. This was one phase of the Papen Plan, which was a failure; unemployment continued to mount. One thing to be learned from that experience is that plans which are merely static stimulants may not work. To implement fixed, one-time subsidies or tax allowances for hiring new employees requires arbitrary standards as to when the hiring was done and for what minimum period. Injustice between individual firms must result, depending on their recent history of hiring and laying-off. Thus such a plan cannot be made powerful enough to assure its operation without also becoming intolerably inequitable. As with some medicines, the side effects of employment subsidies necessitate weak prescriptions.[5]

If competition had been more prevalent in Germany, this phase of the Papen Plan might have been effective. As it happened, monopoly conditions generally prevented the fear that any competitors would accept the subsidy and lower their selling prices.[6] But the existence of effective competition will doubtless multiply the effectiveness of money pumps, perhaps decisively. Employers can hardly avoid acquiring them when their competitors are doing so and getting paid for it.

Hours or Dollars

The Papen Plan does suggest an alternate method of implementing the money-pump program. Could *hours* of work rather than dollars be made the criterion of compliance? Why couldn't a "pump" be rated in hours instead of dollars, obligating an employer to spend for 250 hours of employment per quarter, whatever number of dollars that would come to? There seems to be no compelling reason why either method could not be made to work.

Hour-rating of money pumps might be considered preferable to dollar-rating on the ground of the changing price level. Although corresponding adjustments could be made in the number of money pumps outstanding, perhaps the main counterargument is the presumptive ease and safety with which the price level could be controlled within an adequate program of money-pump contracts, as discussed earlier.

In favor of the dollar-rating plan, canceled checks are more convenient to

[4]*Cf.* A. C. Pigou, *The Economics of Welfare*, 4th ed. (London, 1932), p. 703.

[5]*Cf.* K. E. Poole, *German Financial Policies, 1932–1939* (Cambridge, Mass., 1939), pp. 40–41.

[6]*Cf.* G. Colm, "Why the Papen Plan for Economic Recovery Failed," *Social Research*, Feb. 1934, I, 83–96, esp. 90–93.

verify than wage-and-hour records. On the other hand, the mass of figures currently collected by government and unions would render foolhardy any falsification of either hours worked or of sums paid. Yet I would like to think that the policing of business on such matters as wage rates and hours would ultimately be rendered obsolete under a program of money-pump contracts.

Incentive Taxes

It is instructive to apply the money-pump metaphor to other plans of this general class. In one early proposal an incentive tax was to be applied to a plant's deficiency in employment as related to its physical capacity to employ. Here the money pumps would in effect be attached to productive equipment wherever located. Other plans have proposed taxes on money or on idle money. Thus the pumps would be attached to the units of money themselves. These proposals vary as to the certainty and regularity of the resulting flow of income. They vary as to the direction of the flow induced—that is, as to whether the expenditure would immediately enter the flow of national income payments or dissipate itself in other ways.

In the present money-pump plan it may be said that the "pumps" are not affixed to anything, but rather are distributed about in a manner determined by individuals freely bargaining among themselves, imposing no limitations on liquidity, and granting but negligible capricious relative advantages to different firms. Thus the essential elements of control are separated from the nonessential and troublesome. The attainable result of this general approach, one may hope, would be a certainty of income flow fully compatible with flexibility and with freedom.

AUTHOR'S EPILOGUE

It has been suggested that "money pumps" be renamed *employment incentive contracts*. The foregoing plan, to be either feasible or economical, will require careful education of all the employers in the land. Remember that the negative price is the *marginal* negative price—that which will induce the more balky, shaky, or economically naive employers to buy the contracts. The attraction of this simpler way of arbitrarily assigning permanent though transferable obligations to employ is that it is more readily explainable and, since it is cost-free to government, certain never to run out of allotted funds.

Money to finance payrolls will need to be made available to employers generally during periods of delayed consumer demand or dislocations, such as an oil or mineral crisis. Here, I suggest that the rationale of monetary policy will become clear only when it is no longer tangled with problems that should be controlled by other means.

The spirit of money pumps or employment incentive contracts goes back to Silvio Gesell, a German-Argentinian merchant. In his 1916 book, *The Natural Economic Order*, he clearly anticipated the general theory of John Maynard Keynes, most pointedly in his discussion of the theory of interest. Though partly dated and visionary, Gesell's book has enough undetonated dynamite in it to serve as a catalyst for change in that area also.

Richard Hazelett, March 1981

Public Management of Private Employment—A Comment

ALBERT HART

Albert Hart is one of the most original and insightful economists living. His Ph.D. dissertation at the University of Chicago, titled "Uncertainty and the Theory of the Firm," is a classic that foreshadowed many of the later developments in economic theory. He has worked extensively on the theory of business cycles and expectations and is currently Professor Emeritus at Columbia University.

COMMENT

Mr. Hazelett's suggestion of a control-instrument (his money pump) which would be bought and sold by private parties, and would serve as an instrument for open-market operations by public authorities, is extremely suggestive. In content, it is one of the most hopeful-looking of the long series of policy proposals designed to meet J. M. Clark's celebrated difficulty that labor cost, though an overhead for society, is a variable item for the individual employer. In form, it suggests a widely adaptable linkage of control instruments with market mechanisms.

It is very common to carry on economic-control operations by buying and selling on an existing market. But this is a proposal to create both the market and the commodity it is to deal in, so that the commodity itself becomes an instrumentality of control.

Once we look at the proposal in this way, we can see that it represents a broad class of control possibilities. Some of these are familiar as academic examples, others as bits of economic history; but something is added when we see them as a class.

To begin with academic examples, we often present in the classroom cases where use of market mechanisms might forestall the creation of certain sorts of vested interests. Grazing rights in the national forests, for example, tend to become vested, and to attach an extra element of value to property in ranches which have enjoyed such rights. Since the grazing privilege must be rationed, economists ask, should the rationing not be by price, rather than by a procedure which sets up discrimination between a favored few and excluded many? Or in a city concerned with traffic congestion, the limited number of "medallions" evidencing permission to have taxis on the streets become pieces of transferable property, with a market value exceeding that of a new cab in many cities, recognized as vested in the successors of those who had cabs when the number was closed. If such an element of value is to be created by anticongestion measures, economists ask, should it not be captured for the city as a whole by

Albert Hart, "Public Management of Private Employment—A Comment," *American Economic Review*, 47 (1957), 148–52.

charging for it? And (to go a step further) might not the most suitable charge be found by holding an annual auction of one-year permits?

Historically, an interesting control-instrument market has existed in recent years in the Brazilian auctions of foreign exchange with which to buy imports. Economists have noted that in cases such as the British quota on Danish bacon, a gap is opened between the British demand price and the Danish supply price, inviting dealers on one side or other of the market to form a monopolistic organization and capture the difference. If import quotas are to be limited, economists ask, why not capture this difference for society by auctioning the permits? Once a multiple-currency system is adopted, an exchange auction serves this purpose. A less obvious historical example of a control-instrumentality market is the gold standard. Genetically, of course, the gold market predated control. But in the last few decades, the "commodity" gold has evolved into a control instrument, and the market (more and more clearly centered around government operations) has adapted itself. Commodity-reserve schemes propose to create a market in a commodity-bundle of fixed composition (designed to function as a control instrument analogous to gold); their working would hinge largely on the interplay between control operations and the evolution of the bundle-market and the related markets in single commodities.

A step closer to the Hazelett type of proposal are monetary devices suggested about the time of the Korean war by Jacob Viner[1] and E. A. Goldenweiser.[2] Viner pointed out that in the evolution of our monetary institutions, reserves had changed from being a safeguard for depositors to being an instrument to control the volume of money. Since the initiative in creating or destroying money lies not in accepting deposits but in making or collecting loans, why not link reserves with loans rather than with deposits? Goldenweiser pointed out that if control was sought through a security-reserve (then a very popular suggestion), it would be more effective to require a small percentage in a special type of security issued and regulated for the purpose and held exclusively by banks, rather than a large percentage in an already-issued type largely held outside banks. Putting the two ideas together,[3] it becomes evident that aggregative control of total loans, or of total earning assets of banks, or of categories of credit otherwise defined could be attained by setting up loan-reserve requirements to be met by special securities. These securities would then become in effect transferable loan-permits, which in times of credit restriction would reflect the special value of being able to carry on the restricted activity. Such a device would socialize the windfalls from restriction (like an ideally determined excise on restricted items in a war economy) while using market allocation machinery.

Hazelett's proposal not only dramatizes the fact that some controls can be seen as the creation of markets in control instruments. It also suggests that the one-way effectiveness of some controls might be turned into two-way effectiveness by redesign. The existing markets for control instruments, as far as I have

---

[1] See the commentary by the Federal Reserve Board in Joint Committee on the Economic Report, *Monetary Policy and the Management of the Public Debt, Replies to Questions* (Washington, 1952), pp. 482–89.

[2] *American Monetary Policy* (New York, 1951), p. 63.

[3] Some of these possibilities are worked out in my *Defense and the Dollar* (New York, 1953).

identified them, are all restrictive devices. But Hazelett is suggesting two control devices—not only his money pumps themselves, but his permits to hold excess reserves—which would be capable of setting up incentives toward economic expansion. Perhaps monetary policy "cannot push on a string." But would it be possible to run the string around a snubbing-post, so that it could pull toward expansion in a depression?

For economic-control strategy in the broad, to set up a market in instruments of control offers a most desirable kind of feedback. Proposals for control by such techniques as excise taxes, subsidies, policy toward price discrimination, interest-rate manipulation, regulation of credit terms, all look very workable when we assume that the controllers are perfect forecasters, and all become much less likely to serve the proposed ends as soon as we allow for errors of forecasting. If a market can be created in the control-instrument, however, we have essentially a market mechanism for feeling out the level of tax or subsidy that it takes to get a specified quantitative effect. If the control is redundant, its operation will send back a signal to this effect by bringing the price to zero. If tension of the sort the control is aimed at is building up, its operation will send back a signal by pulling the price farther from zero. Thus this type of mechanism offers a control pattern that will adjust itself to the intensity needed to carry out an assigned job, and beyond that is capable of registering some of the pressures against which (or with which) policy must work.

Interest in this family of control possibilities is bound to vary with our faith or skepticism about the merits of regulating components of economic activity. From the standpoint of dyed-in-the-wool interventionists, here is a choice collection of possible methods of handling components that are refractory to available controls. From the standpoint of confirmed anti-interventionists, here is perhaps a Pandora's box of new ways to get in trouble. But even the free-market enthusiast cannot afford to look only at this aspect. In the first place, some of his own proposals really call for setting up markets in control instruments.[4] In the second place, there will always be situations where the free-market purist has lost the battle as to *whether* a component should be controlled and yet may have some chance of influencing the way it is controlled; the greater impersonality and automaticity of the control-instrument-market technique as against most alternatives should then recommend it. In the third place, the free-market enthusiast in the Henry Simons tradition recognizes the need for monetary and fiscal stabilizers. While he may well object to the ramification of sector controls of this or any other type, he should not overlook the possibility that the Hazelett technique, with its direct applicability to money flows, might be transformable into a general monetary scheme of maximum breadth and impersonality.[5]

[4]The proposal that defense planning should rely on free markets to do the jobs assigned during the second world war to priorities and allocations is a notable example. "Priority" is a temporal concept. If there were in fact two interlinked steel markets—one in tons of steel and another in delivery dates—the proposal might be workable. But the normal market has no machinery for reallocating delivery dates as among customers. In a mild emergency "gray markets" may take over this role; but the market would not have the right kind of flexibility for a real war emergency unless dealings in delivery dates were systematized.

[5]The "contracts" involved—contrary to those suggested in such schemes as Mordecai Ezekiel's *$2500 a Year* (New York, 1936)—are nondiscriminatory. They are not tailored to individuals by negotiations with officials who have discretionary powers, but offered impersonally to those who choose to buy them.

While he has taken pains to present his proposal as a possible additional tool in stabilization policy, rather than as an all-sufficient stabilizer, Hazelett seems to me too casual about the interplay of stabilization measures. If his scheme were adopted, the need for other measures might be less reduced than he suggests; but the conditions for their application might be more improved than he suggests.

Serious as the problem might prove, I pass over the question how the scheme would work in the face of a chronic "cost-push"—that is, a tendency for wage rates to outpace productivity and push up the price level. I have not been able to satisfy myself as to how the cost-push would develop under his policy suggestions. But since this difficulty is common to almost all discussions of stabilization strategy, Hazelett's proposal can be put reasonably well in context by discussing it on the assumption that the cost-push is kept under control through labor policy (private or public).

On this optimistic assumption, Hazelett's scheme has one obvious shortcoming as a self-sufficient stabilizer: it can underwrite payrolls (and presumably employment and production); but, to invert Mill's famous dictum, demand for labor is not demand for output. Even though employers maintain production, employment, and payrolls, their sales may fluctuate. The forces which otherwise would have set up a fluctuation in employment and output will therefore set up a fluctuation not only in the price of money pumps but in the state of inventory. The increasing inventory-risk that would arise in case of serious "involuntary" inventory accumulation makes it likely that recessive forces might sometimes produce a really stiff "negative price" for money pumps.

The logic of the money-pump scheme requires the government to pay whatever price it must to keep enough pumps in circulation. To keep the price from going outrageously high, other policy measures must be able to relieve the inventory situation before involuntary accumulation goes too far. If we regard the money-pump mechanism as the basic defense against deflation, other measures must at least be strong enough to keep inventory from growing too much.

On the other hand, if the scheme were once well established, we would expect business to absorb the early stages of an involuntary inventory accumulation with equanimity. The forces which otherwise would quickly initiate a cumulative decline in output and employment would express themselves at first in a stiffening of the money-pump price. Those responsible for policy would thus gain time to turn around. Tax cuts to stimulate sales, notably, could be withheld till it was clear that involuntary inventory growth was appreciable, and yet come in time to keep the money-pump price from rising to outrageous heights.

A corollary, which Hazelett also draws, is that on the upswing there could be an energetic use of tight money and tight fiscal policy to insure against inflation, without inhibitions arising from the fear of setting off a downswing. If restrictive policy were overdone, the fact would register itself in a stiffening of the money-pump price, and in reports from business that sales were not rising enough to validate the existing output-inventory position. In this case, a downturn would be in the making. But, for the reasons just mentioned, there would be time to diagnose the situation and adapt monetary-fiscal policy to it before substantive damage was done. If the adaptation was overdone, furthermore, the inventories accumulated before it started would be an anti-inflationary cushion, and their depletion would again give time for a turn-around of policy.

Perhaps Hazelett's scheme is too outlandish ever to have a chance. Perhaps its loopholes are broader than they look, and its incidental ill-effects deeper. Certainly I would not be willing to testify that it was sound practical policy (in case it became of political interest) till these matters had been much more thoroughly thrashed out. Yet the argument just presented suggests that such a scheme would have huge advantages. Under almost any other stabilization strategy I have seen suggested,[6] the interplay of inventory position, business expectations and employment is capable of giving a downswing some momentum before the situation is recognized and corrected. The fear of such a result inhibits stabilization measures to check possible inflation in a period of prosperity. The ideal policy would be one so designed that we would always have at the beginning of a downswing what Keynes termed a "breathing-spell"—a period long enough for it to be possible to see clearly that activity was tending to sag, yet not so long that real damage had yet happened, or that the downswing had gathered momentum. Hazelett's proposal offers a mechanism that should make such a breathing-spell a regular feature of business peaks. If this proposal proves objectionable, who can devise an alternative proposal with the same virtue?

[6]A policy combination including a commodity-reserve currency, *if* the latter could be made workable on a broad enough base, would have the same advantages. But most students of commodity reserve feel that at best it could cope with the raw-material aspect of inventory, leaving inventory of finished products as a destabilizer.

Soviets Find Job for Every College Grad

DAN FISHER

Dan Fisher is currently assistant financial editor for the *Los Angeles Times.* Before coming to the *Times,* he covered the automobile industry for *Industry Week* magazine. Since joining the *Times,* he has covered the energy industry and has served as the Moscow Bureau Chief.

MOSCOW—"It's like their wedding day," the university rector said happily.

A graduating senior disagreed. "It's terrible," he said. "Everyone is taking tranquilizers."

The occasion was the Day of Distribution, which is far more emotional than Graduation Day at the 900 or so institutions of higher learning in the Soviet Union. On the Day of Distribution, graduates get their first job assignments.

By the end of June, virtually all of the 800,000 young men and women graduating from universities and other university-level institutions will have met with a placement commission and will know which job is waiting for them.

The system is a creature of this country's planned economy.

In the United States, collegians choose their specialties and take their chances in the job market after graduation. In the Soviet Union, the system cranks out cars, bombs and paper clips according to government decree, and it produces diplomas the same way.

"They give us money, we give them specialists," Arnold Koop, rector of Tartu University in Soviet Estonia, summed up.

Most Soviet students, even though they would probably balk at trading their security for what they see as the chaotic rough-and-tumble of the American job market, are not entirely happy with their system.

Eager to begin enjoying the good life that a college degree virtually assures in this society, many see the first job assignment as a way station at best.

When they scrawl "I consent" at the bottom of the placement commission's decision, Soviet graduates technically commit themselves to work at their first job for at least three years, repaying the state for a free education.

But they resent the fact that many assigned jobs are far from home, in the provinces, where life is often primitive and their talents are sometimes not appreciated. And many wind up with jobs only remotely related to their studies.

There are no nationwide figures available, but judging from scattered information about last year's graduating class as well as a spate of recent articles in the press, tens of thousands of this year's graduates will demonstrate their displeasure by simply not showing up for their assigned jobs.

The Young Communist League newspaper Komsomolskaya Pravda reported at the end of May that while 316,000 engineers graduated last year, "annually thousands of (them) just disappear, as if the earth swallowed them up."

Earlier this year the Ministry of Education bemoaned the "widespread failure of new teacher-training institute graduates to take teaching jobs in 1979" and revealed that, as a result, 28% of the openings went unfilled.

Horror stories like that of young Olga Golubenko illustrate the problem.

Golubenko, an English teacher, is a 1976 graduate of Chernovtsy State University in the Ukraine. While she was aware of the difficulties that young teachers often face in rural schools, she went off dutifully to the village of Iosifovka, where she was assigned to teach at the secondary school.

The stories she had heard, she said, "didn't scare me. I was sure that I had sufficient desire to work and enough knowledge."

When she showed up, she found that her classroom had "gaping cracks in the doors, the stove was rickety and the flue was stopped up. Several times I went to the principal and said, 'Ivan Vasilyevich, come and see what I have to put up with.'"

The principal laughed at her, she said.

In the fall, her classroom was often only half-full since the students were called out of school to help with the harvest.

When she gave 20 of her students the D grades she felt they deserved, the school administration and her fellow teachers criticized her.

"Now I was a poor teacher and was trying to compromise the school," she said. Her colleagues urged her to think of the school's reputation, but she complained to the district department of education, which reprimanded the principal. That only made matters worse.

"I became the object of petty fault-finding," she said.

The principal accused her of being headstrong and too soft to handle life in the village. He told her that her predecessor "used to pass everyone in English," she related.

Golubenko lasted only six months in Iosifovka before she went back to the city, using as an excuse the fact that her mother was ill.

Graduates find many ways to beat the system. Women in their final two years of school often get pregnant since they know that mothers are not required to go to the countryside.

"There are many ways around the system," Natalya, a third-year student at Moscow State University, said conspiratorially. "Everybody tries to use them."

Bribery and nepotism are rampant. Placement, commission members are just one set of targets for under-the-table payments, according to Soviet sources.

Also, Soviet organizations can request the assignment of certain graduates, and such requests are usually honored. And some students use family connections.

Some complain that while they have prepared for careers in the humanities or the sciences, they are assigned jobs as teachers. Up to 90% of the university graduates in the humanities and 60% to 70% of those in the natural sciences are sent to teach.

"We were deceived," a group of graduating students from Tyumen University complained not long ago. "The instructors repeatedly told us that participation in the departments' work opens the path to a scientific career, but now they're suggesting that we go to rural schools."

Only the very top college and university students have any real freedom of choice about where they will work. The head of the Ulan Ude Agricultural Institute in Siberia once told a group of visitors that of 520 graduates the previous year, only 30 got straight A's and therefore won the right to choose their first job.

The privilege is known as "the right of the first night" at Tartu University, Koop, the rector, said.

For others, the system varies slightly from college to college, apparently with a student's ranking in his graduating class playing a greater or lesser role depending on the institution.

According to the law, no enterprise can hire a college graduate who has been assigned to some other job. In fact, however, the law is routinely ignored. There is a labor shortage here—primarily because of the inefficiency of the Soviet economy. Also, the Soviet system has so many built-in incentives for plants, offices and other unnecessary employees that bosses pay little attention to the laws on hiring.

All this makes a farce of what is supposed to be a rigidly controlled procedure designed to tie the Soviet higher education system to the country's economic needs.

The placement commissions work from lists of personnel requirements supplied by ministries, factories, farms and research organizations. The lists evolved from plans drafted up to 15 years ago, plans that determined what kinds of college teachers the country would require, what kind of facilities they would need, how many students would be admitted each year and in what specialties.

One reason the Soviet government can promise a job for every graduate is that only about one of every three students who wants to go to college is admitted.

Soviet officials are becoming increasingly concerned about the job assignment process. But they see it as a planning problem; they do not question the basic idea that Moscow can coordinate the needs of an increasingly complex society of 260 million people.

"Today we have an overproduction of chemical engineers," said S. M. Muratov, rector of the Kuibyshev Polytechnic Institute.

At the same time, there are not enough engineers in some other areas. "We need to significantly increase flexibility in the higher education system, especially when it comes to planning," Muratov said.

Job assignments are the result of a four-stage process that takes two years to filter through the bureaucracy. Each educational institution gathers information that is assembled by the various government ministries and departments. They pass it on to the planning committees for the 15 Soviet republics, and then it is passed up to the Soviet Union's State Planning Committee.

At the same time, enterprises, organizations and institutions submit statements of requirements that follow the same path. The State Planning Committee coordinates the two lists, produces a consolidated plan and passes it back down through the system.

A Guaranteed Jobs Proposal

DAVID C. COLANDER

One of the problems an editor has is finding objective statements from all sides of a position. Although there is nothing necessarily liberal about guaranteed jobs proposals, I could not find a conservative statement of this position. To remedy the situation, I wrote one.

The complaints about the present unemployment compensation system are well known: It destroys individual initiative, provides incentives for people not to work and income for those who do not really need it, and it simultaneously does not provide enough support for those who do. Because most proposals to reform the system focus on restructing incentives by reducing the level of support, they consequently involve an unpleasant equity–efficiency trade-off.

In this article I suggest a simple approach to the unemployment problem that finesses that unpleasant trade-off and improves both the equity and the efficiency of the system. This approach is simply to guarantee a job to all individuals who want to work, thereby directly eliminating all true unemployment and the need for unemployment policy. This guaranteed jobs proposal will:

1. direct the support to only those who need it most
2. eliminate the need for a minimum wage, thereby eliminating the inefficiencies associated with it
3. eliminate many of the negative incentives of our present unemployment compensation system
4. do all of the above at a reasonable cost

WHAT ARE GUARANTEED JOBS PROGRAMS?

A guaranteed jobs program is one in which the government guarantees employment for individuals. "Employment" is a vague term and any specific proposal must spell out the complete characteristics of the job, such as the wage rate, the nature of the work, the location, and the hours of work.

The relative characteristics of the guaranteed job are important since they place a minimum on the type of job the private sector must offer in order to attract workers. Unless the private jobs are overall more attractive in wage rates, work satisfaction, potential or lack of potential, and all other characteristics, individuals will not choose them. Since the guranteed jobs provide the minimum acceptable characteristic-adjusted wage (hereafter referred to as the Wage), that overall attractiveness cannot be set at a relatively high, or even an average, Wage. The reason is simple logic—the minimum cannot also be the average. Thus, any realistic guaranteed jobs proposal must merely set the minimal level job that society finds acceptable.

WHY GUARANTEE JOBS AND NOT INCOME?

The arguments in favor of a government-run guaranteed jobs program are the same ones used to support both guaranteed minimum income proposals and our present system of unemployment insurance. For some, they are simply ethical duties of government; for others, they are a necessary evil—individuals without a means of support will soon be looking to replace the system.

Although the two arguments are fundamentally different, they lead to the same conclusion—the government has a responsibility for providing individuals with a means of supporting themselves. The difficulties come in implementing this responsibility. Guaranteeing income reduces individuals' incentives to work while simultaneously creating inequities between those who are and those who are not working. Such inequities and negative incentives limit these programs to low levels of support with some people receiving too much and others too little. If that same money could be directed at only those who need it, the system would be fairer and the support level could be raised. The primary advantage of a guaranteed jobs program is that it does precisely this; it directs the income to those who need it.

The problem with guaranteeing income, whether in the form of a negative income tax or unemployment insurance, is that the focus is on *money* income not *real* income, which is the measure of fairness. For example, if two identical individuals each receive $200/week, but one must sweep streets for his money while the other merely collects it from the government, the two individuals are not being treated equally. Their real income—their monetary income adjusted for the effort they put into earning that income—is not equal. Guaranteed jobs programs guarantee *real*, not monetary, income, thereby avoiding the inequities and negative incentives of the guaranteed income proposals.

The need to guarantee monetary income for individuals develops for one of three reasons: (1) they are physically or mentally unable to work; (2) they cannot find work; or (3) they choose not to work. Guaranteed income proposals either do not separate these groups or rely upon separating them administratively in a highly imperfect way; and most of the complaints about these programs focus on the resulting inequities among these groups. A guaranteed jobs program by its very nature separates individuals who cannot find work from individuals who choose not to work by providing a job for all individuals who want to work.[1]

The value judgment embodied in a guaranteed jobs program is that every individual who is willing to supply his effort has a right to a minimum standard of living and that in order to have that right one must supply a minimum level of effort. Under a guaranteed jobs program every individual able to work has the right to *earn* an income, not the right to *have* an income. The program is based upon the premise that individuals who are able have a duty to contribute to society if they make claims to the product of society; and the harder someone works, the more he should receive. This does not mean that hard work is in any

---

[1]Since those physically or mentally unable to work are a small percentage of the total, their problems can be addressed in programs designed specifically for them. Such individuals as handicapped and mentally retarded are both able and willing to work, and it is important for their own self-worth that they do work. Their output might not be great, but work is measured in terms of input, not output.

sense noble; there is nothing necessarily noble about hard work. Nor does it mean that a person who works has more inherent moral claims upon the product of society than one who does not. The guaranteed jobs concept is based upon practicality. Without hard work, there would be little or no product to distribute, and thus a society that desires a large total product must encourage its members to exert work effort. If that could be done in such a way as to have "sufficient" product without tying distribution to effort, work and claims to product need not be connected. If, however, it cannot be (and at present in our society I suspect that it cannot), work effort and the total amount received must be related.[2] By maintaining this connection between effort and income, guaranteed jobs proposals achieve higher levels of equity and efficiency than does the present system.

DESIGNING A GUARANTEED JOBS PROPOSAL

The above arguments are general; the true test of the proposal lies in the ability to design a proposal that is both economically and administratively feasible and can be perceived as fair by a broad spectrum of the society. In this section I outline a proposal that, in my view, meets these essential conditions.

All previous attempts at guaranteed jobs have failed because they attempted to solve too many of society's problems in one program. My proposal is to start with a far more modest proposal directed at the most immediate problems that can feasibly be solved by the program. Proposals to address other significant problems should be treated as complements, not substitutes. One limitation that greatly enhances feasibility is to concentrate on providing activities in which individuals can translate their time into income rather than to attempt to provide meaningful, self-satisfying jobs. The reason is twofold. First, many jobs in society are, unfortunately, lacking in meaning. While it is nice to think of a world in which all jobs are meaningful, I know of no way to accomplish this end. Moreover, by making it a government responsibility to provide meaning to individuals' lives we infringe upon individuals' rights to find their own.[3] While these positions are subject to serious debate, given the negative experience of past attempts, focusing initially on a minimal objective of providing the possibility for all to earn a fair income seems necessary.

Thus I argue that, initially, the primary concern of a guaranteed jobs proposal should be to create an institution in which *individuals can translate their time into income at a reasonable money wage*—what some would call work activities, not jobs. Ideally, these work activities would be highly productive—creating benefits for society higher than their costs. But again, realistically, such high goals will probably only destroy the entire proposal. Even though our system works in a highly imperfect manner, it does work, and the more productive the jobs, the more likely it is that either a public or private group is already

---

[2]There is nothing necessarily fair about this connection; one individual might totally enjoy work while another might totally enjoy leisure, but since there is no way of separating individuals according to these preferences, individuals' specific enjoyment of work cannot be taken into account. When all individuals believe that a specific job is more pleasant, the market tends to compensate by reducing the wage for that job. This proposal differs from the market in that it ties minimum rewards to input and not to output.

[3]Obviously this argument can be easily misused; a meaningful search for meaning has certain minimum requirements.

involved in attempting to supply them. These groups will fear replacement and unfair competition and make implementation of the proposal exceptionally difficult. This, at least, has been the experience with previous attempts. Thus, initially at least, it seems desirable to concentrate on activities that are individually beneficial and are not necessarily productive. These might include "jobs" or activities such as grammatical, writing, mathematical, and physical exercises. The program would provide a job from 8:00 A.M. to 5:00 P.M. five days a week consisting of a rigorous set of physical exercises interspersed with writing and grammatical exercises. Requirements would be based upon an individual's capabilities. Individuals would be subject to a set of work rules similar to those in a factory; failure to follow these rules would result in discharge and ineligibility for a period.

These activities have three attributes:

1. They are easily monitored.
2. They are beneficial for the individual.
3. They are not especially enjoyable.

The first is necessary for administrative reasons; these programs can be coordinated with existing school programs and be made available for individuals at the school in their district. This means that the "jobs" are physically accessible for all individuals.

Although the jobs mentioned are not meaningful in some philosophical sense, they are beneficial for the individuals. All of us could benefit from such exercises, and our failure to undertake such programs generally reflects our lack of discipline to do tedious but beneficial activities.

The jobs mentioned are tedious and unpleasant for the simple reason that many necessary jobs in our society are tedious. If these guaranteed jobs were pleasant or offered significant training, these existing jobs could not compete. The fact that these jobs are tedious means that they can have a higher money wage associated with them and a trade-off would be possible between the job characteristics and the money wage. The actual "jobs" listed here are not fundamental to the proposal and were selected merely as examples. The fundamental part of the program is that individuals must earn their right to a minimum income through the input of effort and time. Any "job" that maintains that connection will be acceptable.

The rate of pay for these jobs is a matter for political debate, as are all the characteristics. A possible figure is $4/hour, which would provide $160/week of taxable income for a 40-hour week. Since any individual can get a job at $4/hour, this program will replace the minimum wage. If an individual can get work at a guaranteed job for $4/hour but chooses to work at another job for $3/hour, either because he enjoys it or because he is receiving training from that job, that is his prerogative. By providing a minimum job rather than a minimum wage, the program eliminates the negative effects of the minimum wage law while still maintaining its positive effects.

Much of the funding for the proposal could come from a major modification of unemployment insurance. Since there will be no unemployment, much of the present system can be simply eliminated. Perhaps 40 to 50 percent of those presently eligible for unemployment insurance would choose not to work at these minimum jobs, preferring their free time, while as many as another 4 to 5 million individuals currently ineligible may choose to work.

Thus, the net cost would only increase slightly.[4] The ones who would choose not to work are the ones who need help least while the new participants will be precisely the ones who need help most. Thus, the program will be more equitable and efficient than our present program. An additional benefit of the program is that, having eliminated the unemployment, the tremendous demand for new government proposals to deal with the unemployment will be reduced. Relative to the estimated costs of the likely jobs-creation proposals, the guaranteed jobs proposed is a bargain, and it helps most those who need the most help.

Not all people will benefit from this proposal. If the present system is modified and replaced with this proposal, many people will find themselves worse off and will be required to fend for themselves. But it is precisely such redistributions to those who are most needy that is necessary to maintain a belief in the fairness of the system. This proposal treats all individuals looking for a job equally, whereas our present system favors those who presently have a job and who are better off.

The program presented makes hard choices, some of which you may agree with and others of which you may not. For example, if a college economics professor is laid off, he is unlikely to find the guaranteed job to his liking. He will probably choose not to work. The question of whether he should have more rights to assistance than does an individual who did not finish high school is an open one, and such assistance programs should not be confused with unemployment programs. Is an individual who once had a good job entitled to more than an individual who never had one? What rights do his training give him? These are complex questions, but their complexity should not interfere with society's ability to fairly provide a job for all.

CONCLUSION

Obviously the above proposal is only a sketch, which thus raises innumerable questions that have been ignored or only touched up. There is not space here for deeper consideration of the issues, and, too, this article is designed more to stimulate thought and discussion than to provide a final answer. It demonstrates that there is nothing necessarily liberal about a guaranteed jobs proposal, and that the unemployment problem can be solved by separating unemployment from other issues of social policy. Thus, while it is not a pleasant solution, it may be the best we have.

---

[4]By making the pay lower, say $3.50/hour, the cost could be significantly reduced.

Government Should Be the Employer of First Resort

MICHAEL HARRINGTON

Michael Harrington played a significant role in the development of U.S. social policy, and the publication of his book *The Other America* in 1963 started a major governmental attack on poverty. Since then he has been in the forefront of the socialist movement in the United States, both as an editor of numerous publications and as an author of hard-hitting books and articles.

On July 12, 1971, Richard Nixon became the first President since Franklin D. Roosevelt to sign a general public-employment law: the Emergency Employment Act, which calls for an investment of $2.25-billion in the creation of 150,000 public-service jobs. Nixon had vetoed a similar measure only eight months earlier, with appropriate conservative scorn for Rooseveltian "W.P.A.-type" jobs; in retrospect, his sudden fondness for his own W.P.A. program can be interpreted as having been a portent of his dramatic conversion—or opportunistic accommodation—to Democratic party Keynesianism. That came a month later, in August, with the wage-price freeze. And then in the last few months there have even been unconfirmed reports, usually described as coming from the President's chief economic adviser, Treasury Secretary John Connally, that the Administration is going to come up with an even more sweeping, New Deal-type, program.

Though Mr. Nixon has made punditry a high-risk occupation during his three years in office, there is nothing mysterious about why, in his New Economic Policy, he has become consistently inconsistent with what once was his traditional Republicanism. In fact, his endorsement of the concept of public-service jobs is part of the basic strategy of Nixon's approach to the economy, and symptomatic of an emerging fact of current political life: Proposals of impeccably leftist origins—radical or liberal—are now being systematically redesigned to serve the cause of sophisticated conservatism. Such adaptations date at least as far back as Bismarck, a conservative *Junker* who co-opted socialist ideas. But rarely has the reversal been so thoroughgoing: the dollar devalued, pervasive controls over wages and prices imposed, and a huge outlay for Government jobs approved—all at the hands of an orthodox Republican, all in a single year.

In his spectacular *volte-face* on the job bill, Nixon was embracing an idea, belatedly and without much ardor, that has been loitering in the corridors of Socialist thought for at least 145 years. Louis Blanc, a French historian and, briefly, a Government official, first formulated the concept of governmentally guaranteed work in 1836. It was tried in Paris during the Revolution of 1848

Michael Harrington, "Government Should Be the Employer of *First* Resort," *The New York Times Magazine*, 26 March 1972, ©1972 by The New York Times Company. Reprinted by permission.

and, until the philosophical ascendance of Marxism in the last quarter of the 19th century, it was what most Europeans understood to be Socialism. The concept was imported to the United States when the Great Depression forced Roosevelt to put about 10 per cent of the labor force on Federal payrolls. In 1944, he and organized labor fought for a legally binding right to work (a proposal that would mean what it said and has nothing to do with the antilabor, state legislation packaged dishonestly under the same name), but conservatives expunged that commitment from the Employment Act of 1946. In its place they put the pious wish that every American should have a job, an incantation which did nothing to prevent five major unemployment crises in 25 years.

The president had good reason to change his mind about the wisdom of the Federal Government's creating jobs. It is clear—much clearer than Mr. Nixon can bring himself to admit publicly—that the private sector of the economy has failed to generate the jobs that are needed. Worse still, the data all suggest that the inadequacies are structural and that their negative effects will intensify.

The evidence has been accumulating rapidly since the halcyon days of the Johnson Administration, when the National Commission on Technology, Automation and Economic Progress reported that the expanding economy harbored no inherent trend toward technological unemployment; America, the commission said, could cope with any rate of technological innovation as long as the economy was intelligently managed. But even while it kept the faith with the Keynesian denomination of free marketry, the commission noted that, from a social point of view, there were more than five million jobs, largely in the public or nonprofit sectors, which could be funded out of tax revenues. A few years later, with whole neighborhoods of Detroit and Newark in ruins, the National Advisory Commission on Civil Disorders took up that suggestion with a much greater sense of urgency. The private sector, it said, should generate a million new jobs, and the Government should commit itself to financing another million jobs in public service, over a three-year period; in the first year alone, the report urged, the Government should aim at providing 250,000 openings.

The Johnson Administration responded to the proposal for an effort by the private sector but backed off from direct Federal job funding in the public sector. At the urging of the White House, the National Alliance of Businessmen joined in a program called JOBS (Job Opportunities in the Business Sector). It was supposed to yield 338,000 jobs by June, 1970, and 614,000 by June, 1971. According to an audit by the General Accounting Office, the cumulative total of trainees on June 30, 1970, was actually 48,351. The current number of trainees, according to the Department of Labor, is 69,000—slightly more than 10 per cent of the 1971 goal.

A similar record of failure was established by the WIN (Work Incentive) program set up by a 1967 amendment to the Social Security Act, a fact of some significance since it involves an approach not unlike the "workfare" scheme in Mr. Nixon's welfare reform plan. WIN has provided educational and job training for welfare recipients with the aim of preparing them to compete in the private sector. But there are only 100,000 participants in the plan instead of the 280,000 estimated at the outset. Only 20 per cent of its trainees have found jobs. And, as a survey by the Ohio Bureau of Employment showed in April of this year, the WIN graduates could mainly hope for employment as cooks, salad girls, waitresses, nursemaids—jobs which paid only a little more than welfare.

It is certainly true that the dismal showing of these experiments was facilitated by the recession brought about by Mr. Nixon's Old Economic Policy. When corporations are laying off organized workers with previously marketable skills there is practically no hope for welfare recipients who had been unable to get jobs during a period of relatively full employment. But that does not mean that the problem will cease to exist as soon as the economy gets moving again.

The deep-going structural transformations in the economy to which Mr. Nixon is responding demand something more than reliance upon the mechanism of a free market. In 1980, according to Department of Labor projections, there will be more professional, technical and kindred workers, most of them with college or postgraduate degrees, than assembly-line workers, truck drivers and bus drivers (15.5 million as against 15.4 million). The number of people in the professional category is expected to increase by 50 per cent during this decade while the semiskilled operatives will go up by only 10 per cent; the nonfarm laborers will decline by 2 per cent and the farm workers by 33 per cent. In other—and more portentous—words: the semiskilled and unskilled jobs which have been the traditional exit from poverty and point of entry into the industrial system will be the jobs in short supply. And, at the same time, a dramatically increased number of poor young people, particularly young blacks, will be gathering at the exit door, ready to compete for the dwindling number of job openings.

The problem is not confined to the bottom of the economic and class structure. In the sixties, there were extraordinary outlays for space, education and Vietnam, all of which improved the relative position of organized workers (who are neither poor nor affluent), scientists and technicians at all levels, and the educated in general; society's investment per student in higher education accelerated faster than the growth in the Gross National Product, and resulted in an enormous increase in the college population. Then the Federal programs which animated these trends were cut back; suddenly unemployment rose, not simply among the unskilled, but among engineers and scientists as well.

Despite the disintegration at each end of the economic ladder, Mr. Nixon did not abandon the traditional wisdom hastily. Though he spoke of "workfare," he did not make a move to generate a single job. Therefore, he was simply proposing to force the most marginal members of the labor force—unskilled women for the most part—into a market where the very best they could hope for would be competition with one another for menial, low-paying jobs. "Workfare" was, and is, so contradictory a proposal that one Presidential adviser has been known to suggest that it is simply rhetoric designed to calm down reactionary Congressmen who would not otherwise vote in favor of Nixon's income floor for welfare recipients. I suspect that this assessment is unfair to the President. He is, I think, sincerely deluded on this point.

Mr. Nixon stressed the same theme in his Labor Day address to the nation and his speech on the New Economic Policy to the Congress: "Labor is good in itself"; "no job is menial if it leads to self-reliance, self-respect and individual dignity." But forced labor in a Soviet camp, or even the abrasive routine of an automobile assembly line, is not "good in itself." And I am quite sure that the President is not sanguine about the prospect of careers in migrant labor camps for Julie and David and Tricia and Ed. The best that can be said for his windy, old-fashioned nonsense is that a good many of the jobs in the economy, given the limitations of scarcity and technical ingenuity, may be a miserable necessity.

Even if he cannot fairly be accused of honorary Socialism, Mr. Nixon has at least allowed himself to face up to some of the facts. In December, 1970, when he vetoed the Employment and Manpower Act, he was still sticking by the letter of the old faith: He was, he said, against any program that "would relegate a large number of workers to permanent, subsidized employment." In July, when he reversed himself, he explained that he did so because the jobs to be funded by the legislation are only temporary.

That qualification allows the President to pretend that there will soon be jobs aplenty in the business sector for all who need them, an optimistic assumption contrary to all the trends. And how, precisely, is a state or city supposed to structure a "temporary" position? As Edward Hamilton, the former budget director of New York City and now its Deputy Mayor, put the problem: "What if we moved those people into permanent city jobs and then Washington ended the program because national unemployment was down again? We'd be left holding the bag with X number of people built into our financial structure and no more Federal money."

Clearly, Mr. Nixon based his reversal on a distinction without a difference, and the conventional interpretation of this and all his other shifts in economic policy is that he has made a 180-degree turn in order to look the problems of re-election in the eye. And yet, even though the political rationalization is only thinly disguised in the President's rhetoric, it is important to say a word in defense of his sincerity and consistency. I would argue that he has simply moved from an utterly obsolete conservatism to a much more sophisticated, though still completely inadequate conservatism. He is not Saul on the road to Damascus in the throes of an overpowering conversion experience but a wily helmsman who has changed a disastrous course by about 15 or 20 degrees. He is still sailing the same ship.

In the New Economic Policy as a whole, Mr. Nixon has been won, not to Keynesianism, but, in John Kenneth Galbraith's phrase, to reactionary Keynesianism. In the fundamentalist free-market model in which Mr. Nixon believed until almost yesterday, the corporation is central because the maximization of its self-interest mysteriously leads to the common good. In his three years in the White House, Mr. Nixon has learned that economic providence is not quite so benign in the rewards it bestows upon a passive President. So he has shifted slightly. The corporation remains central; now, in accepting the carrots which a hopeful nation thrusts upon it, it is stimulated to accomplish the common good. So it is that Mr. Nixon proposed in August to give business $9-billion worth of encouragement, the consumer $2.5-billion, and the poor an I.O.U. on welfare reform.

This same pattern of reactionary Keynesianism is apparent in the details of all his employment proposals. First of all, there is the question of numbers. The bill Mr. Nixon vetoed in December, 1970, would have created more than 400,000 jobs through both accelerated public works and public-service employment. The bill he signed last July is supposed to yield 150,000 jobs and, at the current rate of expenditure, will apparently fund only 130,000 of them. This does not simply mean that Mr. Nixon embraced the principle of Federal responsibility in this area and then reduced a very modest application of it by about two-thirds. That is true enough, but there are qualitative consequences of that quantitative change that are also extremely important.

With the very limited number of jobs authorized by the President in a time of high unemployment, the new openings will have to be spread paper-thin over the entire country. The Administration anticipated that almost all 130,000 jobs would have been filled by Christmas; in November, Mr. Nixon himself rather plaintively wrote to 14,000 state and local officials asking them to hurry up— only 31,000 unemployed had actually been put to work. And some reports from the field indicate that many of those being hired are neither the very poor nor the professionally dislocated, but those from an in-between category whose new jobs pay up to $8,000 a year. That group obviously has its problems too, and deserves help. But the very fact that such a choice has to be made with limited funds shows that the program, far from being an exercise in manpower planning and careful social investment, is the merest of stopgaps. Indeed, Nixon's own reduction of Federal employees might cancel out the entire employment efforts of the bill he signed. And in his letter, the President himself referred to a special group of unemployed who could not be handled even with a bill providing twice the number of jobs: 350,000 jobless veterans of the war in Vietnam.

Second, the President clearly regards these public-service jobs as second-class in character. The crucial instrument for the generation of employment, as befits Nixon's reactionary Keynesianism, is the tax incentive for the big corporation. The Employment Act of 1971 is a temporary, and reluctant, expedient. But the President, unfortunately, is not alone in this attitude. There are dedicated liberals who also talk of the Government as the "employer of last resort." The implication of that phrase, and of the Administration's present policy, is that the best possible use for labor is always to be found in the private sector; when Washington's help is sought, it is to mount an occasional rescue operation, but that is all.

To pose the issue in that fashion is to place public-service employment in a perpetually negative light, an unwelcome deviation from normality. But then, given the minimal, unplanned program which he approved, the President could not possibly have been thinking in any positive way about the issue. For he has not changed his basic faith that the private corporation provides the way to social happiness.

Finally, there is the issue of menial labor as it relates to welfare reform. It is, I take it, obvious that the President's Labor Day homily on the Protestant ethic was not an exercise in philosophical speculation but an endorsement of the "get tough" measures of Governors Reagan and Rockefeller, which force able-bodied welfare recipients to work as ordered by the authorities. It is hard to imagine an approach more contrary to the rhetoric which rationalizes it. "No work is demeaning or beneath a person's dignity," the President told the Congress in September, "if it provides food for his table and clothes and shelter for his children. The thing that is demeaning is for a man to refuse to work and then to ask someone else who works to pay taxes to keep him on welfare."

Lurking just behind all that talk about the nobility of menial labor is another, and more basic, attitude: Work is the punishment which is going to be meted out to the welfare malingerers. It is an axiom of basic pedagogy that one does not make a child atone for misbehaving by forcing him to read or write or do other things the school system has all along claimed are good and valuable activities. Yet that is just what the President and Reagan and Rockefeller are doing: They want to instruct some of our most abused, and sometimes marginal, citizens in the glories of work by using legal compulsion to rub their noses in menial labor. In saying this I am not trying to psychoanalyze these leaders, to deal with their interior motives. The plain fact is that they do not propose to provide welfare recipients with well-planned, useful work at decent pay but to force them to work in order to get a welfare check.

That official attitude, I would suggest to Mr. Nixon, is really demeaning and destructive to a person's dignity. Society has failed to give him a chance to work like everyone else; it has stigmatized him as lazy for not having found employment in the middle of a recession; and now Government forces him into a new category of secondclass citizenship where Americans labor, not for a wage, but for a welfare check. (The male chauvinism of English grammar somewhat obscures my point, for the real object of this chastisement is not the generalized "him" which stands for both men and women, but a "her," most likely a welfare mother.) In reality, the imposition of reactionary Keynesian values on welfare reform is the opposite of what it claims to be: It does not ennoble what is unalterably base, but it creates a kind of peonage where people must work simply for their keep. That violates even the Protestant ethic.

There is thus no need for quaking in the boardrooms; Mr. Nixon has kept the conservative faith that private economic power is the best instrument for promoting the public good, and what has seemed like a dramatic conversion is merely melodrama for tactical advantage. The forms have changed—he has moved from Herbert Hoover to Arthur Burns—yet the basic values are very much intact.

But times change, and Presidents certainly do. If, as this analysis has suggested, the private sector of the American economy becomes less and less able to absorb available manpower and, perhaps more importantly, less and less able to make a socially desirable allocation of that manpower, what then? What programs and what politics provide Mr. Nixon and his successors with alternatives?

The central proposal for dealing with these problems is, I think, quite obvious. There should be a formal Federal guarantee of a right to work for every employable citizen. (The corollary is a right to a livable income for all those who cannot work, which I support enthusiastically, but will not argue for here.) The right to work would operate in two ways: negatively in that the Government would be obliged to offer meaningful employment to all those who cannot find it in the private sector; positively in that the Government should undertake comprehensive manpower planning and, wherever indicated, establish itself as an employer of first resort.

Even without a Government commitment, organized labor has already begun to confront the question that Presidential rhetoric cannot banish: Why, in a nation more and more dependent on the application of science to the manufacturing process, must grinding, demeaning occupations exist at all? Or, where they do, why are they not recognized for what they are and their effects minimized? Automobile assemblyline workers spend their laboring lives in an environment so dehumanized it could be its own caricature. And the last time the United Automobile Workers Union negotiated a contract, its leadership adopted a demand that had arisen spontaneously from the membership—"30 and out," retirement at the end of 30 years no matter what the worker's age. In their last contract, the United Steelworkers won a 13-week sabbatical once every five years for men with 15 or more years on the job.

Even Senator George McGovern, who stands to the left in the line-up of Democrats seeking the Presidential nomination but is nevertheless clearly in the traditional mold of American political figures, has come close to the concept of planned, Government employment. McGovern has proposed that the Government contract with private industry to guarantee jobs in socially desirable fields for any adult who wants to work. And, in general, there is more movement toward the four-day work week.

All of these reactions are profoundly commonsensical attempts to minimize the indignities associated with so many jobs in the United States. This mood has spread among the poor as well. In New York City, as Nathan Glazer reported in The Public Interest, women on welfare are reluctant to take menial jobs which pay only a little bit more than their benefits. I am sympathetic with the hard-working Americans, particularly those directly engaged in production, who are outraged at this attitude, even though I do not share their anger. I am not at all sympathetic toward those executives, including the President, who, from the vantage point of their creative and well-paid jobs, lecture the poor about the joys of menial labor. And I think that the welfare mothers who balk at such employment are right, morally as well as economically.

In a society with the technological capacity of the United States, it is somewhat obscene to celebrate low-paying, menial employment. It should be a national goal to abolish such jobs by creating machines that will progressively eliminate all the routine tasks that are now dulling the lives of men and women. But, to pose the hoary, generic question: who will then collect the garbage? There are obviously some onerous jobs which can't be done away with in the near future, and a smaller number which perhaps can never become the work of a machine. For those jobs that must be done by humans, the pay, instead of being miserly, should be handsome. That, conservatives will say, would price them out of competition and provide industry with the incentive to find a way to mechanize them. Fine. For there are many more important jobs that need to be done, from the building of new cities to the improvement of medical care. And if some drudgery persists even in these new jobs, it will at least be in the satisfaction of real social needs—especially the needs of the human drones who now work in the harness of an inattentive technology.

If we adopted such a positive and creative approach we would also discover that a good many of the people who seem capable only of lowly work have hidden talents. Paraprofessionals in the school and health systems have already demonstrated that the rejects of a free labor market can make a positive contribution to society when jobs are consciously designed to make use of their natural aptitudes. These paraprofessionals provide valuable services, for which people are more than willing to pay. And since an upgrading of skills is involved, their higher wages would even satisfy the current crucial measurement: They would not be inflationary. The initial Federal outlay would be a social investment, not a handout, and in the not-so-long run such investments would pay for themselves.

The work thus generated would be primarily in the public and nonprofit sectors. That does not mean that Washington would put millions on the payroll, since most of the jobs would be at the state and municipal levels and in nonprofit institutions like hospitals. But the funding of a good many of them will have to come from the nearest thing to a progressive tax we have, the Federal income tax. And even though all this could be done without disturbing the capitalist structure of the economy—the corporations would, alas, remain in control of their billions even after such sweeping reforms—it is clear that there would be a significant shift from private, profit-oriented work to public and not-for-profit occupations.

In the long run, the implementation of a legal right to work would require careful planning. As our current experience demonstrates, it is no simple thing even to phase engineers out of aircraft production and into environmental protection—and they are educated, mobile people, less in need of government's benign attention than the economically depressed, but numerically superior, unskilled working force. Investments and decisions will have to be made well in advance of times of crisis.

Strangely enough, the short run would be easier to deal with. There is already a backlog of requests from communities for Federal funds to help build more than 6,000 waste-treatment plants, water and sewerage systems, hospitals, nursing homes, public health centers and the like; they would cost $13-billion, including $6-billion in Federal money.

Organized labor would logically be the vanguard of any political movement for a guaranteed right to work. Unions fought for that very demand almost 30 years ago, and since then have battled for a whole range of manpower programs which would stimulate the economy, not by passing out windfalls to the corporations, but by putting men and women to work satisfying the urgent needs of society. Labor cannot, of course, prevail alone, but it has natural allies in the middle class; and the issue also is one on which the interests of black and white workers most obviously converge. The formation of such a coalition around the demand for a guaranteed right to work would have ramifications for the entire society.

Such a realignment is no longer the impossibility it may once have seemed. American politics has been in the process of redefining the meaning of right and left for some time. The fundamental confrontation of the thirties between the liberal advocates of state intervention in the economy and its conservative opponents, which for so long has conditioned political debate, is now played out. That really is what Richard Nixon was telling us this summer when he proclaimed his own W.P.A. and initiated Government controls over wages and prices, and he is quite right.

By now, as Milton Friedman himself once said, we are all Keynesians. The crucial question remaining is: What kind of Keynesian? The arguments over what used to seem like only the details of economic policy—how should a tax reduction be apportioned between corporations and the poor? How much should the shipping industry be subsidized?—are becoming central. Mr. Nixon's reactionary Keynesianism is clear; he clings to the faith that private greeds somehow vector into a public good, and he therefore still looks to corporations as the real leaders of the American economy—even when, as President, *he* is leader. His honor as a consistent conservative is quite intact; it is only his policies which are intolerable.

But even he has had to do something, in his own constricted terms, in the face of our geometrically increasing social needs: the great cities coming unstuck, the environment deteriorating, the large numbers of marginal workers accumulating outside the margins of the private sector. It is apparent that Louis Blanc's 1836 idea—that society must guarantee each citizen a right to work, and make good the guarantee—has more than reached the fullness of its time. We need the constructive use of the energies of the unemployed, the underemployed and the misemployed. All that is required is a militant mass movement to prod the dawdling spirit of history into action.

Full Employment and Balanced Growth Act of 1976

U.S. CONGRESS

Before any important bill becomes a law, hearings will be held in which experts and interested parties are asked to testify. Those hearings are then published with the act.

The article below is a reprint of a version of the Full Employment and Balanced Growth Act of 1976, commonly known as the Humphrey-Hawkins Act. Following that is a summary of the comments of Leon Keyserling, one of the most influential supporters of the act.

The Full Employment and Balanced Growth Act is designed as the legislative foundation for America's economic policy and program in the decades ahead.

Under it, business, labor, agriculture and government at all levels would work cooperatively to formulate goals, policies and programs for promoting the healthy growth of the private sector and the more efficient provision of those services that only government can supply. The expanded production of useful goods and services would translate into practical reality the right of all adult Americans to opportunities for useful paid employment at fair rates of compensation. By 1980, at the latest, unemployment would be reduced to the minimum level of frictional unemployment consistent with efficient job search and labor mobility and in no event more than 3% of the civilian labor force.

A major provision of the bill provides for a "Full Employment and Balanced Growth Plan," which the President is to send to Congress every year. This plan is to include: Specific targets for full employment, production and purchasing power; priority policies and programs for energy, transportation, food, small business, environmental improvement, health care, education day care, housing and other vital areas; fiscal and monetary policies to promote full employment and balanced growth and to balance the Federal budget at full employment levels of Federal revenue; comprehensive policies and programs to prevent or combat inflation; an active role in full employment and balanced growth policy for the Board of Governors of the Federal Reserve System; and the promotion of more governmental economy and efficiency through intensive reviews of government regulations and the gradual introduction of zero-base budgeting.

A 12 person Advisory Committee on Full Employment and Balanced Growth would assist the Council of Economic Advisers in helping prepare the President's Economic Report and Full Employment and Balanced Growth Plan.

More specifically, the bill also provides for: Comprehensive counter-cyclical policies, including a counter-cyclical grant program for State and local governments; special provisions for assistance to depressed regions of the country and inner city areas; integration, improvement and expansion of existing youth

U.S. Cong., Committee on Education and Labor, *Hearings on Equal Opportunities*, 94th Cong., 2nd sess. (Washington, D.C.: GPO, 1976), L, 154–203.

employment programs; and supplemental (or last resort) provision of employment opportunities for those not able to find work elsewhere. This is to be done under Presidential direction by the Secretary of Labor through a new Full Employment Office in the Department of Labor and using reservoirs of federally operated public employment projects and private nonprofit employment projects.

Throughout the bill, first emphasis is placed on expansion of private employment opportunities, encouraged by improvements in monetary and fiscal policies. The second line of defense against unemployment is public activity at the State and local level. Federal employment projects are last resort.

The Bill also mandates a more active role for the Congress—including its Joint Economic Committee and the Budget Committees of each House in reviewing the required reports and proposals of the President and the Federal Reserve System and in determining the specifics of goals, policies and programs for full employment and balanced growth. Each year the Congress is to debate and vote on a Concurrent Resolution approving, modifying or disapproving the President's Full Employment and Balanced Growth Plan. With the help of the Joint Economic Committee, the annual Concurrent Resolution on the Budget is to deal specifically with the employment, production and purchasing power goals implicit in its recommendations concerning the levels of Federal expenditures and revenues. To assist in these efforts, a new Division of Full Employment and Balanced Growth is set up in the Congressional Budget Office.

In general, the Bill extends and amplifies the economic planning policies and machinery established by the Employment Act of 1946.

Full Employment and Balanced Growth Act of 1976

SUMMARY AND SECTION-BY-SECTION ANALYSIS

Summary

The Full Employment and Balanced Growth Act of 1976 establishes the right of all adult Americans able, willing, and seeking to work to opportunities for useful paid employment at fair rates of compensation. To support that right, the act commits the U.S. Government to fundamental reform in the management of the economy so that full employment and balanced economic growth are achieved and sustained. This includes the creation of a permanent institutional framework within which the President, the Federal Reserve Board, and the Congress are systematically encouraged to develop and establish the economic goals and policies necessary to provide productive employment for all adult Americans, as well as the mandating of specific employment programs to achieve the goal of 3 percent unemployment as promptly as possible, but within not more than 4 years after the date of the enactment of this act.

Section-by-Section Analysis

SECTIONS 1 AND 2. These sections include the title, table of contents, and general findings. Among the most important general findings are: (1) the high social and economic costs of unemployment; (2) the need for explicit economic goals and a coordinated economic policy among the President, the Federal Reserve and Congress; (3) that inflation is often aggravated by high unemployment; and (4) that there must be direct employment and anti-inflation policies to supplement aggregate monetary and fiscal policies to achieve and maintain full employment and balanced growth.

TITLE I—ESTABLISHMENT OF GOALS, PLANNING AND GENERAL ECONOMIC POLICIES

SEC. 101.—STATEMENT OF PURPOSE. The purpose of this title is to declare the general policies of the act, to provide an open process under which annual economic goals are proposed, reviewed, and established; to provide for the development of a long-range Full Employment and Balanced Growth Plan, to provide for economy in government measures, to insure that monetary, fiscal, anti-inflation and general economic policies are used to achieve the annual economic goals to support the long-range goals and priorities of the Full Employment and Balanced Growth Plan, and generally to strengthen and supplement the purposes of the Employment Act of 1946.

SEC. 102—DECLARATION OF POLICY. The Employment Act of 1946 is amended to declare that all adult Americans able, willing, and seeking work have the right to useful paid employment at fair rates of compensation. Moreover, the Congress further declares that the Federal Government use all practical means, including improved anti-inflation polices, to promote full employment, production and purchasing power.

SEC. 103—ECONOMIC GOALS AND THE ECONOMIC REPORT OF THE PRESIDENT. The Employment Act of 1946 is amended to require the President in each annual Economic Report to recommend numerical goals for employment, production, and purchasing power, as well as policies to support these goals and achieve balanced growth and full employment of the Nation's human and capital resources as promptly as possible.

SEC. 104—FULL EMPLOYMENT AND BALANCED GROWTH PLAN. The Employment Act of 1946 is amended to establish a process of long-range economic planning, through the Council of Economic Advisers, to analyze developing economic conditions, to recommend long-term goals for full employment, production, and purchasing power, and to propose priority policies and programs to achieve such goals and to meet national needs. A long-term full employment goal is set at 3 percent adult unemployment, to be attained as promptly as possible, but within not more than 4 years after the date of the enactment of this act.

SEC. 105—ECONOMY IN GOVERNMENT. This section establishes policies and procedures to improve the effectiveness of the Federal Government through the comprehensive planning framework established under this act. In conjunction with the submission of each Full Employment and Balanced Growth Plan, the President shall submit proposals for improving the efficiency and economy of the Federal Government, including, but not limited to, a review of existing Government rules and regulations to determine if they still serve a purpose, and an annual evaluation of 20 percent of the dollar volume of existing Federal programs.

SEC. 106—FISCAL AND MONETARY POLICIES. The Employment Act of 1946 is amended to require that monetary and fiscal policies be utilized in the optimum manner necessary to achieve full employment and balanced growth, including the requirement that the President determine the extent to which fiscal policy can be relied upon to achieve our economic goals and priorities, so that it becomes possible to estimate what supplementary job creation and anti-inflation policies must be utilized to achieve the objectives of this act.

This section also requires the Federal Reserve Board to make an independent report to the President and Congress, in conjunction with each Economic Report, identifying the extent to which the Federal Reserve will support the economic goals recommended in the President's Economic Report and, if the Federal Reserve Board does not support such goals, to provide a full justification of why and to what extent its policies will differ from those recommended by the President. If the President determines that the Board's policies are inconsistent with proposed economic goals and priorities, the President shall make recommendations to the Board and Congress to insure closer conformity with the purposes of this act.

SEC. 107—ANTI-INFLATION POLICIES. The Employment Act of 1946 is amended to require that each Economic Report contain a comprehensive set of anti-inflation policies to supplement monetary and fiscal policy, including, but not limited to, analyzing inflationary trends in individual economic sectors; actions to increase the supply of goods, services, labor, and capital in tight markets, particularly food and energy; provision for an export-licensing mechanism for critical materials in short supply; recommendations to increase productivity in the private sector; recommendations to strengthen and enforce the antitrust laws; and recommendations for administrative and legislative actions to promote reasonable price stability if situations develop that seriously threaten national price stability.

SEC. 108—COUNCIL OF ECONOMIC ADVISERS. The Employment Act of 1946 is amended to require the Council of Economic Advisers to prepare the Full Employment and Balanced Growth Plan, to consult with the Advisory Committee, and to meet other requirements under this act.

SEC. 109—ADVISORY COMMITTEE ON FULL EMPLOYMENT AND BALANCED GROWTH. The Employment Act of 1946 is amended to establish a 12-member private Advisory Committee on Full Employment and Balanced Growth to advise and assist the Council of Economic Advisers on matters relating to the Economic Report and this act. The members of the committee shall be appointed proportionately by the President, the Speaker of the House of Representatives, and the President pro tempore of the Senate in a manner broadly representative of the Public.

TITLE II—COUNTERCYCLICAL, STRUCTURAL AND YOUTH EMPLOYMENT POLICIES

SEC. 201—STATEMENT OF PURPOSE. This title establishes supplementary employment policies to close the employment gap, if one should exist, between the levels of employment achieved through aggregate monetary and fiscal policy and the employment goals established in sections 103 and 104. Accordingly, this title establishes a system of comprehensive and flexible employment policies to create jobs in both the private and public sectors of the economy. These supplementary employment policies shall vary according to economic conditions and the other actions taken under this act, but focus broadly upon reducing cyclical, structural, regional, youth unemployment, and unemployment due to discrimination. This title also establishes a Full Employment Office within the Department of

Labor to use special means for training, assisting, and providing employment for those people who are otherwise unable to find employment. Finally, this title mandates improved integration of income-maintenance programs and full employment policies.

SEC. 202—COUNTERCYCLICAL EMPLOYMENT POLICIES. This section requires the development and submission by the President, within 90 days of the enactment of this act, of a coherent and flexible countercyclical program to reduce high unemployment arising from cyclical movements in the economy. This comprehensive program shall include, as appropriate, public service employment, standby public works, antirecession grants for State and local governments, skill training in both the public and private sectors, and other programs. Moreover, this program shall be automatically implemented during periods of high unemployment, allocate employment assistance to areas of highest unemployment, provide for a well-balanced combination of job creation and related activities in both the private and public sectors, and incorporate transitional mechanisms to aid individuals in returning to regular employment as the economy recovers.

SEC. 203—COORDINATION WITH STATE AND LOCAL GOVERNMENTS AND PRIVATE SECTOR ECONOMIC ACTIVITY. This section requires the development of policies that facilitate harmonious economic action between the Federal Government, regions, States, localities and the private sector. As a primary effort to achieve these ends, the President is required to submit legislation, within 90 days of the enactment of this act, creating a permanent, countercyclical grant program that will serve to stabilize State and local budgets during periods of recession and high unemployment. This program shall be automatically implemented when the national unemployment exceeds a specified level and distribute its funds to those areas of most serious unemployment.

SEC. 204—REGIONAL AND STRUCTURAL EMPLOYMENT POLICIES. This section requires the establishment of comprehensive employment policies designed to reduce the chronic underutilization of human and capital resources in certain areas of the country and in specific groups within the labor force. As a primary effort to reduce unemployment in chronically depressed areas, the President is required within 180 days after the date of enactment of this act to submit legislation providing an insitutional means to make credit available: (1) for public and private investment in economically depressed regions, inner cities, and economic sectors; and (2) to provide an alternative source of capital funds for local and State governments to finance public facilities.

SEC. 205—YOUTH EMPLOYMENT POLICIES. This section requires the development and submission by the President, within 90 days of the enactment of this act, of a comprehensive youth employment program to: (1) foster a smoother transition from school to work; (2) prepare disadvantaged youths with employment handicaps for self-sustaining unemployment through education, training, medical services, counseling and other support activities; (3) develop methods for combining training with work, including apprenticeship and on-the-job training in the private sector; and (4) provide job opportunities in a variety of tasks including conservation, public service activities, inner-city cleanup and rehabilitation and other jobs of value to States, local communities, and the Nation.

SEC. 206—FULL EMPLOYMENT OFFICE AND JOB RESERVOIRS. To insure that full employment is achieved under this act, the President, through the Secretary of Labor, shall develop policies and programs to provide job opportunities to adult Americans who, despite a serious effort to obtain employment, are unable to do so in the general economic environment, or through any of the other provisions of this act. There is established within the Department of Labor a Full Employment Office to assist the Secretary of Labor in providing such job opportunities through counseling, training, and referral to job opportunities in the private sector and in positions drawn from sections 202, 204, and 205 of this act. Additional job opportunities will be provided, subject to regulations on job need and eligibility, through reservoirs of federally operated or approved employment projects, to be phased in by the President in conjunction with the annual employment recommendations required under section 3 of the Employment Act of 1946, and to achieve 3 percent unemployment within 4 years of enactment of this act.

SEC. 207—INCOME MAINTENANCE AND FULL EMPLOYMENT POLICIES. This section requires that full employment policies: (1) provide quality jobs that strengthen income and eliminate substandard earnings; (2) integrate existing income maintenance policies with the full employment policies established by this act; and (3) substitute work for income maintenance to the maximum extent feasible.

Highlights of Prepared Statement of Leon H. Keyserling, on Humphrey-Hawkins "Full Employment and Balanced Growth Act of 1976"

Mr. Keyserling sets forth the highlights of his testimony as follows:

"(1) H.R. 50 will help to reduce current unemployment below the current level, 7.6 percent officially reported and 10.5 percent when fully counted. But the central purpose is to restore full employment—3 percent unemployment—by the end of calendar 1980. Even more vital, the purpose is to end the repeated cycles of ups and downs which have caused us to forfeit more than 3.3 trillion 1975 dollars of total national production and 61 million man- and woman-years of employment opportunity during 1953–1975, and to reform national economic policies which threaten forfeiture of another 1.1 trillion 1975 dollars and another 17 million man- and women-years of employment opportunity during 1976–1980. The current "recovery" is entirely consistent with this dismal outlook, and such an outlook is forecast by many.

"(2) H.R. 50 is not primarily a 'public employment' measure. It proposes improved fiscal and monetary policies, and other policies, to promote expansion of jobs in the private sector. It proposes Federal aid to a wide variety of specialized employment programs—including those for youth—most of which would be in the private sector or administered at State and local levels. Only as a last resort, to assure useful jobs at fair compensation for all adults (probably 18 and over) it provides for Federal conduct of or aid to reservoirs, of public and nonprofit private job products. My estimate is that, of 13.1 million more jobs in 1980 as a whole than in 1975 as a whole, there would be 9.4 million additional private jobs, 3.2 million State and local, and 0.5 million Federal.

"(3) When costs are properly stated, H.R. 50 would involve no net costs, and immense benefits. I estimate that the incremental increases in Federal Budget outlays (i.e. increases above projections of the President's fiscal 1977 Budget), required to implement H.R. 50 in its entirety would not be more than those in line, over the years, with the very recent recommendations by a majority of the Joint Economic Committee that the President's Budget for fiscal 1977 be increased by 24–28 billion dollars. I further estimate that the incremental increases in G.N.P. resulting from H.R. 50 would yield, at existing tax rates, incremental increases in Federal Revenues larger than the incremental increases in Federal Budget outlays, so that even the Budget would be a net gainer. Infinitely more important, I estimate that G.N.P. during the four calendar years 1977–1980 would by 897 billion fiscal 1977 dollars higher under H.R. 50 than under even an optimistic projection of G.N.P. under current national policies and programs. This 897 billion is the net benefit, not cost, of H.R. 50 through calendar 1980.

"(4) Most of the increased Federal Budget outlays under H.R. 50 would unite employment with attention to our neglected national priority needs as specified in H.R. 50—energy, resource development, food supply, environment, mass transportation, housing, health, education, with proper allowance for national defense and other international. Only a small portion would go to the supplemental employment programs set forth in H.R. 50.

"(5) H.R. 50, through higher G.N.P. would reduce the Federal deficit from an annual average of 32.4 billion dollars during fiscal 1971—1977 to an annual average of 10.5 billion during fiscal 1977–1980, with a balanced Budget by fiscal 1979 and a 13.9 billion dollar surplus by calendar 1980.

"(6) H.R. 50 would bring Federal Reserve policies to the support of H.R. 50 objectives, through a more expansionary and steady monetary policy and lower interest rates.

"(7) H.R. 50 would enormously reduce inflation because, over long years, we have learned from all empirical experience that high idleness of workers and other productive resources is far more inflationary than a healthy economy.

"H.R. 50 would substitute limited planning under freedom for conflicting, duplicating, improvised, and wasteful economic policies and programs. Toward this end, H.R. 50 provides for annual goals under the President's Economic Reports, long range goals udner the Full Employment and Balanced Growth Plan, and coordinated efforts among the President, the Federal Reserve, the Joint Economic Committee, the Budget Committees of the Senate and the House, the Congress at large, and State and local governments, functioning economic groups, and the private sector."

The Humphrey-Hawkins Act since Its 1978 Enactment

LEON KEYSERLING

Leon H. Keyserling was chairman of the Council of Economic Advisers under President Truman and is currently president of the Conference on Economic Progress. He originally went to Washington as part of the New Deal brain trust and was a principal author of the Employment Act of 1946. He has remained an active participant and critic of governmental policies ever since and was the principal author of the Humphrey-Hawkins Act.

Developments since enactment of the Full Employment and Balanced Growth Act of 1978 include events which must be of towering significance to all those who recognize that, with national policies being made by the Executive and Legislative Branches of the Federal Government, there can be no meaningful separation between political action so defined and economic and related social policies as narrowly and customarily defined. From enactment of the law in the fall of 1978 and the current writing, and for as far ahead as we can see, what has been in process and is now in prospect in the view of this writer represents the most flagrant, complete, unjustified, deliberate, and explicit violation of law in the twentieth century history of the American Republic. All this is accentuated in that the Humphrey-Hawkins Act, after 4 years of intensive debate and discussion within the Congress, in the media, and otherwise throughout the nation, was put into effect by a majority vote of more than a hundred in the House of Representatives and about 4 to 1 in the Senate, and then signed by Jimmy Carter in a highly advertised gathering at the White House with a promise to pursue it vigorously and immediately toward attainment on schedule of its goals and promises. This is shocking to all who believe—a belief essential to the successful processes of democracy—that confidence among the functioning nonpublic economic community in its various parts and among the people at large in what their Government is promising through law to do must be gravely impaired when the Government persistently and without any articulated claim of justification, or at least only with meretricious and unconvincing claims, does exactly the opposite of what was promised. And this travesty becomes in addition a tragic burlesque, when the Convention Platform of the Party in power in August 1980 promised again to do what it is not doing, by writing into the Platform an express prohibition against attempting to promote more unemployment in the battle against inflation, a prohibition already written into the 1978 law and blatantly repudiated by continuous policy actions since then.

What has just been stated would be cause for concern even if the 1978 law were gravely defective, in which case the proper course would be to change the legislation through normal and well-considered methods. But the evil is

Leon Keyserling, "Humphrey-Hawkins Act since 1978 Enactment." Reprinted by permission.

heightened immensely when the Act in all its essentials has been proved to be even more valid and necessary as at the time of this writing than it was two years ago.

The Humphrey-Hawkins Act did not spring full-blown from the brow of Job, nor was it a "new" experience except in the minds of those who persistently refused to examine or benefit by the experience of the preceding 40 years at least in the trend of U.S. economic developments and the course of national economic policies. The core feature of the Act was to substitute what I have frequently written about during the past 30 years as the substantive equivalent of a long-range *Nation's Economic Budget* or *American Economic Performance Budget* for the fragmentary, disconnected, improvised, *ad hoc*, and unsuccessful national policies which have increasingly come to the fore during the past decade to date. Such a Budget would set forth comprehensive and integrated long range, specific, and quantitative goals for national economic performance, in the context of full use of our potentials when properly galvanized, and blending into the compound due consideration to those social and national economic priorities which we need to serve, and are able to afford. These priorities are not to be divorced from economic performance narrowly conceived, but instead are imperative to the achievement of optimum performance for reasons based upon empirical observation which I have not the space to develop fully in this discussion.

Why was Humphrey-Hawkins not "new," nor derived from reckless experimentation instead of the lessons of experience? It was not "new," in this sense, because it adopted processes used during World War II to achieve miracles of economic and social performance, involving specific methods which, with appropriate modifications, should have been used after the war ended. It was not "new," because the process of goal-making and conformity of national policies to their achievement was used vigorously during the seven years when I was Vice Chairman and then Chairman of the first Council of Economic Advisers. During these years, the policies of the Truman Administration, despite a variety of domestic and international difficulties exceeding in the aggregate any which have occurred since, averaged on a properly weighted basis a far better record of real economic growth, restraint of inflation, attention to national priorities, and (for whatever it is worth) an average 7-year surplus in the Federal Budget, compared with almost nothing but deficits since. It was not "new," in that the Kennedy-Johnson years, primarily under the economic leadership of Walter Heller—during 1961–1966 though less later on—followed albeit in moderated form the same scale of values and purposes which had marked the Truman Administration. It was not "new," in that it was based fundamentally upon experience both successful and unsuccessful under the Employment Act of 1946. And the diametrical departure from the Employment Act's mandates and intent during the Eisenhower Administration 1953–1961 under the economic leadership primarily of Arthur F. Burns, during the Nixon-Ford years 1969–1977, and even more so from 1977 forward during the Carter Administration, has been accompanied by progressive and chronic deterioration, albeit with some undulations, of the average real economic growth rate; a chronic rise in unemployment; a chronic and horrendous increase in inflation; a progressive neglect of the great national economic and related social priorities; and the chronic emergence of staggering Federal deficits.

Space will permit discussion only of the record from 1977 forward. In late 1977, President Carter announced a program to deal primarily with our international economic problems, such as balances of trade and payments and the inordinate rise in the price of gold, to which were improperly attributed excessive responsibility for the alarming increase in domestic inflation. The heart of the effort, fiscal and monetary, was deliberately to increase unemployment and idleness of other production resources in the name of fighting inflation under the so-called "trade-off." Even at that time, I and others interested in the pending Humphrey-Hawkins Bill warned publicly through many channels that this would aggravate rather than restrain inflation; that it was in any event immoral to fasten the main burden of fighting inflation upon the backs of the unemployed and others in need of public help; and that it represented a sad distortion in economic thought and action to hold that very marginal restraint of inflation (which did not in effect result) was worth the gigantic forfeitures in production and employment which, from the start of 1953 to the end of 1980 aggregated loss of more than 8 *trillion* 1979 dollars worth of GNP and loss of more than 83 million years of civilian employment opportunity. This meant also loss of above 2 trillion dollars in Federal, State and local tax revenues at existing tax rates, toward gross neglect of the great national priorities and virtual bankruptcy of some of our largest cities.

The farrago of policy misdirection began to intensify with the President's Economic Report and Budget Message in January 1979, *after* the commitments explicit in the 1978 Humphrey-Hawkins Act. In the name of fighting inflation, which was given the top priority, the goal was a specified increase in unemployment, a result achieved by January 1980, plus the contrived use of fiscal and monetary policies (in which the Federal Reserve more than cooperated) toward the reduction of the real rate of economic growth to only 0.8 percent from the fourth quarter of 1978 to the fourth quarter of 1979, plus the progressive underservice of great national priorities, plus the eventual emergence for fiscal 1980 of a Federal deficit of about 60 billion dollars although the President earlier said that it would be less than half that. Throughout this farrago, I and others dedicated to Humphrey-Hawkins protested in vain, and insisted correctly that the President's declaration that the Act's goal of reducing unemployment to 4 percent by mid–1981 would still be attained was perfectly ridiculous, assuming actual and projected policies.

Then came the President's Economic Report and Budget Message in January 1980. It set the goal of further increases in unemployment, and projected for the first time in history the avowed goal of bringing on a recession, all in the name of fighting inflation. Here again, the President's goals in violation of plain economic common sense, in defiance of moral principles, and in flagrant disregard for the law of the land, were not as bad as what actually happend and what is still happening. The unspeakable record on inflation is too commonly known to be discussed further here. And through all this, I and others committed to Humphrey-Hawkins because it is right protested in vain. The President's proposed Budget revisions later on in 1980, and Federal Reserve policies, moved from the frying pan into the fire. The President's actions at the August 1980 Democratic Convention, despite some shenanigans in connection with Platform "concessions," evidenced his adamant determination, and that of his economic wizards, to persist "courageously" in their "unpopular" but "righteous" course.

The President's January 1980 Economic Report did other things which should disturb all those who have some regard for obedience to law. On his own initiative, the President "modified" the Humphrey-Hawkins Act by extending the goal for the reduction of unemployment to 4 percent overall and 3 percent for those aged 18 and over from 1983 to 1985 and the goal for reducing the rate of inflation to 3 percent from 1983 to 1988. The law authorizes no such action. It merely authorizes the President, as of the 1980 Economic Report, to review progress made, and if necessary to propose new programs to attain the original goals, including if necessary use of so-called "last resort" reservoirs of public service jobs. Only after this is done, the Act then authorizes the President to *recommend to the Congress* modifications in the timetables for achieving the goals. And quite apart from violation of law, the President's early 1980 actions were unrealistic if not disingenuous; if the President did not believe that unemployment under his policy commitments could be reduced from 5.9 percent at the end of 1979 to 4 percent by 1983, how could he believe that it could be reduced from his avowed goal of *increasing* it to the neighborhood of 8 percent by 1981 to 4 percent by 1985? And it appears unspeakable to ask the country to wait until 1988 to get inflation down to 3 percent.

The alibis offered by the Administration for its course of policy action also require examination. Mostly, these alibis cluster around the assertion that OPEC price actions explain almost everything that goes wrong. But the chronic rise in unused resources, with some undulations, and the chronic rise in inflation have been going on at least since 1966, commencing long before the first serious OPEC strike against us. Even today, about two-thirds of the rate of inflation is to be explained by reasons other than what the Arabs have done. Examples are food, housing, and medical care. A majority of the six economic recessions since 1953 occurred because of maladjustments in the economy quite obvious long before serious OPEC actions.

In fact, all six of the recessions have been caused primarily by the lack of planning and consistency in national programs and policies, the absence of goals to guide policies, the use of tax monetary policies to redistribute incomes and allocation of resources in a manner both economically unsound and socially unjust, the failure to be guided empirically by the long lessons of experience, and blind adherence to use of the so-called "trade-off" between unemployment and inflation. These aberrations have been progressively inexcusable since the Humphrey-Hawkins Act of 1978 which was directed against all of them.

Executive mistakes have been compounded by Congressional actions, both before and after enactment of the Humphrey-Hawkins Act. But since its enactment about two years ago, the relevant committees of the Congress and the Congress itself have ignored the Act's explicit mandate to reconstruct Administration programs and policies inimical to the Act's purposes, and instead have predominantly approved the President's proposals and on significant occasions gone him one better. This is also true of the Federal Reserve, mandated under the law to help implement its purposes. The national policies of the Reagan administration at the time of this writing are fundamentally similar to those during the past decade or so, the most recent example being the excitement about "supply-side" economics, a new and attractive name for wrongful reallocations of resource use and incomes or watering the economic tree at the top, and the still pernicious level of the prime rate and home mortgage rates.

The economics profession in academia as well as in Government, and especially the preponderance of its recognized "establishment" leadership, bears a sobering share of responsibility for all that I have described. It has not been empirical, it has clung to outworn ideologies, and above all it has largely bypassed the ultimate or moral values which our economy is rich enough to afford and should be sensible enough to honor. It has not even protested adequately against the most egregious departures from earlier intelligence, especially in acquiescence in attempts to balance the Budget at the expense of the national economy, to fight inflation by fantastic increases in the burden of interest rates, to impose the burden of "sacrifices" upon those who suffer even when times are good, to act defensively and late on a short-range basis instead of affirmatively and early on a long-range basis, and to substitute forecasts of what is going to happen for available correction of what is actually happening. An economy and people who can achieve much more are being told that we "cannot afford" to do even what is most essential.

The evolution of events since the Employment Act of 1946, and now since the Humphrey-Hawkins Act of 1978, have lifted the economics profession to new levels of responsibility and opportunity. May it at long last begin to rise to the challenge.

ADVANCED ANALYSIS OF MOTOR DEVELOPMENT

Kathleen M. Haywood

University of Missouri–St. Louis

Mary Ann Roberton

Bowling Green State University

Nancy Getchell

University of Delaware

Human Kinetics

Library of Congress Cataloging-in-Publication Data

Haywood, Kathleen.
  Advanced analysis of motor development / Kathleen M. Haywood, Mary Ann Roberton, Nancy Getchell
        p. ; cm.
  Includes bibliographical references and index.
  ISBN-13: 978-0-7360-7393-6 (hard cover)
  ISBN-10: 0-7360-7393-0 (hard cover)
  I. Roberton, Mary Ann, 1942- II. Getchell, Nancy, 1963- III. Title.
  [DNLM: 1. Motor Skills. 2. Human Development. 3. Motor Activity.   WE 103]
  LC-classification not assigned
  612.7'6--dc23

                                                    2011029667

ISBN-10: 0-7360-7393-0 (print)
ISBN-13: 978-0-7360-7393-6 (print)

The web addresses cited in this text were current as of May 2011, unless otherwise noted.

Acquisitions Editor: Myles Schrag; **Developmental Editor:** Melissa J. Zavala; **Assistant Editor:** Kali Cox; **Copyeditor:** Jocelyn Engman; **Indexer:** Betty Frizzell; **Permissions Manager:** Dalene Reeder; **Graphic Designer:** Joe Buck; **Graphic Artist:** Denise Lowry; **Cover Designer:** Bob Reuther; **Photographer (interior):** © Human Kinetics, unless otherwise noted; **Photo Production Manager:** Jason Allen; **Art Manager:** Kelly Hendren; **Associate Art Manager:** Alan L. Wilborn; **Art Style Development:** Joanne Brummett; **Printer:** Thomson-Shore, Inc.

Printed in the United States of America   10 9 8 7 6 5 4 3 2 1

The paper in this book is certified under a sustainable forestry program.

Human Kinetics
Website: www.HumanKinetics.com

United States: Human Kinetics, P.O. Box 5076, Champaign, IL 61825-5076
800-747-4457
e-mail: humank@hkusa.com

Canada: Human Kinetics, 475 Devonshire Road Unit 100, Windsor, ON N8Y 2L5
800-465-7301 (in Canada only)
e-mail: info@hkcanada.com

Europe: Human Kinetics, 107 Bradford Road, Stanningley, Leeds LS28 6AT, United Kingdom
+44 (0) 113 255 5665
e-mail: hk@hkeurope.com

Australia: Human Kinetics, 57A Price Avenue, Lower Mitcham, South Australia 5062
08 8372 0999
e-mail: info@hkaustralia.com

New Zealand: Human Kinetics, P.O. Box 80, Torrens Park, South Australia 5062
0800 222 062
e-mail: info@hknewzealand.com

E4416

Thanks to my family. When push comes to shove, family is there for you. I would also like to dedicate my work on this book to two master teachers I first encountered as an undergraduate: Dr. A. Gwendolyn Drew and Mrs. Jo Garrison. Undoubtedly, without them, I would be doing something else today!

Kathleen Haywood

I was able to study with "giants." I thank them for their kindness to a young student with whom they enthusiastically shared their knowledge and passion for the study of motor development: Larry Rarick, Anna Espenschade, Helen Eckert, Vern Seefeldt and, especially, Lolas Halverson. I can only hope that I have deserved their generosity.

Mary Ann Roberton

To my parents, Walter L. and Susan D. Getchell, for giving me endless, unconditional encouragement over many years. In particular, thanks to my mother, who provided the block off of which I became a chip.

Nancy Getchell

Contents

Preface

You've heard the saying that nothing in life is simple. People who have studied motor development would say instead that nothing about the development of life is simple. The range of influences on developing beings is enormous, and the fact that these influences interact with one another paints a picture of rich complexity.

Just consider one example: physical growth. Physical growth and physiological maturation proceed according to a genetic blueprint. Yet, a host of environmental factors ranging from nutrition to carcinogens to climate to disease influence growth and maturation. The psychosocial environment across childhood and throughout adulthood can also affect physical status, either directly or through other environmental factors. These factors can support or impede growth and maturation. Their effect on physical status changes the interaction between the person and the environment, and so a complex interplay between the changing physical person and the environment's many factors continues.

The process of motor development is equally complex. Yet, this complexity is exactly what captures our interest. Each person is unique. Each person's context is unique. A small difference early in development can result in a large difference later in life. What intrigues us is finding the keys that unlock the mystery of understanding a person's developmental status. The deeper we delve into the complex interaction of person, context, and purpose in movement, the more we appreciate the need to consider additional influencing factors. In this textbook, we examine many of the factors associated with and related to motor development. Furthermore, we explore where research within the field has been, where it is now, and where it might be in the future.

PURPOSE

This book is written for graduate or advanced students interested in both a broader and a deeper examination of the field of motor development. In this book, we focus on the ways in which both theoretical perspectives and research paradigms have influenced the understanding of developmental phenomena. This advanced text in motor development is designed to stimulate students to reach a deeper understanding and synthesis of the process and course of motor development and the great range of factors affecting that development. It is aimed at those who may have already studied the basic aspects of motor development and want greater in-depth knowledge and understanding. While graduate study in motor development traditionally has been approached through a variety of readings sometimes supplemented by an undergraduate text, this advanced text meets the need for in-depth study in a more cohesive way. It presents parallels and highlights relationships in a way that individual readings might not. It also provides a foundation in the theoretical underpinnings within the field as well as demonstrates how these theories drive contemporary research.

A unique approach in this text that is consistent with its focus on an advanced audience is that when analyzing research about the various categories of movement skills, this book not only surveys the research findings on a topic but also highlights a smaller number of landmark studies or lines of research to discuss in depth. Advanced students must appreciate the process of research as well as learn to analyze research methods and results for themselves so that they can become both critical consumers of research and researchers themselves. Students can further expand the horizon of study on a particular topic, but they will benefit from exposure to the process and the detail of research studies addressing specific questions.

Such analytical skills will prepare any student for selecting and exploring their own research topic. This text will help them transition into the role of engaging in motor development research, either as part of a research team or in the context of a thesis or dissertation. Moreover, for a student in an area other than motor development, this emphasis on critical analysis will help them to think about their own area in more sophisticated ways.

Another popular saying is that the devil is in the details. For those who want to know more about motor development than can be covered in an undergraduate course, the *fun* is in the details. Learning the details of research and hence the complexities of motor development will increase your engagement, challenge, and excitement. It will also position you to frame your own research questions as you learn more about the process of developmental research.

ORGANIZATION

The text has been organized into three parts. Part I, which is entitled What Is Motor Development? Theoretical Perspectives, explores the meaning of the phrase *lifespan motor development* from both a historical and a contemporary context. After introducing the field of motor development, chapter 1 examines the roots of motor development in describing motor behavior through the research of early developmentalists such as Gesell and McGraw. Chapter 1 also examines inter- and intratask motor skill sequences within the developmental sequence theory. Chapter 2 describes the movement of developmentalists toward considering developing beings in their context or environment. It reviews the transition from indirect to direct perception in specifying the relationship between perception and action. Chapter 3 parallels this paradigm shift in discussing dynamic systems perspectives, especially research studying the emergence and self-organization of movement from interacting subsystems. Finally, chapter 4 reviews the research methods and tools commonly used in motor development research. It also shows how to use inductive reason and strong inference (Platt, 1964) in the research process.

Part II, which is entitled, What Perspectives Do Researchers Use to Study Motor Development? Contemporary Research, examines research agendas within specific classes of motor skills (posture, foot locomotion, ballistic skills, and manipulative skills). Each chapter in part II provides an overview of the research on two or three specific skills to demonstrate how research agendas can help answer specific questions about skill development. Chapter 5 explores postural control. Chapter 6, on locomotion, covers walking and hopping. Chapter 7, ballistic skills, focuses on research on the overarm throw, striking, and kick-

ing. Finally, an examination of manipulative skills focuses on reaching, grasping, and catching (chapter 8).

eBook
available at
HumanKinetics.com

In addition to surveying past and current research on particular skills, each chapter in part II delves more deeply into a few individual studies or lines of research. This rich description illustrates the specifics of research—that is, not only what a research study found but also how the research study found it. Graduate students might well take an interest in some of the approaches to the study of motor development described with these studies and design their own investigations around them. Tips for Novice Investigators included throughout these chapters will help you to think about the research process.

To help you, as a present or future practitioner, see ways to use research in the real world, part III, entitled How Do Practitioners Adopt a Developmental Perspective? Applying Research, describes applications of motor development research within the fields of physical education, early childhood education, gerontology, special education, and physical therapy or rehabilitation sciences. Most of those who have studied motor development over the years have been devoted to acquiring this information for use by clinicians. Chapter 9 examines how practitioners in fields such as adaptive physical education or occupational therapy can apply motor development research to special populations, such as children with Down syndrome, autism spectrum disorders, developmental coordination disorder, or physical or learning disabilities. Another unique aspect of this text is the provision of practical applications of motor development research in chapter 10, using specific examples from the fields of physical and occupational therapy and physical education. An emphasis is how practitioners have used research to create developmentally appropriate practices such as a motivation mastery climate for typically developing children and adults.

This text does not encompass the entire breadth and depth of the body of knowledge within motor development. Rather, it presents major topics and landmark studies and then encourages readers to use their newly found procedural knowledge and analytical skills to explore their own interests. This text is as much about how to locate, distill, and integrate motor development information as it is about specific facts and relationships.

In choosing a finite number of critical discussions, this text focuses on the processes of motor development that have intrigued scholars for years. Doing so brings to light themes that surface in those discussions, such as continuity and discontinuity in motor development as young humans explore reaching (chapter 8) and locomotion (chapter 6). Themes such as these are identified throughout the text so that advanced learners can take note of them as they explore their own motor development interests.

CONCLUSION

This book is intended to guide advanced students to a deeper understanding of lifespan motor development research. The topics discussed are engaging and relevant to both practitioners and future researchers alike. Hopefully you will situate yourself as both a practitioner and a researcher as you move forward in your respective profession and in your personal life as a parent, aunt, uncle, or cousin.

Acknowledgments

Following the trail of e-mails back to the earliest mention of an advanced motor development book leads to a message dated March 18, 2004. Indeed, the writing of this book has been a long haul! There are a good many ways this book could have been written, and we considered all of them, but hopefully the time it took to arrive on this approach was worth the effort. This book would not have been possible without the support of Judy Wright, who made sure this project was well under way before retiring. We would also like to acknowledge the input of our acquisitions editor, Myles Schrag, and our developmental editor, Melissa Zavala, and all the rest of the Human Kinetics staff for their work on this book.

We would also like to acknowledge the support and encouragement of our peers, who convinced us that future generations of motor development students would benefit from a text written for upper-level undergraduate and graduate students. In particular, we would like to thank Linda Gagen, PhD, Jackie Goodway, PhD, Mary Rudisill, PhD, Leah Robinson, PhD, Noreen Goggin, PhD, Crystal Branta, PhD, Patricia Shewokis, PhD, Jennifer Romack, PhD, Kathleen Young, PhD, Jane Clark, PhD, and Karl Rosengren, PhD, for their help during the process of writing this book. It seems as if motor development researchers are truly a community of scholars, and as part of that community, it is hard not to find some way that each and every one has helped us arrive at this point.

We are grateful for the photo contributions of Dr. Tammy Burt from losethetrainingwheels.org and Dr. Jody Jensen from the University of Texas at Austin, both of whom recognize and share the joy of bicycling for all.

What Is Motor Development?

Theoretical Perspectives

Areas of scholarly study are not static and fixed. They evolve as more information is gathered from research, more viewpoints are expressed, and various scholars interpret what is known. In addition to benefitting from new information, areas of study also undergo shifts in perspective or approach. While one approach to the study of a field might have dominated for decades, the shift to another approach may result in new insights and advance our understanding of the field. The new approach might come with new tools that allow researchers to gather not only new information but also different kinds of information.

In part I of this text we review the perspectives that have shaped the field of motor development and form its foundation. We look at how the perspectives have influenced researchers and guided them to advance our understanding of motor development. Reviewing the concepts and perspectives that have shaped motor development is more than a history lesson. This knowledge also helps us understand contemporary thought, because contemporary thought is built on the ideas debated over the past 100 years.

We begin with the first perspective that guided the field: the descriptive perspectives. We examine the ideas of the early pioneers in motor development, especially those ideas that affect current thinking. Also, we see how early methods of recording movement have provided rich descriptions of change and how these methods have evolved into what is used today.

In chapter 2 we discuss perspectives that addressed perception and drew the attention of developmentalists toward the end of the 20th century. Again, beyond the history lesson, we see that at the heart of this discussion are fundamental questions about how performers plan actions and how actions are controlled

as they are ongoing. We see how these discussions contributed to our current ideas and models in motor development.

Chapter 3 reviews how the ideas of researchers from many different fields who studied naturally occurring events and behaviors culminated in systems theory and how the tenets of this theory are applied to motor behavior in general and motor development in particular. We see how the systems approach addresses two fundamental questions in development: (1) how completely new behaviors can emerge and (2) how initial conditions influence actions. This approach also addresses another fundamental concern, which is how the brain can effectively control complex movements in an ever-changing context.

The last chapter in part I provides a foundation for understanding how motor development researchers design their research studies. This chapter will help you appreciate and understand the research described later in the book. It also reviews the various dependent variables seen in developmental research and provides an example of how researchers plan a sequence of studies to build knowledge of particular aspects of motor development.

Part I provides a foundation on which to build an understanding of motor development concepts as the field continues to evolve. It will also help you address increasingly complex questions about the development of motor behavior.

CHAPTER 1

Descriptive Perspectives

For thousands of years human parents have undoubtedly delighted in watching their infants stand and then take their first steps. In the first year of life a child's motor development is so clear, her motor accomplishments so obvious, that even in our sophisticated 21st century, infant motor development remains a source of parental interest and pride.

Because of this interest, at some time hundreds of years ago a parent began recording a child's motor progress. This act was the informal beginning of the field of study called *motor development*. When this beginning occurred, we do not know. We do know that written baby biographies have existed since at least 1787 (Cairns, 1998). Early scientists and educators, such as Darwin (1877), Pestalozzi (as cited in De Guimps, 1906), and Shinn (1900), also recorded the development of their own children or the children of relatives (Irwin & Bushnell, 1980). In all cases, they focused considerable attention on describing progressive changes in the youngsters' motor behavior—that is, their motor development. To this day, descriptions of motor skill acquisition remain the largest portion of the motor development literature. This chapter explores the historical background of those descriptions.

DEFINITION OF MOTOR DEVELOPMENT STUDY

The field of motor development can be described as "the study of lifespan change in motor behavior" (Roberton, 1989b, p. 216). Some people, however, have argued that a definition should clarify what is meant by *the study of*. So, there have been expanded definitions ranging from "motor development is the changes in motor behavior over the lifespan and the process(es) which underlie these changes" (Clark & Whitall, 1989b, p. 194) to "motor development is the sequential, continuous age-related process whereby movement behavior changes" (Haywood & Getchell, 2009) to "motor development is the study of change in motor behavior over time, including typical trajectories of behavior across the lifespan, the processes that underlie the changes we see, and factors that influence motor behavior" (Ulrich, 2007, p. 78). As we shall see, many of the key words in these definitions originate in the descriptive perspectives addressed in this chapter.

HISTORY OF MOTOR DEVELOPMENT IN THE UNITED STATES

The baby biographers were really interested in their children's overall development; thus, they spawned not only the field of motor development but also the field of child development. Changes in motor behavior are an especially dramatic part of an infant's overall development, and so motor behavior took a prominent place in early descriptions of infant behavior. As the study of child development grew more scientific in the early 1900s, the field of motor development grew with it. To this day, child psychologists remain among the most famous names connected with the study of motor development. These scientists were primarily associated with the child study institutes (see Cairns, 1998) established across the United States in the 1920s: Arnold Gesell, Henry Halverson, Louise Ames, and Frances Ilg (Yale University); Nancy Bayley (University of California, Berkeley); Wayne Dennis (Brooklyn College); Myrtle McGraw (Columbia University); Mary Shirley (University of Minnesota); and Beth Wellman (University of Iowa).

Child psychologists lost interest in motor development after World War II. Motor development publications started to come almost exclusively from researchers in physical education, with occasional articles coming from medicine and physical therapy. In contrast to the child psychologists, many of whom studied infancy, these new scholars primarily studied childhood and adolescence. Very few of them produced more than one or two studies, in contrast to the child psychologists and their systematic publication records; however, two physical education scholars did stand out during this time: Anna Espenschade at the University of California, Berkeley and G. Lawrence Rarick at the University of Wisconsin–Madison. These researchers employed longitudinal as well as cross-sectional methodologies and contributed enviable publication records. Early on, both of their universities created graduate courses specifically in the field of motor development. In 1952 Rarick published the first motor development text for the students in his classes. *Motor Development During Infancy and Childhood* reviewed the literature on motor development through middle childhood. Although Rarick revised the text in 1961, he never distributed it nationally. He eventually published an edited text on motor development in 1973.

Meanwhile, in the early l960s the child development scholars associated with the longitudinal studies at the child study institutes realized that their participants, although no longer children, were still interesting. The participants were still developing—that is, changing their behaviors—even into adulthood. Coupled with the growing influence of the new field of gerontology, this realization that behavioral change was the real phenomenon of interest spawned the field of lifespan developmental psychology (Baltes, Reese, & Lipsitt, 1980). A 1963 article by Bayley entitled "The Life Span as a Frame of Reference in Psychological Research" was particularly influential in the birth of the lifespan perspective. Bayley was known for her motor development studies of infants and children, which made her recognize that the field should consider the entire lifespan an important event. Even more importantly for the field of motor development, the

first nationally disseminated textbook on motor development, published 4 years later by Anna Espenschade and Helen Eckert, covered the lifespan. Espenschade knew Bayley through the Institute of Human Development on the Berkeley campus where Bayley worked. Thus, although developmental psychology and its subdiscipline, motor development, had grown apart, the first nationally available text in motor development reflected the new lifespan perspective being adopted in its parent field.[1]

Today most scholars in motor development have backgrounds in kinesiology, the study of human movement. Many trace their scholarly lineage to Rarick or Espenschade or to their associates Ruth Glassow, Helen Eckert, Lolas Halverson, and Vern Seefeldt. The latter are the grandparents of the current students in the field, who are themselves now teaching the next generation of developmental kinesiologists.[2]

Starting in the 1970s the field of motor development began receiving renewed interest from developmental psychologists. Respected scholars, such as Connolly (1970) and Bruner (1973), revisited the explanations posed by the descriptive scholars, suggesting that information-processing models might better explain motor development. Clark and Whitall (1989b) marked these suggestions as the beginning of a **process-oriented period** in the motor development field. Interest in describing motor development began to decline and interest in explaining motor development began to rise. Most important for contemporary thinking were the efforts of Esther Thelen (see Thelen & Smith, 1994), a psychologist who reenergized the study of infant motor behavior with a new theoretical framework called *dynamic systems*. This framework continues to affect both the field of motor development and the field of developmental psychology (see Damon, 1998). Thelen's perspective is discussed in chapter 3.

A number of kinesiologists adopted the information-processing paradigm for the study of motor development (e.g., Clark, 1982; Thomas, 1980; Wade, 1976). They published a considerable body of work describing children's ability to process incoming stimuli and then move in response. Their work is described in chapter 2. A few kinesiologists have also adopted the dynamic systems explanation for motor development (see Clark & Whitall, 1989b; Roberton, 1993; Thelen & Ulrich, 1991). Their work is described in later chapters.

CONCEPT OF DEVELOPMENT

While knowing the names of people connected with an area of study is interesting, the history of a field is best told through its ideas and methods. Viewing the field of motor development as a series of historical periods supplanting each other (see Clark &Whitall, 1989b) is also useful, but ideas and perspectives from one period often extend into subsequent periods. For instance, the definitions of motor development presented earlier reflect ideas distilled over the past 100 years.

The heyday of both motor development description and motor development explanation took place during the first half of the 1900s. Almost without exception the child psychologists of that time implicitly or explicitly adopted a viewpoint of motor development that we now call *organismic* (see Langer, 1969).

That is, they used the biological study of developing organisms as their model for studying children. For this reason they saw their scientific role as to both describe and explain the changing motor behaviors of infants and young children. In contrast to their colleagues in experimental psychology, they preferred to describe the child in a natural setting without manipulating the environment. Particularly influenced by the strides being made in embryology at the time, they used ideas about the developing embryo as a model to help them interpret their own observations.

For instance, embryologists, notably Coghill (1929), saw that development in the embryo occurs in specific directions: The embryo develops from its head to its feet (cephalocaudal), from its trunk to its limbs (proximodistal), and from the ulnar side to the radial side of its arms. Another key aspect of embryo development is differentiation, the development of cells from an unspecialized and global state to a state of specialization. Other ideas from embryology that were incorporated into the study of motor development are morphogenesis, referring to the formation of organs, and integration, referring to the coordination of the specialized cells within the body. Several of these concepts permeate major models of developmental psychology today (see Valsiner, 1998).

As the early child psychologists watched infant motor development, they were reminded of differentiation when they saw children's initial attempts to grasp objects change from global arm sweeps to specialized use of the fingers. They were reminded of ulnar-to-radial development as they saw children change from corraling an object with the ulnar side of the hand to picking up the object with the thumb and index finger. As they watched a child acquire a series of novel locomotor forms, from scooting to crawling to creeping to walking, they felt they were seeing the shape, or morphology, of motor development. As they saw a child first throw with no step and then later incorporate a step into the throw, they thought of integration—different movements being coordinated together to form a larger whole. And finally, as they watched the baby raise the head and push up on the arms long before beginning to walk, they thought they saw cephalocaudal development.

THREE EARLY PIONEERS OF MOTOR DEVELOPMENT

Every field has its giants—investigators who influence subsequent researchers or whose findings are still critical to basic understanding in their field. Motor development research is no exception. Three pioneers in motor development generated many of the questions asked in the field as well as the data collection techniques used to answer these questions. Their influence is still felt today.

Gesell

Key among the child psychologists was Arnold Gesell. His laboratory at Yale University was among the first to use cinematography to document the behaviors of the babies being studied. He and his colleagues wrote many books and

articles describing the acquisition of novel motor behaviors as well as novel cognitive and social behaviors. In fact, he was the cultural infant guru of his day, giving information to lay parents as well as to scholars (Thelen & Adolph, 1992). In his statements about motor development we see the strong influences of embryology and, in particular, morphology:

> *The action systems . . . undergo orderly changes of pattern, which are so consistent that we may be certain that these changes are governed by mechanisms of form regulation comparable with those which are being defined by the science of embryology. (Gesell & Thompson, 1934, p. vi)*

> *Behavior has shape. . . . The shapes which behaviors assume can be investigated in their own scientific right. A morphological approach leads to the description and measurement of specific forms, the systematic study of topographical relations and correlations of such forms, their ontogenetic progression and involution, their comparative features among individuals and among species. (Gesell, 1954, p. 337)*

This perspective on motor development as morphology continues in the work of dynamic systems theoreticians such as Peter Kugler (1986).

Another key idea from the embryology and biology of the time was the belief that maturation, particularly neural maturation, is the driving force that causes movements to change. Gesell was the main proponent of this view. He felt strongly that the mechanisms of infant developmental morphology are genetically driven and receive only slight assistance from the environment (Gesell, 1933, 1939, 1954; Gesell & Thompson, 1934). We understand now that because the developmental progressions that he described were common to most of his infant participants, and because he did not document the environment within which these behaviors occurred, Gesell assumed the changes that he saw arose from an internal, neural cause. However, he also conducted an influential experimental study pitting heredity against environment using the **co-twin method** (Gesell & Thompson, 1929). He and Helen Thompson gave one twin (labeled *T* for trained) 10 minutes of practice for 6 days a week in crawling up four stairs and in manipulating cubes. These sessions started when T was 46 weeks of age and continued for 6 weeks. Meanwhile, they did not allow the other twin (labeled *C* for control) to experience the two activities. Thus, while the twins shared the same heredity, only one received environmental stimulation to practice.

At the end of the training, when both children were 53 weeks old, T was able to climb the stairs in 10 to 18 seconds. C could also climb the stairs but took 40 to 45 seconds to do so. Gesell and Thompson then trained C for 2 weeks; this training shortened her climbing time to that of T's. Moreover, the researchers claimed that C's performance at 55 weeks was far superior to T's performance at 52 weeks: "The maturity advantage of 3 weeks of age must account for this superiority" (Gesell & Thompson, 1934, p. 315). Thus, they felt that maturation had to be the main reason this skill developed. It is interesting, however, that an investigator blind to which twin had received the training felt that T was superior in cube handling. Moreover, Gesell and Thompson (1929) admitted

that compared with C, T remained more agile, was less afraid of failing, and walked faster for several months after the study, but they did not emphasize this result in their report.

In 1946 McGraw commented that Gesell and Thompson were really studying the relative effects of practice when it was introduced at one point in time or 6 weeks later. In 1989 Newell, Scully, Tenebaum, and Hardiman argued that the different forms of cube manipulation are highly dependent on the ratio of hand size to cube size. That is, children whose hands are small relative to the cube are likely to scoop the cube or use two hands to pick it up. Children whose hands are large relative to the cube are more likely to use their forefinger and thumb. Thus, in contrast to Gesell, Newell et al. suggested that physical growth (hand size) rather than neural maturation was the salient factor in the development of prehension.

In addition to his descriptions of infant motor development and his belief in maturation, other ideas of Gesell influenced the field of motor development for years. For instance, Gesell used the term *stage* to describe the "series of postural transformations" (1946, p. 302) that occur in the acquisition of prone progression. This term remains popular today (but see Roberton, 1978b). He also believed that the developmental trajectory of all motor skills follows the developmental directions of embryology, such as cephalocaudal and proximodistal. This belief still appears as a developmental law in many motor development textbooks, despite obvious exceptions to that generalization. For instance, in all forms of foot locomotion, the arms follow the feet in their development due to the constraints of balance; thus, locomotor development, once on the feet, is caudalcephalo rather than cephalocaudal. Newell and van Emmerik (1990) gave other examples both supporting and refuting Gesell's generalizations about developmental direction. Lastly, Gesell's influence is still felt through his developmental norms, which continue to be used in fields such as medicine even though the norms were based almost exclusively on white, middle-class socioeconomic groups. While behavioral norms can be useful, as Thelen and Adolph (1992) indicated, Gesell's portrait of the typical child has slowly morphed into a portrait of the desirable child.

Shirley

Another early student of motor development was Mary Shirley (1931) at the University of Minnesota. A psychologist, she and Edith Boyd, a pediatrician, observed 25 babies weekly during the first year and biweekly during the second year of life. From their own written observations and from the mothers' checklist of items, the two women attempted to trace stages in the development of walking. In addition to describing the babies' movements, the investigators put olive oil on the babies' feet and had the babies walk on white, unglazed wrapping paper. They then brushed the footprints with a powder of lampblack, graphite, and powdered acacia to make the prints stand out. This allowed them to measure variables such as length and width of stride. Each walking session was also timed so that the number of steps per unit of time could be studied as the babies developed.

Shirley (and Boyd) found five distinct skill groupings, or orders, in the development of walking. Each contains several stages; these are listed in table 1.1.

Shirley postulated that within each major order of locomotor development, some shifting of stages might occur for an individual child, but that no stage occurs outside of its major order. The major orders are (1) passive postural control, (2) postural control of the entire trunk and undirected activity, (3) active efforts at locomotion, (4) locomotion by creeping, and (5) postural control and coordination for walking. Shirley also noted many characteristics in speed, length of step, width of step, and angle of foot placement as the babies grew older. The frontispiece of volume II of her study showing some of the stages (see figure 1.1) is still frequently displayed in child development texts (Shirley, 1931).

Table 1.1 Shirley's (1931) Table of Stages in the Development of Walking

		Age in weeks			
Description of stage	Number of cases	Q_1	Median	Q_3	Q
First-order skills					
On stomach, chin up	22	2.0	3.0	7.0	2.5
On stomach, chest up	22	5.0	9.0	10.0	2.5
Held erect, stepping	19	11.0	13.0	15.0	2.0
On back, tense for lifting	19	14.0	15.0	18.0	2.0
Held erect, knees straight	18	13.0	15.0	19.0	3.0
Sit on lap, support at lower ribs and complete head control	22	15.0	18.5	19.5	2.2
Second-order skills					
Sit alone momentarily	22	20.5	25.0	26.0	2.7
On stomach, knee push or swim	22	22.0	25.0	27.0	2.5
On back, rolling	19	25.0	29.0	32.0	3.5
Held erect, stand firmly with help	20	29.0	29.5	33.0	2.0
Sit alone 1 min	20	27.0	31.0	34.0	3.5
Third-order skills					
On stomach, some progress	17	32.5	37.0	41.0	3.7
On stomach, scoot backward	16	34.0	39.5	45.5	5.7
Fourth-order skills					
Stand holding to furniture	22	41.0	42.0	45.0	2.0
Creep	22	41.0	44.5	45.0	2.0
Walk when led	21	37.5	45.0	45.5	4.0
Pull to stand by furniture	17	42.0	47.0	49.5	3.7
Fifth-order skills					
Stand alone	21	56.0	62.0	66.0	5.0
Walk alone	21	59.0	64.0	67.0	4.0

Q_1 and Q_3= first and third quartile; Q=semi-quartile.

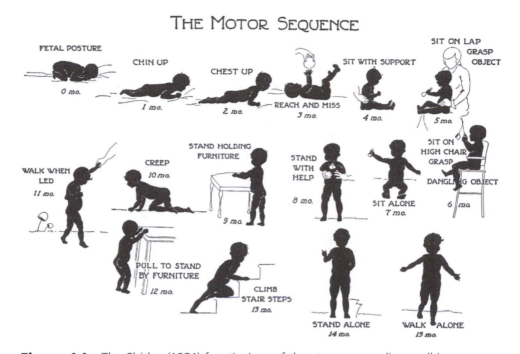

Figure 1.1 The Shirley (1931) frontispiece of the stages preceding walking.

Like Gesell, Shirley concluded that motor development is best accounted for by maturation, and she generalized this conclusion to the development of all motor skills. She justified her reasoning on two characteristics of the locomotor developmental sequence that she had studied: (1) The development was orderly and (2) new skills made sudden appearances.

> *A coordinated act appears suddenly; it is not the culmination of a patient piling up of small motor increments (p. 177) . . . behavior springs forth fully formed or integrated and breaks up into reflexes later (p. 190). . . . The law of integration first and individuation into reflexes later probably applies to babies as well as to lower vertebrates. (Shirley, 1931, p. 191)*

Again, the terminology from embryology is apparent. The word *individuation*, for instance, is a synonym for *differentiation*.

McGraw

A third scholar of this era was Myrtle McGraw, who worked in the Neurological Institute at Columbia University. She also studied the motor development of babies, contributing significant descriptive information to the field. In contrast to Shirley, who looked at the acquisition of different skills on the way to walking, McGraw tended to study changes within a particular skill, such as creeping

or swimming. She based her descriptions on mixed longitudinal data, usually of 40 to 80 babies, depending on the skill. Like Gesell, she frequently used cinematography and co-twin methodologies.

McGraw's (1945/1963) original purpose in studying infant development was to correlate overt motor patterning to its neural substrate. Frederick Tilney was a histologist who had correlated neural development with behavior in animals. He and McGraw planned to do the same with human babies. McGraw would supply "schedules of developmental changes" (1945/1963, p. vii) in infant behavior and Tilney would study brain material from deceased babies of the same age. Thus, McGraw's descriptive work was to be in the service of explanation. Unfortunately, Tilney died, so the correlational analyses were never completed.

McGraw (1945/1963) subsequently published her developmental descriptions as stand-alone information, accompanying them with a hypothesized neurological explanation that was widely accepted in medical and therapeutic circles. She suggested that the neonatal reflexes she had studied, such as the stepping reflex and the swimming reflex, were a product of subcortical parts of the brain. She saw that the reflex behavior died away, to be followed by a time of disorganized behavior. This phase[3] was then followed by movements that she deemed to be under cortical control (see figure 1.2). Thus, she argued that the cortex must have inhibited the output of the subcortex, damping out the manifestation of the original reflex and subsequently allowing integration of all brain areas needed to control the voluntary activity. While accepted for years, this interpretation relative to the developmental sequence for stepping behavior was later revisited by Thelen and Fisher (1982), who proposed a dynamic systems explanation. Their work is examined in chapters 3 and 4.

a

b

c

Figure 1.2   Three phases in swimming behavior from McGraw (1945/1963, p. 34). *(a)* Reflex swimming movements; *(b)* disorganized behavior; *(c)* voluntary or deliberate movements.

Reprinted from M. McGraw, 1963, *The neuromuscular maturation of the human infant* (Hafner Press), 34.

In contrast to Gesell and Shirley, McGraw was not a maturationist. Rather, she was a firm interactionist about the relative contributions of maturation (heredity) and learning (environment) to development. Unfortunately, she used the word *maturation* in the title of several of her articles and books (see, for instance, McGraw, 1945/1963, 1946), so she is frequently labeled as such. Yet, even in the book *The Neuromuscular Maturation of the Human Infant*, McGraw (1945/1963) made the following statement:

> *Most of the neuromuscular functions discussed in the preceding pages are considered to be the result of a maturational process, yet it is obvious that many of them assume at a certain period the fundamental qualities of learning. (p. 122)*

She used as exemplars the acquisition of toilet training and riding a tricycle, arguing that in both cases a certain level of neural *maturation* had to occur to enable the child to have the cognitive understandings required to *learn* the skill. Thus, she believed that the motor development of infants reflects both maturation and learning.

McGraw made this argument even more strongly in her famous co-twin study of Johnny and Jimmy, twins from the Irish ghetto of New York City (McGraw, 1935/1975). For 5 days a week, a laboratory assistant picked up the babies from their home and took them to McGraw's laboratory, where they stayed from 9 a.m. until 5 p.m. Since the family had five other children, this service provided caretaking relief. The study took place for the first 22 months of the twins' life. Because Jimmy appeared to be the stronger child at birth (which McGraw had filmed), he became the control twin and was not given practice on the various skills of infancy that McGraw was studying. Johnny, on the other hand, received stimulation relevant to the skill. For instance, the researchers stimulated Johnny's Moro reflex by slapping a small stick on the mattress where he lay (which we now recognize would also stimulate the startle reflex). This stimulation started when he was 20 days old and occurred at 2-hour intervals, 4 times a day, 5 days a week. This practice continued until Johnny was 9 months old. At each trial his motor response was recorded. Meanwhile, Jimmy's response was tracked once a week.

Through the course of the study, Johnny, the trained twin, received stimulation in all kinds of activities, including swimming, locomotion, getting off of pedestals up to 6 feet (1.8 m) tall, climbing up onto the same pedestals to obtain lures, skating, riding a tricycle, and more. Newspapers and magazines heard of these seemingly bizarre activities and began featuring the study in their coverage, much to McGraw's dismay.[4] In addition to publishing her results, McGraw made available to scholarly groups excerpts from the 16 mm films she used to collect her data. These excerpts are as amazing to watch today as they were in the 1930s.[5]

The Johnny and Jimmy study revealed that certain skills (such as skating) are much more affected by practice than other skills are. In 1975 McGraw reported an amusing sidelight to this fact. When Gesell heard her presentation of the Johnny and Jimmy results at the annual meeting of the Society for Research in Child Development, he was quite upset, feeling that her study "negated [his] famous maturational theory. Of course I knew it didn't; it merely modified it" (McGraw, 1935/1975).

The modification to which McGraw (1935/1975) was referring was to distinguish between the development of **phylogenetic** motor behaviors, which are characteristic of the species, necessary for normal functioning, and therefore less affected by practice, and **ontogenetic** activities, which are characteristic of the individual, not necessary for normal functioning, and therefore more affected by practice. These terms are drawn from other words used by developmental psychologists: *Phylogeny* refers to the study of a species' evolutionary history and *ontogeny* refers to the study of an individual over time.

Most of the behaviors observed on the way to upright locomotion are what McGraw would call *phylogenetic*. Skating and bicycling are ontogenetic skills. This distinction actually supports Gesell's belief that maturation affected the infant skills that he studied. In McGraw's view his main problem was generalizing maturation to be the cause for the development of all motor skills.

In actuality, however, it is hard to distinguish between McGraw's two types of skills once a child is beyond walking (Roberton, 1984). For instance, Espenschade and Eckert (1967) at first categorized throwing as phylogenetic, but in the second edition of the same book they called it *ontogenetic* (Espenschade & Eckert, 1980). To complicate matters more, Langendorfer and Roberton (2002a) hypothesized that early levels of the developmental sequence for throwing may be phylogenetic while later levels may be ontogenetic. They explained that most people reach intermediate levels of the throw with relatively minimal practice, but only considerable practice takes a person to advanced levels of the skill. McGraw implied this possibility herself in the developmental sequences she described as starting with reflexive movement, such as swimming. Hellebrandt, Rarick, Glassow, and Carns (1961) further speculated that the leg action in the development of jumping is phylogenetic and the arm action ontogenetic. Finally, even the phylogenetic motor skills of infancy can be affected by an extreme lack of practice. Dennis (1960) observed infants in an Iranian orphanage who were confined to their cribs with minimal stimulation day after day. He found considerable motor retardation in these children. For instance, only 15% of the children who were 3 to 3.9 years of age were able to walk alone.

Newell and van Emmerik (1990) have suggested that the developmental descriptions of Gesell (and we would add Shirley and McGraw) are better explained by considering changes in the constraints acting on and within children as they attempt a motor task at different ages. We explore this suggestion in more depth in chapter 3. Interestingly, McGraw herself presaged this systems view:

> *Any activity is composed of many ingredients, some of which may for convenience be considered as external and others as internal with respect to the organism, but none of these factors can be considered external to the behavior. It is their relationship to each other which gives the activity pattern and form. A watch in the visual field is just as much an integral part of the activity of reaching and prehension as is the flexor-extensor movement of the arm. Although retaining their own identity, these factors unite in the formation of a behavioral pattern which is distinct from the summation of its parts. (McGraw, 1935/1975, p. 303)*

STAGE VERSUS AGE

While Shirley, Gesell, and McGraw were primarily interested in charting the developmental sequences of infancy, both Shirley and Gesell were also interested in the ages at which most children acquire the skills they charted (see, for instance, Gesell & Armatruda, 1941). Interestingly, McGraw was quite against establishing normative data and purposely used *days* to represent age on the horizontal axis of her developmental sequence graphs (see figure 1.3). She did this to make it more difficult for the reader to determine the children's ages, as she wanted to emphasize the sequence of development rather than the age of acquisition.[6] A number of investigators, however, followed the lead of Shirley and Gesell. They wanted to assist parents and educators in assessing whether children were on course in motor development. Bayley led the way in 1936 with the publication of the California Infant Scale of Motor Development, which is still in use today and better known as the *Bayley Scales* (Bayley, 2005). Others who studied motor skills with a primary focus on abilities at specific ages were McCaskill and Wellman (1938) at the University of Iowa and Jenkins (1930) and Gutteridge (1939) at Columbia University.

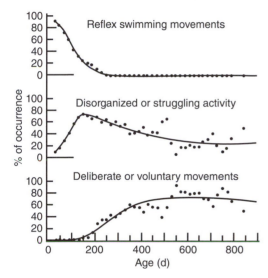

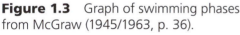

Figure 1.3 Graph of swimming phases from McGraw (1945/1963, p. 36).

Reprinted from M. McGraw, 1963, *The neuromuscular maturation of the human infant* (Hafner Press), 36.

As most parents and teachers know, interest in ages of acquisition and normative information about motor skills has both strengths and weaknesses. Considerable delay in the motor skills of infancy can be an early sign of disease or damage to the nervous system. Observing a lack of progress through the motor milestones of infancy is often the stimulus for parents or physicians to begin suspecting neurological dysfunction. The unanswered question, however, is how considerable the delay needs to be. Because normative data emphasize average ages of acquisition, less attention is paid to the individual differences or normal variability across youngsters of the same age. These differences increase considerably as children move into middle school, high school, and beyond. Thus, paying too much attention to age norms rather than to the variability within age can cause undue concern for adults and children alike. As McGraw emphasized, knowing the sequence of development is more important than knowing ages of attainment.

PHYSICAL EDUCATORS AND KINESIOLOGISTS IN THE FIELD

As indicated earlier, after World War II psychologists' developmental interests moved elsewhere and the field of motor development was dominated by researchers

in physical education, medicine, and physical therapy. Some, like Keogh (1965), continued establishing norms for childhood motor behavior. Others, like Halverson (1966) and Seefeldt (Seefeldt & Haubenstricker, 1982), were interested in the pedagogical implications of motor development. They conducted longitudinal descriptive studies that have contributed to the literature in the field.

Particularly prominent physical educators who continued describing childhood motor development were Rarick, Espenschade, and Glassow. Both Rarick and Espenschade primarily used outcome scores to measure their participants' motor behavior. They were both interested in causation, primarily in the role that growth might play in motor development. Thus, they correlated outcomes of motor tasks, such as the distance children could throw a ball at a given age, with height, weight, and muscular strength. Gender differences were also of interest to both scholars. In addition, Rarick studied the effect of mental retardation on motor development. Glassow focused on using kinematic measures to describe the movement of children. While she published relatively little, the students under her direction created a large body of thesis and dissertation work that ultimately was summarized and published by Ralph Wickstrom under the title *Fundamental Motor Patterns* (Wickstrom, 1970, 1977, 1983). This text is still one of the most cited references on the development of childhood motor skills.

LEGACIES FROM THE DESCRIPTIVE PERSPECTIVES

It is somewhat fashionable to downplay the contributions of those who provided (and still provide) descriptions of motor development by implying that these investigators were not interested in causation. Clearly, however, most were interested in the mechanisms of development. The problem is that there are different levels of explanation (Lightfoot & Folds-Bennett, 1992). Which is the ultimate level? Gesell, for instance, talked frequently about causation but invoked an internal force that he called *maturation*. McGraw was keenly interested in the neural substrate of motor behavior. Many developmental psychologists have even coined explanations in terms of processes that they have conceptualized rather than measured. Piaget (1970), for example, explained the cognitive developmental sequence through a process he called *assimilation and accommodation*. All of these are explanations logically consistent within the theoretical framework of the researcher but residing at different levels of measurement and reasoning. Do all have validity? Overton (1998) argued that they are, in a sense, all valid, at least internally.

The key point is that those scholars who are known for description in motor development did have strong interests in ultimately explaining the behaviors they described. They worked within a theoretical framework and within the models and technologies of the day. Many of the elegant descriptions that they left behind were so carefully crafted that scholars of today can still use those descriptions to speculate on causation at whatever level of explanation they choose. Chapter 3 illustrates this point further.

> ## Tips for Novice Investigators
>
> The key word in scientific research is *why*. If we see a child crawling by moving her arms and legs in a certain way and then a month later see the child using a different method, our first thought is, why? What caused the change? Have her legs grown? Has she gotten stronger? Is she on a different surface? Are her caretakers challenging her too much or too little? Our descriptions of her movement lead us to generate potential explanations that we can then test systematically.

SPECIFIC CONTRIBUTIONS OF THE DESCRIPTIVE PERSPECTIVES

A number of key ideas from the descriptive perspectives of the 20th century have helped shape the field of motor development into the 21st century. We shall explore several of these.

General Developmental Perspective

The foremost contribution is called the *general developmental perspective* (Asendorpf & Valsiner, 1992). This is the belief that there are universal developmental changes—that is, changes that are characteristic of most individuals in the population. This perspective permeates all of developmental psychology and its subfield of motor development. Thus, in her definition of the field of motor development (quoted earlier in the chapter), Ulrich (2007) emphasized that the field studies "typical trajectories of [motor] behavior" (p. 78).

> ## Tips for Novice Investigators
>
> The search for universal developmental changes has guided motor development research for nearly a century and has yielded a wealth of description. Many questions remain, however. The following are a few examples:
>
> - Most developmental description comes from cross-sectional data. To what extent do differences among people of various ages mimic the changes that occur in one person passing through those ages?
> - How variable is typical behavior? Is it displayed 60% of the time? 100%?
> - If the available descriptions are of typical behavior, to what extent does atypical behavior occur? When is atypical development shown? Who shows it?

Qualitative Changes

An important subset of the general developmental perspective is the notion that developmental change goes through an orderly progression of qualitatively different, or novel, discontinuous behaviors. The description of these behaviors

as they occur across time forms a developmental sequence. The developmental sequence is thought of as a series of transformations that together form the morphology of development (Overton, 1998). This idea is the origin of the word *sequential* that appears in the definition of motor development by Haywood and Getchell (2005) quoted earlier in the chapter.

The notion of a transformation connotes the appearance of something new (Roberton & Halverson, 1984). Developmentalists have particularly been drawn to studying the transformations or qualitative changes that occur with development. This is clearly true in motor development research, perhaps because transformations in posture and movement are relatively easy to see compared with transformations in cognition, for example. As we mentioned earlier, some investigators in the early 20th century, such as Shirley (1931), believed that qualitative changes appear suddenly in a person's behavior. Such a perspective probably stems from the frequency with which participants are observed and the degree of detail sought in the observations as well as in the choice of dependent variable. Contemporary students of qualitative change have suggested that increased variability in the dependent variable predicts imminent qualitative change (Kelso, 1995) and that change would not seem sudden if this variability were studied. Chapter 3 discusses this issue in more detail.

Quantitative Changes

Developmental change can also be continuous and quantitative as opposed to discontinuous and qualitative. Each motor behavior may show change that expands, for example, the range of movement at a joint but does not change the type of behavior. Or, a baby may crawl faster even though he is still crawling and not creeping or walking. Chapter 3 explores how quantitative change may presage qualitative change. This phenomenon suggests that both types of change may reflect parts of the same underlying process.

Continuity Versus Discontinuity

Throughout the history of developmental psychology there has been a tendency to pit the question of whether development is a series of quantitative changes (more of the same) against the notion that it is a series of qualitative changes (something new). This is often called the ***continuity versus discontinuity argument***. Over the last two decades, a group of scientists who are essentially neomaturationists have focused on what they call *core competencies* exhibited by infants. These investigators argue that some infant behaviors are innate and form the core for subsequent behaviors that occur later in development. Thus, they maintain that development is essentially a linear process with continuity between infant skills and adult skills. They deny that important nonlinear behavioral transformations occur along the way (see, for instance, Spelke & Newport, 1998; Liben, 2008).

Clearly, some of this issue is due to how a behavior is measured. If an investigator repeatedly measures the distance a child can traverse without assessing changes in the movements the child is using to travel, then that investigator will say that the change over time has been linear and continuous. If the investigator

studies the movement, however, then transformations or qualitative changes will be observed, and that investigator will argue that development is qualitative and discontinuous.

Besides being a potential measurement problem, either–or dichotomies in science are frequently misleading. Indeed, the general developmental perspective argues that both forms of change occur within an individual's development.

Tips for Novice Investigators

Probably the most misleading either–or dichotomy in developmental research is the historical battle between maturation theorists and learning theorists. Because the pioneers in motor development thought that development was caused by *either* an internal force (maturation) *or* an external force (learning), they missed the possibility that multiple factors or relationships between factors may cause behavioral change. The best approach for an investigator is to generate as many potential causes of a phenomenon as possible and then systematically test those hypotheses. This approach is discussed in detail in chapter 4.

Role of Age

Another aspect of the general developmental perspective is the use of age as a marker variable (Wohlwill, 1973) or the horizontal axis on developmental graphs (refer back to figure 1.3). Developmentalists understand, however, that age does not *cause* motor development. Age represents the passage of time. The variables that cause motor development are variables that coact over that same passage of time.

Although the lifespan is now seen as the potential length of time over which development is studied, vestiges remain from the era when the study of motor development focused only on children. For instance, the label *mature level* is still used in textbooks to refer to the most advanced level in a motor development sequence. Yet, as Roberton (1989b) asked, what is maturity when the referent is the entire lifespan?

Measures of Movement

A second inheritance from the descriptive perspectives is the belief that movement can be described both by measuring outcomes of the movement, frequently called *product scores*, and by describing the spatiotemporal aspects of the movement itself. Both Gesell and Shirley used outcome measures as well as verbal descriptions in their work. Glassow and her students (Wickstrom, 1970, 1977, 1983) frequently used product scores to identify poor and skilled performers and then relied on kinematics to describe their motor development. Halverson, who worked with Gesell, also used kinematics to study the acquisition of prehension (Gesell & Thompson, 1929). More recently Caldwell and Clark (1990) suggested further advancements in the use of kinematics and kinetics

to describe movement, and Jensen (2005) demonstrated their use in answering motor development questions.

Researchers have been divided on which behavioral measure best represents motor development. While some work has described the relationship between outcome measures and movement descriptions (Roberton & Konczak, 2001), little is known about their relationship for most motor skills. Roberton and Konczak reported a further complication: The relationship may change over time.

Clark and Whitall (1989b) expressed the view held by a number of contemporary scholars that all measures of motor behavior, whether verbal descriptions or outcome scores or kinematics, should be viewed as products of an underlying process. This view explains some of the differences among the descriptions of the field of motor development presented earlier. Those scholars who specifically added the study of the *process of motor development* to their definition of the field (see Clark & Whitall, 1989b; Haywood & Getchell, 2005) wanted to emphasize that motor development researchers are interested in explaining the movement changes that have been described. Explanation, of course, is understood to be part of science, but many feel the maturation and learning perspective spawned by the descriptive tradition prevented advances in understanding the actual underlying processes of motor development.

In their definition of motor development Haywood and Getchell (2005) also said that the developmental process is continuous. They were implying that even though the products of development may be discontinuous, the underlying process causing those products is continuous. Ulrich's (2007) definition of the study of motor development further distinguished between the underlying process and the factors that affect motor development. She was emphasizing that different factors may be elements in the same process at different points in time. Indeed, the one-factor (maturation or heredity) and two-factor (heredity and environment) models of causation provided by the descriptive tradition may be supplanted by a multifactor model. Chapter 3 presents contemporary thinking about a continuous and potentially multifactor process that may be an alternative to the maturation or maturation and learning explanations adopted within the descriptive perspectives.

Developmental Function

Regardless of the dependent variable chosen for study, another methodological contribution from the descriptive perspectives was the developmental function— a graph representing the acquisition of motor behaviors over time, measured either quantitatively (continuous curve) or qualitatively (staircase graph or a succession of curves). A distinguishing characteristic of developmentalists is that they make and study these graphs of data rising and falling over the lifespan (refer back to figure 1.3). Wohlwill (1973) even conceptualized the study of causation as the experimental attempt to change the naturally occurring developmental function. If by manipulating variables the investigator can modify the shape of the function, then the manipulated variable may be a causative factor in normal development.

> ## Tips for Novice Investigators

Find a copy of Myrtle McGraw's (1935/1975) *Growth: A Study of Johnny and Jimmy.* You'll find that in many respects it reads like a novel. Share with classmates the specifics of the activities that McGraw provided for Johnny. Describe Jimmy's role in the study. Then discuss how this study is an example of a researcher trying to change the developmental function for those particular motor skills.

Recording Movement

Another contribution to contemporary thinking from the descriptive perspectives was the careful methodology employed by the scholars of the time. Many used slow-motion films to document the movements they observed. Issues of objectivity and reliability were carefully assessed before data reduction began. The films and now videos of their data are also an accessible legacy that can be reviewed by subsequent investigators for different interpretations. The weakness of their methodology, however, was their failure to document with equal care the environment surrounding their participants; they rarely attempted to replicate in the laboratory the environmental situations potentially related to the movement transformations they observed in natural settings (Roberton, 1989a). This weakness created a vacuum in the motor development literature regarding the role of context in affecting an individual's behavior. For example, will the movements a person displays when kicking a ball a long distance also be displayed when that same person kicks for accuracy or for a shorter distance? Contemporary research is only beginning to address this question.

Models of Development

The use of models to help investigators crystallize their thinking was another contribution of the descriptive perspectives. Models have an important influence on a field. The descriptive perspectives used the developing embryo as a model for motor development. This model stressed transformations, or the appearance of novel forms. In the 1970s, students of motor development began to adopt information processing as an explanation for changes in motor behavior and implicitly changed the model of development from the embryo to the computer. Computers at that time did not have the capacity to create new forms; thus, the historical emphasis on the sequential appearance of new forms in the movement repertoire was lost to those investigators. Chapter 2 demonstrates this point further. Interestingly, dynamic systems theory again addresses the appearance of new forms. This theory is presented in chapter 3.

Motor Development Sequences

The emphasis on the sequential appearance of new forms is the most lasting contribution of the descriptive perspectives to contemporary study in motor development. While the different types of motor coordination are some of the clearest examples of novel forms in developmental behavior, most of the theorizing

about the characteristics of developmental sequences did not occur in the motor development literature. Instead, the theorizing occurred in the field of developmental psychology in the last half of the 20th century. Stimulated by Jean Piaget's (1970) monumental stage descriptions of cognitive development, developmental psychologists in the 1960s and 1970s, including Kohlberg (1963), Pinard and Laurendeau (1969), Flavell (1971; Flavell & Wohlwill, 1969), Turiel (1969), and Wohlwill (1973), reviewed and critiqued the rules of sequential development, particularly the rules of stage development. Their work ultimately influenced Roberton (1977, 1978a, 1978b, 1982) to examine available motor development sequences for evidence of validity. As Roberton pointed out, the main criterion for a valid developmental sequence stems from the general developmental perspective: Evidence must show that most people go through the sequence in the order indicated. This means that researchers need to have randomly sampled many people and then followed them longitudinally. Few motor development sequences have this support.

Intertask Motor Sequences

In the 1970s motor development investigators (Halverson, Roberton, & Harper, 1973; Seefeldt, Reuschlein, & Vogel, 1972) began to distinguish between two types of motor development sequences: intertask and intratask. Intertask sequences are what Shirley (1931) investigated; the researcher creates these sequences by ordering different motor tasks according to the age at which most persons achieve some criterion level of the task. For example, the baby lifts the head off the surface before rolling over, which in turn precedes crawling (see figure 1.1). Intratask sequences are what McGraw (1945/1963) investigated. Within one task, such as sitting, the researcher charts how movement in that task changes, traditionally until adultlike movement is demonstrated (see figure 1.4).

Still today the most recognized motor sequence is the intertask sequence Gesell studied (Gesell & Thompson, 1934) and Shirley (1931) charted using longitudinal data (see figure 1.1). It follows a child's development from chin up to walk alone (see table 1.1). Newell and van Emmerik (1990) called this sequence "*the* [italics added] motor development sequence," as though it were the only one in motor behavior. The charting of intertask sequences associated with infancy greatly promoted the view that motor development is maturationally determined and that the ages associated with the appearance of the various tasks are the most important piece of knowledge.

Figure 1.4 Development of sitting from McGraw (1945/1963, p. 64).

Reprinted from M. McGraw, 1963, *The neuromuscular maturation of the human infant* (Hafner Press), 64.

From a theoretical standpoint, however, the order of the tasks in an intertask sequence is of greater interest than the age of task acquisition, as the order hints at why one task precedes another chronologically. In fact, the tasks Shirley (1931) included in her well-known sequence are somewhat arbitrary (see table 1.1). For instance, there seems no compelling reason for scooting backward to be a prerequisite to walking. It simply occurs in the time before walking. As Wohlwill (1973) indicated, the problem with most intertask developmental sequences is that they are really no more meaningful than the order of "places on the itinerary of a bus line" (p. 193). To be of theoretical interest there must be an underlying connection for why certain tasks precede others in time. Again, however, as arbitrary as the tasks chosen for observation seem to be, the strength of the infant intertask sequences is the longitudinal study that documented their order.

Theoretically stronger research includes the attempts to determine the intertask sequence for the foot locomotor forms that develop after walking (Clark & Whitall, 1989a; Roberton & Halverson, 1984). For instance, balance and leg strength relative to weight are two likely reasons why two-foot jumping appears before one-foot hopping. The relationship between the development of striking and the development of throwing has also been studied (Langendorfer, 1987a). Unfortunately, this work is cross sectional. No longitudinal research has examined intertask sequences beyond infancy.

Intratask Motor Sequences

More theoretical scrutiny has focused on the intratask sequences of motor development. Because of their presumed relevance to pedagogy, contemporary motor development textbooks carry pages of these sequences, usually organized within categories such as locomotion and object manipulation. Little longitudinal research backs most of the sequences; those that are based on longitudinal research frequently are also based on relatively small numbers of participants. The overarm throw for force has received the most longitudinal study with the largest number of participants across the longest portion of the lifespan (Halverson, Roberton, & Langendorfer, 1982; Roberton, 1978a; Roberton & Langendorfer, 1980; Williams, Haywood, & VanSant, 1998). It has also been supported with cross-cultural (Ehl, Roberton, & Langendorfer, 2005) and generational cohort (Runion, Roberton, & Langendorfer, 2003) studies.

Two types of intratask sequences are described in the motor development literature. One type describes changes that occur across the whole body at once. These whole-body changes were primarily described in unpublished material from Seefelt and Haubenstricker (1982) at Michigan State University and in a cross-sectional study of the overarm throw published by Wild (1938). The other approach is the component approach, in which developmental sequences are tracked within sections or components of the body. This approach, suggested by Roberton in 1977, has been supported by longitudinal evidence from throwing (Roberton, 1978a; Roberton & Langendorfer, 1980) and hopping (Roberton & Halverson, 1988). Tables 1.2 and 1.3 illustrate these two approaches. Langendorfer and Roberton (2002a) have argued that the whole-body perspective captures a few but not all of the profiles, or combinations, of developmental

Table 1.2 Whole-Body Approach to Intratask Developmental Sequences: The Overarm Throw for Force

Stage	Description
Stage 1	The throwing motion is essentially anteroposterior in direction. The feet usually remain stationary during the throw. There is little or no trunk rotation in the most rudimentary pattern at this stage, but performers at the point of transition between stages 1 and 2 may demonstrate a slight trunk rotation in preparation for the throw and extensive hip and trunk rotation in the follow-through. The force of projection comes primarily from hip flexion, shoulder protraction, and elbow extension.
Stage 2	The distinctive feature of this stage is the rotation of the body about an imaginary vertical axis, with the hips, spine, and shoulders rotating as one unit. The performer may step forward with either an ipsilateral or a contralateral pattern, and the arm is brought forward in a transverse plane. The motion may resemble a sling rather than a throw due to the extended arm position during the course of the throw.
Stage 3	The distinctive characteristic is the ipsilateral arm and leg action. The ball is placed into a throwing position above the shoulder by a vertical and posterior motion of the arm at the time that the ipsilateral leg moves forward. There is little or no rotation of the spine and hips in preparation for the throw. The follow-through phase includes flexion at the hip joint and some trunk rotation toward the side opposite the throwing hand.
Stage 4	The movement is contralateral, with the leg opposite the throwing arm striding forward as the throwing arm moves in a vertical and posterior direction during the windup phase. The motion of the trunk and arm closely resembles that of stages 1 and 3. The stride forward with the contralateral leg provides for a wide base of support and greater stability during force production.
Stage 5	The weight shifts entirely to the rear leg as it pivots in response to the rotating joints above it. The throwing hand moves in a downward arc and then backward as the opposite leg moves forward. Concurrently, the hip and spine rotate into position for forceful derotation. As the contralateral foot strikes the surface, the hips, spine, and shoulder begin to derotate in sequence. The contralateral leg begins to extend at the knee as the shoulder protracts, the humerus rotates, and the elbow extends, thus providing an equal and opposite reaction to the throwing arm. The opposite arm also moves forcefully toward the body to assist in the equal and opposite reaction to the throwing arm.

Reprinted, by permission, from V. Seefeldt and J. Haubenstricker, 1982, Patterns, phases, or stages: An analytical model for the study of developmental movement. In *The development of movement control and coordination. Descriptive stages of throwing*, edited by J.A.S. Kelso and J. Clark (Oxford, UK: Wiley-Blackwell) 312-313.

levels across components that actually occur across a group of individuals. Seefeldt and Haubenstricker (1982) have argued that their approach is easier for students to use.

Contemporary views of intratask component sequences are that they are probabilistic (Roberton & Langendorfer, 1980; Roberton, 1982). Each level in the sequence has a certain likelihood of appearance, depending on the age of

Table 1.3 Component Approach to Intratask Developmental Sequences: The Overarm Throw for Force

Component	Description
	Trunk Action
Step 1	***No trunk action or forward-backward movements.***
	Only the arm is active in force production. Sometimes, the forward thrust of the arm pulls the trunk into a passive left rotation (assuming a right-handed throw), but no twist-up precedes that action. If trunk action occurs, it accompanies the forward thrust of the arm by flexing forward at the hips. Preparatory extension sometimes precedes forward hip flexion.
Step 2	***Upper trunk rotation or total trunk "block" rotation***
	The spine and pelvis both rotate away from the intended line of flight and then simultaneously begin forward rotation, acting as a unit, or "block." Occasionally, only the upper spine twists away and then toward the direction of force. The pelvis then remains fixed, facing the line of flight, or joins the rotary movement after forward spinal rotation has begun.
Step 3	***Differentiated rotation***
	The pelvis precedes the upper spine in initiating forward rotation. The child twists away from the intended line of ball flight and then begins forward rotation with the pelvis while the upper spine is still twisting away.
	Forearm action
Step 1	***No forearm lag***
	The forearm and ball move steadily forward to release throughout the throwing action.
Step 2	***Forearm lag***
	The forearm and ball appear to "lag" —that is, to remain stationary behind the child or to move downward or backward in relation to the body. The lagging forearm reaches its farthest point back, deepest point down, or last stationary point *before* the shoulders (upper spine) reach front facing.
Step 3	***Delayed forearm lag***
	The lagging forearm delays reaching its final point of lag until the moment of front facing.

Adapted, by permission, from M.A. Roberton and L.E. Halverson, 1984, *Developing children - Their changing movement* (Baltimore, MD: Lea and Febiger). Copyright M.A. Roberton.

the person. Figure 1.5 shows a typical probability, or population, graph of a hypothetical intratask developmental sequence. Each curve on the graph represents a developmental level (sometimes called a *step*) in the sequence. The horizontal axis is age. The vertical axis is the percentage of people displaying the behavior represented by that level. This kind of graph, first popularized by McGraw (1945/1963; see figure 1.3), shows nicely the coming to be and the passing away that characterizes development: Level 1 dies away, level 2 builds up and then dies away, and level 3 builds up. If figure 1.5 were based on real data, the original construction of the graph would have come from data in which 40% of the 20-year-olds showed level 2 behavior, 60% showed level 3 behavior, and 0% showed level 1 behavior. When the data are based on a sufficient number of people, the graph can be used as a graph of probabilities estimating future

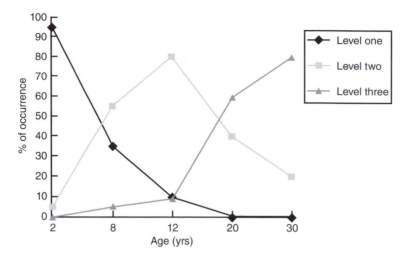

Figure 1.5 A hypothetical probability graph.

expectations. That is, someone using the graph would estimate that the probability that an unknown 30-year-old will show level 2 behavior is 20%. Most
likely, the unknown 30-year-old will display level 3 behavior; it is very unlikely
that the 30-year-old will show level 1 behavior.

Figure 1.5 also demonstrates that the sequence is not age determined but rather
is age related (Roberton & Halverson, 1984). That is, age does not determine
how a person's movement looks. There are probabilities associated with several
ways that the movement may look at any given age. Thus, the graph shows the
variability that occurs across a group of people of the same age. We should also
stress that these types of graphs depict behavior in a consistent environment.
All participants are assessed the same way during each testing session.

While conceptually an intratask developmental sequence is more characteristic
of a population than of an individual, some sequences, such as throwing for
force, are quite robust for the individual. Roberton and Langendorfer (1980)
have showed staircase graphs of individuals going through one of the throwing
component sequences (figure 1.6) as well as a population graph for some of the
same individuals (figure 1.7).

When studying individual progress, however, context needs to be considered. Fischer and Silvern (1985) made an important distinction between a person's functional level in a sequence and a person's optimal level in that same
sequence. The optimal level is the movement that a person can display when
necessary; the functional level is what a person shows as everyday behavior. For
instance, opposition of the arms is the most advanced level of arm action in
walking. Adults late for an appointment often display opposition while hurrying
down the street. When not in a hurry, however, those same adults may display
semiopposition. Semiopposition is the developmental level adjacent to opposition. Only one arm completes a forward and backward swing; the other arm
hangs fairly stationary (Roberton, 1984). When assessing behavior related to a

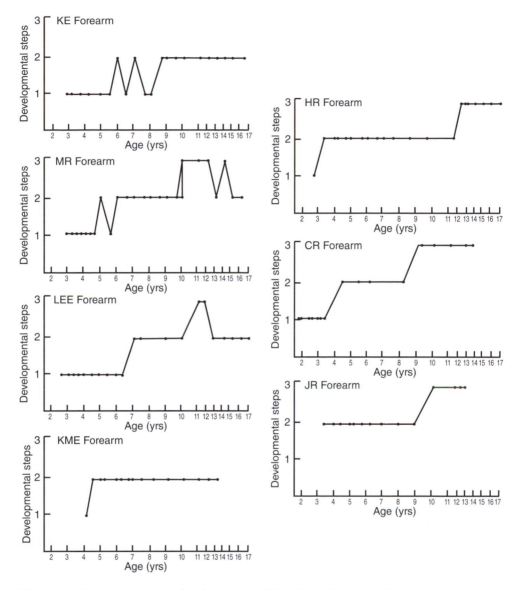

Figure 1.6 Staircase graphs showing individual development through the sequence for forearm action in the overarm throw for force (from Roberton & Langendorfer, 1980).

Reprinted, by permission, from M.A. Roberton and S. Langendorfer, 1980, Testing motor development sequences across 9-14 years. In *Psychology of motor behavior and sport - 1979*, edited by C. Nadeau et al. (Champaign, IL: Human Kinetics), 274.

developmental sequence, investigators must determine which level they want to elicit. That is, context is important. Traditionally, developmental sequence researchers have focused on eliciting and describing the optimal level that participants can demonstrate. Contemporary research is only beginning to explore the effect that varying contexts have on the developmental level an individual may display.

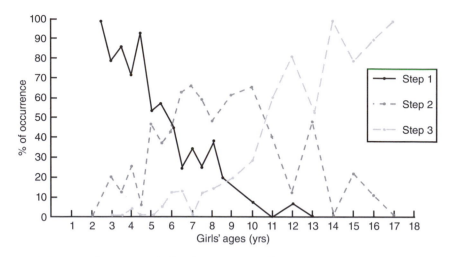

Figure 1.7 Population graph for the sequence for humerus action in the forceful overarm throw (from Roberton & Langendorfer, 1980).

Reprinted, by permission, from M.A. Roberton and S. Langendorfer, 1980, Testing motor development sequences across 9-14 years. In *Psychology of motor behavior and sport - 1979*, edited by C. Nadeau et al. (Champaign, IL: Human Kinetics), 276.

Motor development and the sequences characterizing it have been studied mainly in childhood and infancy. The work of Williams et al. (1998) that examined throwing in older persons is one exception to this statement. Another is the work of VanSant (1997) on the developmental sequences associated with rising from supine. Through cross-sectional studies VanSant has gathered the only truly lifespan data that exist on any motor sequence. Her studies included participants ranging from 4 to 83 years of age. In the process of gathering these data she discovered new behaviors occurring toward the end of the lifespan that had not been observed at younger ages. In other words, there is no final or advanced level in her sequences—there are only changing probabilities for what may be observed at different times in a person's life.

Concept of Regression

Motor development researchers of the 20th century frequently referred to the phenomenon of regression—that is, backward development within an intratask developmental sequence. For example, persons typically showing level 2 of a sequence might, under certain circumstances, begin using level 1. Usually the regression was temporary unless it was due to nervous system damage. The phenomenon was observed in children (1) who regressed in one skill during the emergence of a new skill (McGraw, 1935/1975), (2) whose body parts grew, particularly in length (McGraw, 1945/1963), (3) whose attitude toward the task was unfavorable (Gutteridge, 1939; Shirley, 1931), (4) who found task demands too stressful or too difficult (Gutteridge, 1939; Halverson, 1966; McGraw, 1935/1975), (5) who perceived failure in a task (Halverson, 1966), or (6) who became ill or experienced temporary or permanent nervous system damage (Hooker, 1952;

Paulson & Gottlieb, 1968). Regression is difficult to explain from the theoretical perspective that maturation of the nervous system causes motor development. Chapter 3 addresses this phenomenon from a new perspective.

Inter- and Intraindividual Variability

Traditionally, the general developmental perspective has focused on typical behaviors rather than on deviations, or variability, in those behaviors. As mentioned earlier, this fact has been one of the key problems in using age norms. Moreover, focusing on stability rather than variability may have contributed to the assumption that qualitative change jumps from one stable state to another stable state with no intermediate transitions.

Contemporary authors in developmental psychology have suggested that research should place more emphasis on the study of behavioral variability. Siegler (2007) and Adolph (Adolph & Berger, 2006; Adolph & Robinson, 2008) have emphasized that considerable intraindividual variability is involved in skill acquisition. Adolph (Adolph & Robinson, 2008) argued further that sampling behavior too infrequently has led developmental psychologists to focus on the stability of behavior and to miss the equally important variability in behavior. As chapter 3 discusses, intraindividual variability is an important theoretical construct in dynamic systems theory. As noted earlier, understanding the levels of sequential development as probabilistic (figures 1.5 and 1.7) stresses the interindividual variability present in motor development at any age.

On the other hand, data on the intraindividual variability displayed in forceful throwing show a different story. Roberton (1977, 1978a; Halverson et al., 1982) consistently found that forceful throwers aged 5 to 13 years display the same developmental level in 80% to 90% of their trials, dependent on the component. Lisy (2002) found a similar result for forceful place kicking by college students. It may well be that compared with nonballistic skills, motor ballistic skills are performed with less intravariability.

What Happened to Motor Development Stages?

At some time or another, most investigators of motor sequences have lapsed into *stage* terminology to describe the appearance of novel forms. Shirley (1931), for instance, called each of the motor tasks in the motor milestones of infancy a *stage*. Clearly, these motor tasks are simply different tasks that develop in a certain order chronologically. Even within intratask sequences, no stages have been validated for motor behavior. As Roberton (1978b, 1982) pointed out, a stage requires horizontal structure (Wohlwill, 1973), meaning that there must be generalization across tasks at one point in time. The term implies that every motor task a person attempts when in a stage should show similar movement behaviors. For instance, a child who kicks a ball with a minimal backswing of the foot should throw with a minimal backswing of the arm and strike a tennis ball with a minimal backswing of the racket. The literature contains little evidence for this possibility. The inter- and intratask developmental sequences discussed in this chapter show vertical structure (i.e., they change in an orderly way with time or age) but no horizontal structure. This is why Roberton (1978a, 1978b)

has argued that the novel forms in intratask sequences should be called *levels* or *steps* rather than *stages*. Both Langendorfer (1987a) and Roberton (1982) conducted initial studies of the horizontal structure between throwing and striking, but the question has not been pursued further. The work of Langendorfer and Roberton is discussed in chapter 7.

Vocabulary

The last gift made by the scholars representing the descriptive perspectives has been much of the technical vocabulary still used in the field. This vocabulary, with phrases ranging from *developmental morphology* to *developmental sequences*, is a primary legacy to the contemporary study of motor development.

ROLE OF DESCRIPTION WITHIN MOTOR DEVELOPMENT RESEARCH

Approximately 40 years ago, Joachim Wohlwill (1973) suggested a scheme for conceptualizing research in developmental psychology. His framework organized the seemingly disparate research studies that had been conducted in his field. Of lasting importance is that it also provided a road map for the systematic steps that should occur in developmental research. Description, the focus of motor development research in the 20th century, is the second of five systematic steps in Wohlwill's research framework. Without descriptions of the developmental functions and sequences that form the core of motor development, there would be no basis for subsequent study. Hopefully, this chapter has demonstrated the rich heritage of information—the basic core of concepts and dependent variables upon which future generations can build—that the descriptive perspectives provided.

SUMMARY

The study of motor development, or lifespan change in motor behavior, has been associated with the field of developmental psychology since their joint beginning in the 1700s. Since then, child and developmental psychologists, kinesiologists, and physical therapists have dominated research in the field. Different paradigms have guided these researchers with the most dominant being the descriptive perspectives. From this orientation have come key ideas that still frame the study of motor development. Chief among these are the views that change in motor behavior can be both qualitative and quantitative, continuous or discontinuous. Particularly unique is the motor development research emphasis on qualitative change, an emphasis reflected in the study of both intratask and intertask developmental sequences.

Footnotes

[1]Eckert received her doctorate at the University of Wisconsin–Madison, where she encountered Rarick's monograph. She credits its influence on the Espenschade and Eckert (1967) book. Personal communication from Eckert, 1968.

[2]Both M.A. Roberton (1972) and Frank Smoll (1982) used this term, but it never caught on.

[3]McGraw rarely used the term *stage* because she didn't believe suddenness was characteristic of the appearance of new movements. The sudden appearance of skills had been used as a criterion for a stage by Shirley. Personal communication from McGraw, 1976.

[4]Personal communication from McGraw, 1976.

[5]DVDs made from films that McGraw edited for public consumption are available from S. Langendorfer, division of kinesiology, Bowling Green State University. Her original research films are available for study at the Wisconsin State Historical Society, Madison, Wisconsin 53706.

[6]Personal communication with McGraw, 1976.

CHAPTER 2

Perspectives on Perception and Action

The human body can move to accomplish amazing feats. It can move with speed, with precision, and with artistry. How humans control the musculoskeletal system to achieve such a wide range of movements is fascinating. No less mysterious is how we successfully make those moves within the constraints of the environment.

A jump shot in basketball can be a flawless movement and still be of little value to the team if the ball misses the basket. A tennis forehand can be quick and powerful but to no avail if the ball sails out of bounds. We probably don't even want to think about what results from mismatches between movement and the environment in gymnastics or platform diving! Ouch!

We have long realized that we cannot fully appreciate how we control movement unless we understand how movement control incorporates the environment. What does it really mean to *know about* the environment? What is perception of the environment in the context of movement or action? The case of vision illustrates the complexity of this question. Movers who possess vision rely heavily on visual information to move in the environment and to perform many movement tasks. Yet, we are able to see the environment by virtue of light rays falling on our retinas, which are two-dimensional surfaces (see figure 2.1). How does the brain not only construct a three-dimensional environment from two-dimensional information but also construct it so quickly that we can respond in fractions of a second? This is an important issue for the understanding of motor control.

When the study of development from a descriptive perspective started to wane, interest grew in the role the environment plays in developmental change. Actually, scientists had been interested in how humans and animals integrate environmental information with movement control for centuries. We naturally want to

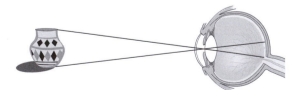

Figure 2.1 Three-dimensional objects are projected onto our retinas as two-dimensional objects, and yet our brains perceive objects as being three dimensional.

understand how we perceive surfaces and objects in the environment and how we use those perceptions when we move. The 1970 publication of *Mechanisms of Motor Skill Development*, edited by K. Connolly, provided an impetus for using a new model, the ***information-processing model***, which gives the environment an important role in motor development. This approach addresses developmental change through hypothetical processes based on computers. Perception, especially perception of the environment, is a major component of the model. The environmental stimulus, the processing of information to perceive the context and to choose an action, and the response are similar to the input fed to a computer, the sequential processing by a computer program, and the computer's output, respectively.

We will see in this chapter that the information-processing model stimulated a great deal of research about both motor learning and motor development, although we will also discuss shortcomings of the model and alternatives that conceptualize the role of the environment in yet another way. Thus we will examine the role of the environment in movement control from two broad perspectives on the relationship between perception and action. One perspective can be called an *indirect* or *stimulus–response perspective*. Generally the scholars working from this perspective use the information-processing model. The other perspective is called a *direct* or *ecological* perspective. It suggests ways the environment can be perceived directly without a linear processing of information. Let's consider the indirect perspective first.

INDIRECT PERSPECTIVE

The indirect perspective has dominated research on perception and action (see table 2.1). Much more of the empirical work performed in psychology and its subsets of motor learning and motor development is rooted in the indirect perspective compared with the direct perspective.

Features of Indirect Perspective

The indirect perspective is a *dualistic* framework in which the environment and the person are considered to be separate or disjointed. In this framework, a person perceives an object in the environment and then develops a mental representation of the object. The representation of the object stands between the object and the person. Objects, then, have a duplicity because they exist in the physical world and they also exist mentally as representations. For example, a dualistic approach to the experience of reading this book would suggest that the room and this book are out in the environment and that representations of them are in the mind.

The information-processing approach is an indirect perspective because the processing of information comes between a stimulus in the environment and the response to it. From the indirect or stimulus–response perspective, action (the response) follows perception (the stimulus), typically after the perceptual information is transformed (calculations are performed on the perceptual information). The perceptual *information* is *processed* so that the appropriate action can be selected and carried out. Knowing must always *follow* perception.

Table 2.1   Indirect Perspectives

Perspective	Major features	Development
Von Helmholtz	Dualistic Distance perception in three dimensions from two-dimensional retinal images requires processing to enhance two-dimensional information	Learning to better process information and use previous experience
Mechanistic	Dualistic Environmental objects known to perceivers by physical energy Impoverished input that must be extensively processed to recreate reality Stimuli defined by physical variables	Learning to better process impoverished input
Behaviorist (Watson, Skinner)	Dualistic Environmental antecedents to behavioral consequences, with reinforcers subsequently increasing (positive reinforcement) or decreasing (negative reinforcement) the probability of the behavior Data-based observation of behavior	
Information processing/cybernetic (Connolly)	Dualistic Sequential processing steps between input and behavior, many involving memory Motor programs	Learning to better process input as individual processes become more adultlike.

Consider a teenager playing first base in baseball or softball. The player sees the batter strike the ball and sees the ball bouncing until it is within reach. According to the stimulus–response perspective, the player perceives the ball at successive moments in time and the brain uses these discrete perceptions to calculate the future position of the ball. At the point when the ball is on course to bounce up and hit the player in the face, the player is able to move the hands to intercept the ball. Knowledge of where to intercept the ball is built from perceptions that arrive in succession. Thus the stimuli are like individual frames of a movie film that must be processed in order to be viewed as an event (see figure 2.2).

In the indirect perspective, stimuli are impoverished. They do not provide complete information about events and objects in the environment. Cognitive operations embellish the input, adding to it to enrich the mental representation of the event or object. In talking about visual stimuli, Neisser (1967, p. 3) stated that patterns of light arriving at the retina "bear little resemblance to either the real object that gave rise to them or to the object of experience that the perceiver will construct as a result." Researchers who adopt the perspective of indirect perception typically hold that *memory* is the primary source of the embellishments to impoverished stimuli. Memory must be involved in order for the person to know that discrete stimuli are actually events and that two-dimensional images on the retina are three-dimensional objects in the environment.

Figure 2.2 Indirect modeling of an approaching ball features a large number of successive snapshots, the information from which is combined (processed) centrally to project an interception point.

Photo courtesy of Kathleen Haywood.

The indirect perspective partitions stimuli. The various senses provide an example of this concept. When an event occurs, such as when a tennis ball is hit to a player, the player has perceptions in more than one sense. The tennis player sees the moving racket strike the ball and the ball start on an approaching trajectory, so there is a visual sensation and resulting visual perception. The player also hears the racket hit the ball, so there is an auditory sensation and resulting auditory perception. How are the separate perceptions connected such that the player knows they come from a single event? Psychologists have examined this question and their results have implications for understanding motor development. This research area examines how infants integrate perceptions from different senses into one event. An important feature of the indirect perspective, then, is the separateness of stimuli and the requirement that the

perceiver act upon, or mentally process, separate stimuli to bring them together when appropriate.

Another feature of the indirect perspective is that the validity of what a person knows is determined by how accurately a mental representation maps onto the environment. A person's conceptual scheme is good if it corresponds to the actual external world. *Meaning* in this dualistic framework involves relative correspondence between a person's idea of an object or event and the actual environmental object or event (Heft, 2001).

Historical Roots

The indirect perspective reflects the influence of Hermann von Helmholtz's 19th century writings (Heft, 2001) on 20th-century psychology. Von Helmholtz had a particular interest in the perception of distance. He recognized that judgments of the distance between a perceiver and an object involve a three-dimensional world and a two-dimensional image of that world on the retina. Von Helmholtz argued that people judge distance by going beyond the information from the two-dimensional retinal image and processing the information to add to the two-dimensional information. Development of distance perception is a matter of learning how to become better at processing information. Distance judgments use previous experiences.

The roots of dualism date to the early 17th century and to the Cartesian perspective. The Cartesian perspective is a worldview based largely on the work of great scientists such as Descartes (after whom the perspective is named), Galileo, Kepler, and Newton. These scientists took a natural science approach that sought to identify the universal principles for the natural order (Berlin, 1980; Heft, 2001). Their perspective is dualistic because they viewed the physical laws that govern the environment as separate from mental processes, which they believed do not follow physical laws.

Objects and inert matter of the environment can be located with respect to the three Cartesian coordinates and an abstract time dimension (Burtt, 1954). Objects are known to perceivers by physical energy, such as light energy in the case of vision, mechanical energy in the case of audition or touch, and so on. Hence, the objects of the environment interact mechanically and follow natural laws. The natural order, as reflected in the laws of the physical and biological sciences, explains the environment. Psychologists today describe the environment in much the same way that Galileo, Descartes, and Newton described it; this approach is called a *mechanistic viewpoint*. For a good part of the history of psychology, researchers have modeled experimental methodologies after the physical science approach.

Of course, the mechanistic view of the environment emphasizes the separateness of body and mind. The limited nature of stimuli coming to the perceiver (i.e., the impoverished input) requires the mind to use extensive processing to recreate the reality of the world.

Behaviorism

The major principles of behaviorism, one of the most influential schools of psychology, are well known. The behaviorist perspective, as articulated by the

father of behaviorism, John B. Watson, emphasizes the objective measure of behavior. Mental states, introspection, and consciousness are dismissed as entities of study. Watson described psychology from the behaviorist perspective as "a purely objective experimental branch of natural science. Its theoretical goal is the prediction and control of behavior" (1913, pp. 158-177). He felt that a person can study only what a person can observe.

How does behaviorism relate to our discussion of perception and action? Interestingly, Watson did not address perception in his articulation of behaviorism. This omission might have doomed behaviorism as a perspective that overlooked something as important as perception if not for the revisions of B.F. Skinner. Skinner stressed the relationship between environmental antecedents and behavioral consequences. He promoted the notion of a positive reinforcer that increases the probability of behavior that precedes it and a negative reinforcer that reduces the probability of behavior preceding it.

Behaviorism also encompasses a dualistic perspective. Watson rejected unobservable mental entities, such that only observable physical entities remained. Yet, psychology for Watson became the study of the physical world and bodily processes, or observable behaviors. The behaviorists thus helped the persistence of the dualistic perspective, through the separateness of the physical world, even if their support was unintended.

An important legacy of behaviorism is the observation of behavior through data-based methods. Data-based experimental methods had been used earlier in psychology, but in the decades following the publication of Watson's seminal works in 1913, 1925, and 1930, psychologists embraced the data-driven study of human behavior. This aspect of behaviorism is consistent with the Cartesian approach of applying experimental methodologies from the natural sciences to human behavior. Boosted by Skinner's work in operant conditioning, psychologists embarked on decades of empirical work using data-based observation of human behavior and its development.

Information-Processing Models

Models of behavior based on the indirect or stimulus–response perspective typically are labeled *information-processing* or *cybernetic* models. The similarity between this view of human behavior and the way early computers worked is the reason for using the word *cybernetic*. The stimuli perceived by humans are similar to the input fed to a computer. A computer processes the information, or input, in stages and then generates output. In humans, information must be processed between the stimulus input and the behavior output. That is, sequential processing steps, many involving memory, intervene between input and output. These sequential steps are akin to a computer program. Hence the notion of programs that control movement, or motor programs.

In the late 1960s and the 1970s it was popular to picture more and more elaborate information-processing models. Simple models started with representations for stimuli, responses, and perceptual feedback resulting from responses, which subsequently becomes new input (see figure 2.3). These simple models were often called *black box models* because all the intervening cognitive processing

was represented by one box between input and output, without a proposition for the various sequential steps involved in processing.

Models became more elaborate as psychologists attempted to explain how perceivers add to the impoverished input to recreate the real world comprising the environment, its features, and its objects. Often depicted were filtering mechanisms for the sensory input, memory (iconic, short term, and long term), attentional mechanisms, and choice-of-response functions (see figure 2.4; Broadbent, 1958; Fitts, 1962, 1964; Marteniuk,1976; Stallings, 1973, 1976; Welford, 1960, 1968, 1976; Whiting, 1970, 1972). These depictions were of functions rather than anatomical centers in the nervous system, although ultimately researchers sought to link functions to anatomical structures. These more elaborate models also depicted the sequential processing stages, ordered in time, necessary to arrive at a response.

Information-processing models drove much of the research on human behavior and its development during this time. Stimuli were varied so that the effect on the response could be observed. For example, in researching the relatively simple behavior of reaction time, researchers varied the strength (loudness, brightness, and so on) of the stimulus to see if a reaction would be faster or slower. Or, they gave a warning signal to observe how that warning affected speed of reaction. Another reason why researchers systematically manipulated stimuli was to observe how responses changed so that they could hypothesize about the intervening central processes (recall that brain imaging tools were not available at the time). For example, they hypothesized that information is sent back and forth to a long-term memory center so that the sensed object or event can be identified. They also hypothesized the existence of a choice delay that represents the time required to select the appropriate response. Researchers also

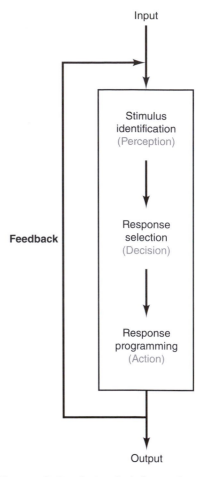

Figure 2.3 A simple information-processing model. This kind of model is sometimes called a *black box model* because the central box represents a large number of central nervous system functions and locations thought to be necessary for processing so that action can be taken.

Adapted, by permission, from R. Schmidt and G. Wrisberg, 2007, *Motor learning and performance*, 4th ed. (Champaign, IL: Human Kinetics), 30.

studied variations in feedback and the resulting effect on responses. For example, feedback could be restricted by blindfolding performers or embellished by supplementing feedback with additional information.

One of the hypothesized central functions drew much attention. This was the function of selecting a response appropriate for the sensory information forming the input. Researchers quickly saw that there are an almost infinite

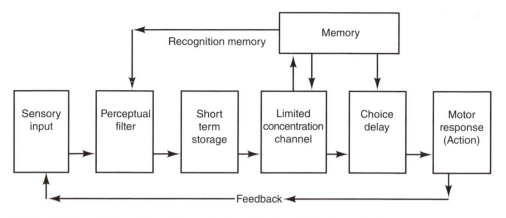

Figure 2.4 Researchers elaborated on the simple black box information-processing models. Although they lacked tools of today, such as magnetic resonance imaging (MRI), by varying stimuli and observing the response, they could hypothesize functions of the brain involved in processing information to develop elaborated models such as the one shown here.

Reprinted from *Motor Learning from Theory to Practice,* L.M. Stallings, Copyright 1982, with permission from Elsevier.

number of stimuli and an almost infinite number of responses and often very little time to link a stimulus with the appropriate response. This led researchers to hypothesize, consistent with the cybernetic model, that performers possess motor programs akin to computer programs. A motor program was envisioned as a set of commands within the motor system that provides the detail for muscle activity and hence the performance of a movement response without much modification. Some theorists hypothesized that there are hierarchical motor programs containing subprograms, or central pattern generators, that are specific neural circuits for a type of movement, such as walking. For a given stimulus an executive function in the brain selects the correct motor program and the program controls the response. The executive function in this process came to be called the *homunculus* (see figure 2.5). The roots of the word *homunculus* come from the Latin word for "little man."

The root of differences in movement over the lifespan lies largely in the hypothesized central functions. Hence, the information-processing model provided a straightforward paradigm for studying motor development.

Developmental Study

Without tools to observe cognitive processing directly, researchers commonly approached developmental research from the indirect perspective by varying the stimulus or the response of a motor task presented to performers of differing ages. The researchers then compared the responses of children, adults, and older adults as the task and feedback about performance were changed. They then hypothesized which central processes likely accounted for the differences. For example, they might attribute performance differences to richer memories

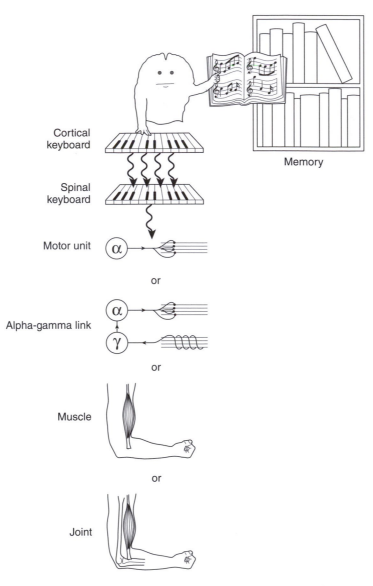

Figure 2.5 Information-processing models feature the notion of an executive function or a homunculus that directs muscle activity as if playing a cortical keyboard.

Reprinted from "Human Motor Behavior: An Introduction" by J.A.S. Kelso (Ed.), 1982, p. 240. Copyright 1982 by Lawrence Erlbaum Associates.

of performance conditions in adults compared with children, to slowness in memory retrieval in older adults compared with younger adults, or to age-related differences in response programming.

Often, the limits of perception were explored. For example, researchers compared the responses of infants, young adults, and older adults to a range of sound frequencies. The researchers could then identify the range of stimuli that could

be perceived at certain ages. A common assumption of the indirect perspective is that infants initially experience pieces of information from each sensory system separately as an unorganized array of stimuli. The task of developing infants is to learn how to integrate information from the various systems.

Let's consider several studies conducted from the indirect perspective. Clark (1987) compared kindergartners, fourth graders, and adults on a choice reaction time and movement time task with two stimulus choices and three levels of response complexity. In the easiest response, participants depressed two response keys, one with the right index finger and one with the left. They were to lift the finger corresponding to one of two stimulus lights. In the moderate task, participants lifted the appropriate key and then moved to press a second key. In the most complex task, participants lifted the appropriate key, moved to press the second key, and then moved to press a third key. Clark found that fourth graders were slower than adults in reaction time, but there was no difference between these two age groups for complexity of the response. Kindergartners were always slower than the fourth graders and the adults, but they were much slower in the most complex task.

The fourth graders were also slower than the adults in movement time, and they again took slightly longer to move in the most complex condition. The kindergartners, as expected, were slower than the other groups, but they were slower in the moderate condition than they were in the most complex condition. In the complex condition the kindergartners took longer to react but moved more quickly to the second response key. They traded off reaction time and movement time depending on the response complexity. Clark suggested that these results demonstrated an increased capacity with age to program complex movements before initiating them. The youngest children appeared to preplan movement only when the task was the most complex. Hence, Clark manipulated a task's stimulus and its response complexity to address age-related differences in response programming.

Clark and colleagues (Clark, Lanphear, & Riddick, 1987) also used an information-processing model to examine the response speed of older adults. Age-related declines in speed had become a general observation. Clark et al. pretested older adults on a two-choice reaction time task under two levels of stimulus–response compatibility. In the compatible condition participants lifted the finger under the light that came on but in the low compatibility condition lifted the finger on the opposite side of the light that came on. Some of the older adults followed the pretest with 7 weeks of video game practice; the others did not practice. The researchers found that adults who practiced were faster when tested again, especially in the low compatibility condition. They suggested that these results reflect an improvement in response selection by older adults who practiced—that is, the researchers related an aspect of information processing in a portion of the lifespan to a variation in the task and to practice.

Thomas, Mitchell, and Solmon (1979) compared second and fourth graders on their use of knowledge of results—that is, feedback about performance. The children performed an arm-positioning task while their view of their arm was blocked, and the researchers provided knowledge of results that varied from no

information to general information (only directional information, long or short) to precise information (how far long or short). The children of each age were divided into three groups, and each group received one of the three levels of knowledge of results. They then had 40 trials to learn the task and 20 additional trials without any knowledge of results. Compared with the younger children, the older children were better able to maintain their performance when knowledge of results was no longer available. Precision of knowledge of results made little difference to the younger children, but the older children who received more precise information maintained performance at a higher level compared with those who received general information. Thomas et al. suggested that their results reflected the fourth graders' superior ability to label and code the knowledge of results information for long-term memory. They also suggested the younger children could not process the precise information they received during the learning phase as well as the older children could. This study demonstrated how varying knowledge of results that became input for subsequent performances could address the central processes—that is, the processing of information between stimulus and response. Thomas (1980) reviewed much of the existing literature on applications of the information-processing model to performance differences between children and adults and related the information to a range of central processes involving memory, including rehearsal, labeling, grouping, and coding.

▶ Tips for Novice Investigators

No doubt you can see how relatively easy it is to conduct research on development from an information-processing perspective. There are numerous stimuli that can be presented to performers of various ages so that response differences can be recorded. Performance feedback that might strengthen or weaken a response can also be varied in numerous ways, such as by precision or timing. After considering the Clark et al. (1987) and Thomas et al. (1979) studies, you could probably design two or three additional studies related to theirs. As we continue our discussion, though, consider the disadvantages of indirect approaches, starting with the notion that studies from this perspective are in fact indirect. Behavior control is not observed directly but rather inferred. Note, too, the singular emphasis on the central nervous system in the control of movement.

Researchers soon began to question information processing as an adequate model for several reasons. First, there is the homunculus notion (Tuller, Turvey, & Fitch, 1982). Who directs the little man in the head in selecting the appropriate response or motor program? It's possible to hypothesize that there is a little man within the little man, but obviously there is no logical end to this chain. Second, there is the storage problem. Memory capacity would have to be vast in order to store motor programs for what seems like an infinite number of movements produced by humans in response to an infinite number of environmental conditions.

A third issue is the novelty problem. Humans obviously perform new movements or new variations of learned movements, and they often do so successfully. If movements are executed via motor programs, how do we get the program for the first executed movement and how can our initial attempt sometimes be successful? The computer analogy leaves unanswered questions, and thus the information-processing approach became problematic in the views of more and more researchers. The unanswered questions were particularly problematic for developmentalists, especially the novelty issue in studies of infants and toddlers. The information-processing approach to motor learning and control did advance the field and should by no means be considered a poor model. Nevertheless, by the late 1980s many researchers were ready for new approaches to both questions about the role of the environment and questions about how movement is controlled.

As we now turn to discuss direct perception, remember that much of the available information about human behaviors and their development was gathered from research conducted from the indirect perspective. Understanding this perspective and its underlying assumptions allows us to more effectively interpret the results of research studies built on the indirect approach.

DIRECT PERSPECTIVE

The direct perspective, or ecological view, of perception and action differs fundamentally from the indirect perspective, especially regarding the nature of stimulation and the role that memory might or might not play in giving meaning to perception. The performer perceives environmental objects, events, and places directly from sensations impinging on the sensory receptors. Less research on human behavior and development has been conducted from this perspective. Yet, the direct perspective provides an intriguing view of perception and action.

Historical Roots

The roots of direct perception and ecological psychology can be found in William James' philosophy of radical empiricism (see table 2.2). We mentioned earlier that von Helmholtz, in writing about distance perception, greatly influenced the thinking of psychologists. William James was one of a few psychologists who thought differently than von Helmholtz. James argued that distance is an inherent quality of vision, is perceived immediately, and is available without the need for processing of visual stimulation.

James used radical empiricism to deal with some of the problems, as he saw them, imposed on psychology by the Cartesian tradition and to provide a perspective more compatible with evolutionary theory. He adopted a biological and evolutionary perspective that attempted to tie analyses of mental functioning to biological, especially brain, processes. James embraced reciprocity between animal and environment and attributed their interdependency to their mutual evolutionary history. In his later writings James clearly rejected dualism.

James and his seminal works, *The Principles of Psychology* (1890) and *Essays in Radical Empiricism* (1912/1976), drew a great deal of attention from psycholo-

Table 2.2   Direct Perspectives

Perspective	Major features	Development
James	Ecological Perceiving distance is an inherent quality of vision Interdependent performer and environment evolved mutually through history	
Gestalt	Metaphysical dualism Environmental objects convey meaning to individuals Mind transforms and organizes sensory data	
Gibson	Ecological Stimuli defined by information for action Information a performer needs is available in the stimuli and does not need embellishment Affordance is the individual perception of the functional significance of objects, events, or places and is specific to the perceiver Events are perceived in unified space-time	Detecting affordances, exploring movement capabilities in relation to the environment, and learning and remembering the consequences of movements

gists in the early 1900s. However, his works did little to change the thinking of the vast majority, whose viewpoint remained the Cartesian perspective. Edwin B. Holt was a student of James, though, and Holt later mentored James J. Gibson (see figure 2.6), who is considered to be the father of direct perception (the ecological view; Gibson, 1950, 1960, 1966, 1979).

Gibson began formulating his ideas toward the end of World War II. During the war, psychologists intensified their study of depth and distance perception in aviation. Estimating the distance to the ground when landing an airplane was a major challenge to pilots in training. Psychologists realized that typical measures of depth and distance perception administered in the dark or against a homogeneous background didn't predict a pilot's success or failure in landing a plane. The notion began to emerge that perception of space requires perception of a continuous background surface (Gibson, 1950). When Gibson later

Figure 2.6   James J. Gibson.
Photo courtesy of Division of Rare and Manuscript Collections, Cornell University Library.

articulated ecological psychology, though, he was mostly a lone voice given little, especially empirical, attention for many years. Gibson considered his wife, Eleanor Gibson, a partner in developing ecological psychology.

Eleanor Gibson in particular focused on developmental issues from this perspective. We will explore some of her work later.

Features of Direct Perspective

According to the direct perspective the performer perceives environmental objects, events, and places directly from sensations impinging on sensory receptors. This requires a very different notion of stimulus when compared to that of the indirect perspective. Gibson (1950, 1960, 1966, 1979) articulated this difference. While indirect or traditional researchers defined stimuli by physical variables, Gibson defined stimuli in terms of information for action, or structures that specify the environment to a performer in terms of actions that can be performed upon it. These structures are complex and perceived over time. Consider a park bench, for example. A researcher holding the indirect perspective defines a visual stimulus associated with a park bench in terms of wavelength and intensity, while a researcher holding the direct perspective focuses on the changing image of the park bench on the retina as the performer walks toward it (thus specifying distance from the bench) and the actions (such as sitting) the bench makes possible due to its height and width in relation to the size of the performer.

From the direct perspective, stimulation is rich and unambiguous from the outset. The information a perceiver needs to know about acting on the environment is available in stimulation without any embellishment or processing on the part of the perceiver. Also, stimulation is a continuous event, an ongoing occurrence, rather than a series of discrete stimuli later assembled by processing. In fact, from the direct perspective, perception is of events rather than isolated objects (Michaels & Carello, 1981). Events are nested, and longer events are perceived by detecting continuity of briefer events rather than by adding together discrete parts.

One of Gibson's most intriguing ideas was that of the *affordance*. An affordance is an individual's perception of the *functional* significance of an object, event, or place in the environment—that is, what can the person do with the object? It is also defined as the action or actions that objects, events, or places in the environment *permit*. Imagine a parking lot with a black asphalt surface. On a summer day it allows a driver to sprint across the asphalt to a parked car. On a damp winter day with freezing temperatures, that same lot might not afford sprinting but rather careful walking. A second example is a golf club that affords, or permits, a tall man to strike a golf ball. The same golf club would not afford striking a golf ball to a 6-year-old (see figure 2.7). On the other hand, a golf club scaled down in length and weight does afford striking to the 6-year-old. A chair with a knee-high seat affords sitting for adults but not necessarily toddlers (for whom the seat is at chest height), and it would not afford sitting for adults if someone mounted that chair on 6-foot (1.8 m) stilts (the seat is now at head height)! Affordances are specific to individuals (although groups of like individuals share affordances), and it is the affordance that an individual perceives. That is, individuals perceive what actions are possible in the environment.

Note that affordances reflect a system involving both person and environment. Affordances defy dualism. They imply an active perceiver. Meaning is a feature of perceiving rather than something attached to stimuli *after* information is processed, as in the indirect perspective. We can use the term *ecosystem* to describe the person and environment taken together. Gibson also used the term *niche*, saying that "in ecology a niche is a setting of environmental features that are suitable for an animal, into which it fits metaphorically" (1979, p. 129). Also, "a niche refers more to *how* an animal lives than to *where* it lives. I suggest that a niche is a set of affordances" (1979, p. 128). Living creatures and the environment evolved together. Thus, people and animals evolved to detect affordances—the information *useful* to acting and surviving in the environment, the information that has meaning. Performers, or as Gibson termed them, *actors*, can alter the affordances of the environment but must remain within the environment.

Figure 2.7 An implement that affords an action to a person of large size might not afford that action to a person of small size.

Photo courtesy of Kathleen Haywood.

The notion of an affordance is a controversial aspect of direct perception because of its relational feature: By definition, an affordance is specific to the perceiver. A sledgehammer affords striking to a large, strong individual but not to a small, slight individual. Traditionally, researchers studying perception have considered environmental objects, places, and events and their properties to be constant. That is, researchers have held that shape, mass, location, and so on are invariant across perceivers, so that the attributes of an object or surface are independent of an individual. For those who prefer the indirect perspective, the relational aspect of affordances, wherein attributes are a function of an active perceiver, is problematic.

Dualism is rejected in the direct perspective. The individual and the environment each owe their identity to the other. The relationship between them is one of mutuality and reciprocity (Gibson, 1979; Heft, 2001). It is also a dynamic relationship because the individual can both seek out certain aspects of the environment and adjust features of the environment, often to better fit with a desired action. Features of the environment can lead to the individual making adjustments in the environment, and those adjustments in turn change the environment. According to Gibson, "the words animal and environment make an inseparable pair. Each term implies the other" (1979, p. 8). Note that

in describing this dynamic relationship Gibson generalized actors to include animals as well as humans.

Reaching to grasp an object provides a good example of reciprocity. While it is possible for humans to execute a reaching and grasping movement without the intention of obtaining an environmental object, functionally that is not what we do. Rather, we reach and grasp with the goal of obtaining or adjusting objects. We reach *toward* something, thus adapting the biomechanics of the reach. The size, shape, weight, and texture of the object form a structure, and we perceive the structure in order to determine that the object is graspable and that our hand needs to be oriented in a particular way to grasp it.

The relational nature of actor and environment is also demonstrated in Gibson's articulation of another feature of direct perception—*optical flow*. Optical flow is the visual streaming of environmental features that occurs as an individual moves in the environment. If the performer moves forward in a stable environment, an outward flow pattern, or expansion, of optical textures is perceived (see figure 2.8). This pattern is called an *expanding optical array*. If the performer moves backward in a stable environment, the optical textures flow inward, or contract. If the performer rotates, the borders of the field of view change but the size of optical texture units remains constant (Fitch, Tuller, & Turvey, 1982).

Figure 2.8 Optical flow. As we approach objects their images expand on our retinas.
Photo courtesy of Kathleen Haywood.

Stand in the middle of a room and focus on a point on the far wall. Walk toward that point and notice how the images of objects in the room expand. Walk backward and watch how they shrink. Now rotate in place and notice how the sides of the room on the edge of your view slide, while the images of objects in the room remain constant. If you stand still as an object approaches, the optical array at the location of the object expands while the optical texture of things behind the approaching object is deleted. Thus, transforming optical arrays provides information about the mutuality of perceiver and environment. Gibson noted that parts of the actor's body are in the field of view and occlude environmental features in unique ways. The optical information about self *"accompanies* the optical information to specify the environment. The two sources of information co-exist" (Gibson, 1979, p. 116). The optical array provides direct information

about movement in and of the environment. There need not be any processing of sensory information through successive stages to identify the nature of movement. Again, we can see how direct perception rejects the notion of dualism, in which the individual and environment are separated by mental processing.

Another interesting aspect of direct perception involves the information contained in the energy patterns of stimuli. If processing of stimulus information is not required, as proponents of direct perception hold, then the information a person needs in order to know the environment must be in those energy patterns. The patterns must be uniquely linked to the objects, events, and locations in the environment, and they must not be changed by certain transformations. Hence, these patterns of stimulation are termed *invariants*. They are left unchanged by transformations. For example, while you are viewing a square picture of a friend on your computer screen, you can change the dimensions to make the picture taller than wide or wider than tall. Though doing so transforms your friend into a taller, thinner person or a shorter, broader person, you are still able to recognize your friend.

Or, imagine you are standing on one end of a basketball court and looking at a basketball on the far end line. As you walk the length of the court toward the ball, the image of the ball occupies a larger and larger space on the retina of your eye. Yet, you don't assume the ball is getting bigger; you assume you are getting closer. This phenomenon is called *perceptual constancy*. Direct perceptionists attribute perceptual (in this case, size) constancy to invariants, patterns of stimulation conveying surface brightness and intensity of illumination that are in turn related to the inclination or orientation of surfaces. This complex structure of stimulation conveys information that is the basis for size constancy. Note that indirect perceptionists conceive of a simpler pattern of stimulation that involves just the amount of light from the ball reaching the retina. It is the experience of the perceiver combined with the stimulus that is processed and allows the perceiver to know that the size of the ball remains constant.

Time is viewed differently from the direct perspective than it is from the indirect perspective. We saw earlier that, from the indirect perspective, perceptions are assembled from discrete stimuli—that is, slices of time are assembled such that events are constructed. There are past, present, and future stimuli. Traditional researchers, then, study only the stimuli in the present; they view perceivers as dealing with a succession of nows. Space and time are separated in order to understand how perceivers gain knowledge of the environment through successive assemblies of discrete time slices.

From the ecological perspective, perceivers know the environment from events over time; change itself is what is perceived. Rather than perceiving space and perceiving time and then integrating the two, as the indirect perspective proposes, individuals perceive events in unified space-time (Michaels & Carello, 1981). Perception and the information it provides are available continuously rather than in snatches of time that must be assembled into events.

This has been a necessarily brief overview of direct perception. Far more information is available elsewhere (see Heft, 2001; Michaels & Carello, 1981). In summary, within the direct perception perspective the unit of analysis is

the ecosystem, which is a system comprising person and environment. People have evolved in the environment, and the natural (ecological) condition of the environment is paramount; people perceive the environment in terms of action; and people are active rather than passive actors in their environments.

Gestalt Psychology

You might wonder about the relationship between the Gestalt perspective and the ecological perspective, perhaps noting similarities between the two. Psychologists working in the Gestalt tradition influenced the direct perspective notion of affordances, as they, too, were influenced by the radical empiricism of William James. Gestalt psychologists hold that environmental objects convey meaning to individuals. Koffka and Lewin were particularly influential in articulating notions similar to the notion of affordance in ecological psychology (Gibson, 1979). For example, Koffka (1935, p. 7) wrote that "a fruit says, 'Eat me'; water says, 'Drink me.'" We can see the similarity to the notion of an affordance.

Gestalt psychology features mental categories by which sensory data become organized perceptions. Gestalt psychologists emphasize the mind's role in transforming and organizing experienced sensory data. That is, they view perception as the interaction between physical characteristics of stimuli and mental laws that follow an observer's experiences (Robinson, 1995). Much of the early experimental work conducted by Gestalt psychologists involved apparent movement. For example, we can see movement when viewing frames that are rapidly presented in succession with small changes in image position. The movement is not in the stimulus; rather, the observer creates the movement. The Gestalt emphasis on structure in perceptual experience and the pursuit of meanings and values in experience overlaps with Gibson's ecological psychology.

There also are critical differences between Gibson's ecological perspective and the Gestalt perspective. Gestalt psychologists generally accept some type of metaphysical dualism or distinction between mind and world (Heft, 2001). Koffka made a distinction between the geographical environment and the behavioral environment. Gibson clearly rejected this mind–world distinction in articulating direct perception. Also, the empirical work of Gestalt psychologists is based on physical science, while the empirical work of ecological psychologists is based on biological science.

Perception and Action

Gibson's fundamental notion of person–environment reciprocity eventually resulted in increased research attention on how perceptual information modulates action. This work is described as the study of perception and action. A perception–action perspective takes on certain features distinct from the information-processing perspective of movements generated by motor programs. Bertenthal and Clifton (1998) outlined these features, which we review in brief here.

The perception–action perspective allows for the slight variations in movement that occur from response to response. These variations can be due to starting positions of the limbs, loads on the limbs, inertia of the moving limbs,

and reactive forces. Yet, the same goal-directed behavior can be achieved consistently despite these variations. The perception–action perspective holds that this is possible because perceptual information can modulate the active muscle forces during movement. Coordinated actions are viewed as functional units or action systems rather than movements uniquely controlled from response to response (Reed, 1982).

Since change always occurs as movement is carried out, meaning that movement always creates disequilibrium, it is unlikely that actions are just a series of reactions to intermittent stimuli. Perception and action must be coupled throughout a movement. Moreover, perceptual information must be prospective in the control of movement. Obviously there is some time lag for neural conduction, and moving limbs possess inertia. These factors dictate anticipation of future movement (von Hofsten, 1993).

Recall Gibson's notion of an affordance. The environment and its objects are functionally defined in terms of an observer's body size and characteristics as well as level of motor skill. Whether an action should be executed depends on an observer perceiving both environment and self. For example, people determine whether the riser height of the staircase in front of them affords walking up the stairs with an alternate step pattern based on their body proportions (Warren, 1984).

Traditional information-processing models assume that different sensory systems gather different sources of perceptual information. Exteroceptors such as those in the eyes and ears gather sensations from the external environmental while proprioceptors such as those in the joints, muscles, and tendons detect information about the self. From the perception–action perspective most perceptual systems provide exteroceptive and proprioceptive information (Gibson, 1966). The implication for development is that infants and children must learn to differentiate perceptual information specifying the self from information specifying the environment (Gibson & Schmuckler, 1989).

Proponents of direct perception consider the development of perception and action to be mutual and reciprocal (Bertenthal, 1996). Greater perceptual differentiation gives children more precise information for controlling action. Improvements in coordinating movements and scaling movements appropriately demand greater perceptual differentiation (Bertenthal & Clifton, 1998).

Developmental Study

As empirical work from the perception–action perspective has increased, so has the portion of that work focusing on development, even of infants. The early work of James J. and Eleanor Gibson included a focus on how infants coordinate their movement with concurrent perceptual information (Gibson, 1982, 1988; Gibson, 1979; Lockman, 1990). A central question became how infants acquire affordances. Eleanor Gibson and her colleagues began a line of work to address this question. They explored the texture and slope of surfaces in studies with crawling and walking infants (Gibson et al., 1987; Adolph, Eppler, & Gibson, 1993). We examine this empirical work in more detail later; it suggests that even infants detect affordances and that they explore their movement capabilities in

relation to their environment, learning and remembering the consequences of their movements (Thelen, 1995).

Empirical work from the direct and perception–action perspective on the integration of sensory modalities also suggests that infants possess integrated **multimodal perception**. This finding implies that the nervous system is made to integrate information from different sensory modalities (Damasio, 1989; Stein & Meredith, 1993). If so, our perceptions are coherent in time and space from the start. This idea contrasts with the indirect perspective notion that the initial experience of infants is a confusing, unorganized array of light, sounds, and feels. The task for infants in this latter case is to learn to integrate the various perceptual systems. Piaget (1952, 1954) also proposed that infants must learn to coordinate sensory information across modalities.

An example of the evidence for integrated, multimodal perception in infants comes from studying postural control. Visual, proprioceptive, and vestibular information provide redundant sensory input for postural control. A commonly used paradigm in studying infant postural control is to place infants on a stationary floor in a room (within a room) whose walls and ceiling can be moved. If the room is moved, the associated visual information can elicit a postural compensation. Lee and Aronson (1974) first showed that standing infants can make an appropriate response. Bertenthal and Bai (1989) then demonstrated that infants just capable of independent sitting can also respond appropriately. Jouen (1990) even showed that newborns make postural compensations of their heads in response to visual flow information. These studies indicate that at very young ages infants make a single motor response to multiple sensory inputs and show no evidence of needing to learn how multiple sensory inputs are related to one another. We consider the research on postural control in more detail in chapter 5.

▶ Tips for Novice Investigators

The debate over how perceptions from our various sensory systems come together for the same objects or events illustrates the difference between the indirect and direct perspectives. You can more closely examine how the differences between the two perspectives play out in experimental studies by doing some additional reading. To better appreciate indirect perception, search a psychology database of journal articles for sensory integration in infants. To better appreciate the direct perspective, read some of the studies on infants in moving rooms referenced in this chapter.

Another example of multimodal perception occurs when newborns imitate the facial gestures adults make to them (Anisfeld, 1991). The newborns can see the adults' gestures but can feel only their own face. It appears that actions are typically guided by multimodal information. This allows infants to rapidly develop adaptive behaviors such as sitting, reaching, and walking. The redundant

information is available to modulate actions in response to a changing context for movement (Bertenthal, 1996).

The perception–action model of development, then, proposes an actor who generates perceptual experiences through action, exploring the environment and selecting experiences and retaining correlated perceptions and actions to function in the world (Thelen, 1995). In subsequent chapters we go beyond these few examples of developmental research from a direct or perception–action perspective and consider how the adoption of this perspective informs research on the development of posture and manipulative skills.

A RESOLUTION?

If you expect the two perspectives on the relationship between perception and action to provide different answers to the same questions, you likely will be disappointed. In many cases, the researchers adopting each perspective ask very different questions. The great value of understanding and appreciating each perspective is putting the empirical work from each perspective into a context. Researchers might use the term *perception and action* for a range of differing perspectives, so readers must recognize the fundamental positions and assumptions of each perspective to put research results into a context and identify the limitations of those results.

Is a resolution beyond hope? Melvyn Goodale and David Milner have provided interesting research information that could shed some light on how the two fundamentally different perspectives might be resolved. Their work has stimulated others to consider what are now termed ***dual-processing theories***.

Dual-Processing Theories of Visual Processing

In their text *Sight Unseen*, Goodale and Milner (2005) describe work with several individuals. The first, Dee F., experienced carbon monoxide poisoning. The accident left her with visual form agnosia. She could see the color and texture of objects but not their form or shape.

To understand the implications of visual form agnosia, consider a test Goodale and Milner conducted with Dee F. They presented Efron rectangles that all had the same surface area but had different lengths and widths (see figure 2.9) to Dee F. in pairs, and she was to say if they were the same or different. Dee F. performed at a chance level for all but the most extreme rectangle, which was very long in length and short in width. One day during their work Goodale and Milner realized that Dee F. could reach for and grasp an object just as a person without visual form agnosia would, orienting her hand to both the shape and the orientation of the object. Thus, when Dee F. *acted*, she could do so based on the shapes of objects. She performed just like healthy participants when picking up blocks shaped like the Efron rectangles, orienting her hand in the most efficient direction (Carey, Harvey, & Milner, 1996). Likewise, Dee F. performed like healthy participants when walking over obstacles of varying height, raising her leg just enough to allow her foot to clear each obstacle. Yet she could not look at the obstacles and estimate their heights.

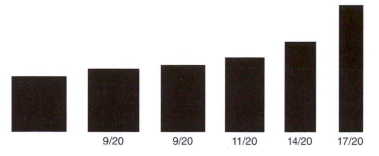

9/20   9/20   11/20   14/20   17/20

Figure 2.9   Efron rectangles that have the same area but vary in lengths and widths. In their experiment, Goodale and Milner showed Dee F. pairs of shapes—such as a square and a rectangle—and asked whether the two were the same or different. Shown below each rectangle is the number of correct responses out of 20 Dee F. gave after comparing each of these rectangles to the reference square on the far left. For rectangles similar to the square, Dee responded approximately at the level of chance.

Reprinted from *Sight unseen* by M. Goodale and A. D. Milner, 2004, p. 15, fig. 1.4. By permission of Oxford University Press. Copyright 2004 by Oxford University Press. www.oup.com

Goodale and Milner also worked with Ruth V., a subject who had experienced two strokes, one on each side of the brain, and was left with optic ataxia. Optic ataxia is a deficiency in visually guided movements. Ruth V. did not adjust her hand when reaching for objects (Goodale et al., 1994). She always opened her hand wide. Many individuals with optic ataxia have intact visual perception, and Ruth V. was one of them. She could use her finger and thumb to show researchers how big she thought an object was. She also performed reasonably well when asked whether two shapes were the same or different. Thus Ruth V. performed in nearly the opposite pattern of Dee F.

The opposite patterns of ability and disability observed in Dee F. and Ruth V. provide a **double dissociation** (see table 2.3). Brain damage that affects one kind of task but not another cannot be attributed to one task being easier than the other. The other half of the double dissociation rules out that explanation. Goodale

Table 2.3   Double Dissociation Suggesting Quasi-Independent Brain Systems

Patient	Behavior	Neural pathway
Dee F.	Patient has difficulty with judgments of rectangles that are the same or different in length and width yet orients her hand to the shape and orientation of an object when reaching for it.	Primate work suggests this behavior occurs with damage to the ventral stream (primary visual area to inferior temporal cortex).
Ruth V.	Patient performs well in judging whether two shapes are the same or different but does not orient her hand when reaching for objects.	Primate work suggests this behavior occurs with damage to the dorsal stream (primary visual area to posterior parietal cortex).

and Milner (2005, p. 28) addressed the two opposing viewpoints of perception and action: "What a double dissociation can also suggest—but cannot prove—is that different, quasi-independent brain systems (or brain 'modules' as they are sometimes called) are handling each of the two abilities that are dissociated."

Goodale and Milner discussed work from many other areas of study that supports the proposal of two brain systems. First, work with primates has shown that damage to the **dorsal stream** results in a pattern of abilities and disabilities much like those of Ruth V. (Glickstein et al., 1980; Glickstein, Buchbinder, & May, 1998). The dorsal stream, or neural pathway, proceeds from the primary visual area of the brain to the posterior parietal cortex of the brain. In contrast, lesions of the **ventral stream** in monkeys produce symptoms of visual agnosia similar to those of Dee F. (Klüver & Bucy, 1939). The ventral stream proceeds from the primary visual area of the brain to the inferior temporal cortex of the brain.

Second, experimental work using electrical activity recordings of individual neurons has demonstrated that neurons in each stream code visual information differently. For example, some neurons in the dorsal stream fire only when a monkey actually responds (such as by reaching) to a target (Hyvärinen & Poranen, 1974; Mountcastle, Lynch, Georgopoulos, Skata, & Acuna, 1975). Some neurons in the ventral stream respond only when a monkey is shown a picture of a face (Gross, Rocha-Miranda, & Bender, 1972; Gross, Desimone, Albright, & Schwartz, 1985). In fact, the visual streams appear to be subdivided into smaller modules that have a specific function or extract a specific type of information from visual signals. Neurons in the two visual streams seem to function in a way that is consistent with the patterns of abilities and disabilities of patients with specific symptoms.

These types of experimental findings, as well as others (for a more complete discussion see Milner & Goodale, 2006), suggest that there is one visual system—the ventral stream of visual processing—that primarily translates visual stimuli to perceptions and a second visual system—the dorsal stream of visual processing—that primarily allows primates and humans to translate visual signals into action (see figure 2.10). Of course, the two systems are not completely independent. They must interact seamlessly.

It is possible that the behaviors explored by researchers working from an information-processing perspective are those that use the ventral stream of visual processing. That is, these researchers study behaviors that follow perception, such as reacting to a signal. They study the limits of sensation and the effects of blocking a perceptual system, such as the effects of performing a task blindfolded.

On the other hand, the behaviors explored by researchers working from a direct or perception–action perspective may tend to involve the dorsal stream of visual processing. These researchers study actions that require a dynamic

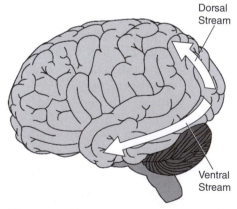

Figure 2.10 The ventral and dorsal streams.

interaction between the actor and the environment. For example, they might study adaptations to dynamic changes in the environment.

Thus the two streams of visual processing might account for how the two perspectives on the relationship between perception and action, although fundamentally different, have both yielded valuable information about behavior. They involve two separate but interactive processing systems in the brain that evolved to meet the need to control different types of behavior.

▶ Tips for Novice Investigators

After researchers began attending to the direct perspective and appreciating aspects of behavior that the direct perspective better explains, there was still the fact that the indirect perspective was valuable in explaining other aspects of behavior. Studies from the indirect perspective have yielded valuable information about behavior and development. Researchers face a dilemma if they must reject one perspective and favor the other.

The quasi-independent systems for visual processing suggest that the very behaviors researchers explored from the indirect or information-processing perspective were the very types processed through the ventral stream. The exact opposite is true for the behaviors studied from the direct perspective. Novice researchers can benefit from realizing that researchers typically study a particular type of behavior from a chosen perspective. A complete understanding eventually requires studying all types of behaviors from multiple perspectives. Researchers are not right or wrong in choosing a behavior to study or a perspective to adopt but are wise in remembering that each choice has its limitations.

Glover (2004a, 2004b) also has articulated two models of vision for action: the **planning–control model** and the **perception–action model**. The latter is similar to the hypotheses of Goodale and Milner. Both models propose that a ventral stream terminating in the inferotemporal cortex of the brain serves perception. But the planning–control model proposes that action planning involves the medial visual stream that terminates in the inferior parietal lobes while online control relies on the dorsal stream. The perception–action model proposes that both planning and control involve the single visual system located in the dorsal stream. While these two models have sparked debate (see Glover, 2004a and the following open peer commentary), the distinction between the planning of actions and the online control of actions could be a useful distinction in the study of motor development.

Interestingly, an area of developmental research on **scale errors** in young children might highlight the distinction between action planning and online control. Let's consider this area of research and what it suggests about the development of perception and action.

Scale Errors in Children

A group of researchers noted an occasional and interesting behavior in young children. They informally observed young children attempting an action on an

object even though the action was impossible because of the great size difference between the child and the object. For example, a child might try to sit in a doll's chair that was much too small, even for a young child. DeLoache, Uttal, and Rosengren (2004) tried to investigate these scale errors systematically. They let normally developing 18- to 30-month-olds play with three large objects—an indoor slide, a child-sized car, and a child-sized chair. They then replaced these objects with miniature replicas identical to the originals except for size.

The researchers then watched for any attempt at an action that constituted a scale error, such as an attempt to sit on the miniature chair, go down the miniature slide, or step into the miniature car. An action was considered to be a scale error only if the attempt was serious and persistent—that is, not a pretend action. They found that 25 of the 40 children made a scale error; the most errors were made by those in the 20.5- to 24-month-old age range. Follow-up research demonstrated that scale errors can be observed not just in laboratory settings but also in preschool classrooms (Rosengren, Carmichael, Schein, Anderson, & Gutiérrez, 2009) and home settings (Rosengren, Gutiérrez, Anderson, & Schein, 2009; Ware, Uttal, & DeLoache, 2010).

Ware, Uttal, Wetter, and DeLoache (2006) wondered whether scale errors occur not only when actions involve the child's body but also when actions involve playing with two objects. They had children aged 16 to 40 months play with a 16.5-inch (42 cm) doll and five pairs of objects: bathtubs, beds, rocking chairs, hats, and wagons. One object of the pair was an appropriate size for the doll, while the other was much too small for the doll. Over half of the children made at least one scale error involving the doll. The 35- to 40-month-old group made more errors than the young children made, perhaps because they were more engaged in playing with the doll and had more opportunities to make errors. Rosengren, Gutiérrez, et al. (2009) later distinguished these types of scale errors as body scale errors and object scale errors.

Ware et al. (2006) suggested that scale errors in children demonstrate a dissociation between action planning and action control. Visual information regarding the size of an object is occasionally not integrated into a decision to act on an object. A child's representation of a larger object and appropriate actions on it override the visual perception of the miniature object. So, visual information for planning an action is not integrated with visual information for online control of an action.

The findings on scale errors suggest that dual-processing theories of visual processing are applicable to children as well as to infants and adults. They also address the distinction between planning and online control using real objects as opposed to the visual illusions used in many research studies, and they demonstrate the behaviors in the same individual.

SUMMARY

In this chapter we have outlined two broad and very different approaches to how environmental and perceptual information is used in the control of action. The indirect approach, represented most often by information-processing models, hypothesizes a sequential processing of the input information and execution of

a selected action by a motor program. The direct or perception–action approach proposes that perceptual information modulates the ongoing action. There is a close reciprocal relationship between environment and action.

The dual-processing theories of visual processing suggest that there is a distinction between the planning of action and the online control of action, with different streams in the brain involved in each. This idea suggests that there is value in appreciating the different perspectives on the relationship between perception and action and recognizing the assumptions that each perspective brings to the study of the development of any type of motor behavior.

CHAPTER 3

Systems Approach

We saw in chapter 1 that early motor development researchers tended to emphasize the role of maturation, especially the maturation of the nervous system, in driving development. Then in chapter 2 we saw that movement and behavioral science researchers in the 1970s emphasized the role of the environment in driving behavior and development. This emphasis resulted in greater interest in sensory-perceptual systems and in cybernetic models describing how information delivered by the sensory-perceptual systems is processed and leads to a decision to move (act). Cybernetic models eventually gave way to models that allow for a more direct relationship between perception and online control of movement.

Central to the study of development is explaining the appearance of new behavioral forms (Wolff, 1987). An infant placed supine remains supine until one day when she rolls onto her stomach. A toddler says one word at a time until one day when he first puts words together in a short sentence. During development, new behaviors emerge from precursors that do not contain the new patterns (Thelen & Smith, 1998).

The maturationists looked for the source of new behaviors within the person, searching for neural or genetic code, or stored instructions, that turn on and direct new behavior. The environmentalists looked for the source in interactions between the developing person and the structure and pattern of the environment. Many developmentalists combined these two approaches to propose that nature and nurture both provide sources of new behavioral forms. Fundamental to any of these approaches, though, is the assumption that the source preexists the emergence of the new form (Oyama, 1985).

There is a difficulty with this assumption of preexistence (Thelen & Smith, 1998). Who turns on a gene so that it gives the necessary instructions? Who decides what in the environment should be absorbed? The answer must be some agent who evaluates information and makes decisions, an agent reminiscent of the homunculus in the cybernetic models discussed in the previous chapter. We arrive at the same logical impasse here: Who directs the homunculus? Even the proposal that an interaction between genes and environment is the causal agent fails to answer the question. It merely places the preexisting plans in two sources rather than one (Thelen & Smith, 1998).

Thus the traditional explanations for the driving entity in development— nature, nurture, or interaction between the two—were left wanting. In the late

1970s and early 1980s, however, the attention of developmentalists shifted to an approach that first emerged in the 1930s. This was the **general systems theory**. Systems theory explains the emergence of new forms by the process of self-organization. Consider a living organism, such as a person, as a complex system of component subsystems. These component elements can interact to give rise to new patterns without receiving explicit instructions from either genes or the environment. As Thelen and Smith (1998, p. 564) said, "self-organization—processes that by their own activities change themselves—is a fundamental property of living things."

The biologist Ludwig von Bertalanffy is credited with originating the fundamental notions of general systems theory in the 1930s and continuing to articulate its basic components in the decades following (von Bertalanffy, 1933, 1968). Von Bertalanffy resisted reductionist approaches to biological systems wherein smaller and smaller parts of systems were identified. He proposed that it is the *relationship* among parts that can inform our understanding of the behavior of biological systems. He saw the component parts as complex and heterogeneous but coming together to result in behavior that is more than the sum of its parts. Von Bertalanffy ascribed certain principles to systems. Self-organization was one. Another was a disequilibrium or openness to seek stimulation. This is an important notion in development since this property allows for change, and change is at the core of development.

The chemist Ilya Prigogine (1978; Prigogine & Stengers, 1984) was instrumental in furthering general systems theory with the study of systems in nonequilibrium. In such systems fluctuation can cause a shift to a new order of organization. Developmentalists quickly appreciated the relevance of such a notion. For example, they realized they could use self-organization and disequilibrium to explain a shift from one developmental step to another. They proposed that perhaps a system (or systems) in a state of nonequilibrium plays a role in the emergence of new behavior by causing a shift to a new organization of components.

Adolph and Robinson (2008) identified additional benefits of a systems approach for developmentalists. They stressed that a systems approach focuses on the process rather than the end products of developmental change. For example, a traditional approach to studying development is to document a behavior at a time 1, at which point the behavior tends to be simple or inadequate, and then to document the same behavior at a time 2, at which point the behavior is more advanced in some way. A systems approach, however, is more likely to focus on what happens between times of stable behavior, identifying the underlying mechanisms that shape developmental change. In fact, Adolph and Robinson proposed that there are no special time 1s and time 2s in development and that there is no privileged factor that is core to driving development. Rather, there is just process. Instead of studying beginning and end points, developmentalists with a systems perspective study the relationship among the many critical factors that bring about developmental change.

A systems approach, then, has many features with implications for the study of development. Self-organization is one; others include nonlinearity and sensitivity to initial conditions. In this chapter we consider these and other features of

systems, as well as their implications for development, in more detail. First, we take up a model that emphasizes the relationship among component elements. This model is particularly helpful in demonstrating how a behavior changes as the component elements change, in turn altering the interaction among components. In the second part of this chapter, we consider a special class of systems, **dynamic systems**, that evolve over time (hence our interest in their application to development).

MODEL OF CONSTRAINTS

General systems theory emphasizes the interaction, or relationship, of component elements of a system. No one element is predetermined to be more important than any of the others. Karl Newell (1986) proposed a model that shows how component elements can interact to give rise to a movement (see figure 3.1). In this model he used a triangle to emphasize three broad categories of components: the organism (in our case, the human), the environment, and the task. These broad categories can be broken down further into component elements or subsystems.

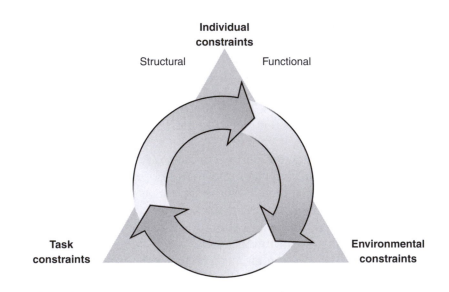

Figure 3.1 Newell's model of constraints.

Reprinted, by permission, from K. Haywood and N. Getchell, 2009, *Life span motor development,* 5th ed. (Champaign, IL: Human Kinetics), 6.

Model Components

First, let's consider the individual. In the context of movement, we can think of the individual performer as having both structural and functional components. The structural components can be divided further into subsystems that make up the physical body, such as the nervous system, the skeletal system, the muscular system, and so on. The functional components can be divided into subsystems related to behavior, such as motivation, fear, and attentional focus.

Tips for Novice Investigators

One key aspect of the general systems model is examining the whole organism rather than the individual parts. In terms of developmental research, this translates into looking at many different characteristics of individuals. For example, a researcher may be interested in the effect that a motor skill intervention has on young children. The researcher must look not only at output measures (such as the Test of Gross Motor Development, Ulrich, 2000) but also at characteristics of the population under study (such as socioeconomic class, race, developmental status), contexts under which the intervention took place (such as in a gym, on a playground, with a large group), and other factors that affect children during an intervention. This requires looking beyond the simple cause-and-effect relationships of reductionist research.

For any particular movement that emerges, we can discuss the numerous relevant elements at several levels and how they interact to give rise to that movement. None of the elements is designated as more important than the others. It is the relationship that is critical.

The environment plays a role in the emergent movement as well. The relevant elements of the environment can be physical, including the distance between and arrangement of structures, surfaces, and objects; temperature and humidity; gravity; and so on. They can also be sociocultural, including gender role stereotypes and game preferences. The third category, the task, can include task goals for the movement and even rules the individual is challenged to follow in executing the task.

Take as an example the movement that arises from the task goal of throwing a ball through a horizontal ring (such as when shooting a basketball). The size of the individual, influenced largely by the skeletal system; the strength of the individual, influenced largely by the muscular system; the weight of the object (basketball); the height of the basket; the cultural influence that makes the task desirable; and other factors all interact to produce the movement of shooting the basketball. A change in any element changes the interaction among the components and potentially changes the movement outcome. Let's say that the components are at certain levels: The individual is short in stature and the basketball is relatively heavy for the individual. The movement that emerges to meet the task goal might be a two-hand shot starting with the ball at waist level. If the components change—for example, if the basket height is lowered and the ball is replaced with a lighter one—the performer might be able to use a one-hand jump shot to achieve the goal. Thus, the model demonstrates a system whose resultant movement arises from the relationship among many elements, and if one thing or two changes, the resultant movement might change.

Newell's Model and Development

It is easy to see why Newell's model can be useful for developmentalists. First, individuals at any point of the lifespan—that is, at any point on a developmental

continuum—can be placed into the model. The status of the individual subsystems at a given point of development can be observed as interacting with task and environment. The effect of change in any of the systems can be studied. This is exactly what our basketball example illustrates: A new movement to achieve a specific goal is made possible by lowering the basket and providing a lighter ball.

Second, the components or subsystems can be time evolving or dynamic. By applying the model to our basketball example over time, we can see that if the individual grows taller and stronger, the interaction among the systems involved in shooting a basketball changes. In fact, if our desire is to make a certain movement pattern possible as an individual grows, we can use the model to see how environmental and task factors can be changed to maintain a given relationship among the relevant systems. The model also shows how new task goals become possible as components change over time. For example, a new task goal might be to use the same movement pattern to shoot the basketball from a longer distance.

Later in this chapter we explore the characteristics of time-evolving systems. For now, we can foreshadow some of these characteristics and emphasize the importance of physical growth and aging as individual structural components in Newell's model. Physical growth and aging, whether considered in terms of overall body size or as subsystems making up the body, are not linear. For example, stature largely reflects change in the skeletal system. Humans grow rapidly in height during early life, settle into a stage of steady growth during childhood, grow rapidly again during the adolescent growth spurt, and then gradually taper off in late adolescence or early adulthood. Change in other systems follows a nonlinear pattern particular to each system. The nervous system does most of its growing very early in life, with smaller increases over childhood and adolescence. The muscular system has a pattern of growth similar to that of the skeletal system but with different timing. For example, it lags behind the skeletal system during the adolescent growth spurt, substantiating the common observation that adolescents grow up and then fill out.

The structural components continue to change throughout the lifespan, though not as rapidly as they do during youth. For example, loss of stature and muscle tissue is a common experience in aging; these changes continue to emphasize the interaction of individual, environment, and task. Rates of change and the timing of change vary widely among individuals and can be related to environmental and task factors, such as diet, exercise, injury, or disease.

From the systems perspective, the emergence of new behaviors must be observed in the context of not just one but many elements and their interaction. Newell's model accommodates both the interaction among component elements and the change in elements over time. Hence the value of the model for researchers who study motor development.

A third benefit of Newell's model for developmentalists is an additional notion that accounts for how even gradual change in elements leads to the emergence of a totally new behavior. This is the notion of **constraints** (Newell, 1984, 1986). The relationship of the component elements can function as a

constraint to behavior—that is, it restrains or permits a given movement when at a given level.

Let's return to the basketball example. At a given stature and level of leg strength, an individual is constrained to scoring a basket by projecting the ball upward so that it falls down into the basket. A given type of movement pattern is dictated by the individual's stature and strength—these attributes constrain the movement to a certain pattern. Of course, the structural subsystems can change. Let's say that the individual's stature changes over time. Even if it does so gradually, and even if strength remains constant, at some point the individual might reach a height from which it is possible to throw the ball down through the basket (a dunk). The interaction among the components at the new level of stature permits a new movement pattern. Thinking of the relationship among components as a constraint illustrates how the relationship channels movement into certain forms or patterns. With change, the relationship can channel the movement into a new form or pattern. Note that constraints can act in both ways: At one point in time they might *restrict* movement to a certain form, but, with change, at another point in time they might *permit* a new form.

The developmental descriptions of the motor milestones viewed initially from the perspective of the maturing neurological system (as discussed in chapter 1) might be better explained by considering all the components as constraints (Newell & van Emmerik, 1990). Take standing independently as an example milestone. Development in the muscular and postural system likely plays a role in infant standing. Yet, the development of these subsystems might be influenced by parents who hold their infant upright so that the infant can practice standing with support. The ages at which motor tasks appear might reflect change in many elements of the movement system.

Newell's triangular model of organism, task, and environment is often called the *model of constraints*. This name emphasizes how the relationship among elements can function as a constraint to influence the emergent movement. It further illustrates how change in one of the many elements might result in a different movement. When even one system changes, the interaction among the systems changes and the movement can change. This leads to two additional but important concepts that are illustrated in the model of constraints.

▶ Tips for Novice Investigators

Newell's model of constraints offers a systematic way to examine the influence of task and environment on movement. Although researchers have modified these two constraints in past research, they often did not manipulate them systematically, and doing so may uncover key relationships. Scaling up or down on one key task or environmental constraint may lead to insights on constraint interactions. For example, by systematically changing ball size when studying throwing skills of children, a researcher could determine at what critical ratio between hand size and ball size a child moves from two- to one-hand throwing.

Rate-Limiting Systems and Multileveled Causality

One characteristic of systems that is illustrated in the model of constraints is the influence that an element or subsystem can have on the rate of movement pattern development. A subsystem that behaves in this way is called a *rate-limiting subsystem* (usually shortened to *rate-limiting system*) for a given task or movement (Soll, 1979; Thelen & Ulrich, 1991). If a movement outcome cannot change to a new pattern until a component subsystem reaches a certain level, then that particular subsystem is controlling *when* the new pattern can emerge. The controlling subsystem may be the slowest-developing subsystem in the group of multiple subsystems interacting to give rise to the movement. If the movement that arises from the interaction of subsystems is considered a developmental marker—that is, as an indicator of the rate of development—then the rate-limiting system influences the rate of development. Note, though, that the new behavior is emerging due to the interaction of element subsystems rather than a directive from genetic code or stored instructions. The change in a subsystem brings about a change in the relationship of the components, and then a new movement emerges.

A second notion emphasized by the model of constraints is **multileveled causality**. Developmental advancement does not rely on the same subsystem for every advancement or developmental marker. There is no one subsystem more important than the others (Abraham, Abraham, & Shaw, 1992; Kelso, 1995; Newell, 1984; Smith & Thelen, 2003), though a given subsystem can be the rate-limiting system for the development of a particular movement. Another subsystem might be the rate-limiting system for another movement, and so on. It should be no surprise that researchers adopting a systems perspective are interested in identifying the subsystem (or subsystems) that influences the emergence of new behaviors—that is, the rate-limiting system. In later chapters we see this to be the case as we consider the research on the emergence of various skills.

Development concerns change over time. Newell's model of constraints is a helpful way to illustrate how change in the relationship among components can influence movement skills. As mentioned earlier, time-evolving systems have unique characteristics. Since developmentalists are interested in change over time, we next turn to learning more about time-evolving or dynamic systems.

DYNAMIC SYSTEMS

Recall that a challenge for the cybernetic or mechanistic (indirect) approaches to motor behavior is the computational load borne by the brain in responding to perceptions. As impressive as brains are, it is still hard to accept that the brain can perform the large amount of computation needed when the environment changes rapidly and the task requires a quick response. While the direct perception approach addresses the computational load issue in the relationship between the environment and the person, the computational load dilemma still exists in the control and coordination of movement.

Researchers grappled with the suggestion that the brain controls each neuromuscular unit involved in complex and especially whole-body movements

on an individual level. Movement scientists began to explore models providing more economy in the control of movements by the brain and nervous system.

Interestingly, the models they began to explore had roots in the many different scientific fields dealing with naturally occurring systems that evolve over time, or dynamic systems. James Gleick (1987) wrote about this work in *Chaos: Making a New Science*. Gleick found a common stimulus behind the work of each scientist he wrote about. Each had found that the prevailing viewpoints in a given field were very successful for studying orderly events and behaviors but weren't very good at explaining discontinuous, random, irregular, or erratic phenomena, such as changes in wildlife populations, the disorder of the atmosphere, or turbulent oceans (Gleick, 1987). In other words, the prevailing modes of analysis did not explain chaotic events or events representing the appearance of new forms. The prevailing approaches were reductionist, focusing on order while ignoring irregularity. The multidisciplinary approach that came to be known as **chaos theory** took a different stance by focusing on differences (even tiny differences) in initial conditions and on variability rather than order.

Chaos is the name given to the irregular and unpredictable time evolution of nonlinear systems. James Yorke and T.Y. Li are credited with using the term *chaos* for the first time in their 1975 paper. Their use of the word did not quite match common usage. It is not that chaotic systems are disorderly. In fact, they are orderly in the sense that they are deterministic. However, they also show a degree of unpredictability. So, *chaos* in this context is referring to irregularity or unpredictability. A chaotic or dynamic system consists of a state space (a collection of coordinates that gives a complete description of the system), a set of times, and a rule for evolution (Meiss, 2007).

The chaos approach to studying dynamic systems addressed several concerns related to movement control. Movement scientists had come to realize that it is unlikely that one subsystem, be it the nervous system and its maturation or the environment by virtue of its sensory-perceptual information, drives development. Rather, *multiple subsystems* are probably important in motor behavior and development. Researchers became increasingly aware that the mechanistic notion of an executive controller of muscle action in the brain likely lacked efficacy and that more attention must be given to the interaction of multiple subsystems. The study of dynamic systems demonstrated that component subsystems can self-organize. It became clear to researchers that some of the fundamental characteristics of dynamic systems studied from the chaos perspective could be useful in modeling the control and coordination of movement.

Yet, why did a theory emerging from the study of dynamic systems specifically change the study of motor *development*? At first glance a theory that looks for mathematical order in irregular phenomena seems far removed from the behavior of a toddler learning to walk. As we will see in the following discussion, work on irregular, chaotic systems addresses a number of issues that motor developmentalists were discussing at the time, such as these:

➤ How do totally new movement forms emerge in development?
➤ How can a movement be successful the very first time it is executed?

> ➤ How do individuals adapt movements in an environment that can be subtly different every time a movement pattern is executed?

> ➤ Can the nervous system actually make decisions to move immediately and quickly by processing, bit by bit, the sensory-perceptual information from the environment and the body itself? If it can't, what could be an alternative explanation?

> ➤ Does the suggestion that the body uses motor programs (similar to computer programs) solve the problem of explaining how the body responds immediately and quickly, or does the storage room needed in the brain for such programs create another problem?

The available approaches to the study of motor development could not provide satisfactory answers to these questions, and by the 1980s researchers were ready to embrace the potential solutions offered by the study of dynamic systems. To appreciate how the study of these systems energized motor development research with a new perspective, let's review the fundamental characteristics of dynamic systems.

FUNDAMENTAL CHARACTERISTICS OF DYNAMIC SYSTEMS

Compared with the information-processing approach, the study of dynamic systems is based on a very different set of assumptions. The basic model is not of a computer but of irregular systems that evolve with time—that is, dynamic systems. These systems are nonlinear and do not repeat past behavior. Although such unpredictable systems are irregular and chaotic, they follow deterministic equations (Baker & Gollub, 1990). Dynamic systems are deterministic because their future dynamics can be fully defined by their initial conditions and without any random elements.

Information on the mathematics of dynamic systems and the deterministic equations they follow is available elsewhere (Abraham & Shaw, 1984a, 1984b; Briggs & Peat, 1989; Gleick, 1987). Our interest is in considering how movement and movement development can be modeled using multiple dynamic systems. Our first step is to define the fundamental characteristics of dynamic systems that might be used to model the systems involved in motor development. We begin with the topic of self-organization and then go on to discuss the nonlinear nature of dynamic systems, the sensitivity to the initial set of conditions from which a system evolves, and the entrainment of systems.

Self-Organization

Self-organization of systems addresses two of the persistent issues of movement development. One is the emergence of new movement patterns. The other is the capacity to control degrees of freedom in movement—that is, to control the joints, muscles, and numerous neuromuscular motor units involved in a complex movement. We consider these issues one at a time.

Emergence of New Movement Patterns   A common question asked by scientists is how patterns in nature emerge from randomness. The developmental parallel to this question asks how new forms of behavior arise (Thelen & Ulrich, 1991). The ability of elements of dynamic systems, be they physical, biological, or mathematical, to organize spontaneously into patterns is central to the systems approach. These patterns do not exist in the individual elements of the system; rather, they emerge under certain conditions. Thelen and Ulrich (1991) offered the example of a pot of water placed on a stove. At room temperature the water molecules move around randomly. As heat is applied, the bottom layer of water gets hotter and hotter. At a critical point the warmer water begins to rise. When conditions are right, this water convection forms into a pattern of rolls. A new pattern has emerged.

The individual elements of a dynamic system are free to move independently. Potentially, there is a large number of degrees of freedom of movement for individual units. Under certain conditions, though, the degrees of freedom can be restricted, and the individual units participate in a pattern, such as the convection rolls in the pot of heated water. The elements are no longer independent. They have self-organized. No entity has directed each element to move in a certain way. It is this self-organizing pattern formation of systems that initially drew the interest of motor behavior researchers trying to explain the control of movement and the emergence of new behaviors.

Self-organization of elements in systems can explain how the degrees of freedom for a movement are reduced to a manageable number. Thus self-organization addresses the computational load concern: If elements of movement systems can self-organize, then the brain (including the developing brain) has a more manageable task in controlling movement. Thelen (1989, p. 497) put the notion of self-organization specifically within the context of motor development:

> Development proceeds not as the progressive revelation or elaboration of already existing schemata, programs, or plans, but as the opportunistic marshaling of the available components that best befit the task at hand. Development is function driven to the extent that anatomical structure and neurological mechanisms exist only as components until they are expressed in a context. Once assembled in context, behavior is, in turn, molded and modulated by its functional consequences.

Hence, the emergence of new behaviors and their immediately successful performance by developing individuals can be explained by the self-organization of dynamic systems.

Degrees of Freedom Problem   Russian neurophysiologist Nikolai A. Bernstein addressed some of the most important questions facing movement scientists and is often credited with establishing the field of biomechanics. Yet, the Western world became aware of his work only after his death in 1966 because his writings were not translated into English until the late 1960s. The 1967 translation of his book, *The Coordination and Regulation of Movements*, identified pivotal questions about the control of movement.

In particular, Bernstein addressed the degrees of freedom problem, now known as *Bernstein's problem* (Kugler, Kelso, & Turvey, 1982). Every joint is free to move in a number of ways. This results in a huge computational load for the hypothesized executor (homunculus) described earlier. How can the brain possibly make so many choices in such a short time and then direct each individual neuromuscular unit to fire as needed?

Think of a movement choice as a degree of freedom. Now, consider a simple motor action such as reaching out to grasp a glass of water. To keep the action simple, consider only the reach and not the grasp. There are at a minimum three joints involved in this action (shoulder, elbow, and wrist). For each joint, choices must be made about how to move. The shoulder joint has a variety of anatomical joint positions that are mutually exclusive. For example, it can be flexed *or* extended (one degree of freedom), abducted *or* adducted (one degree of freedom), and internally *or* externally rotated (one degree of freedom). Therefore, the shoulder joint has three degrees of freedom that must be controlled. Fortunately, the elbow has only one degree (we will ignore supination and pronation for now), and the wrist has two. Consequently, at the joint level, there are six degrees of freedom that the brain must control during the reaching action. This seems very possible, but the choices do not end here.

Tips for Novice Investigators

The notion that the brain controls all levels of movement creates various difficulties for researchers. If all explanations of movement lead back to the brain, then what levels of analysis are important to study? Furthermore, from where does the brain acquire its instructions for movement? A reductionist perspective makes movement a problem for the brain to overcome. Yet, a skilled athlete demonstrates an efficiency of movement that would not be possible if the brain had to attend to millions of details. A systems perspective acknowledges that much of movement comes from interactions between brain and body within a movement context.

Controlling the shoulder joint is a series of muscles responsible for each joint action. The function of some muscles may be position dependent. For example, the clavicular fibers of pectoralis major are responsible for adduction, medial rotation, and flexion of the arm if the arm starts at the side of the body, whereas the sternocostal fibers are responsible for extension of the arm if the arm starts overhead (see figure 3.2). Each muscle crossing the shoulder joint adds another degree of freedom that must be controlled in coordinated action—and the number of degrees of freedom does not end at the muscle level. Consider that each muscle is made up of hundreds of muscle fibers grouped into motor units, each of which is innervated by a single motor neuron. Depending on distance, force, timing, and so on, a unique pattern of on and off must be provided to each motor unit during a successful reaching action. There are thousands of degrees of freedom that must be controlled to perform this simple action—and

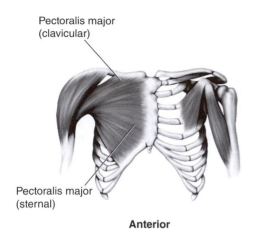

Pectoralis major
(clavicular)

Pectoralis major
(sternal)

Anterior

Figure 3.2 The pectoralis major.

Reprinted from R. Behnke, 2005, *Kinetic anatomy*, 2nd ed. (Champaign, IL: Human Kinetics), 47.

if the initial position of the arm is changed, each degree of freedom must be adjusted as well. Now the reach no longer looks so simple!

Bernstein hypothesized that coordinated movement would be impossible if the brain had to control all these individual degrees of freedom. Yet, humans perform tasks such as reaching every day. Coordination is *not* a problem in reality. Bernstein concluded that each level (motor unit, muscle, joint, and so on) must somehow interact in an integrated fashion. He argued that degrees of freedom cannot be controlled individually but must be constrained in a functional unit specific to a particular action.

Constraints   A group of scientists working at Haskins Laboratories in Connecticut addressed how the number of free variables, executive instructions, and decisions involved in movement control could be minimized by functional units. Kugler, Kelso, and Turvey (1980) proposed that the human body can organize spontaneously into functional units. Turvey et al. (Turvey, Fitch, & Tuller, 1982) then demonstrated how a constraint can be applied to achieve a functional unit.

Consider a two-dimensional space with x and y axes, and let's say that there are two elements (points) within the space (see figure 3.3a). Two coordinates are needed to identify the position of each element (x_1 and y_1 for element A and x_2 and y_2 for element B). Since two coordinates are needed to describe each of the two elements, the system has four degrees of freedom. Now, if the two elements are connected by a steel bar of length L (see figure 3.3b), then the two elements are constrained. The position that element A occupies determines the position of element B. The length L constrains the position of element B relative to the position of element A. This relationship can be expressed as an equation: $(x_2 - x_1)^2 + (y_2 - y_1)^2 = L^2$. This equation is called an *equation of constraint*. Note that the degrees of freedom are reduced from four to three: Once x_1, y_1, and x_2 are specified, y_2 is fixed. Thus, applying a constraint to the system reduced the degrees of freedom. It follows that if elements of the neuromuscular system can be constrained, then the degrees of freedom—and hence the instructions and decisions involved in controlling movement—can be reduced.

Thelen and Bates (2003, p. 381) noted how important such solutions are to the problems of movement control in general as well as movement control in infants and children:

> *Here was the brilliant solution to Bernstein's degrees of freedom problem. Rather than the degrees of freedom being a curse, a computational load to be overcome, they become the very source of organization and indeed, of change. Patterns emerge from the complexity of the system and its energetic status. As such, no component or element has priority or privilege, since it is the particular*

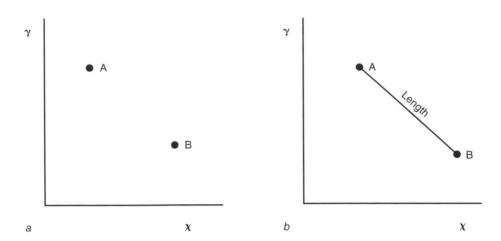

Figure 3.3 These simple graphs demonstrate how linking two elements can reduce the number of degrees of freedom within a system. In *a*, the two points each have two degrees of freedom—that is, they can vary along both the vertical and horizontal axes. Thus the system has a total of four degrees of freedom. In *b*, a bar links the two elements so that they move together. This reduces the degrees of freedom to three.

Adapted from J.R. Hillsdale, 1982, *Human motor behavior: An introduction book*, edited by J.A. Scott Kelso (Lawrence Erlbaum).

coalition of elements from which coherence arises. Thus, movements need not be "represented" in the nervous system in all their detail. The details are created in their assembly.

Thus self-organization provides a way to model the acquisition and control of movement patterns wherein the number of free variables, executive instructions, and decisions in controlling movement is minimized.

Nonlinearity

Another characteristic of dynamic systems that is of interest to developmentalists is the nonlinearity of dynamic systems. Nonlinearity appears to be a hallmark of development. Smith (2006, p. 87) described development as "a series of evolving and dissolving patterns of varying dynamic stability rather than an inevitable march towards maturity." Dynamic systems alternate between times of stability and times of instability. What is particularly relevant to developmentalists is what prompts the change. Why does a stable behavior become less stable? What influences the transition from one behavior to another? Why do new behaviors emerge? Dynamic systems theory proposes a new way to think about these questions.

A first step in examining transitions is to consider the nature of the period of stability. Then we can consider what pushes behavior from one period of stability to another.

Attractor States A period of stability can be thought of as a period of preference for certain patterns. Not all patterns are observed during this time, but the preference is not dictated by a homunculus. Rather, a preferred pattern or state reflects cooperation among the component elements of the developing

individual in a particular set of conditions (Thelen & Ulrich, 1991). The preferred behaviors emerge from the interaction among the components and are called *attractor states*.

To provide an example of attractor states in development, Kugler, Kelso, and Turvey (1982) reexamined the longitudinal findings of Halverson, Roberton, et al. (e.g. Halverson, Roberton, and Harper, 1973; see also Roberton, 1977, 1978; Roberton & Langendorfer, 1980) on the developmental sequences of the over-arm throw (see table 7.4 in chapter 7). These data show that individuals exhibit stable performance within a developmental level for a period of time. That is, they fall into an attractor state, which is followed by a brief period of instability and then the emergence of a new stable motor pattern constituting another attractor state. So, we might think of development as involving transitions from one attractor state to another.

Attractor states are referenced to their current dynamic status. Behavior can be pushed out of the attractor state. Kugler et al. acknowledged this developmental trajectory:

Under certain scale changes the dynamic qualities of the system will remain invariant, while under critical scale changes the previously stable organization of the manifold may suddenly break down and be replaced by a new organization. The important feature of this sequence of events is that a continuous change in a single variable (or combination of variables) may bring about a sudden qualitative change in the macro structure. . . .

What is the nature, then, of these variables that can bring about change? We consider this next.

Tips for Novice Investigators

Be aware of the unexpected influences that different variables within your research may have on behavior outcomes. You might decide to use a specific distance to a target in order to control for absolute distance in a reaching experiment. However, doing so will backfire if you don't account for relative distance—that is, the arm length of the participant divided by the absolute distance. By keeping relative values constant, you can avoid sudden (and unwanted) shifts in behavior that are unrelated to your study!

Control Variables and Phase Shifts   What pushes behavior out of a preferred pattern or attractor state? That is, what brings about a transition? The transitions between attractor states are called *phase shifts*. A phase shift may seem gradual or abrupt, depending on the timescale of observation (Thelen & Ulrich, 1991). Phase shifts can be brought about by a change in one or more components of a subsystem. Recall that subsystems are interdependent. Small changes in one level may result in large changes at another level. Remember from our discussion on the model of constraints that a small change such as

an increase in bone length or density, muscular strength, neural connections, and so on may result in new behaviors. The component that changes to bring about a phase shift is called a control parameter or control variable. It is a control variable changing to a critical value that pushes a behavior out of its stable attractor state. The change leading to attainment of the critical value can be quantitative or qualitative, steady and gradual or sudden. What follows attainment of the critical value is a period of instability that allows the system to seek a new stable attractor state.

Sensitivity to Initial Conditions

French mathematician, physicist, and theoretical astronomer Henri Poincaré was the first person to recognize the importance of sensitivity to initial conditions in the evolution of nonlinear systems. He realized that small differences in initial conditions could produce very large differences in final phenomena (Baker & Gollub, 1990). A small initial difference between two linear systems grows linearly with time, but a small initial difference between two dynamic nonlinear systems grows exponentially with time. Poincaré realized that this made the prediction of dynamic systems impossible, and he laid down the foundation for the modern mathematical principles of dynamic systems (Holmes, 2005).

The Butterfly Effect   Poincaré's work on initial conditions early in the 20th century was followed by Edward Lorenz's work in the middle of the 20th century. Although Edward Lorenz was a mathematician, his interests shifted to meteorology after he served as a weather forecaster during World War II. Lorenz used an early computer to model the weather in hopes of learning how to predict weather long range. One day he wanted to repeat the last part of a simulation of the evolution of a weather system. So, he restarted the simulation in the middle by typing in values from the computer printout of the first run. He was astonished an hour later to observe an entirely different end result for the simulation. He traced the cause of this difference to the fact that the computer stored six decimal places in its memory but he had the printouts rounded to three decimal places to save paper, which meant that he typed in a value from the printout that was 0.000127 different from the value used by the computer in the first simulation run. Somewhat by accident, Lorenz had demonstrated that a very small difference in starting conditions can make for large differences later as chaotic systems evolve over time. Lorenz's finding came to be known as the *butterfly effect*, "the notion that a butterfly stirring the air today in Peking can transform storm systems next month in New York" (Gleick, 1987, p. 8). More formally, the butterfly effect is known as *sensitive dependence on initial conditions*. Coincidentally, the butterfly effect made it obvious that long-range prediction of naturally occurring systems such as the weather can be very difficult. More importantly for our discussion of motor development, the butterfly effect illustrates why the environment in which a movement takes place can so greatly affect the emergent movement, as does the initial position of body and limbs.

Context-Conditioned Variability   Recall our earlier mention of the clavicular and sternocostal fibers of the pectoralis major. In one position, fibers of this muscle can shorten to flex the arm, while in another position fibers of the same muscle can extend the arm. This is an example of **context-conditioned variability**. If activation of a muscle always had the same result, it would be easier for a homunculus to control muscles. Activation of muscles could be commanded without regard to context. But, this isn't the case. The result of muscle activation depends on the context. The pectoralis major is an example of context-conditioned variability from an *anatomical* source.

Another source of context-conditioned variability is *mechanical* variability (Turvey et al., 1982). The forces acting on a limb are not just muscular forces. Nonmuscular forces are also at work. An excellent example of a nonmuscular force is gravity. If a person standing with the right arm held out to the side at shoulder height wishes to lower the arm, both muscular forces and gravity operate. Changes in the moments of inertia of a limb are another example of nonmuscular force. Any system for controlling movement must recognize that both muscular and nonmuscular forces influence movement. The homunculus model does not do a very good job of accounting for nonmuscular forces.

Context-conditioned variability is an important issue for both the learning and development of motor skills. Children and even novice adults tend to hold many parts of their bodies rigid when attempting a new skill, such as striking a ball with a racket. This can be thought of as freezing some of the degrees of freedom in body movement to simplify the task at hand. It is largely the control of nonmuscular forces that is simplified with this strategy. Yet, to become more effective at the task, the performer must figure out how to incorporate nonmuscular forces into the movement. Allowing additional degrees of freedom is necessary to give power to the stroke, in part by using a step and weight transfer, trunk rotation, shoulder rotation, and so on. This might be seen in increased variability. The performer unfreezes and becomes less rigid before a qualitative change in the movement pattern occurs and the pattern becomes stable. Ultimately, forces available in the context must be exploited and more degrees of freedom controlled.

Coordinative Structures   The dynamic systems model accommodates sensitivity to initial conditions and context-conditioned variability in the control of movement since movement emerges from component systems as they exist in a context. Functional units might be another way in which context variability is accommodated. Kugler et al. (1982) were instrumental in suggesting that movement control involves functional units called *muscle linkages* or *coordinative structures*. Over the short term, muscles can be constrained to function as a unit. A coordinative structure, then, is a group of muscles spanning multiple joints constrained to act as a single functional unit.

Kugler et al. (1982) provided a simple example of a coordinative structure with locomotion. The muscles of the ankle, knee, and hip are distinct and can act individually but also act as a unit during walking. In one collective, the hip flexors, knee flexors, and ankle plantar flexors work together as the recovery leg starts to swing forward, and then in another collective the hip extensors, knee

extensors, and ankle dorsiflexors prepare for heel strike. The locomotion coordinative structures work in this predictable way even when the walking speed or the terrain changes. That is, the locomotion coordinative structures are *scale independent*. Coordinative structures adjust automatically to changing external conditions, reaching the same final position from any initial position (Tuller, Turvey, & Fitch, 1982). Kugler et al. suggested that equations of constraint coordinate these structures. The two muscle collections used in locomotion reduce the degrees of freedom involved in controlling a leg for walking.

Entrainment

Balthasar van der Pol was a Dutch electrical engineer born in 1889 who also worked on nonlinear systems early in the 20th century. He focused on oscillating frequencies, using vacuum tubes to examine the behavior of electrical circuits. He determined that electrical circuits demonstrate stable oscillations, now called *limit cycles*, with specific dynamic properties. He found that electrical circuits can **entrain** to a driving signal whose frequency is close to that of the limit cycle. Van der Pol eventually extended his work on entrainment to model the human heart and investigated how to stabilize arrhythmias. Our interest here is not oscillating frequencies but rather the modeling of movement as an oscillator.

Oscillators as a Model   The two types of oscillators used in modeling movement are the mass–spring system and the pendulum. Consider a spring that is attached to a fixed surface such as the ceiling at one end and has a mass attached at the opposite end. If the mass is pushed or pulled so that it compresses or stretches the spring and is let go, the mass and spring will oscillate, eventually returning to an equilibrium position. The *mass–spring system* achieves the equilibrium position determined by the length and stiffness of the spring as well as the weight of the mass regardless of the initial conditions—that is, regardless of how much or little the spring was compressed or stretched. In other words, it achieves equilibrium regardless of the context (the initial conditions). This simple system arrives at the equilibrium position without any executive controller or homunculus. Calculations on the initial conditions and independent regulation of a large number of degrees of freedom are not necessary (Tuller et al., 1982). Thus an oscillatory system can provide the model for muscles that are linked by equations of constraint.

Consider that the arm and leg movements are cyclic during walking. The arms and legs each function like a pendulum: They are attached to the body and swing back and forth. It is interesting to model the arms and legs as a special class of oscillators called **limit-cycle oscillators**. These oscillators are mutually synchronizing so that when two or more interact they can influence each other to behave as one (Tuller et al., 1982).

This mutual synchronization is called *entrainment*. Huygens first observed entrainment in the 18th century. He found that two clocks (clocks having oscillatory mechanisms) mounted on a board that transmitted vibration synchronized and kept identical time. The legs in walking can be modeled as limit-cycle oscillators that can entrain in one-half cycle out of phase.

When humans walk, the two legs are always opposite each other in the walking cycle. That is, a leg moves in a continuous cycle: toe-off, swing forward, heel strike, support weight, toe-off, and so on. If we know the position in the cycle of one leg, we know the position in the cycle of the other. If one leg is at toe-off, the other is at heel strike. If one leg is at support, the other is at swing forward. This relationship is said to be *one-half cycle out of phase*. If the two legs are constrained to maintain this relationship, the result is a reduction in the degrees of freedom needed to control walking.

The arms can be added to this model as additional limit-cycle oscillators that entrain to each other and the legs. An advantage gained in modeling collections of muscles as limit-cycle oscillators is that entrainment provides a means of achieving coordination between the limbs without the burden that cybernetic models place on an executive function to control numerous individual muscles, joints, and limbs. The degrees of freedom that must be controlled in order to walk are greatly reduced.

APPLYING THE DYNAMIC SYSTEMS MODEL TO A MOTOR DEVELOPMENT PROBLEM

Perhaps the best way to appreciate how the characteristics of dynamic systems can be used to model motor development is to see how a research team used dynamic systems to address a particular developmental issue. Let's consider the case of the reflexes seen in infancy. Recall that a reflex is a particular automatic response to a specific stimulus. It is a response that is carried out without thought or intention. Developmentalists have long observed the existence of reflexes that disappear later on in infants.

Developmentalists have been particularly interested in the walking or stepping reflex for its similarity to voluntary walking (see table 3.1). The reflex is elicited by holding an infant upright and lowering the infant to a horizontal surface.

Table 3.1   Infant Reflexes

Study citation	Key concept	Noteworthy findings	Comparative comments
Zelazo, Zelazo, & Kolb, 1972	Reflexes transform into mature walking patterns through practice.	Infants who practiced reflex stepping on a treadmill walked sooner.	All studies challenge the notion that reflexes must disappear before voluntary walking begins. The second and third suggest that all systems (rather than just the maturing brain) must be considered when examining developmental change.
Thelen & Fisher, 1982	Changing a subsystem can make a reflex disappear.	Adding weights to young infants' legs decreased their step reflex.	
Thelen, Fisher, & Ridley-Johnson, 1984	Interacting subsystems can change the emergence of reflexes.	Putting infants in a reduced-gravity environment increased the step reflex.	

The reflexive response is stepping movements of the legs. The stepping reflex is typically observed up to 5 months of age, so it appears much earlier than voluntary walking and disappears months before voluntary walking.

Developmentalists have offered several explanations for the disappearance of the stepping reflex. The maturationists suggested that the disappearance reflects the maturation of the cortex. These researchers proposed that as higher brain centers mature they are able to inhibit the lower brain centers that mediate reflexes. With continued maturation, the centers control voluntary walking. The existence and disappearance of reflexes reflect the status of nervous system development.

Peiper (1963) suggested instead that reflexes have a purpose because they allow practice of movement patterns before the higher brain centers are mature enough to control those patterns. Zelazo et al. (Zelazo, 1983; Zelazo, Konner, Kolb, & Zelazo, 1974; Zelazo, Zelazo, & Kolb, 1972) offered yet another viewpoint. They purposely increased the number of times the stepping reflex was elicited in a small group of infants. Later, these infants were observed to start walking at a younger age than average. The researchers concluded that reflexes can be subsumed into voluntary movements. For example, the walking reflex is transformed into voluntary walking.

Unconvinced by these various hypotheses, Esther Thelen and her colleagues (Thelen & Fisher, 1982; Thelen, Fisher, & Ridley-Johnson, 1984) developed an ingenious series of experiments to examine different potential causes for the disappearance of the stepping reflex. They began with the notion that multiple systems—rather than just one system—play a role in the disappearance. They had observed that one of the changes in infants correlating with the disappearance of the stepping reflex is an increase in subcutaneous fat that occurs during infancy. Could this gain in fat and the resultant change in the strength required to move heavier legs be related to the disappearance of the stepping reflex? In order to test whether the muscle and adipose tissue systems are involved, the researchers had to find a way to make a light and stepping infant resemble a nonstepping and heavier infant and, just as importantly, to get a non-stepping, heavier infant to resemble a lighter, stepping infant. The only variable that could be changed was leg strength. In a first experiment, the researchers added tiny weights to the legs of lighter infants. The added weight was proportional to the amount of weight the infant would add between 4 and 6 weeks of age. If maturation of the nervous system were the only cause of reflex stepping, then the infants should continue to step regardless of the small weights. Actually, the infants reduced the number of reflex steps taken while wearing the weights.

The next experiment was designed to regress the leg weight of heavier infants to that of younger, lighter infants. The researchers achieved this by holding the infants upright in an aquarium filled with water up to their hips. The water reduced the pull of gravity on the legs and made them relatively lighter. The water was room temperature, and the researchers noted that often the infants did not respond in any way to being held in the water. When the infants' feet touched the bottom surface of the tank, though, the number of steps increased (Thelen & Fisher, 1982). If maturation of the nervous system is the only explanation

for the reflex disappearing, then nothing should have been able to increase the rate of stepping, as the higher brain centers would have inhibited it. Thus the researchers demonstrated that change in other systems plays a role in the disappearance of the stepping reflex.

Thelen et al. demonstrated that the systems approach can be used to examine the processes underlying development. While maturation of the nervous system is important in motor development, other subsystems are important to the change observed in the stepping reflex. As well as studying multiple subsystems, Thelen et al. demonstrated that change in a subsystem can function as a control variable. The role of a control variable in bringing about change is another characteristic of dynamic systems. More of Thelen's work will be discussed throughout the text.

SUMMARY

The systems approach has much to offer researchers interested in understanding developmental change. Dynamic systems evolve over time and undergo change that is not linear. These characteristics describe the body as it grows and ages. Dynamic systems evolve by transitioning from times of stability, or attractor states, through times of instability to other attractor states. We observe this pattern in motor development, too. Dynamic systems are sensitive to the conditions initially in place when they begin to evolve. Movement scientists have long realized that models of movement control must allow for the same movement goal to be achieved from variable environmental conditions and different starting positions of the body and limbs. Most importantly, dynamic systems have been shown to self-organize and to use methods of control such as entrainment and the application of constraints. The demonstration of these possibilities is important, as they provide explanations for how the large number of degrees of freedom in movement can be reduced for the reasonable control of complex movements.

The systems approach provided a heuristic function for movement scientists by focusing researchers' attention on new ways to solve existing questions in motor development. There is value in examining multiple theories. Researchers using differing approaches all serve to gain from alternative views, as both theorists and empiricists are forced to question behaviors their theories can't account for and improve their models until a satisfactory explanation can be found (for example, see Schmidt & Lee, 2011 on generalized motor programs). Ultimately, these challenges and changes serve to enhance our understanding of motor development.

CHAPTER 4

Motor Development Research Approaches

Developmental research is unique in the questions it asks and in the way it is designed. This uniqueness stems from the definition of motor development as *change* over the lifespan. Such a definition requires research designs that measure change directly or allow change to be inferred from the data. In this chapter we examine the strengths and weaknesses of various developmental research designs and look at the common methods of measuring motor development. We conclude with several suggestions for strengthening research in this field.

RESEARCH DESIGNS

There are various research designs appropriate for examining developmental change. What has long been considered the gold standard for developmental research is the longitudinal research design, in which several individuals are observed over long lengths of time. Understandably, many graduate students are interested in studies that can be completed in shorter amounts of time. Alternative methods that provide a window on development include cross-sectional studies, mixed longitudinal studies, and prelongitudinal screening.

Longitudinal Design

The hallmark of developmental research is the longitudinal design. Researchers using this method track the same participants over time using repeated measures; thus, the researchers directly watch the behavior changes occurring in the participants. For example, a researcher interested in the development of walking might examine young children repeatedly from the time before they can walk until the time they can walk without assistance.

Longitudinal studies may last months or even years; ideally they last over the lifespan. As noted in chapter 1, many of the early researchers in motor development conducted longitudinal studies, usually of infants who could be followed over several months or a few years. In more recent times, Halverson and Roberton examined the development of a variety of fundamental motor skills by filming seven children as they developed from approximately 3 years of age to 18 years

of age (see Halverson, 1966; Roberton & Halverson, 1984, 1988). In addition, these same investigators filmed 73 other children throwing for force from ages 5 to 7 and then refilmed 39 of the children when they were 13 years of age (see Halverson, Roberton, & Langendorfer, 1982; Langendorfer & Roberton, 2002b).

Once longitudinal data are collected, they are graphed with time on the horizontal axis and the dependent measure on the vertical axis (see figure 4.1). The traditional measure of time has been age, so the data are frequently graphed over months or years. A number of these longitudinal graphs appear throughout this book. They are the distinguishing feature of motor development research because they are the only way that change in the movement of individuals can be viewed directly. For this reason they are highly prized.

As we indicated in chapter 1, age is not the cause of the data and therefore is not an independent variable. Wohlwill (1970, 1973) suggested that age be called a *marker variable*, meaning a variable against which developmental data are traditionally plotted. He went on to say that the real focus of developmental research is the *developmental function* (the curve) formed in the graph. Figure 4.1 shows a developmental function for a hypothetical variable measured on a continuous scale. Variables measured on ordinal or nominal scales, such as levels in motor development sequences, yield a staircase function (see figure 1.6) or a series of curves, each representing the percentage of the participants displaying a particular developmental level at each age (see figure 1.7). Regardless, the question of interest to a developmental researcher is the *shape of the function plotted across time.*

Wohlwill (1970, 1973) argued that once the developmental function has been studied and, ideally, replicated, it should become the focus of experimental manipulation. That is, the investigator should try to change the shape of the function by subjecting new participants from a targeted age range to some form of intervention. Successfully manipulating the function (meaning that the new data yield a differently shaped graph) gives a strong sense of what may cause natural change. In this way, too, the descriptive work of motor development researchers becomes directly tied to their experimental work.

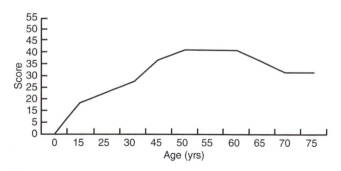

Figure 4.1 A traditional longitudinal graph with the dependent variable measured on a continuous scale. The resulting developmental function is the focus of motor development research.

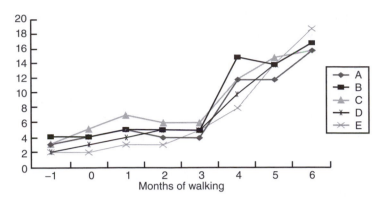

Figure 4.2 A longitudinal graph using months of walking rather than age as the horizontal axis.

As scholars better recognized the role of experience and practice in the acquisition of motor skills, a new way of graphing time appeared. Figure 4.2 shows a hypothetical data set from a longitudinal design examining balance in children before, during, and after they begin to walk. The measure under examination is a score on a dynamic balance test. The researcher began testing five infants several months before they developed the ability to walk. She continued to test them through their first steps and for a total of 6 months after each began to walk. She then graphed the data at monthly intervals calculated from the time at which they first stepped. Thus, at any particular walking age the infants are at different chronological ages. This method de-emphasizes age while still emphasizing the change over time that is the focus of motor development. It also stresses the role of practice or experience. Clark and colleagues have used this approach in their contemporary studies of infant walking (see Clark & Phillips, 1993; Clark, Whitall, & Phillips, 1988).

For all its strengths, longitudinal research has its drawbacks. First, if the study is long enough, it is possible that the original researchers will not live to see the results! Longitudinal studies in developmental psychology, such as those started by Nancy Bayley (see chapter 1) from the Institute of Human Development at the University of California, Berkeley, often outlive their originators. Second, due to the length of time involved, longitudinal research amasses considerable data, some of which are never analyzed because the scientists are overwhelmed by the sheer volume. Although being overwhelmed by data is less likely in the computer age, it has been a frequent problem in past studies of motor development. Third, longitudinal research requires a lengthy commitment to the study not only on the part of the researchers but also on the part of the participants. For this reason participant dropout is always a serious concern.

For all these reasons, longitudinal studies tend to have smaller numbers of participants and to use participants who are not randomly selected; thus, the generalizability of the data from these studies should be verified using other samples. Another generalizability question raised about participants in longitudinal

studies is the degree to which the repeated measures change the participants so that they are no longer typical individuals.

Finally, if the timing of the repeated measures performed in a longitudinal study is arbitrary, which it typically is, then the "Whoops, I missed it!" phenomenon can occur. That is, if a subject who is measured at 3-month intervals displays a behavior at month 4, the researchers won't see and record that behavior until month 6. Or, if the behavior is short lived and disappears at month 5, the investigators will never see it at all.

> ## Tips for Novice Investigators

There are several ways to avoid missing critical behaviors, particularly when working with infants and young children. If feasible, the researcher can reduce the time intervals between data collection sessions, particularly during times of rapid change. Another solution is to have parents fill out a behavioral log or checklist that helps identify new movements as they emerge. Such a checklist should be quick and easy to fill out. Parents can e-mail computerized checklists back to the researcher on a weekly basis.

Cross-Sectional Design

A less time-consuming alternative to the longitudinal design is the cross-sectional design. In a cross-sectional study, researchers choose groups of individuals at selected points within the age range of interest. For example, researchers interested in change during adolescence might measure a group of 13-year-olds, a group of 15-year-olds, and a group of 17-year-olds (see figure 4.3). When the measurements of each group are plotted using age as the horizontal axis, the differences between age groups are assumed to reflect the change that might be observed in a single group followed over the time frame from 13 to 17 years of age. The advantage of this method is that researchers can study development in a relatively short time. The disadvantage is that this snapshot of the age range does not directly observe change; the investigators have to *infer* change from the age group *differences*. The assumption is that the 17-year-olds were once like the 13-year-olds and that the 13-year-olds will one day be like the 17 year-olds. If a cohort effect exists, these age differences could suggest change where none exists.

A cohort or generational effect occurs when one age group is exposed to something

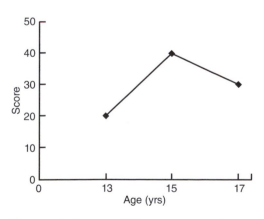

Figure 4.3 A traditional cross-sectional study comparing participants of different ages. Development must be inferred from such data.

that others are not exposed to. This exposure could be to particular teaching practices, environmental differences, equipment changes, societal changes, and so on that have a strong influence on that specific age group. For instance, Runion, Roberton, and Langendorfer (2003) wondered if the onset of Title IX in the United States affected the gender differences typical in the overarm throws of children. They compared data on 13-year-olds after Title IX with data on 13-year-olds collected 20 years earlier, before Title IX. Thus, the children's ages were constant but their generations differed. If this cohort comparison had not been made, then the assumption would have continued that the gender differences described in the 1980s are still true in the 21st century. (Chapter 7 gives the results of this study.) This type of design, which compares different cohorts of the same age, has been called a *time-lag design* (Schaie, 1965).

Convergence Design

For many researchers, a longitudinal design may not be feasible, and a cross-sectional design might be inappropriate if cohort effects are likely. In another type of experimental design, variously known as a *cross-sequential*, *time-lag*, or *convergence design* (Baltes, Cornelius, & Nesselroade, 1979; Schaie, 1965, 1970; Wohlwill, 1973), several different age groups are selected as in a cross-sectional design and then are observed longitudinally over a relatively shorter time frame. Change is inferred from the initial age of the youngest group to the final age of the oldest group. If the ages of the different groups overlap, then cohorts can be compared as in a time-lag design.

Consider an investigator interested in swimming speed. Because of his concern about cohort effects, he uses a convergence design. Instead of observing four groups of 6-, 7-, 8-, and 9-year-olds at one point in time, he measures two groups (6 years of age and 7 years of age) every 6 months over the course of 2 years, so that he has observations for the 6-year-old group at 6.0, 6.5, 7.0, 7.5, and 8.0 years of age and for the 7-year-old group at 7.0, 7.5, 8.0, 8.5, and 9.0 years of age. The cohorts overlap at 7.0, 7.5, and 8.0 years of age, which allows a check for cohort differences, and in the 24 months the researcher also captured longitudinal data over the age range of interest (see figure 4.4). If the different cohorts performed similarly at the overlapping ages, as is the case in figure 4.4, the researcher can infer developmental change over the 6- to 9-year-old age range with more confidence.

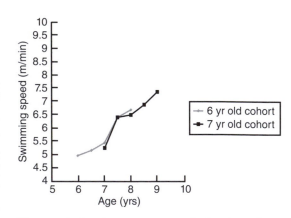

Figure 4.4 A convergence design based on both cross-sectional and longitudinal data. It allows for cohort comparisons and lengthens the age range under study. Data are hypothetical.

Mixed Longitudinal Design

Occasionally a developmental study uses the term *mixed longitudinal* to describe its research design. What the authors mean by this is that they measured a group of participants longitudinally but added additional data from some people who were perhaps studied at only one age (or two). The results are interpreted as if all the participants had been studied longitudinally, and there is no effort to separate out the data of those who were not studied longitudinally. The only way that the reader can tell what was going on in the study is by looking at the sample sizes for each age (if cited) and noting if those sample sizes differ from testing time to testing time. The strength of the mixed longitudinal design is that the sample size can be larger than what might be possible with a straight longitudinal design since the participants show up for only one or two testing sessions as opposed to many sessions. The weakness of such an approach is that the data misrepresent the actual change observed in the sample. In contrast to a convergence design, in which the nature of the sample is clear and is studied for differences between the longitudinal and cross-sectional groups, the mixed longitudinal design treats all the participants as though they had been studied over time.

While longitudinal data are the most prized data in motor development research, cross-sectional designs are used more frequently because of their practicality. Convergence designs, on the other hand, have rarely been used in motor development research but will hopefully become more frequent in the future.

We close this section with a unique developmental design that employs a two-step approach of screening hypothesized developmental sequences before beginning the necessary longitudinal research needed for validation. This approach, proposed by Roberton, Williams, and Langendorfer (1980), is called *prelongitudinal screening.*

Prelongitudinal Screening: Cross-Sectional Data

In prelongitudinal screening, the researcher first envisions a graph of the longitudinal progression of a group of people traveling through a hypothesized but accurately ordered developmental sequence. At 8 years of age, for instance, some participants will be at an early level of development, some will be in the middle levels of development, and some will be advanced. At 10 years of age, fewer participants will be at the early and middle levels, and more will have progressed to advanced behavior. The investigator then collects cross-sectional data on the developmental levels of participants, graphing the percentages of people at each age who show each level. If the proposed sequence is correct, the resulting cross-sectional graph should reflect some portion of the hypothesized longitudinal graph: The curves for each developmental level should mimic the order and shape of the curves (increasing or decreasing percentages) predicted for the longitudinal graph (see figure 4.5). If the results do mimic a portion of the predicted longitudinal graph, then the investigator can conclude that the data have supported at least part of the hypothesized sequence. If enough of the sequence receives support, then the investigator should proceed with an actual longitudinal study to validate the sequence.

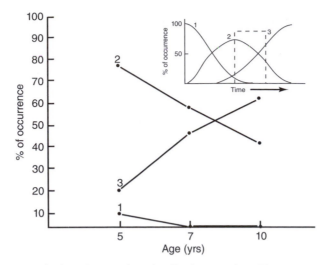

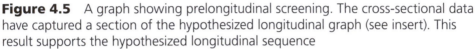

Figure 4.5   A graph showing prelongitudinal screening. The cross-sectional data have captured a section of the hypothesized longitudinal graph (see insert). This result supports the hypothesized longitudinal sequence

Reprinted with permission from *Research Quarterly for Exercise and Sport,* Vol. 51: 729, Copyright 2002 by American Alliance for Health, Physical Education, Recreation and Dance, 1900 Association Drive, Reston, VA 20191.

Prelongitudinal Screening: Across-Trials Variability

Another way to screen a hypothesized developmental sequence is to examine the variability across trials that study participants show when they are categorized on each trial using the developmental sequence. The criteria by which the variability is judged are as follows: (1) If the proposed developmental sequence is correct, each participant should vary across trials only to adjacent levels in the sequence. If a proposed sequence has four levels, for example, and a participant demonstrated level 1 behavior on five trials, level 3 behavior on two trials, and level 4 behavior on three trials, then the sequence order should be rejected since the participant skipped from level 1 to level 3. This reasoning is based on stringent developmental sequence theory, which argues that all persons (or almost all) go through valid sequences without skipping developmental levels. (2) At least 50% of a person's trials should be in one developmental level if that person really is in a sequence level. The sample participant just described would pass that criterion. Too much variability should make the researcher suspicious that the levels being tested do not really tap into steady-state behavior.

The advantage of screening a sequence before beginning a longitudinal study is obvious. If the hypothesized developmental sequence is poorly constructed, it is best to learn this before spending time and money on longitudinal study. If the cross-sectional or across-trials data reveal problems with the sequence, the investigator simply goes back to the drawing board, revamps the hypothesized sequence, and performs another prelongitudinal screening. Developmental sequence studies that have employed screening procedures include those of Roberton (1977); Halverson and Williams (1985); Messick (1991); and Barrett, Williams, McLester, and Ljungkvist (1997).

> ## Tips for Novice Investigators

What design is right for you? Often, a graduate student may be tempted to use a cross-sectional design for the sake of convenience and time. However, a convergence design does not take much more time and offers a much better picture of what is occurring developmentally. A researcher could observe children several times over the span of a year, providing a 1-year longitudinal window within each age cohort.

DEVELOPMENT SIMULATION

Prelongitudinal screening involves looking at data that are not longitudinal with the hypothesized longitudinal actuality in mind. Several other techniques have been used in developmental study that are not longitudinal themselves but can allow the investigator to infer what longitudinal analysis might reveal. Ultimately, as we indicated earlier, only longitudinal study can validate developmental phenomena.

Microgenesis

Heinz Werner (1957), a well-known developmental psychologist associated with Clark University in the middle of the 20th century, proposed a technique to allow scientists to observe development in a compressed time frame. He called this technique *microgenesis*. By displaying perceptual phenomena to participants in shorter and shorter durations, he caused participants to behave perceptually in ways characteristic of the developmental levels that they had already passed through. Thus, using microgenesis, the researcher revealed more primitive developmental levels without actually measuring participants going through those levels.

The term *microgenesis* applies to a useful, broad category encompassing all methods that cause regression or backward development in a compressed time frame. For instance, while it has not been used in motor development research, hypnosis is a potential method in this category.

Another method of microgenesis involves manipulating constraints to evoke regression. For instance, in natural circumstances, regression occurs in an intratask sequence when a person is constrained by some kind of task or environmental change. An example is walking on ice. When on ice, most people modify their gaits into a developmentally earlier form, such as holding the arms in low guard, even though they normally use opposition or semiopposition when walking. (See chapter 6 for definitions of these terms.) The investigator can create regression to reveal forms that occurred earlier in development by purposely manipulating the constraints surrounding the mover. Raising a person's height, such as by putting the person on an elevated balance beam, can elicit locomotor regression, while moving a person closer to a target can elicit regression in ballistic skills. Observing behaviors in such situations allows researchers to infer that these responses represent more primitive developmental levels.

Another way for investigators to infer parts of an intertask developmental progression is to watch what people do when they cannot yet perform the requested skill. This behavior is called *substitution* because it consists of substituting one skill for another in an intertask sequence (Roberton & Halverson, 1984). For instance, when asked to skip, children who cannot yet skip frequently gallop instead. This fact tells the investigator that galloping precedes skipping in the intertask developmental sequence for locomotion. Chapter 6 presents more examples of substitution in locomotion.

Asymmetrical Development

The last method that we describe for simulating development is particular to motor development research. This method takes advantage of the fact that an individual's dominant side often shows more advanced motor development than the nondominant side shows. For example, people throwing with their nondominant side show more primitive developmental levels than they show when throwing with their dominant side. By having participants throw with each arm, the investigator controls for body characteristics while studying the developmental differences across sides.

Getchell and Roberton (1989) explored the reason why children progress from one level of hopping to the next by taking advantage of the fact that hopping children tend to progress on their dominant foot before they progress on their nondominant foot. These researchers found children who were one developmental level ahead on their dominant foot than they were on their nondominant foot. By studying these children as they hopped with each foot on a force platform, the researchers were able to deduce the possible cause for advancement between these two levels. This study is discussed in more detail in chapter 6.

DEPENDENT VARIABLES

The best research design is wasted if an investigator chooses an unwise dependent variable. Throughout its history motor development research has used a variety of dependent measures to reflect changing motor behavior. We shall review the strengths and weaknesses of several of these measures.

Product Scores

Product scores are the outcomes of movements. They indirectly reflect the movements that participants display. Footprints have been a favorite product score in the study of walking. In 1931, Mary Shirley used lampblack on olive oil to preserve her toddler's footprints; 70 years later Adolph, Vereijken, and Shrout (2003) were still using footprints (this time made with colored ink) to study toddler walking. Myrtle McGraw used another ingenious approach (McGraw & Breeze, 1941) in which she poured milk on a glass plinth, covered the milk with a rubber mat, and then had children walk across the plinth. A 16 mm camera, pointed upward from underneath the plinth, filmed the children's footsteps as they showed through the milk.[1]

Other product scores used in motor development research include ball velocity, distance thrown or kicked, running speed, and so on. The advantages of product scores are that they (1) are usually easier and quicker to measure compared with direct measures of movement and (2) tend to be continuous data, which makes them available for analysis with most parametric statistical techniques. Their disadvantages are that they (1) do not indicate the kind of movement used to produce them, (2) are generally correlated to anthropometric measures, and (3) frequently do not reflect movement discontinuities. The distance a ball is kicked, for example, tends to increase gradually over time as a person grows regardless of whether that person's kicking movements have actually changed.

Tips for Novice Investigators

When using product scores as your dependent measure, be careful to select a score that accurately reflects what you are trying to measure. For example, researchers interested in motor coordination may be tempted to use time spent on an agility test as their dependent measure. However, this measure is a better reflection of quickness than of motor coordination.

Movement Description

Throughout the history of motor development research, investigators have used checklists and anecdotal records to describe the movement of their participants directly, especially when validating developmental sequences that they wished to use as their dependent variable. Such real-time assessment takes considerable practice, however, in order to achieve both intra- and interobserver objectivity.

Since the 1920s most researchers studying motor development have preferred to use data collection methods that permanently and directly record at least some aspects of participants' movements. These records allowed the researchers to revisit the data when the participants were no longer present in order to quantify the results or describe them verbally. To capture the data, most researchers during the 20th century used slow-motion 16 mm film. They then replayed the film as many times as needed to reduce the data—that is, to describe what their participants were doing. Videography has now replaced filming for verbally describing movements.

Kinematics

Early on, biomechanical measurements were made from 16 mm film by scholars such as Henry Halverson in Gesell's lab at Yale University. Mary Pat Murray (Murray, Drought, & Kory, 1964) used another method called interrupted light photography. While a strobe light flashed 20 times a second, a 35 mm camera photographed participants as they walked in semidarkness with reflective markers placed on key joints. The position of the reflectors was recorded on the film, gradually creating a white stick figure on a black background (see figure 4.6).

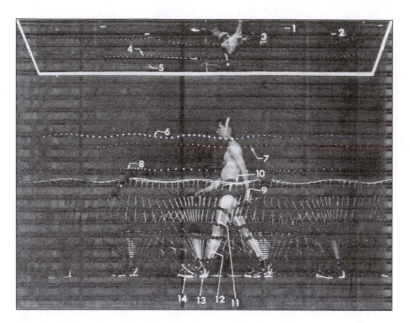

Figure 4.6 A 35 mm photograph (interrupted light photography) of a participant walking in semidarkness with reflective markers. Note the overhead mirrors. Kinematic data were obtained from the resulting stick figures.

From M.P. Murry, A.D.B. Drought, and R. C. Kory, 1964, "Walking patterns of normal men," *Journal of Bone and Joint Surgery* 46:335-360. Reprinted with permission from The Journal of Bone and Joint Surgery, Inc.

Kinematic measurements (displacement, velocity, and acceleration) were then made from enlargements of the pictures.

Under the direction of Ruth Glassow at the University of Wisconsin–Madison, most of the early developmental kinematic descriptions of basic motor skills and sporting skills (see Wickstrom, 1970) were created by measuring joint angles and segmental inclinations from projections of each film frame onto the platen of a Kodak Recordak, a microfilm viewer modified to project 16 mm film. Now video records, which are digitized, are used to obtain kinematic data, although more frequently motion analysis camera systems are used to collect the spatial coordinates of joints marked with reflective material. The advantage of these systems is that they can provide data quickly and perform three-dimensional analyses fairly easily; their disadvantage is the lack of a visual record of the movement.

Kinetics

While kinematics give a more precise picture of movement and its change over time, kinetics are now routinely used by several scholars who are attempting to tease out the source of the forces that shape the way a movement looks (see Holt, 2005; Jensen, 2005; Ulrich & Kubo, 2005; van Soest & Ledebt, 2005). Using the equation

$$NET = MUS + GRAV + MDT + ENV,$$

where *NET* = net torque, *MUS* = net effect of all muscles spanning a joint, *GRAV* = the torque created by gravity, *MDT* = motion-dependent torques, and *ENV* = external forces that may be acting on the body, these biomechanists use inverse dynamics to partial out the general muscle torques generated by the central nervous system (Jensen, 2005). Holt (2005), in addition, has been interested in other dynamic resources or potential sources of energy that are part of the organismic constraints affecting movement. In addition to the active muscular forces, these resources include passive elastic energy from soft tissues and energy from the pendulum-like transfers of swinging body parts. Holt's work on atypical development has shown how differences in these dynamic resources can explain why atypically developing children show different gait patterns (Holt, Obusek, & Fonseca, 1996). From this work Holt has developed the theory that a good part of the challenge of acquiring advanced motor development is being able to take advantage of the passive dynamics of the body system (Holt, 2005).

Contemporary Tools

As interest shifts to kinetics, the use of force recorders is gradually increasing in motor development. Ground reaction forces can be determined for various gaits by using force plates; ergometers have been used by Jensen (2005) to measure pedaling forces. Electromyography (EMG) will also gradually increase as a window into muscle action. Renewed interest in the nervous system will likely lead to use of MRI and computed tomography (CT) as their availability increases and their cost decreases. As with all research tools, investigators must train carefully in their use and interpretation and must establish their reliability.

▶ Tips for Novice Investigators

Do not underestimate the amount of time it may take to become proficient at a particular research tool. Although technological advances (such as automatic digitizing by computer programs) have made certain aspects of data collection, reduction, and analysis easier, other issues creep up that cannot be ignored. Computer programs provide researchers with many different options for setting up acquisition and so on, and the researcher must select from these options knowledgeably. By far the easiest way to learn how to use this equipment is to volunteer time assisting others with their research!

Motor Development Scales and Tests

We would be remiss if we closed this section on dependent variables without addressing the use of established motor development tests and scales. The main difference between these scales and the variables we have been discussing is that scales and tests attempt to measure a construct (usually motor development but sometimes coordination or another related term). Assessing the validity of a test of a construct is quite involved. First, what does the test creator mean by the

construct? For example, what is the whole of motor development? Is there really such a thing or is motor development made up of a variety of discrete skills? Second, if there is a whole, then how can we measure it? Usually, construct validity in the motor realm is established through correlation with another test that purportedly measures the same construct. Clearly, if that other test isn't valid, then subsequent tests correlated with it will also not be valid.

The next aspect of validity specifically related to motor development scales and tests is the question of whether the instrument is developmental. On the surface this question is easily answered: Do scores on the test change over time? At a deeper level, however, is the question of how the test is scored. Is the test really assessing the changing ways in which people move as they develop? Many current motor development scales are actually assessing how close the performer comes to an adult model of performance. The test developer describes adult or elite performance (often without reference to current biomechanical studies of adult performance) and then gives points for each attribute of the adult performance displayed by the person taking the test. Movements that are somewhere on the continuum between primitive and adult are not given credit unless they are the adult movement. A child at level 5 of a six-step sequence, for instance, still receives a 0 in the scoring for that characteristic. This type of scoring is sometimes called an *error model* in contrast to a *developmental model*. The performer is in error unless he shows the movement the test creator deemed as adult performance. A developmental test, on the other hand, gives credit for levels between beginning and advanced—in other words, it measures the developmental sequence of movements that occur over time in that test.

Researchers like motor development scales and tests that are already designed because they are ready to use straight out of the box, so to speak. The consumer of such tests, however, needs to study them carefully to see whether they are really measuring the construct the researcher wants to measure and whether they are evaluating the performer's movement in a developmental way.

Tips for Novice Investigators

Make sure that the motor development test you select actually measures what you want to measure. Some tests include several different subtests that may or may not relate to your primary question. For example, the Movement Assessment Battery for Children assesses manipulative skills, ball skills, and balance and is primarily used for children with disabilities (Henderson & Sugden, 1992). It is not the most appropriate test if you are interested in examining gross motor coordination in children; for that, you should use a scale such as the Test of Gross Motor Development (Ulrich, 2000).

ANTHROPOMETRIC MEASURES

Often the study of development is grouped with that of growth; however, these are not the same. The study of anthropometrics relates to the measurement of human anatomy in relation to body dimensions. Such measurements include

height, weight, and limb length, among others. Growth examines the change in anthropometrics over time and is most closely observed during childhood.

Growth as a Constraint

In the latter half of the 20th century, developmentalists often collected anthropometric measures in order to study physical growth. These measures were generally reported separately from movement data. Newell's model of constraints (see chapter 3), however, highlights the importance of physical growth as an individual structural constraint on the development of movement. Since the physical body changes over the lifespan, developmentalists who have information about body size can better attribute changes in movement to the individual, the task, the environment, or their interaction. In addition, researchers can make the task in a research study more equivalent for participants of all ages and sizes by adapting the equipment to body size (see figure 4.7).

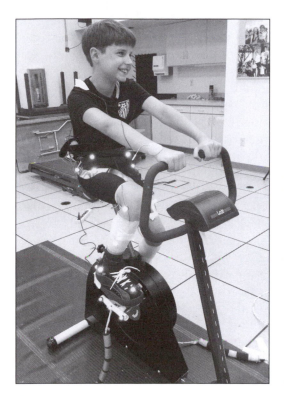

Figure 4.7 This bicycle has been adapted in size for children.

Courtesy of Jensen Lab, University of Texas, Austin.

Useful Measures

Anthropometric measurements of length, such as standing height, sitting height, or the length of any body segment, reflect skeletal growth in youths or age-related changes in the skeletal system. Relating measurements of length to each other, such as when calculating the ratio of shoulder breadth to hip breadth, can also provide information about body shape and how it changes over time.

Another measure of size is weight. Whole-body weight has the disadvantage of representing both fat and nonfat tissue, thus limiting its usefulness as a measure of growth or even maturation. Yet, body weight can be apportioned into fat and nonfat weight to provide very useful measurements. Sometimes developmentalists are more interested in the mass of a body segment than in weight per se. For example, researchers interested in studying the coordination of bicycling over age have to determine the mass of the leg so that the torque generated by cyclists can be apportioned into torque due to muscle, motion, and gravity (see figure 4.8).

Normalizing Product Scores

Growth measures can be used to *normalize* product scores. For instance, a researcher interested in studying vertical or long jumping from childhood through adolescence would do well to measure standing height. As children become taller, they can reach higher and jump farther, so product scores should be made relative to this anthropometric measure. An additional use for measures of segment length is to normalize a distance across individuals of varying size. For example, a researcher studying the speed and accuracy of reaching across short versus long distances in participants aged 1 to 8 years might employ normalization to place the target at 25% of arm length for the short reach and 75% of arm length for the long reach. Otherwise, if absolute distances were used, any age differences might actually be caused by differences in body size rather than changes in the coordination and control of the reaching movement.

Figure 4.8 This bicycle measures forces through an ergometer in the pedal.

Courtesy of Jensen Lab, University of Texas, Austin.

As with all research measures, investigators using anthropometric measurements for intraindividual comparisons over time or interindividual comparisons at one time must train to take their measurements with consistent methods and markers. Intraobserver and interobserver reliability should be assessed periodically.

MOVING THE FIELD FORWARD: STRONG INFERENCE RESEARCH

While contemporary research is often associated with sophisticated statistical methods, John R. Platt argued that the best and most efficient research is based on clear logic applied as solid inductive and deductive thinking. Platt, a biophysicist at the University of Chicago, wrote a classic article on this topic that appeared in *Science* in 1964. He titled it "Strong Inference." The purpose of this article was to stimulate rapid advances in science by urging investigators to follow a series of steps similar to but expanded on those found in the scientific method. The field of motor development could profit from this approach.

In strong inference research, a scientist generates a series of interrelated studies, each designed to rule out alternative explanations for the phenomenon of interest. Platt (1964) suggested the following steps:

1. Devise alternative hypotheses.
2. Devise crucial experiments to exclude one or more of the hypotheses.
3. Carry out the experiments cleanly.
4. Recycle the procedure.

While Platt's description of strong inference has not been without criticism (see Davis, 2006; McDonald, 1992; O'Donohue & Buchanan, 2000), it has two key strengths that could contribute considerably to motor development research. The first is step 1: the generation of *multiple alternative* hypotheses. By generating more than one hypothesis, the experimenter is not wedded to one answer to a problem. Sometimes researchers seem to be trying to prove or support their own hypothesis. Having multiple hypotheses lessens this bias. The second strength is the emphasis in step 2 of trying to refute hypotheses rather than support them. This also takes personal bias toward a particular hypothesis out of the picture. The true scientist tries to eliminate hypotheses (regardless of who dreamed them up) until, ideally, a clear solution survives.

Figure 4.9 shows an example of using Platt's strong inference to attack a problem in motor development. The question under study is why some children practice throwing on their own hour after hour while other children rarely practice. Again, rather than trying to prove a pet hypothesis, the motor development researcher should try to generate as many answers to the question as possible. Figure 4.9 shows eight possible answers that can be hypothesized. The right side of the figure shows two experiments designed to refute some of the generated hypotheses. One experiment would try to refute a hypothesis dealing with gender stereotypes by giving children questionnaires designed to elicit their views of throwing as either masculine or feminine. Runion, Roberton, and Langendorfer (2003) actually conducted such an experiment. Their results are discussed in chapter 7.

The second experiment in figure 4.9 pits two hypotheses against each other: If obesity is held constant, would youth sport participants practice more than nonparticipants practice? Of course, for this experiment the researchers would have to be able to find youth sport participants who are also obese. If such participants cannot be found, then this particular design would not work. The point for our purposes, however, is that through a series of studies a research question can be examined systematically and alternative hypotheses can be refuted until a clear answer emerges.

The strong inference approach suggests that motor development research should begin with a substantial amount of time spent carefully considering the problem and developing testable hypotheses. What are the great unanswered questions in motor development? What are the possible answers to these questions? Brainstorming such answers as hypotheses is the most important preparation for doing developmental research but is a step frequently omitted.

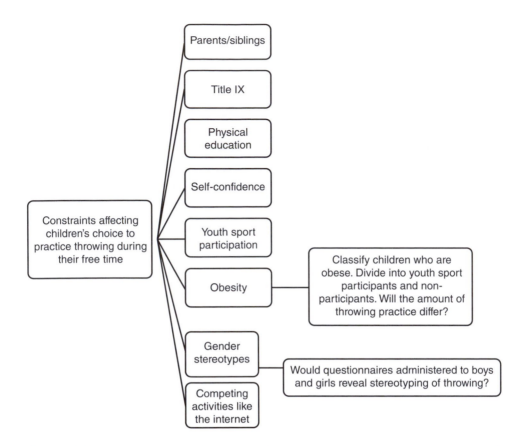

Figure 4.9   A hypothetical flowchart or logical tree with possible hypotheses and initial studies testing why children do not practice overarm throwing.

Once a hypothesis is chosen for testing, careful selection of independent and dependent measures as well as careful experimental design should lead to unambiguous conclusions based on the clear logic of the thought processes. Platt (1964) called this type of thinking *"catch[ing] phenomena in a logical box"* (p. 352). He argued that logical analysis is the key to scientific progress. He further argued that every scientist should keep a notebook of the great unanswered questions in the field and work out logical trees of hypotheses and crucial experiments:

Tips for Novice Investigators

Strong inference is important to novice researchers for several reasons. First, it forces the researcher to really think through the problem and its potential explanations before performing research. Doing this will lead to better empirical designs. Second, it provides a framework for future studies, depending on the outcome of the first. The researcher will then have a viable research line, which is an essential component of promotion and tenure at many institutions of higher education.

"Devote a half hour or an hour to analytical thinking every day, writing out the logical tree and the alternatives and crucial experiments explicitly in a permanent notebook" (p. 352). If every motor development researcher followed this practice, the field would surely advance much faster than it has in the past.

MOVING THE FIELD FORWARD: WOHLWILL'S DEVELOPMENTAL RESEARCH SCHEMA

In 1973 Joachim Wohlwill published a textbook devoted to analyzing the research techniques used in developmental psychology. He conceptualized developmental research into a framework that even today can act as a road map for motor development researchers. Our summary here does not substitute for a careful reading of his book, *The Study of Behavioral Development*, but it does act as both a summary of this chapter and a challenge to young motor development researchers.

Wohlwill (1973) organized developmental research into five categories that were meant to be developmental—that is, he meant for researchers to start at the top and work their way down through the categories. His path represents a life time of research or the total output of a laboratory across several decades. The categories, however, also help place even a single study into the steady progress being achieved in a particular research focus.

I. Discovery and Synthesis of Developmental Dimensions

In simple language this step consists of deciding what to study and how to measure it. The researcher needs to search for dimensions that are developmental rather than situational and to create a way to measure this variable. The importance of this step—of asking, "What am I going to measure?"—cannot be overemphasized. Coming from a dynamic systems perspective, the question would be, "What is my collective variable?"

II. Descriptive Study of Age Changes

Here the researcher collects the data to create a developmental function (if the data are quantitative) or a developmental sequence (if the data are qualitative). This allows the researcher to create a developmental curve or narrative of how changes occur over time.

III. Correlational Study of Age Changes

In this step, the researcher looks at two developmental functions (either two dependent variables or a dependent variable and another variable) to see how they interrelate. Or, the researcher looks at the relationship across developmental sequences to find evidence of stages (behaviors common across several tasks at the same point in time).

IV. Study of Determinants of Developmental Change

At this point Wohlwill suggests that the researcher should attempt to manipulate variables to change the developmental function or sequence in order to understand its cause. This is the experimental level of developmental research.

V. Study of Individual Differences in Development

Most developmental study is focused on the average or the modal way of behaving at a certain age. This final level of developmental research, however, focuses on the exceptions to the rule, the deviations from typical development, and the causes for such interindividual variability.

Wohlwill's road map of research allows us to organize the many motor development studies that are reported in this text and elsewhere. More importantly, along with Platt's challenge to do strong inference research, Wohlwill's developmental research schema challenges all of us to see the possibilities and conduct the studies that will push the field of motor development forward.

RESEARCH METHODS IN PRACTICE: ESTHER THELEN AND REFLEX STEPPING

An excellent example of using strong inference in motor development research lies in the series of studies by Thelen and colleagues described in chapter 3. In these studies we can also see progression through parts of Wohlwill's research framework. Thelen began her research by describing the rhythmical movements called *stereotypies* in infants (Thelen, 1979, 1981). From these observations she selected spontaneous leg kicking for further description and observation using videotape. By timing the various phases of kicking, Thelen, Bradshaw, and Ward (1981) thought they saw similarities between the infant kicks and the adult walking cycle. (For a challenge to this interpretation, see Janzen, 1989.) Regardless of the accuracy of this comparison, Thelen's argument that some stereotypies are continuous with subsequent voluntary movement made her wonder if primitive reflexes might also be connected to voluntary movement. As noted in chapter 3, the prevailing view at the time was that neuromaturation makes primitive reflexes disappear in order for voluntary movements to develop. This view had been promoted by McGraw's (1945/1963) extensive observations that primitive reflexes always disappear before homologous voluntary movements appear. Although McGraw was implying causation from correlation in time (reflex stepping disappearing, then voluntary movement appearing), her views were still widely accepted in the field of motor development and in applied fields such as physical and occupational therapy.

In contrast to this prevailing zeitgeist, Thelen saw McGraw's view as a hypothesis that could be tested empirically. Thelen continued her descriptive work, looking for alternative hypotheses in the events that occur at the same time that the stepping reflex disappears in most babies. In 1982 she and Fisher observed that spontaneous kicking and reflex stepping of 2-week-old infants (see figure 4.10a-b) share similar kinematics and EMG patterns and therefore reflect the same muscle synergies. This finding suggested continuity rather than discontinuity between primitive reflex and voluntary movement. Next, Thelen, Fisher, and additional colleagues examined 63 infants, finding that the reflex stepping rate was directly related to levels of arousal and that chubbier infants stepped less (Thelen, Fisher, Ridley-Johnson, & Griffin, 1982). This observation

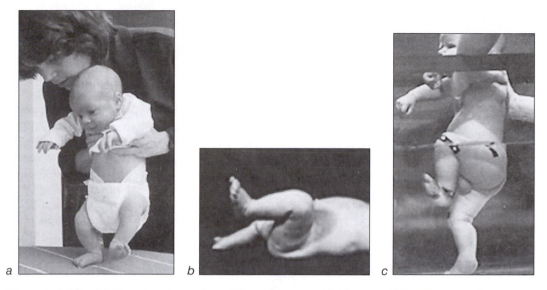

a b c

Figure 4.10 (a) The stepping reflex, (b) spontaneous kicking, and (c) reflex stepping in a tank filled with water.

Reprinted, by permission, from J.O. Spencer et al., 2006, "Moving toward a grand theory of development: In memory of Esther Thelen," *Child Development* 77(6):1521-1538.

supported two alternative hypotheses to neuromaturation: increased arousal and increased weight.

As described in chapter 3, Thelen and colleagues then designed a series of studies pitting these hypotheses against each other (Thelen, Fisher, & Ridley-Johnson, 1984). First, they conducted another descriptive study, counting the number of steps that infants took at 2, 4, and 6 weeks of age and measuring the infants' arousal state, ponderal index, leg volume, and body fat at each age. Again they found that arousal was the best predictor of number of steps, but they also found that the infants who had gained the most weight at 4 weeks actually stepped less.

Now, in order to determine if weight truly affects stepping, the researchers needed to design an experiment in which arousal remained constant while weight was either increased or decreased. Thelen et al. manipulated leg weight by adding small weights to the legs of 12 4-week-old infants. When the weights were added, the infants began to step less, going from an average of 14 steps to less than 10 steps, a statistically significant change. At the same time, there were no arousal differences between weighted and nonweighted conditions, thus ruling out that alternative hypothesis.

The final experimental manipulation to eliminate competing explanations was to see if reducing weight in heavier infants who already had reduced reflex stepping would lead to the infants increasing their steps. They held 4-week-old infants in a small tank of water (see figure 4.10c). The water was warm, so placing the infants in the tank did not increase their arousal, again controlling for

that alternative hypothesis. Indeed, when in the tank, the infants increased their steps twofold, going from 10 to 20 steps in the 1-minute collection time.

Thus, Thelen et al. were able to conclude from this series of studies (some descriptive, some correlational, and some experimental) that infant stepping movements during upright posture decline in normal development as a result of the changing ratio between leg weight and the hip flexor strength. The full effect of Thelen's systematic studies has been described elsewhere (e.g., Clark, 2002; Corbetta & Ulrich, 2008; Spencer et al., 2006); the point we wish to make in this chapter is how each of her studies scaffolded onto the next, ruling out specific alternative hypotheses and driving the next study. Starting with descriptive studies, her data helped formulate hypotheses that subsequent correlational and experimental studies could test. Esther Thelen's careful use of strong inference illustrates the contribution that this kind of thinking can make to solving the great unanswered questions in motor development.

SUMMARY

Many different types of experimental designs exist that researchers interested in studying motor development can adopt. The gold standard for developmental research is the longitudinal design, in which several participants are observed over long time periods. Of course, such a design may not be efficient for graduate students who hope to finish their degree within 2 – 3 years! In this case, other designs, such as cross sectional, cross longitudinal, or convergence designs can be adopted. Researchers may examine a variety of dependent measures, such as kinematics, kinetics, or scores on assessment tests. These should be well thought out so that they accurately reflect the developmental question under study. Finally, researchers should try to develop a framework under which to study their developmental problem rather than attempting a "one off" experiment. Using Platt's strong inference or Wohlwill's developmental schema will provide a novice researcher with a series of questions to answer which, in turn, can develop into a viable research line.

Footnotes

[1]McGraw produced a short 16 mm film of this procedure. It is available on videotape or DVD from S. Langendorfer, division of kinesiology, Bowling Green State University, Bowling Green, Ohio 43403.

PART

II

What Perspectives Do Researchers Use to Study Motor Development?

Contemporary Research

Part II focuses on relatively recent research within the context of several motor skills. We explore not only the development of particular skills but also how research on skill development contributes to our fundamental understanding of motor development. At times, we also see the gaps in knowledge that remain and we identify unanswered questions that need more research attention.

The first chapter in part II, chapter 5, addresses postural control. Obviously, for any complex motor skill—not to mention any activity of daily living—postural control is necessary for successful action. Through research studies we look at how postural control develops and we identify factors that might compromise postural control in older adulthood.

Chapter 6 examines locomotion—specifically, foot locomotion. Our focus is on developmental sequences, but we also consider contemporary research that addresses neural control of walking and hopping.

Chapter 7 considers the class of skills we call *ballistic*—those movements that require a rapid, all-out forceful movement. Striking, throwing, and kicking are the activities examined closely by research reports.

In chapter 8 we take up manipulative skills, which are skills involving use of the hands, often to attain an object. We first look at research on the development of reaching and grasping and on the development of tool use. Then we examine what is involved in intercepting objects not coming directly to us and look at how catching might develop.

Motor skills are varied in type and large in number. We do not consider every motor skill that has been examined through research. Instead, we focus on those skills that have received the most research attention and on areas of research that provide the most information about the nature of motor development.

CHAPTER 5

Development of Postural Control

The internationally acclaimed dance troupe Pilobolus is known for its unique pair and group poses and transitions. Weight bearing is shared among the dancers: They balance on just about any body part, on the floor, or on another dancer. Watching these dancers is a good reminder of the many body systems required to maintain postural control and balance or to let go of balance in order to move to a different position (see figure 5.1).

When we say *balance*, we are typically referring to maintaining a position, whether stationary or moving, to avoid crashing to the floor! That is, we are typically referring to maintaining equilibrium. Stationary balance is labeled static balance while moving balance is labeled dynamic balance. One aspect of balance is *aligning body segments* such that we attain and maintain equilibrium, and another aspect is *righting the body*—that is, bringing the body into alignment as we move from one position to another. A common example of righting is moving from lying down to upright standing. Aligning the body segments and righting the body together can be termed *posture*. Notice that posture is not just maintaining a static position such as upright sitting or standing. It also includes righting the body, maintaining a body shape, and maintaining equilibrium as we move—that is, orientation control. Here, the term *postural control* is used for both balance and orientation control.

Figure 5.1 Two dancers from Pilobolus balance on a third dancer.

Photograph by Howard Schatz, courtesy of Pilobolus.

It is good to remember what information our bodies use to control posture. We need only to stand on one foot and close our eyes to realize that visual information is useful to balance. Somewhat more complicated are the many proprioceptors that, coupled with the vestibular apparatus, provide information about the body's position in relation to gravity; the relative position of the head, limbs, and trunk; the movement of the head; and the support of body parts on surfaces. Certainly a great deal of integrated information from multiple sensory-perceptual systems is necessary for balance. This in itself makes postural control complicated, but the dozens of muscles involved in maintaining alignment of the head, trunk, and limbs and adapting to perturbations to balance rapidly before equilibrium is lost make postural control complicated indeed!

Chapter 1 described Shirley's (1931) intertask sequence of motor milestones acquired in the first 12 to 18 months of life. Many of these milestones involve acquiring a new posture, such as rolling over, sitting, standing, and walking. It is no wonder that developmentalists are interested in how postural control develops in early life. Part of our discussion in this chapter focuses on postural control in infancy and childhood.

In this chapter we also consider postural control within the whole of the lifespan. Changes in posture and balance can reflect parallel changes in other body systems. For example, a loss of leg muscle makes balancing more difficult. Identifying body systems that influence postural control while undergoing age-related change is a way for researchers to identify the role that these systems play in postural control. There is also a practical side to studying loss of postural control in older adults. Even the popular press has reported on the frequency of falls among older populations. Such falls can be costly and very detrimental to the overall health of an individual. In addition, there are disabilities that become more prevalent in older adulthood, and many of these disabilities affect postural control. Loss of postural control might dictate the end of independent living for an older adult. It is no surprise, then, that developmentalists have focused on postural control in older adults.

Before we begin looking at segments of the lifespan, however, we should first consider the theoretical perspectives that developmentalists have used to explore postural control. This is where our discussion begins.

THEORETICAL PERSPECTIVES

There are two major perspectives on postural control. One dominated the thinking of developmentalists for most of the last century. The second has received increasing attention over the last quarter century.

Reflex Hierarchy Approach

The perspective that guided work on postural control for most of the 20th century is called the *reflex hierarchy approach*. This approach focuses on what reflex responses, especially righting and postural responses, imply about the neurological control of posture. To review, a reflex is a specific automatic response to a specific sensory stimulus. It is made without thought. Specific reflex responses can be made at various anatomical levels of the central nervous system, includ-

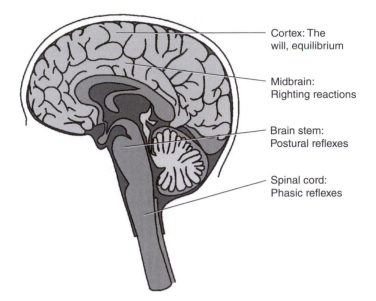

Figure 5.2 The reflex hierarchy.

ing the spinal cord, the brain stem, the midbrain, and the cortex (see figure 5.2). The reflex hierarchy approach sees posture as a reflex response to sensory inputs to motor centers in the central nervous system. Recall that the maturationists studied the disappearance of reflexes in infancy and assumed that this disappearance results directly from the maturation of the central nervous system (the central nervous system can inhibit reflexes in favor of voluntary movement).

The reflex hierarchy approach to postural control is rooted in the work of Sherrington (1906). Sherrington took a Cartesian approach (see chapter 2) to investigate systematically the neural control of behavior by studying reflex responses in animals. He viewed reflex behavior strictly as a mechanical response to stimuli (Reed, 1989). Magnus (1926a, 1926b) later applied Sherrington's work on reflexes to the study of posture (see table 5.1).

Magnus transected the nerves of four-legged animals at various anatomical levels and systematically noted the resultant posture of the animal and the animal's

Table 5.1 Key Theorists in the Reflex Hierarchy Tradition

Theorist	Key concept
Sherrington and Magnus	CNS centers mediate specific reflexes following specific stimuli.
McGraw	Maturation of the cerebral cortex allows infants to inhibit reflexes and gain voluntary control of movement.
Weisz	With development, righting reflexes fade and equilibrium reactions emerge.
Schaltenbrand	Lack of development of righting reflexes is associated with neurological dysfunction.
Bobath	Abnormal postural reflex mechanisms are associated with neurological dysfunction.

response to a change in position. He noted that decerebrated animals demonstrate tonic or postural reflexes: the tonic neck reflex, the tonic labyrinthine reflex, and the positive supporting reaction. The tonic reflexes are elicited with changes in head position relative to the body or relative to gravity, respectively. The positive supporting reaction is evoked when stretch or pressure is applied to the soles of a decerebrated animal's feet. In animals without a functioning cortex, the appropriate stimulus always yields a reflexive response. Proceeding in this way, Magnus was able to hypothesize which central nervous system centers mediate which reflexes.

Developmentalists with a maturation viewpoint, working at about the same time in history, linked Magnus' work to motor development. They argued that as the higher centers of the nervous system mature and exert control over lower levels of the central nervous system, infants gain progressive control over reflexive behavior. McGraw (1945/1963) assumed that the maturation of the cerebral cortex in infants allows inhibition of the reflexes and volitional control of motor skills. Weisz (1938) noted that righting reflexes fade while equilibrium reactions emerge during the course of motor development. Schaltenbrand (1928) also promoted the notion that righting reflexes are eventually brought under the control of the developing higher centers of the nervous system. He further hypothesized that a lack of development of righting responses can be associated with neurological dysfunction in children. Bobath (1965) later built her theory of abnormal motor development on this notion. Many educators and therapists came to associate abnormal motor behavior in children with a neurological dysfunction characterized by an abnormal postural reflex mechanism: dominating tonic reflexes and absent righting reflexes (VanSant, 1995). Magnus' work influenced developmentalists not only during his time but also during the decades following.

The reflex hierarchy perspective was well accepted for most of the 20th century but ultimately was found wanting in regard to several aspects of behavior (Reed, 1989). First was the tendency of the researchers taking this approach to view posture as static, as a summation of antigravity stretch reflexes used to maintain balance. Recent research, however, has suggested that the mechanisms controlling posture and the mechanisms controlling movement are tightly integrated rather than separate systems.

In addition, the reflex hierarchy perspective focused on gravity as the single outside force with which postural control must contend. It is now evident that self-generated reactive forces are also a factor in the maintenance of equilibrium. Reaching out to pick up a pitcher of water is an example. Trunk muscles and possibly even lower-limb muscles must activate to stabilize the body as a heavy weight is lifted at a distance away from the trunk.

A third complication for the reflex hierarchy perspective is that many postural responses involve most of the body. A reflex is typically defined as a local response to a specific sensory input. Yet, to achieve postural control many joints otherwise free to move must be maintained at a specific angle, and maintaining equilibrium often involves anticipating the forces that will act on the body or a body part. Cordo and Nashner (1982) established that postural activity *precedes* action, anticipating the need to counterbalance the forces generated in carrying out a task. This finding clearly does not fit the model of posture

as a set of reflex responses. One reason why the reflex hierarchy perspective is insufficient for explaining all aspects of postural control is that it was rooted in studies of animal behavior performed under unnatural conditions (VanSant, 1995). Developmentalists recently have turned to another, more functional perspective to explain aspects of postural control not addressed by the reflex hierarchy approach.

Systems Approach

The emergence of systems theory late in the 20th century provided a new perspective on posture. Nikolai Bernstein was one of the first to address the link between maintaining posture and making a limb movement. He introduced the notion of **postural synergy**, the combination of control signals to multiple muscles to assure stability of either a limb or the whole body in *anticipation* of a perturbation.

While the reflex hierarchy approach focused on a specific stimulus for a specific reflex neurological loop, a systems approach recognizes that even infants use multimodal perceptual information to maintain equilibrium (Gibson, 1987). All perceptual systems can contribute information simultaneously used to control posture (Reed, 1982a; VanSant, 1995).

Furthermore, perceptual information is not contributing merely to the maintenance of a stable state but rather to a dynamic process of continuously changing forces that act on the body so that it can move. Gravity is not the only force monitored. Reaction forces to surfaces as well as self-generated forces resulting from movement are also being monitored. From the systems perspective, posture is synonymous with the control and flexible use of all the forces acting on a body. This view is in contrast to the traditional approach, which regards posture as the response to gravity used to achieve stability.

Using the systems approach, researchers began focusing on the integration of systems in postural control. With the emergence of the systems perspective in the early 1980s, work by several researchers demonstrated that posture can influence movement possibilities. Amiel-Tison and Grenier (1980) observed that supporting the head of infants increases their reaching movements. Fentress (1981) showed that young mice can produce more grooming movements with the forepaws when provided with postural support. Researchers recognized that when compared with the reflex hierarchy perspective, systems theory better accommodates a link between posture and movement skills.

As mentioned earlier, the body must anticipate counterbalancing the forces that accompany a desired movement. A decreased ability to make anticipatory postural adjustments is a characteristic of movement disorders such as Parkinson's disease or traumatic brain injury. This fact highlights the close integration of posture and movement.

When researchers shifted from the reflex hierarchy theory to systems theory, they freed themselves to study postural control in more natural environments and with more natural tasks. This shift will be evident as we consider recent advances in our understanding of the emergence of postural control in infancy and of meeting the challenges to postural control that accompany aging.

Tips for Novice Investigators

As you reflect on the connections between the foundational chapters of this text and the topic of postural control, you no doubt recognize that the reflex hierarchy approach focuses on a single system (the neurological system). Just as developmentalists began to realize the importance of multiple systems, researchers studying postural control likewise looked more extensively at the role of multiple systems in postural control. The importance of perception and especially the role of the visual and kinesthetic systems was quickly identified. Developmentalists also identified the need for anticipatory use of the muscles. For example, skilled movers stabilize the body as the arm reaches out to lift a heavy object. Postural control obviously requires many systems of the body to cooperate in a highly interactive way. A novice researcher with an interest in the body's systems can find many questions to explore in the area of postural control. Note that many of the research methods used to explore the interaction of multiple systems in postural control vary information to one or more systems. You might apply this approach to your study of postural control.

EARLY DEVELOPMENT

Infancy is a time when many new postures are acquired in a relatively short time frame. Naturally, infants have attracted the attention of researchers wanting to know more about how posture, especially upright posture, is controlled. One measure of postural control that provides information is **body sway**.

Body Sway

Upright standing in humans is never motionless at any age. We sway when standing, although the movement might not be noticeable to the naked eye. The downward projection of the body's center of gravity moves around in a small area ahead of the ankle joints, within the base of support. Excursions of this point can be measured if a person stands on a force platform. The smaller the excursions, the more stable the stance. So, quiet stance is often used to study sensorimotor control of posture.

Before we look at body sway in infancy, let's review what is known about adult body sway. Researchers have found that adult sway during quiet stance has two components; these two components likely reflect two different control mechanisms. There is a slow drift that might be attributed to small errors in estimating postural state (Kiemel, Oie, & Jeka, 2002, 2006) and a fast-damped oscillation that might reflect control of body sway over the base of support. In the latter case the body is somewhat like an inverted pendulum of a clock, wherein there is weight at a distance from the point of rotation.

Adult sway increases during the performance of a challenging task (Woollacott & Shumway-Cook, 2002) but decreases when additional sensory information is provided (Jeka, Oie, & Kiemel, 2000). In fact, even a light touch of a stationary surface reduces sway (Jeka & Lackner, 1994). Likely, the additional information

from the touch is used to anticipate postural adjustments—that is, it provides *prospective* postural control.

A group of researchers from the University of Maryland recently studied early postural control in nine infants exhibiting typical development (Chen, Metcalfe, Jeka, & Clark, 2007; Chen, Metcalfe, Chang, Jeka, & Clark, 2008; Metcalfe, Chen, et al., 2005; Metcalfe, McDowell, et al., 2005). The researchers observed the infants monthly from the time when they could sit independently to the time when they had been walking independently for 9 months (see table 5.2). The infants were positioned on a saddle-shaped chair for sitting trials (see figure 5.3) and in parallel stance on a pedestal for standing trials. The pedestal, which discouraged the infants from moving their feet, was mounted on a force platform. The force platform measured **center of pressure (COP)** excursions (see figure 5.4) so that sway direction, amplitude, velocity, and variability could be derived.

The infants were also videotaped so that times of quiet stance when the infants were not making vigorous movements, bouncing, or holding onto a parent or

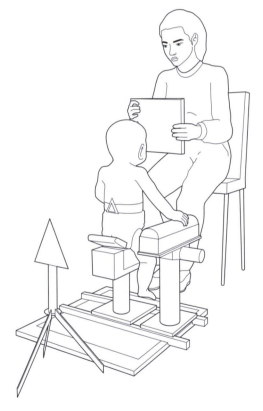

Figure 5.3   Chen et al. (2007) used a saddle-shaped chair affixed to a force platform for the seated trials in their study on infant postural control. Note the bar used in the touch condition. Markers helped identify on the video recordings the segments when there was no falling, bouncing, or vigorous movement.

Table 5.2 Studies of Postural Control Over the Lifespan

Study citation	Key topic or concept	Noteworthy findings	Comparative comments
Metcalfe, McDowell, et al. (2005)	Observed nature of sensorimotor modalities and integration in earliest times of upright stance. Six infants were measured monthly from 1 mo before onset of walking to 9 mo of walking experience. Infants stood on a pedestal on a force platform with a touch bar at the side. Conditions analyzed in this study were a stationary touch bar and a touch bar oscillating at 0.3 Hz.	By 6 mo of walking experience, infants adopted a temporally consistent relationship with oscillating bar. With walking experience postural responses were increasingly stable.	Walking experience allows active tuning of sensorimotor relations for estimating body position in space and refining temporal control of postural sway.
Metcalfe, Chen, et al. (2005)	Described the temporal organization of infant postural sway in quiet stance in first year of walking. Six infants were measured as described previously. Conditions analyzed in this study were standing independently (no touch) and touching a stationary bar.	Low-level touch forces attenuated sway. With increased walking experience, infants learned to make less frequent postural corrections.	Early postural development involves calibrating sensorimotor relations for estimating self-motion and identifying and tuning control system properties.
Chen, Metcalfe, Jeka, & Clark (2007)	Observed any changes in sitting posture at the time of learning to walk. Nine infants were measured monthly from the onset of sitting to 9 mo of walking experience. Infants sat on a saddle-shaped chair mounted on a force platform. Conditions included sitting independently (no touch) and touching a stationary bar.	Infants swayed more at time of transition to walking. Light touch attenuated sway only during the transition time.	Transitioning to a new skill might involve recalibrating an internal model for sensorimotor control of posture.
Chen, Metcalfe, Chang, Jeka, & Clark (2008)	Described development of infant posture in quiet upright stance in first year of walking and the influence of light touch. Nine infants were measured as described previously. Infants stood on a pedestal on a force platform with a touch bar at the side. Conditions included standing independently and touching the stationary bar.	With experience, postural sway lowered in frequency and was slower and less variable in oscillation velocity. Touch stabilized postural sway.	Infants sway differently with upright experience; presumably this finding reflects a refinement of sensorimotor dynamics that improves estimations of self-motion.
Bair, Kiemel, Jeka, & Clark (2007)	Described multisensory reweighting in children. Forty-one children aged 4 to 10 y were measured. Children stood in modified heel-to-toe stance looking at a front screen with the index finger lightly touching a bar. Visual scene and touch bar were simultaneously oscillated while postural sway was recorded.	Intramodal reweighting was observed as young as age 4 y but intermodal reweighting was observed only in older children. Amount of reweighting increased with age.	Development of multisensory reweighting contributes to stable but more flexible control of upright stance. (Reweighting is defined on page 111.)

Study citation	Key topic or concept	Noteworthy findings	Comparative comments
Jeka et al. (2006)	Determined whether sensory reweighting is related to stimulus amplitude with both sinusoidal and translational stimuli. Young adults, healthy elderly, and elderly prone to falls were measured. Participants stood in front of a visual display while standing on a force platform. The visual display oscillated at different amplitudes or a single amplitude with translation at different speeds. Frequency used was known to produce a strong sway response.	Nervous system processed more than stimulus velocity to determine postural response. Postural control mechanisms compensated for visual scene translation.	Little evidence was found that elderly prone to falls are deficient in sensory reweighting.
Jeka, Allison, & Kiemel (2010)	Observed whether reweighting of visual stimuli occurs more slowly in older adults versus younger adults and even more slowly in adults prone to falls		
Logan et al. (2010)	Studied multiple roles of vision in controlling trunk when changing from standing to walking		

For instructions on how to complete table 5.2, see Tips for Novice Investigators on page 124.

experimenter could be isolated and analyzed. In some trials the infants sat or stood independently, while in others they touched a bar to their right that was either stationary or moving (see figure 5.3). The bar was constructed so that the infants could touch it but not grab onto it.

Chen et al. (2007) examined infant sitting longitudinally and focused on sitting posture at the time each infant began to walk. They found that sitting infants swayed more at the age when they transitioned to walking than they swayed at any other age—that is, when they acquired a new posture. Sway was attenuated by touching the bar but only during this transition to walking. The researchers suggested that increased sway at the transition age reflects an adjustment to using sensory information to control posture in the *new* postural position. That is, learning to walk requires a recalibration of sensorimotor control of posture. The supplementary sensory information gained from touching the bar helps control posture during this recalibration process.

Chen et al. (2008) next longitudinally examined changes in body sway during standing as the infants acquired more and more walking experience. The amount of sway did not decrease as the infants acquired walking experience, a somewhat unexpected finding since older children demonstrate less sway than infants demonstrate (Riach & Hayes, 1987). Yet, the nature of the body sway did change, becoming slower with experience. The researchers suggested that this reflects the infants using sensory feedback in estimating and adjusting their posture and hence preventing excessive movements. The key

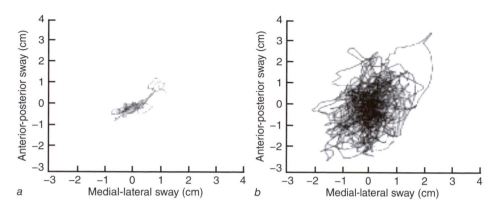

Figure 5.4 Examples of COP calculations from the ground reaction forces measured by a force platform. Anteroposterior movement is plotted on the vertical axis while mediolateral movement is plotted on the horizontal axis. These recordings were made during a trial with an oscillating touch surface. The left graph is from a performer who exhibited greater stability than the performer recorded on the right graph exhibited.

Reprinted, by permission, from by J.S. Metcalfe et al., 2005, "Development of somatosensory-motor Integration: An event-related analysis of infant posture the first year of independent walking," *Developmental Psychobiology*, 46: 27.

features of postural development in the months after learning to walk, then, are better integration of perception and action and more prospective control of posture.

Chen et al. (2008) found that allowing infants to lightly touch the stationary bar reduced their amount of sway, as it does for children and adults (Riach & Hayes, 1987; Jeka & Lackner, 1994). They suggested that light touch reduces the corrective actions that infants need to make to maintain upright posture.

In another phase of this work, six infants were recorded while standing with a stationary touch bar or a moving touch bar (Metcalfe, McDowell, et al., 2005). The moving bar oscillated mediolaterally at one of three frequencies and one of three small amplitudes. The infants were tested from 1 month before to 9 months after the onset of walking.

When touching the oscillating bar, infants showed increasing temporal consistency between bar movement and body sway as they gained walking experience. This finding is consistent with the suggestion that as infants acquire walking experience, sensorimotor control of posture is improved and body position in space is better estimated. Furthermore, control of the temporal aspects of postural sway is improved.

In summary, this line of work on upright postural control tells us that infant postural development is more than just reducing sway. There is a change in the nature of sway toward lower frequency and slower, less variable velocity. Sensory information is used more efficiently in estimating posture so that appropriate responses can be made. The rich sensorimotor experience acquired with walking apparently improves upright postural control.

Sensory System Priorities in Development

Earlier we indicated that postural control is based on input from many sensory receptors throughout the body. Naturally, developmentalists asked which system—visual or proprioceptive (the vestibular system plus the somatosensory system)—is more important to postural control. They also asked whether the weighting of sensory information changes with development. Research into this topic generally adopted the technique of putting visual and proprioceptive information into conflict and then noting how postural control was affected.

A common research paradigm used to implement this strategy is the **moving room paradigm**. An individual is placed in a room within a room. The inside room typically consists of a front wall, two sidewalls, and a ceiling. It is placed on a track and controlled by a servomotor so that it can be moved in a single large movement or in small back-and-forth movements. The participant is placed on a force platform and typically is asked to face the front wall and look at a target on that wall. The force platform records body sway, including movements in which the center of balance shifts so much that the participant would fall if not prevented from doing so by a harness or experimenter.

Lishman and Lee (1973) first demonstrated that moving the walls could disrupt the balance of standing adults. Moving the walls creates an optic flow of the walls sliding past on the periphery and suggests to persons positioned in the moving room that they are swaying off balance and should respond with a postural correction in the opposite direction. Of course, their proprioceptive information indicates no such thing. Hence, the visual and proprioceptive information is put into conflict. Infants and children respond in the same way. Thus, beginning in the first months of life we use visual information to maintain posture (Bertenthal & Bai, 1989; Butterworth & Hicks, 1977; Delorme, Frigon, & Lagacé, 1989; Lee & Aronson, 1974).

In order to manipulate both vision and proprioception, researchers have placed children on a movable platform (under the force platform) inside the moving room. Then they moved the room, moved the platform, or moved both. They found that only children 7 years of age and older can maintain upright postural control when the two types of sensory information conflict (Forssberg & Nashner, 1982; Shumway-Cook & Woollacott, 1985). Other research, though, places attainment of adultlike postural control at older ages, such as 12 years (Peterson, Christou, & Rosengren, 2006) or 15 years (Hirabayashi & Iwasaki, 1995).

Differences between children and adults probably involve differences in how precisely the postural control system adapts when sensory information is in conflict. Adults are capable of very precise reweighting of sensory information when necessary. If one sensory system provides unreliable information, the postural control systems of adults can decrease the emphasis on information from this system and increase emphasis on information from the other, more reliable system. This reweighting process involves decreasing the weighting of irrelevant information and increasing the weighting of relevant information, even when stimulus characteristics may be changing. It is likely that children cannot reweight sensory information as precisely as adults can, but little is known about when children acquire adultlike precision.

Godoi and Barela (2008) used a moving room paradigm in a cross-sectional study of 4-, 6-, 8-, 10-, 12-, and 14-year-olds plus young adults to address this very issue. We highlight this study here to learn about the development of postural control in children and adolescents as well as more about postural control in general. Godoi and Barela employed a methodology in which the moving room oscillated back and forth a small distance. Previous research had shown that infants and children sway along with room movement—that is, they have sensory–action coupling, but the coupling strength is weaker and more variable than that shown by adults (Barela, Godoi, Freitas Júnior, & Polastri, 2000; Barela, Jeka, & Clark, 2003). Godoi and Barela hypothesized that this fact reflects children's inability to reweight sensory information precisely.

The moving room used by Godoi and Barela had a pattern of black and white vertical stripes and a visual target on the front wall. The researchers analyzed nine trials lasting 60 seconds each. One was a baseline trial without room movement, and the rest were moving trials in which the room moved at two frequencies (0.2 and 0.5 hertz) combined with four distances (0.25, 0.50, 1.0, and 1.5 meters) between the front wall and the participants. None of the participants reported that they were aware the room moved.

Room movement induced sway in all the participants, and young children swayed more than older participants swayed. In the baseline trial with no room movement, the 4-year-olds swayed more than all the older participants swayed, and the 6- and 8-year-olds swayed more than young adults swayed. When the room oscillated, the 4-year-olds swayed more than all the older participants swayed, and all of the young groups swayed more than the young adults swayed (see figure 5.5). That young children swayed more than older children or adults swayed was expected, but these results also suggested that *when* children become adultlike in their postural response is task dependent because the age groups were differentially influenced by the various room movement conditions. As age increased, body sway was more tightly linked to room movement, but room movement induced less sway (see figure 5.6a). The influence of room movement on the strength of coupling between perception and action decreased as distance from the front wall increased for the 4-, 6-, 8-, and 10-year-olds but not for the older participants (see figure 5.6b).

So, even though the young children had weaker coupling to the visual information about room movement, they were more influenced by the movement than the older children and adults were. The young children could not adapt to changes in characteristics of the visual information as well as adults could. It is still possible that other factors, such as an immature visual system, a greater sensitivity to optic flow, or an inability to handle conflicting sensory inputs, are involved. Any of these factors could be a rate-limiting factor in the development of postural control.

Within this limitation, however, Godoi and Barela's (2008) results do suggest that the development of postural control in childhood is related to reweighting sensory cues from the environment to control body sway. More adultlike adaptation, or an improved ability to emphasize relevant information and de-emphasize irrelevant information, seems to come in the second decade of life. Overall, in infancy and childhood there is an improving ability to use sensory-perceptual information in postural control.

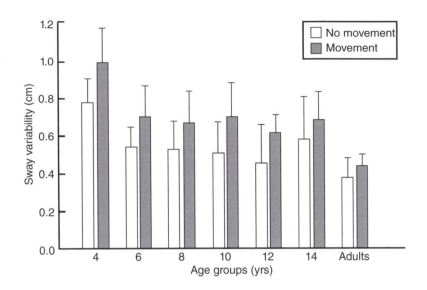

Figure 5.5 Godoi and Barela (2008) plotted sway variability in the anteroposterior direction for all age groups. The T bars represent one standard deviation from the mean. Sway variability was greater when the room was oscillating than when it was not moving, and there were age-related differences in sway variability.

Reprinted, by permission, from D. Godoi and J.A. Barela, 2008, "Body sway and sensory motor coupling adaptation in children: Effects of distance manipulation," *Developmental Psychobiology* 49: 82.

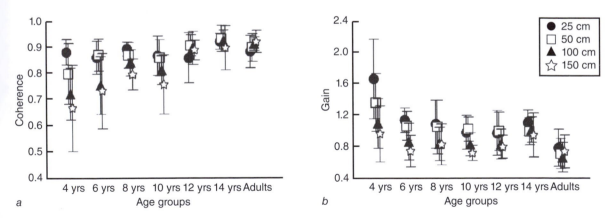

Figure 5.6 Godoi and Barela (2008) plotted (*a*) mean coherence values, which represent the strength of body sway relative to room movement (coupling of body sway to visual stimulus), and (*b*) gain, a measure of the dependence of induced body sway on stimulus motion, across age. The movement frequencies of 0.2 and 0.5 hertz are combined here.

Reprinted, by permission, From D. Godoi and J.A. Barela, 2008, "Body sway and sensory motor coupling adaptation in children: Effects of distance manipulation," *Developmental Psychobiology* 49: 82.

RISING TO STAND

When it comes to collecting data over the lifespan, posture and balance should be easier to study when compared with tasks difficult for young children or older adults to perform. However, there are few posture or balance skills for which we have a true lifespan of data (even cross-sectional data). An exception is Ann VanSant's work on rising to stand. In this task, an individual lies supine on the floor and then rises to a standing position. By studying individuals from 4 to 83 years of age, VanSant proposed lifespan developmental sequences for rising. She took a component approach and identified sequences for the arms, the legs, and the head and trunk (see table 5.3).

Individuals going through the early developmental steps typically rotate the trunk and push on the floor with one or both hands to assume a kneeling or half-kneeling position. They then rise to standing from this kneeling position. Individuals in the early levels also assume an asymmetrical squat before standing. Asymmetry is a theme of the early levels. Children are often observed at these levels (see table 5.4).

Table 5.3   Developmental Sequences for Rising to Stand

Step	Description
Upper-limb region	
Step 1	**Push and reach to bilateral push**
	One hand is placed on the support surface beside the pelvis. The other arm reaches across the body and the hand is placed on the surface. Both hands push against the surface to an extended elbow position. The arms are then lifted and used for balance.
Step 2	**Push and reach**
	One or both arms are used to push against the support surface. If both arms are used, there is asymmetry or asynchrony in the pushing action or a symmetrical push gives way to a single-arm push pattern.
Step 3	**Symmetrical push**
	Both hands are placed on the surface. Both hands push symmetrically against the surface before the point when the arms are lifted synchronously and used to assist with balance.
Step 4	**Bilateral reach**
	The arms reach forward, leading the trunk, and are used as balance assists throughout the movement. A front or slightly diagonal facing is achieved before the back extends to the vertical.
Step 5	**Push and reach with thigh push**
	One or both arms are used to push against the support surface. If both arms are used, there is asymmetry or asynchrony in the pushing action or a symmetrical push gives way to a single-arm push pattern. The other arm is then placed on one knee and pushes, assisting in extension of the trunk or legs to the vertical.
Step 6	**Push and reach to bilateral push with thigh push**
	One hand is placed on the support surface beside the pelvis. The other arm reaches across the body and the hand is placed on the surface. Both hands push against the surface to an extended elbow position. One or both arms are then lifted and placed on the thighs and push, assisting in extension of the trunk or legs to the vertical.

Step	Description
Axial region	
Step 1	**Full rotation with abdomen down**
	The head and trunk flex and rotate until the ventral surfaces of the trunk contact the support surface. The pelvis is then elevated to or above the level of the shoulder girdle. The back extends up to the vertical, with or without accompanying rotation of the trunk.
Step 2	**Full rotation with abdomen up**
	The head and trunk flex and rotate until the ventral surface of the trunk faces, but does not contact, the support surface. The pelvis is then elevated to or above the level of the shoulder girdle. The back extends from this position up to the vertical, with or without accompanying rotation of the trunk.
Step 3	**Partial rotation**
	Flexion and rotation bring the body to a side-facing position with the shoulders remaining above the level of the pelvis. The back extends up to the vertical, with or without accompanying rotation.
Step 4	**Forward with rotation**
	The head and trunk flex forward with or without a slight degree of rotation. Symmetrical flexion is interrupted by rotation or extension with rotation. Flexion with slight rotation is corrected by counterrotation in the opposite direction. One or more changes in the direction of rotation occur.
Step 5	**Symmetrical**
	The head and trunk move symmetrically forward past the vertical; the back then extends symmetrically to the upright position.
Lower-limb region	
Step 1	**Kneel**
	Both legs are flexed toward the trunk and rotated to one side. A kneeling pattern is assumed. One leg is then flexed forward to assume a half-kneeling position. The forward leg pushes into extension as the opposite leg moves forward and extends.
Step 2	**Jump to squat**
	The legs are flexed and rotated to one side. Both legs are then lifted simultaneously off the support surface and derotated. The feet land back on the surface with the hips and knees flexing to a squat or semisquat position. The legs then extend to the vertical.
Step 3	**Half kneel**
	Both legs are flexed toward the trunk as one or both legs are rotated to one side. A half kneel is assumed. The forward leg pushes into extension as the opposite leg moves forward and extends.
Step 4	**Asymmetrical squat**
	One or both legs are flexed toward the trunk, assuming an asymmetrical, crossed-leg, or wide-based squat. Internal rotation of the hips may cause the feet to be placed on either side of the pelvis. Asymmetry of hip rotation is common. The legs push up to an extended position. Crossing or asymmetries may be corrected during extension by stepping action.
Step 5	**Symmetrical squat**
	The legs are brought into flexion with the heels approximating the buttocks in a narrow-based squat. Stepping action may be seen during assumption of the squat, or balance steps (or hops) may follow the symmetrical rise.

Reprinted, by permission, from A.F. VanSant, 1997, A lifespan perspective of age differences in righting movements. In *Motor development: Research & reviews,* Vol. 1, edited by J.E. Clark and J.H. Humphrey (pp. 46-63). (Reston, VA: National Association for Physical Education and Sport), 46-63.

Table 5.4 Developmental Sequences for Rising to Stand and Percent of Trials at Each Step by Cross-Sectional Age Group

Developmental step	Age group (in years)						
	6	17	28	35	45	55	71
Upper-limb region							
Step 1: Push and reach to bilateral push	16	3	12	11	26	35	50
Step 2: Push and reach	61	41	38	52	55	29	14
Step 3: Symmetrical push	22	56	47	30	12	18	6
Step 4: Bilateral reach	0	1	0	3	0	0	0
Step 5: Push and reach with thigh push	0	0	0	4	7	8	17
Step 6: Push and reach to bilateral push with thigh push	0	0	0	3	1	15	13
Axial region							
Step 1: Full rotation with abdomen down	<1	0	0	0	0	0	0
Step 2: Full rotation with abdomen up	8	3	14	7	10	21	48
Step 3: Partial rotation	16	3	20	17	17	35	38
Step 4: Forward with rotation	61	42	20	40	56	34	9
Step 5: Symmetrical	15	50	46	36	16	10	5
Lower-limb region							
Step 1: Kneel	2	0	0	3	8	21	20
Step 2: Half kneel	6	1	3	17	20	8	6
Step 3: Jump to squat	26	7	13	17	20	27	46
Step 4: Asymmetrical squat	58	59	58	53	62	41	25
Step 5: Symmetrical squat	9	34	26	27	10	2	2
Number of subjects	120	120	32	32	34	30	60
Number of trials	1,200	120	320	318	337	298	300

Reprinted, by permission, from A.F. VanSant, 1997, A lifespan perspective of age differences in righting movements. In *Motor development: research & reviews,* Volume 1, edited by J.E. Clark and J.H. Humphrey (Reston, VA: National Association for Physical Education and Sport), 53-54.

With development, more symmetry is observed. Adolescents, for example, often use a symmetrical hand push and trunk flexion with an asymmetrical squat. The most efficient pattern for rising is a symmetrical push with the hands against the floor. The arms are then raised for balance. The head and trunk come forward past vertical and then the back extends to upright. The legs flex to bring the heels near the buttocks so the individual can squat and then extend the legs to stand.

Some developmental levels are characteristic of older adults. The arms reach forward for balance. There may be some trunk rotation to a diagonal position. One or both hands push on the thighs to help extend the trunk and legs to vertical (see steps 5 and 6 described for the upper-limb region in table 5.4).

VanSant's work shows that unique movement patterns can emerge in older adulthood. Pushing on the thighs to rise is not observed in children or adolescents. The movement patterns of older adults are not simply regressions to the patterns used

by children. In fact, older adults appear to break the task into segments so they can achieve balance in each segment. It is likely that loss of strength or flexibility, perhaps due to arthritis, plays a role in the patterns used by older adults, but the role played by other factors, especially the use of sensory information, requires further research for a fuller appreciation of the lifespan development of rising.

POSTURAL CONTROL IN OLDER ADULTHOOD

Developmentalists are interested in postural control in older adults for many of the same reasons they are interested in postural control in infants and children. Age-related changes in postural control can tell us much about how posture is controlled and what information is important to control processes. Knowing the crucial information systems and processes can suggest areas in which to design interventions to help older individuals who have compromised postural control. So, there are both theoretical and practical reasons for studying postural control and balance in older adults.

There are various age-related differences in balance and postural control observed between young and old adults. Older adults sway more than young adults sway (Newell, Slobounov, Slobounova, & Molenaar, 1997), especially when somatosensory information is perturbed (Forth, Metter, & Paloski, 2007; Manchester, Woollacott, Zederbauer-Hylton, & Marin, 1989; Teasdale & Simoneau, 2001) or the balance task becomes more difficult (Wolfson et al., 1992). This discovery has led researchers to investigate several specific aspects of postural control in older adults. First, older adults may have to devote more attention to maintaining postural control. Facing a balance challenge while performing another task can force older adults to shift more of their attention to maintaining balance. Thus, performing a balance task concurrently with another (usually cognitive) task has been studied in older adults. Second, researchers have examined the effects of disturbing the various sensory systems, or channels of sensory information, and have looked at how effectively older adults reweight sensory information when given inaccurate information from one system. Being able to recover balance quickly when it is disturbed is crucial to stability. Just by looking at the number of falls in older adults, we can see that quick responses are compromised with aging. So, third, researchers have examined the reaction times to balance perturbations and the sequencing of muscle responses to maintain balance in older adults. Let's examine a key research study dealing with each of these types of age-related differences in postural control.

Dual-Task Performance

Age-related changes in the various systems involved in maintaining postural control might cause older adults to devote more of their attention to maintaining equilibrium. It is important to know if this is the case, since diverting an older adult's attention might compromise stability. Attentional demands are sometimes studied with a **dual-task paradigm**. Doumas, Smolders, and Krampe

(2008), for example, used a dual-task paradigm to examine the role of cognitive resources in postural stability. These researchers asked participants to balance while concurrently performing a cognitive task such as recalling digits. They were particularly interested in the effects of increasing the difficulty of the balance task by compromising sensory information. They selected 18 young adults with a mean age of 21.7 years and 18 older adults with a mean age of 70.9 years. The participants self-reported no neurological or orthopedic disorders and were not taking medications known to affect balance. Several screening tests, such as a digit symbol substitution test and digit span test, were given so that individuals scoring far below the mean could be eliminated from the study.

The cognitive task used in this study was a working memory task known as the *n-back task* (Dobbs & Rule, 1989). A series of digits was successively presented on a computer screen, and participants were challenged, starting with the third digit, to name the digit presented two cycles previously (a 2-back task). Task difficulty could be adjusted by changing the time between digit presentations. Participants whose performance was nearly perfect on the 2-back task were asked to do a 3-back task. In the first session with the participants, the researchers determined the conditions yielding 80% correct performance for each individual, and this was the difficulty level used for that individual in the dual-task condition.

The postural control task was to maintain an upright stance with the eyes open while on a force platform with a three-sided surround (a small version of the room in a room described earlier). In the baseline condition the platform and surround were stationary. To make the postural control task more difficult, the researchers slightly moved either the surround or the force platform by rotating in the sagittal plane. The first condition was known as *visual sway referencing* and the second was known as *somatosensory sway referencing*. As with the cognitive task, baseline single-task performance was measured in the first session with the participants.

In the second session, which was held on a subsequent day, the participants performed the tasks singly or together. The *n-back task* was presented on a screen built into the surround of the balance task. Counterbalanced blocks of trials were presented, with each block consisting of nine trials: three single-task trials followed by four dual-task trials followed by two single-task trials.

Anteroposterior and mediolateral sway of the COP was measured by the force platform. Imagine a plot of the COP excursions in these dimensions constructed over the time of the trial. An ellipse can be fitted over the COP excursions to include 88% of the COP trajectories, eliminating outliers (see figure 5.7). The area of the ellipse reflects stability: A larger size is associated with more sway and less stability.

Both groups improved from session 1 to session 2. There was more sway in the referencing conditions, especially the somatosensory sway referencing condition. In the latter condition the older adults were less stable than the younger adults were. In dual-task trials with a stable platform, the young adults were just as stable as they were in single-task trials, but the older adults increased almost 40% in instability in dual-task conditions compared with single-task conditions (see figure 5.8). Interestingly, in dual-task trials with somatosensory sway referencing, instability did not increase for older adults; rather, cognitive task performance declined 15%.

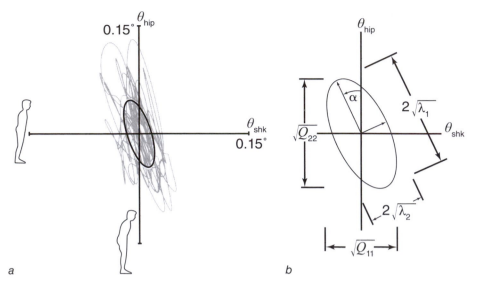

Figure 5.7 (*a*) An ellipse fitted onto a plot of ankle motion (movement of the shank over the foot) on the horizontal axis and hip motion on the vertical axis. The larger the ellipse, the more movement observed. (*b*) The length of the major axis of the ellipse (λ_1) represents use of a hip strategy, while the length of the minor axis (λ_2) reflects an ankle strategy. The correlation of the joints is represented by the angle α.

Reprinted from *Gait and Posture,* Vol. 16, R.A. Speers, A.D. Kuo, and F.B. Horak, "Contributions of Altered Sensation and Feedback Responses to Changes in Coordination of Postural Control Due to Aging," pg. 24. Copyright 2002, with permission of Elsevier.

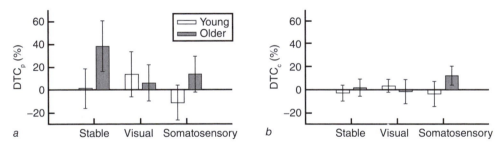

Figure 5.8 Doumas et al. (2008) plotted the proportional dual-task costs (DTCs) by condition to represent the additional cost to performance imposed by the dual-task setting. DTCs are the difference between single-task and dual-task scores divided by the single-task score and then multiplied by 100 to form a percentage. DTCs in posture are shown in (*a*) and DTCs in cognition are shown in (*b*). Error bars represent ±2 standard errors of the mean.

(*a*) Reprinted from *Experimental Brain Research,* Vol. 187, M. Doumas, C. Smolders, and R. Krampe, "Task prioritization in aging: effects of sensory information on concurrent posture and memory performance," pg. 279. Copyright 2008 by Elsevier. Experimental brain research by SPRINGER-VERLAG. Reproduced with permission of SPRINGER-VERLAG in the format Journal via Copyright Clearance Center.

(*b*) Reprinted from *Experimental Brain Research,* Vol. 187, M. Doumas, C. Smolders, and R. Krampe, "Task prioritization in aging: effects of sensory information on concurrent posture and memory performance," pg. 279. Copyright 2008 by Elsevier.

These results suggest that when balance conditions are relatively stable, older adults can afford an increase in instability to maintain a cognitive task. When the balance task becomes more demanding, however, the older adults reprioritize, emphasizing postural stability over cognitive performance. This finding suggests that older adults can be flexible in resource allocation. Flexibility probably develops gradually over the lifespan to compensate for age-related sensorimotor and cognitive declines. From these results we can also see that increasing the demands on older adults while they are balancing can create a challenging situation.

The limitations of research on dual-task performance should be acknowledged. The choice of tasks is an important aspect of research design. It is difficult to establish the level of difficulty of the tasks, especially when they are in different domains (motor, cognitive), and it is difficult to know how changing difficulty levels in one domain affects difficulty levels in another domain.

Relative Weighting of Sensory Information

We have already encountered the ongoing discussion (within the study of postural control) on the various sensory systems and the relative importance of the input from these systems. One way to study how individuals integrate sensory information from different systems is to limit or change information from one system and observe whether information from another system is given a higher priority—that is, whether sensory reweighting occurs. When researchers began using the moving room paradigm with infants, they quickly found that infants seem to rely more on vision than on somatosensory information, but they also noted that this effect diminishes with standing experience. When can children reweight sensory information? Forssberg and Nashner (1982) were among the first to emphasize the importance of sensory integration in the development of postural control. They suggested that children younger than 7.5 years cannot reweight sensory inputs, but little investigation of this hypothesis took place until a new experimental method became available. Bair, Kiemel, Jeka, and Clark (2007) used this method to observe children aged 4 to 10 years. They had the children face a limited (by goggles) visual field of lights in a darkened room. The children stood in a slightly staggered stance with an index finger lightly touching a bar. Postural sway was recorded with a three-dimensional tracking system. The visual scene and the touch bar were oscillated simultaneously but at different amplitudes. Three amplitudes (2, 4, or 8 millimeters) for each modality resulted in five combinations (test conditions).

The investigators found evidence of intramodal reweighting in children as young as 4 years, but intermodal reweighting was observed only in older children. The extent of reweighting increased with age, suggesting that there is a developmental trend in adaptive ability that eventually results in adultlike stability and flexibility to control upright stance. By adulthood disturbances in somatosensory information actually seem to be more disruptive than disturbances in visual information when it comes to maintaining balance.

Naturally, researchers carried this interest in the relative weighting of sensory information to older adulthood. There are age-related changes in vision (especially a decreased sensitivity to low-frequency spatial motion); in the vestibular apparatus,

due to a decrease of hair cells in the canals and otolith organs of the inner ear; and in proprioception, due to decreased cutaneous and joint sensation. Jeka et al. (2006) extended some of the research methods described earlier for studies on infant development to examine sensory reweighting in older adults (see table 5.2). They found no evidence that sensory reweighting is deficient in older adults, but they also recognized that the speed of processing of sensory information must be considered. Hence, researchers have manipulated visual, vestibular, and proprioceptive information to observe the effect on balance in older adults.

Speers, Kuo, and Horak (2002) conducted a sensory reweighting study by comparing older adults aged 60 to 79 years with younger adults aged 20 to 29 years on performance of the **Sensory Organization Test (SOT)**. The SOT evaluates the use of visual, vestibular, and proprioceptive sensation during quiet standing by altering available visual and proprioceptive information. This is accomplished by making the visual surround (miniature room within a room) or support surface sway *with* the participant's body sway—that is, through visual or somatosensory sway referencing. Sway referencing results in inaccurate sensory information. For example, when a person sways forward, the usual visual feedback reflects objects expanding on the retina. If the visual display or surround sways with the individual, the images do not expand. Table 5.5 shows the six conditions of the SOT that result from varying either visual or somatosensory information.

Table 5.5 Conditions in the Sensory Organization Test (SOT)

Condition number	Visual information	Proprioceptive information
1	Normal	Normal
2	Absent (eyes closed)	Normal
3	Sway referenced	Normal
4	Normal	Sway referenced
5	Absent (eyes closed)	Sway referenced
6	Sway referenced	Sway referenced

Participants in the Speers et al. (2002) study stood on a force platform wearing a safety harness. COP was measured while the participants stood as still as possible for 20 seconds. One trial each of condition 1 and 2 and three trials each of conditions 3 through 6 were performed. A trial was ended early when participants took a step, touched the surround, or opened their eyes in an eyes-closed condition.

Speers et al. (2002) also used optical encoders and sway bars to measure the joint angles of the lower limbs and to measure changes in the body's **center of mass (COM)** from upright in the sagittal plane. A small balance perturbation might result in increased sway, while a larger perturbation might result in individuals moving the joints of their lower limbs to maintain their COM over their base of support. Thus shank and hip angles provide information about the coordination and use of joint movements to control posture.

The researchers used covariance matrices to quantify how individual joints varied, how the joints covaried, and how the COM varied during the trials. Plots of the change in shank angle against the change in hip angle were fitted with an ellipse, as described previously. The size of the ellipse reflects the amount of overall motion, while the direction of the ellipse reflects the correlation of the hip and ankle motion. Different characteristics of the ellipse provide still more information (see figure 5.7). For example, the major axis of the ellipse (λ_1) represents ankle and hip motions that reflect changes in hip angle used to maintain balance, while the minor axis (λ_2) reflects changes in ankle angle. The orientation of the ellipse (α) reflects the extent motion of the joints is coordinated.

Speers et al. (2002) found that the older adults swayed significantly more than the younger adults swayed in conditions 1, 2, 4, 5, and 6. Both COP and COM measures reflected this increase in sway. Differences between the age groups in the coordination of joint movements were found in conditions 2, 4, 5, and 6 (see figure 5.9). By examining the various types of information provided by the covariance measures, the researchers were able to describe which measures contributed to age group differences in the various SOT conditions.

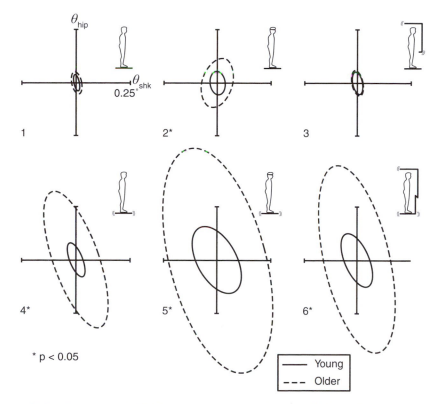

Figure 5.9 Speers et al. (2002) compared the ellipses of hip and ankle movement for young adults (solid line) with ellipses for older adults (dotted line) for each condition of the SOT. There were significant differences in conditions 2, 4, 5, and 6.

Reprinted from *Gait and Posture*, Vol. 16, R.A. Speers, A.D. Kuo, and F.B. Horak, "Contributions of altered sensation and feedback responses to changes in coordination of postural control due to aging," pg. 26. Copyright 2002, with permission of Elsevier.

SOT conditions with normal or absent vision were associated with age-related differences in ankle strategy, while SOT conditions with visual sway referencing were associated with age-related differences in hip strategy and joint coordination. This tells us that inaccurate visual information leads older adults and younger adults to change the coordination pattern of sway in different ways. Older adults appear to be more dependent on visual information. That is, in older adulthood there is a sensory reweighting to visual information.

The amount of sway increased greatly in conditions 4, 5, and 6, in which the proprioceptive information was sway referenced. In these conditions, the older adults were able to generate sufficient ankle torque to maintain stability, so the increased unsteadiness is more likely to be associated with decreased proprioception—that is, decreased ability to detect the platform's small movements, increased sensory noise (neurological static), or even increased efferent noise. Thus older adults experience a degradation of proprioceptive information and place more emphasis on vision. If visual information is absent or inaccurate, steadiness decreases significantly. This reweighting of sensory information is likely a normal aspect of aging, but an increased reliance on visual information is a factor in susceptibility to loss of balance. Likely, the visual information cannot fully compensate for the proprioceptive information that is lost.

Rosengren et al. (2007) performed a spectral analysis of SOT results for 20 older women. In the more difficult, sway referencing conditions, the women improved in equilibrium scores between the first and second trials. This suggests that the older women could change strategies and make greater use of an ankle strategy in subsequent trials. The ankle strategy is discussed in more detail in the following section.

Movement Responses in Older Adults

The tendency toward slower movements in older adults is well known, whether the hypothesis is that slowing reflects caution so that balance can be maintained or that slowing reflects age-related degenerative changes in the various body systems. We know that maintaining equilibrium often requires a rapid response when that equilibrium is challenged. It is not surprising, in light of the increased incidence of falling in older adulthood, that an inability to react quickly to a balance threat is problematic for older adults.

Beyond reacting quickly to regain balance, individuals must coordinate the various joints in the most efficient way to regain balance. Nashner and colleagues (Nashner, 1977; Nashner & Woollacott, 1979; Horak & Nashner, 1986) have described three characteristic patterns of muscle activity, called *muscle synergies*, associated with postural movement strategies for recovering balance. These are the ankle strategy, the hip strategy, and the stepping strategy. They can be used to control the amount of body sway forward and backward and regain equilibrium. The ankle strategy moves the entire body as a unit, in the same direction, around the ankle joint. The figure next to the horizontal axis in figure 5.7 shows an ankle strategy. This strategy is efficient when we are in upright stance or when we experience a small perturbation in balance. In the hip strategy the larger hip muscles are activated, moving the upper body in the direction opposite the lower body.

The figure next to the vertical axis in figure 5.7 shows a hip strategy. The hip strategy is useful when we need to control larger sway movements or when we are standing on a surface narrower than the length of the feet. The stepping strategy involves taking one or more steps to establish a new base of support. The stepping strategy might be the preferred strategy under normal circumstances. It is also likely that in naturally occurring conditions, we use combinations of the strategies to regain our balance (Spirduso, Francis, & MacRae, 2005, p. 133).

Tips for Novice Investigators

The research teams from the University of Maryland built on issues and research techniques to address many aspects of postural control (see table 5.2 on pages 108 and 109). Two more recent studies appear at the end of table 5.2. You can choose either one study or both studies for further reading to expand your knowledge of postural control. Complete the table entries to help place the individual studies in the bigger context of the research sequence.

From table 5.2 you can generate topics that could be addressed with future research. For example, are there other transitions from one movement skill to another (other than sitting to walking) that are of interest to developmentalists? What are some of them? Notice that researchers have addressed many age groups in the lifespan. What additional research is needed to give us a more complete understanding of the development of postural control over the lifespan?

Age-related changes can affect the strategy used. Compared with young adults, older adults tend to use the hip strategy more often (Horak, Shupert, & Mirka, 1989; Manchester et al., 1989). Decreased sensation in the feet or ankles could make it difficult for older adults to employ an ankle strategy. This preference might also reflect ankle muscle weakness. When an individual is on a slippery surface, using the hip strategy might make a fall more likely since the surface cannot resist sheer forces of the feet (Horak et al., 1989).

Tucker, Kavanagh, Barrett, and Morrison (2008) compared healthy young and older men performing a balance task for both reaction time and the pattern of response coordination. These researchers asked the men to stand on a force platform so that COP could be measured. To gather information about how the body segments moved to maintain stability, the researchers mounted accelerometers on participants' heads and lower trunks (see figure 5.10). These devices detected motion in three planes. Participants began trials either in quiet stance or in voluntary (self-driven) anteroposterior or mediolateral sway. During the trial a two-choice auditory cue was given: "forward" or "backward" and "left" or "right." After participants initiated sway in the direction cued, they continued voluntary sway in that plane at their preferred frequency (see table 5.6). In some conditions, participants changed from voluntary sway in one direction to voluntary sway in the other direction.

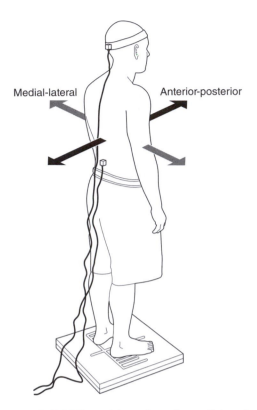

Figure 5.10 Tucker et al. (2008) positioned study participants on a force platform and placed accelerometers on their backs and heads.

Reprinted from *Human Movement Science,* Vol. 27, M.G. Tucker, J.J. Kavanagh, R.S. Barett, and S. Morrison, "Age-related differences in postural reaction time and coordination during voluntary sway movements," pg. 731, Copyright 2008, with permission of Elsevier.

Table 5.6 Experimental Conditions in Tucker et al. (2008)

Initial condition		Two-choice audio cue	Sway response
Static	Quiet standing	Forward or backward	Anterior-posterior sway
	Quiet standing	Left or right	Medial-lateral sway
Dynamic	Anterior-posterior sway	Left or right	Medial-lateral sway
	Medial-lateral sway	Forward or backward	Anterior-posterior sway

Participants were instructed to use ankle movement for anteroposterior sway and to sequentially shift their weight from one leg to the other for mediolateral sway. Their arms were at their sides. The order of presentation was randomized, and catch trials were used to discourage anticipation.

The investigators found that the older men reacted more slowly to the cues to initiate or switch voluntary sway, either when starting in quiet stance (static conditions) or when starting in voluntary sway (dynamic conditions). This finding

was not a surprise, but it did demonstrate that the slower reaction carried over to whole-body balance and stability responses.

The reaction time was slower when participants in either age group started in the dynamic condition compared with the static condition (see figure 5.11). This likely reflects the increased attentional demands of the dynamic condition. In analyzing COP, trunk, and head motion, the researchers noted that the older men were closer than the young men to making simultaneous movements. Moreover, the young men tended to respond in a coordinated sequence that was bottom up (COP, then trunk, then head) rather than respond in the more synchronous coordination pattern used by the older men. The older men, then, adopted a more rigid movement strategy to meet the challenge of maintaining stability while initiating or changing movement.

While increasing postural rigidity is a strategy the older men used to maintain stability when challenged with a change in movement, this rigidity might contribute to their slower reaction time. Thus rigidity may prove to be a hindrance to dynamic postural stability.

Overall, we see that older adults can be flexible in allocating their resources when balancing but that challenging balance conditions force them to devote more attention to postural stability. With aging, there is likely a reweighting of sensory information toward using more visual information, and anything that affects the availability of visual information can prove a challenge for balance. A natural response of older adults to changing balance conditions is to become

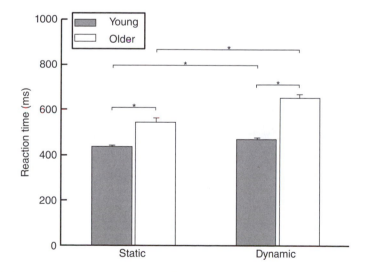

Figure 5.11 Mean reaction times for Tucker et al.'s (2008) participants in the static and dynamic conditions. Error bars represent 1 standard error of the mean. The horizontal lines with an asterisk indicate mean scores that were significantly different at $p < .05$.

Reprinted from *Human Movement Science*, Vol. 27, M.G. Tucker, J.J. Kavanagh, R.S. Barett, and S. Morrison, "Age-related differences in postural reaction time and coordination during voluntary sway movements," pg. 731, Copyright 2008, with permission of Elsevier.

more rigid. This strategy might slow the reaction to regain balance when it is compromised.

While there is a loss of balance in many older adults, there are also older adults whose balance is equivalent to that of young adults, and there is indication that certain interventions can improve balance in older adults. Consider some of the factors that affect balance: decreased function in the neural systems, such as loss of sensory information, sensory noise, or reweighting of sensory information, and decreased function in the musculoskeletal systems, especially loss of strength. Interventions that address these factors might improve balance function.

It is likely that interventions must be specific to a loss of function affecting balance if they are to improve balance. Lichtenstein, Shields, Shiavi, and Burger (1989) put older women in a general exercise program for 1 hour three times a week for 16 weeks, but found that the exercising women did no better than those in a control group on several balance tests. In contrast, Fiatarone et al. (1990) put a group of frail elderly in a nursing home on a resistance training program focused on improving leg strength and saw both significant strength and balance improvements.

Hu and Woollacott (1994a, 1994b) found success with balance retraining programs focusing on using different sensory inputs and their integration when sensory input was altered. In their first study (1994a), they trained 12 healthy adults aged 65 to 90 years with 10 hours of visual, vestibular, and somatosensory input manipulation. The trained adults demonstrated less body sway than controls demonstrated on five of eight training conditions. The researchers retested the older adults 4 weeks after training ended, and the program participants still performed better than the controls on several balance tests.

In a second study (1994b), 24 adults aged 69 to 90 years were measured on muscle and kinematic response characteristics before and after balance retraining. Tests consisted of displacing the support surface and measuring response characteristics. Multisensory balance retraining resulted in less coactivation of antagonist muscles, facilitating balance control. It seems, then, that sensory training programs in balance control can improve balance and that the benefit can transfer to other balance tasks. Overall, interventions that specifically address one or more functions whose loss leads to balance difficulties can be successful.

Effect of Stroke on Postural Control

Stroke is a major cause of permanent disability. While stroke can strike throughout the lifespan, two-thirds of people who experience stroke are older than 65 years. There are many consequences of stroke, including sensory, motor, and cognitive impairments, but certainly impaired postural control is a significant consequence that in turn affects activities of daily living and locomotion (Geurts, de Haart, van Nes, & Duysens, 2005). The site of the brain lesion affects the type and extent of postural control impairment and might affect the extent of balance recovery following stroke. It is important for researchers to identify the mechanisms underpinning postural control recovery and compensatory strategies so that rehabilitation programs can maximize stroke recovery.

The ways in which stroke can affect postural control are many. The effect on unperturbed stance is often increased body sway and weight-bearing asymmetry in favor of the nonparetic (not paralyzed) leg. There may be an impaired ability to withstand balance perturbations and a delayed response of the leg muscles to perturbation, especially on the paretic side. This might lead to compensatory activation of leg muscles in the nonparetic leg. People who have experienced stroke characteristically limit the speed and extent of their movements in response to this impaired ability. Of course, voluntary weight displacement or shifting is necessary for locomotor activities as fundamental as walking or rising from a chair. People who have experienced stroke often demonstrate impaired weight shifting, including slow or directionally imprecise weight shifts and difficulty shifting from weight bearing on two legs to weight bearing on one leg.

Compared with age-matched healthy peers, stroke patients tend to rely more on vision to balance (Marigold & Eng, 2006). This can contribute to increased COP excursions. Additionally, postural control seems to demand relatively more attention in stroke patients, the likelihood being that more attention is given to weight bearing on the paretic leg.

Rehabilitation programs typically address many of these postural control issues. In order to help stroke patients better maintain their standing balance and improve their weight-bearing symmetry, COP and postural sway feedback during upright standing has been used (Shumway-Cook, Anson, & Haller, 1988), as has COP feedback during more dynamic tasks such as sit-to-stand transfers, weight shifting, and stepping (Winstein, Gardner, McNeal, Barto, & Nicholson, 1989). Shoe adaptations and canes have also been introduced. Perturbation training with moving platforms has been used to improve response to stance perturbations (Hocherman, Dickstein, & Pillar, 1984). To facilitate weight shifting, interventions have had patients make rhythmic weight shifts with visual feedback provided on a monitor (de Haart, Geurts, Dault, Nienhuis, & Duysons, 2005), engage in repetitive sit-to-stand training with visual feedback and correction mirrors (Cheng, Wu, Liaw, Wong, & Tang, 2001), and engage in lower-limb strength training (Weiss, Suzuki, Bean, & Fielding, 2000). Interventions to address an overreliance on vision have included balance exercises performed while blindfolded, which is vision deprivation training (Bonan, et al., 2004). Practicing balance while completing another task (a dual-task paradigm) is suggested to improve the automaticity of balance (de Haart, Geurts, Huidekoper, Fasotti, & van Limbeek, 2004).

It is not clear what rehabilitation intervention is the best. In a review of the literature, Geurts et al. (2005) concluded that there is little indication that feedback training during unperturbed stance results in significant improvement, although repetitive sit-to-stand training is effective. Balance training with visual deprivation has been found to be more effective than training with full vision. Aids such as canes contribute positively to the rehabilitation of postural control, at least for unperturbed standing. The value of training under dual-task conditions in order to regain automaticity of balance skills needs more investigation. While it seems clear that normal sensory integration is important to balance recovery,

much more research on the best interventions to improve sensory integration is needed. Certainly, the search for effective interventions illustrates the many systems involved in postural control and the importance of integrating information from these systems to maintain equilibrium.

SUMMARY

Studying postural control over the lifespan has identified the rich number of factors involved in maintaining equilibrium. Balance depends on visual, vestibular, and proprioceptive information. Infants seem to rely heavily on vision, but by adulthood it is a loss of proprioceptive information that is most problematic for maintaining balance. With aging there appears to be a natural loss of some proprioceptive information, leading older adults to rely more heavily on visual information. This reweighting of sensory information has been an area of interest for researchers and demonstrates the remarkable ability humans have to adapt to available information.

Providing additional information can be helpful to stability. Even light touch of a surface allows individuals to better anticipate adjustments in their posture. When balance is lost, a quick response is needed to regain stability. The pattern of coordination of responses may undergo age-related changes. Slower and perhaps less efficient movement patterns put older adults at risk of falls, but training interventions might compensate for this risk. Interventions following stroke address a number of aspects of postural control, including those related to the sensory, motor, and cognitive systems.

While this review has covered many aspects of postural control, it does not include all aspects of investigating postural control. Nor have all aspects of postural control been thoroughly investigated. Few of the tasks in the research studies surveyed involved dynamic movement. The results of investigations using very different methodologies, some focusing on static balance, others on dynamic tasks, and still others on perturbations to balance, are sometimes difficult to integrate. Also, little research deals with the relative orientation of body segments. Consider what the topic of postural control involves for an astronaut in space or for gymnasts and divers as they execute somersaults and twists. There is certainly much that remains for us to learn about postural control at different points in the lifespan.

CHAPTER 6

Development of Locomotion

The term *locomotion* comes from Latin. *Locus* means "place" and *movere* means "to move," and thus the noun *locomotion* means "movement from place to place." The human body is so versatile that human locomotion encompasses activities as diverse as crawling, rolling, swimming, and, of course, moving on foot. This chapter focuses on how foot locomotion develops.

While many foot patterns can be used to locomote, American movement taxonomies[1] usually recognize eight basic patterns: jumping, walking, skipping, running, hopping, leaping, galloping, and sliding. As noted in chapter 1, the development of these forms can be studied in relation to each other (an intertask developmental sequence), or the development of each form can be studied separately (an intratask developmental sequence).

INTERTASK DEVELOPMENTAL SEQUENCE

Although the motor milestones that lead to walking have been studied in detail, the sequence of locomotor tasks that develop after walking has not been validated. We can gain some sense of the sequence, however, by examining how each of the eight patterns is defined. For instance, we can distinguish between locomotor patterns that involve flight and patterns that do not involve flight. Indeed, of the eight basic foot patterns, only walking does not contain a moment of flight. Walking is defined as moving through space by shifting weight between alternating feet with one foot always on the ground. Of the seven locomotor tasks that contain flight, three are combinations of other foot patterns. These are the gallop, skip, and slide. The gallop comprises a step and a leap, while the skip comprises a step and a hop. The slide, a sideways gallop, is the only foot pattern for which the direction of movement is specified. All the other patterns may be performed forward, backward, sideways, or diagonally.

Thus, five locomotor forms contain flight and are not made up of other forms. Hopping is defined as taking off into the air from one foot and landing on the same foot. Jumping is defined only by its landing: It is taking off into the air from one or two feet and then landing on two feet simultaneously.

The run is defined as taking off from one foot and landing on the other in an alternating fashion with a moment of flight during which neither foot is on the ground. Leaping is a run that exaggerates the moment of flight by making it last longer and that frequently propels the body higher when compared with the run.

Hypothesizing the Developmental Sequence

Defining the locomotor patterns can aid in hypothesizing the developmental sequence of these patterns, based on when they first appear in primitive form in a child's repertoire. The word *primitive* is used in developmental study to mean "early or first level." Although primitive forms of a motor task may appear when a child is rather young, the child may not become skillful in that task for many years, if at all.

Everyone knows that walking is the first foot locomotor pattern to develop. Its definition should suggest why: Walking is the only foot locomotor task that does not contain a moment of flight. For this reason it demands the least amount of leg strength to move the body's center of gravity forward, because a person can walk with relatively little projection from the supporting leg. Since it lacks a moment of flight, walking is also the most stable foot locomotor pattern. Having both feet on the ground between leg swings makes it easier for the walker to maintain balance.

The ratio of leg strength to body weight is a rate limiter for walking and all other foot locomotor skills. This ratio is the lowest for walking. Balance is the other important rate limiter for walking and foot locomotion. Recall that a rate limiter is a constraint that holds back the development of a motor task until the constraint reaches a certain value. The complete system needed for the development of walking is considered later in this chapter.

The second foot locomotor pattern to develop is an extension of the walk: running. At first the child merely walks fast, but eventually a moment of flight appears between alternating takeoffs and landings. The child becomes able to project against gravity, if only momentarily, to push their body weight off the ground. Clark and Whitall (1989a) reported a case study in which a child's run appeared 7 months after walking.

Logically, if a person can run, then a harder push-off should produce a leap. Meanwhile, landing on two feet from a one- or two-foot takeoff (a jump) should occur around this time as well. If a step and a leap can occur, then they can be combined into galloping and sliding. The task demanding the most strength relative to body weight and the greatest balance seems to be hopping. Therefore, hopping should be a late-developing locomotor task. Since skipping requires the ability to hop on each foot, it should occur after hopping. This logical order, then, is our hypothesis about the intertask developmental sequence for foot locomotion.

Substitutions

As mentioned in chapter 4, one way to discern parts of an intertask developmental sequence is to watch for substitutions when children attempt a task (Roberton &

Halverson, 1984). If children cannot perform a task, they frequently substitute a skill they already have in their repertoire for the one that is not in their repertoire. In the case of foot locomotion, children who cannot skip may substitute the gallop instead. Children who cannot hop may substitute bounce jumping. Children who cannot jump down may step down. These substitutions indicate that during development galloping precedes skipping, jumping precedes hopping, and stepping precedes jumping.

Checking the Literature

So, what do researchers say about this developmental sequence? Roberton and Halverson (1984) used anecdotal information from a longitudinal study of seven children to propose a sequence of walk, run, leap, jump (jump down and bounce jump in place), gallop, hop, skip, and slide. They indicated that they did not have a sense of the order among leap, jump, and gallop. Clark and Whitall (1989a) ordered five of the foot patterns: walk, run, gallop, hop, and skip. They also speculated from Fortney's (1983) data that rate limiters for the run are the ability to generate peak takeoff and landing forces of about two times body weight and the ability to control balance given these forces. In the same case study in which running emerged 7 months after walking, galloping emerged 6 months after running. Clark and Whitall felt that the rate limiter for galloping is the ability to uncouple the alternating phasing of the walk and run to produce the asymmetry of one foot leading and the other catching up. They defined the gallop as a step and run, which is the primitive form of the more advanced step and leap.

Performing a Prelongitudinal Screening

How can we test all these speculations? Developmental sequences require longitudinal validation, but the first (and quicker) method is to perform prelongitudinal screening using cross-sectional data (Roberton, Williams, & Langendorfer, 1980). As described in chapter 4, in prelongitudinal screening data are collected on children of various ages. The ages are selected based on literature speculations on the ages when the primitive forms of the various skills appear. For our screening, we might choose 12-month-olds, 19-month-olds, 25-month-olds, 36-month-olds, and so on. (The first three age groups are based on the ages in the case study of Clark and Whitall, 1989a.) Next we would evaluate each group of children to see what locomotor patterns they could perform, and then we would graph each pattern according to the percentages of children in each age group who displayed at least a primitive form of the pattern. As the percentages are graphed across the age groups, the typical order of pattern acquisition should become apparent. Ultimately, validation of the sequence will require longitudinal study, but prelongitudinal screening is a faster and less expensive way to begin (Roberton et al., 1980).

During our prelongitudinal screening, we would try to create optimal conditions for eliciting the developmental pattern. For instance, most people would not believe that leaping occurs before the age of 3, and yet Roberton and Halverson (1984) showed film illustrating a 34-month-old leaping over a roll of towels (see figure 6.1).

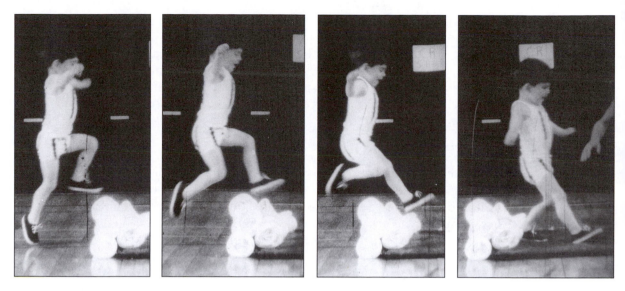

Figure 6.1 This 34-month-old child displayed a beginning leap when asked to run, get over the rolled towels, and keep on running.

Reprinted, by permission, from M.A. Roberton and L.E. Halverson, 1984, *Developing children - their changing movement* (Philadelphia, PA: Lea and Febiger). Copyright M.A. Roberton.

The task was to run, get over the towels, and keep on running. By presenting the task in this manner, the researchers kept cognitive processing to a minimum so the child did not need to understand what constitutes a leap. The movement occurred naturally from the run and the additional height demanded by the towels. The third part of the task, to keep on running, encouraged the landing on one foot that is part of the leap.

INTRATASK DEVELOPMENTAL SEQUENCES

Intratask developmental sequences of varying validity appear in the motor development literature. Developmental validity requires longitudinal study, which few of the published sequences for foot locomotion have received. Two locomotor skills, however, have been studied in considerable detail, if not always developmentally. We focus on these two here while encouraging you to explore the data available on the other patterns. We will examine what is known about the developmental sequences and product scores (outcome measures) of these two skills and then look at contemporary research that may illuminate why these sequences occur in the way that they do.

Walking

Walking has been studied extensively with product scores as well as verbal and biomechanical descriptions of the movement. This literature on walking reflects the tools and observations of the early maturationists as well as the tools and interpretations of contemporary dynamic systems scholars.

Developmental Sequence

While a developmental sequence for walking has not been validated, Roberton hypothesized a sequence in 1984 based on the literature of the time. A modification of it appears in table 6.1. The sequence describes development in three components: leg action, trunk action, and arm action. Of particular interest are the change from single-knee lock to double-knee lock and the change in the arms from high guard through semiopposition and opposition. Semiopposition is probably the functional arm level of most adults, while the optimal level, opposition, emerges in vigorous walking.

Leg Action

Product scores (Adolph, Vereijken, & Shrout, 2003; Shirley, 1931) have indicated that beginning toddlers take short steps with their legs relatively wide apart. They tend to point their toes laterally. When combined with the lateral spread between the feet, pointing the toes out enlarges the base of support. With time, toddlers lengthen their steps, decrease the lateral distance between their feet, increase the distance they travel before falling, and increase the velocity with which they cover that distance. In a study of 309 children, Sutherland, Olshen, Biden, and Wyatt (1988) found that between 1 and 7 years of age the average step length increased from 22 to 48 centimeters. The correlation between step length and leg length was .91, suggesting that these increases were primarily due to increasing leg length. These data are an example of how a developmental trend in product scores may reflect body size changes as well as (or sometimes even more than) movement changes.

Ivanenko, Dominici, and Lacquaniti (2007) described the early levels of leg action (table 6.1) as a combination of stepping in place with forward progress. They speculated that toddlers sacrifice energy efficiency in order to maintain upright posture. Gabell and Nayak (1984) have argued that two product scores, stride width and time spent in double support, reflect balance control during walking. Both decrease as skill increases. Bril and Breniere (1993; Breniere & Bril, 1998) extensively developed the thesis that balance dominates early walking development. They felt that during the first 3 to 6 months of walking experience, children learn the postural requirements for gait. Afterward, children move into a second phase of fine-tuning the other aspects of walking, such as muscle activation, head control, and head–trunk coordination. In line with this thinking, Clark and Phillips (1993) reported that phase planes of the thigh and shank begin to look adultlike after 3 months of walking experience.

Ivanenko et al. (2007) described adult leg action in walking as "vaulting over an inverted pendulum of the stance limb" (p. 67) while simultaneously swinging the contralateral limb forward. These researchers felt that this **pendular walk** develops through experience, an argument that directly contrasts with the view of early maturationists (see chapter 1). Adolph et al. (2003) presented data supporting the experience hypothesis. They found that walking experience accounted for 19% to 26% of additional variance across several product measures, such as step length and width, after controlling for age and body size (see table 6.2).

Table 6.1 Hypothesized Developmental Sequences for Walking

Level	Description
Leg action	
Level 1	***Flat-footed, single-knee lock***
	The toddler's primitive leg movements are characterized by short, wide steps, with excessive leg lift due to flexion of the thigh at the hip. Little ankle action occurs, and stepping is flat-footed. The knee is partially flexed when the foot strikes the ground, and it locks into extension during the support phase.
Level 2	***Unclear heel strike***
	Flexion of the thigh at the hip decreases while hip extension at the end of the stance increases, producing longer strides. The base of support narrows. Stepping is still primarily flat-footed.
Level 3	***Heel strike, double-knee lock***
	The heel strikes first as the foot contacts, and then the body weight rides over the rest of the foot. As the heel strikes, the knee locks into extension. It flexes as the weight rides onto the foot and then extends (locks) again at midstance.
Trunk action	
Level 1	***No pelvic rotation***
	The toddler's walk contains no pelvic rotation.
Level 2	***Pelvic rotation***
	The pelvis rotates forward on the side of the leg that is swinging while rotating backward with the supporting leg.
Arm action	
Level 1	***High guard***
	The arms do not participate in walking movements. Hands are held about shoulder high. Sometimes laterally rotated arms are abducted at the shoulder with the elbows flexed, causing the hands to ride even higher.
Level 2	***Middle guard***
	Lateral rotation decreases, allowing the hands to be held about waist high. The hands remain motionless, except in reaction to shifts in equilibrium.
Level 3	***Low guard***
	The elbows are extended so that the hands hang down at the sides or slightly ahead of the body. The arms still do not swing except in reaction to equilibrium shifts.
Level 4	***Semiopposition***
	Flexion at the elbow occurs in response to forward movement of the opposite leg. Extension occurs when the leg on the same side steps forward. Excursion of the hands forward and backward may be unequal and irregular. Sometimes both hands may be in front of the body simultaneously.
Level 5	***Opposition***
	During vigorous walking, each arm swings forward from the shoulders and elbows in time with forward stepping of the opposite leg. The arm swings back as the leg on the same side steps forward. Relaxed arms swinging forward and backward pass each other at the coronal midline; thus, the arms are never in front of or behind the body at the same time.

These sequences, slightly modified from those hypothesized by Roberton (1984), have not been validated.

Reprinted, by permission, from M.A. Roberton, 1984, Changing motor patterns during childhood. In *Motor development during childhood and adolescence*, edited by Jerry Thomas (Minneapolis: Burgess Press), 56. Copyright by Jerry Thomas.

Table 6.2 Contemporary Studies of Walking

Article	Purpose	Method	Result	Relevance
Adolph, Vereijken, & Shrout (2003)	Looked at the contributions of body size, age, and walking experience to the development of walking in children aged 9-17 mo (n = 210) with comparisons to children aged 5-6 y and college students	Replicated the product score results of earlier studies using a variant of Shirley's (1931) oil and lampblack technique (see chapter 1) and then compared the ability of the three variables to predict changes in the product scores	Found that walking experience (practice) is the best predictor of walking development (in contrast to early maturation theories)	An example of contemporary research that replicated and then tried to explain past developmental findings
Ivanenko, Dominici, & Lacquaniti (2007)	Reviewed a series of their own studies using pendulum mechanics as a model for the leg action in walking	Compared kinematic analyses of toddlers and adults to see which group better fits the pendulum model	Found that toddlers do not immediately exploit pendular mechanics in their walking; use of this mechanism gradually develops	An example of using biomechanical analyses and models to study motor development

Tips for Novice Investigators

From a research standpoint, walking experience is a more informative variable than age alone. By standardizing the different times walking begins across individuals, walking experience creates a similar timeline across children who may have started walking at different ages. By holding age constant, this timeline gives a rough estimate of time spent in practice.

Jeng, Liao, Lai, and Hou (1997) used the pendulum model to predict the preferred walking frequency of children aged 3 to 12 years. The model was accurate for children from age 7 on and for adults. The authors also found that the children's lowest energy costs occurred at their preferred walking frequency and that intra- and interlimb coordination was less variable at this same frequency. Thus, it seems that the physical characteristics of the legs, such as length and mass, have to be considered as part of the dynamic system from which the developmental levels of walking emerge.

Black, Chang, Kubo, Holt, and Ulrich (2009) have also used the pendulum model to study the physical and mechanical characteristics of this dynamic system. They found that global stiffness (a measure of resistance to landing force) and angular impulse values in the sagittal plane increase in toddlers during the first 6 months of walking experience, with stiffness values beginning to plateau as early as 3 months of walking. Concomitant muscle firing becomes more efficient over the 6 months (Chang, Kubo, & Ulrich, 2009). Black et al. also found that stiffness values increased when the babies were forced to walk faster on a treadmill. Interestingly, the stiffness values shown by these toddlers were higher than those shown by preadolescents. Thus, learning to regulate stiffness in an efficient, energy-sparing manner is part of the underlying challenge in learning to walk and, as we shall see, in learning to perform other locomotor tasks as well.

In a series of studies using interrupted light photography (a technique described in chapter 4), Murray (Murray, Drought, & Kory, 1964; Murray, Kory, & Clarkson, 1969; Murray, Kory, & Sepic, 1970) tracked adult walking into old age, giving us the data for a lifespan view of this skill. From both product measures and kinematic descriptions of men older than 67 years and women older than 60 years, Murray found less vertical displacement of the head; less flexion and extension at the shoulder, elbow, knee, and ankle; and less pelvic rotation (when compared with younger adults). At the end of the stance phase there was less push-off due to reduced plantar flexion of the ankle, which probably explains the lessened vertical head displacement. At the same time, older adults exhibited more lateral displacement of their heads, a finding that suggests increased lateral sway. Product scores indicated that the 60- to 65-year-old men had shorter strides and turned their toes out more than the 20- to 25-year-olds did. In 1969 Murray et al. confirmed that older men (this time aged 67-87 years) took significantly shorter strides than younger participants took.

Gabell and Nayak (1984) compared the within-participant variability of step length, stride width, time spent in double support, and stride time between younger and older adults. Interestingly, they found that while the means of older adults changed (as reported by Murray), participants older than 64 years with no pathologies were not more variable in their performance than participants aged 21 to 47 years were. These authors argued that any increased variability with age was due to pathology rather than the aging process per se.

In figure 6.2 we have combined the data from several studies of boys and girls and (primarily) adult men to create a speculative lifespan graph for step length. The graph suggests that step length increases until about age 20, when it plateaus, and then at age 60 gradually shortens again.

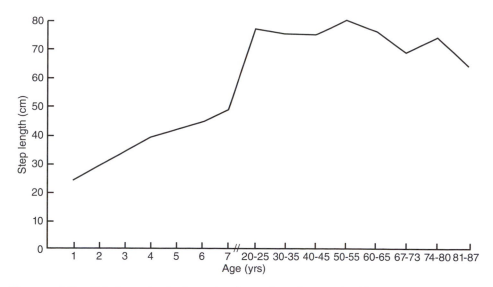

Figure 6.2 This hypothetical graph of step length over the lifespan was estimated from data reported by Adolph et al. (2003), Sutherland et al. (1988), and Murray et al. (1964, 1969).

A study in 1983 by Swedish authors Lundgren-Lindquist, Aniansson, and Rundgren emphasized the real-life implications of such lifespan data. They measured the abilities of 112 women and 93 men in a longitudinal study that began when the participants were 70 years old. The authors found that when the participants were 79 years old, the average comfortable walking speed was 1.03 meters per second for men and 0.92 meters per second for women. The speed required to cross the street at traffic lights in Sweden is 1.4 meters per second. The maximum walking speed for the average 79-year-old woman was 1.18 meters per second, meaning that many of these participants could not cross the street in time. This is a clear example of the need to design the environment around the developmental abilities of the people living in that environment.

Arm Action

In 1967 Murray, Sepic, and Barnard focused on the arm action of 30 men grouped into age categories from 21 to 66 years. These researchers documented the optimal walk of adulthood (see level 5 in table 6.1), in which the shoulder and elbow reach maximum flexion at the time of **contralateral heel strike** and maximum extension at the time of **ipsilateral heel strike**. They found that even during fast walking, the level 5 arm movements of the 60-year-old participants showed decreased amplitudes of shoulder and elbow flexion.

Figure 6.3 comes from a study by Murray et al. (1969; see table 6.3) conducted with participants in their 80s. It suggests that range of motion continues to

Table 6.3   Examples of the Systematic Descriptive Work of Mary Pat Murray

Article	Purpose	Method	Result	Commentary
Murray, Drought, & Kory (1964)	To develop a simple, inexpensive, and reproducible method of recording limb segment displacements in walking and to establish data for different age groups	Used interrupted light photography (see chapter 4) to collect data on 60 men placed into age groups of 20-25, 30-35, 40-45, 50-55, and 60-65 y	Described differences across age in the walking cycle and its components and in movements of the pelvis and trunk	Researchers often need to develop their own methodology and assess its reliability and validity before they can answer the questions they pose.
Murray, Sepic, & Barnard (1967)	To identify the range of normal variability in arm action patterns during fast and self-chosen walking speeds	Used interrupted light photography to collect data on six men in five age groups: 21-25, 32-35, 42-48, 53-58, and 63-66 y	Began to describe arm–leg coordination during walking as well as basic kinematics of the shoulder and elbow	In addition to giving basic descriptions, this study provided one of the first descriptions of double swinging.
Murray, Kory, & Clarkson (1969)	To confirm previous findings that men aged 60 y and older differ in several gait components when compared with younger men	Used interrupted light photography to describe the walks of 64 men in age groups from 20-87 y	Found, among other things, that men older than 65 y tend to have shorter and broader strides, walk more slowly, and show less forward shoulder flexion and less backward elbow extension in their arm swing	This study continued to build a body of data that forms the foundation of what we know today about the development of walking.

decrease in the arm movements as well as in the stride of the older walker. When compared with the developmental descriptions in table 6.1, figure 6.3 may be demonstrating semiopposition, in which both swinging arms may appear in front of the body at the same time, or, more likely, **low guard**, in which the arms do not swing but are held in a low position where they are ready to extend for protection (see table 6.1). In either case, this is an example of the movement regression that can occur with aging or with different environmental contexts. In support of the low guard hypothesis, Murray et al. (1969) stated that

> *the walking performance of the older men gave the impression of a guarded or restrained type of walking in an attempt to obtain maximum security. The walking of the older men resembled that of someone walking on a slippery surface or of someone who lacks sensory information, such as when walking in darkness. (p. 176)*

An interesting observation by Murray et al. (1967) was that during preferred walking speed some adult participants showed "a small accessory wave of flexion superimposed on the extension excursion" (p. 276). Several papers have followed up on this observation of double swinging (Jackson, Joseph, & Wyard, 1983; Webb, Tuttle, & Baksh, 1994), finding that it occurs even in young

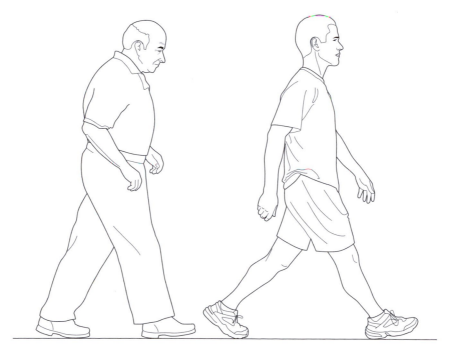

Figure 6.3 The 80-year-old walker (on the left) shows decreased range of motion in the arms and legs when compared with a younger walker (on the right). The arm action of the older adult is likely low guard (see table 6.1).

Based on Murray, Kory, and Clarkson 1969.

and middle-aged adults. Craik, Herman, and Finley (1976) determined that it occurs at walks slower than 0.75 hertz. They described it as a phase shift from 1:1 (arms-to-leg cycle) to 2:1 in which shoulder flexion of both arms is tied to each step. Some of their participants did not demonstrate the double swing but held their arms in prolonged shoulder extension, which may be a description of low guard position (see table 6.1).

Scholars have modeled this particular phase shift using dynamic systems analysis. For instance, Wagenaar and van Emmerik (2000) have accurately predicted the actions of the arms from their resonant frequencies. They also located the occurrence of the phase shift at a stepping cadence of 0.7 to 0.8 hertz in most adults, supporting the earlier observation of Craik et al. (1976). The pendular model of the arms was also used by Webb et al. (1994), who added an experimental aspect to their research on double swinging. First they confirmed that double swinging tends to occur when a participant's stride frequency falls below the natural pendular frequency of the arms. Then they placed weights in their participants' hands. The weights changed the distribution of the arm's mass relative to its fulcrum (the shoulder joint) and thus changed the arm's natural frequency. Indeed, the weighted trials lowered the participants' natural arm frequency. This, in turn, lowered the stride frequency at which each participant began double swinging.

These studies show that during adult walking, the arm action is tied to the frequency of the legs. This observation suggests that some of the developmental arm actions described in table 6.1 may be due to the cadence of the walk. As children and elders walk, their more primitive arm movements may reflect the slow cadence of their legs. The leg movements, in turn, may reflect additional constraints on the walker, an idea we will explore later.

Interlimb Coordination

Studying the arm action during walking is essentially studying the interlimb coordination between the arms and the legs. Another aspect of interlimb coordination in walking is the coordination between the two legs. Clark, Whitall, and Phillips (1988) studied the development of the temporal and spatial phasing between the two legs. Temporal phasing is the timing relationship between the legs, while spatial phasing refers to their relative position in space. These authors looked at new walkers who walked both independently and while supported and at toddlers who had been walking for 0.5, 1, 3, and 6 months. New walkers were those who could make at least three steps without falling. Clark et al. found that the average temporal phasing of all the groups was the same, roughly 50%. The variability around the temporal phasing, however, declined until 3 months of walking, at which point the average variability matched that of adult walkers. Spatial phasing showed no differences across the walking groups with the exception of the supported walkers, who were closest to 50% phasing. Spatial phasing had more variability than temporal phasing had. This variability also declined until 3 months of walking.

Most scientists feel that a **spinal central pattern generator (CPG)** controls the alternating movement of the legs. Although Clark et al. (1988) did not

address this point, their temporal data suggest that this CPG is functioning at the beginning of walking. Indeed, that same pattern generator is probably active in the leg kicks of the supine baby and in the reflex stepping and swimming movements observed soon after birth (Forssberg, 1985). The pattern generator seems a necessary but not sufficient condition for voluntary walking.[2]

In addition to showing support for a pattern generator, Clark et al. (1988) illustrated the importance of balance as an additional constraint on walking development as a whole and on interlimb coordination in particular. When their beginning walkers were supported, the variability in the temporal and spatial relationships between the two legs began to approach adult values. Ledebt and Bril (2000) noted a considerable decrease in head and trunk oscillations during the first weeks of walking, an indication of the increasing stability of the upper trunk in relation to the rest of the body. Kubo and Ulrich (2006) argued that the longer double stance seen in the step cycle of toddlers reflects the struggle to couple the anteroposterior and mediolateral oscillations present in independent walking.

An interesting study of interlimb coordination in walking was one in which researchers added mass to the wrists or ankles of adults during treadmill walking (Donker, Mulder, Nienhuis, & Duysens, 2002). Using EMG, these scientists found that adding mass to one wrist altered the muscular activity and movement of the other arm. Even more dramatic was the finding that adding mass to an ankle caused changes in both arm actions. Very clearly the arms and legs are tied together in walking, with the legs acting as forcing oscillators that drive the arm action.

Most investigators feel that part of the coordination between and across limbs is inherited from the quadripedal organization of the mammalian spinal cord (Jackson et al., 1983). In addition, most agree that arm movements counteract the rotations of the upper spine and pelvis that are produced by the legs during walking. This may be another reason why the young walker and the slow or careful walker use middle and low guard: These slow walkers do not produce the trunk rotation that semiopposition and opposition help counteract. A further speculation about guard positions is that they place the arms in a position of readiness in case the arms need to parachute (extend) if balance is lost.

Dynamic Systems View of Walking

In 1989 Thelen, Ulrich, and Jensen explicated the dynamic system that produces walking behavior. We have already mentioned some of its components. It is worth taking a moment, however, to see in its totality the complex system from which any developmental level of walking emerges at any point in the lifespan. This systems view is in direct contrast to the unidimensional view held by the motor development pioneers, who focused almost exclusively on the nervous system as the sole cause of walking behaviors.

Thelen et al. (1989) argued that the *spinal CPG* that facilitates the alternating stepping actions of the legs and the *sensory processing* that integrates knowledge of the environment with "knowledge of self-movement" (p. 43) are two necessary components of the system that produces walking. Both develop before the

appearance of walking. *Sensitivity to optic flow* is part of this integration of body and environment. Added to these three components is the ability to *balance* both in a bipedal position and on one foot as the other moves forward. Also needed are the *strength* to counteract gravity *relative to supporting body weight* in an upright posture and the ability to *control the relationships among multiple body segments* while vertical. Moreover, there must be *motivation* to move toward a distant object or place. Children who are visually impaired, for instance, are delayed in any type of locomotion primarily because they cannot see the potentially interesting stimuli in their environments (Levtzion-Korach, Tennenbaum, Schnitzer, & Ornoy, 2000). This latter example shows how any of the system components can be a rate limiter for an individual child. In babies exhibiting typical development, however, strength and balance are the critical rate limiters for walking. Toward the elderly end of the lifespan, balance and strength may once again become critical rate limiters for maintaining an optimal level of walking.

A final and important component of this dynamic system is the *context* or environment surrounding the individual attempting to walk. As Murray et al. (1969) mentioned, a slippery surface, an elevated surface, and a surface dotted with obstacles can constrain the movements displayed by the walker and make it less likely that the walker will use the optimal levels described in table 6.1.

Contemporary Research

The development of walking continues to be of considerable interest to motor development researchers; however, their questions now tend to address causation: Why does walking develop the way that it does? Over time, what factors cause changes in walking? In addition, verbal descriptions have given way to biomechanical analyses, some of which have been influenced by the dynamic systems perspective. For instance, contemporary investigators are attempting to model walking as the interaction of up to six nonlinear oscillators: each leg, each arm, the pelvis, and the thorax (e.g., Wagenaar & van Emmerik, 2000).

Lastly, interest in the neural control of walking has returned. As mentioned earlier, investigators generally agree that the early stepping patterns of newborns reflect the existence of spinal CPGs (Forssberg, 1985). This viewpoint refutes the developmental discontinuity that the disappearance of the stepping reflex was once thought to represent. As discussed in chapter 1, the original assumption was that the reflex was controlled by the subcortical areas of the brain. As higher brain centers developed, they inhibited the reflex, causing it to disappear (McGraw, 1945/1962). Zelazo (Zelazo, Zelazo, & Kolb, 1972) and Thelen (Thelen, Fisher, & Ridley-Johnson, 1984) have demonstrated that the reflex can be maintained and that it disappears when the strength-to-mass ratio of the leg changes with growth. Thus, the neural aspect of stepping is now viewed as continuous from reflex stepping to adult walking.

Hopping

Hopping, or projecting the body into the air from one foot and landing on the same foot, is one of the bouncing gaits (Farley, Blickhan, Saito, & Taylor, 1991). While adults do not often hop for its own sake, the hop is an integral part of

dance (in steps such as the schottische) and in the locomotor task of skipping. In robotics, it has served as a model for hopping machines (see Raibert, Brown, & Chepponis, 1984). A reflex form of hopping, the limping reaction (Peiper, 1963), is present in a number of species. If an animal's body is displaced away from its supporting limb and base of support, the animal will flex that limb to lift it off the ground and then extend to replace it under the body. Forward, backward, and sideways hopping reflexes can be elicited in animals, including humans. Herdman et al. (1983) found that the hopping response was slowed but not extinguished in cats after complete spinal cord transection. They suggested that the basic neural circuitry for the hopping reflex lies in the cord and that supraspinal influences fine-tune the response. To date, no research has assessed whether the hopping reflex is developmentally continuous with voluntary hopping. As can be seen in table 6.4, however, the movements used in level 1 leg action in voluntary hopping appear to be similar to those described for the hopping reflex.

Developmental Sequences

Although voluntary hopping has received considerably less study than walking has received, developmental sequences have been validated for hopping over distance—that is, for hopping to travel somewhere. Halverson and Williams (1985) first hypothesized and studied the hopping sequences in a prelongitudinal screening of 63 3-, 4-, and 5-year-olds. The sequences were then validated by Roberton and Halverson (1988) in seven children, each of whom was filmed longitudinally for 15 to 17 years.

Of particular interest in the developmental sequence for the leg action is the qualitative change between level 2 and level 3 (see table 6.4). In level 2 the nonhopping leg, or swing leg, is held in a stationary position, usually in front of the body. In level 3 that same leg begins pumping forward and backward to help project the body. Level 3 is probably the functional developmental level for this skill, while level 4 is used for hopping forcefully.

The sequence for arm action also shows a dramatic change between level 2, in which the arms are used for balance, and level 3, in which they swing up and down bilaterally to assist in force production (see table 6.4). This pattern again changes qualitatively when only one arm swings in unison with the pumping leg (level 4). Level 4, semiopposition, is likely the functional arm level for most advanced individuals unless they are trying to produce forceful travel. Then they will display opposition (level 5). In this way, the functional and optimal behavior of the arms in hopping is similar to the functional and optimal behavior of the arms in walking.

Interlimb Coordination

As with walking, all four limbs are active and coordinated in advanced hopping. Figure 6.4 illustrates the limb relationships in the advanced hop as averaged across seven children when they were 15 to 18 years of age (Roberton & Halverson, 1988). The four horizontal bars show the relative timing (normalized) data for each limb during one hop cycle, which lasts, on average, 506 milliseconds. The bottom bar represents the hopping leg from foot touch of the first landing to

Table 6.4 Developmental Sequences for Hopping Over Distance

Level	Description
Leg action	
Level 1	***Momentary flight*** The support knee and hip quickly flex, pulling (instead of projecting) the foot from the floor. The flight is momentary. Only a hop or two can be achieved. The swing leg is lifted high and held in an inactive position to the side or in front of the body.
Level 2	***Fall and catch with swing leg inactive*** Forward lean allows gravity to combine with minimal knee and ankle extension to help the body fall forward of the support foot. Through quick knee and hip flexion in the support leg, balance is recovered in the landing, or catch. The swing leg is inactive and is usually held in front of the body. Repeated hops are achieved.
Level 3	***Projected takeoff with assisting swing leg*** Perceptible extension occurs in the support hip, knee, and ankle before takeoff. There is little delay in changing from knee and ankle flexion upon landing to takeoff extension. The swing leg now pumps up and down to assist in projection, but range is insufficient to carry it behind the support leg when viewed from the side.
Level 4	***Projection delay with leading swing leg*** Upon landing, the weight of the child is smoothly transferred to the ball of the foot before the knee and ankle extend to take off. The swing leg begins forward action well before initiation of knee extension in the support leg. The range of pumping action in the swing leg increases so that it passes behind the support leg when viewed from the side.
Arm action	
Level 1	***Bilateral inactive*** The arms are held bilaterally, usually high and out to the side, although other positions behind or in front of the body may occur. Arm action is slight and not consistent.
Level 2	***Bilateral reactive*** Arms swing forward briefly, then move downward and backward through medial rotation at the shoulder in a winging movement before takeoff. This movement appears to be in reaction to loss of balance.
Level 3	***Bilateral assist*** The arms pump up and down together, usually in front of the trunk. Any downward and backward motion of the arms occurs after takeoff. The arms may move parallel to each other or be held at different levels as they move up and down.
Level 4	***Semiopposition*** The arm on the side opposite the swing leg swings forward and upward in synchrony with the forward and upward movement of that leg. The action of the other arm is variable, often moving through a short forward and backward cycle or moving up and down out to the side of the body or held relatively inactive at the side.
Level 5	***Opposing assist*** The arm opposite the swing leg moves forward and upward in synchrony with the forward and upward movement of that leg. The other arm moves in the direction opposite the action of the swing leg. The range of the arm action may be minimal unless the task requires speed or distance.

The term *inactive* means there is little or no movement assisting in force production.

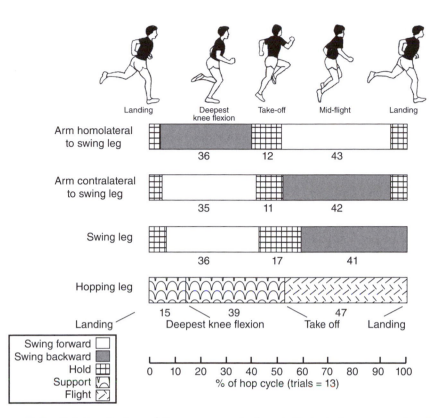

Figure 6.4 Relative timing of the movement of each limb during one cycle of advanced hopping. Data were averaged across 13 trials from seven children aged 15 to 18 years. Each bar represents the action of one limb for one cycle of the hop. From Roberton and Halverson (1988).

foot touch of the next landing. Within this action are the support phase, which takes up about 53% of the hop cycle, and the flight phase. The support phase, in turn, can be divided into two parts: from foot touch to the point of deepest knee flexion and from deepest knee flexion until takeoff. This latter part consumes the greatest amount of support time.

Superimposed on the action of the hopping leg is the movement of the swing leg. The swing leg moves through a range of approximately 120° both forward and upward and then downward and backward. The swing forward begins about 6% (30 milliseconds) into the hop cycle and ends roughly 10% (50 milliseconds) before takeoff. The backward swing starts about 7% (35 milliseconds) into the flight phase and ends simultaneously with the end of the cycle at foot touch.

Concomitant with the leg actions are the swinging actions of the arms (see figure 6.4). The arm contralateral to the swing leg pumps forward with the swing leg and moves for the same duration. The arm homolateral to the swing leg begins backward movement that again lasts for approximately the same duration: 36% of the cycle. The reverse swings of the arms and the swing leg are again tied and last

similar durations. The coordination of the arms and swing leg seems to be most tight in the duration of the movement. The two arms, however, are closely tied both in terms of duration and in terms of initiation and cessation of movement.

Developmentally, these timing relationships take years to emerge. Figure 6.5 shows the longitudinal record of one boy as he progressed from level 3 to level 4 leg action (Roberton & Halverson, 1988). Each data point represents the relative timing difference between the beginning of forward movement in the swing leg and the beginning of knee extension in the hopping leg. The negative percentages mean that the swing leg began its forward movement ahead of knee extension. When the child's hops were first filmed at age 3 years and 10 months, his leg action was at level 2, in which the swing leg does not move. Thus, the graph begins at age 4 with the first instance of level 3 leg action. It demonstrates that this particular timing relationship between the swing leg and the hopping leg took 5 years to develop. The timing relationship then remained fairly constant until the end of the study, when the child was 18. Using phase planes derived from these data, Roberton and Halverson (1988) argued that the hopping leg acted as an external forcing oscillator to which the swing leg ultimately entrained.

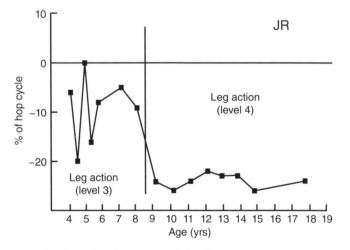

Figure 6.5 Longitudinal development of the timing relationship between the start of forward movement in the swing leg and the start of knee extension in the hopping leg. The child's (JR's) knee extension began at 0. Negative numbers indicate movements that began ahead of knee extension. In level 3 (see table 6.4) the swing leg began its forward movement closer to the start of knee extension and was more variable from year to year; in level 4 the swing leg regularly began forward movement over 20% of the hop cycle ahead of knee extension.

Mass–Spring Model

Roberton and Halverson (1988) also found a timing relationship in the hop that, in contrast to the developing relationship between the swing leg and the hopping leg, was invariant from the first primitive hops. Regardless of the child's age or

developmental level, the relative time from landing to fullest knee extension stayed the same. The authors called this a *bouncing invariant* and suggested that it represents an equation of constraint or coordinative structure that maintains relative relationships within the leg despite developmental changes in mass and landing force. Such a mechanism is able to use the force developed eccentrically in the landing to help propel the body for the next hop. Roberton and Halverson (1988) hypothesized that, as children take advantage of the potential storage and recovery of elastic energy in their muscles and tendons, they begin to operate like simple mass–spring systems (see Farley et al., 1991). A mass–spring system operates according to Hooke's law: Changes in the spring are proportional to the force acting on it (Alexander, 1997). The authors calculated knee stiffness in their participants' hops, stiffness being the slope of the force–displacement relationship. As demonstrated in figure 6.6, they found that level 2 hops had much greater stiffness than level 3 or 4 hops had. Recall that Black et al. (2009) found greater stiffness in early walkers as well. Greater stiffness is associated with coactivation of muscles surrounding a joint.

Getchell and Roberton (1989) confirmed that level 2 hoppers exhibit greater stiffness than level 3 hoppers exhibit. These authors eliminated body size as an explanation for this phenomenon by studying children who showed a level 2 hop on one leg and a level 3 hop on the other leg. This is a common developmental asynchrony in locomotor skills such as hopping and skipping. One leg, presumably the dominant leg, precedes the other in progressing to the next developmental level. By studying children who exhibited two different developmental levels at the same time, the researchers were able to show that the swinging of the swing leg, rather than body size, is the cause of the softer (less stiff) landing. Moreover, their values for average whole-body stiffness (20 kilonewtons per meter for level 2 and 9 kilonewtons per meter for level 3) were the same as those calculated by Roberton and Halverson (1988) for knee stiffness.

By using cinematography and a force plate, Getchell and Roberton (1989) were also able to demonstrate differences in the instantaneous stiffness of the two types of landings (see figure 6.7). They speculated that stiffness acts as a control parameter in the hop. To protect the joints during the jarring landings of level 2 hops, the system immediately defaults upon touchdown to soften the landing (see the top graph in figure 6.7). In level 3 the system adjusts before

▶ Tips for Novice Investigators

Research involves continual verification of previous findings. This verification is strengthened when multiple methods yield the same result. A good example is the confirmation of stiffness values in the development of hopping. Roberton and Halverson (1988) reported values based on kinematics digitized from 16 mm films. Getchell and Roberton (1989) then confirmed these values using landing forces measured by a force plate.

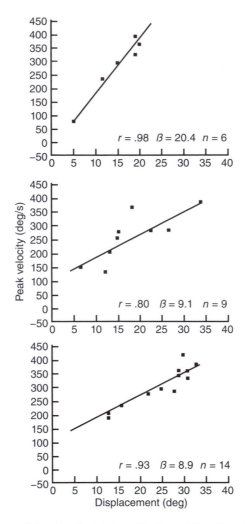

Figure 6.6   Stiffness of the landing leg in the hop (β) estimated by the ratio of the peak velocity of knee flexion at landing to its displacement. The top graph shows level 2 leg action, the middle graph shows level 3 leg action, and the bottom graph shows level 4 leg action. Stiffness decreases as hopping develops over time.

landing to achieve the softer, safer, more functional movement. Thus, at some stiffness level between 20 and 9 kilonewtons per meter may lie the critical value at which the system reorganizes to produce level 3 movements.

Austin, Tiberio, and Garrett (2002, 2003) and Austin, Garrett, and Tiberio (2002) studied 10 adult males hopping in place. They found that hopping at a frequency 20% faster than the preferred frequency (2.03 hertz, or hops per second) yielded stiffness values close to 23 kilonewtons per meter, which

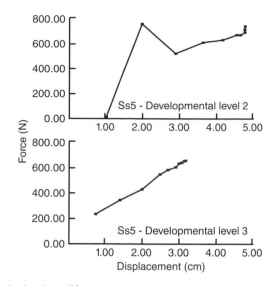

Figure 6.7 Whole-body stiffness measured on a force plate from the point of landing (first point on the left) to the point of the lowest center of gravity (on the right). The top graph shows a child's landing on one leg, which displayed a level 2 hop, while the bottom graph shows the same child's landing on the other leg, which displayed a level 3 hop.

Reprinted from N. Getchell and M.A. Roberton, 1989, "Whole body stiffness as a function of developmental level in children's hopping," *Developmental Psychology* 25: 920-928. By permission of M.A. Roberton.

are considerably higher than the adult preferred stiffness level of about 14 kilonewtons per meter. This finding fits in well with the frequencies of the children tracked by Roberton and Halverson (1988). The latter authors found that the children's preferred hopping frequency decreased over time from 3 to 2.06 hertz, a decrease that is perceptible to adults. At the same time, stiffness levels decreased from 20 to 9 kilonewtons per meter. Thus, hopping at higher frequency is related to higher stiffness levels in both children and adults. The same finding has been reported for bipedal hopping (two-foot jumping; Farley et al., 1991).

Austin et al. (2002) also obtained adult instantaneous stiffness recordings at frequencies 20% less than the adult preferred frequency. These recordings looked quite similar to those of Getchell and Roberton (1989) for level 2 hopping (see figure 6.7). Austin et al. speculated that this nonlinear deviation from the linear mass–spring behavior suggests that the nonhopping leg functions as a second mass, creating a mass–spring system with two masses. Their suggestion makes sense in light of the position in which the swing leg is held in level 2 hopping. An alternative or companion hypothesis, however, is that at these slow frequencies in adults the stretch reflex operates after landing to promote further flexion of the hopping leg. This hypothesis also fits in with the comment by Getchell and Roberton (1989) that the level 2 hopper was not able to adjust stiffness levels before landing and so defaulted after landing.

FURTHER STUDY

We hope this overview of developmental work on walking and hopping whets your appetite for learning more about the development of the various locomotor forms. It is interesting to watch the human body acquire the versatility in locomotion displayed by adult movers and to observe the gradual decline in locomotor facility that many people experience with aging. Galloping (Whitall, 1989), jumping (Clark & Phillips, 1985; Hellebrandt, Rarick, Glassow, & Carns, 1961), and running (Fortney, 1983) have received developmental study, as have forms of locomotion that do not take place on the feet, such as crawling and creeping (Sparrow, 1989) and swimming (Erbaugh, 1986; Langendorfer & Bruya, 1995). In addition to learning about locomotor development for its own sake, understanding these developmental processes can be helpful in rehabilitation after accident or stroke, in helping youngsters acquire these skills, and in helping older adults maintain their confidence and competence in these basic patterns of everyday life.

▶ Tips for Novice Investigators

Chapter 4 of Langendorfer and Bruya (1995) provides developmental sequences for a number of components of aquatic readiness, such as water entry, buoyancy, body position in the water, and arm actions. Some of these sequences have received preliminary validation; others are simply hypothesized. Any novice investigator interested in aquatics might enjoy contributing to this literature by providing developmental research on one or more of these components.

SUMMARY

Despite their ubiquity in the human repertoire, locomotor tasks need considerably more developmental study. Although aspects of the intertask sequence for foot locomotion are known, the entire sequence still awaits validation, as does the intratask sequence for walking. However, cross-sectional product data and descriptions of walking movements do exist for some parts of the lifespan. This descriptive information has enabled attempts to model walking as a dynamic system. In particular, researchers have used the pendulum as a model for both leg and arm action in walking. In contrast to the walking research, the developmental sequence for hopping has been extensively studied. In addition, developmental researchers have used a mass-spring model to study changes in both whole-body and knee stiffness values. These changes seem to parallel changes in both hopping frequency and leg action. Hopefully, developmental knowledge will continue to grow about these two skills as well as the many others that comprise human locomotion.

Footnotes

[1]See, for instance, Winters (1975). Other taxonomies, such as Laban's (see Russell, 1987), use slightly different definitions.

[2]It is possible to walk with alternating steps without a pattern generator. McGeer (1990) described a functional walking robot that relied only on gravity, inertia, and a stance leg that rotated as an inverted pendulum. While this passive walking could occur only on an incline, McGeer argued that adding a motor to generate energy would allow the robot to walk on a flat surface. On the other hand, Raibert (1990) has pointed out that just because a machine can walk in a certain way does not mean that living systems walk in the same way.

CHAPTER 7

Development of Ballistic Skills

Movements can be classified by their EMG and force curve signatures. Three movement categories are (1) ramped movements in which force is gradually and steadily applied through continuously graded muscle firing; (2) discontinuous, slow movements that accelerate gradually, then decelerate, and then accelerate again, such as when tracking an object with a hand; and (3) ballistic movements that are rapid, all-out, forceful movements that reach peak acceleration within milliseconds of their initiation (Brooks, 1983; Desmedt, 1983).

In simple ballistic movements, such as a rapid reach for an object, the motion is started by an initial strong impulse in the agonist muscle. The agonist firing then stops, but the movement continues due to the momentum of the limb. A burst by the antagonist muscle subsequently causes the limb to decelerate. In targeting tasks, there may be a second burst in the agonist to correct the limb placement. This creates a signature triphasic pattern of muscle activation: agonist, antagonist, agonist (Palmer, Cafarelli, & Ashby, 1994).

In contrast to single-limb movements, ballistic skills involving the total body are quite complex. Typical sport skills are examples of ballistic skills. Of these, movements in which the performer projects an object have been of considerable interest to both biomechanists and developmentalists. Striking (as in batting and swinging a racket), kicking (as in football and soccer), and throwing (as in handball and baseball or softball) have all received study. These complex movements tend to begin proximally with action of the trunk muscles; energy is then passed from segment to segment of the open kinetic chain until it reaches the distal effector, usually the hand or foot. During striking, kicking, and throwing, this energy exchange is superimposed on a running or stepping base of support.

Another interesting commonality across these complex projectile skills is that they employ a backswing to place the body segments in position to move forward. In the advanced form of striking, throwing, and kicking, the backswing and forward swing partially overlap, and proximal segments begin to move forward while more distal segments are still moving backward. The advanced form of these movements also involves strong acceleration of the distal segment just milliseconds before contact or release, which yields high distal angular

velocity. This acceleration seems to result partially from the inertia of each distal segment against the motion of adjacent proximal segments. The lagging segment stretches the agonist muscles of the distal segment, which may in turn excite reflexes that augment the muscular contractions in the distal segment (Roberts & Metcalfe, 1968). As we will see, lag is one aspect of object projection that develops only gradually over time. It is so important for effective ballistic movement that Southard (2002a, 2002b) used lag as a collective variable in his studies of throwing.

In this chapter we focus on the development of striking, throwing, and kicking. Most developmental studies on ballistic projectile skills have been based in developmental sequence theory, although a few studies are beginning to address issues from a dynamic systems perspective. At the close of this chapter we discuss future directions in this area.

> Tips for Novice Investigators

In this and other chapters you will find same or adjacent graphs that include data from different studies. Combining data from different studies helps us to visualize and hypothesize change over a larger portion of the lifespan. Using graphs to see data is always a good way for researchers to understand their results and to generate additional hypotheses or studies.

INTERTASK DEVELOPMENTAL SEQUENCE

The only ballistic skills that have been studied in relation to their intertask development are overarm throwing and striking. The approach used in this research is quite different from the intertask approach used to study locomotion (see chapter 6). For locomotion, the developmental sequence is formed by ordering each locomotor skill according to its initial appearance in the movement repertoire. For throwing and striking, the two tasks are compared to see where participants are located within a component developmental sequence at the same point in time in each skill. Do the participants show the same developmental level in the two skills, or do they develop faster in one skill than they do in the other?

Langendorfer (1987a) compared the development of trunk and humerus action in overarm throwing with development of the same action in overarm striking. He asked 58 boys aged 1.5 to 10.3 years to throw a ball forcefully and to strike a tennis ball suspended 6 inches (15 cm) above their head forcefully with a lightweight racket. He then looked at side and rear film views to categorize the boys' movements in each skill. Figure 7.1 shows his results. From the cross-sectional data we can infer how the longitudinal data might look. The data on trunk action (see figure 7.1a) suggested that children advance in throwing before they do in striking: The boys started out at a primitive level in both skills and then advanced to level 2 throwing before achieving level 2 striking and advanced to level 3 throwing before reaching level 3 striking. The cross-sectional data on humerus action

(see figure 7.1*b*) suggested that children begin at level 1 in both skills and then move ahead in either skill until they reach level 2 in both skills. Then, however, they progress to level 3 in throwing before they progress to level 3 in striking.

Langendorfer (1987a) learned from his data that he could not compare forearm action between striking and throwing. Rather, the action of the racket, which is the distal segment in striking, was more comparable to the forearm action of throwing. Figure 7.1*c* shows the developmental comparison for forearm action. While some children exhibited different relationships early on, more progressed in striking before they progressed in throwing. Then throwing took the developmental lead for more children.

The finding on forearm action demonstrates how equipment can affect a person's developmental level. Using Newell's notions of person constraints (see chapter 3),

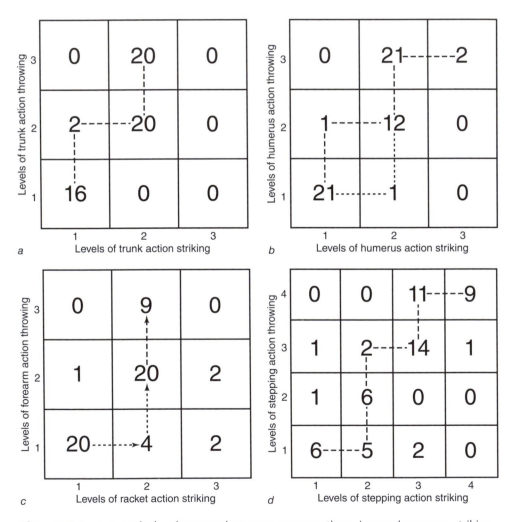

Figure 7.1 Intertask development between overarm throwing and overarm striking.

Reprinted with permission from *Research Quarterly for Exercise and Sport*, Vol. 58: 21-29, Copyright 1987 by the American Alliance for Health, Physical Education, Recreation and Dance, 1900 Association Drive, Reston, VA 20191.

we can think of equipment as an extension of the body. Comparing hammering with a hammer with pounding with a fist demonstrates how an implement changes the inertial characteristics of the arm and hand. This analysis also applies to prosthetic limbs. In both cases the performer needs to learn how to incorporate the implement into the actual movement pattern. Langendorfer's (1987a) data suggest that at first the implement assists the child in achieving a higher developmental level in the distal component, probably because its greater inertia causes lag. Later, though, the handle length may hinder change to a higher developmental level by making it more difficult to delay that lag until the body has reached front facing (see tables 7.1 and 7.4).

The last component that Langendorfer (1987a) compared across the two skills was stepping. As we can see in figure 7.1d, the developmental relationship for stepping was less clear. Langendorfer attributed this result to a degree of unreliability in the component sequence: Stepping tended to be variable across trials in both throwing and striking, making intertask comparisons unreliable.

The arrows in figure 7.1 reflect Langendorfer's (1987a) speculation on the longitudinal course that these two tasks might display while developing. The only actual longitudinal information that we have regarding this question was reported by Roberton (1982). She compared the development of trunk action within sidearm striking (as opposed to overarm striking) and overarm throwing. Interestingly, the trunk action of four children did follow the developmental path that Langendorfer's cross-sectional overarm data suggested: The children progressed one level in their throwing trunk action and then caught up to that same level in their striking trunk action. Then they progressed again in throwing before catching up in striking.

▶ Tips for Novice Investigators

Langendorfer's (1987a) work was based in motor stage theory. This theory guided a number of motor development researchers during the 1970s and 1980s. Since motor development research frequently uses the notion of developmental sequences, it is worth studying Langendorfer's article to get an understanding of the different possibilities for sequential development. Here are a few questions to answer:

- What did Langendorfer mean when he said that "all stages represent developmental change, but not all developmental changes are stage-like" (p. 21)?

- Examine a couple of undergraduate motor development texts. Do the stages they describe satisfy the criteria mentioned by Langendorfer? If not, where did these book stages come from?

- What are vertical structure and horizontal structure? Can development demonstrate one without the other?

- What might explain Langendorfer's finding that several components in throwing and striking show synchronous development at primitive levels but asynchronous development at more advanced levels?

Table 7.1 Hypothesized Developmental Sequences for Overarm Striking for Force

Level	Description
Trunk action	
Level 1	No trunk action *or* extension or flexion of the trunk
Level 2	Spinal rotation only *or* spinal and then pelvic rotation *or* block rotation (with or without lateral trunk flexion)
Level 3	Differentiated (pelvic and then spinal) rotation (with or without lateral trunk flexion)
Humerus action	
Level 1	Oblique (or obtuse) humerus–trunk angle
Level 2	Humerus aligned horizontally (90°) but independent
Level 3	Humerus lag
Forearm action	
Level 1	No lag
Level 2	Lag
Level 3	Delayed lag
Stepping action	
Level 1	No forward step
Level 2	Forward step with ipsilateral leg
Level 3	Forward step with contralateral leg
Level 4	Long forward step with contralateral leg
Elbow angle (at initiation of forward movement)	
Level 1	20° or less *or* greater than 120°
Level 2	21°-89°
Level 3	90°-119°
Spinal range of motion	
Level 1	Spine (at shoulders) rotates through less than 45°
Level 2	Spine rotates between 45° and 89°
Level 3	Spine rotates more than 90°
Pelvic range of motion	
Level 1	Pelvis (below the waist) rotates less than 45°
Level 2	Pelvis rotates between 45° and 89°
Level 3	Pelvis rotates more than 90°
Racket action	
Level 1	No racket lag
Level 2	Racket lag
Level 3	Delayed racket lag

Reprinted, by permission, from S. Langendorfer, 1987, Prelongitudinal screening of overarm striking under two environmental conditions, In *Advances in motor development research*, Vol. 1, edited by J. Clark. J. Humphrey (Brooklyn, NY: AMS Press), 17-47.

Clearly, more research is needed on the intertask developmental relationships across projectile skills as well as across other ballistic skills. Understanding the development between skills would assist parents and teachers in knowing which tasks to introduce first to learners and in understanding the degree to which transfer might occur across tasks. From a theoretical point of view, the developmental asynchronies between components common to two tasks might cast light on the arguments of specificity versus generality that occur periodically in the literature (see Henry, 1958/1968).

INTRATASK DEVELOPMENTAL SEQUENCES

The rest of this chapter focuses on the separate development of ballistic tasks. First we will look at the two tasks Langendorfer (1987a) studied: overarm striking and throwing. Then we will examine what is known about the development of another form of striking: placekicking.

Overarm Striking

Two investigators have used cross-sectional data to screen the developmental sequences for overarm striking (see table 7.1). Using the same children from his studies on intertask development, Langendorfer (1987b) found that trunk action, humerus action, racket action, elbow action, spinal range of motion, and pelvic range of motion passed the prelongitudinal screening for overarm striking and were ready for longitudinal testing. Figure 7.2 displays his data for racket action.

In 1991 Messick followed up on Langendorfer's (1987b) work, studying the tennis serve in 60 experienced male and female players aged 9 to 19 years. Her cross-sectional data also supported the sequences in the elbow and racket components as well as in a new component, preparatory trunk action. This latter component, hypothesized by Messick, is listed in table 7.2.

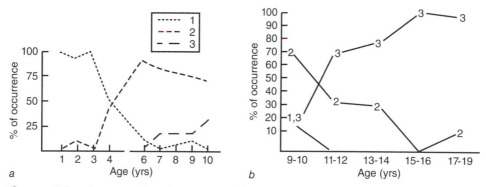

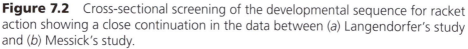

Figure 7.2 Cross-sectional screening of the developmental sequence for racket action showing a close continuation in the data between (a) Langendorfer's study and (b) Messick's study.

(a) Reprinted, by permission, from S. Langendorfer, 1987, Prelongitudinal screening of overarm striking under two environmental conditions, In *Advances in motor development research*, Vol. 1, edited by J. Clark. J. Humphrey (Brooklyn, NY: AMS Press), 17-47.

(b) Reprinted with permission from *Research Quarterly for Exercise and Sport*, Vol. 62: 31, Copyright 1991 by the American Alliance for Health, Physical Education, Recreation and Dance, 1900 Association Drive, Reston, VA 20191.

Of particular interest is how well Messick's data line up with Langendorfer's data. For instance, figure 7.2 also contains Messick's data for racket action. Approximating from the graphs, we can see that both investigators found that less than 20% of their 9- to 10-year-olds displayed level 1 development. Around 70% of that same age group showed level 2 development, and 20% to 30% displayed level 3 development. More importantly, the direction of the three curves, in terms of falling or rising over the ages studied, was the same. Clearly, these sequences are ready for longitudinal study.

Both Langendorfer (1987b) and Messick (1991) asked additional and interesting questions of their data. Langendorfer compared his participants' performance when the ball was suspended in a stationary position with their performance when the same ball was swinging. He found no significant differences in the developmental levels displayed. This question is an example of asking what happens when the constraints between performer and task are changed. We shall look further at constraints in our discussion of throwing. Messick (1991), on the other hand, asked whether graphing her data by experience would make the curves look different from when the data were graphed by age. She found that age and experience covaried in the tennis serve such that the experience graphs for each component were quite similar to the age graphs. Both led to the same conclusions about the validity of the proposed sequences.

Table 7.2 Developmental Sequence for Preparatory Trunk Action in the Tennis Serve

Level	Description
Level 1	No trunk action or flexion or extension of the trunk
Level 2	Minimal trunk rotation (<180°)
Level 3	Total trunk rotation (>180°)

Reprinted with permission from *Research Quarterly for Exercise and Sport*, Vol. 62: 249-256, Copyright 1991 by the American Alliance for Health, Physical Education, Recreation and Dance, 1900 Association Drive, Reston, VA 20191.

Kicking

Despite its popularity due to its use in soccer and football, placekicking (the soccer instep kick) has been largely ignored in developmental study. Early on, Halverson (1940), who specialized in motor development research at Yale University under Gesell, reported that 18-month-olds kick a ball only by stepping into it while 2-year-olds can actually kick the ball. Roberts and Metcalfe (1968) subsequently claimed that kicking is an extension of running, thus suggesting that if a child can run, a child can kick. Deach (1950) proposed four stages of kicking in her dissertation study of 2- to 6-year-olds, but, unfortunately, she placed the children in her study directly behind the ball, thus preventing them from taking an approach. Since her pioneering work, few investigations have examined kicking from a developmental perspective. Two studies are described here with the hope that you might be the researcher to conduct the next logical study stemming from their work.

Bloomfield, Elliott, and Davies (1979) filmed 56 boys aged 2 to 12 years as they performed a soccer kick for both force and accuracy. The researchers then grouped the children according to the whole-body patterns they displayed:

Group 1 (ranging from 2 years, 4 months to 5 years, 1 month) displayed a limited backswing and follow-through and took no more than a one-step approach, if any. Arm movement was not "co-ordinated" (p. 157).

Group 2 (ranging from 3 years, 8 months to 7 years, 1 month) had a modified backswing and follow-through. They used balancing actions of the arms and did not use an approach step.

Group 3 (ranging from 2 years, 10 months to 5 years, 4 months) also did not use an approach step but showed a degree of thigh hyperextension and leg flexion during the backswing and some follow-through after ball contact. One arm moved in opposition to the kicking leg but primarily acted to balance the body during vigorous kicks.

Group 4 (ranging from 3 years, 11 months to 11 years, 9 months) on average used a five-step approach before kicking the ball but did not have an extensive backswing despite the run-up. Both arms swung in opposition to the leg action, but the arm swing was minimal.

Group 5 (ranging from 4 years, 11 months to 12 years) averaged 4.1 steps as they approached the ball. Their shank flexed at the knee as the thigh swung forward. The follow-through after ball contact was "well-developed" (p. 157). The arm action was in opposition to the leg action.

Group 6 (ranging from 9 years, 1 month to 12 years, 3 months) averaged 3.9 steps for the approach and often used an angled run-up. They had a large backswing due to their approach as well as a full follow-through. The arm action was opposition.

Bloomfield et al. (1979) described group 6 as approaching the advanced kick, which they described as having the following characteristics: At the end of the approach, the performer leaps onto the support foot, which is placed level with or slightly in front of the ball. The forward swing of the kicking leg begins before the support foot contacts the ground and is characterized by flexion of the knee and hip. The shank begins extending as the thigh decelerates. At contact, the shank is almost perpendicular to the ground. The trunk leans slightly backward and to the side. The opposite arm swings forward with the kicking leg. During follow-through the kicking leg swings to approximately waist height while the support leg forcefully extends at the knee.

The six groups of Bloomfield et al. (1979) had a large age range associated with each of the patterns. The authors acknowledged that a component approach to their whole-body descriptions might better accommodate the individual differences associated with a given age and might yield tighter developmental sequences.

Lisy (2002) focused on components in her study of kicking, but she took a different approach to prelongitudinal screening. She grouped 22 female and male college students according to their ball velocities, which ranged from less than 25 miles per hour (40 kph) to greater than 53 miles per hour (85 kph). She then graphed the occurrence of the levels of her proposed developmental sequences using the percentages displayed by the different velocity groups. Her proposed sequence for preparatory hip action (see table 7.3) held up quite well. Figure 7.3 shows her data for levels 3 through 5. She had no college student in the first two levels, so this sequence still needs further study before longitudinal research

begins. In contrast to Messick (1991), who found that experience was a useful screening variable for striking, Lisy found no relationship between experience and her proposed levels of kicking.

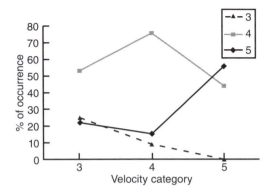

Figure 7.3   Differences in developmental levels for preparatory hip action when screened using levels of ball velocity displayed by college students. Level 3 = 36 to 44.5 miles per hour (58-72 kph), level 4 = 45 to 52.5 miles per hour (72-84 kph), and level 5 = 53+ miles per hour (85+ kph).

Reprinted, by permission, from M. Lisy, 2002, *Testing developmental sequences for the forceful kick.* Unpublished master's project. (Bowling Green: OH: Bowling Green State University). 23.

Table 7.3   Hypothesized Developmental Sequence for Preparatory Hip Action in Placekicking

Developmental levels	Definitions
Level 1	*No leg backswing*
	The kicking leg or foot does not move away from the direction of the kick before contacting the ball.
Level 2	*Backswing as a result of approach*
	The kicking leg or foot moves away from the direction of the kick, but the heel does not elevate to the height of the knee.
Level 3	*Straight backswing*
	The heel of the kicking leg reaches the height of the knee (i.e., shank is parallel to surface) but not the height of the hip (i.e., greater trochanter).
Level 4	*Circular backswing*
	The heel of the kicking leg elevates to the height of the knee (i.e., shank is parallel to surface) or beyond while appearing to cross the midline of the body.
Level 5	*Large circular backswing*
	The heel of the kicking leg elevates equal to or higher than the greater trochanter of the hip.

Reprinted, by permission, from M. Lisy, 2002, *Testing developmental sequences for the forceful kick.* Unpublished master's project. (Bowling Green: OH: Bowling Green State University). 14.

> ## Tips for Novice Investigators

The developmental study of kicking needs considerable work. The ideas of Bloomfield et al. (1979) could be broken into components and screened using cross-sectional data. Lisy's (2002) preparatory hip action component is also ready for cross-sectional screening. Since ball velocity covaries with age, ball velocity is another variable to examine in such a study.

Of additional interest might be studies on support (plant) foot placement relative to the ball and studies on the role of balance in producing a kick. Descriptions in the literature vary considerably as to where the foot is placed in the advanced kick. Bloomfield et al. (1979) indicated that it was placed even with or slightly ahead of the ball; however, the most careful study thus far found that elite Australian junior soccer players (mean age 16.8 years) placed their plant foot 37.3 centimeters to the side of the ball and 8.1 centimeters behind the ball (McLean & Tumilty, 1993). When the same players kicked with their nondominant foot, they placed it farther to the side of the ball, which the authors inferred was less skillful.

In terms of the role of balance in kicking, Butterfield and Loovis (1994) found no relationship between their measures of balance and their definition of kicking skillfulness in 716 children aged 4 to 14 years. On the other hand, Anderson, Chew-Bullock, Kim, Mayo, and Sidaway (2006) were able to explain more than 50% of the variance in the kicking velocities of university students by various measures of balance. Clearly, we need more work on this interesting question.

Throwing

In contrast to striking and kicking, throwing has received considerable developmental research. Developmental sequences for the overarm throw for force have been validated longitudinally and are now used as dependent variables in studies on gender differences, constraints on throwing (such as distance and accuracy demands), aging effects, and relationships between the developmental sequences and their product scores. Indeed, the throwing literature is an exemplar of the kind of research that can be accomplished once the developmental sequences for a task are validated so they can be used as dependent variables.

Developmental Sequences

Table 7.4 contains the validated sequences for three components of the overarm throw. In 1977 Roberton first screened these components using an across-trials methodology that has since proved quite useful. She filmed 73 first graders as they made 10 forceful throws. She then assessed the sequences using the following criteria: For the sequence to be accurate, each child's variability across trials could only encompass adjacent levels in the sequence, and at least 50% of each child's trials had to be within that child's modal category. In 1978 Roberton reported 2 to 3 years of longitudinal support for the sequences that had survived the across-trials screening in the same children, and in 1980 she and Langendorfer reported 9 to 14 years of supportive longitudinal data on seven other children.

Table 7.4 Validated Developmental Sequences for Overarm Throw for Force

Step	Description
Humerus action during forward swing	
Step 1	**Humerus oblique** The humerus moves forward to ball release in a plane that intersects the trunk obliquely above or below the horizontal line of the shoulders. Occasionally, during the backswing, the humerus is placed at a right angle to the trunk, with the elbow pointing toward the target. It maintains this fixed position during the throw.
Step 2	**Humerus aligned but independent** The humerus moves forward to ball release in a plane horizontally aligned with the shoulder, forming a right angle between humerus and trunk. By the time the shoulders (upper spine) reach front facing, the humerus (elbow) has moved independently ahead of the outline of the body (as seen from the side) via horizontal adduction at the shoulder.
Step 3	**Humerus lag** The humerus moves forward to ball release horizontally aligned, but at the moment the shoulders (upper spine) reach front facing, the humerus remains within the outline of the body (as seen from the side). No horizontal adduction of the humerus occurs before front facing.
Forearm action during forward swing	
Step 1	**No forearm lag** The forearm and ball move steadily forward to ball release throughout the throwing action.
Step 2	**Forearm lag** The forearm and ball appear to lag (to remain stationary behind the child or to move downward or backward in relation to the child). The lagging forearm reaches its farthest point back, deepest point down, or last stationary point *before* the shoulders (upper spine) reach front facing.
Step 3	**Delayed forearm lag** The lagging forearm delays reaching its final point of lag until the moment of front facing.
Trunk action during forward swing	
Step 1	**No trunk action or forward and backward movements** Only the arm is active in force production. Sometimes, the forward thrust of the arm pulls the trunk into a passive left rotation (assuming a right-handed throw), but no twist-up precedes that action. If trunk action occurs, it accompanies the forward thrust of the arm by flexing forward at the hips. Preparatory extension sometimes precedes forward hip flexion.
Step 2	**Upper trunk rotation or total trunk (block) rotation** The spine and pelvis both rotate away from the intended line of flight and then simultaneously begin forward rotation, acting as a unit, or block. Occasionally, only the upper spine twists away from and then toward the direction of force. The pelvis, then, remains fixed, facing the line of flight, or joins the rotary movement after forward spinal rotation has begun.
Step 3	**Differentiated rotation** The pelvis precedes the upper spine in initiating forward rotation. The child twists away from the intended line of ball flight and then begins forward rotation with the pelvis while the upper spine is still twisting away.

Reprinted from M.A. Roberton and L.E. Halverson, 1984, *Developing children: Their changing movement* (Philadelphia: Lea and Febiger), 103, 107. By permission of M.A. Roberton.

Since then the sequences have been widely used. Their developmental validity remains quite robust. Kinematic support for the developmental levels within trunk, humerus, and forearm action has been supplied as well (see Stodden, Langendorfer, Fleisig, & Andrews, 2006a, 2006b).

Table 7.5 contains two proposed sequences for throwing that have not yet been validated. Each needs additional cross-sectional or across-trials screening and longitudinal study. Stepping has received kinematic support (Stodden et al., 2006a), but its reliability and developmental validity have been questioned (Langendorfer, 1987a).

Table 7.5 Hypothesized Developmental Sequences for Overarm Throw for Force

Step	Description
	Preparatory arm backswing
Step 1	**No backswing**
	The ball in the hand moves directly forward to release from the arm's original position when the hand first grasped the ball.
Step 2	**Elbow and humerus flexion**
	The ball moves away from the intended line of flight to a position behind or alongside the head by upward flexion of the humerus and concomitant elbow flexion.
Step 3	**Circular upward backswing**
	The ball moves away from the intended line of flight to a position behind the head via a circular overhead movement with the elbow extended, or an oblique swing back, or a vertical lift from the hip.
Step 4	**Circular downward backswing**
	The ball moves away from the intended line of flight to a position behind the head via a circular down and back motion that carries the hand below the waist.
	Stepping action
Step 1	**No step**
	The child throws from the initial foot position.
Step 2	**Homolateral step**
	The child steps with the foot on the same side as the throwing hand.
Step 3	**Contralateral short step**
	The child steps with the foot on the opposite side from the throwing hand.
Step 4	**Contralateral long step**
	The child steps with the opposite foot for a distance greater than half the child's standing height.

Reprinted from M.A. Roberton and L.E. Halverson, 1984, *Developing children: Their changing movement* (Philadelphia: Lea and Febiger), 106, 118. By permission of M.A. Roberton.

Lifespan Perspective

In 1982 Halverson, Roberton, and Langendorfer used the Roberton developmental sequences to track 39 children from age 6 to age 13. In 1990 Williams, Haywood, and VanSant studied the overarm throws of 21 adults who were, on

average, 71 years of age. Figure 7.4 is a set of composites made from these two research groups' data for trunk, humerus, and forearm action (see table 7.4 for written descriptions). To form the composites, we used the data on the girls from the Halverson et al. study, since 16 of the participants used by Williams et al. were women. These cross-sectional data, of course, may be misleading since none of the participants in either study were randomly selected and since the older throwers may never have reached the levels of the younger throwers due to cohort differences. The data also tell us nothing about the lifespan between age 13 and age 71. The graph is only a teaser to challenge you to obtain more data that can eventually create a clear lifespan graph for motor skills of interest.

With those caveats, however, it is fun to speculate on the potential meanings of the data in figure 7.4. For instance, the graph on trunk action implies that many women may never develop level 3 differentiated rotation and that regression from level 2 to level 1 may occur with aging. Of the participants in the Williams et al. (1990) study, 2% used no movement of the trunk when they threw (level 1). This level totally disappeared by 8 years of age in the data from Halverson et al. (1982). Regression also seems to have occurred in humerus development. The incidence of level 3 humerus action declined in the elderly, while the incidence

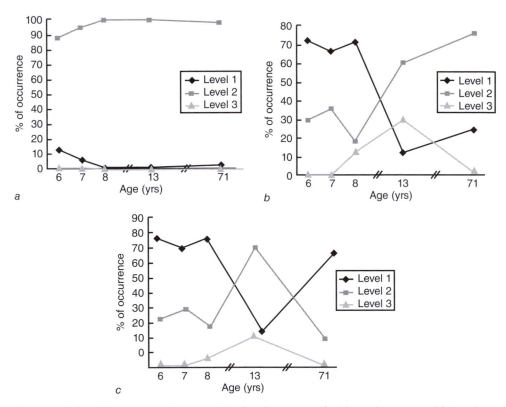

Figure 7.4   Lifespan development in the throwing of girls and women. (*a*) Trunk action, (*b*) humerus action, and (*c*) forearm action.

Hypothesized and redrawn from the data of Halverson, Roberton, and Langendorfer 1982; and Williams, Haywood, and VanSant 1990.

of levels 1 and 2 increased. Similar signs of regression can be seen in the forearm action. Again, we want to emphasize that this teaser exercise may be showing cohort differences rather than regression, but it gives an example of how data from various studies can be put together to generate new hypotheses.

Fortunately, Williams, Haywood, and VanSant (1998) continued to study eight of their participants for 7 years. These longitudinal data showed surprising stability during the years when the participants were in their 70s. Some of the participants even progressed in one or another component, suggesting that disuse had originally affected their movement or that there were cohort differences, as suggested earlier. Several participants reduced their range of movement over time; this reduction did not necessarily change their developmental level but did reflect the overall forcefulness of their throw. Such change within a developmental level is considered a quantitative rather than qualitative change. It would be interesting to see if a certain amount of quantitative change predicts subsequent qualitative change, as suggested by dynamic systems theory.

Developmental Profiles

Confidence in the developmental validity of several of the throwing component sequences has progressed to the point where investigators are now studying the profiles formed across components. A profile is a listing of the developmental levels observed in a person in each component at a given point in time. For instance, the profile T2-H2-F2 (level 2 trunk action, level 2 humerus action, level 2 forearm action) describes a thrower who displays block rotation of the trunk, an aligned but independent humerus, and a lagging forearm (see table 7.4 and figure 7.5).

Langendorfer and Roberton (2002a) studied the throwing profiles displayed by the 39 children followed longitudinally by Halverson et al. (1982). Of the 27 profiles theoretically possible, only 14 were expressed during this 7-year time frame. Langendorfer and Roberton speculated that anatomical and biomechanical constraints eliminated the unobserved movement combinations. They also studied the changing attractor strengths of the observed profiles by

Figure 7.5 The T2-H2-F2 throwing profile (see table 7.4 and text for descriptions).

Reprinted from *Motor Development: Research and Reviews*, with permission from NASPE (National Association for Sport and Physical Education), 1900 Association Drive, Reston, VA 20191.

locating them on a graph formed by the average stability of the profile over 10 trials and by the frequency with which the profile was observed in the sample (see figure 7.6). While many attractors changed strength over the 7 years, as would be expected developmentally, several remained strong in the sample across the same time frame. In particular, the profile T2-H2-F2 (figure 7.5) was displayed by 37 of the 39 children at some point in the 7 years. This observation led Langendorfer and Roberton (2002a) to speculate that most children achieve this profile with some minimal degree of experience. This suggests that the profile is phylogenetic, meaning that it is characteristic of the human species. Profiles beyond T2-H2-F2 might be ontogenetic, meaning that they are characteristic of individuals who become skillful in throwing.

The same authors (Langendorfer & Roberton, 2002b) then tracked the changing profiles of the 2002a study participants as they grew from 5.7 to 8 years of age. The resulting data (figure 7.7) showed the children progressing

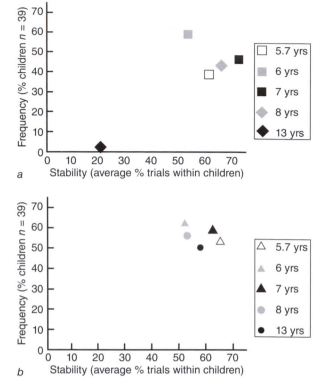

Figure 7.6 A comparison of the longitudinal strengths of two throwing profiles studied in a sample of children as they developed from age 5.7 to age 13. (a) T2-H1-F1 (b) T2-H2-F2.

Reprinted from *Motor Development: Research and Reviews*, with permission from NASPE (National Association for Sport and Physical Education), 1900 Association Drive, Reston, VA 20191.

and sometimes regressing from profile to profile. Figure 7.7 shows that many children progressed along common developmental pathways; for instance, T2-H1-F1 frequently led to T2-H2-F1, which then commonly led to T2-H2-F2. For children who progressed that far, T2-H2-F2 seemed to be a gateway to more advanced movements, although only 12 children had progressed beyond that profile by 8 years of age. At the same time, however, some children took individual paths shared with few or no others. Thus, the data nicely illustrate the common paths of development as well as the individual differences that occur as children attempt to execute the same task at different points in their development.

Knowing which components commonly change before other components change may provide clues to the mechanism causing the change. For instance, the fact that T2 (block rotation of the trunk) preceded or occurred simultaneously with arm action development led Langendorfer and Roberton (2002b) to hypothesize that achieving a certain level of trunk acceleration might be necessary to elicit intermediate and advanced levels of arm action. These researchers noted that children often increase the range or speed of their trunk rotation when

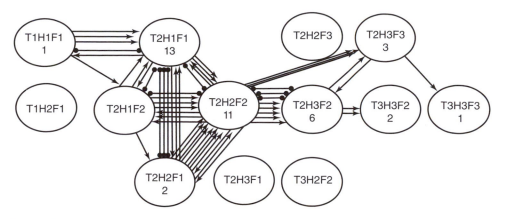

Figure 7.7 Longitudinal pathways through modal profiles of throwing of individual children. The arrowheads indicate direction of change. The numbers in ovals represent the number of children showing that profile at the close of the study.

Reprinted with permission from *Research Quarterly for Exercise and Sport*, Vol. 53: 198-205, Copyright 2002 by American Alliance for Health, Physical Education, Recreation and Dance, 1900 Association Drive, Reston, VA 20191.

trying to increase ball velocity. Thus, as Southard (2002a, 2002b) argued, ball velocity may well be a control parameter in forceful overarm throwing.

Langendorfer and Roberton (2002b) further hypothesized that differentiated rotation of the trunk may result from the inertia developed by the lagging arm. They noted that advanced arm action always seemed to precede advanced trunk action. Thus, intermediate trunk action may be a developmental precursor to advanced arm action, which in turn may be a precursor to advanced trunk action.

Several studies have extended the Langendorfer and Roberton (2002a, 2002b) profile descriptions (see table 7.6). Barton and French (2004) found that the most primitive profile in 108 male Little Leaguers aged 6.5 to 9.5 years was T2-H2-F2. Thus, in general, these youngsters were developmentally ahead of the Langendorfer and Roberton participants. Moreover, the fact that T2-H2-F2 was the most primitive profile observed supports the suggestion by Langendorfer and Roberton (2002a) that development beyond this profile is characteristic only of more skillful throwers. Most frequently exhibited by the Little Leaguers was T2-H3-F3. Only 5% of these youngsters had reached T3-H3-F3. When Barton and French added the backswing and stepping to the profiles, they found that the movements most frequently displayed were a circular downward backswing combined with a contralateral long step, block rotation of the trunk, humerus lag, and delayed forearm lag (B4-S4-T2-H3-F3). These data supported the Langendorfer and Roberton observation that advanced humerus action developmentally preceded advanced trunk action. Since not all the participants with an advanced backswing had differentiated trunk rotation, Barton and French suggested that the mechanical cause of differentiated rotation was possibly the timing relationship between backswing and forward trunk rotation.

Jones and Barton (2008) continued the Barton and French (2004) idea of studying children in more advanced sport settings. They examined the throwing

Table 7.6 Studies Focusing on Developmental Profiles of Throwing

Article	Description	Data Collection Methods
Langendorfer & Roberton (2002a, 2002b)	Categorized 39 children followed longitudinally over ages 5.7, 6, 7, 8, and 13 years (boys and girls)	Slow-motion 16 mm film taken in a controlled setting
Barrett & Burton (2002)	Categorized throws of 100 collegiate baseball players (males)	Video taken from the stands during game play
Barton & French (2004)	Categorized throws of 108 Little Leaguers aged 7-10 years (boys)	Video taken in a controlled setting
Robinson, Goodway, & Williams (2007)	Categorized throws of 16 preschoolers (mean age = 4.5 years; boys and girls)	Video taken in a controlled setting
Lorson & Goodway (2008)	Categorized throws of 105 children aged 6-8 years (boys and girls)	Video taken with two stationary cameras during a throwing game
Jones & Barton (2008)	Categorized throws of 38 U14 ASA softball players (mean age = 13.75 years; girls)	Video taken in a controlled setting

Controlled setting = a stable testing environment using a set placement of cameras (usually to the side and rear of the performer).

profiles of U14 Amateur Softball Association (ASA) girls aged 13.75 years. Again, the most common profile observed was T2-H3-F3, while 20% of the girls ($N = 38$) displayed T3-H3-F3. Halverson et al. (1982) did not examine profiles but reported that no 13-year-old girl displayed T3, differentiated rotation; only 12% showed F3, delayed forearm lag; and only 29% showed H3, humerus lag (see figure 7.4). Thus, as expected, girls playing U-14 ASA softball were more skillful than the typical schoolgirl.

Another study supporting some of the Langendorfer and Roberton (2002b) profile observations was conducted by Robinson, Goodway, and Williams (2007). These authors observed the profiles of 16 preschoolers (mean age = 54 months) after each of seven instructional sessions. Individual profile graphs indicated that contralateral stepping preceded block rotation of the trunk and that the development of block rotation preceded developmental changes in arm positioning.

Movement Process and Product Relationship in Throwing

A number of investigators have studied a product (outcome) of throwing, usually either ball velocity or the distance the ball has traveled (see figure 7.8). Less studied is the relationship between the developmental sequences and their product scores at different points in the lifespan. Roberton and Konczak (2001), again using the Halverson et al. (1982) longitudinal data, found that the components were very good predictors of ball velocity. The children's location in the developmental sequences explained 68% to 86% of the variance in ball velocity each year of the study (ages 6, 7, 8, and 13 years). They also found that the best movement predictor changed each year, although humerus or forearm action always accounted for considerable variance. At age 13, however, stride length was the best predictor of ball velocity.

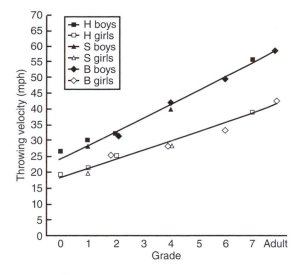

Figure 7.8 A compilation of ball velocities from children throwing in three different studies.

Reprinted, by permission, from A. Burton and R. Rodgerson, 2003, The development of throwing behavior. In *Development of movement co-ordination in children*, edited by G. Savelsbergh et al. (New York: Routledge), 230.

Constraints on Throwing

Most of the research on the development of overarm throwing has focused on throwing for force. Targets have been absent or minimal (such as a wall). Moreover, this research has occurred under controlled conditions. Generally, participants take their time to throw for a certain number of trials. Only film or video cameras and the investigators are present. The data collected under these conditions, however, have now made it possible to ask what happens in other situations. As constraints are changed, how does movement change during the attempt to throw? Are there lawful relationships across differing constraints that allow prediction from one condition to another? Moreover, as Manoel and Oliveira (2000) pointed out, the effects of task, environmental, and person constraints may vary depending on where in the lifespan an individual is. Task constraints may differentially affect the movement of a 3-year-old compared with a 75-year-old. And, as these authors suggested, if the participant does not perceive a change in task demands, then one's behavior may not change across conditions.

Study after study have noted the developmental consistency of throwers from trial to trial in the forceful, minimal target condition. Yet, Garcia and Garcia (2002) indicated that in an instructional setting young children throw with considerable variability. Most likely this is because the instructional setting tends to be a very open environment—other children are moving about and balls are flying everywhere. The constraints of task and environment may be continuously changing, leading to movement variability. But, we don't know if this is really true, since these interesting questions are only beginning to be studied. Following is an overview of the questions concerning constraints that investigators are currently asking.

Games

Two papers have used the component developmental sequences for overarm throwing to look at performance in game situations. The game context is composed of (1) what the performer is specifically trying to do (the task) and (2) the pressures and excitement of the game (the general environment in which the task is performed). Barrett and Burton (2002) categorized 3,684 throws made by collegiate baseball players in actual games. The researchers simplified the throw sequences since, in the game, camera angles often occluded some of the criteria needed for categorizations. Using modified sequences for forearm action,

backswing action, and stepping action (in which they focused on the relative positioning of foot and knee), Barrett and Burton noted a variety of throwing profiles, depending on the distance the ball was thrown and whether the throw was an active part of the game or an inactive return made between times of game action. Pitchers used alternatives to an advanced profile in only 4% of their active throws, and outfielders used alternatives in only 13% of their active throws. Catchers and infielders most often showed alternatives to an advanced profile. Catchers, in particular, rarely used the most advanced pattern. Their most frequent alternative was no or mistimed forearm lag, a circular upward backswing, and a contralateral foot or knee forward. The investigators noted that inactive and short throws were frequently made using alternative profiles. Thus, the distance the ball had to travel, the amount of response time available, and the initial posture of the thrower were constraints that shaped the overarm throws of collegiate baseball players.

Lorson and Goodway (2008) examined the throws of children in a game. These researchers also used modified developmental sequences due to the difficulty of seeing certain criteria for category placement during game play. The game involved 6- to 8-year-olds throwing yarn balls to the opposing team's side of the court. Thus, the specific task was a throw for force (depending on how far the thrower was from the half-court line); minimal accuracy was needed. The children were also required to move through space before throwing the ball. Lorson and Goodway (2008) found that both before and after instruction, the profile displayed most frequently by the boys was a contralateral step, trunk rotation, and delayed forearm lag. Instruction in throwing increased the number of boys showing this profile to slightly more than half. For the girls, the most frequently displayed profile before instruction was an ipsilateral step with no trunk rotation and no or mistimed forearm lag. After instruction, the most frequently displayed profile progressed to a contralateral step, trunk rotation, and no or mistimed forearm lag. The authors felt that the profiles observed were similar to those seen in controlled situations demanding force but little accuracy. Thus, the game environment did not seem to affect the children's throws, at least for the group as a whole.

Gender

It may seem odd to call gender a constraint, but in the case of throwing it may act as one. Of all the basic sport skills, the overarm throw shows the largest difference between genders (Thomas & French, 1985). Figure 7.8 is a composite created by Burton and Rodgerson (2003) showing gender differences in ball velocities taken from several studies on the overarm throw. The figure supports the data of Halverson et al. (1982), who reported that by age 13 (seventh grade) girls were throwing 21.66 feet per second (6.60 m/s) slower than boys. They did point out that the top girl thrower, who threw 87 feet per second (26.5 m/s), was only 5 feet per second (1.5 m/s) slower than the top boy thrower, who threw 92 feet per second (28 m/s). Thus, while gender need not be a constraint for every individual, as a group, boys are much more successful in throwing for force than girls are. These differences seem to persist across the lifespan. Williams, Haywood, and VanSant (1991) reported that in their sample of 65- to 76-year-olds

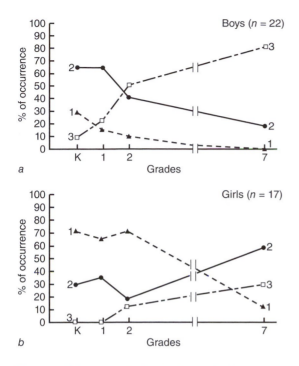

a

b

Figure 7.9 Longitudinal change in humerus action from 5 to 13 years of age by gender.

Reprinted with permission from *Research Quarterly for Exercise and sport*, Vol. 53: 198-205, Copyright 1982 by American Alliance for Health, Physical Education, Recreation and Dance, 1900 Association Drive, Reston, VA 20191.

the men were throwing almost 16 feet per second (4.9 m/s) faster than the women were throwing.

Women and men also differ in the developmental levels they display. Figure 7.9 compares the longitudinal changes in humerus action of boys and girls in the Halverson et al. (1982) study that followed young throwers from kindergarten through seventh grade (5-13 years of age). By seventh grade almost 80% of the boys displayed level 3 humerus action, while only 28% of the girls displayed this level. This difference held for trunk action and forearm action as well (see figure 7.4). For instance, by seventh grade not a single girl displayed differentiated rotation, while 46% of the boys showed this advanced behavior.

Unanswered is the question of what gender represents. Many have argued that it is essentially an American social phenomenon in which girls and women are not encouraged to engage in throwing. Indeed, some would argue that girls and women have been actively discouraged from throwing. Consequently, they do not practice throwing as much as boys do. Indeed, Halverson et al. (1982) found that the boys in their study reported both more organized league experience and more throwing practice than the girls reported. Williams, Haywood, and Painter (1996) reported that boys and girls were not statistically different in their ball velocities and were only slightly different in their developmental levels when all of them threw with their nondominant hand. Since the participants showed the typical gender differences when throwing with their dominant hands, the authors argued persuasively that differential levels of practice must cause the gender difference in throwing.

Runion, Roberton, and Langendorfer (2003) initially argued in favor of practice effects as well. They said that the Halverson et al. (1982) data described youngsters who were pre–Title IX. Even the data on the 13-year-olds had been collected in 1979, when Title IX still had little effect on the public schools. Runion et al. (2003) felt that post–Title IX boys and girls would show less difference in throwing, if such differences were due to practice effects. Therefore, Runion et al. collected data on a 1999 cohort of boys and girls 13 years of age. When they compared their results to those of Halverson et al., they found that boys were still throwing almost 23 feet per second (7 m/s) faster than the girls were and that there was no difference between the 1979 and 1999 cohorts in the movements displayed.

Moreover, the 1999 boys and girls reported the same amount of practice that the 1979 cohort reported. Title IX had not affected the typical schoolchild.

A subsequent cross-cultural study provided further evidence that gender differences in throwing may not be due solely to societal expectations. Ehl, Roberton, and Langendorfer (2005) compared throwing data on 50 German 13-year-olds with the data from Runion et al. (2003). Because German teens are more likely to play soccer than to play throwing games, the investigators expected that gender differences would be less evident in Germany. Unbelievably, the ball velocity difference between German boys and German girls was 23 feet per second (7 m/s)—the same difference found in the Runion et al. data! The investigators had also hypothesized that German girls would trail German boys in fewer movement components when compared with American girls and boys. Again, they were wrong: German girls trailed German boys developmentally in more—not less—components. The fact that girls were developmentally behind boys in a country where throwing was less popular refuted the authors' assumption that social pressures alone caused girls to lag boys in the United States. The authors speculated that girls may have a biological tendency to move less vigorously than boys move, a tendency that is then magnified by societal pressures on skills such as throwing.

While unique in focusing on vigorous movement, this speculation is in general agreement with a growing body of literature arguing that evolution may have shaped males to be, on average, better throwers (see Watson, 2001). Moreover, some evolutionary scientists have argued that over the millennia the act of throwing has actually shaped subsequent brain development and specialization, hand structure, lateralization, and even language capacity (Burton & Rodgerson, 2003; Wilson, 1998; Young, 2003). For instance, Young (2003) argued that the precision grip (named by Napier in 1956) evolved through the natural selection of hominids more successful with their throwing behaviors. Among kinesiologists, Thomas and French (1985; see also Thomas, 2000) have concluded that biological differences overlaid by practice effects are the cause of gender differences in throwing. Using meta-analysis, they calculated effect sizes from throwing studies, finding a 1.5 standard deviation difference between boys and girls as early as age 3. The Ehl et al. (2005) hypothesis that less vigorous movement is the main cause of gender differences adds another layer of interpretation to this interesting literature on throwing and provides a testable hypothesis for future study.

Tips for Novice Investigators

As a field of study, motor development is now well over 100 years old; yet, the basic data collected on motor skills during that time have tended to be from white, middle-class Americans or Europeans. Clearly, cross-cultural studies of ethnic groups within countries as well as across countries are needed. The Ehl et al. (2005) study of throwing is a nice beginning in this vein. Equally needed are studies of cohort differences, such as the Runion et al. (2003) study of children before and after Title IX. The results of both studies challenged our basic assumptions about the role of environmental influences.

Force Versus Accuracy

If ball velocity is indeed a control parameter for throwing, then what developmental level do throwers show when throwing for accuracy rather than force? The question of force versus accuracy has been studied for years but not from a developmental perspective. One of the first to look at the question developmentally was Roberton (1987). She used a framework developed by Gentile, Higgins, Miller, and Rosen (1975) to expand accuracy demands to include whether the target was moving or stationary and whether conditions were constant from trial to trial. She had 22 children aged 3.25 to 8.1 years throw beanbags at a lighted circle projected on a sheet hanging 8 to 11 feet (2.4-3.4 m) away (the distance depended on age). The children also threw for force with no target. When the target appeared, it was either stationary or moving slowly at 2 miles per hour (3.2 kph). Sometimes the initial location of the target changed from trial to trial; sometimes it did not. As a whole, the children did not change developmental levels across conditions, and they were not more accurate in one condition over another. They did reduce the velocity of their throws when the target was moving from a variable starting location. The few children who did change developmental levels across conditions tended to be more variable across trials in the throw for force. Children showing primitive humerus or forearm movements when throwing for force were not responsive to the changing target conditions.

Langendorfer (1990) had young adults and 9- to 10-year-olds throw for accuracy, for force, and for both force and accuracy. Male adults and children displayed lower developmental levels in the accuracy condition compared with the force condition. Female adults did not change across conditions, and female children changed only their stepping, using more advanced levels in the force condition. Langendorfer speculated that the distance between target and thrower, which was 33 feet (10 m) for adults and 20 feet (6 m) for children, was really a force-plus-target condition for the adult women. He also noted that, while not changing developmental levels, some throwers did lessen their range of movement within a developmental level. This is the same quantitative change that Williams et al. (1998) noted in their senior throwers.

Two subsequent studies defined distance from the target in relative terms rather than the absolute terms used by Roberton (1987) and Langendorfer (1990). Manoel and Oliveira (2000) asked 7-year-olds to throw 10 times for maximum distance. They then used half of each child's average distance as the distance the child stood from a target. They found that the children showed 31 regressive changes and only 3 progressive changes in developmental levels across various components when switching from the distance throws to accuracy throws. Every component except stepping was affected in at least 1 of the 18 children studied.

Hamilton and Tate (2002) defined distance from the target in units of standing height. They asked third graders (mean age 8.25 years; $N = 26$) to throw hard at three targets (small, medium, and large) from distances 2, 4, and 6 times their body height. Under these conditions, the target size did not affect the developmental levels of the throws, but the distance away from the targets did. For the group as a whole, the components affected were stepping action, trunk action,

and humerus action. As target distance increased, progression appeared in those components. This finding, as well as that of Barrett and Burton (2002), essentially suggests that the closer people get to a target, the more likely they are to regress from the movements used to produce maximal force.

The developmental research is still not clear on the relative effects of accuracy demands and target distance. Each of the studies cited used different age groups and different conditions in terms of the distance from the target, the definition of distance, and the size of the target, as well as whether the target was moving or stationary and whether the throwers were urged to throw hard even when throwing for accuracy. Moreover, several of the studies used parametric analyses to detect change in developmental levels, which are ordinal, nonparametric data. Thus, it is frequently unclear how many participants actually changed developmental levels when group means changed. Moreover, basement effects seem to be present in primitive throwers. As Langendorfer (1990) noted, primitive movers may not have other movement options available to allow them to respond to changing constraints. Or, as Manoel and Oliveira (2000) noted, some movers may not perceive the constraints or their relevance.

Some researchers have argued against using the term *regression* to describe change over a short time frame, saying that this change is not backward development but simply an appropriate response to changing constraints (see Manoel & Oliveira, 2000). As we indicated in chapter 1, however, the term *regression* has been used since the inception of the study of motor development to describe either long-term or short-term backward change in a developmental sequence. Regression is not considered a bad thing; rather, use of this term recognizes that motor development provides a repertoire of sequential movement options that can be displayed at any time in the lifespan, depending on the task, person, and environmental constraints.

DEVELOPMENTAL RESEARCH

We conclude this chapter by restating the obvious: The amount of developmental research available on ballistic skills varies considerably across those skills. Numerous questions remain about the development of the three tasks addressed in this chapter as well as about the development of all the other tasks

▶ Tips for Novice Investigators

Recently, Mally, Battista, and Roberton (2011) showed that distance (or force) may be a control variable for some components of kicking. They demonstrated that the number and type of forward steps in the approach, the distance between the feet in the final foot position of the approach, the position of the shank in the forward leg swing, and the leg action of the follow-through were all significantly affected by the distance children (mean age of 8 years) were asked to kick. The authors also provided an observation tool for forceful kicking that could become the basis for potential developmental sequences in this skill.

in the ballistic category. Traditionally, developmental study of ballistic skills has focused on asking performers to kick, strike, or throw for maximal force since that is the definition of *ballistic*. It is natural, of course, to wonder what happens to the developmental level of movers when they are asked to produce less force. As we have seen, the components of throwing are affected to some degree when the task demands change, depending on the initial developmental level of the thrower. How kicking and striking are affected remains to be studied. Presumably, force will prove to be a control variable for all ballistic skills.

These questions are basically contextual. They are focused on understanding more clearly the basic constraints shaping task performance. It is our hope that the information provided in this chapter has sensitized you to the exciting work that remains to be done and will encourage you to find a problem you yourself could investigate.

SUMMARY

Total body, ballistic skills are characterized by rapid acceleration that starts proximally, then is passed across body segments until it reaches the distal effector. In advanced striking, throwing, and kicking each segment of the open kinetic chains lags behind its proximal segment. Acquiring this lag is the key challenge in the development of these skills. Several components of throwing and striking may share common developmental sequences although development between the two skills tends to be asynchronous. Developmental sequences for the forearm, trunk, and humerus have been validated for forceful throwing using several longitudinal data sets. Because of their validation, the sequences have become variables in studies of product-process relationships and the effect of constraints on throwing. Kicking and striking await more developmental study although they have received preliminary investigation.

CHAPTER 8

Development of Manipulative Skills

Many animals can run faster, swim faster, or jump higher than humans can, but animals do not have the manual dexterity of humans. Even compared with other primates, humans are unique in their ability to manipulate objects with fine and precise coordination. Think of a concert pianist playing a complicated and fast-moving piece of music. Humans are alone in their ability to execute such tasks.

We can glimpse the importance of manipulative skills to humans by considering people who have lost upper limbs. Approximately 650,000 people worldwide have had an upper limb amputated, and even with state-of-the-art prosthetic arms and hands these people find it difficult or impossible to pursue many careers and hobbies (Boykin, 2008). Most people today are still fitted with a version of the Trautman hook (see figure 8.1). Invented in 1925, this hook consists of a single fixed finger and a single moving finger to give users some ability to grasp objects. Prototypes of advanced prosthetics that feature nerve control, movement of individual fingers, or the ability to grasp small objects such as pencils are still not available to most people. It is, of course, fine and flexible control of individual finger movements that distinguishes the skills humans are capable of performing from those that animals or even machines can perform. Injuries or diseases that affect the ability to finely manipulate objects indeed influence our quality of life. Manipulative skills are fundamental for humans.

Developmentalists are interested in the emergence of manipulative skills. Most of their research has focused on the development of reaching and grasping in infancy and the development of **interception skills** used in physical activities such as catching.

Figure 8.1 A Trautman hook.

Photo courtesy of J.R. Salzman, The Open Prosthetics Project.

The latter skills are usually acquired in childhood but can be perfected throughout the lifespan. The development of reaching and grasping represents the first manipulative skill that involves the infant's environment, while the development of a manipulative skill such as catching represents acquisition of a fundamental skill essential in many sports and some everyday activities. What skills such as reaching and catching have in common is an element of prospection. Action must be planned so that the hand is in the right place at the right time to interact with an environmental event. The reach to grasp results in obtaining an object and a catch is made to possess and control an object. The prospection involved in these skills makes studying their development both complex and intriguing.

At the other end of the lifespan (advanced age) a loss of hand strength is common. This loss makes even the activities of daily living problematic. Individuals with loss of hand strength cannot grasp support bars and railings, open containers, or cook meals.

This chapter reviews the research on reaching and grasping tasks and interception tasks, two broad but important categories of manipulative skills. We start with reaching and grasping and then move on to intercepting objects with the hands.

REACHING AND GRASPING

We obtain an object in our environment with a smooth, seamless reach and grasp. The reach and grasp are adapted to the location of the object as well as to the object's specific characteristics such as size, shape, and even anticipated weight. An obvious prerequisite for this movement is sensory-perceptual information, especially visual observation of the object and proprioceptive information about the position and orientation of the arm, hand, and fingers. It is not surprising that much of the research on the emergence of manipulative skills deals with the relative roles of the various sensory-perceptual systems and neuromuscular control of the upper limbs. Even though humans execute the reach and grasp as a seamless movement, researchers often have focused on reaching and grasping separately to better understand each component of the movement. With this in mind, our first discussion is on the development of reaching.

Reaching

We all have seen young infants thrash their arms about, usually when excited or agitated. Arm movement increases when a particularly exciting object or familiar person enters the near visual field. The issue under study is how infants progress from these early movements to reaching *toward* and eventually *to* specific objects at 3 to 5 months of age.

Before turning to contemporary research, we should recognize the history of developmentalists' thinking on the emergence of reaching and why we no longer find some of these explanations useful. In the era when the maturation perspective dominated, the appearance of intentional reaching was believed to

reflect maturation of the cerebral cortex. This hierarchical approach focused on movement as a matter of the brain commanding and the body responding. Once the brain was mature enough to command a reach, the movement of reaching to a target could be executed. This view overlooked the roles played by properties of the body itself, environmental supports, and task demands. These factors should seem familiar, as they are factors represented in Newell's (1986) model of constraints (which was introduced in chapter 3). By including all of these factors we can better address the uniqueness of each reach as a different, fluid, and flexible solution to a unique reaching task.

When use of the maturation perspective waned, developmentalists began applying a constructivist view that recognized the role of vision in reaching. Piaget (1952) was among the first to propose that once infants bring a hand near the general location of an object, they construct a match between the seen object and the seen and felt hand. With repeated matches and mismatches, infants learn how to reach a seen object. Bruner and Koslowski (1972; Bruner, 1973) proposed a slightly different type of construction, but it was still one that emphasized visually guided arm movements. Note that visually guided reaching distinguishes infant reaches from visually elicited reaches made by adults. Adults can see a target object and successfully reach for it even while looking away to another part of the visual field. A challenge to these constructivist views of reaching development came when Clifton, Muir, Ashmead, and Clarkson (1993) demonstrated that infants are perfectly good at reaching for glowing targets or sound sources in the dark and without sight of the hand.

More contemporary approaches to studying reaching focus on multiple causes for movement and how components interact to achieve the resultant movement (Thelen, 1995). Bertenthal and von Hofsten (1998) directed attention to the importance of support and stability of the eyes, head, and trunk to allow reaching with the arms. Compared with a nonsupportive posture, facilitative postural support can elicit more reaching activity. Postural support must always be a consideration in analyzing reaching activity.

Research has also focused on the components of the reaching motion. Infants' first reaches are jerky and inaccurate. Infant reaches consist of many accelerations and decelerations (von Hofsten, 1979), whereas adult reaches comprise one acceleration and one deceleration to arrive in the vicinity of the target and a small final correction to reach the target with precision. Adult reaches are smooth and as straight as possible. The segments of acceleration and deceleration within the reach are called *movement units*. The multiple movement units in infant reaching have attracted the attention of researchers.

Thelen and colleagues (Thelen et al., 1993; Corbetta & Thelen, 1996; Thelen, Corbetta, & Spencer, 1996) undertook a series of studies focusing on the problem of controlling the arms as the fundamental challenge for infants learning to reach (see table 8.1). The research team was interested in what multiple movement units could tell us about the development of reaching. The researchers studied

Table 8.1   Comparing Studies on Control of Early Reaching

Study Citation	Key Concept	Noteworthy Findings	Comparative Comments
Thelen et al. (1993)	Determined age at which infants transitioned to reaching. Observed four infants every week from 3-30 wk of age and then every other week until 52 wk of age; recorded IREDs on shoulder, elbow, wrist, and knuckles; recorded EMGs; videotaped reaches	First reaches were made between 12 and 22 wk of age. Early reaches were inaccurate and muscles were often coactivated.	Infants arrive at the solution of reaching in different ways. This finding is termed *soft assembly*. Infants learn to reach by reaching.
Thelen, Corbetta, & Spencer (1996)	Observed role of movement speed in acquisition of reaching. Observed same infants using same method described for previous study	Infants needed experience to better control speed and trajectory of reaching, with this improved control coming at 30-36 wk of age. Each infant had a speed preference.	Infants may explore speed and how to stabilize reaches during self-generated movements of the other limbs or the trunk.
Corbetta & Thelen (1996)	Observed bimanual reaching since judgments seem to lag accurate hand configuration in single-arm reaching. Observed same infants using same method described for previous two studies	Found that tendencies in unimanual or bimanual reaching were related to nonreaching arm activity. Infants switched back and forth between unimanual and bimanual arm movements.	Development may include the ability to inhibit general movements across limbs as well as the influence of many developing subsystems.

four full-term infants, observing them every week from 3 to 30 weeks of age and then once every 2 weeks until 52 weeks of age.

Recording Infant Reaches

To study infant reaches, the researchers placed infrared light-emitting diodes (IREDs) on the infants at each recording session (see figure 8.2). These IREDs marked the shoulder, elbow, and wrist joints as well as the knuckles on the hands. Four video cameras were positioned from multiple angles to record the positions of the IREDs, thus providing time and place information. Two additional video cameras recorded the infants' actions, and EMG signals were recorded from the muscles involved in elbow flexion and extension, shoulder elevation and retraction, shoulder flexion and elevation, and trunk extension. All of the information was synchronized (Thelen et al., 1993).

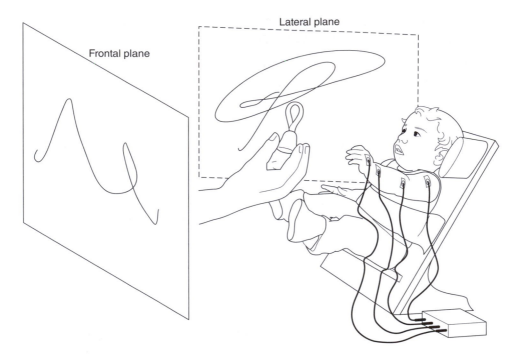

Figure 8.2   The setting used by Thelen et al. (1993) to study infant reaching. IREDs were placed on infants' shoulders, elbows, wrists, and knuckles. Four cameras that recorded the IRED positions gave the researchers information about movement trajectories in both the frontal and lateral planes.

Reprinted from "The transition to reaching: mapping intention and intrinsic dynamics," by E. Thelen et al., 1993, *Child Development*, 64(4), p. 1063. Copyright 1993 by Blackwell Publishing.

The infants were placed in a narrow chair so that they could move their arms freely. The chair was reclined back 30° from vertical. The chair and a wide strap placed around the infants' trunks provided stability and a consistent trunk position each time the infants reached. The researchers recorded 8 to 12 trials at each session, during which the infants reached for 8 to 10 colorful, attractive toys small enough to be grasped with one hand. The trials were 14 seconds long. The toys were presented individually and in random order at the trunk midline and at shoulder height to encourage reaching. The presentation was either from a parent, a researcher, or an apparatus. About 10% to 20% of the recording time contained reaches that the researchers could analyze. These added up to about 300 reaches per infant over the length of the study.

The researchers collected information about the path, or trajectory, of arm movements; the speed of the arm movements; the movement units; the unimanual or bimanual nature of the reach; and muscle activation. They then analyzed the information and presented their results in three publications, which we discuss next.

Tips for Novice Investigators

As you compare the studies in table 8.1, you can see how each successive study addressed an additional issue not covered in the first study. There are still many other issues or questions that could be addressed. Identify three aspects of the development of early reaching control that you would like to know about that weren't covered in these studies. Then, read the study that Clearfield, Feng, and Thelen published in 2007. What additional issues did Clearfield et al. address? Did any of these issues overlap with the ones you identified?

Transition to Reaching

Thelen et al. (1993) first looked at the transition to reaching. They found that each of the four infants made the transition—that is, their first reaches—at a different age within the range of 12 to 22 weeks. Also, the infants each had their own activity levels and a preferred movement pattern. Two of the infants who characteristically moved with large, vigorous movements seemed to damp down their movements to reach. The other two infants characteristically made quieter movements. In order to lift their arms to reach they had to apply more muscle power to make larger, more vigorous movements.

The early reaches were not very accurate, and the infants often activated muscle extensors and flexors simultaneously (coactivation) to move their arms (see figure 8.3). The intention to reach a toy was evident. The trajectories, speeds, and durations of these early reaches were highly variable. The infants seemed to arrive at the solution of reaching in unique ways. This phenomenon has been termed *soft assembly* of a movement because the movement response is assembled for a particular task in a particular context rather than based on a memory or motor program.

From these observations, Thelen et al. (1993) suggested that the movement pattern was chosen flexibly. It was self-organized movement, a solution discovered through exploration. The reaching movements observed within the first year did not seem to be the result of an innate program housed in the central nervous system. Clearfield et al. (2007) confirmed this conclusion by studying reaching in pairs of twins and finding that monozygotic twins were no more similar to each other than unrelated infants were.

Nor did reaching appear to reflect visual mapping. Rather than matching visual images, infants matched their natural dynamics and the task. They learned to reach by reaching.

Movement Speed

Corbetta and Thelen (1996) considered the role of movement speed in the acquisition of reaching by the four infants. They found that after reaching began there was a time frame for each infant when reach trajectories were unstable and poorly controlled. The infants needed 10 to 18 weeks of reaching experience before they could better control the speed and trajectory of their reaches,

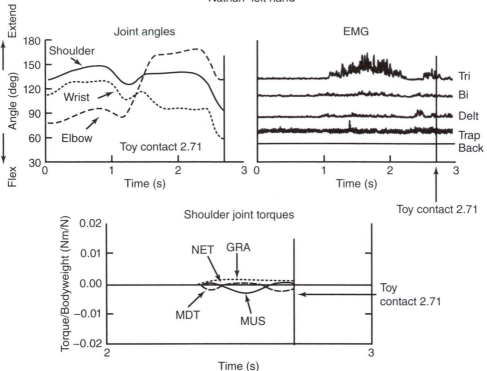

Figure 8.3 Information generated by a 3-second segment of reaching made by one of the infants in the study of Thelen et al. (1993). The top left graph shows rotations of the various joints. The top right graph shows EMGs of five muscle groups and illustrates tonic coactivation. The bottom graph shows torques at the shoulder. Net torque (NET) is partitioned into torque due to gravity (GRA), muscle torque (MUS), and motion-dependent torque (MDT).

Reprinted from "The transition to reaching: mapping intention and intrinsic dynamics," by E. Thelen et al., 1993, *Child Development*, 64(4), p. 1066. Copyright 1993 by Blackwell Publishing.

which happened at approximately 30 to 36 weeks or 8 months. Practice didn't necessarily account for the improvement since the four infants had such variable amounts of reaching experience before achieving stable reaching. More stable sitting posture at 6 to 8 months could contribute to the stability of reaches, as could the experience with alternate arm movements in crawling and creeping that the infants acquired around that age.

The four infants had individual speed preferences. Each alternated between times of faster or more variable movements and times of more stable, or similar, movements. The researchers did observe that by the second half of the year all of the infants had quieter arm movements right before they reached.

In time spans when the infants' reaches were fast (but less straight), their nonreaching movements were also fast, suggesting enhanced speed exploration. This active time of faster movements might allow infants to find an appropriate speed for both reaching and nonreaching movements. Indeed, the multiple

movement units observed in early reaching might reflect movements in other limbs or in the trunk that disturb the reach. Eventually infants can stabilize the path of reaches even during other self-generated movements.

Bimanual Reaching

Corbetta and Thelen (1996) specifically examined bimanual reaches made by the infants. Their work was based on the perplexing observation that long after the infants showed evidence of adapting unimanual reaches to the properties of objects—for example, shaping the hand depending on whether a rod was vertical or horizontal (von Hofsten & Fazel-Zandy, 1984)—they did not necessarily demonstrate bimanual coordination in reaching for objects of various sizes and shapes. Even though by 9 months of age the infants shaped their hands in anticipation of the object being grasped, at the end of the first year the infants could still be seen to reach with both arms when only a unimanual reach was needed (Corbetta & Mounoud, 1990). Early hand use appeared to be changeable and idiosyncratic. Indeed, Corbetta and Thelen confirmed that the interlimb coordination of reaching during the first year was extremely variable and inconsistent.

Corbetta and Thelen (1996) wondered if early bimanual reaching was an interaction between the spontaneous coordination tendencies of infants and learning to perform reaches adapted to the task at hand. These researchers compared reaching activity to nonreaching interlimb activity in the arms. They found that the two were related, in that during the times when infants showed bimanual reaching, other bilateral but nonreaching arm activity was synchronized. The more synchronized the spontaneous movements were, the more likely the infants were to reach bimanually. During times when the infants predominantly reached with one arm, interlimb activity did not appear to be coordinated. These time spans were not age related. Infants switched back and forth between times of unimanual and independent arm movement and times of bimanual and synchronized arm movement. Ultimately, developmentalists would like to know what factors influence these shifts back and forth.

Corbetta and Thelen (1996) suggested several factors. One difference between infants and adults is that infants move all their limbs when excited, while adults easily inhibit movement in all of their limbs but one. The results of this study on bimanual reaching perhaps reflect the developmental process of inhibiting general responses across the limbs—that is, inhibiting an overflow of movement to a nonfunctioning limb. Speed was discussed previously, and the researchers noticed that interlimb activity was more synchronized during times of high energy, when infants made faster, stronger, and more forceful movements. It is also possible that acquiring new skills in manipulating two objects (one in each hand) encourages a return to bimanual reaching after a time of unimanual reaching. The parallel development of other postural and locomotor skills might also be relevant to the coordination shifts. Corbetta and Thelen suggested that the shifting coordination patterns observed during the first year most likely reflect the influence of many developing subsystems.

Grasping

Reaches bring the hand close to an object so that it can be grasped. *Prehension* is another term for grasping an object with the hand. Interest in the development of grasping dates to the 1930s, and its continued study provides information not only on how grasping proceeds with development but also on how infants can shape the hand in anticipation of the grasp. Consider various objects in the environment and how you position your hand to pick them up. Without thought, you position or shape the hand on its way to the target object so that you can quickly and accurately grasp the object once the hand arrives. The following discussion focuses on these two aspects of grasping.

H.M. Halverson, who worked in Gesell's lab at Yale University, published a description of grasping development in 1931. This work was a classic study in infant development. Halverson filmed infants between 16 and 52 weeks of age grasping a 1-inch (2.5 cm) cube. He was able to identify a progression in grasping development—that is, he saw the emergence of specific types of grips at average ages (see figure 8.4). For example, Halverson found a squeeze

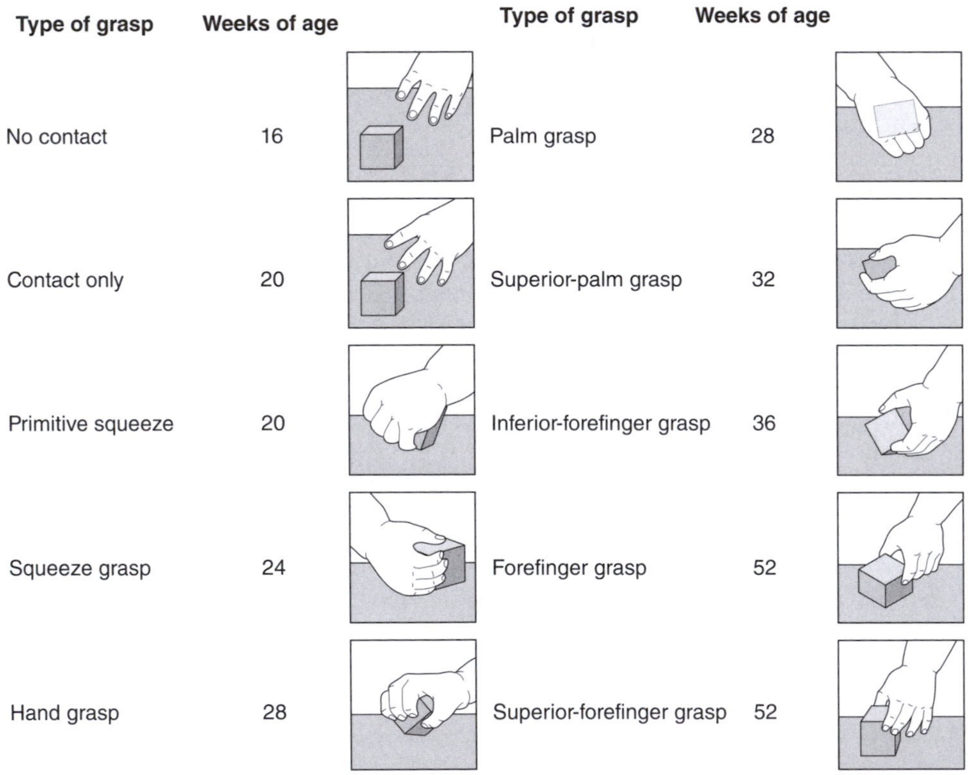

Type of grasp	Weeks of age		Type of grasp	Weeks of age	
No contact	16		Palm grasp	28	
Contact only	20		Superior-palm grasp	32	
Primitive squeeze	20		Inferior-forefinger grasp	36	
Squeeze grasp	24		Forefinger grasp	52	
Hand grasp	28		Superior-forefinger grasp	52	

Figure 8.4 The types of grasps Halverson identified while watching infants grasp a 1-inch (2.5 cm) cube.

Reprinted from H.M. Halverson, 1931, "An experimental study of prehension in infants by means of systematic cinema records," *Genetic Psychology Monographs* 10: 212-215, a publication of the Helen Dwight Reid Educational Foundation.

grasp to emerge at an average age of 24 weeks. Overall he identified 10 different types of grasps.

Napier (1956) later suggested that prehensile movements could be categorized as **power grips**, in which an object is grasped by partly flexed fingers and the palm with counterpressure from the thumb, and **precision grips**, in which an object is pinched between the flexed fingers and the opposing thumb. Adults use either grip depending on the shape, size, and other characteristics of the object and the force required. For example, we might begin with a power grip on the large lid of a tightly closed jar and then switch to a precision grip once the lid is loosened and simply must be twisted off the jar. If we apply Napier's categories to Halverson's 10 grips, we find a transition from using power grips at younger ages to precision grips at older ages. The transition comes at approximately 9 months of age. The consistency of the progression across infants led developmentalists of the time to view it as strong support for the maturation perspective.

The shortcomings of the maturation explanation became obvious by 1982, when Hohlstein repeated Halverson's study but used different shapes and sizes of target objects. She found that the age of transition from power grips to precision grips depended on the object characteristics. This finding stressed the role of the environment and task in grasping development. A study that went beyond the first year (between 6 and 20 months) of age and used cubes and spheres of different sizes demonstrated that 6- to 8-month-olds use almost all of Halverson's grips, depending on the object (Butterworth, Verwerj, & Hopkins, 1997). Object size more than object shape seems to influence grip selection. By early in the second year, the infants used precision grips much more than they used power grips. It appears that even though there is a transition from power grips to precision grips over the first year of life, use of a particular grip is not just a matter of age. Infants use a wide range of grip types in response to the target object.

Newell, Scully, Tenebaum, and Hardiman (1989) proposed that the type of grasp used to pick up an object as well as the choice between a unimanual or a bimanual grasp depends on the size of the hand relative to the target object. Our own experience tells us that sometimes we anticipate that an object is so large or heavy that we decide to reach for and pick it up with two hands rather than one. What Newell et al. proposed, though, is that a change in grip type or a switch to using two hands instead of one occurs at specific ratios of hand size to object size. This is one tenet of ecological psychology we discussed in chapter 2—body scaling.

Body scaling is founded in the notion that environmental objects are defined to us not so much by their absolute size but by their relative size to our bodies. Recall from chapter 2 Gibson's notion of affordances. In the case of grasping, the function of an object for us is relative to size. Newell, Scully, Tenebaum, and Hardiman (1989) proposed that the relative size between toddlers' hands and objects was a factor in toddlers adapting their grasp types. These researchers found that at a critical ratio of hand size to cube size of 0.6, the toddlers switched from a one-hand grasp to a two-hand grasp. This ratio of 0.6 was invariant over the age range of 3 to 5 years and was similar to the ratio for adults. Van der Kamp, Savelsbergh, and Davis (1998) found a ratio that was very similar (0.7) at 5, 7, and 9 years of age. While grasping small objects with one hand and large

> ## Tips for Novice Investigators

Notice that the work of Newell, Scully, Tenebaum, and Hardiman (1989) and van der Kamp et al. (1998) on body scaling focused on the size of the object relative to the size of the hand. Other characteristics of the object and of the hand can be considered in body scaling. As you read about other research on grasping, take note of the characteristics explored. You should be able to identify some additional characteristics not observed in these studies. These could be the focus of additional research studies, perhaps in combination with characteristics that have been observed in published research.

objects with two hands appears to be body scaled in children and young adults, we have little information about infants younger than 2 years or older adults. These studies need to be duplicated with the goal of providing more lifespan information on body scaling!

While there are few data on body scaling in infant grasping, researchers have found that infants begin to orient their hand to a target object between 5 and 7 months of age (Witherington, 2005). For example, 5-month-olds align their hand vertically to grasp a vertically oriented object only after contacting the object. After reaching 7 months of age, however, they can align their hand during the reach. By 9 months of age infants are quite good at shaping their hands to the target object as their reach approaches it (Lockman, Ashmead, & Bushnell, 1984; Newell, Scully, McDonald, & Baillargeon, 1989; Pieraut-LeBonniec, 1985). Infants use visual information, the seen object, to shape their hands. Realize that as early as 2 months of age, infants can explore held objects visually and orally, so starting then they are learning how visual and haptic information match.

Barrett, Traupman, and Needham (2008) recently explored infants' anticipation of object structure in planning a grasp based on visual information. The researchers had infants grasp four round balls of similar size; however, two of the balls were hard and rigid and two of them were soft and compressible (see figure 8.5). The researchers observed 5-, 9-, 12-, and 15-month-olds, expecting that infants within the 7 to 9 month age range might use a precision grasp with the nonrigid balls and a power grasp with the rigid balls based on their visual inspection of the target ball (the infants did not handle the balls before reaching for them). The researchers found that all of the infants, even the 5-month-olds, shaped their hands appropriately, readying a power grip for the balls that appeared rigid (see figure 8.6). All of the infant groups

Figure 8.5 The four balls, two rigid (left) and two compressible (right), used by Barrett et al. (2008).

Reprinted from *Infant Behavior and Development*, Vol. 31, T.M. Barrett, E. Traupmann, and A. Needham, "Infants' visual anticipation of object structure in grasp planning," p. 2, Copyright 2008, with permission of Elsevier.

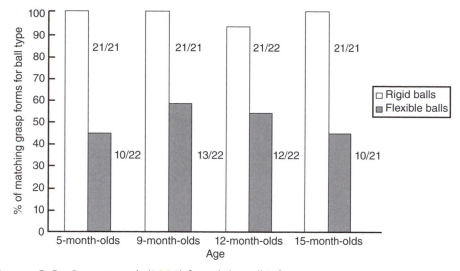

Figure 8.6 Barrett et al. (2008) found that all infant age groups used a power grip for the rigid balls on almost every trial (the numbers next to the bars represent the number of times the relevant grip was used out of the total possible trials). The infants used a precision grip for the flexible balls on about half the trials.

Reprinted from *Infant Behavior and Development*, Vol. 31, T.M. Barrett, E. Traupmann, and A. Needham, "Infants' visual anticipation of object structure in grasp planning," p. 6, Copyright 2008, with permission of Elsevier.

prepared a precision grip for the balls that appeared compressible about half of the time, and all of the infants tended to use fewer fingers to grasp the nonrigid balls compared with the rigid balls. The youngest infants were not as successful in their grasps, but the researchers proposed that this had more to do with factors such as hand size and strength than hand shaping. This work supports the suggestion that young infants use visual information to orient and shape the hand during a reach, regardless of whether they can actually grasp the object.

Of course, once the hand reaches adult size, it remains constant at that size over the balance of the lifespan. Hand strength, however, does not remain constant, and this can affect manipulative skills. Additionally, arthritic conditions can affect individuals, with the incidence and extent of arthritis tending to increase with age. Other age-related factors that can affect manipulation are a decline in sensation from the hands and a deterioration of muscle fibers.

Jansen et al. (2008) conducted a cross-sectional study of men and women in 5-year increments between 65 to 70 years and 85+ years. They measured both grip force and pinch force in three orientations of the hand. Grip and pinch force declined in successive age groups. Hand strength in men was markedly stronger than it was in women at younger ages, but as age increased it declined more steeply in men. By age 85, the difference between the genders was relatively small (see figure 8.7). Of course, Jansen et al. compared group means. There are a number of factors that could vary among individuals. Many studies could be designed to consider the habitual activities of participants or exercise interventions to improve hand strength.

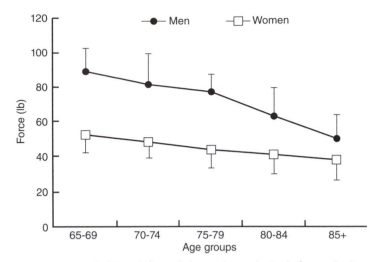

Figure 8.7 Jansen et al. (2008) found that grip and pinch force decline with age. Grip force for the right hand is shown here. Notice that in the younger age group, the men had much more strength than the women had, but with aging the strength declined more sharply in men. The men were only a little stronger than the women were in the oldest age group.

Reprinted, by permission, from C.W.S. Jansen et al., 2006, "Hand force of men and women over 65 years of age as measured by maximum pinch and grip force," *Journal of Aging and Physical Activity* 16(1): 24-41.

Reach to Grasp

Consider the practice of studying reaching and grasping separately. While there is good reason for separating them, there is also good reason for studying them together. Grasping requires a goal-directed reach! In addition, the research reviewed thus far told us only that by the end of the first year infants adjust the opening of their hand to the size of the object during their reach. That does not necessarily mean that their grip formation is adultlike. In fact, research by Kuhtz-Buschbeck, Stolze, Jöhnk, Boczek-Funcke, and Illert (1998) with children aged 4 to 12 years suggested that only the oldest participants were very precise in scaling their grip to an object when visual control of movement was lacking. Young children used a wide opening on approach, as if to provide a higher safety margin.

Zoia et al. (2006) compared the reach to grasp of 5-year-olds with that of adults. In this study, 10 participants in each age group, both male and female, reached for cylinders of three different diameters placed at two different distances from the starting position (see figure 8.8). The researchers used shutter glasses to provide two viewing conditions. Shutter glasses can be quickly switched from clear to opaque. In the vision conditions, participants could see the target object throughout the reach and grasp. In the no-vision conditions, the glasses were opened for 400 milliseconds and then closed, at which time the individual was to reach and grasp the target cylinder.

Movement duration, trajectory, and velocity were recorded, as was the distance between the thumb and index finger. Participants took longer to reach for the

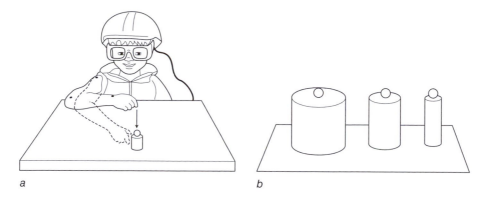

a   b

Figure 8.8 (a) The position of participants, the helmet with shutter glasses attached, and the markers recorded by cameras in the study by Zoia et al. (2006). (b) The three sizes of red wooden cylinders to be grasped. The cylinders were 1.5, 3.0, and 5.0 centimeters in diameter and were placed either 15 or 30 centimeters from the starting point.

smallest cylinder, and the researchers found a direct relationship between the object size and the maximum opening of the hand during the reach. Obviously, it took participants longer to reach the farther distance, but the decelerative phase of the reach was proportionally longer for these longer reaches. Grip opening was wide when participants were reaching for farther objects. Compared with the vision condition, the no-vision condition was characterized by increased movement duration, a longer decelerative portion, a wider grip opening, and an earlier grip opening.

The 5-year-olds tended to have a longer movement duration and a wider grip (relative to hand size). The decelerative phase of the children's reach was long at the longer distance (see figure 8.9). All together, the Zoia et al. (2006) study demonstrated that increasing the distance of the reach affected the timing and formation of the grasp. Object size and distance did not affect the reach and the grasp independently. Object characteristics affected both reach kinematics and grip formation. The children in the study could scale their grip according to object size in the no-vision condition but, compared with adults, used a strategy that provided a larger safety margin via a wider grip opening. The researchers suggested that since the corticospinal tract is not mature until age 6, the process of selecting a grasp that precisely matches the object properties might still be forming in 5-year-olds.

The Zoia et al. (2006) study addressed the reach and grasp as a unit, which provided a more authentic analysis than isolating the reach and the grasp. There are other aspects of a reach to grasp that are encountered in everyday life and have been studied. You can expand your knowledge of manipulative skill development by reading about them. Some suggestions for further research are reaching in peripersonal versus extrapersonal space (Gabbard, Cordova, &

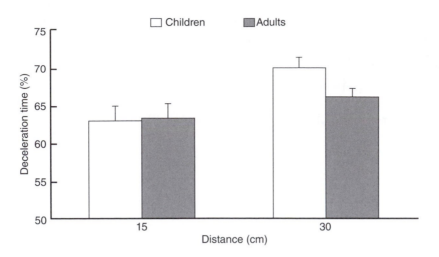

Figure 8.9 Deceleration time was longer for the children compared with the adults but only at the longer distances. The "T" bars represent one standard deviation around the mean deceleration time percentage.

Reprinted, by permission, from S. Zoia et al., 2006, "A comparison of the reach-to-grasp movement between children and adults: A kinematic study," *Developmental Neuropsychology* 30:731. Developmental neuropsychology Copyright 2006 by TAYLOR & FRANCIS INFORMA UK LTD - JOURNALS. Reproduced with permission of TAYLOR & FRANCIS INFORMA UK LTD - JOURNALS in the format Textbook via Copyright Clearance Center.

Ammar, 2007), reaching to grasp objects in a cluttered space (Tresilian, Mon-Williams, Coppard, & Carson, 2005), grasping point compared with center of mass (Duemmler, Schoeberl, & Schwarzer, 2008), and the effect of end-state comfort on unimanual and bimanual reaching (Zhang & Rosenbaum, 2008).

Tool Use

At the beginning of this chapter we acknowledged the uniqueness of humans in their manual dexterity. A particularly good way to appreciate that dexterity is to consider how humans use environmental objects, and sometimes even surfaces, as tools to accomplish specific goals. Of course, there are some animals that both use and make tools, often very proficiently. In contrast to animals, though, even human children conceptualize tools in terms of function. They consider functional representations of tools—that is, they know tools exist to achieve a particular goal, even when they are not being used to achieve that goal (Hernik & Csibra, 2009). Kemler Nelson, Egan, and Holt (2004) observed that when preschoolers are told either the name or the function of a tool, the ones who are told only the name tend to ask follow-up questions to get more information about the tool. The researchers concluded that when preschoolers, even as young as 2 years of age, ask "What is it?" they are asking more about what an object is for than what it is called.

So unique and special is the use of tools by humans that the development of tool use has received much research attention. Tool use has been a means to study goal-directed behavior, action-planning sequences, flexibility to solve various movement challenges, the role of previous experience, functional under-standing of tools, perseveration, and grip configuration. Frequently studied

tools have been the spoon during infancy and writing implements during early childhood. It is beyond the scope of this chapter to consider all of these topics, so we consider just two.

Grip Configuration

Earlier we discussed the research on grasping that led developmentalists to appreciate the importance of the environment and task in grasping development, to explore the concept of body scaling, and to examine the role of prospection in shaping the hand for a grasp, even by infants. Now let's consider the development of grip configurations in using tools.

You shouldn't be surprised to learn that early research on how tools are grasped described developmental progressions in children and attributed change to maturational factors (Connolly & Elliott, 1972; Rosenbloom & Horton, 1971; Saida & Miyashita, 1979). During the development of grasping a writing utensil, a shift from using a power grasp to using a tripod grasp (holding the utensil between the thumb and first two fingers) was observed. By 4 to 6 years of age, children used a dynamic tripod grasp that allowed for small movements of the thumb and fingers.

As you might also have anticipated, recent research has placed more emphasis on the environment and task, applying a model such as Newell's model of constraints to writing tool use. This was the approach of Braswell, Rosengren, and Pierroutsakos (2007), who observed 3- and 4-year-olds copying shapes (circle, cross, square, and triangle), making quick vertical lines, making quick horizontal lines, and drawing freely with a pencil. From videotape, the researchers coded the grip configuration, the hand position (along the pencil), the implement orientation, and any hand switching or changes made from one grip to another. The grip configurations coded were a palmar grip (pencil in palm), a digital grip (pencil against four fingertips with thumb opposing), a modified tripod grip, and a tripod grip (distinguished by the finger positions and number of fingers contacting the pencil). The quality of the shapes drawn was coded from 1 to 4.

A notable result of this research study was that the children varied their grip configurations widely and displayed numerous variations within grip types. About half of the children in the study had more than two grip changes. One child changed his grip 27 times in the session, and two children used all four grip types. In contrast, children did not change position, orientation, or hand very frequently. Children with stable grip configurations copied shapes more accurately compared with the children who widely varied their grips. The variability in overall grip configuration is not something predicted by a maturation approach. The variability is more consistent with the notion that the task and environment also influence the grip used, even in children.

Braswell et al. (2007) considered task demands by analyzing the effects of the seven different drawing tasks on the grip. Their drawing freely condition was unique since much of the previous research had focused on copying tasks. The researchers found that grip changes occurred significantly more often in free drawing than in any other task, suggesting that task demands can lead children to vary their grips. Overall, grip configurations in this age group were flexible and adaptive. They did not appear to change as a function of age or maturation.

It is likely that with development, though, factors other than grip become increasingly important, and these factors need more research (Braswell et al., 2007). Examples include person constraints such as hand strength and finger coordination and environmental constraints such as implement size and weight.

Tool Selection

Smitsman and Cox (2008) suggested that tasks involving tool use require choices regarding the following:

> ➤ The goals that can be attained (potential end states)
> ➤ The means that can be employed to accomplish end states (use of body segments and tools)
> ➤ The parameter settings to sequence movements

These authors emphasized that the study of action selection is a key to understanding how goal-directed behaviors develop. So, they designed two experiments with 3-year-olds to learn more about how children select a tool for a task. Both experiments allowed Smitsman and Cox (2008) to observe whether children persevere to use a tool in ways consistent with their previous experience, even when a new task calls for using the tool in another way.

The first experiment examined tool-to-target relationships by providing the children with a cane with a right angle (a basic hook). Children were to use the cane to either push or pull an object to a target location. The starting position of the target dictated whether pushing the object with the outside of the hook or pulling the object with the inside of the hook was more appropriate. The results indicated that when the target location was switched, the children tended to persevere. They tried to use the tool in the manner that was appropriate for their initial experience, even when switching to a new mode of tool use would have been more efficient.

The second experiment focused on the relationship between actor (child) and tool. In this case the tool was a spoon with a deep bowl used to carry food to a puppet. The children were given initial experience in which grasping the spoon's handle with the right or left hand was promoted by placement of the tool in front of the corresponding shoulder. The side, right or left, reflected a child's preferred hand use. Then, the spoon was presented at body midline with the handle pointing toward the children, and the hand used to grasp the tool handle was observed. Again, children persevered in using the hand they had initially used, and there was no influence by whether the initial training was on the right or left side.

Thus task information and experience on earlier trials influenced action selection. Perseverative behavior is generally observed in children. It is not confined to particular ages or tasks. The process of action selection is influenced by multiple factors. The work of Smitsman and Cox (2008), in addition to other work on perseveration in tool use (Thelen, Schöner, Scheier, & Smith, 2001), suggests that action selection reflects multiple influences coming together from moment to moment during task performance rather than simple cause-and-effect associations.

Summary

These selected areas of research on the development of reaching and grasping help us to understand the information that infants use to acquire new skills. While infants might not acquire reaching skills by matching the position of the seen and felt hand to a seen object, they use visual information about the target object to prepare their grasp. Likely, the visual information obtained becomes increasingly important as grasping tasks become more demanding—for example, extracting a small object from a collection of many objects. Learning to control the arms through experience seems to be the challenge of reaching.

The study of action planning in tool use suggests that children arrive at an insight on what to do once motor, perceptual, and cognitive influences cooperate in selecting where to look, reach, and attend (Thelen et al., 2001; Thelen & Smith, 1994; Thelen & Whitmeyer, 2005). Clearly, recent researchers have taken an approach to the developmental landscape of manipulative skills that emphasizes task dynamics as much as the changing individual.

There are other aspects of manipulation that researchers have addressed. Of interest are hand-to-mouth movements of young infants (Lew & Butterworth, 1997) and hand preference (Fagard, Spelke, & von Hofsten, 2009; Marschik et al., 2008). In addition, there are other aspects of tool use that have been studied (Barrett, Davis, & Needham, 2007; Lockman, 2008). With advancing age, rapid aiming movements are acquired (Vercruyssen, 1997), and in the older portion of the lifespan the challenge is to maintain precise manual performance (Hughes et al., 1997; Ranganathan, Siemionow, Sahgal, Liu, & Yue, 2001). All of these topics may be of interest to you, and surveys of these topics can highlight additional questions in need of research.

INTERCEPTION SKILLS

We label the second broad category of manipulative skills *interception skills*. Catching is probably the first interception skill that comes to mind, but these skills go far beyond catching in their nature and scope. In this category we include catching with the hands as in many ball games, trapping with the feet as in soccer, fielding with a stick as in field or ice hockey, catching with an implement as in lacrosse, and intercepting objects as in volleyball (when receiving a serve). Skill in avoiding collisions such as when playing basketball or driving a car is included, as is attempting collisions such as when playing American football. The common aspect of all these skills is judging a moving object or moving to avoid or promote interception—that is, prospection of a future event. These skills are obviously common in a large number of sport activities as well as in activities of everyday living.

Catching Development

Let's begin by considering what is pertinent to the study of catching development. There is obviously a perceptual aspect to catching: There is a need to predict where a moving object will be located so actions can be planned. Then, movements must be executed so that the object can actually be obtained. We do not expect

children to play the outfield with the skill of a professional baseball player, but it is interesting to see that the bases of such catching skills develop early in life.

As early as 2 months of age infants can stabilize their gaze on a moving object, and their eye movements predict the upcoming motion rather than lag behind it (von Hofsten & Rosander, 1997). Around 4 months of age infants can even move their eyes to a reappearance point when part of the moving object's path is occluded (Rosander & von Hofsten, 2004; von Hofsten, Kochukhova, & Rosander, 2006). Recall that at this age infants can grasp objects within reach. A long line of research by Claes von Hofsten et al. has demonstrated that infants also begin to reach for moving objects successfully by this age. By 18 weeks, they can intercept an object moving at 30 centimeters per second (von Hofsten, 1980, 1983; von Hofsten, Vishton, Spelke, Feng, & Rosander, 1998; see table 8.2). On the other hand, infants of this age still miss the object fairly often, especially when the speed of the object varies (Van Hof, van der Kamp, Caljouw, & Savelsbergh, 2005).

Table 8.2 Von Hofsten Studies Relevant to Infant Catching

Study Citation	Key Concept	Noteworthy Findings	Comparative Comments
Von Hofsten, Feng, & Spelke (2000)	Observed predictive head tracking of moving objects that traveled behind a small occluder. Observed infants aged 6 mo and varied linearity of the path of object	There was no predictive head movement on the first trial, but the infants quickly learned to anticipate on successive trials. Anticipation of nonlinear motion was slower and less consistent.	Representations of objects persist during temporary occlusion and are somewhat biased toward inertial motion. Occlusion reduces the precision of object representation.
Spelke & von Hofsten (2001)	Observed effect of occluding part of an object's path on reaching for a moving object. Observed infants aged 6 mo and varied length of the path that was occluded	Reaching was less successful when the path of the moving object was partially occluded.	Representation of hidden objects becomes more precise with development.
Jonsson & von Hofsten (2003)	Recorded effect of occluding part of a moving object's path or blacking out room lights on reaching. Observed infants aged 6 mo and varied the extent of occlusion or blackout	In all conditions infants moved their heads on a path extrapolating from previous motion. Reaching was more severely affected by nonvisibility than eye tracking was. Blackout inhibited reaching, but this lessened with practice. Longer blackout had more effect. Reaching was more severely inhibited with occlusion.	Representations of infants are similar to those of adults and are likely graded in the sense that mode of representation changes when the nonvisibility time is long.

(continued)

Table 8.2 *(continued)*

Study Citation	Key Concept	Noteworthy Findings	Comparative Comments
Rosander & von Hofsten (2004)	Observed eye and head movements of infants watching an oscillating object. Measured infants aged 2-5 mo and varied the point on the path occluded and velocity	Over the age span, observed the infants, progressed from no prediction to consistent prediction, but there were large individual differences.	By 5 mo of age representations of occluded objects in motion can incorporate dynamics of the motion, such as differences in velocity.
Von Hofsten, Kochukhova, & Rosander (2007)	Recorded eye and head movements in response to an oscillating object on a horizontal trajectory with an occluded place at the center of the path. Observed infants aged 4 mo and varied occluder width, oscillation frequency, and motion amplitude	Infants shifted their gaze to the opposite side of the occluder before the object reappeared.	When the object is behind the occluder, the object's velocity is represented. Infants track objects in their mind's eye.
Fagard, Spelke, & von Hofsten (2009)	Observed the effect of the direction of motion on aspects of grasping. Observed infants aged 6, 8, and 10 mo	With development, the infants used increasingly diverse strategies by grasping and reaching with the ipsilateral hand in both directions of motion.	Infants demonstrate diverse strategies for dealing with the task of intercepting motion in various directions.

Van Hof, van der Kamp, and Savelsbergh (2008) attempted to learn more about the control strategy infants use to reach a moving object. They studied infants in three age groups: 3- to 5-month-olds, 6- and 7-month-olds, and 8- and 9-month olds. Their apparatus made it possible to send a ball on a straight path at constant speeds between 10 and 200 centimeters per second toward and just above the shoulder of a seated infant. Three cameras recorded when and how the infant responded to the approaching ball. Ball speeds were presented in a staircase method in order to determine the highest ball speed that would elicit a reach by an infant. This allowed the researchers to analyze the infants' perceptions of whether the ball was catchable.

Van Hof et al. (2008) found that perceptions of balls as catchable improved dramatically over the age span studied. Moreover, they were able to associate this improvement with a shift in movement control strategy. The youngest infants were not very accurate in intercepting balls, and they were not very good at perceiving which speeds they were more likely to intercept. In fact, a higher proportion of 3- to 5-month-olds were excluded from the study because they did not attempt to intercept the ball even once. So, the youngest infants did not always perceive the ball as something to be caught. They tended to initiate their

movement when the ball was a constant distance from the point where it could be intercepted, no matter what speed the ball was traveling.

In contrast, the 6- to 7-month-olds were better at catching and were better at judging whether balls were catchable, although they often overestimated their ability to intercept fast-moving balls. The number of infants who used the distance strategy was comparable to the number of infants who switched to a time strategy in which they started moving at a fixed time before interception. Infants in the oldest group rarely reached for balls moving too fast to be caught. If anything, they were conservative in their judgments of whether balls were catchable. A clear majority in this group used the time strategy. This suggests that the use of temporal information is an important advancement in the interception of moving objects.

Tips for Novice Investigators

Read the sequence of studies conducted by von Hofsten et al. described in table 8.2. Answer the following questions to better understand how these researchers progressed from one study to another to build a clearer picture of infant catching behavior.

- How did the purpose of the studies evolve over time?
- How did the methods change over the course of the studies?
- When were new aspects of behavior added to the line of studies, and why were they were added?
- What are two or three other research questions that you could ask to build on the work of these researchers?
- Would you use similar methods to answer these questions or would you introduce different methods?

Von Hofsten's more recent research has observed the effect of occluding a portion of the moving object's path on predictive action (von Hofsten, Feng, & Spelke, 2000; Spelke & von Hofsten, 2001; Jonsson & von Hofsten, 2003). Fagard et al. (2009) also considered how direction of motion interacted with hand preference, crossing the midline, bimanual interception, contralateral grasping, and hand switching. They observed 6-, 8-, and 10-month-old infants and found that reaching became more proficient with age, starting with the left-to-right direction of motion. Younger infants frequently reached with the contralateral hand, but older infants demonstrated more diverse strategies and could better intercept with the ipsilateral hand or use a bimanual grasp. It appeared that, with development, infants better adapted movement for spatial compatibility and hand preference. We revisit this theme of motor constraints as we consider skillful catching later in this chapter.

Of course, to be a skilled ball player, a person must be successful at considerably more difficult catching tasks. A moving object's path can be quite

complicated, and the interception point can be in many places relative to the body, including points distant to the catcher. It would be helpful to know if a developmental sequence exists for catching so that the landscape for development under challenging task conditions could be observed. Several investigators (Haubenstricker, Branta, & Seefeldt, 1983; Seefeldt, Reuschlein, & Vogel, 1972; Strohmeyer, Williams, & Schaub-George, 1991) have hypothesized a developmental sequence for two-hand catching, both for the whole task and for components of the task. Let's look closely at the Strohmeyer et al. sequence since these authors took a component approach.

Strohmeyer et al. (1991) filmed children aged 5 to 12 years attempting to catch a soft, 10-centimeter ball tossed directly at the torso, at forehead height, or slightly above the head. A subset of participants also attempted to catch a ball tossed within reach to the right or left. The throws were underhand, made at moderate speed, and had an arc that peaked about 2 meters above ground. The researchers first determined movement components of catching and categorized the catches of the study participants into developmental levels. They began with components and developmental levels suggested by Harper in 1979 (as cited in Roberton & Halverson, 1984) and then adapted the sequences to be more comprehensive based on pilot work. The levels identified for four components—arm preparation, arm reception, hand, and body—are shown in table 8.3.

When Strohmeyer et al. (1991) categorized the catches of their study participants, they found that the hand component generally met the criteria for a developmental sequence, especially when the tosses varied from straight at the torso to the right or left of the torso. Children with more advanced catching adjusted their hands to the flight and size of the ball, putting their little fingers or thumbs together depending on the height of the flight path. The researchers found that a developmental level added in the pilot work did not hold up, so they revised the suggested sequence by combining levels 2 and 3, resulting in a total of three steps for the development of the body component. Generally, the developmental progression is from (1) not adjusting the body to ball flight to (2) beginning to adjust awkwardly to ball flight to (3) moving the feet, trunk, and arms to adjust for ball flight.

Harper originally divided arm action into a preparation component and a reception component, but Strohmeyer et al. (1991) did not find that the arm preparation component followed an age-related pattern of change. While the levels of arm action were age related, the researchers found that steps 1 and 2 as well as steps 3 to 5 could be combined. The portion of children at each age within a given developmental level depended on whether the throws were to the body or to the right or left of the body. This finding emphasizes how task constraints affect performers' movements and therefore how they are categorized into developmental steps. The percentage of catches categorized into each arm reception step for each age is shown in figure 8.10. Note the similarity of steps 1 and 2 in both conditions, but note that fewer children were categorized into step 5 when the throws were to various locations versus when they were to the body.

Unfortunately, little additional work has been done on catching. Questions remain even after the work of Strohmeyer et al., and many studies could be

Table 8.3 Developmental Levels of Catching

Component	Description
Arm preparation	
Step 1	The arms await the ball outstretched with elbows extended.
Step 2	The arms await the ball with some shoulder flexion still apparent and flexion apparent in the elbows.
Step 3	The arms await the ball in a relaxed position at the sides of the body or slightly ahead of the body. The elbows may be flexed.
Arm reception	
Step 1	The arms remain outstretched and the elbows are rigid. Little to no give occurs, so the ball bounces off the arms.
Step 2	The elbows flex to carry the hands upward toward the face. Initially ball contact is with the arms, and the object is trapped against the body.
Step 3	Initial contact is made with the hands. Children unsuccessful in using the fingers may still trap the ball against the chest. The hands still move upward toward the face.
Step 4	The arms are transversely adducted in a clapping motion to attempt catching the ball in the hands. The elbows flex and the shoulders extend to bring the ball down and toward the body.
Step 5	Ball contact is made with the hands. The elbows flex and the shoulders extend to bring the ball down and toward the body.
Hand	
Step 1	The palms of the hands face upward. (Rolling balls elicit a palms down, trapping action).
Step 2	The palms of the hands face each other.
Step 3	The palms of the hands are adjusted to the flight and size of the oncoming object. The thumbs or little fingers are placed close together, depending on the height of the flight path.
Body	
Step 1	No adjustment of the body occurs in response to the flight path of the ball.
Step 2	The arms and trunk begin to move in relation to the flight path, but the head remains erect, creating an awkward movement to the ball. The catcher seems to be fighting to remain balanced.
Step 3	The feet, trunk, and arms all move to adjust to the path of the oncoming ball.

designed to answer these questions. There is certainly a need for a more complete understanding of catching development.

Newell's model of constraints is useful in considering how task constraints affect catching. Certainly the flight of the object can vary considerably. The distance of flight can be short or long. The trajectory can be low or high, and the direction can vary. The speed of the ball can range from slow to fast, but it can also be constant or variable, either during a given flight or from flight to flight. Finally, the object to be caught can vary in size or shape. Clearly, some

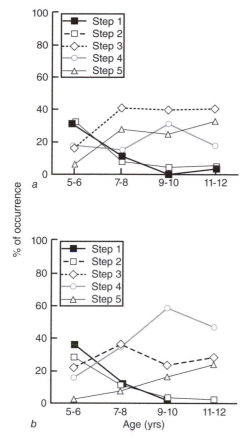

Figure 8.10 Percentage of catches at each developmental step for arm action across age. In *a*, tosses were directed at the torso while in *b*, they were directed at the head and various locations.

combinations of flight path, speed, and object characteristics make for more difficult tasks, while others make for easier tasks. As catchers are developing their proficiency, their categorization into steps on the developmental sequence for a given component might depend on the constraints of the particular catching task. Strohmeyer et al. (1991) found indications of this for arm action in catching based on the direction of ball flight. It is certainly important for researchers assessing individuals' developmental levels to consider the task constraints for any particular catching task.

How is it that we learn to intercept objects at locations away from our starting point and traveling in high trajectories? This topic has been addressed in recent research, and this is the body of work we review next.

Object Interception Models

Before we discuss the research on interception, let's think back to chapter 2 and our discussion of the contrasting theoretical perspectives on perception. Perception plays a large role in the action of catching, so it should be of little surprise that the indirect and direct perspectives on perception influence the investigation of how we intercept objects.

Researchers adopting an indirect perspective assume that skilled catchers are able to observe the initial part of an object's flight and extrapolate from that information to predict where the object will land. As long as the catcher is able to move fast enough to arrive at that location before or as the ball arrives and position the hands as needed, the catcher can intercept the object. Cues such as depth and distance and knowledge of flight trajectories are used to make the extrapolation accurate. In contrast, researchers adopting a direct perspective assume that skilled catchers use information available in the visual display to arrive at the interception point. Perhaps catchers keep some relationship between themselves and the object constant as they approach the interception point. Let's consider a line of research driven by each of these perspectives, starting with the indirect perspective.

Indirect Perspective and Coincidence Anticipation

The importance of skill in intercepting objects was recognized early on, but good methods of investigating this behavior have depended on the develop-

ment of new technologies. Initially, investigators made devices that moved objects, such as balls, a given distance in a given time. Participants in research studies were directed to anticipate the arrival of the object at a designated place and to operate a switch to coincide with the arrival—hence the term *coincidence anticipation* (Belisle, 1963). Timing devices allowed the researchers to compare the time the object actually took to travel to the target point with the performer's operation of the switch; thus, the researchers knew whether the performer acted early or late and by how much (e.g., Haywood, 1980; Haywood, Greenwald, & Lewis, 1981). To act at the same time the object arrives at the target location, performers must take into account their own reaction time delay and the movement time of the action, meaning that they must estimate the interception time and place and begin movement ahead of the object's arrival.

Eventually, Stanley Bassin designed a device that was manufactured and distributed by Lafayette Instrument Company (Lafayette, Indiana): the **Bassin Anticipation Timer**. The Bassin timer simulates movement by sequentially lighting LEDs mounted in a straight or curved line on a long narrow box. Sections of these boxes can be assembled to vary the distance traveled by the simulated light. The lighting of the LEDs can also be varied to simulate an object moving at various speeds. The boxes can be positioned in various ways so that the simulated object approaches the performer, moves from the performer's right to left (or left to right), and so on. These features provide a great advantage over most of the constructed devices. The most recent models of the Bassin timer allow investigators to study constant versus accelerating or decelerating speeds and the effect of occluding the performer's view of the lights at various places along its path.

Research studies using a variety of apparatuses, but especially the Bassin timer, have identified factors that influence the accuracy of anticipating interception. Speed influences accuracy. Faster objects are more difficult to judge, especially if the path of the object is also short. A common observation is that compared with adults, children tend to respond too early to slowly moving objects and too late to fast-moving objects.

Benguigui, Broderick, Baurès, and Amorim (2008) designed a study to determine why this phenomenon exists in children's coincidence anticipation. These investigators observed children aged 6, 7.5, 9, and 10.5 years as well as adults on a coincident timing task in which the researchers could occlude the moving object over the last portion of its path toward the target of interception. They had the light representing the moving object travel at one of two speeds and used 25 different occlusion durations. Each participant completed 50 trials in random order. The researchers determined whether participants relied on distance or time information by plotting the time from movement start to an individual's estimate of arrival time against the time and distance the light was occluded. Individuals relying on distance information estimated the occluded time as a function of occluded distance—that is, the longer the occluded distance, the longer their time estimation. Benguigui et al. confirmed the later responses for faster velocities in children and further found that the younger groups of

children tended to rely on distance rather than time information or to switch back and forth between the two. The latter resulted in great variability. The oldest children and adults tended to rely on time information and overall were more consistent and accurate (see figure 8.11). It would certainly be interesting to know if reliance on distance cues by younger children generalizes across other types of tasks.

Research using devices such as the Bassin Anticipation Timer has identified many factors that influence the performance and development of interception skills, but such studies have a major shortcoming as far as direct, or ecological, researchers are concerned. This shortcoming is simply that the movement observed is often simulated and not very similar to the movement of the objects we have evolved to intercept in real life. Mechanical devices that actually use an object often are restricted to slow speeds or to straight, two-dimensional movement pathways. Again, this is not much like the real-world task. Daish (1972) described the real-life problem of catching a ball thrown or batted in a high trajectory. Consider the trajectories of three balls, all projected at an angle of 45° and traveling at varying velocities: 22.3, 24.0, and 25.7 meters per second. Each ball decelerates due to aerodynamic drag proportional to the square of its velocity. So, the balls follow three different trajectories and land 5 meters apart

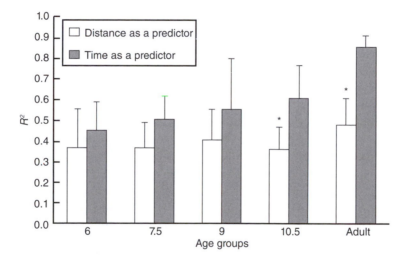

Figure 8.11 Benguigui et al. (2008) analyzed their data by calculating two linear regressions for each participant. This yielded two regression coefficients, one for the slower velocity and one for the faster velocity. Regression coefficients were transformed to Fisher's z-scores for the analyses. The bars indicate the intra-group variability. Post hoc tests on R^2 values were done to follow up on a significant main effect of age. The oldest children and adults tended to rely on time information, which was a better predictor than distance information. Younger children relied on distance information or switched back and forth between using distance and time.

Reprinted from "Motion prediction and the velocity effect in children," by N. Benguigui, M.P. Broderick, R. Baurès, and M.-A. Amorim, 2008, *British Journal of Developmental Psychology*, 26, p. 400. Copyright 2008 by British Psychological Society.

from one another. Yet, the initial portions of each trajectory are very similar. Could a catcher arrive at the correct location to catch a ball by extrapolating from the cues provided in the initial phase of a ball's flight? Researchers with a direct perspective suggest that the answer is no, that information regarding projection angle, velocity, and wind resistance is not precise enough to accomplish the task in this way. They suggest an alternative way in which catchers might arrive at the correct place. We examine their hypothesis next.

Direct Perspective and Catching Fly Balls

Researchers adopting a direct or ecological perspective prefer to study interception skills as they occur naturally. Filming technology has made it possible not only to record successful or unsuccessful interceptions but also to compare the performer's position to the object's position throughout the task. This is key because researchers adopting the direct perspective assume that all of the information the performer needs to intercept an object is available in the visual display; therefore, the performer does not need to predict or extrapolate where to intercept the object from information available only during the early part of the object's flight. Researchers studying direct perception, then, have focused on identifying what information performers might use to arrive at the correct location for interception.

If we apply Gibson's notion of **optical flow** (see chapter 2) to the task of catching, we can see that the image of a ball directly approaching a catcher expands in size on the retinas and occludes more and more of the background as it approaches (see figure 8.12). A catcher might use this information to know when the ball will arrive. If the ball approaches at a constant rate, its image expands at an accelerating rate, eventually looming in the visual field and indicating imminent arrival. So, the rate of an image's expansion and its location in the visual field could be information used to catch.

Lee and Young (1985) suggested that the pattern of optical flow and the rate of expansion provide information about the time remaining until an approaching object reaches the plane of an observer's eye. The faster an object approaches, the faster the rate of expansion of the retinal image. An optical variable can be determined that is related to the rate of image expansion and the time to contact. This variable is named *tau*. It is defined as the retinal image size divided by the rate of the image's change in size. Tau could be a relationship that both people and animals use for various interception tasks. For example, people might use tau when catching balls or braking to avoid a motor vehicle collision, and birds might use tau when folding the wings back when diving into water or simply landing on a perch.

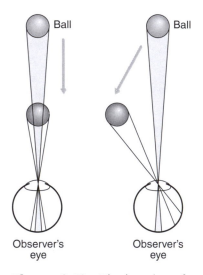

Figure 8.12 The location of a ball in the visual field could be information used to catch the ball.

Reprinted, by permission, from R. Schmidt and C. Wrisberg, 2008, *Motor learning and performance*, 4th ed. (Champaign, IL: Human Kinetics), 94.

Lee and Young's suggestion regarding tau allows for *prospective* control of movement. That is, tau allows for actions to be made before interception (Lee, 1998). Lee's continued work on tau led to a general theory that has drawn much attention from researchers on a variety of interception behaviors (e.g., Pepping & Grealy, 2007). Refinement and expansion of the original theory have led to a more global theory addressing action control and interactions between organisms and their environments. This could certainly be a topic for further reading and research!

Of course, catching is considerably more difficult when a ball is projected high into the air (rather than directly projected straight at us), from far way (rather than from nearby), and perhaps aimed toward a distant location (rather than to our location). Chapman (1968) first considered what visual information a catcher could use to intercept a ball in parabolic flight. His goal was to identify an equation reflecting a consistent relationship that a catcher could use for interception. He demonstrated that an object in parabolic flight will land at a catcher's location if a particular mathematical relationship equals 0. The relationship is based on the angle of elevation of gaze (see figure 8.13) and is $d^2(\tan \alpha)/dt^2$, where α is the angle of elevation of gaze and t is time. If the relationship does not equal 0, the catcher must move. Of course, researchers with the direct perspective are not suggesting that catchers compute this relationship but rather that experienced catchers directly perceive the relationship and subconsciously move to the point where the relationship is 0. A difficulty with Chapman's work is that in the real world objects do not travel in true parabolic trajectories because of air resistance.

McLeod and Dienes (1993) stimulated a series of research studies on catching when they built on Chapman's work by publishing a short study of one catcher (see table 8.4). They videotaped a catcher running to a ball projected into the air at an angle of 45° and a speed between 20 and 25 meters per second. The catcher was required to run forward 5.6 or 8.4 meters or backward 2.9 meters but was not required to run left or right in order to catch the ball. McLeod and Dienes analyzed five successful catches at each distance and found that the catcher, after about a half second, started to run, accelerating until he reached the velocity where Chapman's (1968) relationship equaled 0. The catcher would speed up or slow down to maintain a speed at which Chapman's relationship was close to 0. He was always moving when he caught the ball; he did not arrive at the interception point early and wait for the ball.

McLeod and Dienes (1993) concluded that this strategy puts a catcher on a course to interception and does not require a catcher to extrapolate or predict the future location of the ball. It is not a conscious strategy; rather, it is a strategy whose effectiveness is discovered unconsciously by catchers. There is a factor that is implicit in this strategy: If catchers keep their angle of gaze between 0° (which translates to the ball dropping to the ground in front of the catcher; see figure 8.13) and 90° (which translates to the ball going over the catcher's head) throughout the flight, it is still possible to catch the ball. When the catcher moves to keep $d^2(\tan \alpha)/dt^2$ close to 0, $\tan a$ is positive and the angle of gaze α is between 0° and 90°, so the ball will be intercepted. This strategy is called the **optical**

Table 8.4   Comparison of Studies on Catching Strategies

Study Citation	Key Concept	Noteworthy Findings	Comparative Comments
Chapman (1968)	Identify the visual information a catcher can use to intercept a ball. Used objects traveling in a true parabolic flight path	Found that a relationship based on the angle of gaze elevation resulted in a ball landing at a catcher's location if the relationship equaled 0.	Such a relationship could be directly but subconsciously perceived.
McLeod & Dienes (1993)	Determine whether a relationship can be identified for authentic ball flights that are not parabolic. Videotaped a catcher running to a ball projected at 45° and between 20 and 25 m/s; catcher ran forward or backward	Confirmed Chapman's notion. Keeping the relationship equal to 0 and the angle of gaze between 0° and 90° resulted in interception.	Using a strategy of moving to catch the ball rather than predicting its end point works. This strategy is called *optical acceleration cancellation (OAC)*.
McLeod & Dienes (1996)	Repeat 1993 study with more participants and higher trajectory. Projected balls at 64° and 24 m/s	Catchers moved to catch the ball rather than predicting where it would land, running there, and waiting.	The OAC model was confirmed.
Lenoir, Musch, Janssens, Thiery, & Uyttenhove (1999)	Identify the visual information a catcher can use to intercept a ball when required to move side to side. Asked performers to ride a cycle on a path to intercept a moving ball	Performers maintained their angular position to the moving ball.	This strategy was labeled the *constant bearing angle (CBA) strategy*.
McBeath, Shaffer, & Kaiser (1995)	Identify a strategy for intercepting balls that require both vertical and horizontal movement. Observed the paths of two catchers when the catcher's angle of gaze elevation and horizontal angle of gaze varied	Catchers moved in a curved path, as if they were monitoring a relationship rather than predicting the landing point ahead of time.	This strategy was labeled the *linear optical trajectory (LOT)*. Like the OAC method, this is an error-nulling strategy.
Chohan, Verheul, Van Kampen, Wind, & Savelsbergh (2008)	Determine if children use a CBA strategy. Observed walking speed children used to intercept balls moving at two angles and three speeds	Found evidence that children used the CBA strategy, although older children used it more.	There might be a developmental trend to become better at using error-nulling strategies for interception.

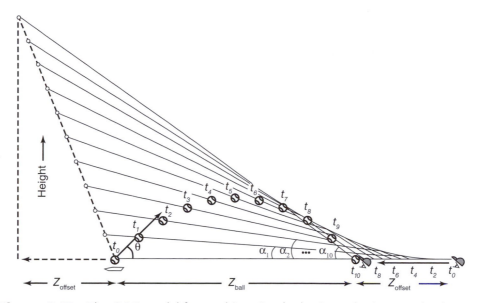

Figure 8.13 The OAC model for catching. On the horizontal axis, t_0 marks the starting position of the ball (see left) and the catcher (see right). α is the catcher's angle of gaze. As time progresses from t_1 to t_{10}, the optical path of the ball rises with constant velocity for ideal parabolic trajectories. If the catcher moves to keep $d^2(\tan \alpha)/dt^2$ close to 0, the ball is caught.

Reprinted, by permission, from M.K. McBeath, D.M. Shaffer, and M.K. Kaiser, 1995, "How baseball outfielders determine where to run to catch fly balls," *Science* 268: 570. Science by American Association for the Advancement of Science. Reproduced with permission of AMERICAN ASSOCIATION FOR THE ADVANCEMENT OF SCIENCE in the format Journal via Copyright Clearance Center.

acceleration cancellation (OAC) model for catching. The moving catcher keeps the optical ball speed constant, canceling any acceleration or change in velocity relative to the catcher's position.

McLeod and Dienes (1996) later repeated their study with additional participants and obtained the same results. They also projected a ball at 64° and 24 meters per second, such that the ball was in the air longer and catchers would have more time to run to the interception point and wait for the ball's arrival, if that were their strategy. The researchers found that catchers did not use the spare time in this way but instead arrived at the interception point at the same time as the ball. McLeod and Dienes titled their 1996 article, "Do Fielders Know Where to Go to Catch the Ball or Only How to Get There?" The answer was that catchers know how to get to the interception point. They don't decide where the ball will land based on information from the early flight of a ball. They monitor relationships with the environment to arrive at the correct place at the correct time.

The OAC model provides a good explanation of how we run forward or backward to catch a fly ball, but it doesn't address how we catch balls to the right or left of us as well as in front or back of us. Lenoir et al. (Lenoir, Musch, Janssens, Thiery, & Uyttenhove, 1999) examined a simplified version of this task by isolating how we might intercept objects moving only horizontally. Sport examples of such a task include ice hockey goalies moving sideways to intercept a puck

sliding along the ice and soccer goalies moving sideways to intercept a rolling ball. Lenoir et al. suggested that goalies could use the strategy of a **constant bearing angle (CBA)** to arrive at the interception point at the correct time. That is, goalies could move to keep their angle to the puck or ball (β) constant, and doing so would take them to a point to intercept the object. They would not need to know where the object was aimed, the final distance it would travel, or its velocity in order to intercept it.

Tips for Novice Investigators

The studies in table 8.4, which were conducted on the use of error-nulling strategies for catching balls or intercepting moving objects, used adults. The researchers began studying this topic by using accomplished performers and discovering how they went about performing. We are interested in how such skill develops. Only the study by Chohan, Verheul, Van Kampen, Wind, and Savelsbergh (2008) involved children. Identify several research questions that you could ask about how children develop strategies for intercepting moving objects and design a study that could answer one of your questions.

Lenoir et al. (1999) tested their notion by having individuals ride a cycle on a path representing one side of a triangle to intercept a ball moving along a track on the other side of the triangle. The investigators found that performers did maintain the angular position—that is, they used the CBA strategy. The investigators further suggested that performers allow for intercepting the object with the part of the body that is going to do the interception. They keep the intercepting limb's (or intercepting implement's) angular relationship to the moving object constant. Hockey goalies, for example, keep their hockey stick or skates at the constant angle, while soccer goalies might keep their feet at the constant angle.

The more common and challenging interception task must take into account not only horizontal movement but also vertical movement. An example of such a task is when a ball is thrown high into the air, to the side of a catcher, and in front of or behind the catcher's starting position. This is the task facing an outfielder in baseball. McBeath et al. (McBeath, Shaffer, & Kaiser, 1995; Shaffer, 1999; Shaffer & McBeath, 2002) suggested a strategy that catchers might use for this type of task. They proposed that a catcher moves along a path that maintains a **linear optical trajectory (LOT)** for the ball relative to its starting location (home plate in baseball) and the background scene. This strategy incorporates both the catcher's angle of elevation of gaze α and the horizontal angle of gaze β as in the constant bearing angle strategy. In figure 8.14a, α and β specify an optical (observed) trajectory projection angle ψ. Figure 8.14b shows that if the catcher moves along a path from time one, t_1, through time four, t_4, and if the tangents of α and β remain constant, ψ remains constant. This is denoted in figure 8.14b by the straight line that connects all of the projections of the optical, or observed, angle in three dimensions.

More simply put, the catcher must move continuously and more directly under the ball. If the optical trajectory that the catcher observes begins to curve down, the ball might fall in front of the catcher. If the optical trajectory appears to be arcing past the catcher, then the ball might go over the catcher's head. The catcher uses an error-nulling strategy to move such that the ball stays overhead without curving down or arcing up. This allows the catcher to adapt to changes in the ball's path due to ball spin, air resistance, or wind!

McBeath et al. (1995) filmed two catchers to confirm that they actually moved in this way. Shaffer (1999) also confirmed the LOT strategy and additionally demonstrated that catchers were not very good at predicting the apex of a ball's trajectory or the ball's final landing spot if they only observed the first half of the ball's flight. Observing the path of the catcher provided further evidence that catchers monitor

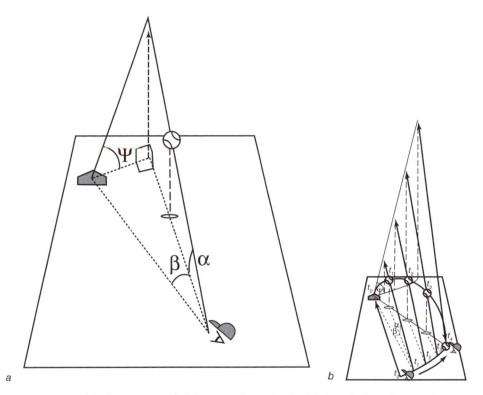

a   b

Figure 8.14 (a) The LOT model for catching. The ball is headed to the catcher's right. α is the angle of gaze, β is the lateral optical angle, and ψ is the picture plane optical angle, or the observed trajectory projection angle. (b) If the catcher runs such that lateral optical ball movement stays proportional to vertical optical ball movement, the ball will be caught. Note the running path curves slightly.

(a) Reprinted, by permission, from M.K. McBeath, D.M. Shaffer, and M.K. Kaiser, 1995, "How baseball outfielders determine where to run to catch fly balls," *Science* 268: 570. Science by American Association for the Advancement of Science. Reproduced with permission of AMERICAN ASSOCIATION FOR THE ADVANCEMENT OF SCIENCE in the format Journal via Copyright Clearance Center.

(b) Reprinted, by permission, from M.K. McBeath, D.M. Shaffer, and M.K. Kaiser, 1995, "How baseball outfielders determine where to run to catch fly balls," *Science* 268: 571. Science by American Association for the Advancement of Science. Reproduced with permission of AMERICAN ASSOCIATION FOR THE ADVANCEMENT OF SCIENCE in the format Journal via Copyright Clearance Center.

information in the visual display. Rather than moving in a straight line, as catchers would do if they knew ahead of time where the ball would land, the catchers moved in a curved path, as they would do if keeping a relationship with the ball constant. McBeath et al. also suggested that the LOT strategy explains why catchers feel it is easier to catch balls headed to their side than to catch balls headed straight toward them. The lateral angle, β, is information added to the angle of gaze, α, to provide the spatial cue of linearity (Shaffer, McBeath, Roy, & Krauchunas, 2003). Balls headed directly toward the catcher provide only information about α.

Both the OAC and LOT strategies are error-nulling strategies—that is, catchers are making constant adjustments to errors in their relationship to the ball. Yet, the OAC and LOT strategies differ in the type of cue a catcher uses. The OAC model predicts that catchers rely primarily on temporal information (speeding up or slowing down to keep a certain relationship) while the LOT model emphasizes that catchers rely on spatial and temporal cues. You may be interested in reading the continued debate in the literature between these two research teams regarding the relative merits or possible complementary usage of the OAC and LOT strategies (McLeod, Reed, & Dienes, 2001; Shaffer & McBeath, 2002; McLeod, Reed, & Dienes, 2002; Shaffer et al., 2003). These researchers have also studied animals (Shaffer, Krauchunas, Eddy, & McBeath, 2004) and robotic modeling (Sugar & McBeath, 2001).

Of course, the study of the strategies used for catching balls that move in complex paths has largely involved adult catchers. So how does moving to catch develop? McLeod and Dienes (1993, 1996) suggested that children might learn to move to catch balls thrown toward them from their experience with watching such balls. If children are stationary, only balls with $d^2(\tan \alpha)/dt^2 = 0$ (or close to 0) come to them. Once they start moving, they only get close to those balls with a low value of $d^2(\tan \alpha)/dt^2$. So, perhaps in childhood we discover the strategy unconsciously.

Chohan et al. (2008) recently studied 5- to 7-year-olds and 10- to 12-year-olds and whether they adhered to a CBA strategy to intercept a ball. The researchers placed a tennis ball on a platform that could be moved right to left at three different constant speeds. The children started at one of two starting points. Both starting points were 4 meters from the interception point, but one was at 90° to the ball's path and the other was at 45° to the path. The children were told to start walking when the ball started moving and to intercept the ball within a marked target area. While moving, they were free to adjust their walking speed. Use of the CBA strategy required a near-constant walking speed. While both age groups sometimes deviated from a CBA strategy, the older children moved more consistently with a CBA strategy. The younger children deviated from the CBA strategy to a greater degree in some task conditions than in others. They deviated from the strategy especially when the ball velocity was slow and the approach was angled, perhaps because they prepared ahead of the start for the faster velocity. While there are limitations to this initial study, Chohan et al. provided some indication that children can use and perhaps become more proficient at using such strategies for interception.

Earlier we acknowledged that an important developmental trend for infant reaching to intercept a moving object might be motor constraints and the ability to adapt movements so they are spatially compatible with the interception task.

This might continue to be the case with the development of moving to catch, and certainly this is one topic deserving of more research attention. Anecdotally, some baseball experts suggest that the very best outfielders are those who can best configure their bodies to catch a ball in the hand once having arrived in the vicinity to intercept the ball. Devising a way to test this hypothesis across the age span when catching can develop to a proficient level would be an interesting challenge for those interested in this topic.

The important message is that information is available to catchers in the visual display, and this information can be monitored to help catchers arrive at an interception point at the same time the object arrives. Furthermore, this can be done without computing data cues from the early flight path to extrapolate the time and place of interception. This holds true for the other interception tasks listed earlier.

SUMMARY

Manipulative skills are wide ranging. Some are very fine movements, others are larger movements, and still others are routinely combined with movements such as locomotion. The evidence from developmental studies of manipulative skills is consistent with the more ecological views of movement: Reaching movements can be soft assembled, even in infancy, and information in the visual display is sufficient to allow catchers to intercept objects by keeping certain relationships in that visual display. Recent research has provided explanations of how manipulative skills are executed without requiring the existence of a motor program.

How Do Practitioners Adopt a Developmental Perspective?

Applying Research

To this point, most of our discussion has been of typical development. Yet, not all individuals develop typically. In chapter 9 we discuss atypical development and center our discussion around whether the cause of atypical development is associated with genetic etiologies, experience-dependent etiologies, or multiple or unknown etiologies. Research on atypical development not only helps professionals work with people who are developing atypically but also informs our broad understanding of development, including what and how certain factors change the course of development.

One reason why motor development is so interesting to a large number of people is our interactions with changing individuals, including ourselves. Many people work in a professional role that involves facilitating development. Our last chapter examines the research on interventions for development. While the research on this topic is limited, an appreciation can be gained for research-based approaches to facilitating motor development.

CHAPTER 9

Atypical Motor Development

Thus far in this text, we have focused on typical motor development—changes we might expect in people who do not have unique individual constraints and who are moving in typical environments performing normal tasks. Basically, this is motor development on average. In chapter 1, we described the general developmental perspective, which suggests that identifiable changes occur with fairly predictable timing in most individuals (Asendorpf & Valsiner, 1992). At the same time, we discussed the notion of developmental functions, and different developmental functions exist for different people. These can deviate from the average developmental course in a variety of ways; in some instances, development is advanced (motor skills appear sooner than expected), while in others, it is delayed (motor skills appear later than expected). In still others, development is actually different (the person moves in unique ways). In this chapter, we focus on the latter two situations. Intuitively, we know that structural and functional individual constraints can lead to atypical developmental trajectories. For example, a child with cerebral palsy may be delayed in the acquisition of fundamental motor skills due to muscle spasticity, or an adult with multiple sclerosis may see motor proficiency diminish as a result of deteriorating myelin sheaths in the brain and spinal cord. In certain conditions, people may exhibit motor coordination delays that can be overcome with enhanced practice or experience, as is the case of some children with specific learning disabilities; in other conditions, people may never move typically, as is often the case of individuals with developmental coordination disorder.

Part of the challenge for practitioners who wish to remediate conditions that lead to differences in motor control is that they must not only understand the nature of the disease state and how that disease state affects movement in real time but also understand how the disease state acts as a constraint or rate limiter in the development of motor skills. Furthermore, the practitioner must consider what new movement forms might emerge from the confluence of constraints. Over time, the underlying condition may no longer directly influence movement (e.g., individuals with low muscle tone at birth may improve their

muscle tone over time), but it still may have led to a drastic shift in a person's everyday movement (low muscle tone may delay the onset of locomotion, which may affect social and cognitive development). In this chapter, we explore atypical development from this point of view: What are the characteristics of certain disabilities or disease states, and how do they influence movement over time?

IDENTIFYING ATYPICAL DEVELOPMENT BY UNDERSTANDING TYPICAL DEVELOPMENT

In order to be able to identify atypical development, we must first understand typical development. As described in chapter 1, most people hold the general developmental perspective. We believe that most human beings develop in a similar, species-specific way, a concept that has been described as *universality* (Thelen & Ulrich, 1991). If we asked 100 parents to describe the ways in which their children changed over time, we would find many common descriptions of the development from infancy through childhood and beyond. Without such homogeneity in progression, we would not be able to identify the emergence of specific behaviors and corresponding developmental sequences, as we have already done in previous chapters. As described throughout this book, researchers such as Bayley (1966) and Shirley (1931) have studied common patterns in infancy and toddlerhood (see chapter 1); others have examined developmental sequences in children and adults (Halverson, Roberton, & Harper, 1973; Roberton & Halverson, 1984; Seefeldt, Reuschlein, & Vogel, 1972). Knowing these sequences is beneficial to many different types of practitioners, as they provide roadmaps outlining typical development within a variety of domains. Such universality exists within a species in part because of species-specific anatomical constraints.

At the same time, a great deal of developmental variability exists in these sequences, particularly in their timing but also in their order. Furthermore, individuals may take a variety of different pathways to achieve a motor goal. Consider bipedal locomotion (Piek, 2002). Some infants begin to walk early, perhaps as young as 7 months, spending little time creeping or crawling and sometimes even skipping earlier forms of locomotion altogether, whereas other infants may walk as late as 18 months, spending months favoring crawling as the preferred mode of locomotion. Although humans share many physical and environmental characteristics, we each have our own distinct individual constraints, and these

▶ Tips for Novice Investigators

When investigating any type of atypical development, be sure to get a representative sample of participants who are typically developing to perform the task under study. Further, be sure to match these participants on whatever the most important characteristics are of the atypical population, whether it is age, gender, weight, strength, IQ, or another characteristic.

interact with each other as well as with the environment and task in a unique way. Furthermore, this interaction changes over time—constraints act upon and thereby change each other, creating a new context in which the form and influence of constraints change as well. Two individuals, no matter how similar they may be, will differ in their developmental courses. Motor development, therefore, is marked by variability (Deutsch & Newell, 2005).

These two concepts, universality and variability, may seem in opposition to each other. However, every typically developing person shows predictable progression through developmental sequences while at the same time showing individual differences in timing and even sequencing of behaviors. For example, young infants raise their heads in prone, prop themselves up, roll over, sit up, pull to stand, and walk with support. These movements represent a universal sequence of motor milestones that infants must obtain in order to walk upright on their own. However, if we compare the progression of two infants through these milestones, two distinct developmental paths will emerge. Thus, universality and variability coexist; together, they provide a range of values for developmental variables that indicate what typical development is.

Individual constraints in the form of anatomical similarities account for some of the similarities seen in movement patterns, but other constraints are important as well. In fact, experience plays a vital role in development. Consider experience as the confluence of constraints related to perception and action rather than a stimulus–response reaction. Individuals do not have experiences superimposed on them; rather, their individual constraints mediate the ways in which they perceive and act on the environment. Certain environmental experiences are both highly probable and necessary for typical development; that is, these experiences are universal. The resulting development is termed *experience expectant* and accounts for many of the similar behaviors we see in infants and children, such as language acquisition (Anderson et al., 2000).

On the other hand, *experience-dependent* development accounts for many individual differences (Kail & Cavenaugh, 2010). The unique experiences of an individual, particularly within the first 3 years of life, when brain development is at its zenith, promote new brain growth while at the same time cultivating that which already exists. But what happens if something changes? What if a person passes through a critical time without experiencing something specific and necessary for development during that time? What if the building blocks of development, DNA, are different? What if an individual experiences some sort of trauma early in life? How will these individuals move, and how will their movement change over time? Finally, what can practitioners and parents do to intervene?

MOTOR DEVELOPMENT THAT IS NOT AVERAGE

The general developmental perspective expects most humans sharing similar genetics and environmental constraints to develop a broad range of motor skills over time, and we define this development as *typical motor development.*

There is robust evidence supporting typical sequences of motor patterns, such as Bayley's motor milestones (chapter 1), the progression of walking (chapter 6), and the progression of throwing (chapter 7). At the same time, changes in initial conditions (genetics, environment, or both) can lead to atypical motor development. For example, the notion of critical or sensitive time frames (specific time frames in which certain tissues may be sensitive to external stimuli) suggests that certain time frames carry more weight in terms of the developing motor system. In some instances, environmental influences occurring during a sensitive time frame can lead to atypical motor development; in other instances, atypical development may be adjusted or corrected by providing experiences during a critical time frame. Furthermore, an infant may be born with a genetic abnormality, and environmental differences will have a differing effect on the course of development.

Atypical motor development, therefore, cannot be simply or easily categorized. Rather than providing an exhaustive list of conditions that lead to atypical development, we will discuss three general ways in which atypical development may occur and then provide specific examples that illustrate the resulting effects on movement in the developing system. This is somewhat of an oversimplification of how disabilities that lead to differences in motor skill occur; however, it should provide a basic framework from which you can explore different types of motor impairments from a developmental perspective. In this framework, we will categorize atypical motor development as initially stemming from (1) genetic differences, (2) environmental or experiential influences, or (3) a combination of the two. When we discuss interventions in chapter 10, it will be clear that, as always, genetics and environment interact with and change each other, so that they always have a profound influence on each other in a way that can sometimes alter an individual's developmental.

Atypical Motor Development With Genetic Etiologies

Atypical motor development may stem from genetic abnormalities that influence movement (such as Huntington's disease) or from abnormalities that influence the specific anatomy that an individual has (such as Down syndrome), which in turn influences movement. Genes, which are made of DNA, provide instructions related to the production of a protein or enzyme within the cell. Prenatally, these genes direct the differentiation of cells (e.g., into cardiac, epidermal, or nervous cells) so that they have specific characteristics and develop into organ systems. Sometimes, something goes amiss in this process. A gene may show a variation (a mutation) or an extra gene may exist, both of which can produce an atypical developmental trajectory. The study of genetic disorders is expansive, and our description here is both short and simplistic.

In many cases, atypical development stemming from genetic differences cannot be altered by environmental or experiential modifications (although the field of genetic modification is growing), and developmental differences persist throughout the lifespan. This is not to say that experiences after birth will not modify an individual's developmental trajectory (see chapter 10). However,

individuals who have a genetic anomaly have a different starting point as well as developmental path compared with their typically developing peers.

Down Syndrome

Down syndrome (DS), also known as *trisomy 21*, is an example of a genetic disorder that affects general development as well as motor development. Within the United States, approximately 1 in 733 infants is born with DS each year, making it a prevalent genetic disorder (National Down Syndrome Society, 2011). Individuals born with DS share a variety of characteristic anatomical features. These include a round face with a small chin, widely spaced and slanted eyes, shorter limbs and digits, a smaller head, hypotonia, and hyperflexible joints. Another congenital condition that often exists in people with DS is heart defects. People with DS often experience intellectual disabilities as well. All of these can be considered individual movement constraints and have a profound effect on how motor development proceeds within this population.

Causes of Down Syndrome

People with DS are born with an extra portion of chromosome 21, which leads to an altered developmental trajectory. This genetic condition is the result of an abnormality in the chromosome arrangement that occurs during meiosis. The abnormality occurs at conception and is not related to any environmental condition such as maternal alcohol or drug use. However, it should be noted that as a mother's age increases, so does the incidence of DS in her offspring, which rises from less than 1 in 1,000 in mothers younger than age 30 to 1 in 12 in mothers who are age 49 (National Institute of Child and Human Development, 2011).

Motor Development Differences in Down Syndrome

The anatomical differences present at birth due to trisomy 21 create a unique movement context for infants with DS; this in turn creates atypical developmental trajectories. In fact, trisomy 21 serves as an example of Poincaré's sensitivity to initial conditions playing out in developmental time. In particular, hypotonia and joint laxity have a cascading effect on the development of a variety of skills, both motor and cognitive.

Early in development, infants with DS often experience hypotonia, which is best described as a lack of muscle tone. Infants with DS have often been characterized as floppy. Later in development, hypotonia often improves. However, the initial lack of muscle tone usually results in delayed acquisition of motor milestones throughout infancy, including grasping, sitting, rolling, and pulling to stand (see table 9.1; Joblin & Virji-Bula, 2004). Because these milestones require a certain degree of strength, hypotonia can be considered a rate-limiting factor in their acquisition. Furthermore, infants acquire many of these milestones in a sequence that leads to the ability to maintain an upright posture. Delays in milestones lead to delays in the attainment of fundamental motor skills such as walking and activities of daily living such as eating (Reid & Block, 1996; Ulrich, Ulrich, & Collier, 1992). One of the key differences in motor development between children with and children without DS that in children with DS, delays can be significant, and the age ranges in which motor skills are achieved

Table 9.1 Research on Attainment of Motor Milestones in Children With Down Syndrome

Motor milestone	Cunningham & Sloper (1978)		Berry et al. (1980)		Winders (1997)	
	Range (months)	Average age (months)	Range (months)	Average age (months)	Range (months)	Average age (months)
Rolls	4-11	8	2-12	6-7	2-10	5
Sits steadily without support	8-16	11	7-16	11	5-9	7
Pulls to standing	10-24	17	8-28 (or more)	17	7-12	8
Stands alone	16-36	22	—	21	9-16	11
Walks without support for three or more steps	16-42	24	14-36	26	9-17	13
Grasps cube	4-10	7	—	—	3-7	5
Passes object from hand to hand	6-12	8	—	—	4-8	5
Puts three or more objects into box	12-34	19	—	—	9-18	12
Builds a tower of two 1 in. (2.5 cm) cubes	14-32	20	—	—	10-19	14

Adapted, by permission, from A. Jobling and N. Virji-Babul, 2004, *Motor development in Down syndrome: Play, move and grow* (Burnaby, BC, Canada: Down Syndrome Research Foundation).

are fairly broad. Some of the delays in this population may also be related to heart abnormalities (Sacks & Buckley, 2003). However, many children with DS eventually acquire these motor skills (Block, 1991).

Predictably, individuals with DS differ from their typically developing peers in balance and postural stability (Butterworth & Cicchetti, 1978; Jobling, 1999; Sacks & Buckley, 2003). As discussed in chapter 5, postural control is the ability to maintain balance or equilibrium (either static or dynamic). Several of the constraints seen in DS, including joint laxity and low muscle tone, have a significant influence on the ability to maintain postural control.

Ligamentous laxity results in hypermobile joints. This in and of itself may not act as a rate limiter for postural control (as evidenced by successful gymnasts, ice skaters, and wrestlers). The difference between a successful gymnast and a person with DS, however, is having sufficient strength to control the trunk and limbs throughout an expanded range of motion. When joint laxity interacts with low muscle tone, the result is difficulty with postural stability and control. Several studies have shown that infants with DS are more likely to exhibit a greater degree of postural sway as well as difficulty with balance. These issues last throughout infancy and into childhood and adulthood and lead to motor pattern differences designed to improve dynamic stability (Smith & Ulrich, 2008).

Delays in obtaining upright posture translate into delays in the onset of locomotion. Children with DS often begin walking much later (on average, about a year later) than their typically developing peers (who, on average, walk between 12 and 15 months of age; Kubo & Ulrich, 2006b; Smith & Ulrich, 2008; Ulrich

et al., 1992). Early walking patterns (short, wide steps taken with toes out and arms in high guard) preserve balance, as balance is the primary rate limiter that an infant must overcome in order to take independent steps. In children with DS, not only are the motor milestones necessary to obtain an upright posture delayed but also balance is compromised by low muscle tone and joint laxity.

There is some debate over the consequences of these delays, which often linger well past the age ranges identified in typically developing children. Motor development and early movement influence both social and cognitive development. For example, infants begin to explore their environment by reaching and grasping objects; this exploration allows for a human–object interface involving multiple sensory systems (vision, tactile, and possibly taste). Such movements help create neural pathways in the brain that are critical within the first 3 years of life (Kail & Cavenaugh, 2010; Ulrich et al., 1992). If infants (either with or without DS) are significantly delayed in these experiences, they miss out on some or all of these opportunities to learn to integrate sensory information (Ulrich, Lloyd, Tiernan, Looper, & Angulo-Barroso, 2008). Part of this learning is discovering cause-and-effect relationships in the surroundings. Furthermore, independent locomotion provides infants and toddlers with a means to control and explore their environment as well as an opportunity to interact socially (Lynch, Ryu, Agrawal, & Galloway, 2009). Therefore, delayed motor skill acquisition can have a far more profound effect than just delayed movement; it can influence the entire developmental process, leading to greater cognitive disabilities than those that would exist if movement opportunities had been possible (Ulrich et al., 2008).

Given the potential for delayed motor development to augment motor and cognitive differences over time, it is important to determine the effectiveness of intervention in remediating, reversing, or changing developmental trajectories in individuals with DS. Do differences in constraints caused by trisomy 21 mean that individuals with DS cannot change their motor patterns over time with interventions? That is, by accounting for rate-limiting constraints, can we shorten the delays seen in DS? Additionally, can we change the differences in motor patterns? A cadre of research studies suggests that individuals with DS can, in fact, improve with practice—sometimes as much as or more than typically developing individuals can (Lafferty, 2005; Perán, Gil, Ruiz, & Fernandez-Pastor, 1997; Smith, Kubo, Black, Holt, & Ulrich, 2007; Wang & Ju, 2002).

Much of the recent research on walking in individuals with DS has come from the laboratories of Ulrich, Ulrich, and colleagues at the University of Michigan (this research is more extensively reviewed in chapter 10). This research team has taken a systematic strong inference approach to answering questions related to motor development in this population. In one study (Smith et al., 2007), the researchers wanted to investigate the influence of task-specific practice (by providing a task constraint focused on improving balance) on walking ability in children who had at least 6 years of walking experience to see if the children would change their dynamic strategy (reduce high levels of stiffness and impulse). The researchers hypothesized that increased stiffness, which was noted in previous research, resulted when participants overcompensated for laxity and lower muscle tone in what they perceived as an unstable context (Ulrich, Haehl,

Buzzi, Kubo, & Holt, 2004). The researchers tested 16 preadolescents (8 with and 8 without DS) as they walked over ground (on a GAITRite mat and over a force plate) and then on a treadmill at 40%, 75%, and 110% of their speed over ground. Next, participants practiced walking at 75% maximum velocity for four practice sessions. Practice focused on balance as well as providing experience on the treadmill and included 12 60-second trials in which the participants held onto the railing with both hands for 15 seconds, held with one hand for 15 seconds, and then held with no hands for 30 seconds. After completing four practice sessions, all participants repeated the protocol of the first session.

▶ Tips for Novice Investigators

When working with a population with intellectual disabilities, researchers need to spend time planning and piloting different ways in which to administer task instructions. In other words, researchers must be sure that they provide simple, unambiguous instructions that participants can understand. This helps to control interpretation of task instruction as a variable that might change movement.

The researchers found that participants with DS had, as anticipated, higher values of stiffness and impulse in their initial trials when compared with the typically developing (TD) group. Practice did not provide a radical change in walking form; after practice, the participants with DS did not walk kinematically similar to the TD group. However, they improved the efficiency of gait by reducing both stiffness and impulse. In fact, these values improved more in the DS population, such that their posttest values resembled the pretest values of the TD group. This result showed that participants with DS can improve and optimize the ways in which they allocate dynamic resources (stiffness and impulse) through a change in task constraint over time.

Other studies have had similar results (see table 9.2). For example, children with DS were asked to practice jumping over a 6-week time frame (Wang & Ju, 2002). Each of the 30 practice sessions (3 per week) involved both practice and instruction on jumping. After the intervention, the group with DS improved more than their TD peers improved on both horizontal and vertical jumping as well as on floor and beam walking. Again, the DS group did not look the same as the TD group, but the intervention led to improvement. This was also the finding in a study by Lafferty (2005), who found that five children with DS who participated in a 12-week stair-climbing intervention showed improvement over time. The same held true in studies of fine motor skills (Dulaney & Tomporowski, 2000) and running (Perán, et al., 1997).

To summarize, individuals with DS have different individual constraints. Their limbs and digits tend to be short, and many have coexisting heart defects and intellectual disabilities. People with DS often have hypotonia during infancy and joint laxity across the lifespan. Infants and young children often experience motor delays in the acquisition of motor milestones; however, with intervention,

Table 9.2 Gait Interventions for Children With Down Syndrome

Study citation	Key concept or topic	Intervention	Comparative comments
Lafferty (2005)	Stair-climbing	12 wk	In all studies, children with DS improved performance as a result of intervention. In several studies, the DS children improved more than their typically developing peers
Peran, Gil, Ruiz, & Fernandez-Pastor (1997)	Running	Endurance, speed, and strength exercises 2-3 times per week in four 3 mo blocks	
Smith, Kubo, Black, Holt, & Ulrich (2007)	Walking	Walking at different velocities and with different balance accommodations in four practice sessions on a treadmill	
Wang & Ju (2002)	Jumping	Practice and instruction on horizontal and vertical jumping 3 times per week for 3 wk	

these delays can be diminished in older children and adults. At the same time, it is difficult to know what long-term differences in cognitive and social development are stemming from early delays in locomotion and other exploratory behaviors. Qualitatively, individuals with DS may move differently from those without DS, but these differences may not have a profound effect on function.

Atypical Development With Experience-Dependent Etiologies

Experiences or environmental influences during embryonic and fetal development form a group of experience-dependent disabilities or disorders. As we discussed earlier in the chapter, typical development depends on individuals receiving particular experiences or environmental stimuli during specific times in development (Kail & Cavenaugh, 2010). At the same time, atypical development can be related to an altered or lack of experience or environmental stimulus. Atypical motor development can emerge from a specific experience or environmental event during a short, critical time frame of fetal development. For example, if a fetus loses oxygen to its brain, cerebral palsy will likely result. Atypical motor development can also result from general experiences sustained over a longer duration, such as in fetal alcohol syndrome, in which the embryo and fetus receive repeated exposure to alcohol throughout prenatal development. Alcohol exposure affects many systems during their critical times of differentiation and growth. Disabilities in this group do not exist at conception and are not the result of a genetic abnormality, as in DS; rather, some event or experience causes the condition.

Cerebral Palsy

Cerebral palsy (CP) is a neurological disorder resulting from nonprogressive lesions to the brain that occur at or near the time of birth; as such, CP is experience dependent rather than expectant (National Institute of Neurological

Disorders and Stroke, 2011). The difficulties that exist in motor control and coordination do not worsen over time (Krageloh-Mann & Horber, 2007). No damage occurs directly to the muscles or nerves; rather, movement difficultly stems directly from the brain lesion. Because brain injury must occur within a sensitive time frame during brain development, the majority of children with CP are born with it. Rarely, infants develop CP after birth as a result of head injury or brain infection. After a few months of development in the term-born infant, the window for CP starts to close; after this point, any brain lesions are classified as something other than CP (Kulak, Sobaniec, Kuzia, & Bockowski, 2006). However, many symptoms are noticed most clearly during voluntary movement, and so it may take months or years to identify and diagnose CP. The rate of diagnosis in the United States is about 2.4 out of 1,000 children, with a higher incidence in males than in females. Premature infants are more likely to acquire CP, as their brains have not fully developed and are highly susceptible to injury.

Causes of Cerebral Palsy

CP is caused by brain lesions, most typically from hypoxic ischemia, or damage to the brain cells caused by lack of oxygen. This particular pathway is typically responsible for the neurological condition known as *periventricular leukomalacia (PVL)*, which is a type of brain injury affecting infants in which small areas in the white matter in the ventricles die (Riddle et al., 2006). PVL occurs from lack of oxygen to the brain between weeks 24 and 28 of gestation. In general, the global blood flow to the brain is lowered. This becomes significant in the periventricular area of the brain, as it receives too little blood to support the tissue. After 30 minutes of this ischemia, white matter begins to deteriorate. This injury pathway is responsible in many cases of CP (Krageloh-Mann, 2007). Other causes of CP include exposure to radiation or infection during fetal development, asphyxia before birth, trauma during labor and delivery, and complications in perinatal life or early childhood. CP is more frequently observed in multiple births.

Motor Development Differences in Cerebral Palsy

Several types of motor coordination or control deficiencies exist in populations with CP. Spasticity is the most common characteristic of CP, affecting approximately 70% of all individuals diagnosed with the condition. Spasticity presents as high muscle tone, rigid musculature, and exaggerated reflexes. It results from overfiring of motor neurons due to an inappropriate balance of excitatory and inhibitory signals from the upper neurons integrated and distributed at the spinal column (Granata, Ikeda, & Abel, 2000; O'Sullivan et al., 1998). Spastic CP can be divided into diplegia (legs and some impairment in both arms), hemiplegia (either right or left side), and quadriplegia (arms and legs). Monoplegia and triplegia also exist but are far less prevalent in individuals with spastic CP.

Several other types of CP exist. Athetoid CP, characterized by slow and uncontrolled movement in the limbs, affects 10% to 20% of individuals diagnosed with CP and is caused by damage to the basal ganglia during pregnancy. Individuals with athetoid CP have mixed muscle tone, which results in involuntary writhing movements, often in the hands, feet, arms, and legs. In certain cases, speech is

affected as well. Another type of CP is ataxic CP, which is the least common form. It is diagnosed in 5% to 10% of cases. Ataxic CP is caused by brain damage to the cerebellum and is characterized by limb coordination and balance difficulties. Individuals may also have some form of tremor that is exacerbated when attempting voluntary movements such as reaching and grasping.

Over the past two decades, a group of researchers (Russell et al., 1989, 1993) developed the Gross Motor Function Measure (GMFM), a tool designed to assess motor function and how it changes over time (see table 9.3). Created by a group of Canadian physical therapists, the GMFM consists of 88 items grouped into five dimensions: (1) lying and rolling; (2) sitting; (3) crawling and kneeling; (4) standing; and (5) walking, running, and jumping (Russell et al., 1989). Items were selected to represent the motor functions typically performed by 5-year-olds without motor impairments and are scored on a 4-point Likert scale ranging from 0 (cannot do) to 3 (task completion). The researchers used the GMFM to evaluate 111 individuals with CP (ranging in age from less than 3 to 20 years but with

Table 9.3   Gross Motor Function Measure Used With Children With Cerebral Palsy

Four-point position	Standing	Walking
18. Creeps on stomach >6 ft	51. Pulls to standing at furniture	63. Cruises, two hands on rail, 15 steps each way
19. Maintains a four-point position (10 s)	52. Stands momentarily alone for 3 s	64. Walks, two hands held by one person, >10 steps
20. Achieves sitting from four-point position	53. Stands holding, lifts right foot (13 s)	65. Walks, one hand held, 10 steps
21. Attains four-point position	54. Stands holding, lifts left foot (13 s)	66. Walks alone 10 steps
22. Four-point extends right arm	55. Stands independently (20 s)	67. Walks, stops, turns 180°, returns
23. Four-point extends left arm	56. Stands independently on right leg (10 s)	68. Walks backward >10 steps
24. Crawls or hitches >6 ft (1.8 m)	57. Stands independently on left leg (10 s)	69. Walks carrying an object
25. Crawls reciprocally forward >6 ft (1.8 m)	58. Stands from small stool	70. Walks between parallel lines 8 in. (20 cm, >10 steps)
26. Crawls upstairs 14 steps	59. Stands from high kneel	71. Walks a straight line >10 steps
27. Crawls downstairs backward 14 steps	60. Lowers to floor	72. Steps over stick knee high, right foot leading
	61. Squats in play	73. Steps over stick knee high, left foot leading
	62. Picks up object from floor	74. Runs
		75. Kicks ball with right foot
		76. Kicks ball with left foot
		77. Jumps high 12 in. (284 cm)
		78. Jumps distance >12 in. (30 cm)
		79. Hops on right foot independently 10 times
		80. Hops on left foot independently 10 times

Scoring key: 0 = cannot initiate; 1 = initiates independently; 2 = partially completes; 3 = completes independently

Adapted, by permission, from D.J. Russell et al., 1989, "The gross motor function measure: A means to evaluate the effects of physical therapy," *Developmental Medicine and Child Neurology* 31: 341-352.

101 participants between 3 and 9 years old), 25 individuals with brain injury (between 3 and 20 years old), and 34 typically developing children (between 4 and 6 years old). All participants were assessed twice, with 4 to 6 months lapsing between assessments, by 1 of 14 experienced physical therapists. Correlations were found between change assessed by the GMFM and change assessed by parental and therapist function ratings as well as evaluations from therapists blinded to the assessment session. The researchers found that the GMFM was valid and sensitive to both improvement and deterioration in movement. This was a significant finding, for it provided physical therapists with a tool for measuring change in motor skill performance.

Because individuals with CP often differ dramatically in the level of CP involvement as well as in the degree to which motor control is compromised, it has been difficult to characterize a general developmental trajectory for this group as a whole. However, such information would aid practitioners in assessing and assisting this population. Rosenbaum, along with colleagues from several different institutions in Canada and the United States, undertook this challenge, examining 657 children with CP aged 1 to 13 years and following these children from 1996 to 2001. The investigators assessed motor function with the GMFM and severity of CP with the Gross Motor Function Classification System (GMFCS; see table 9.4). From the results, the investigators were able to create a series of average curves for each of the different classifications in the GMFCS. These curves provided a basis for what individuals at each of the different levels achieved in terms of their gross motor function. The authors cautioned that these curves do not address quality of movement (or as the authors described it, *motor control*). However, they do provide a basis for the developmental trajectory of individuals with various degrees of CP.

In CP, individual constraints such as spasticity cast a strong influence on emergent movement. For example, people with spastic CP often walk with a characteristic scissors gait, which is accompanied by a propensity for greater stiffness and muscle coactivation. For many years, interventions focused on

Table 9.4   Examples of Locomotion using the Gross Motor Classification System for Children with Cerebral Palsy

Level	Description
Level I	Individual can walk in any environmental context without restrictions or need for assistive devices.
Level II	Individual does not require assistive devices to walk, but walking is limited when there are objects in the environment (e.g., crowded sidewalks, uneven surfaces).
Level III	Individual requires assistive devices to walk, and locomotion is limited in environments outside or within the community.
Level IV	Individual has limits on self-mobility, although it is still possible indoors. He or she must use a power mobility device (e.g., motor-powered wheelchair) outdoors or in crowded environments.
Level V	Individual has difficulty with self-mobility, even when using power mobility devices.

Based on Rosenbaum et al. 2002.

modifying these patterns to make them resemble typical gait patterns. However, Holt and associates began to rethink this intervention strategy, which had met with limited success and focused on impairment over function (Holt, Obusek, & Fonseca, 1996; Holt, Fonseca, & LaFiandra, 2000; Fonseca, Holt, Fetters, & Saltzman, 2004)). Using a dynamic systems approach, these authors explicitly defined individual, environmental, and task constraints; examined their inter-relationship through dynamic laws; and used these laws to develop better inter-ventions (Holt, Fonseca, & LaFiandra, 2000). They began by modeling stiffness in human locomotion using a mass–spring pendulum system—an escapement driven, damped hybrid pendulum and spring model—in an attempt to capture the "global spring-like behavior of the musculoskeletal system without identi-fying the specific structures that produce those forces" (Holt et al., 2000; see figure 9.1). After laying out a strategy based on understanding the allocation of dynamic resources for walking in individuals with spastic CP, the authors tested their model on five children with mild spastic hemiplegic CP and five typically developing controls matched in age, gender, height, and weight. Using their model, the researchers predicted that the children with CP would have higher global stiffness on the affected side and they made other predictions related to oscillation characteristics as well. Participants walked at their preferred frequency around a track and then walked for an additional four trials at ±10% and ±20% of their preferred frequency, during which time kinematics and global stiffness were calculated.

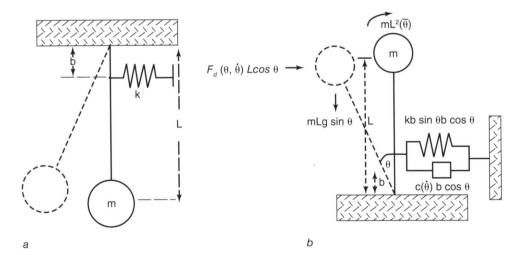

a   b

Figure 9.1   Models of (a) regular pendulum and spring and (b) inverted, (F) escapement-driven, (c) damped, (mL) pendulum, and (k) spring. A linearized version of (b) was used in the Holt, Fonseca, & LaFiandra (2000) experiment to derive estimates of the stiffness value of the spring from the natural frequency of the system.

As predicted, the children with CP differed in their kinematic variables and demonstrated greater stiffness as well as a greater ratio of stiffness to gravitation (elastic to gravitational restoring torque) in their affected limb. They also showed a greater ratio of stiffness to gravitation when compared with their typically developing counterparts. These results validated the use of the mass–spring model in the task of walking. More importantly, Holt et al. (2000) provided a theory-based explanation of the gait patterns seen in children with spastic hemiplegic CP that used individual constraints and indicated the functional significance of the walk:

> In clinical research in CP it is often claimed that a plantar-flexed foot is the direct result of the neurological insult. . . . Alternatively, a plantar flexed foot on ground contact is an effective biomechanical adaptation because it provides a mechanism for loading the body mass in a spring-like fashion, and thereby improves the ability to load the stiff Achilles/triceps surae spring. The plantar-flexed foot may not be a direct result of the insult but an adaptation that facilitates use of the available dynamic resources. (p. 397)

Thus the authors suggested that the plantar flexion exhibited by children with CP during walking is a *functional* adaptation—it is a resultant movement pattern emerging from the interacting constraints within a context, and it allows for the successful completion of the task of locomotion. These results were confirmed in additional research that showed that gait patterns of children with CP emerged from the dynamic interaction of the resources available to them (Fonseca, Holt, Fetters, & Saltzman, 2004).

In sum, individuals with CP can differ vastly in their motor development depending on the type of CP (spastic, ataxic, athetoid), the number and location of limbs impaired (diplegia, hemiplegia, quadriplegia), and the degree of impairment (levels I through V on the GMFCS). Over time, movement emerges based on the resources available to individuals. Because CP is nonprogressive, motor impairment does not deteriorate over time, and it may improve with therapy, surgery, or other treatments.

Atypical Development From Multiple or Unknown Etiologies

The third general source of atypical motor development comes from a unique combination of genetics and environment, the exact weighting of which may be unknown. That is, a fetus may be genetically predisposed to a condition, which may manifest itself due to exposure to an environmental agent at a certain point during pregnancy. There is a unique interweaving between environment and individual that results in atypical development; because of this, the root cause cannot be traced to one source. Such atypical development may frustrate parents and practitioners, who wish to understand the underlying cause of the disease.

Autism Spectrum Disorders

Autism spectrum disorders (ASD), a group of developmental disorders associated with social, behavioral, and communication issues, have frequently made the news over the past decade owing to the dramatic increase in their rate of occurrence within the United States. For example, in 2007, the Centers for Disease Control and Prevention (CDC) estimated that approximately 1 in 150 children had ASD or a closely related pervasive developmental disorder (PDD). The CDC revised this statistic to an astonishing 1 in 110 children in 2009 (CDC, 2009). This was a substantially higher rate than had been recorded previously. Autism ranks as the sixth most common category for which children receive special services, and approximately 1% of the population will eventually be diagnosed with the disorder. Without a doubt, ASD have become a concern to parents and practitioners around the country because of their growing prevalence in children.

Individuals with ASD can exhibit a broad range of symptoms, but those most generally associated with ASD are difficulties in social situations and interactions (e.g., avoiding interpersonal contact), communication issues (e.g., delayed language acquisition or lack of speech), and stereotypical or repetitive movements (e.g., hand flapping or body rocking; World Health Organization, 2007). Other symptoms may include sensory system difficulties (either over- or underloading or integration issues), obsessive interests, lack of empathy, and echolalia (repeating others' words or phrases over and over). In addition to autism, PDDs include Asperger's syndrome (AS), Rett syndrome (RS), pervasive developmental disorder not otherwise specified (PDD-NOS), and disintegrative disorder. Children as young as 2 years can be reliably diagnosed with ASD; however, children are often not diagnosed until after the age of 3, primarily because the diagnostic criteria involve delayed language acquisition and impaired social interaction (Pope, Lynch, Liu, & Getchell, 2010).

Causes of Autism Spectrum Disorders

As neurodevelopmental disorders, ASD occur when typical brain and nervous system development is somehow disrupted. Perhaps the most mysterious and frustrating issue surrounding ASD is the cause. To date, no one has isolated a cause of the disorders, although some evidence suggests that genetic predispositions exist. In a small percentage of individuals, genetic abnormalities such as fragile X syndrome and chromosome 15 duplications can be identified. At the same time, environmental agents are likely to play a role in ASD. Unlike CP, however, ASD have no clear environmental origin (e.g., they are not caused by brain injury), despite some contention that vaccination precedes the onset of ASD. The issue of vaccination has been controversial since a research article published in *Lancet* in 1998 describing a relationship between the two (Wakefield et al., 1998). However, the editors of *Lancet* retracted the article early in 2010, citing improper and unethical data collection techniques. Thus at present there is no empirical evidence that vaccination causes ASD. There may be some critical

time frame during gestation in which some teratogen, such as thalidomide, may increase the risk of developing ASD; at the same time, it appears that children develop ASD after birth (CDC, 2009). With no clear cause of these disorders, as well as vast individual differences in how the disorders present, breakthroughs in prevention and treatment have been slow.

Motor Development Differences in Children With Autism Spectrum Disorders

One of the great difficulties facing practitioners and researchers working with individuals with ASD is the degree to which variability supersedes universality in this population (Pope et al., 2010). That is, two individuals with the same diagnosis of ASD will act and react very differently from each other. These individual differences lead to significant challenges for researchers trying to identify and quantify motor development in this population. For example, individuals with ASD may respond differently to a controlled experimental design due to different sensitivity to sensory stimuli or a lack of understanding of the described procedures. Furthermore, each individual responds differently to different interventions. All in all, typical developmental trajectories are all but impossible to determine. However, researchers have identified some general characteristics related to movement and motor development that suggest that individuals with ASD move differently from their typically developing counterparts (Pope et al., 2010). The importance of determining motor differences, particularly in younger children, cannot be underscored enough: If early developing motor differences exist, then assessment of these deficits may aid in identifying children at risk for ASD at a younger age than is currently possible.

Primarily through retrospective video analysis, researchers have identified early motor differences in children with ASD. Kanner (1943), who first identified ASD, noted that the infants exhibited hypotonia, or low muscle tone (similar to infants with DS). Other researchers have also observed hypotonia (Adrien et al., 1993; Ming, Brimacombe, & Wagner, 2007). For example, Ming et al. (2007) reviewed the clinical records of 154 children diagnosed with ASD in an attempt to determine the types and prevalence of motor impairments in this population, particularly hypotonia, delayed motor milestones, coordination issues, and toe walking. Children ranged in age from 2 to 18 years, with a mean age of 6 years. Reflecting the gender differences within the ASD population, there were 126 males and 28 females within the study. All of the children were on the autism spectrum: 74 were diagnosed with autism, 70 with PDD-NOS, and 10 with AS. The researchers determined that 51% of the group demonstrated hypotonia as infants; the prevalence of hypotonia decreased over time to 38% in the age range of 7 to 18 years. Not all retrospective studies have indicated that infants with autism have hypotonia. Saint-Georges et al. (2010) performed an exhaustive research review using retrospective video analysis and determined that across the 41 studies reviewed, hypotonia was not a consistent finding.

Given that at least a percentage of children with ASD exhibit hypotonia, subsequent issues with the acquisition of motor milestones may exist (as in

children with DS). Low muscle tone affects infants' ability to raise the head while in the prone position, which affects the ability to sit supported, and so on. In fact, another consistent finding among individuals with ASD is a delay in achieving motor milestones and fundamental motor skills as young children. Acknowledging the limitations of looking back at records after diagnosis, Landa and Garrett-Mayer (2006) performed a 2-year longitudinal prospective study in which they followed a group of 84 infants who were either high ($n = 60$) or low ($n = 27$) risk for ASD.

Infants were tested at 6, 14, and 24 months using the Mullen Scales of Early Learning (MSEL), a standardized developmental test for children aged 0 to 69 months. The MSEL consists of five subscales: gross motor, fine motor, visual reception, receptive language, and expressive language. At 2 years, all children were given the Autism Diagnostic Observation Schedule (ADOS), which is a semistructured, play-based interview that provides systematic probes for symptoms of autism in social interaction, communication, play, and repetitive behaviors. Of the 60 children deemed at risk, 21 met the ADOS algorithm criteria for ASD as well as received a clinical diagnosis of ASD; 2 children from the low-risk group met the criteria and were included in the high-risk group. Early on, no statistical differences existed between groups. However, by 24 months, the high-risk group showed delays in both gross and fine motor skills, and group members were significantly different from the typically developing group in all domains.

In related research, a group of investigators assessed motor development in children younger than 3 years of age (Provost, Lopez, & Heimerl, 2007). In this study, 19 children with ASD, ranging in age from 21 to 41 months, were examined with the Bayley Scales of Infant Development II (BSID II; Bayley, 1993) and the Peabody Developmental Motor Scales, Second Edition (PDMS-2; Folio & Fewell, 2000). The researchers determined that 84% of the children were significantly delayed on the BSID II and PDMS-2. In a similar study, Ozonoff et al. (2008) examined the early movement behavior of children later identified as ASD and reported a delay in the appearance of motor milestones, including lying in prone and supine position, rolling, sitting, crawling, and walking, with the most significant delay occurring in walking onset. Therefore, it appears that delays in motor milestones exist in many of the children diagnosed with ASD.

Tips for Novice Investigators

One of the characteristics of ASD is a hypersensitivity to stimuli. In order to accommodate for this within the laboratory setting, a researcher should take care to remove or reduce as much extraneous stimuli as possible. This includes visual (such as flickering computer monitors), auditory (conversations among individuals), but also tactile (Velcro straps) and olfactory (perfumes, lotions, and so on that have a heavy smell) stimuli.

Acknowledging that delays appear to exist in the ASD population, Ozonoff et al. followed strong inference (see chapter 4) and asked the next logical question: Can motor delays differentiate children with autism from children who have more general developmental delays? If motor delays could be used for differentiation, then practitioners could use motor delays to identify infants at risk for ASD. In the resulting study, Ozonoff et al. (2008) placed 103 children between 24 and 60 months of age in 1 of 3 groups: children with ASD, children with developmental delays (DD), or children with typical development (TD). Home videotapes of the participants were analyzed and coded with the Infant Motor Maturity and Atypicality Coding Scales (IMMACS), which rate six motor milestones (lying in prone and supine position, roll, sit, crawl, walk) as well as protective skills (e.g., righting the body after losing balance). What Ozonoff et al. (2008) found, in contrast to earlier reports and speculation, is that the only group that differed in terms of number of movement abnormalities and protective skills was the DD group; the ASD and TD groups were not significantly different. The ASD and DD groups both showed motor delays, but they were not significantly different from each other. Therefore, the notion that motor delays can be used to identify children at risk for ASD was not supported in this research. Obviously, a prospective study examining both qualitative and quantitative variables is necessary as a next step to confirm this finding.

Are individuals with ASD merely delayed in motor skill acquisition, or do they differ in the ways in which they move? Several research studies (see table 9.5) have found at least one consistent difference between children with ASD and children without ASD, and that is their walking patterns. Over three decades ago, researchers found that children with ASD demonstrate abnormal limb movements, shortened steps, and persistent toe walking (Damasio & Maurer, 1978; Vilensky, Damasio, & Maurer, 1981). More recently, Ming et al. (2007), in their retrospective study, determined that nearly 20% of children with ASD walked on their toes rather than on their entire foot. Esposito and Venturi (2008) used retrospective video analysis as well as an observational scale to examine 42 children with ASD who had been walking at least 6 months and also found differences in early walking patterns. Vernazza-Martin et al. (2005) found significant differences in gait when comparing 15 children aged 4 to 6 years with and without ASD, as did Woodward (2001) in a study of children with ASD aged 3 and 10 years. One consistent finding is that the gait cycle is slower and less consistent in children with ASD.

Dewey, Cantell, and Crawford (2007) compared the performance of children with different disabilities on the Bruininks-Oseretsky Test of Motor Proficiency-Short Form. Participants included 49 children with ASD, 46 children with developmental coordination disorder (DCD) and attention-deficit/hyperactivity disorder (ADHD), 38 children with DCD, 27 children with ADHD, and 78 children with typical development. The results indicated that although all the atypical groups displayed significant impairment of motor skills, children with ASD were significantly more impaired compared with their cohorts with specific motor skill deficits. They were also the only group to show impairment on gestural skills. Several researchers have found deficiencies in fine motor skills

Table 9.5 Current Research on Gait Differences in Children With Autism Spectrum Disorders

Study citation	Motor skill observed	Noteworthy findings	Comparative comments
Ming, Brimacombe, & Wagner (2007)	Walking	20% of children with ASD toe walked (retrospective).	Mixed methods are often used, but regardless of experimental design, children with ASD tend to walk differently from and less consistently than their neurotypical peers.
Esposito & Venturi (2008)	Walking	Toddlers with ASD who had been walking at least 6 mo showed differences from typically developing gait.	
Vernazza-Martin et al. (2005)	Walking	Children aged 4-6 y with and without ASD differed in gait patterns.	
Woodward (2001)	Walking	Children aged 3-10 y with and without ASD differed in gait patterns.	

in children with ASD. These range from delays in manual dexterity (Miyahara et al., 1997) and graphomotor skills (Mayes & Calhoun, 2003) during early and middle childhood to motor control issues in prehension (Mari, Castiello, Marks, Marraffa, & Prior, 2003). Such fine motor skill deficits influence handwriting as well as many functional activities involving the hands and arms. Across these studies, it appears that individuals with autism do move differently when compared with their typically developing counterparts and that deficits range from fine to gross motor skills.

In sum, although motor deficits are not listed as part of the *DSM-V* diagnostic criteria for ASD, individuals with these disorders tend to exhibit motor skill deficiencies as well as differences in motor development. Infants with ASD may exhibit hypotonia (although this finding is not as robust as it is in infants with DS). In addition, delays may exist in the acquisition of motor milestones and fundamental motor skills. Differences in skills such as gait and manual dexterity persist into childhood.

Developmental Coordination Disorder

Another disorder with an unknown etiology that has garnered considerable empirical attention as of late is DCD (Wilson & Larkin, 2008). DCD, also known as *developmental dyspraxia*, is characterized by extreme lack of motor coordination and by other movement deficits in the absence of neurological defects. DCD has been calculated to affect as much as 6% of the elementary school population (American Psychiatric Association, 1994; Barnhart, Davenport, Epps, & Nordquist, 2003; Barnett, Kooistra, & Henderson, 1998). Although the disorder was described as early as 1937, it took until 1994 for a group of 43 experts in various movement disorder fields to come to a consensus on a name and description for DCD in order to facilitate both research and diagnosis (see the sidebar for the *DSM-V* description of DCD). Individuals characterized as having DCD

fall into the 0 to 10th percentile of performance on the Movement Assessment Battery for Children (M-ABC), a standardized motor skills test used to assess motor proficiency in children with disabilities (Geuze, Jongmans, Schoemaker, & Smits-Engelsman, 2001; Henderson & Sugden, 1992; Miyahara & Möbs, 1995). Because DCD is categorized as a learning disability, it also may influence a child's ability to perform academically. Motor difficulties can range from gross to fine motor to balance skills and can include motor planning deficits and visual or spatial difficulties (Cermak & Larkin, 2002; de Castelnau, Albaret, Chaix, & Zanone, 2007; Kaplan, Wilson, Dewey, & Crawford, 1998; Przysucha & Taylor, 2004; Whitall et al., 2006). Table 9.6 provides examples of functional motor issues that children with DCD may have.

DSM-5 Diagnostic Criteria for Individuals With DCD

A. Motor performance that is substantially below expected levels, given the person's chronologic age and previous opportunities for skill acquisition. The poor motor performance may manifest as coordination problems, poor balance, clumsiness, dropping or bumping into things; marked delays in achieving developmental motor milestones (e.g., walking, crawling, sitting) or in the acquisition of basic motor skills (e.g., catching, throwing, kicking, running, jumping, hopping, cutting, coloring, printing, writing).

B. The disturbance in Criterion A, without accommodations, significantly interferes with activities of daily living or academic achievement.

C. The disturbance is not due to a general medical condition (e.g., cerebral palsy, hemiplegia, or muscular dystrophy).

(APA, 2011)

Causes of Developmental Coordination Disorder

The nature and mechanisms underlying the coordination deficits of children with DCD are poorly understood, despite several decades of study. There is much speculation—but no clear answer—regarding the cause (or causes) of DCD. In fact, when a child is diagnosed with DCD, practitioners must carefully rule out other conditions, such as intellectual disabilities, mild CP, muscular dystrophies, and seizure disorders, as well as neuropathologies such as spasticity, tremors, or pronounced hypotonia (Polatajko & Cantin, 2005). As with ASD, there appears to be a complex interplay between genetic predisposition and environmental or experiential factors at the root of DCD. Recently, in a study designed to look at genetic and environmental components of ADHD and DCD, Martin, Piek, and Hay (2006) examined 1,285 Australian twin

Table 9.6 Examples of Motor Difficulties in Children With Developmental Coordination Disorder

At home	At school	At play
Dressing, putting on socks, fastening fasteners, zipping a coat, putting on shoes or boots, tying shoelaces Using utensils Bathing, showering, washing hair	Printing and handwriting (slow or messy) Using scissors, glue Drawing (immature drawings) Grasping pencil Performing in physical education Falling off chair in class, bumping into things	Running (awkward gait) Balancing Climbing onto play structures Riding a bicycle Skating, in-line skating Skipping Playing sports Throwing, catching, kicking balls

Adapted, by permission, from S.E. Henderson and D. Sugden, 1992, *Movement assessment battery for children* (London: The Psychological Corporation).

pairs between 5 and 16 years of age. The researchers found that for DCD there was a substantial genetic component as well as a frequent family environmental component (this includes shared peri- and postnatal experiences). Several hypotheses exist on the mechanism of DCD, including neurological (Sigmundsson, Ingvaldsen, & Whiting, 1997; Wilson, Maruff, Ives, & Currie, 2001) or cerebellar (Cantin, Polatajko, Thach, & Jaglal, 2007) dysfunction. In a recent review of DCD and coexisting conditions, Zwicker, Missiuna, and Boyd (2009) found that the preponderance of evidence pointed to involvement of the cerebellum and associated networks, potentially coming from premature birth. At the same time, these authors acknowledged that other structures such as the basal ganglia, parietal lobe, and corpus callosum may have influenced development, which in turn may explain the heterogeneity of the condition. Frequently, other conditions coexist with DCD, including learning disabilities such as dyslexia, ADHD, and sensory integration issues.

Part of the difficulty in understanding DCD is that there is no one clear test of diagnostic criteria. Diagnostic criteria are rather broad: The American Psychiatric Association (2011) defines these as "motor performance that is substantially below expected levels, given the person's chronologic age and previous opportunities for skill acquisition" (see sidebar on page 232). Yet, no standardized way in which to measure differences in motor performance has emerged, despite nearly 30 years of study. Geuze et al. (2001) explored this issue by conducting a meta-analysis of 176 DCD studies performed from 1965 to 1999 (the majority of which were published after 1980). They found that although most studies used an inclusion criterion that was related to some measure of motor functioning, there was no consensus on which standardized test to use; while 50% of the studies used the M-ABC (Henderson & Sugden, 1992), several other tests were also used. In addition, no standard cutoff score existed. Identification of DCD, therefore, is somewhat of a moving target and is difficult to quantify.

Motor Development Differences in Developmental Coordination Disorder

One difficulty in describing motor development differences as a function of DCD is that in the past DCD has fallen under the auspices of *learning disability*, which means it was not often identified in children until a disparity between intellectual ability and academic performance was observed (Miyahara & Möbs, 1995). Therefore, there is not a lot of information on motor deficits in infancy and early childhood; in general, studies have involved children aged 4 or older, since the diagnostic term *DCD* is not used until age 6. Many of the deficits are therefore functionally age dependent and cannot be identified in young children. That is, difficulties with handwriting or dressing do not exist in the absence of handwriting or dressing. Children younger than age 6 may be described as at risk for DCD if they exhibit delays in the acquisition of motor milestones, difficulties with gross or fine motor skills, and incoordination (such as bumping into objects, difficulty grasping, and tripping). During early childhood, people at risk for DCD often experience moderate hypotonia, which (unlike hypotonia in ASD or DS) generally persists throughout infancy and childhood and results in difficulties with postural control and balance (Barnhart, Davenport, Epps, & Nordquist, 2003; Geuze, 2003, 2005; Hadders-Algra, 2003). Remember that *pronounced* hypotonia actually contraindicates DCD.

Individuals classified as having DCD generally exhibit deficits in three categories: postural control, motor learning, and sensorimotor coordination (Gueze, 2005). Often, individuals with DCD respond with inappropriate postural responses, and balance and postural control remain lifelong issues.

In terms of motor skills, children with DCD demonstrate a variety of coordination deficits that interfere with activities of daily living. Particular attention has been paid to difficulties with fine motor coordination, as these are more clearly related to academic difficulties. Common deficits include difficulty with handwriting or drawing as well as functional problems with manual dexterity (gripping objects, buttoning clothing, zipping); these may be due, in part, to issues with motor planning (Barnhart et al., 2003; Smits-Engelsman, Niemeijer, & van Galen, 2001; Wilson et al., 2001). Additionally, children with DCD often have difficulty with gross motor skills. Children with DCD may have awkward walking and running patterns and have difficulty throwing and catching (Clark, Getchell, Smiley-Oyen, & Whitall, 2005; Wilson & McKenzie, 1998). These differences, although not impervious to intervention, tend to persist even in the face of extensive practice.

One fundamental motor skill that has received empirical attention is two-hand catching. Researchers have examined catching in part because the M-ABC includes ball catching as an item on the Ball Skills subtest; however, administrators of this test evaluate number of catches only and do not look at movement form. Soon after DCD was defined in the *DSM-IV*, researchers realized that children with DCD have difficulty catching; the goal became to understand *how* catching differs within this population. Early research by Lefebvre and Reid (1998) examined the perceptual skill needed for catching. The authors compared

40 children with DCD with 46 children without DCD (all between 5 and 7 years of age) on an interception task in which the children made spatial and temporal judgments on ball trajectories. The results suggested that children with DCD may have perceptual issues that affect catching. In 2004, Van Waelvelde et al. attempted to gain more clarity on how movement form differs for catching in children with DCD. Their study included 43 children with DCD between the ages of 7.5 and 9.5 years who were age- and gender-matched to a group of typically developing children. Since one of the primary interests of the researchers was to determine if children with DCD are delayed or different, they added a unique control group: They gender matched to a group of typically developing children who were at least 1 year younger than the DCD group but who scored similarly on a ball catching test. The authors reasoned that if the DCD group was delayed, members of this group would catch similarly to the children in the younger group. The participants were tested on the M-ABC, the Test of Gross Motor Development (TGMD; Ulrich, 2000), and a long ball catching test. Test scores as well as a ratio of grasping errors on the long ball test were compared. Results showed that the DCD group significantly differed from the age-matched group on all measures. When compared with the younger group, the DCD group had the same number of caught balls (scored the same value on the M-ABC) but showed significantly lower scores on the TGMD and demonstrated more grasping errors. The researchers concluded that children with DCD not only are developmentally delayed but also move differently.

In an attempt to better understand movement differences in two-hand catching as well as in interlimb coupling in this population, researchers from the University of Leeds performed a pair of studies (see table 9.7) using both quantitative and qualitative methods (Astill & Utley, 2006; Utley & Astill, 2007). In the first study, the authors used three-dimensional kinematic analyses to examine two-hand catching in 16 children with and without DCD. They determined that the children without DCD not only caught significantly more balls but also had higher levels of interlimb coupling, which suggests a reduction in the degrees

Table 9.7   Strong Inference in Studying Two-Hand Catching

Study citation	Key concept	Noteworthy findings	Comparative comments
Roberton & Halverson (1984)	Developmental sequences exist for two-hand catching in typically developing children.	Hypothesis of developmental sequences for two-hand catching	This series of studies shows the importance of understanding sequential developmental change. The studies flow from hypothesis through validation of developmental sequences in typically developing children and subsequent comparison to children with DCD.
Strohmeyer, Schauber-George, & Williams (1991)	Developmental sequences exist for two-hand catching in typically developing children.	Prelongitudinal screening of two-hand catching sequence	
Astill & Utley (2006)	Children with DCD catch differently compared with typically developing children.	Less variability, more inflexibility with DCD	
Utley & Astill (2007)	Developmental sequences can be validated and children with and without DCD compared.	Lower developmental levels in arms; lower overall developmental profile	

of freedom. In the children with DCD, this reduction made their catching *too* inflexible, in that they could not make necessary adjustments to variability in catching conditions (see chapter 3 for more detail on degrees of freedom).

Utley and Astill (2007) followed this research with an investigation using the catch developmental sequence in which they measured developmental levels of the catch. Previous research provided the hypothesized developmental sequences (Roberton & Halverson, 1984) as well as prelongitudinal screening of the sequences (Strohmeyer, Williams, & Schauber-George, 1991); however, the resultant levels were not validated. Therefore, Utley and Astill first performed a prelongitudinal screening using modified components (Haywood & Getchell, 2005), which consisted of analyzing videotapes of 360 catching trials from 36 participants aged 7 to 10 years and classifying participants in terms of their arm, leg, and body actions. These developmental sequences were evaluated according to across-trials and cross-sectional screening criteria and were supported, although longitudinal study is necessary to confirm their validity (see chapter 4 for a more complete description of the process of validating developmental sequences).

After screening the two-hand catching developmental sequences, Utley and Astill (2007) set out to determine if children with and without DCD differed on these sequences. The researchers recruited an additional 20 participants between 7 and 8 years of age (10 with DCD and 10 age-matched controls). Each child performed 30 catching trials; from these 600 videotaped trials, the researchers classified arm, hand, and body components. Modal sequence levels were calculated, as were developmental profiles, which were analyzed using chi-square statistics. Results showed that compared with children without DCD, children with DCD performed at a statistically lower developmental level in the arm and body actions. Furthermore, the children with DCD were significantly lower and more inconsistent in their developmental profiles. Interpreting these results from a constraints perspective, the authors suggested that the differing individual constraints in DCD affect catching by providing shallow attractor states (more typically associated with younger children) that in turn account for instability in profiles.

The research on two-hand catching in DCD provides a good example of researchers using strong inference to direct their studies by following up on previous research to get closer to the answer of both how and why differences exist. Using this information along with other research paradigms, researchers discovered that part of the underlying difficulty relates to sensory–motor or per-ception–action coupling (described in detail in chapter 2), which is the mapping of sensory information to movement (Ameratunga, Johnston, & Burns, 2004; Mackenzie et al., 2008; Piek & Dyck, 2004; Whitall et al., 2006; Zoia, Pelamatti, Cuttini, Casotto, & Scabar, 2002; Zoia, Castiello, Blason, & Scabar, 2005). In general, these studies indicated that children with DCD process information differently, and this leads to motor difficulties, particularly increased variability in performance.

In sum, individuals with DCD have a wide variety of motor deficits that exist early in life and persist throughout development. These deficits affect motor coordination as well as balance and postural control. They may seriously impede

function in fine motor skills, such as handwriting and grasping objects. They also affect gross motor function, such as throwing and catching, which makes sport participation difficult for individuals with DCD.

COMBINING THEORY AND PRACTICE

For practitioners working with individuals with disabilities—individuals who have developed atypically—Newell's notion of constraints offers a novel way to approach movement. When we think about disabilities, it is easy to slip into the habit of comparing people with atypical development with people with typical development, focusing on how they differ and what they cannot do. You may recognize this as using an error model, as discussed in chapter 4. This type of error model treats disability and differences as characteristics that hold individuals back from moving normally. Intervention based on this model focuses on getting individuals with disabilities to mirror typical movement as closely as possible. In this chapter, we would like to present an alternative developmental model based on Newell's constraints. Recall that the difference between an error model and a developmental model is that the developmental model requires observing where individuals are now, where they have been, and where they are going. Intervention focuses on moving individuals to a higher developmental level, rather than trying to force people into the perfect, most advanced movement pattern. To consider disabilities as constraints, we must first look carefully at the disability and see how it affects movement within the human system. Holt et al. (2000) took this approach in their research on CP, in which they examined walking in CP as dynamically distinct from typical walking. Ulrich et al. used this strategy as well, identifying stiffness as a measure of interest in DS.

After identifying individual constraints that affect movement, we must look at how individuals developed early in childhood so we can have a better understanding of the source of the movement pattern. In the case of DS, for example, hypotonia and hypermobility in infancy have a strong effect on the attainment of motor milestones, so that fundamental movement patterns such as walking can be substantially delayed. Understanding early movement helped researchers determine that people with ASD or DCD likely move differently from their typically developing peers (as opposed to being delayed in their motor development). The implications for intervention are quite important: Practitioners should not expect children with motor differences to perform the same way as typically developing individuals. Practitioners using an error model stand to become extremely frustrated as their interventions fail over time.

Finally, practitioners need to understand what the next developmental step is for each individual: How should the movement patterns change? Using the constraints model, the practitioner must consider how to change either individual constraints (with strengthening, stretching, and so on) or task or environmental constraints to make movement more advanced. The resultant movement form may not resemble that of typically developing individuals. However, it will combine the individual, environment, and task to allow for more efficient movement patterns to emerge.

SUMMARY

Typical motor development shows a measure of universality, which includes species-specific progression through a common set of motor milestones. At the same time, humans have many individual differences, which account for the variability in the expression of motor behavior we see every day. Experience influences both universality and individuality. Some behaviors require specific experiences that are common among a species (experience expectant), whereas other behaviors emerge from unique experiences of the individual (experience dependent). Atypical development can result from differences in these two types of experience, from genetic differences or disorders, or from an interaction of genetic predisposition with specific experience.

Within this chapter, we discussed various types of atypical motor development. Individuals with DS have a genetic disorder that influences physical development. They have shorter limbs, hypotonia, lax joints, and often heart defects, and they experience delays in the achievement of motor milestones and fundamental motor skills. Conversely, CP results when a brain lesion occurs during fetal development or just before birth. There are various types of CP, such as spastic, athetoid, and ataxic, and individuals with CP may show muscle spasticity, rigidity, and other movement difficulties. Although etiologies for both ASD and DCD are not clear, it appears that in these cases genetic predisposition couples with certain environmental stimuli. Infants with ASD may experience hypotonia, and children with ASD may encounter difficulties with gross and fine motor skills. Individuals with DCD experience significant difficulty with motor coordination; these difficulties affect both gross and fine motor functional ability.

CHAPTER 10

Motor Development Interventions

From the start, many of the people who studied motor development wanted to apply their findings to parenting, therapy, and education. Researchers wanted to understand what factors affect motor development in a positive way by providing the most effective, developmentally appropriate instructional or therapeutic techniques to both typically developing individuals and individuals with special needs, such as people with disabilities or children at risk of developing disabilities in the future. We use the term *intervention* to describe programs designed to improve motor development. By definition, intervention means "to interfere with the outcome of course of a condition or process". We provide an intervention in motor development in an attempt to modify the rate of change in motor skill acquisition and performance. If we apply an intervention to typically developing individuals, we do so with the purpose of improving qualitative or quantitative measures of performance—preferably both—above and beyond any improvement that might occur without the intervention. Showing an improvement in quantitative measures such as velocity or distance is not sufficient to indicate developmental change; there should be some indication of a change in movement form.

The same holds true for interventions for populations with special needs. What is of critical importance is establishing empirically that the intervention actually works: Within the population under study, those receiving an intervention should improve more than those not receiving the intervention. Such research establishes the validity of an intervention technique. With this in mind, we will review the literature on motor development interventions in both typically and atypically developing populations.

INTERVENTIONS IN TYPICALLY DEVELOPING POPULATIONS

Given the importance of motor skill development to overall levels of physical activity, it is somewhat surprising that there are few empirical studies of motor skill interventions for typically developing individuals. Recall our discussion

of strong inference in chapter 4. To follow a logical tree of empirical questions and answers, we need to establish what effect a particular intervention has in a typically developing population before applying the intervention to an atypical population. We want to establish empirically that we have changed the developmental course of a motor skill or group of skills. However, in the literature on motor development intervention, it is rare to find reports of such studies. Several notable exceptions exist.

Tips for Novice Investigators

Intervention studies, whether conducted in typical or atypical populations, are the next step in developmental research after determining what typical is. These studies allow researchers to test the efficacy of teaching methods in a controlled environment. When planning intervention studies, always remember to give the intervention enough time to be effective.

Overarm Throwing

A set of studies in the 1970s examined the effects of a motor skill intervention on overarm throwing in children. In the preliminary study, Halverson, Roberton, Safrit, and Roberts (1977) wanted to determine the influence of an instructional program focused on progressing the developmental level of the throw. They hypothesized that the instructional program could transition children to a more advanced movement pattern. The authors provided a group of 15 kindergartners with 120 minutes of throwing instruction in 12 physical education classes spread over 8 weeks. The throwing instruction was part of an overall motor skills physical education program. The researchers provided the intervention group with developmentally appropriate force goals for throwing and gave verbal cues that tapped into more advanced developmental actions, such as trunk rotation, foot and hand opposition, and arm lag (see chapter 7 for a review of the developmental sequence for forceful overarm throwing). To examine the effects of the intervention, they compared this group to a group of age-matched children who received the motor skills program but no instruction in throwing. In addition, the researchers examined an additional control group comprising children who did not receive the motor skills program or throwing instruction. They found that instruction did not significantly improve the throwing velocity of the intervention group compared with the two groups of age-matched controls.

What remained was to determine if the intervention influenced motor development and advanced movement form. Therefore, in the follow-up analysis, Halverson and Roberton (1979) examined films from pre- and postintervention assessments and determined the developmental levels of the trunk, leg, and arm (humerus, elbow, forearm) components of the throw. The researchers analyzed 10 trials per participant for both pre- and postintervention and compared modal values of developmental level to see if participants had progressed, regressed, or

stayed the same. Percentages of participants who progressed were compared using chi-square analysis. In three of the actions compared (forearm, trunk, step), the intervention group had a significantly higher number of children who improved compared with the other groups (see table 10.1). Furthermore, the intervention group significantly improved over both control groups in range of spinal rotation and over the second control group in range of pelvic rotation. Humerus and elbow levels did not differ among groups. Therefore, the results of this analysis clearly indicated that children qualitatively improved their throwing proficiency as a result of intervention. When looking across the two studies, we can see what seems to be a paradoxical finding: Movement process improved when movement product did not. This finding suggests that researchers and practitioners cannot rely on quantitative measures to indicate developmental improvement; rather, researchers and practitioners need to examine both to understand the effects of their intervention.

Table 10.1 Percentage of Children Showing Developmental Progress Between Pre- and Posttests

Group	Humerus	Elbow	Forearm lag	Trunk action	Range of pelvic rotation	Range of spinal rotation	Stepping action
Experimental (n = 22)	9	13	36*	27*	32**	54*	55*
Control 1 (n = 23)	0	13	4	4	9	13	13
Control 2 (n = 24)	13	13	0	4	4	4	21

*Significantly different from both control groups at .05.

**Significantly different from control group 2 at .05.

Adapted, by permission, from Halverson and Roberton 1979, The effects of instruction on overhand throwing development in children. In *Psychology of motor behavior and sport*, edited by G. Roberts and K. Newell (Champaign, IL: Human Kinetics), 258-269.

General Motor Skills

There are several other studies indicating that motor skill interventions improve motor proficiency in children (van der Mars & Butterfield, 1988; Forweather et al., 2008; Graf et al., 2005; Ignico, 1991). Unfortunately, for many of these studies, motor development is neither clearly defined nor measured qualitatively. This does not invalidate these studies; however, the absence (or, for that matter, presence) of quantitative change does not prove that developmental change did or did not occur. For example, Graf et al. (2005) examined the influence of a physical activity and motor proficiency intervention on 651 children (460 intervention, 191 control) ranging between 5 and 9 years of age. The purpose of the intervention was to increase energy expenditure and improve fundamental motor skills, particularly coordination and endurance. Daily lessons lasting at least 5 minutes included combinations of 11 exercises on coordination, 7 exercises for posture and balance, 16 relaxation techniques, 8 exercises performed to rhythm and music, 10 exercises using creative movement, 8 games relating to group participation, and 8 exercises for back training. We will focus on the findings regarding coordination performance. The sole measure of coordination

was a score on a lateral jumping test in which participants jumped with two feet over a small line for a duration of 15 seconds. Although the test and control groups proved to be significantly different in terms of the researchers' definition of coordination—a quantitative score—we have no indication whether the children changed their movement form as a result of the intervention.

Several studies have used indicators of developmental change (see table 10.2). For example, van der Mars and Butterfield (1988) compared the effect of a general motor skills intervention on young children between 3 and 6 years of age. The intervention group consisted of 15 children who received a performance-based curriculum that allowed for instruction on an individual basis as well as developmentally appropriate modifications to the task (e.g., changing the distance thrown or the size of the ball). The intervention group was provided with a 40-minute session each week for 8 weeks. The control group of nine children received no instruction. All participants were given a pre- and posttest with the Ohio State University Scale of Intra-Gross Motor Assessment, a criterion-referenced scale focused on qualitative assessment of motor development of 10 object control and locomotor skills. Results were statistically compared. Within the treatment group, there was significant improvement in 5 of the 10 skills (with an additional skill nearing significance). When looking across the groups, the intervention group performed significantly better on throwing and catching, with running approaching a significant difference. Outside of the statistical comparison, the number of children in the intervention group who improved by at least one developmental level from pre- to posttest was at least twice as many as those in the control group in 7 of the 10 skills. For example, five intervention children improved by one level in the hop, whereas only two control children did. Overall, the researchers suggested that their intervention held promise in improving motor skills for young children.

In a related study, Ignico (1991) provided 15 kindergartners with a motor skills intervention focusing on object control and locomotor skills. The children's pre- and posttest scores on the Test of Gross Motor Development (TGMD; Ulrich, 1985) were compared with scores of 15 children who spent the same amount of time in free play. The intervention group received instruction on the 12 skills included on the TGMD. In any given test session, they received instruction on 4 to 6 tasks. These tasks were divided into three stations, and children spent 9 minutes per station, for a total of 28 minutes per session. Intervention occurred twice a week for a total of 10 weeks. After Ignico completed the intervention, she reassessed all participants with the TGMD and then calculated their overall Gross Motor Development Quotient (GMDQ). After statistically adjusting the scores for pretest differences, Ignico found the two groups to be statistically different, with $F(1, 25) = 44.52$, $p = .0001$. The intervention group surpassed the control group by a wide margin on the posttest. In fact, the GMDQ for the intervention group improved by 19 points from pre- to posttest, whereas the control group actually declined by 2 points. Ignico did not look at individual skills within the TGMD to see if the specific skills were affected differently. However, on the whole, the study lends support to the efficacy of a motor skill intervention for young children.

Table 10.2 Motor Skill Interventions for Typically Developing Children

Study Citation	Intervention age group	Intervention type	Success of intervention
van der Mars and Butterfield (1988)	3 – 6 year olds	Eight week individual instruction plus developmentally appropriate modifications	Intervention group significantly better in throwing and catching than controls in posttest
Ignico (1991)	5 – 6 year olds	Instruction on 12 items of TGMD, two times per week for 10 weeks	Intervention group significantly better on TGMD scores than controls in posttest
Foweather et al., 2008	8 – 9 year olds in afterschool recreation program	Nine weeks, two times per week, one hour sessions, basic skill instruction	Significant differences only in balance proficiency, with intervention better than controls.
Barnett, van Beurden, Morgan, Brooks, Zask, & Beard, 2009	Same participants as van Beurden et al., 6 years later.	Long term retesting after original intervention from van Beurden, et al., 2003	Besides catching, the intervention group did not have a large advantage over the control group in mastering skills.

At least one study examined the effect of an intervention in older children. Foweather et al. (2008) wanted to determine if a motor skills intervention administered in an after-school multiskill sport club could improve fundamental motor skills in children aged 8 to 9 years. The intervention group of 19 children received instruction on a variety of skills, including the vertical jump, leap, sprint, kick, catch, throw, and balance. A control group of 15 children received no instruction and did not participate in the club. Intervention occurred twice a week for 9 weeks, and each session lasted 1 hour. Two skills were taught per week. The researchers assessed skill levels using process measures by means of a checklist of skill attributes similar to those of van Beurden et al. (2003). After assessment, each skill received a binary value of either proficient or not proficient. These were then compared using a binary logistical regression that predicted the likelihood of being proficient at a particular skill. Of all the skills, only balance showed a significantly increased likelihood of proficiency in the intervention group over the control group, although trends for differences existed in the kick, catch, and throw. The authors suggested that their research may have been limited by lack of statistical power to detect differences (if a researcher wants power of .80 to detect a medium effect size, a sample size of 300 must be used for logistic regression). Given this limitation, they suggested that there may be practical significance in the kick, catch, and throw in addition to the significance in balance.

Looking at all of these studies, we see that interventions generally have a positive influence on the acquisition of motor skills over the short term. Remember, however, that the study of motor development focuses on change over a longer developmental time, so we also need to determine the long-term effects of an intervention. This is the next logical step for intervention studies. Recently, Barnett et al. asked whether a successful intervention will have a lasting influence

on motor development (Barnett et al., 2009). They followed up their Move It, Groove It intervention from 2000 (van Beurden et al., 2003) with the Physical Activity and Skills Study (PASS), in which they examined motor skills in 276 of the original 1,045 participants 6 years after the intervention. Skills observed for PASS were three object control skills (kick, catch, throw) and three locomotor skills (hop, slide, vertical jump). All skills were assessed on 5 to 6 proficiency features, which were scored as correct or incorrect. These were summed per skill to determine whether the participant performed at mastery or near mastery (MNM: no more than one feature incorrect). The MNM scores were compared with the participants' original postintervention scores on the skills for which the intervention group performed statistically better than the control group. This meant they were compared on all skills but the hop. The authors used logistical regression to determine the probability that the intervention group either maintained or increased MNM levels compared with the controls over the subsequent postintervention years.

The results of the logistical regression indicated that, in the absence of continued intervention, the experimental group did not lose its advantage over the control group in three skills but did lose its advantage in two skills (the throw and kick). The intervention group maintained a slight advantage in the jump and gallop. The notable exception was catching, for which the intervention group was five times more likely to achieve MNM compared with the control group. These results show a mixed influence of the intervention over the long run.

INTERVENTIONS FOR ATYPICAL POPULATIONS

Some research has been conducted on motor development interventions for individuals with special needs. For this chapter, we broadly define individuals with special needs as people who may require complementary or supplementary education or therapy to keep at or near the developmental levels of their peers. This population includes, among others, individuals with learning or physical disabilities, individuals of lower socioeconomic status, individuals of an underserved minority, and individuals who are currently healthy but are at risk of falling behind their peers in motor ability. The developmental trajectory of these individuals may place them below the normative values for the rest of the population. This placement, in turn, may negatively affect their quality of life, activities of daily living, ability to work and play, and so on. Often practitioners want to intercede to improve these individuals' motor proficiency, ability to perform functional motor tasks, or ability to live independently. Therefore, we use the term *intervention* to describe instructional or therapeutic techniques designed to improve some aspect of motor development in individuals with special needs.

The following sections describe specific research studies devoted to motor development interventions for individuals with special needs. We review a range of research studies that include children at risk for developmental delays and individuals with specific disabilities.

Interventions for Disadvantaged Children

As we have emphasized throughout this text, understanding motor development requires a knowledge of change. We must be able to observe movement at one time and consider from where that movement emerged (How did the individual move before?) and in which direction the movement is going in the future (How will the individual move after?). This is particularly important when a child is at risk for developmental delays. At-risk children may not currently perform below norms for other children their age. However, due to biological factors (low birth weight), environmental factors (socioeconomic status), or some combination of both, these children are predisposed to developmental delays (Hamilton, Goodway, & Haubenstricker, 1999). Eventually these children fall below the norm. In these cases, intervention—and the earlier in childhood, the better—helps to counter predisposing factors. With this in mind, a small but growing group of researchers have examined the influence of motor skill interventions on preschoolers defined as at risk or vulnerable to developmental delays.

In one study, Hamilton et al. (1999; see table 10.3) examined the extent to which children enrolled in a Head Start program (a federally funded program designed to promote school readiness for children aged 3 to 5 years who come from low-income backgrounds) benefited from a parent-led, 8-week object control motor skills intervention. The underlying premise was that income level acts as an environmental constraint that negatively affects the acquisition of motor skills over time; by intervening with parents, the researchers hoped to manipulate that environmental context to be more encouraging to emerging fundamental motor skills. The intervention group included 15 children enrolled in a Head Start program. These children were provided with two 45-minute lessons per week delivered by parents who had been trained by the researchers in how to properly instruct their children to perform the specific skills and how to provide appropriate feedback. The lessons were parent directed and focused on throwing, catching, striking, and kicking. Parents taught at least two skills per session, during which the researcher assisted if problems arose with skill delivery. The control group consisted of 12 children who participated in movement songs and activities for the same amount of time but did not receive any object control

Table 10.3   Motor Skill Interventions for At-Risk Children

Study Citation	Intervention age group	Intervention type	Success of intervention
Hamilton, Goodway, & Haubenstricker (1999)	Children aged 3 – 5 years in a Head Start program	Eight week, parental-led, focusing on object control skills	Intervention group improved significantly more than control group.
Goodway & Branta (2003)	Children aged 3 – 5 years in pre – K program for at risk children	12 week, teacher-led, focusing on both locomotor and object control skills	Intervention group improved significantly more than control group on both sets of skills.
Goodway, Crowe, and Ward (2003)	Children aged 3 – 5 enrolled in compensatory Pre-K program for at-risk children	Nine week, teacher-led, focusing on both locomotor and object control skills	Intervention group improved significantly more than control group in all skills.

instruction. All participants were tested before and after the intervention using the TGMD, which includes 10 skills divided into two sections: locomotor skills (run, hop, slide, gallop, standing long jump) and object control skills (catch, throw, strike, kick, roll).

The pretest confirmed that all the children in the study were either at risk of or already experiencing motor development delays. Both groups averaged below the 20th percentile (meaning that 80% of children their age scored higher than they did on the motor skills test), and 59% of the children scored below the 5th percentile. Following statistical analysis, the researchers determined that the intervention group significantly outperformed the control group on object control skills. The increases were dramatic: The mean percentile of the intervention group rose from 19.9 pretest to 67.3 posttest, whereas the control group remained at about the 17th percentile. Thus, the authors suggested that parents providing a structured motor skill intervention mentored by professionals can positively influence change in motor development in their young at-risk children.

Goodway and Branta (2003) followed this study by examining the influence of a teacher-led motor skills intervention in both object control and locomotor skills on at-risk preschoolers. These researchers also used children enrolled in programs specifically designed for children who are disadvantaged and at risk for delays. The researchers compared 31 children who received 12 weeks of an instructional program (two sessions per week, 45 minutes per session) with 28 controls who received regular preschool programming without intervention. The intervention focused on eight fundamental movement skills, including the locomotor skills of hopping, jumping, and galloping and the object control skills of ball bouncing, striking, kicking, catching, and throwing. Each session consisted of 10 minutes of sustained activity, two 10-minute blocks of specific skill instruction in which groups of 5 to 6 children rotated through three stations, and 3 minutes of closure during which key skill components were reiterated. The researchers provided a direct instructional approach, and children were provided with a progression of 3 to 4 activities derived from a developmental task analysis and the children's developmental level. In other words, the researchers matched the tasks and equipment to the specific individual constraints of the children, determined a developmentally appropriate task level, and then progressively changed the task or equipment as children mastered each skill (Herkowitz, 1979). All children were tested with the TGMD before and after the intervention (Ulrich, 1985).

As with the previous study, before the intervention, the control and intervention groups scored similarly to each other and below average on both the locomotor and object control subtests, ranging from the 15th to 27th percentiles on the different subtests of the TGMD. After intervention, the scores from the intervention group doubled on the locomotor skills subtest, whereas the scores of the control group did not, instead remaining at 26% (see figure 10.1). A repeated measures ANOVA revealed that these were significant differences between the groups at $F(1, 57) = 134.23$, $p < .001$, with a large effect size ($\eta^2 = .70$). This suggested that the results were highly meaningful. Object control skills mirrored these results, with the intervention group showing large gains compared with the control group, significant at $F(1, 57) = 161.55$, $p < .001$, $\eta^2 = .74$.

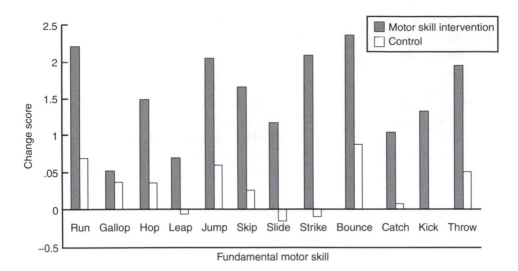

Figure 10.1   Children in the motor skills intervention group improved significantly more than the children in the control group improved in a wide variety of skills.

These results suggested the efficacy of such a motor skill intervention for children from disadvantaged backgrounds.

In a third related study, Goodway, Crowe, and Ward (2003) provided a motor skill intervention over 9 weeks to a group of disadvantaged preschoolers and compared their performance in object control and locomotor skills to the performance of children not receiving the intervention. All the children in the study were either developmentally delayed or at risk for developmental delays and were recruited from a compensatory prekindergarten program for at-risk children. The intervention group consisted of 33 children with an average age of 4.9 years, and the comparison group consisted of 30 children with an average age of 5.0 years. As part of the study, the intervention group was enrolled in the Successful Kinesthetic Instruction for Preschoolers (SKIP) program, which consists of a 9-week program of 35-minute sessions administered 2 days per week. During the 35 minutes, children received 10-minute blocks of skill instruction for three skills. The researchers provided both developmentally and instructionally appropriate practices and taught the group one skill at a time using a direct instructional approach. They then provided a progression of 3 to 4 activities, so that the children could progress at their own rate through the activities. In addition, the equipment, task, and feedback were modified as necessary to match the needs of each individual child. The comparison group was provided with typical preschool activities; no motor skills instruction was provided. All children were tested on the TGMD before and after the program.

The researchers determined that there were significant differences on the TGMD between the two groups after the motor skills program. The motor skills

intervention group improved in locomotor skills (moving from the 7th to the 50th percentile pre- to posttest) and object control skills (moving from the 11th to the 60th percentile pre- to posttest), whereas the comparison group did not significantly change in percentile ranks. Overall, the effect size of the statistical differences was strong, suggesting that the results were not only statistically significant but also meaningful. By the end of the 9-week program, 75% of the children were at or above the 25th percentile in locomotor skills and 85% were at or above the 25th percentile in the object control skills. Thus, Goodway et al. (2003) concluded that applying a developmentally appropriate motor skills intervention successfully improved motor skills in preschool children. They acknowledged that follow-up was necessary to determine the long-term effect of these changes within this group. Nonetheless, the results added support to the notion that programs can assist children with or at risk for developmental delays in learning fundamental motor skills.

The results of these studies suggest that a structured, developmentally appropriate intervention based on motor skills can influence the acquisition of motor skills in a disadvantaged preschool population. This is a particularly significant finding considering that structured physical education (presumably the most easily accessible vessel through which intervention might occur) is rarely mandated in preschools.

Manipulating Intervention Environments

The studies just discussed followed the basic theoretical premise of Newell's constraints: Appropriately altering environmental or task constraints can facilitate the emergence of motor skills in a disadvantaged population. These studies provided evidence that developmentally appropriate interventions targeting motor skills work for preschool children. Another important factor that could affect the acquisition of motor skills is perceived competence. In children, perceived competence—what they believe about their motor skill proficiency in specific tasks—influences engagement in activities. In essence, the higher the child's level of perceived competence in an activity, the more the child engages in that activity (Harter, 1978). Researchers have theorized that perceived competence affects the development of motor competency as well as the levels of physical activity in young children (Stodden et al., 2008).

Given the success of the general motor skill interventions, a group of researchers decided to examine the effects of different types of *instructional* environments on motor skill performance, fundamental motor skill development, and perceived competence. They focused on the differences between teacher-centered approaches that provide low autonomy for children and student-centered approaches that provide high autonomy for children (e.g., Valentini, Rudisill, & Goodway, 1999; Parish & Rudisill, 2006; Robinson & Goodway, 2009; Robinson, Rudisill, & Goodway, 2009). The researchers described the student-centered approach as a high-autonomy *mastery motivational climate* (Parish, Rudisill, & St. Onge, 2007; Robinson & Goodway, 2009). This approach is considered high autonomy for students because they make decisions regarding the level of skill they perform and the amount they practice. Fundamental to this approach is the notion that

effort and outcome are related—that is, when the learning environment is both mastery oriented and highly autonomous, children achieve and learn (in this case, improve in fundamental motor skills). Several research studies have shown that this approach to teaching and learning leads to improvement in motor skills (Valentini & Rudisill, 2004a, 2004b) as well as physical activity levels (Parish, Rudisill, & St. Onge, 2007) and perceived competence (Robinson & Goodway, 2009).

In order to investigate the influence of the instructional environment on the development of motor skills and perceived physical competence in developmentally delayed kindergartners, Valentini and Rudisill (2004a) provided groups of children with developmental delays with either a high-autonomy or low-autonomy movement environment while teaching locomotor and object control skills over 12 weeks. The low-autonomy environment involved fixed time schedules, low variety and challenge, and no variability in task difficulty, whereas the high-autonomy environment provided high variety and challenge, flexible rotation and choice of stations varying in difficulty, no time restraints per station, and a choice of task difficulty. All participants were assessed with the TGMD pre- and posttest (Ulrich, 1985). Results showed that both groups improved similarly on object control skills; however, in locomotor skills, the mastery group improved significantly more than the low-autonomy group improved. The mastery group also showed significantly higher values of perceived physical competence after the intervention, whereas perceived physical competence in the low-autonomy group did not change. A 6-month follow-up found that the mastery group retained both the motor skill improvements and level of perceived competence even after 6 months. Thus, in the researchers' views, the study findings supported the efficacy of a motivational mastery climate for the development of locomotor skills in young children.

Interestingly, object control skills did not differ between groups as a function of instructional environment in the work by Valentini and Rudisill (2004a). In a series of studies, Robinson et al. (Robinson & Goodway, 2009; Robinson, Rudisill, & Goodway, 2009) examined object control skills more extensively, comparing the two instructional climates. In the first study, Robinson and Goodway examined 117 children from disadvantaged backgrounds. The children were divided into low-autonomy, high-autonomy, and control groups. The low-autonomy group ($N = 38$) received a teacher-centered instructional intervention for 9 weeks (2 days a week, 30 minutes per day). In this intervention, the students followed the guidance and direction of the instructors. The high-autonomy group ($N = 39$) received identical lesson content, task progressions, motor skill activities, and critical cue words, but students in this group were able to select skills, level of difficulty within a skill, and amount of time engaged in a skill. Furthermore, their activities were self-paced as they moved through activity stations. Finally, the control group received 30 minutes of unstructured recess twice a week during the 9 weeks. All groups were given a pretest, posttest, and retention test 9 weeks after the termination of the intervention. Testing consisted of the TGMD. Statistical differences did not exist in the pretest scores; in the posttest and retention test, the two intervention groups improved dramatically compared with the control group but did not differ from each other (see figure 10.2a). This confirmed the result of Valentini and Rudisill (2004a) that both

instructional environments improved object control similarly. However, in a follow-up analysis, Robinson et al. (2009) determined that differences between the two interventions did exist in perceived physical competency. Measures of perceived competency improved only in the high-autonomy group, and these values stayed high even after 9 weeks (see figure 10.2*b*). From these two studies, the researchers concluded first that compared with unstructured activity, structured physical activity classes focusing on object control skills, regardless of level of autonomy, are better at improving motor skills . At the same time, a mastery motivational climate has benefits over a teacher-centered approach in terms of the psychological dimension of perceived competency.

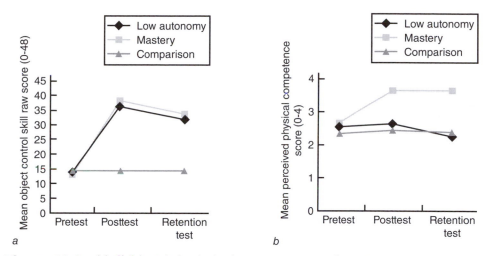

Figure 10.2   (a) Children in both the low-autonomy and mastery intervention groups improved significantly more than the comparison group improved. However, they did not differ from each other in object control skill. (b) Although motor skill scores did not differ between intervention groups, perceived physical competency scores did, with the mastery group scoring higher than both groups in the posttest and retention test.

(a) Reprinted with permission from *Research Quarterly for Exercise and Sport,* Vol. 80, No. 3 pgs, 533-542, Copyright 2003 by the American Alliance for Health, Physical Education, Recreation and Dance, 1900 Association Drive, Reston, VA 20191.

(b) Reprinted with permission from *Research Quarterly for Exercise and Sport,* Vol. 80, No. 3 pgs, 543-551, Copyright 2003 by the American Alliance for Health, Physical Education, Recreation and Dance, 1900 Association Drive, Reston, VA 20191.

Across the previous set of studies, several points are clear. First, young children with or at risk for developmental delays tend to perform motor skills less proficiently than other children their age perform them. This suggests that some form of intervention is necessary to assist their development of fundamental motor skills. Second, developmentally appropriate motor skill interventions can bring the motor skill proficiency level of these children up to or above the level of their peers. While both high-autonomy and low-autonomy intervention approaches boost motor skills, high autonomy appears to better facilitate locomotor skills and perceived competence.

INTERVENTIONS FOR CHILDREN WITH DISABILITIES

Recently, in fields such as adaptive physical education and physical therapy, researchers have created innovative ways in which to improve motor abilities and development as well as critically examine the efficacy of different theoretical models in explaining movement development and predicting change. In chapter 2, we provided background on perception–action perspectives, both indirect (e.g., information processing) and direct (e.g., ecological). In chapter 3, we discussed systems approaches to motor development, focusing on Newell's model of constraints as well as dynamic systems theory and characteristics of dynamic systems, such as nonlinearity, phase shifts, and attractor states. One of the important functions of such perspectives is that they provide researchers with a structure from which to ask questions and create hypotheses, using methods such as strong inference (see chapter 4) or other forms of induction or deduction. This becomes particularly useful when studying atypical populations, because these theories suggest ways in which practitioners can intervene more systematically. Researchers, therefore, design interventions based on a theoretical model and then test the effectiveness of the intervention. From their results, they can make recommendations to practitioners on how best to intervene. In addition, they can use strong inference to develop new questions to enhance future interventions.

Treadmill Interventions for Children With Down Syndrome

As we mentioned in chapters 1 and 3, interest in motor development research has experienced a resurgence since the 1980s, due to several theoretical papers that used dynamic systems theory as a tool to understand developmental change (e.g., Kugler, Kelso, & Turvey, 1982). In a 1991 monograph entitled "Hidden Skills: A Dynamic Systems Analysis of Treadmill-Elicited Stepping During the First Year," Thelen and Ulrich described a series of research studies designed to examine the dynamic characteristics of infant treadmill gait. These authors determined that typically developing infants could step—while being appropriately supported—in a stable and increasingly alternating fashion when provided with experiences on a treadmill. Treadmill stepping emerged well before self-directed walking (between 3 and 5 months of age).

The knowledge that infants step sooner when supported on a treadmill became significant in the context of infants with DS. As we mentioned in the previous chapter, infants with DS often experience delays of up to a year or more in walking (due in part to hypotonia and joint laxity) that can lead to delays in fundamental motor skills and activities of daily living. Furthermore, the delay in walking affects cognitive, social, and other types of development. Therefore, any intervention leading to an earlier onset of walking for children with DS should help reduce the gap between them and their typically developing peers. With the goal of creating a treadmill intervention, Ulrich, Ulrich, and Collier (1992) asked if infants with

DS would step on a treadmill as typically developing infants did. The researchers supported seven 11-month-old infants with DS on a portable treadmill for eight trials lasting 30 seconds each performed at three different speeds. None of these infants had attempted to walk or step on their own at the time of testing. However, all but one of the infants responded by stepping while on the treadmill; the highest percentage of steps were alternating (66%). Other types of patterns were a single step (one step preceded and followed by a nonstepping action in the other leg), parallel step (both feet swinging forward at the same time), and double step (two steps on the same leg within alternating steps). Speed did not influence the number of steps. The researchers concluded that infants with or without DS responded similarly to the treadmill protocol. They suggested that because treadmill stepping and walking have many similar kinetic and kinematic characteristics, treadmill stepping allowed individual constraints such as balance, strength, and coordination (alternating steps) to change enough to allow walking to emerge.

Ulrich et al. (1992) then decided to take a theory-driven, systematic approach to examining treadmill stepping in DS. These authors sought to follow a group of infants longitudinally to understand the self-organization of treadmill stepping. They planned to investigate the emergence of stepping by identifying the attractor state for the skill and then to determine important control parameters and learn how these parameters brought about a transition to new stepping patterns. Ulrich, Ulrich, Collier, and Cole (1995) examined nine infants with DS between the ages of 8 and 11 months, following them for at least 4 months until each infant produced consistent alternating step patterns for 3 months. Each month, they tested the infants with the protocol used in their previous study (Ulrich et al., 1992). The researchers found that relative interlimb phasing between the legs best described the attractor state for treadmill stepping. There was a phase shift toward a great number of steps at .5 (e.g., alternating). A high degree of variability existed throughout. This information provided the necessary theoretical support for using a dynamic systems approach for a treadmill intervention with this population.

In a subsequent study, Ulrich, Ulrich, Angulo-Kinzler, and Yun (2001) randomly assigned 30 infants with DS to either a control or an experimental group. On average, infants began the study at 10 months old (±1.5 months) and began participating when they could sit independently for 30 seconds. All the participants received the physical therapy that infants with DS typically receive. In addition, the intervention infants received in-home practice stepping on a small, motorized treadmill. The intervention consisted of the infants being held over the treadmill, which moved at 0.46 miles per hour (0.74 kph), by the parent. If the infants did not step, the parents repositioned them. This process occurred 8 minutes a day (starting with 1 minute of intervention followed by 1 minute of rest) for 5 days per week until the infant began independent walking. The research team visited participants on a biweekly basis, carefully monitoring motor development and growth.

The results indicated that the experimental protocol was successful (table 10.4). The intervention group could rise to a standing position as well as walk with assistance sooner than the control group could (the former difference not significant at $p = .09$ and the latter difference significant at $p = .03$). In addition, the group with treadmill training learned to walk with assistance sooner and to walk independently significantly sooner (at 19.9 months versus 23.9 months)

Table 10.4 Differences Between Experimental and Control Groups in Length of Time From Entry Into Study to Onset of Selected Locomotor Behaviors

Locomotor behavior	Experimental group	Control group	Mean difference	p value	Effect size
Rises to stand	134 (69.7)*	194 (115.8)	60	.09	0.61
Walks with help	166 (64.6)	240 (102.7)	73	.03	0.80
Walks independently	300 (86.5)	401 (131.1)	101	.02	0.83

*Mean (standard deviation); unit = days.

than the control group. All three of these comparisons had moderate to large effect sizes. The researchers concluded that the treadmill intervention was successful in encouraging the emergence of independent walking in infants with DS.

Bicycle Interventions for Children With Intellectual Disabilities

Learning to ride a bicycle is a rite of passage for many children. The ability to ride requires strength, balance, and coordination, both within and across limbs, applied to a piece of equipment (the bicycle) that is constantly changing position. Given that description, it is hard to believe anyone ever learns to ride! Nonetheless, almost 90% of the population eventually learns to ride a bicycle (Klein, McHugh, Harrington, Davis, & Lieberman, 2005). The use of training wheels controls some of the degrees of freedom, which allows children to master coordination without the constraint of balance acting as a rate limiter. Not all individuals respond well to training wheels, however; individuals with disabilities are among those who may have difficulties learning to bicycle with training wheels (Burt, 2002; Klein et al., 2005).

In response to this problem, Klein et al. (Burt, 2002; Burt, Poretta, & Klein, 2007; DiRocco & Klein, 2001; Klein et al., 2005) developed a bicycle training program for individuals with disabilities. The program uses developmentally appropriate progressions on specialized bicycles that manipulate stability through mechanical modifications. One underlying theoretical approach is to alter the task and environment as constraints, such that a practitioner can coax a motor behavior to emerge (Newell, 1986; Gagen & Getchell, 2004). Since balance is the rate-limiting constraint, the bicycle must be altered to accommodate lack of ability to balance; biomechanically, the way to account for balance is to increase stability. Therefore, the initial bicycle is the most stable, with crowned rollers on the front and back. The design allows riders to gain stability while retaining the dynamic attributes of bicycling (see figure 10.3). After mastering this bicycle, individuals are presented with progressively less stable bicycles that also include gearing changes; these require the rider to progressively take more control of balance (Klein et al., 2005).

Using this theoretical framework, Burt et al. (Burt, 2002; Burt et al., 2007) examined the acquisition of bicycling ability in children with intellectual disabilities. Using Gibson's theory of affordances (Gibson, 1979), these authors theorized that standard bicycles—even with training wheels—would not afford

Figure 10.3 A child participating in the weeklong Lose the Training Wheels program. He is sitting on a bicycle that is modified to allow riding without high balance requirements. If necessary, the volunteer (left) holds the bicycle steady.

Photo courtesy of Tammy Burt.

learning the skill of bicycling in a population of children who have difficulty not only with learning but also with balance and interlimb coordination in complex skills. The researchers accounted for balance by systematically modifying the stability of the bicycle as described earlier. To facilitate change in coordination, they modified speed (slower bicycles allow more time for decision making and feedback from the body and environment and provide less opportunity for crashing).

Burt et al. intervened with seven children aged 7 to 11 years who had mild intellectual disabilities and could not independently ride a conventional bicycle. The researchers provided these children with four different bicycles that were systematically modified to provide specific amounts of stability and speed. The first bicycle, which had two rollers rather than a back wheel, provided the greatest amount of support; with its fixed gear system, it represented the most simple task. The most complex adapted bicycle had a large front tire and a conventional rear tire and drivetrain. The most complex bicycle overall was a conventional child-sized bicycle. Children received individualized instruction for 45 minutes on 3 days a week. During several training sessions, participants rode each of the bicycles, starting with the easiest bicycle and, after meeting specific performance criteria (e.g., riding 12 meters on 3 of 5 trials), advancing to the next, more complex bicycle. After mastering a particular bicycle, the participants had a generalization trial, in which they performed a variation of the initial bicycling task, where they would ride through a series of cones. They continued this process until they were able to ride a conventional bicycle.

Although trial and session numbers varied, all of the participants progressed through the succession of bicycles and were able to ride a conventional bicycle by their last acquisition session. The average number of sessions was 4.9, with a widely varied number of trials per participant and per bicycle. Of the seven participants, five maintained this ability to perform the task after 2 to 3 days, and three could generalize to conventional cycling skill by riding a bicycle through a series of cones. Both the success rate and training sessions were exceptional when compared with a more conventional, instruction-based bicycle training

program in Michigan that was directed at a similar population and lasted 16 weeks but had only about a 50% success rate (Burt et al., 2007).

This model of wheel-free bicycle training has been used extensively with individuals with different types of disability, such as ASD, CP, and DS. The research by Burt et al. (Burt, 2002; Burt et al., 2007) represents the only true experiment testing the efficacy of the adaptive bicycles. At the same time, a growing number of reports suggest that the adaptive bicycle is successful. For example, DiRocco and Klein (2001) reported a 75% success rate in adaptive bicycle training in a camp environment. Furthermore, Klein et al. (2005) described various clinics and camps in which children were successful in learning to ride bicycles. Klein has run his camps since 1999, and approximately 9,000 children have experienced the bicycle intervention. Klein helped form a nonprofit bicycle training organization, called *Lose the Training Wheels* (www.losethetrainingwheels.org), that runs more than 70 camps per year all across the country and caters to individuals with a wide variety of disabilities. Success rates are reported at 80%; success is defined as the ability to ride a bike for a distance of 40 feet (12 m) without intervention (Burt, personal communication, August 2010). Although this does not mean that the children are independent riders (they have not necessarily learned how to brake or start themselves independently), the numbers are quite impressive and suggest that the bicycle intervention is, in the short term, successful. More follow-up needs to occur to examine the long-term effects of this program.

Interventions for Developmental Coordination Disorder

Of the many types of disabilities, DCD poses a particular problem for practitioners because it is difficult to define. In chapter 9, we defined DCD as motor coordination impairment that is significant enough to affect academic performance or activities of daily living and that is *not* caused by a general medical condition. Despite the international consensus on DCD in 1994, many different terms have been used to describe motor coordination issues in children, such as *minimal motor dysfunction, developmental dyspraxia, motor praxis, clumsy child syndrome*, and so on (Hillier, 2007). Furthermore, diagnostic criteria vary. Standard measures have been suggested (under 15th percentile on standardized motor tests along with an IQ score greater than 69; Geuze, Jongmans, Schoemaker, & Smits-Engelsman, 2001), but no international body has adopted standard measures. So, the lack of consistency in defining what DCD is and how it can be identified makes intervention studies difficult due to the heterogeneity of the participant group.

Nonetheless, many researchers have investigated interventions for children with DCD over the past several decades, with mixed results (e.g., Miller et al., 2001; Miyahara, Yamaguchi, & Green, 2008; Wilson et al., 2002). No standard intervention exists. In fact, quite the opposite is true. In a systematic review of intervention studies, Hillier (2007) identified more than 30 unique interventions, from traditional sensorimotor to kinesthetic training to cognitive orientation to daily occupational performance (CO-OP). In an attempt to more systematically

summarize results across studies, Pless and Carlsson (2000) performed a meta-analysis of studies examining the effects of motor skill intervention on DCD. They classified interventions into three general theoretical approaches. The first is a **general abilities approach**. Those using this approach assume that general perceptual motor abilities underlie functional motor skills. Thus, interventions include balance facilitation as well as a focus on general physical abilities. **Sensory integration (SI)** is the second approach, which primarily focuses on sensory integrative therapy. The basic assumption underlying the SI approach is that sensory motor integration abilities underlie functional motor skills (and general cognitive ability). Finally, the **specific skills** approach assumes that specific motor control and learning processes underlie functional motor skills. Pless and Carlsson (2000) sought to determine if any of the approaches is supported by evidence and how different experimental design factors influence outcomes (you may recall from statistics that a meta-analysis is a statistical method of combining research evidence in order to calculate a more accurate, population-based effect size).

Pless and Carlsson (2000) examined 21 DCD intervention studies; 13 of these were used in their meta-analysis. They found that the specific skills interventions yielded the highest mean effect size (1.46, which is considered large). These were followed by the general abilities interventions (0.71) and SI interventions (0.21). Thus, the interventions that focused on task-specific activities derived the best motor outcomes in children with DCD. Another interesting finding was that home (1.41) and small-group (0.96) interventions yielded larger effect sizes than one-on-one interventions (0.45) yielded, although the researchers speculated that this may be due to the greater impairment of those involved in one-on-one interventions. Furthermore, the length of the intervention did not change the effect size, whereas the frequency did, with greater frequency per week (3-5 times) generating greater effect sizes. Pless and Carlsson concluded that practitioners providing interventions for children with DCD should use a task-specific approach in a small-group or home setting, with sessions occurring at least 3 to 5 days per week.

In 2007, Hillier published another systematic review of DCD intervention studies conducted from 1970 to 2004. Unlike a meta-analysis, the purpose of a systematic review is to examine objectively defined high-quality, peer-reviewed literature related to a single or small set of questions in an attempt to synthesize an answer. Hillier's question related to the evidence of the effectiveness of DCD interventions in randomized control studies, controlled clinical trials, and other experimental designs. After a thorough search of many different sources using the different descriptors of DCD, Hillier found 47 studies specifically related to DCD interventions. These were then ranked in terms of level of evidence (from strong to insufficient evidence) and then synthesized to determine the level of evidence for her specific questions. Hillier concluded that the results strongly confirmed the suggestion that interventions (regardless of type) are better than no interventions for children with DCD. Of the different types of intervention, perceptual-motor therapy and sensory integration both had strong evidence of effectiveness (see Table 10.5).

Table 10.5 Systematic Reviews of Motor Skill Interventions for Children With DCD

Study Citation	Number of studies included in analysis	Successful interventions	Comparative comments
Pless and Carlsson (2000)	13	Task specific; home or small group; higher frequency per week	Overall, many different types of interventions with children with DCD are effective.
Hillier (2007)	47	Any intervention was better than none; perceptual-motor therapy and sensory integration more effective	

One general conclusion we can garner from these two research articles is that interventions in children with DCD are effective. Still, we do not have a clear vision of what a DCD intervention looks like. Therefore, we will examine several different intervention studies in detail. The first, a case study by Miyahara and Wafer (2004), compared two different types of intervention programs, a skills theme approach and a movement concepts approach (Graham, Holt/Hale, & Parker, 1993). The skills theme approach focused on improving specific skills and used a more traditional style of teaching skills, which included activities such as throwing, catching, batting, and so on. The movement concept approach focused on improving self-efficacy and confidence and included activities such as movement exploration, creative dance, and so on. Both approaches focused on the specific deficits of the child (e.g., ball skills, balance). The purpose of this investigation was to determine if children respond differently to these different types of interventions.

Miyahara and Wafer (2004) observed seven fourth-year student instructors teaching seven children with DCD over a 5-week block using one teaching style followed by a second 5-week block using the other style. Interventions were specifically matched to the needs of the children; for example, for one child, the skills theme goals were to improve balance, object control, and manual dexterity, while for another child, the skills focused on tying shoelaces along with ball, balance, and locomotor skills. The following is a comparison of the different types of tasks within each teaching style:

> In the first semester, Anne's tutor, Angela, designed a movement concepts program to improve Anne's balance, manual dexterity, and locomotor skills. Throughout the 5 week program, Anne practiced a game of statues, in which she was required to "freeze" and maintain static balance. . . . [During the skills themes during the second semester], Anne practiced the stork balance task from the MABC and received stickers when she achieved targeted times (Miyahara and Wafer 2004, p. 291).

Two measures were taken in pre- and posttests after each 5-week block: the Movement Assessment Battery for Children (M-ABC; motor domain) and the Pictorial Scale of Perceived Competence (affective domain; Harter & Pike, 1984).

Children were also evaluated on a case-by-case basis using a pattern-matching strategy that looked for literal replication to see if teaching styles matched outcomes (skill themes improved skills; movement concepts improved self-efficacy). The authors reviewed videotape from each of the lessons for all of the children. They determined that the skills themes approach did, in fact, lead to an improvement in targeted motor skills, and the movement concepts led to greater movement exploration. Furthermore, four of the children had their skill levels decrease when not working on specific skills. This was perhaps the most important finding of this research: Regardless of teaching style, when children stopped an intervention, their performance tended to decline. On a practical basis, this finding suggests that intervention and monitoring should continue for longer durations. In terms of future research, this finding suggests that research on interventions should include some sort of retention interval to determine if the immediate effects of an intervention actually persist after training stops.

Another example of a DCD intervention comes from Hung and Pang (2010). These researchers wanted to compare group-based versus home-based motor skills interventions for children with DCD. They acknowledged the results of the meta-analysis by Pless and Carlsson (2000), which suggested that group-based therapies have an advantage. However, they were concerned about the diversity of treatment types as well as the heterogeneity of participants across the studies reviewed. Therefore, they wanted to provide a direct comparison between a group and an individual invention. They randomly assigned 23 children with DCD into either a group ($n = 12$; 8.4 ± 1.2 years old) or an individual ($n = 11$; 7.8 ± 1.2 years old) intervention category. All children were given a pretest with the M-ABC. Both groups received 45 minutes of training once per week for a total of 8 weeks. Training included agility and balance, core stability, bilateral coordination, and eye–hand or eye–foot coordination tasks. The researchers progressed tasks in a developmentally appropriate fashion, so that participants were both challenged and successful. In the group-based intervention, the student-to-instructor ratio ranged from 4:1 to 6:1, and all interventions were performed by the same instructor. All participants received a 20-minute home exercise program to complete every day in order to reinforce concepts learned in class, and participants had to fill out a log as a compliance check. Furthermore, the parents were provided with a questionnaire asking them their level of satisfaction with the program. After the 8 weeks, all participants took the M-ABC again.

Statistically, both groups significantly improved from pre- to posttest (figure 10.4). At the same time, no statistical differences existed between the group and individual interventions. Furthermore, six children within each group improved such that their scores were greater than the 15th percentile, which is the cutoff score for DCD. Both groups scored similarly for home exercise compliance (between 50% and 62%), and there were no statistical differences in parental satisfaction. The authors were encouraged by these results, because effective group-based interventions allow more children to receive intervention both from economically and efficiency perspectives.

In another study, Miyahara et al. (2008) observed children who attended the movement development clinic that has existed at the University of Otago at

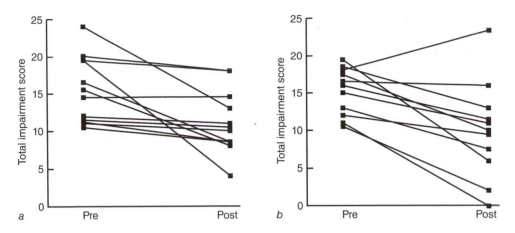

Figure 10.4 Children with DCD who received (*a*) individual or (*b*) group intervention improved similarly on their M-ABC scores after treatment. Note that a lower impairment score indicates better performance.

Reprinted, by permission, from W.W. Hung and M.Y. Pang, 2010, "Effects of group-based versus individual-based exercise training on motor performance in children with developmental coordination disorder: A randomized controlled study," *Journal of Rehabilitation Medicine* 42(2): 122-128. Journal of rehabilitation medicine by European Board of Physical and Rehabilitation Medicine. Copyright 2010 Reproduced with permission of TAYLOR & FRANCIS INFORMA UK LTD - JOURNALS in the format Textbook via copyright Clearance Center.

Dunedin (New Zealand) since 1950 and that has been run by Miyahara since 1996. The clinic does not serve children with DCD exclusively; rather, it caters to children with a broad range of neuromuscular and physical disabilities. The intervention approach adopted by the clinic is a case formulation approach and is administered by third- and fourth-year students. These students first list the movement issues observed in individual children, then hypothesize about mechanisms causing these issues, and finally develop an individualized movement plan that included tasks, instructions, and the teaching environment. The purpose of this research was to determine the prevalence of DCD among the 326 children receiving services at the clinic from the 1990s to 2005 and then to determine the efficacy of the motor skills intervention for these individuals. Miyahara et al. (2008) also wanted to determine if the theoretical knowledge base assumed by the instructors influenced outcomes. Specifically, they wanted to see if instructors who had adopted and taught with an information-processing framework would differ from those adopting a constraints-based approach. The authors reasoned that understanding and manipulating the interaction among individual, task, and environment may lead to better outcomes for children with DCD.

In this retrospective study, the records of 326 children (100 females, 226 males) were observed, and clinical diagnoses were recorded. Miyahara et al. (2008) verified a DCD diagnosis through two levels of analysis: (1) diagnosis from clinical professionals and (2) assessment in the movement development clinic using the M-ABC and *DSM-IV* criteria. Only 28 children were originally diagnosed with DCD by clinical professionals, and the second level of analysis yielded an additional 35 children who could be classified as having DCD. This finding represented a significant underdiagnosis of DCD by clinical professionals.

For the group of 63 children with DCD, the average intervention lasted 12 weeks, and the mean percentile significantly improved from the 9th to the 18th. A closer look at the data showed that, despite these group changes, 38 of the 63 children remained at or below the 15th percentile cutoff for DCD. To examine the effect of theoretical knowledge on outcomes, 10 teacher–student dyads starting before 2002 (representing an information-processing theoretical background) were compared with 10 teacher–student dyads starting after 2002 (representing a constraints-based approach). There were no statistical differences between the outcomes for children whose instructors used an information-processing versus a constraints-based approach. The authors felt that this confirmed the findings of Hillier's research: Intervention of any sort is better than nothing. Although a constraints-based approach did not lead to substantial differences between groups, the authors suggested that, given the equivalence of the two, practitioners may benefit from considering individual, task, *and* environment when developing interventions.

SUMMARY

A variety of research suggests that individuals in typical or atypical populations can benefit from interventions designed to improve their motor development. Researchers have focused much of their intervention research on improving fundamental motor skills in children, particularly young children. This follows a basic premise that improving the developmental course that a child takes (that is, helping children with poor motor skills to perform at or near the levels of peers) early on helps with motor skill development throughout childhood and beyond. In other words, young children will receive a bump that will put them on course to develop typically. Much of the research we have reviewed suggests that, in the short run, children improve performance when administered a developmentally appropriate intervention. What occurs in the long run is not clear. Longitudinal studies must be performed to determine the long-term influence of interventions. Many scenarios exist. An intervention could provide the boost that children need to put them on a similar developmental course as their peers. Alternatively, an intervention could provide a short-term performance enhancement that disappears once the intervention is removed. Some of the lasting influences of intervention might also depend on the population under study (typical or atypical). Investigating the long-term effects of interventions provides a rich area open to researchers and will dictate the types of motor development interventions used in the future.

Glossary

attractor states—Preferred patterns of behavior that emerge from interacting subsystems. In human behavior, walking and running would be considered attractor states.

Bassin Anticipation Timer—Instrument designed by Stanley Bassin that simulates a moving object by sequentially lighting LEDs. Speed can be varied. Performers press a button coincident with the arrival of the light at a designated point. The instrument provides the exact difference early or late between the arrival of the light and the response. Also, an instrument that measures coincidence anticipation.

body sway—Small oscillatory movements of the body around the ankles, like an inverted pendulum, during balanced standing. An alternate term is *postural sway*. Body sway is typically measured by force platforms in the anteroposterior direction or the mediolateral direction.

butterfly effect—When a small change in the initial conditions of one system, such as a flap of a butterfly's wings, has a profound effect on other systems, such as creating a tornado elsewhere.

center of mass (COM)—Point in three-dimensional space at which a body's mass is concentrated.

center of pressure (COP)—Force representing the average ground reaction forces of all parts of the body in contact with the ground, allowing for representation of the forces at a single point. In balanced standing on a force platform, a COP can be calculated and moves as the body leans.

central pattern generator (CPG)—A neural mechanism in the human spinal cord hypothesized to generate alternating EMG leg patterns that may be responsible for stepping movements.

chaos theory—The study of dynamic systems in which the behavior of the system is highly sensitive to initial conditions.

coincidence anticipation—Motor response in which a movement is required to coincide in time, in space, or in time and space with the arrival of some moving object at a designated point. Also, anticipation timing.

constant bearing angle (CBA)—Strategy for intercepting a moving object in which a catcher moves to keep the relative bearing (direction) the same over time.

constraints—Characteristics of the organism, task, or environment that either encourage or discourage certain behavioral patterns.

context-conditioned variability—The behavior of a system depends on its context. Therefore, patterns vary based on initial conditions.

continuity versus discontinuity argument—A dispute in developmental psychology between those who believe development is a linear and continuous process and those who believe it is nonlinear with qualitative transformations occurring along the way.

contralateral heel strike—During locomotion, the point at the end of the forward swing of the leg when its heel contacts the supporting surface. The contralateral heel is that belonging to the leg opposite the arm swinging forward.

co-twin method—A research method in which one member of a set of twins is used as a control while the other member receives an experimental treatment. By using twins, the researcher controls for genetics.

dorsal stream—A visual neural pathway from the retina to the posterior parietal cortex conveying visual signals for action.

double dissociation—Outcome of research results demonstrating opposite patterns of impaired and preserved abilities in individuals with brain damage, suggesting but not proving that different brain systems are involved in dissociated abilities.

dual-processing theories—Theories suggesting that different neurological streams in the brain control action planning and the online control of action.

dual-task paradigm—Experimental method in which any interference with the performance of a task due to a second, simultaneously performed task is recorded.

dynamic system—A system whose complex behavior or pattern emerges over time (i.e., is time dependent).

entrain—Different oscillating systems begin to cycle together with one, unified pattern.

general abilities approach—An intervention approach used for children with developmental coordination disorder that assumes general perceptual motor abilities underlie functional motor skills. These interventions focus on improving general physical abilities and balance rather than specific tasks such as walking or prehension.

general systems theory—Theory that systems exist as a function of their interacting elements. These systems have self-organizing behaviors or principles that can be seen across a wide number of different and complex phenomena, the study of which is directed at finding unity of sciences.

information-processing model—A model for the control of movement in which stimulus information proceeds through a number of successive operations or stages leading to response, somewhat like a computer. The model components are functional rather than anatomical.

interception skills—Fundamental skills that require a performer to catch, gather, block, or strike a moving object. Also included are tackling and blocking another performer.

ipsilateral heel strike—During locomotion, the point at the end of the forward swing of the leg when the heel contacts the supporting surface. The ipsilateral heel is that belonging to the leg on the same side as the referent arm.

limit-cycle oscillators—A special class of oscillators that synchronize to act as a single unit.

linear optical trajectory (LOT)—Strategy for intercepting a moving object in which the catcher moves continuously and directly under the ball such that it neither curves down nor arcs up relative to the catcher, allowing for adjustments due to wind, air resistance, or ball spin.

low guard—A position sometimes observed during locomotion in which the arms do not swing but are held relatively stationary next to the hips.

microgenesis—Research method that allows a researcher to infer development in a compressed time frame by causing regression or backward development in people who have already passed through those levels of development.

moving room paradigm—Experimental method in which the postural stability of individuals is recorded when they are placed in a room within a room. The inner room consists of at least three walls and a ceiling that can be oscillated or moved toward or away from the individual, thus putting visual and kinesthetic information in conflict.

multileveled causality—Development emerges from many different interacting subsystems, all of which contribute to change over time. This is in contrast to attributing change to one subsystem.

multimodal perception—Perceiving objects, surfaces, or other aspects of the environment and events across sensory-perceptual systems rather than perceiving them separately and then matching or integrating the information.

muscle linkages or coordinative structures—Groups of muscles that are constrained together to perform a particular function. There is no structural linkage among the group of muscles.

ontogenetic—A term popularized by McGraw (1935/1975) to describe motor skills that are particular to an individual rather than the species and therefore require specialized practice by that individual.

optical acceleration cancellation (OAC)—Strategy for intercepting a moving object in which the catcher keeps the optical ball speed constant, hence canceling any change in velocity relative to the catcher's position.

optical flow—Visual streaming of environmental objects on the retina as a perceiver moves through the environment that changes predictably over time and provides information about position, motion, and timing.

organismic—A research perspective that uses the biology of developing organisms as a model for the events and processes of motor development.

pendular walk—Walking in which the leg swinging forward mimics the swing of a pendulum (with the foot as the free end) while the stance leg mimics the swing of an inverted pendulum (with the head and trunk as the free end).

perception–action model—A model of motor control in which a single system in the dorsal stream serves in both planning and control.

phase shift—The change from one attractor state to another.

phylogenetic—A term popularized by McGraw (1935/1975) to describe motor skills that are typical of the species—that is, skills that seem to develop similarly in all persons without specialized practice.

planning–control model—A model of motor control in which a ventral stream serves in perception, a medial visual stream serves in action planning, and a dorsal stream serves in online motor control.

postural synergy—Suggested by Bernstein, a postural control strategy in which fixed groups of muscles are activated to maintain posture, thus simplifying motor control of a complex muscle activation pattern.

power grip—Grasping an object in the flexed fingers and palm with counterpressure from the thumb. It facilitates using an implement with force, such as when hammering.

precision grip—Grasping an object between the flexed fingers, often the fingertips, and the opposing thumb.

prehension—A grasp with the hand.

process-oriented period—Era in motor development research defined by Clark and Whitall (1989b) as extending from 1970 to the present. It is particularly marked by interest in the processes underlying behavioral change.

rate limiter—One system or constraint that holds back the rate at which an organism develops as a whole.

scale errors—Action or attempted action on an object even though that action is impossible due to a great size difference between the object and the actor.

sensory integration (SI)—An alternative to the general abilities approach, this intervention approach for children with developmental coordination disorder assumes that the ability to coalesce sensory stimuli with motor function and movement underlies functional motor skills (and general cognitive ability). SI interventions focus on improving the ability to merge senses with movement.

Sensory Organization Test (SOT)—Test of postural control providing six conditions that variously manipulate visual, vestibular, and proprioceptive information. The support surface can be tiled to follow an individual's anteroposterior body sway (sway referenced), thus eliminating orientation information. The eyes can be open or closed to provide additional conditions. The conditions create sensory conflict so that adaptive responses can be studied.

soft assembly—A characteristic of the neurological control of movement in which components come together to address the movement goal. Contrasts with neurological control models based on preprogrammed movements.

specific skills—An intervention approach for children with developmental coordination disorder, this approach assumes specificity in motor learning and control skills. These interventions focus directly on particular skills such as catching or kicking.

spinal central pattern generator (CPG)—A neural mechanism in the human spinal cord hypothesized to generate alternating EMG leg patterns that may be responsible for stepping movements. Same as central pattern generator.

stroke—Interruption of the blood supply to any part of the brain resulting in a rapid loss of brain function. The interruption can be a blockage or a leakage of blood.

tau—Greek letter used to symbolize time until contact. The size of a retinal image divided by the rate of change of the image.

time-lag design—A quasi-experimental design in which individuals born in different years (age cohorts) are observed when they reach the same age. This isolates any effects of generational exposure or experience from the influence of age alone.

ventral stream—A visual neural pathway from the retina to the inferior temporal cortex conveying visual signals for perception.

References

Abraham, F. D., Abraham, R. H., & Shaw, C. D. (1992). *A visual introduction to dynamical systems theory for psychology.* Santa Cruz: Aerial Press.

Abraham, F. D., Abraham, R. H., & Shaw, C. D. (1992). *A visual introduction to dynamical systems theory for psychology.* Santa Cruz: Aerial Press.

Abraham, R.H., & Shaw, C.D. (1984a). *Dynamics—the geometry of behavior. Part One: Periodic behavior.* Santa Cruz, CA: Aerial Press.

Abraham, R.H., & Shaw, C.D. (1984b). *Dynamics—the geometry of behavior. Part Two: Chaotic behavior.* Santa Cruz, CA: Aerial Press.

Adolph, K., Vereijken, B., & Shrout, P. (2003). What changes in infant walking and why. *Child Development, 74,* 475-497.

Adolph, K.E., Eppler, M.A., & Gibson, E.J. (1993). Crawling versus walking in infants' perception of affordances for locomotion over sloping surfaces. *Child Development, 64,* 1158-1174.

Adolph, K.E., Eppler, M.A., Martin, L., Weise, I.B., & Wechsler-Clearfield, M. (2001). Exploration in the service of prospective control. *Infant behavior and development, 23,* 441-460.

Adolph, K.E., & Berger,S. (2006). Motor development. In D. Kuhn & R. Siegler (Eds.), *Handbook of child psychology.* Vol.2, (6th ed., pp. 161-213). New York: Wiley.

Adolph, K., & Robinson, S. (2008). In defense of change processes. *Child Development, 79,* 1648-1653.

Adrien, J.L., Lenoir, P., Martineau, J., Perrot, A., Hameury, L. Larmande, C. & Sauvage, D. (1993). Blind ratings of early symptoms of autism based upon family home movies. *Journal of the American Academy of Child and Adolescent Psychiatry, 32*(3), 617-626.

Alexander, R. (1997). Invited editorial on "Interaction of leg stiffness and surface stiffness during human hopping." *Journal of Applied Physiology, 82,* 13-14.

Ameratunga, D., Johnston, L., & Burns, Y. (2004). Goal directed upper limb movements by children with and without DCD: A window into perceptuo-motor dysfunction? *Physiotherapy Research International, 9,* 1-12.

American Psychiatric Association (2011). Diagnostic and Statistical Manual of Mental Disorders 5, proposed revision. A 16 Developmental Coordination Disorder. http://www.dsm5.org/ProposedRevision/Pages/proposedrevision.aspx?rid=88

American Psychiatric Association. (1994). *Diagnostic and statistical manual of mental disorders* (4th ed.). Washington, DC: Author.

Amiel-Tison, C., & Grenier, A. (1980). *Neurological evaluation of the human infant.* New York: Masson.

Anderson, D. I., Campos, J. J., Anderson, D. E., Thomas, T. D., Witherington, D. C., Uchiyama, I., & Barbu-Roth, M. A. (2001). The flip side of perception-action coupling: Locomotor experience and the ontogeny of visual-postural coupling. *Human Movement Science, 20,* 461-487.

Anderson, D.I., Chew-Bullock, T., Kim, A., Mayo, A., & Sidaway, B. (2006). Do tests of one-legged balance predict kicking velocity? *Journal of Sport and Exercise Science, 28*(Suppl.), S25.

Anderson, D.I., Hubbard, E.M., Campos, J.J., Barbu-Roth, M.A., Witherington, D., & Hertenstein, M.J. (2000). Probabilistic epigenesis, experience, and psychological development in infancy. *Infancy, 1*(2), 245-251.

Anisfeld, M. (1991). Review: Neonatal imitation. *Developmental Review, 11,* 60-97.

Asendorpf, J., & Valsiner, J. (1992). Three dimensions of developmental perspectives. In J. Asendorpf & J. Valsiner (Eds.), *Stability and change in development.* Newbury Park, CA: Sage.

Astill S,. & Utley, A. (2006). Ball catching in children with developmental coordination disorder. *Motor Control* 10: 109-124

Astill, S., & Utley, A. (2006). Two-handed catching in children with developmental coordination disorder. *Motor Control, 10*(2), 109-124.

Austin, G., Garrett, G., & Tiberio, D. (2002). Effect of added mass on human unipedal hopping. *Perceptual and Motor Skills, 94,* 834-840.

Austin, G., Tiberio, D., & Garrett, G. (2002). Effect of frequency on human unipedal hopping. *Perceptual and Motor Skills, 95,* 733-740.

Austin, G., Tiberio, D., & Garrett, G. (2003). Effect of added mass on human unipedal hopping at three frequencies. *Perceptual and Motor Skills, 97,* 605-612.

Bair, W.-N., Kiemel, T., Jeka, J.J., & Clark, J.E. (2007). Development of multisensory reweighting for posture control in children. *Experimental Brain Research, 183,* 435-446.

Baker, G.L., & Gollub, J.P. (1990). *Chaotic dynamics: An introduction.* Cambridge, UK: Cambridge University Press.

Baltes, P., Cornelius, S., & Nesselroade, J. (1979). Cohort effects in developmental psychology. In J. Nesselroade & P. Baltes (Eds.), *Longitudinal research in the study of behavior and development* (pp. 61-87). New York: Academic Press.

Baltes, P., Reese, H., & Lipsitt, L. (1980). Life-span developmental psychology. *Annual Review of Psychology, 31,* 65-110.

Barela, J.A., Godoi, D., Freitas Júnior, P.B., & Polastri, P.F. (2000). Visual information and body sway coupling in infants during sitting acquisition. *Infant Behavior and Development, 23,* 285-297.

Barela, J.A., Jeka, J.J., & Clark, J.E. (2003). Postural control in children—coupling to dynamic somatosensory information. *Experimental Brain Research, 150,* 434-442.

Barker, R.G. (1968). *Ecological psychology: Concepts and methods for studying the environment of human behavior.* Stanford, CA: Stanford University Press.

Barker, R.G. (1978). *Habitats, environments, and human behavior: Studies in ecological psychology and eco-behavioral science.* San Francisco: Jossey-Bass.

Barker, R.G., & Wright, H.F. (1951). *One boy's day.* New York: Harper & Row.

Barker, R.G., & Wright, H.F. (1955). *Midwest and its children.* New York: Harper & Row.

Barnett, A. L., Kooistra, L., & Henderson, S.E. (1998). "Clumsiness" as syndrome and symptom. *Human Movement Science, 17,* 435-447.

Barnett, L.M., van Beurden, E., Morgan, P.J., Brooks, L.O., Zask, A., & Beard, J.R. (2009). Six year follow-up of students who participated in a school-based physical activity intervention: a longitudinal cohort study. *Int J Behav Nutr Phys Act, 6,* 48.

Barnhart, R.C., Davenport, M., Epps, S.B., & Nordquist, V.M. (2003). Developmental coordination disorder. *Physical Therapy, 83*(8), 722-731.

Barrett, D., & Burton, A. (2002). Throwing patterns used by collegiate baseball players in actual games. *Research Quarterly for Exercise and Sport, 73,* 19-27.

Barrett, K.R. (1979a). Observation of movement for teachers—a synthesis and implications. *Motor Skills: Theory Into Practice, 3,* 67-76.

Barrett, K.R. (1979b). Observation for teaching and coaching. *Journal of Physical Education, Recreation and Dance, 50,* 23-25.

Barrett, K.R., Allison, P.C., & Bell, R. (1987). What preservice physical education teachers see in an unguided field experience: A follow-up study. *Journal of Teaching in Physical Education, 7,* 12-21.

Barrett, K.R., Williams, K., & Whitall, J. (1992). What does it mean to have a "developmentally appropriate physical education program?" *Physical Educator, 49,* 114-118.

Barrett, K.R., Williams, K., McLester, J., & Ljungkvist, S. (1997). Developmental sequences for the vertical cradle in Lacrosse: An exploratory study. *Journal of Teaching in Physical Education, 16,* 469-489.

Barrett, T.M., Davis, E.F., & Needham, A. (2007). Learning about tools in infancy. *Developmental Psychology, 43,* 352-368.

Barrett, T.M., Traupman, E., & Needham, A. (2008). Infants' visual anticipation of object structure in grasp planning. *Infant Behavior and Development, 31,* 1-9.

Barton, G., & French, K. (2004). Throwing profiles of 7-, 8-, 9-, and 10-year old Little League baseball players. *Research Quarterly for Exercise and Sport, 75* (Suppl.), A-44.

Bayley, N. (1936). *The California Infant Scale of Motor Development.* Berkeley, CA: University of California Press.

Bayley, N. (1963). The life span as a frame of reference in psychological research. *Vita Humana (Human Development), 6,* 125-139.

Bayley, N. (1966). *Bayley Scales of Infant Development.* New York: Psychological Corporation.

Bayley, N. (1993). *Bayley scales of infant development—Second edition.* San Antonio, TX: The Psychological Corporation.

Bayley, N. (2005). *The Bayley Scales of Infant and Toddler Development* (3rd ed.). San Antonio: Harcourt Assessment.

Belisle, J.J. (1963). Accuracy, reliability, and refractoriness in a coincidence-anticipation task. *Research Quarterly, 34,* 271-281.

Bell, R., Barrett, K.R., & Allison, P.C. (1985). What preservice physical education teachers see in an unguided, early field experience. *Journal of Teaching in Physical Education, 4,* 81-90.

Benguigui, N., Broderick, M.P., Baurès, R., & Amorim, M.A. (2008). Motion prediction and the velocity effect in children. *British Journal of Developmental Psychology, 26,* 389-407.

Berlin, I. (1980). The counter-enlightenment. In H. Hardy (Ed.), *Against the current: Essays in the history of ideas* (pp. 1-24). New York: Viking.

Bernstein, N. (1967). *The coordination and regulation of movement.* London: Pergamon Press.

Berry, P., Andrews, R.J. & Gunn, V.P. (1980). *The early development of Down's syndrome in infants. Final Report to National Health and Medical Research Council.* St Lucia, Qld: University of Queensland, Fred and Eleanor Schonell Educational Research Centre.

Bertenthal, B.I. (1996). Origins and early development of perception, action, and representation. *Annual Reviews in Psychology, 47,* 431-459.

Bertenthal, B.I., & Bai, D.L. (1989). Infants' sensitivity to optical flow for controlling posture. *Developmental Psychology, 25,* 936-945.

Bertenthal, B.I., & Clifton, R.K. (1998). Perception and action. In W. Damon (Ed.), *Handbook of child psychology: Vol. 2. Cognition, perception, and language* (pp. 51-102). New York: Wiley.

Bertenthal, B.I., & von Hofsten, C. (1998). Eye, head and trunk control: The foundation for manual development. *Neuroscience and Biobehavioral Reviews, 22,* 515-520.

Black, D., Chang, C.-L., Kubo, M., Holt, K., & Ulrich, B. (2009). Developmental trajectory of dynamic resource utilization during walking: Toddlers with and without Down syndrome. *Human Movement Science, 28,* 141-154.

Block, M.E. (1991). Motor development in children with Down syndrome: A review of the literature. *Adapted Physical Activity Quarterly, 8,* 179-209.

Bloomfield, J., Elliott, B., & Davies, C. (1979). Development of the soccer kick: A cinematographical analysis. *Journal of Human Movement Studies, 5,* 152-159.

Bobath, B. (1965). *Abnormal postural reflex activity caused by brain lesions.* London: Heinemann.

Bonan, I.V., Yelnik, A.P., Colle, F., Michaud, C., Normand, E., Panigot, B. et al. (2004). Reliance on visual information after stroke. Part II. Effectiveness of a balance rehabilitation program with visual cue deprivation after stroke: A randomized controlled trial. *Archives of Physical Medicine and Rehabilitation, 85,* 274-278.

Boykin, S. (2008, October). With open-source arms. *Scientific American, 299,* 90-95.

Braswell, G.S., Rosengren, K.S., & Pierroutsakos, S.L. (2007). Task constraints on preschool children's grip configurations during drawing. *Developmental Psychobiology, 49,* 216-225.

Breniere, Y., & Bril, B. (1998). Development of postural control of gravity forces in children during the first 5 years of walking. *Experimental Brain Research, 121,* 255-262.

Briggs, J., & Peat, F.D. (1989). *Turbulent mirror.* New York: Harper & Row.

Bril, B., & Breniere, Y. (1993). Posture and independent locomotion in early childhood: Learning to walk or learning dynamic postural control? *Advances in Psychology, 97,* 337-358.

Broadbent, D.E. (1958). *Perception and communication.* New York: Pergamon Press.

Brooks, V.B. (1983). Motor control: How posture and movements are governed. *Physical Therapy, 63,* 664-673.

Bruner, J.S. (1973). Organization of early skilled action. *Child Development, 44,* 1-11.

Bruner, J.S., & Koslowski, B. (1972). Visually pre-adapted constituents of manipulatory action. *Perception, 1,* 3-12.

Burt, T. (2002). Effects of adapted bicycles plus feedback on the acquisition, maintenance, and generalization of conventional cycling skills for children with mild mental retardation. Unpublished dissertation. The Ohio State University.

Burt, T., Poretta, D., and Klein R., (2007)."Use of adapted bicycles on the learning of conventional cycling by children with mental retardation," *Education and Training in Developmental Disabilities.*

Burton, A., & Rodgerson, R. (2003). The development of throwing behavior. In G. Savelsbergh, K. Davids, J. van der Kamp, & S. Bennett (Eds.), *Development of movement co-ordination in children* (pp. 225-240). New York: Routledge.

Burtt, E.A. (1954). *The metaphysical foundations of modern science.* Garden City, NY: Doubleday Anchor.

Butterfield, S., & Loovis, E.M. (1994). Influence of age, sex, balance, and sport participation on development of kicking by children in grades K-8. *Perceptual and Motor Skills, 79,* 691-697.

Butterworth, G., & Cicchetti, D. (1978). Visual calibration of posture in normal and motor retarded Down's syndrome infants. *Perception, 7*(5), 513-525.

Butterworth, G., & Hicks, L. (1977). Visual proprioception and postural stability in infancy. A developmental study. *Perception, 6,* 255-262.

Butterworth, G., Verweij, E., & Hopkin, B. (1997). The development of prehension in infants: Halverson revisited. *British Journal of Developmental Psychology, 15*(2), 223-236.

Cairns, R. (1998). The making of developmental psychology. In W. Damon & R. Lerner (Eds.), *Handbook of child psychology: Vol. 1. Theoretical models of human development* (5th ed.) New York: Wiley.

Caldwell, G., & Clark, J. (1990). The measurement and evaluation of skill within the dynamical systems perspective. In J. Clark & J. Humphrey (Eds.), *Advances in motor development research* (pp. 165-200). New York: AMS Press.

Cantin, N., Polatajko, H.J., Thach, W.T., & Jaglal, S. (2007). Developmental coordination disorder: Exploration of a cerebellar hypothesis. *Human Movement Science, 26*(3), 491-509.

Carey, D.P., Harvey, M., & Milner, A.D. (1996). Visuomotor sensitivity for shape and orientation in a patient with visual form agnosia. *Neuropsychologia, 34,* 329-338.

Centers for Disease Control and Prevention (2011). http://www.cdc.gov/ncbddd/autism/index.html

Cermak, S., & Larkin, D. (2002). *Developmental coordination disorder.* Albany, NY: Delmar Thompson Learning.

Chang, C.-L., Kubo, M., & Ulrich, B. (2009). Emergence of neuromuscular patterns during walking in toddlers with typical development and with Down syndrome. *Human Movement Science, 28,* 283-296.

Chapman, S. (1968). Catching a baseball. *American Journal of Physics, 36,* 868-870.

Chen, L.-C., Metcalfe, J.S., Chang, T.-Y., Jeka, J.J., & Clark, J.E. (2008). The development of infant upright posture: Sway less or sway differently? *Experimental Brain Research, 186,* 293-303.

Chen, L.-C., Metcalfe, J.S., Jeka, J.J., & Clark, J.E. (2007). Two steps forward and one back: Learning to walk affects infants' sitting posture. *Infant Behavior and Development, 30,* 16-25.

Cheng, P.T., Wu, S.H., Liaw, M.Y., Wong, A.M., & Tang, F.T. (2001). Symmetrical body-weight distribution training in stroke patients and its effect on fall prevention. *Archives of Physical Medicine and Rehabilitation, 82,* 1650-1654.

Chohan, A., Verheul, M.H.G., Van Kampen, P.M., Wind, M., & Savelsbergh, G.J.P. (2008). Children's use of the bearing angle in interceptive actions. *Journal of Motor Behavior, 40*(1), 18-28.

Clark, J. (1982). Developmental differences in response processing. *Journal of Motor Behavior, 14,* 247-254.

Clark, J. (1987). Age-related differences in programming a movement. In J.E. Clark & J.H. Humphrey (Eds.), *Advances in motor development research 1* (pp. 95-104). New York: AMS Press.

Clark, J. (1993). A longitudinal study of intralimb co-ordination in the 1st year of independent walking: A dynamical systems analysis. *Child Development, 64,* 1143-1157.

Clark, J.E. (2002). Stepping into a new paradigm with an old reflex. A commentary on "The relationship between physical growth and a newborn reflex by Esther Thelen, Donna A. Fisher, and Robyn Ridley-Johnson. *Infant Behavior and Development, 25,* 91-93.

Clark, J.E., & Metcalfe, J.M. (2002). The mountain of motor development: A metaphor. In J.E. Clark & J.H. Humphrey (Eds.), *Motor development: Research and reviews* (Vol. 2, pp. 163-190). Reston, VA: National Association for Sport and Physical Education.

Clark, J.E., & Phillips, S. (1985). A developmental sequence of the standing long jump. In J. Clark & J. Humphrey (Eds.), *Motor development: Current selected research* (Vol. 1, pp. 73-85). Princeton, NJ: Princeton Book.

Clark, J.E., & Phillips, S. (1993). A longitudinal study of intralimb co-ordination in the 1st year of independent walking: A dynamical systems analysis. *Child Development, 64,* 1143-1157.

Clark, J.E., & Whitall, J. (1989a). Changing patterns of locomotion: From walking to skipping. In M. Woolacott & A. Shumway-Cook (Eds.), *Development of posture and gait across the lifespan* (pp. 128-151). Columbia, SC: University of South Carolina Press.

Clark, J.E., & Whitall, J. (1989b). What is motor development? The lessons of history. *Quest, 41,* 183-202.

Clark, J.E., Getchell, N., Smiley-Oyen, A., & Whitall, J. (2005). Developmental coordination disorder: Identification, issues, and interventions. *Journal of Physical Education, Recreation and Dance, 76,* 49-53.

Clark, J.E., Lanphear, A.K., & Riddick, C.C. (1987). The effects of videogame playing on the response selection processing of elderly adults. *Journal of Gerontology, 42*(1), 82-85.

Clark, J.E., Whitall, J., & Phillips, S. (1988). Human interlimb coordination: The first 6 months of independent walking. *Developmental Psychobiology, 21,* 445-456.

Clearfield, M.W., Feng, J., & Thelen, E. (2007). The development of reaching across the first year in twins of known placental type. *Motor Control, 11,* 29-53.

Clifton, R.K., Muir, D.W., Ashmead, D.H., & Clarkson, M.G. (1993). Is visually guided reaching in early infancy a myth? *Child Development, 54,* 1099-1100.

Coghill, G.E. (1929). *Anatomy and the problem of behavior.* Cambridge, UK: Cambridge University Press.

Connolly, K. (1970). *Mechanisms of motor skill development.* New York: Academic Press.

Connolly, K., & Elliott, J. (1972). The evolution and ontogeny of hand functions. In N. Blurton Jones (Ed.), *Ethological studies of child behavior* (pp. 329-284). London: Cambridge University Press.

Corbetta, D., & Mounoud, P. (1990). Early development of grasping and manipulation. In C. Bard, M. Fleury, & L. Hay (Eds.), *Development of eye-hand coordination across the life span* (pp. 188-216). Columbia, SC: University of South Carolina Press.

Corbetta, D., & Thelen, E. (1996). The developmental origins of bimanual coordination: A dynamic perspective. *Journal of Experimental Psychology: Human Perception and Performance, 22,* 502-522.

Corbetta, D., & Ulrich, B. (2008). Esther Thelen's legacy: A dynamic world that continues to reach out to others. *Infancy, 13,* 197-203.

Cordo, P., & Nashner, L. (1982). Properties of postural adjustments associated with rapid arm movements. *Journal of Neurophysiology, 47,* 287-302.

Craig, R.H. (1976). Interlimb coordination. In S.G.R. Herman (Ed.), *Neural control of locomotion* (pp. 51-64). New York: Plenum Press.

Craik, R., Herman, R.I., & Finley, F.R. (1976). Interlimb coordination. In R. Herman, S. Grillner, P. Stein, & D. Stuart (Eds.), *Neural control of locomotion* (pp. 51-64). New York: Plenum Press.

Cunningham, C. & Sloper, P. (1978). *Helping your handicapped baby.* London: Souvenir Press.

Daish, C. (1972). *The physics of ball games.* London: English Universities Press.

Damasio, A.R. (1989). Time-locked multiregional retroactivation: A systems-level proposal for the neural substrates of recall and recognition. *Cognition, 33,* 25-62.

Damasio, A.R., & Maurer, R.G. (1978). Neurological model for childhood autism. *Archives of Neurology, 35*(12), 777-786.

Damon, W. (1998). *Handbook of child psychology: Vol. 1. Theoretical models of human development* (5th ed., R. Lerner, Vol. Ed.). New York: Wiley.

Darwin, C. (1877). A biographical sketch of an infant. *Mind, 2,* 285-294.

Davis, R.H. (2006). Strong inference: Rationale or inspiration? *Perspectives in Biology and Medicine, 49,* 238-250.

de Castelnau, P., Albaret, J.M., Chaix, Y., & Zanone, P.G. (2007). Developmental coordination disorder pertains to a deficit in perceptuo-motor synchronization independent of attentional capacities. *Human Movement Science, 26*(3), 477-490.

De Guimps, R. (1906). *Pestalozzi, his life and work.* New York: Appleton.

De Haart, M., Geurts, A.C., Dault, M.C., Nienhuis, B., Duysens, J. (2005). Restoration of weight-shifting capacity in patients with post-acute stroke: A rehabilitation cohort study. *Archives of Physical Medicine and Rehabilitation, 86,* 755-762.

de Haart, M., Geurts, A.C., Huidekoper, S.C., Fasotti, L., & van Limbeck, J. (2004). Recovery of standing balance in post-acute stroke patients: A rehabilitation cohort study. *Archives of Physical Medicine and Rehabilitation, 85,* 886-895.

Deach, D. (1950). *Genetic development of motor skills in children two through six years of age.* Unpublished doctoral dissertation, University of Michigan, Ann Arbor.

DeLoache, J.S., Uttal, D.H., & Rosengren, K.S. (2004). Scale errors offer evidence for a perception-action dissociation early in life. *Science, 204,* 1027-1029.

Delorme, A., Frigon, J.-Y., & Lagacé, C. (1989). Infants' reactions to visual movement of the environment. *Perception, 18,* 667-673.

Dennis, W. (1960). Causes of retardation among institutional children: Iran. *Journal of Genetic Psychology, 96,* 47-59.

Desmedt, J.E. (1983). Size principle of motoneuron recruitment and the calibration of muscle force and speed in men. *Advances in Neurology, 39,* 227-251.

Deutsch, K.M., & Newell, K.M. (2005). Noise, variability, and the development of children's perceptual-motor skills. *Developmental Review, 25*(2), 155-180.

Dewey, D., Cantell, M., & Crawford, S.G. (2007). Motor and gestural performance in children with autism spectrum disorders, developmental coordination disorder, and/or attention deficit hyperactivity disorder. *Journal of the International Neuropsychological Society, 13*(2), 246-256.

DiRocco, P., Klein R., (2001). Adapted bicycling and dynamical systems. *International Adapted Physical Education Symposium*, Vienna.

Dobbs, A.R., & Rule, B.G. (1989). Adult age differences in working memory. *Psychology of Aging, 4,* 500-503.

Donker, S.M. (2002). Adaptations in arm movements for added mass to wrist or ankle during walking. *Experimental Brain Research, 145,* 26-31.

Donker, S.M., Mulder, T., Nienhuis, B., & Duysens, J. (2002). Adaptations in arm movements for added mass to wrist or ankle during walking. *Experimental Brain Research, 145,* 26-31.

Doumas, M., Smolders, C., & Krampe, R.Th. (2008). Task prioritization in aging: Effects of sensory information on concurrent posture and memory performance. *Experimental Brain Research, 187,* 275-281.

Duemmler, T., Schoeberl, P., & Schwarzer, G. (2008). Development of visual center of mass localization for grasp point selection. *Cognitive Development, 23,* 370-384.

Dulaney, C.L., & Tomporowski, P.D. (2000). Attention and cognitive-skill acquisition. In D.J. Weeks, R. Chua, & D. Elliott (Eds.), *Perceptual-motor behavior in Down syndrome* (pp. 175-198). Champaign, IL: Human Kinetics.

Ehl, T., Roberton, M., & Langendorfer, S. (2005). Does the throwing "gender gap" occur in Germany? *Research Quarterly for Exercise and Sport, 76,* 488-493.

Erbaugh, S. (1986). Effects of aquatic training on swimming skill development of preschool children. *Perceptual and Motor Skills, 62,* 439-446.

Espenschade, A., & Eckert, H. (1967). *Motor development.* Columbus, OH: Merrill.

Espenschade, A., & Eckert, H. (1980). *Motor development* (2nd ed.). Columbus, OH: Merrill.

Esposito, G., & Venuti, P. (2008). Analysis of toddlers' gait after six months of independent walking to identify autism: A preliminary study. *Perceptual and Motor Skills, 106*(1), 259-269.

Facoetti, A., Lorusso, M.L., Cattaneo, C., Galli, R., & Molteni, M. (2005). Visual and auditory attentional capture are both sluggish in children with developmental dyslexia. *Acta Neurobiologiae Experimentalis, 65,* 61-72.

Fagard, J., Spelke, E., & von Hofsten, C. (2009). Reaching and grasping a moving object in 6-, 8-, and 10-month-old infants: Laterality and performance. *Infant Behavior and Development, 32,* 137-146.

Farley, C.B., Blickhan, R., Saito, J., & Taylor, C. (1991). Hopping frequency in humans: A test of how springs set stride frequency in bouncing gaits. *Journal of Applied Physiology, 71,* 2127-2132.

Fentress, J. (1981). Sensorimotor development. In R. Aslin, J. Alberts, & M. Petersen (Eds.), *Development of perception: Vol. 1. Audition, somatic perception, and the chemical senses.* New York: Academic Press.

Fiatarone, M.A., Marks, E.C., Ryan, N.D., Meredith, C.N., Lipsitz, L.A., & Evans, W.J. (1990). High-intensity strength training in nonagenarians: Effects on skeletal muscle. *Journal of the American Medical Association, 263,* 3029-3034.

Fischer, K., & Silvern, L. (1985). Optimal and functional levels in cognitive development: The individual's developmental range. *Newsletter of the International Society for the Study of Behavioral Development, 2*(Serial No.), 1-4.

Fitch, H.L., Tuller, B., & Turvey, M.T. (1982). The Bernstein perspective: III. Tuning of coordinative structures with special reference to perception. In J.A.S. Kelso (Ed.), *Human motor behavior: An introduction* (pp. 271-281). Hillsdale, NJ: Erlbaum.

Fitts, P.M. (1962). Factors in complex skill training. In R. Glaser (Ed.), *Training research and education.* Pittsburgh: University of Pittsburg Press.

Fitts, P.M. (1964). Perceptual-motor skill learning. In A.W. Melton (Ed.), *Categories of human learning.* New York: Academic Press.

Flavell, J. (1971). Stage-related properties of cognitive development. *Journal of Cognitive Psychology, 2,* 421-453.

Flavell, J., & Wohlwill, J. (1969). Formal and functional aspects of cognitive development. In D. Elkind & J. Flavell (Eds.), *Studies in cognitive development* (pp. 67-120). New York: Oxford University Press.

Folio, M.R., & Fewell, R.R. (2000) Peabody Developmental Motor Scales. 2nd ed. Austin, TX: Pro-ed.

Fonseca, S.T., Holt, K.G., Fetters, L., Saltzman, E. (2004). Dynamic resources used in ambulation by children with spastic hemiplegic cerebral palsy: relationship to kinematics, energetics, and asymmetries. *Phys Ther, 84,* 344-354.

Forssberg, H. (1985). Ontogeny of human locomotor control I. Infant stepping, supported locomotion and transition to independent locomotion. *Experimental Brain Research, 57,* 480-493.

Forssberg, H., & Nashner, L.M. (1982). Ontogenetic development of postural control in man: Adaptation to altered support and visual conditions during stance. *Journal of Neuroscience, 2,* 545-552.

Forth, K.E., Metter, E.J., & Paloski, W.H. (2007). Age associated differences in postural equilibrium control: A comparison between EQscore and minimum time to contact [TTC (min)]. *Gait and Posture, 25,* 56-62.

Fortney, V. (1983). The kinematics and kinetics of the running pattern of 2-, 4-, and 6-year-old children. *Research Quarterly for Exercise and Sport, 54,* 126-135.

Foweather, L., McWhannell, N., Henaghan, J., Lees, A., Stratton, G., & Batterham A.M. (2008). Effect of a 9-wk. after-school multiskills club on fundamental movement skill proficiency in 8- to 9-yr.-old children: An exploratory trial. *Percept Mot Skills* 2008, 106, 745-754.

Gabbard, C., Cordova, A., & Ammar, D. (2007). Estimation of reach in peripersonal and extrapersonal space: A developmental view. *Developmental Neuropsychology, 32,* 749-756.

Gabell, A., & Nayak, U.S.L. (1984). The effect of age on variability in gait. *Journal of Gerontology, 39,* 662-666.

Gagen, L., & Getchell, N. (2004). Combining Theory and Practice in the Gymnasium: Constraints within an Ecological Perspective. *Journal of Physical Education Recreation and Dance,* 75(5), 25.

Garcia, C., & Garcia, L. (2002). Examining developmental changes in throwing. In J. Clark & J. Humphrey (Eds.), *Motor development: Research and reviews* (Vol. 2, pp. 62-95). Reston, VA: National Association for Sport and Physical Education.

Gentile, A., Higgins, J., Miller, E., & Rosen, B. (1975). The structure of motor tasks. In C. Bard (Ed.), *Mouvement: Actes du 7th symposium en apprentissage psycho-moteur et psychologie du sport* (pp. 11-28).

Gesell, A. (1929). Physical education in the preschool years. *American Physical Education Review, 34,* 528-529.

Gesell, A. (1933). Maturation and the patterning of behavior. In C. Murchison (Ed.), *Handbook of child psychology* (pp. 209-235). Worcester, MA: Clark University Press.

Gesell, A. (1939). Reciprocal interweaving in neuromotor development. *Journal of Comparative Neurology, 70,* 161-180.

Gesell, A. (1946). The ontogenesis of infant behavior. In L. Carmichael (Ed.), *Manual of child psychology* (pp. 295-331). New York: Wiley.

Gesell, A. (1954). The ontogenesis of infant behavior. In L. Carmichael (Ed.), *Manual of child psychology* (2nd ed., pp. 335-373). New York: Wiley.

Gesell, A., & Armatruda, C. (1941). *Developmental diagnosis: Normal and abnormal child development.* New York: Psychological.

Gesell, A., & Thompson, H. (1929). Learning and growth in identical infant twins: An experimental study of the method co-twin control. *Genetic Psychological Monographs, 6,* 1-124.

Gesell, A., & Thompson, H. (1934). *Infant behavior, its genesis and growth.* New York: McGraw-Hill.

Getchell, N., & Roberton, M.A. (1989). Whole body stiffness as a function of developmental level in children's hopping. *Developmental Psychology, 25,* 920-928.

Getchell, N., & Whitall, J. (2003). How do children coordinate simultaneous upper and lower extremity tasks? The development of dual motor task coordination. *Journal of Experimental Child Psychology, 85,* 120-140.

Getchell, N., Wei, H. & Mackenzie, S. (2008). Factors affecting motor development. In G. Payne (Ed.), *Introduction to human motor development*. Beijing: Peoples Education Press.

Geurts, A.C.H., de Haart, M., van Nes, I.J.W., & Duysens, J. (2005). A review of standing balance recovery from stroke. *Gait and Posture, 22*, 267-281.

Geuze R.H. (2005.) Postural control in children with Developmental Coordination Disorder. *Neural Plast* 12:111-124.

Geuze, R.H. (2003). Static balance and developmental coordination disorder. *Human Movement Science, 22*(4-5), 527-548.

Geuze, R.H., Jongmans, M.J., Schoemaker, M.M., & Smits-Engelsman, B.C.M. (2001). Clinical and research diagnostic criteria for developmental coordination disorder: A review and discussion. *Human Movement Science, 20*(1-2), 7-47.

Gibson, E.J. (1982). The concept of affordances in development: The renascence of functionalism. In W.A. Collins (Ed.), *The concept of development. Minnesota Symposium on Child Psychology* (Vol. 15, pp. 55-81). Hillsdale, NJ: Erlbaum.

Gibson, E.J. (1987). What does infant perception tell us about theories of perception? *Journal of Experimental Psychology: Human Perception and Performance, 13*, 515-523.

Gibson, E.J. (1988). Exploratory behavior in the development of perceiving, acting, and the acquiring of knowledge. *Annual Review of Psychology, 39*, 1-41.

Gibson, E.J., & Schmuckler, M.A. (1989). Going somewhere: An ecological and experimental approach to the development of mobility. *Ecological Psychology, 1*, 3-25.

Gibson, E.J., Riccio, G., Schmuckler, M.A., Stoffregen, T.A., Rosenberg, D., & Taormina, J. (1987). Detection of the traversability of surfaces by crawling and walking infants. *Journal of Experimental Psychology: Human Perception and Performance, 13*, 533-522.

Gibson, J.J. (1950). *The perception of the visual world.* Boston: Houghton Mifflin.

Gibson, J.J. (1960). The concept of the stimulus in psychology. *American Psychologist, 15*, 694-703.

Gibson, J.J. (1966). *The senses considered as perceptual systems.* Boston: Houghton Mifflin.

Gibson, J.J. (1979). *An ecological approach to visual perception.* Boston: Houghton Mifflin.

Gleick, J. (1987). *Chaos: Making a new science.* New York: Penguin Books.

Glickstein, M., Buchbinder, S., & May, J.L. (1998). Visual control of the arm, the wrist and the fingers; pathways through the brain. *Neuropsychologia, 36*, 981-1001.

Glickstein, M., Cohen, J.L., Dixon, B., Gibson, A., Hollins, M., LaBossiere, E., & Robinson, F. (1980). Corticopontine visual projections in macaque monkeys. *Journal of Comparative Neurology, 190*, 209-229.

Glover, S. (2004a). Separate visual representations in the planning and control of actions. *Behavioral and Brain Sciences, 27*, 3-78.

Glover, S. (2004b). What causes scale errors in children? *Trends in Cognitive Sciences, 8*, 440-442.

Godoi, D., & Barela, J.A. (2008). Body sway and sensory motor coupling adaptation in children: Effects of distance manipulation. *Developmental Psychobiology, 49*, 77-87.

Goldfield, E.C. (1989). Transition from rocking to crawling: Postural constrains on infant movement. *Developmental Psychology, 25*(6), 913-919.

Goodale, M., Meenan, J.P., Bülthoff, H.H., Nicolle, D.A., Murphy, K.J. & Racicot, C.I. (1994). Separate neural pathways for the visual analysis of object shape in perception and prehension. *Current Biology, 4*, 604-610.

Goodale, M., & Milner, D. (2005). *Sight unseen.* Oxford, UK: Oxford University Press.

Goodway, J.D., & Branta, C.F. (2003). Influence of a motor skill intervention on fundamental motor skill development of disadvantaged preschool children. *Research Quarterly for Exercise and Sport*, 74(1), 36-46.

Goodway, J.D., Crowe, H., & Ward, P. (2003). Effects of motor skill instruction on fundamental motor skill development. *Adapted Physical Activity Quarterly*, 20(3), 298-314.

Graf C., Koch B., Falkowski G., Jouck S., Christ H., Staudenmaier K., Tokarski W., Gerber A., Predel H.G., & Dordel S. (2005). Effects of a school based intervention on BMI and motor abilities in childhood. *J Sport Sci Med* 2005 , 4, 291-299.

Graham, G., Holt/Hale, S., & Parker, M. (1993). *Children moving: A reflective approach to teaching physical education* (3rd ed.). Mountain View, CA: Mayfield Publishing.

Granata, K.P., Ikeda, A.J., & Abel, M.F. (2000). Electromechanical delay and reflex response in spastic cerebral palsy. *Archives of Physical Medicine and Rehabilitation*, 81(7), 888-894.

Gross, C.G., Desimone, R., Albright, T.D., & Schwartz, E.L. (1985). Inferior temporal cortex and pattern recognition. In C. Chagas, R. Gattass, & C. Gross (Eds.), *Pattern recognition mechanisms* (pp. 179-201). Berlin: Springer-Verlag.

Gross, C.G., Rocha-Miranda, C.E., & Bender, D.B. (1972). Visual properties of neurons in the inferotemporal cortex of the macaque. *Journal of Neurophysiology*, 35, 96-111.

Gutteridge, M. (1939). A study of motor achievements of young children. *Archives of Psychology*, 244.

H'Doubler, M. (1946). *Movement and its rhythmic structure*. Madison, WI: Kramer Business Service.

Hadders-Algra M. (2003). Developmental Coordination Disorder: Is clumsy motor behavior caused by a lesion of the brain at early age? *Neural Plast 10*, 39-50.

Halverson, H.M. (1931). An experimental study of prehension in infants by means of systematic cinema records. *Genetic Psychology Monographs*, 10, 107-286.

Halverson, H.M. (1940). Motor development. In A. Gesell (Ed.), *The first five years of life* (pp. 65-107). New York: Harper & Row.

Halverson, L. (1966). Development of motor patterns in young children. *Quest*, 6, 44-53.

Halverson, L. (1985). Developmental sequences for hopping over distance: A prelongitudinal screening. *Research Quarterly for Exercise and Sport*, 56, 37-44.

Halverson, L. E., Roberton, M. A., Safrit, M. J., & Roberts, T. W. (1977). The effect of guided practice on overhand throw ball velocities of kindergarten children. *Research Quarterly*, 48, 2, 311-318.

Halverson, L., & Williams, K. (1985). Developmental sequences for hopping over distance: A prelongitudinal screening. *Research Quarterly for Exercise and Sport*, 56, 37-44.

Halverson, L., Roberton, M.A., & Harper, C. (1973). Current research in motor development. *Journal of Research and Development in Education*, 6, 56-70.

Halverson, L., Roberton, M.A., & Langendorfer, S. (1982). Development of the overarm throw: Movement and ball velocity changes by seventh grade. *Research Quarterly for Exercise and Sport*, 53, 198-205.

Halverson, L.E., & Roberton, M.A. (1979). The effects of instruction on overhand throwing development in children. In G. Roberts & K. Newell (Eds.), *Psychology of motor behavior and sport*, 258-269. Champaign, IL: Human Kinetics.

Hamilton, M., & Tate, A. (2002). Constraints on throwing behavior of children. In J. Clark & J. Humphrey (Eds.), *Motor development: Research and reviews* (Vol. 2, pp. 49-61). Reston, VA: National Association for Sport and Physical Education.

Hamilton, M., Goodway, J., & Haubenstricker, J. (1999). Parent-assisted instruction in a motor skill program for at-risk preschool children. *Adapted Physical Activity Quarterly*, 16(4), 415-426.

Harter, S. (1978). Effectance motivation reconsidered: Toward a developmental model. *Human Development*, Vol 21(1), 34-64.

Harter, S., & Pike, R. (1984). The pictorial scale of perceived competence and social acceptance for young children. *Child Dev*, 55(6), 1969-1982.

Haubenstricker, J.L., Branta, C.F., & Seefeldt, V.D. (1983, June). *Standards of performance for throwing and catching.* Proceedings of the Annual Conference of the North American Society for Psychology of Sport and Physical Activity, Asilomar, CA.

Haywood, K.M. (l980). Coincidence-anticipation accuracy across the life span. *Experimental Aging Research*, 6, 45l-462.

Haywood, K.M., & Getchell, N. (2005). *Life span motor development* (4th ed.). Champaign, IL: Human Kinetics.

Haywood, K.M., & Getchell, N. (2009). *Life span motor development* (5th ed.). Champaign, IL: Human Kinetics.

Haywood, K.M., Greenwald, G., & Lewis, C. (1981). Contextual factors and age group differences in coincidence-anticipation performance. *Research Quarterly for Exercise and Sport*, 52, 458-464.

Heft, H. (2001). *Ecological psychology in context: James Gibson, Roger Barker, and the legacy of William James's radial empiricism.* Mahwah, NJ: Erlbaum.

Hellebrandt, F., Rarick, G., Glassow, R., & Carns, M. (1961). Physiological analysis of basic motor skills I. Growth and development of jumping. *American Journal of Physical Medicine*, 40, 14-25.

Henderson, S.E., & Barnett, A. (1998). Developmental movement problems. In J. Rispens, T. van Yperen, & W. Yule (Eds.), *The classification of specific developmental disorders* (pp. 191-213). Amsterdam, Netherlands: Kluver.

Henderson, S.E., & Sugden, D. (1992). *Movement Assessment Battery for Children.* London: The Psychological Corporation.

Henry, F.M. (1968). Specificity vs. generality in learning motor skill. In R.C. Brown & G.S. Kenyon (Eds.), *Classical studies on physical activity* (pp. 331-340). Englewood Cliffs, NJ: Prentice Hall. (Original work published 1958)

Herdman, S.D., Douglas, M., Shell, D., Volz, D., Yancery, S., Chambers,W., & Liu, C. (1983). Recovery of the hopping response after complete spinal cord transection in the cat. *Experimental Neurology, 81*, 776-780.

Herkowitz, J. (1979). Developmentally engineered equipment and playspaces for motor development and learning. In *Psychology of motor behavior and sport.* C.H. Nadeau, W.R. Halliwell, K.W. Newell, and G.C. Roberts. Champaign, IL: Human Kinetics.

Hernik, M., & Csibra, G. (2009). Functional understanding facilitates learning about tools in human children. *Current Opinion in Neurobiology, 19*, 34-38.

Hillier S.L. (2007) Intervention for children with developmental coordination disorder: A systematic review. *The Internet Journal of Allied Health Science and Practice*, 5 (3).

Hirabayashi, S., & Iwasaki, Y. (1995). Developmental perspective of sensory organization on postural control. *Brain and Development, 17,* 111-113.

Hocherman, S., Dickstein, R., & Pillar, T. (1984). Platform training and postural stability in hemiplegia. *Archives of Physical Medicine and Rehabilitation, 65,* 588-592.

Hohlstein, R.E. (1982). The development of prehension in normal infants. *American Journal of Occupational Therapy, 36,* 170-176.

Holmes. P. (2005) Ninety plus thirty years of nonlinear dynamics: More is different and less is more. *Int. J. Bifurcation and Chaos,* 15 (9), 2703-2716.

Holt, K. (2005). Biomechanical models, motor control theory, and development. *Infant and Child Development, 14,* 523-527.

Holt, K.G., Fonseca, S.T., & LaFiandra, M.E. (2000). The dynamics of gait in children with spastic hemiplegic cerebral palsy: Theoretical and clinical implications. *Human Movement Science, 19*(3), 375-405.

Holt, K.G., Obusek, J.P., & Fonseca, S.T. (1996). Constraints on disordered locomotion. A dynamical systems perspective on spastic cerebral palsy. *Human Movement Science, 15*(2), 177-202.

Hooker, D. (1952). *The prenatal basis of behavior.* Lawrence, KS: University of Kansas Press.

Horak, F.B., & Nashner, L.M. (1986). Central programming of postural movements: Adaptation to altered support-surface configurations. *Journal of Neurophysiology, 55,* 1369-1381.

Horak, F.B., Shupert, C.L., & Mirka, A. (1989). Components of postural dyscontrol in the elderly: A review. *Neurobiology and Aging, 10,* 727-738.

Hu, M., & Woollacott, M.H. (1994a). Multisensory training of standing balance in older adults: I. Postural stability and one-leg stance balance. *Journals of Gerontology, 49,* M52-M61.

Hu, M., & Woollacott, M.H. (1994b). Multisensory training of standing balance in older adults: II. Kinematic and electromyographic postural responses. *Journals of Gerontology, 49,* M62-M71.

Hughes, S., Gibbs, J., Dunlop, D., Edelman, P., Singer, R., & Chang, R.W. (1997). Predictors of decline in manual performance in older adults. *Journal of the American Geriatrics Society, 45,* 905-910.

Hughes, V.A., Frontera, W.R., Wood, M., Evans, W.J., Dallal, G.E., Roubenoff, R., & Fiatarone Singh, M.A. (2001). Longitudinal muscle strength changes in older adults: Influence of muscle mass, physical activity, and health. *Journals of Gerontology, Series A: Biological Sciences and Medical Sciences, 56,* B209-B217.

Hung, W.W., & Pang, M.Y. (2010) Effects of group-based versus individual-based exercise training on motor performance in children with developmental coordination disorder: A randomized controlled study. *J Rehabil Med, 42*(2), 122-128.

Hyvärinen, J., & Poranen, A. (1974). Function of the parietal associative area 7 as revealed from cellular discharges in alert monkeys. *Brain, 97,* 673-692.

Ignico A.A. (1991). Effects of a competency-based instruction on kindergarten children's gross motor development. *Phys Educ.* 1991;48 (4), 188–199.

Irwin, D., & Bushnell, M. (1980). *Observational strategies for child study.* New York: Holt, Reinhart, & Winston.

Ivanenko, Y.D., Dominici, N., & Lacquaniti, F. (2007). Development of independent walking in toddlers. *Exercise and Sport Sciences Reviews, 35,* 67-73.

Jackson, K.M., Joseph, J., & Wyard, S.J. (1983). The upper limbs during human walking. Part 1: Sagittal movement. Part 2: Function. *Electromyography and Clinical Neurophysiology, 23,* 425-446.

James, W. (1890). *The principles of psychology* (Vols. 1-2). New York: Holt.

James, W. (1976). *Essays in radical empiricism.* Cambridge, MA: Harvard University Press. (Original work published 1912)

Jansen, C.W.S., Niebuhr, B.R., Coussirat, D.J., Hawthorne, D., Moreno, L., & Phillip, M. (2008). Hand force of men and women over 65 years of age as measured by maximum pinch and grip force. *Journal of Aging and Physical Activity, 16*, 24-41.

Janzen, T. (1989). *Spontaneous kicking in infants: A replication study.* Unpublished master's thesis, University of Wisconsin, Madison.

Jeka, J.J., & Lackner, J.R. (1994). Fingertip contact influences human postural control. *Experimental Brain Research, 100*, 495-502.

Jeka, J.J., Allison, L.K., & Kiemel, T. (2010). The dynamics of visual reweighting in health and fall-prone older adults. *Journal of Motor Behavior, 42*, 197-208.

Jeka, J.J., Allison, L.K., Saffer, M., Zhang, Y., Carver, S., & Kiemel, T. (2006). Sensory reweighting with translational visual stimuli in young and elderly adults: The role of state-dependent noise. *Experimental Brain Research, 174*, 517-527.

Jeka, J.J., Oie, K.S., & Kiemel, T. (2000). Multisensory information for human postural control: Integrating touch and vision. *Experimental Brain Research, 134*, 107-125.

Jeng, S.F., Liao, H.F., Lai, J.S., & Hou, J.W. (1997). Optimization of walking in children. *Medicine and Science in Sports and Exercise, 29*, 370-376.

Jenkins, L. (1930). A comparative study of motor achievement of children of five, six, and seven years of age. *Teachers College Contributions to Education, 414*.

Jensen, J. (2005). The puzzles of motor development: How the study of developmental biomechanics contributes to the puzzle solutions. *Infant and Child Development, 14*, 501-511.

Jobling, A. (1999). Attainment of motor proficiency in school aged children with Down syndrome. *Adapted Physical Activity Quarterly, 16*, 344-361.

Jobling, A., & Virji-Babul, N. (2004). *Motor development in Down syndrome: Play, move and grow.* Burnaby, BC: Down Syndrome Research Foundation.

Jones, L., & Barton, G. (2008). Throwing profiles of U-14 ASA softball players. *Research Quarterly for Exercise and Sport, 79*(Suppl.), A-39.

Jonsson, B., & von Hofsten, C. (2003). Infants' ability to track and reach for temporarily occluded objects. *Developmental Science, 6*(1), 86-99.

Jouen, F. (1990). Early visual-vestibular interactions and postural development. In H. Bloch & B.I. Bertenthal (Eds.), *Sensory-motor organization and development in infancy and early childhood* (pp. 199-216). Dordrecht, Netherlands: Kluwer.

Kail, R.V. & Cavanaugh J.C. (2010), *Human development: A life-span view*, 5th ed: Cengage Learning, Wadsworth.

Kaminski, G. (1997). Roger Barker's ecological psychology. In W.G. Bringmann, H.E. Lück, R. Miller, & C.D. Early (Eds.), *A pictorial history of psychology* (pp. 288-292). Chicago: Quintessence.

Kanner, L. (1943). Autistic disturbances of affective contact. *Nervous Child, 2*, 217- 250.

Kanner, L. (1944). Early infantile autism. *Journal of Pediatrics, 25*, 211-217.

Kaplan, B.J., Wilson, B.N., Dewey, D., & Crawford, S.G. (1998). DCD may not be a discrete disorder. *Human Movement Science, 17*(4-5), 471-490.

Kelso, J.A.S. (1995). *Dynamic patterns: The self-organization of brain and behavior.* Cambridge, MA: MIT Press.

Kemler Nelson, D.G., Egan, L.C., & Holt, M.B. (2004). When children ask, "What is it?" what do they want to know about artifacts? *Psychological Science, 15*(6), 384-389.

Kent, M. (2007). *Oxford dictionary of sports science and medicine.* Oxford, UK: Oxford University Press.

Keogh, J. (1965). *Motor performance of elementary school children.* Los Angeles: University of California.

Keogh, J. (1977). The study of movement skill development. *Quest, 28,* 76-88.

Kiemel, T., Oie, K.S., & Jeka, J.J. (2002). Multisensory fusion and the stochastic structure of postural sway. *Biological Cybernetics, 87,* 262-277.

Kiemel, T., Oie, K.S., & Jeka, J.J. (2006). Slow dynamics of postural sway are in the feedback loop. *Journal of Neurophysiology, 95,* 1410-1418.

Klein, R.E., McHugh E., Harrington S.L., Davis T., and Lieberman L.J., (2005) Adapted Bicycles for Teaching Riding Skills. *Teaching Exceptional Children,* Vol. 37, No. 6, (July 2005), 50-56

Klüver, H., & Bucy, P.C. (1939). Preliminary analysis of functions of the temporal lobes in monkeys. *Archives of Neurology and Psychiatry, 42,* 979-1000.

Koffka, K. (1935). *Principles of Gestalt psychology.* New York: Harcourt, Brace & World.

Kohlberg, L. (1963). The development of children's orientations toward a moral order. I. Sequence in the development of moral thought. *Vita Humana, 6,* 11-33.

Krageloh-Mann, I. (2007). Cerebral palsy. An update. *Monatsschrift Kinderheilkunde, 155*(6), 523-528.

Krageloh-Mann, I., & Horber, V. (2007). The role of magnetic resonance imaging in elucidating the pathogenesis of cerebral palsy: A systematic review. *Developmental Medicine and Child Neurology, 49*(2), 144-151.

Kubo, M., & Ulrich, B. (2006a). Coordination of pelvis-HAT (head, arms and trunk) in anterior-posterior and medio-lateral directions during treadmill gait in preadolescents with/without Down syndrome. *Gait and Posture, 23*(4), 512-518.

Kubo, M., & Ulrich, B. (2006b). Early stage of walking: Development of control in mediolateral and anteriorposterior directions. *Journal of Motor Behavior, 38,* 229-237.

Kugler, P. (1986). A morphological perspective on the origin and evolution of movement patterns. In M. Wade and H.T.A. Whiting (Eds.), *Motor development in children: Aspects of coordination and control* (pp. 459-525). Dordrecht, Netherlands: Martinus Nijhoff.

Kugler, P., Kelso, J.A.S., & Turvey, M.T. (1982). On the control and coordination of naturally developing systems. In J.A.S. Kelso & J.E. Clark (Eds.), *The development of movement control and coordination* (pp. 5-78). New York: Wiley.

Kugler, P.N., Kelso, J.A.S., & Turvey, M.T. (1980). On the concept of coordinative structures as dissipative structures: I. Theoretical lines of convergence. In G.E. Stelmach & J. Requin (Eds.), *Tutorials in motor behavior* (pp. 3–47). New York: North-Holland.

Kugler, P.N., Kelso, J.A.S., & Turvey, M.T. (1982). On coordination and control in naturally developing systems. In J.A.S. Kelso & J.E. Clark (Eds.), *The development of human movement coordination and control* (pp. 5-78). New York, London: John Wiley.

Kuhtz-Buschbeck, J.P., Stolze, H., Jöhnk, K., Boczek-Funcke, A., & Illert, M. (1998). Development of prehension movements in children: A kinematic study. *Experimental Brain Research, 122,* 424-432.

Kulak, W., Sobaniec, W., Kuzia, J.S., & Bockowski, L. (2006). Neurophysiologic and neuroimaging studies of brain plasticity in children with spastic cerebral palsy. *Experimental Neurology, 198*(1), 4-11.

Kulak, W., Sobaniec, W., Smigielska-Kuzia, J., Kubas, B., & Walecki, J. (2006). Metabolite profile in the basal ganglia of children with cerebral palsy: A proton magnetic resonance spectroscopy study. *Developmental Medicine and Child Neurology, 48*(4), 285-289.

Lafferty, M.E. (2005). A stair-walking intervention strategy for children with Down's syndrome. *Journal of Bodywork and Movement Therapies, 9,* 65-74.

Landa, R., & Garrett-Mayer, E. (2006). Development in infants with autism spectrum disorders: A prospective study. *Journal of Child Psychology and Psychiatry, 47*(6), 629-638.

Langendorfer, S. (1980). Longitudinal evidence for developmental changes in the preparatory phase of the ovearm throw for force. Report to the Research Section, National Convention of the American Alliance for Health, Physical Education, Recreation and Dance, Detroit.

Langendorfer, S. (1987a). A prelongitudinal test of motor stage theory. *Research Quarterly for Exercise and Sport, 58*, 21-29.

Langendorfer, S. (1987b). Prelongitudinal screening of overarm striking development performed under two environmental conditions. In J. Clark & J. Humphrey (Eds.), *Advances in motor development research* (Vol. 1, pp. 17-47). New York: AMS Press.

Langendorfer, S. (1990). Motor-task goal as a constraint on developmental status. In J. Clark & J. Humphrey (Eds.), *Advances in motor development research* (Vol. 3, pp. 16-28). New York: AMS Press.

Langendorfer, S., & Bruya, L. (1995). *Aquatic readiness.* Champaign, IL: Human Kinetics.

Langendorfer, S., & Roberton, M.A. (2002a). Developmental profiles in overarm throwing: Searching for "attractors," "stages," and "constraints." In J. Clark & J. Humphrey (Eds.), *Motor development: Research and reviews* (Vol. 2, pp. 1-25). Reston, VA: National Association for Sport and Physical Education.

Langendorfer, S., & Roberton, M.A. (2002b). Individual pathways in the development of forceful throwing. *Research Quarterly for Exercise and Sport, 73*, 245-258.

Langer, J. (1969). *Theories of development.* New York: Holt, Reinhart & Winston.

Latash, M.L. (2000). Motor coordination in Down syndrome: The role of adaptive changes. In D.J. Weeks, R. Chua, & D. Elliott (Eds.), *Perceptual-motor behavior in Down syndrome* (pp. 199-224). Champaign, IL: Human Kinetics.

Ledebt, A., & Bril, B. (2000). Acquisition of upper body stability during walking in toddlers. *Developmental Psychobiology, 36*, 311-324.

Lee, D.N. (1980). Visuo-motor coordination in space-time. In G.E. Stelmach & J. Requin (Eds.), *Tutorials in motor behavior* (pp. 281-285). Amsterdam: North-Holland.

Lee, D.N. (1998). Guiding movement by coupling taus. *Ecological Psychology, 10*, 221-250.

Lee, D.N., & Aronson, E. (1974). Visual proprioceptive control of standing in human infants. *Perception and Psychophysiology, 15*, 529-532.

Lee, D.N., & Young, D.S. (1985). Visual timing of interceptive action. In D. Ingle, M. Jeannerod, & D.N. Lee (Eds.), *Brain mechanisms and spatial vision* (pp. 1-30). Dordrecht, Netherlands: Martinus Nijhoff.

Lefebvre, C., & Reid, G. (1998). Prediction in ball catching by children with and without a developmental coordination disorder. *Adapted Physical Activity Quarterly, 15*, 299-315.

Lenoir, M., Musch, E., Janssens, M., Thiery, E., & Uyttenhove, J. (1999). Intercepting moving objects during self-motion. *Journal of Motor Behavior, 31*, 55-67.

Levtzion-Korach, O., Tennenbaum, A., Schnitzer, R., & Ornoy, A. (2000). Early motor development of blind children. *Journal of Paediatrics and Child Health, 36*, 226-229.

Lew, A.R., & Butterworth, G. (1997). The development of hand-mouth coordination in 2- to 5-month-old infants: Similarities with reaching and grasping. *Infant Behavior and Development, 20*, 59-69.

Li, T.Y., & Yorke, J.A. (1975). Period three implies chaos. *American Mathematical Monthly, 82*, 985.

Liben, L. (2008). (Ed.) Essays on Continuities and Discontinuities. *Child Development, 79*, 1600-1658.

Lichtenstein, M.J., Shields, S.L., Shiavi, R.G., & Burger, C. (1989). Exercise and balance in aged women: A pilot controlled clinical trial. *Archives of Physical Medicine and Rehabilitation, 70*, 138-143.

Lightfoot, C., & Folds-Bennett, T. (1992). Description and explanation in developmental research: Separate agendas. In J. Asendordp & J. Valsiner (Eds.), *Stability and change in development: A study of methodological reasoning* (pp. 207-228). Newbury Park, CA: Sage.

Lishman, J.R., & Lee, D.N. (1973). The autonomy of visual kinaesthesis. *Perception, 2*, 287-294.

Lisy, M. (2002). *Testing developmental sequences for the forceful kick.* Unpublished master's project, Bowling Green State University, Ohio.

Lobo, M.A., Galloway, J.C., & Savelsbergh, G.J.P. (2004). General and task-related experiences affect early object interaction. *Child Development, 75*(4), 1268-1281.

Lockman, J.J. (1990). Perceptual motor coordination in infancy. In C.-A. Hauert (Ed.), *Developmental psychology: Cognitive, perceptuomotor, and neuropsychological perspectives* (pp. 85-111). New York: Plenum Press.

Lockman, J.J. (2008). On tool use, perseveration and task dynamics. *Infancy, 13*(3), 279-283.

Lockman, J.J., Ashmead, D.H., & Bushnell, E.W. (1984). The development of anticipatory hand orientation during infancy. *Journal of Experimental Child Psychology, 37*, 176-186.

Logan, D., Kiemel,T., Dominici, N., Cappellini, G., Ivanenko, Y., Lacquaniti, F., & Jeka, J.J. (2010). The many roles of vision during walking. *Experimental Brain Research, 206*, 337-350.

Lorson, K., & Goodway, J. (2008). Gender differences in throwing form of children ages 6-8 years during a throwing game. *Research Quarterly for Exercise and Sport, 79*, 174-182.

Lundgren-Lindquist, B., Aniansson, A., & Rundgren, A. (1983). Functional studies in 79 year olds. III. Walking and climbing performance. *Scandinavian Journal of Rehabilitative Medicine, 15*, 125-131.

Lynch, A., Ryu, J.C., Agrawal, S., & Galloway, J.C. (2009). Power mobility training for a 7-month-old infant with spina bifida. *Pediatric Physical Therapy, 21*(4), 362-368.

MacCracken, M.J., & Stadulis, R. (1985). Social facilitation of young children's dynamic balance performance. *Journal of Sport and Exercise Psychology, 7*, 150-165.

Mackenzie, S.J., Getchell, N., Deutsch, K., Wilms-Floet, A., Clark, J.E., & Whitall, J. (2008). Multi-limb coordination and rhythmic variability under varying sensory availability conditions in children with DCD. *Human Movement Science, 27*(2), 256-269.

Magnus, R. (1926a). Some results of studies in the physiology of posture. Carmeron Prize Lectures Part I. *Lancet, 211*, 531-535.

Magnus, R. (1926b). Some results of studies in the physiology of posture. Carmeron Prize Lectures Part II. *Lancet, 211*, 585-588.

Mally, K., Battista, R., & Roberton, M.A. (2011). Distance as a control parameter for place kicking. *Journal of Human Sport and Exercise, 6*(1), 122-134. www.jhse.ua.es/index.php/jhse/article/view/174/311.

Manchester, D., Woollacott, M., Zederbauer-Hylton, N., & Marin, O. (1989). Visual, vestibular and somatosensory contributions to balance control in the older adult. *Journals of Gerontology, Series A: Biological Sciences and Medical Sciences, 44*, M118-M127.

Manoel, E.DeJ., & Oliveira, J.A. (2000). Motor developmental status and task constraint in overarm throwing. *Journal of Human Movement Studies, 39*, 359-378.

Mari, M., Castiello, U., Marks, D., Marraffa, C., & Prior, M. (2003). The reach-to-grasp movement in children with autism spectrum disorder. *Philosophical Transactions of the Royal Society of London, Series B: Biological Sciences, 358*(1430), 393-403.

Mari, M., Castiello, U., Marks, D., Marraffa, C., & Prior, M. (2003). The reach-to-grasp movement in children with autism spectrum disorder. Philosophical Transactions of the Royal Society of London, Series B, *Biological Sciences, 358,* 393–403

Marigold, D.S., & Eng, J.J. (2006). The relationship of asymmetric weight-bearing with postural sway and visual reliance in stroke. *Gait and Posture, 23,* 249-255.

Marschik, P.B., Einspieler, C., Strohmeier, A., Plienegger, J., Garzarolli, B., & Prechtl, H.F.R. (2008). From the reaching behavior at 5 months of age to hand preference at preschool age. *Developmental Psychobiology, 50,* 512-518.

Marteniuk, R.G. (1976). *Information processing in motor skills.* New York: Holt, Reinhart & Winston.

Martin, N.C., Piek, J.P., & Hay, D. (2006). DCD and ADHD: A genetic study of their shared aetiology. *Human Movement Science, 25*(1), 110-124.

Mayes, S.D., & Calhoun, S.L. (2003). Ability profiles in children with autism—influence of age and IQ. *Autism, 7*(1), 65-80.

McBeath, M.K., Shaffer, D.M., & Kaiser, M.K. (1995). How baseball outfielders determine where to run to catch fly balls. *Science, 268,* 569-573.

McCaskill, C., & Wellman, B. (1938). A study of common motor achievements in the preschool ages. *Child Development, 9,* 141-150.

McDonald, J. (1992). Is strong inference really superior to simple inference? *Synthese, 92,* 261-282.

McGeer, T. (1990). Passive dynamic walking. *The International Journal of Robotics Research, 9*(2), 62-82.

McGraw, M. (1941). Quantitative studies in the development of erect locomotion. *Child Development, 12,* 267-303.

McGraw, M. (1946). Maturation of behavior. In L. Carmichael (Ed.), *Manual of child psychology* (pp.332-69). New York: Wiley.

McGraw, M. (1963). *The neuromuscular maturation of the human infant.* New York: Hafner Press. (Original work published 1945)

McGraw, M. (1975). *Growth: A study of Johnny and Jimmy.* New York: Appleton-Century/Arno Press. (Original work published 1935)

McGraw, M., & Breeze, K.W. (1941). Quantitative studies in the development of erect locomotion. *Child Development, 12,* 267-303.

McLean, B., & Tumilty, D.McA. (1993). Left-right asymmetry in two types of soccer kick. *British Journal of Sports Medicine, 27,* 260-262.

McLeod, P., & Dienes, Z. (1993). Running to catch the ball. *Nature, 362,* 23.

McLeod, P., & Dienes, Z. (1996). Do fielders know where to go to catch the ball or only how to get there? *Journal of Experimental Psychology: Human Perception and Performance, 22,* 531-543.

McLeod, P., Reed, N., & Dienes, Z. (2001). Toward a unified theory: What we do not yet know about how people run to catch a ball. *Journal of Experimental Psychology: Human Perception and Performance, 27,* 1347-1355.

McLeod, P., Reed, N., & Dienes, Z. (2002). The optic trajectory is not a lot of use if you want to catch the ball. *Journal of Experimental Psychology: Human Perception and Performance, 28,* 1499-1501.

Meiss, J. D. (2007). *Differential Dynamical Systems.* Philadelphia: SIAM.

Messick, J.A. (1991). Prelongitudinal screening of hypothesized developmental sequences for the overhead tennis serve in experienced tennis players 9-19 years of age. *Research Quarterly for Exercise and Sport, 62,* 249-256.

Metcalfe, J.S., Chen, L.-C., Chang, T.-Y., McDowell, K., Jeka, J.J., & Clark, J.E. (2005). The temporal organization of posture changes during the first year of independent walking. *Experimental Brain Research, 161*, 405-416.

Metcalfe, J.S., McDowell, K., Chang, T.-Y., Chen, L.-C., Jeka, J.J., & Clark, J.E. (2005). Development of somatosensory-motor integration: An event-related analysis of infant posture in the first year of independent walking. *Developmental Psychobiology, 46*, 19-35.

Michaels, C.F., & Carello, C. (1981). *Direct perception.* Englewood Cliffs, NJ: Prentice Hall.

Michel, G.F., & Moore, C.L. (1999). *Developmental psychobiology: An interdisciplinary science.* Cambridge, MA: MIT Press.

Miller, L.T., Polatajko, H. J., Missiuna, C., Mandich, A.D., & Macnab, J.J. (2001). A pilot trial of a cognitive treatment for children with developmental coordination disorder. *Hum Mov Sci, 20*(1-2), 183-210.

Milner, A.D., & Goodale, M.A. (2006). *The visual brain in action* (2nd ed.). Oxford, UK: Oxford University Press.

Ming, X., Brimacombe, M., & Wagner, G.C. (2007). Prevalence of motor impairment in autism spectrum disorders. *Brain and Development, 29*(9), 565-570.

Miyahara, M., & Mobs, I. (1995). Developmental dyspraxia and developmental coordination disorder. *Neuropsychology Review, 5*(4), 245-268.

Miyahara, M., & Wafer, A. (2004). Clinical intervention for children with developmental coordination disorder: A multiple case study. *Adapted Physical Activity Quarterly, 21*(3), 281–300.

Miyahara, M., Tsujii, M., Hori, M., Nakanishi, K., Kageyama, H., & Sugiyama, T. (1997). Brief report: Motor incoordination in children with Asperger syndrome and learning disabilities. *Journal of Autism and Developmental Disorders, 27*(5), 595-603.

Miyahara, M., Yamaguchi, M., & Green, C. (2008). A review of 326 children with developmental and physical disabilities, consecutively taught at the Movement Development Clinic: Prevalence and intervention outcomes of children with DCD. *Journal of Developmental and Physical Disabilities, 20* (4), 353-363.

Mountcastle, V.B., Lynch, J.C., Georgopoulos, A., Skata, H., & Acuna, C. (1975). Posterior parietal association cortex of the monkey: Command functions for operations within extrapersonal space. *Journal of Neurophysiology, 38*, 871-908.

Murray, M.K. (1969). Walking patterns in healthy old men. *Journal of Gerontology, 24*, 169-178.

Murray, M.P. (1964). Walking patterns of normal men. *The Journal of Bone and Joint Surgery, 46*, 335-360.

Murray, M.P., Drought, B., & Kory, R. (1964). Walking patterns of normal men. *The Journal of Bone and Joint Surgery, 46*, 335-360.

Murray, M.P., Kory, R.C., & Clarkson, B.H. (1969). Walking patterns in healthy old men. *Journal of Gerontology, 24*, 169-178.

Murray, M.P., Kory, R.C., & Sepic, S.B. (1970). Walking patterns of normal women. *Archives of Physical Medicine and Rehabilitation, 51*, 637-650.

Murray, M.P., Sepic, S.B., & Barnard, E.J. (1967). Patterns of sagittal rotation of the upper limbs in walking. *Physical Therapy, 47*, 272-284.

Murray, M.S. (1967). Patterns of sagittal rotation of the upper limbs in walking. *Physical Therapy, 47*, 272-284.

Napier, J.R. (1956). The prehensile movements of the human hand. *The Journal of Bone and Joint Surgery, 38*, 902-913.

Nashner, L.M. (1977). Fixed patterns of rapid postural responses among leg muscles during stance. *Experimental Brain Research, 30,* 13-24.

Nashner, L.M., & Woollacott, M. (1979). The organization of rapid postural adjustments of standing humans: An experimental-conceptual model. In R.E. Talbott & D.R. Humphrey (Eds.), *Posture and movement* (pp. 243-257). New York: Raven Press.

National Down Syndrome Society (2011). Down Syndrome Fact Sheet. http://www.ndss.org/

National Institute of Child and Human Development (2011). Down syndrome. http://www.nichd.nih.gov/health/topics/Down_Syndrome.cfm

National Institute of Neurological Disorders and Stroke (2011). Cerebral Palsy. http://www.ninds.nih.gov/disorders/cerebral_palsy/cerebral_palsy.htm

Neisser, U. (1967). *Cognitive psychology.* New York: Appleton-Century-Crofts.

Newell K.W., & Roberts, C.G. (1979) *Psychology of Motor Behaviour and Sport.* Champaign, IL: Human Kinetics.

Newell, K. (1984). Physical constraints to development of motor skills. In J. Thomas (Ed.), *Motor Development during Childhood and Adolescence.* Minneapolis, MN: Burgess Publishing Company.

Newell, K. (1986). Constraints on the development of coordination. In M. Wade & H.T.A. Whiting (Eds.), *Motor development in children: Aspects of coordination and control* (pp. 341-360). Dordrecht, Netherlands: Martinus Nijhoff.

Newell, K.M., & van Emmerik, R. (1990). Are Gesell's developmental principles general principles for the acquisition of coordination? In J. Clark & J. Humphrey (Eds.), *Advances in motor development research* (Vol. 3, pp. 143-164). New York: AMS Press.

Newell, K.M., Scully, D.M., McDonald, P.V., & Baillargeon, R. (1989). Task constraints and infant grip configurations. *Developmental Psychobiology, 22,* 817-832.

Newell, K.M., Scully, D.M., Tenebaum, F., & Hardiman, S. (1989). Body scale and the development of prehension. *Developmental Psychobiology, 22,* 1-13.

Newell, K.M., Slobounov, S.J., Slobounova, E.S., & Molenaar, P.C. (1997). Stochastic processes in postural center-of-pressure profiles. *Experimental Brain Research, 113,* 158-164.

O'Donohue, W.O., & Buchanan, J.A. (2000). The weaknesses of strong inference. *Behavior and Philosophy, 29,* 1-20.

O'Sullivan, M.C., Miller, S., Ramesh, V., Conway, E., Gilfillan, K., McDonough, S., & Eyre, J.A. (1998). Abnormal development of biceps brachii phasic stretch reflex and persistence of short latency heteronymous reflexes from biceps to triceps brachii in spastic cerebral palsy. *Brain, 121*(12), 2381-2395.

Overton, W. (1998). Developmental psychology: Philosophy, concepts, and methodology. In W. Damon & R. Lerner (Eds.), *Handbook of child psychology: Vol. 1. Theoretical models of human development* (pp. 107-188). New York: Wiley.

Oyama, S. (1985). *The ontogeny of information: Developmental systems and evolution.* Cambridge, UK: Cambridge University Press.

Ozonoff, S., Young, G.S., Goldring, S., Greiss-Hess, L., Herrera, A.M., Steele, J., Macari, S., Hepburn, S., & Rogers, S.J. (2008). Gross motor development, movement abnormalities, and early identification of autism. *Journal of Autism and Developmental Disorders, 38*(4), 644-656.

Palmer, E., Cafarelli, E., & Ashby, P. (1994). The processing of human ballistic movements explored by stimulation over the cortex. *Journal of Physiology, 481,* 509-520.

Parish, L.E., & Rudisill, M.E. (2006). HAPPE: Promoting physical play among toddlers. *Young Children, 61*(3), 32.

Parish, L.E., Rudisill, M.E., & St. Onge, P.M. (2007). Mastery motivational climate: Influence on physical play heart rate and intensity in African American toddlers. *Research Quarterly for Exercise and Sport. 78*, 171-178.

Paulson, G., & Gottlieb, G. (1968). Developmental reflexes: The reappearance of foetal and neonatal reflexes in aged patients. *Brain, 91*, 37-52.

Peiper, A. (1963). *Cerebral function in infancy and childhood.* New York: Consultants Bureau Enterprises.

Pepping, G.-J., & Grealy\, M.A. (Eds.). (2007). *Closing the gap: The scientific writings of David N. Lee.* Mahway, NJ: Erlbaum.

Peran, S., Gil, J.L., Ruiz, F., & Fernandez-Pastor, V. (1997). Development of physical response after athletics training in adolescents with Down syndrome. *Scandinavian Journal of Medicine and Science in Sports, 7*, 283-288.

Peterson, M.L., Christou, E., & Rosengren, K.S. (2006). Children achieve adult-like sensory integration during stance at 12-years-old. *Gait and Posture, 23*, 455-463.

Peurala, S.H., Könönen, P., Pitkänen, K., Sivenius, J., & Tarkka, I.M. (2007). Postural instability in patients with chronic stroke. *Restorative Neurology and Neuroscience, 25*, 101-108.

Piaget, J. (1952). *The origins of intelligence in children.* New York: International Universities Press.

Piaget, J. (1954). *The construction of reality in the child.* New York: Basic Books.

Piaget, J. (1970). Piaget's theory. In P. Mussen (Ed.), *Carmichael's handbook of child psychology* (pp. 703-732). New York: Wiley.

Piek, J.P. (2002). The role of variability in early motor development. *Infant Behavior and Development, 25*(4), 452-465.

Piek, J.P., & Dyck, M.J. (2004). Sensory-motor deficits in children with developmental coordination disorder, attention deficit hyperactivity disorder and autistic disorder. *Human Movement Science, 23*(3-4), 475-488.

Piek, J.P., Gasson, N., Barrett, N., & Case, I. (2002). Limb and gender differences in the development of coordination in early infancy. *Human Movement Science, 21*(5-6), 621-639.

Pieraut-LeBonniec, G. (1985). Hand-eye coordination and infants' construction of convexity and concavity. *British Journal of Developmental Psychology, 3*, 273-280.

Pinard, A., & Laurendeau, M. (1969). "Stage" in Piaget's cognitive-developmental theory: Exegesis of a concept. In D. Elkind & J. Flavell (Eds.), *Studies in cognitive development* (pp. 121-170). New York: Oxford University Press.

Pirila, S., van der Meere, J., & Pentikainen, T. (2007). Language and motor speech skills in children with cerebral palsy. *Journal of Communication Disorders, 40*, 116-128.

Platt, J.R. (1964). Strong inference. *Science, 146*, 347-353.

Pless, M., & Carlsson, M. (2000). Effects of motor skill intervention on developmental coordination disorder: A meta-analysis. *Adapted Physical Activity Quarterly, 17*(4), 381-401.

Polatajko H.J., & Cantin N. (2005). Developmental coordination disorder (dyspraxia): An overview of the state of the art. *Seminars in Pediatric Neurology 12*(4):250-8.

Pope, M., Lynch, A., Liu, T., & Getchell, N. (2010). Motor development in children with autism spectrum disorders. In F. Columbus (Ed.), *Motor skills: Development, impairment and therapy.* Hauppauge, NY: Nova Science.

Prakash, P. (1984). Second language acquisition and critical period hypothesis. *Psycho-lingua, 14*(1), 13-17.

Prigogine, I. (1978). Time, structure, and fluctuations. *Science, 201*, 777-785.

Prigogine, I., & Stengers, I. (1984). *Order out of chaos: Man's new dialogue with nature.* New York: Bantam Books.

Provost, B., Lopez, B.R., & Heimerl, S. (2007). A comparison of motor delays in young children: Autism spectrum disorder, developmental delay, and developmental concerns. *Journal of Autism and Developmental Disorders, 37*(2), 321-328.

Przysucha, E.P., & Taylor, M.J. (2004). Control of stance and developmental coordination disorder: The role of visual information. *Adapted Physical Activity Quarterly, 21*(1), 19-33.

Raibert, M. (1990). Foreword: Special issue on legged locomotion. *International Journal of Robotics* Research, 9 (2), 2-3.

Raibert, M.B., Brown, H.B., & Chepponis, M. (1984). Experiments in balance with a 3D one-legged hopping machine. *The Internal Journal of Robotics Research, 3,* 75-92.

Ranganathan, V.K., Siemionow, V., Sahgal, V., Liu, J.Z., & Yue, G.H. (2001). Skilled finger movement exercise improves hand function. *Journals of Gerontology, Series A: Biological Sciences and Medical Sciences, 56A,* M518-M522.

Rarick, G. (1952). *Motor development during infancy and childhood.* Madison, WI: College Printing and Typing.

Rarick, G. (1973). *Physical activity—human growth and development.* New York: Academic Press.

Reed, E.S. (1982a). An outline of a theory of action systems. *Journal of Motor Behavior, 14,* 98-134.

Reed, E.S. (1982b). Descartes' corporeal ideas hypothesis and the origin of scientific psychology. *Review of Metaphysics, 35,* 731-752.

Reed, E.S. (1989). Changing theories of postural development. In M.H. Woollacott & A. Shumway-Cook (Eds.), *Development of posture and gait across the life span* (pp. 3-24). Columbia, SC: University of South Carolina Press.

Reid, G., & Block, M.E. (1996). Motor development and physical education. In B. Stratford & P. Gunn (Eds.), *New approaches to Down syndrome* (pp. 309-340). London: Cassell.

Riach, C.L., & Hayes, K.C. (1987). Maturation of postural sway in young children. *Developmental Medicine and Child Neurology, 29,* 650-658.

Riddle, A., Luo, N.L., Manese, M., Beardsley, D.J., Green, L., Rorvik, D.A., et al. (2006). Spatial heterogeneity in oligodendrocyte lineage maturation and not cerebral blood flow predicts fetal ovine periventricular white matter injury. *Journal of Neuroscience, 26*(11), 3045-3055.

Riley, M., & Roberton, M.A. (1981). Developing skillful games players. Consistency between beliefs and practice. *Motor Skills: Theory into Practice, 5,* 123-133.

Roberton, M.A. (1972). Developmental kinesiology. *Journal of Health, Physical Education, and Recreation, 43,* 65-66.

Roberton, M.A. (1977). Stability of stage categorizations across trials: Implications for the "stage theory" of over-arm throw development. *Journal of Human Movement Studies, 3,* 49-59.

Roberton, M.A. (1978a). Longitudinal evidence for developmental stages in the forceful overarm throw. *Journal of Human Movement Studies, 4,* 167-175.

Roberton, M.A. (1978b). Stages in motor development. In M. Ridenour (Ed.), *Motor development: Issues and applications* (pp. 63-81). Princeton, NJ: Princeton Book.

Roberton, M.A. (1982). Describing 'stages' within and across motor tasks. In J. Kelso & J. Clark (Eds.), *The development of movement control and co-ordination* (pp. 293-307). New York: Wiley.

Roberton, M.A. (1984). Changing motor patterns during childhood. In J. Thomas (Ed.), *Motor development during preschool and elementary years* (pp. 48-90). Minneapolis: Burgess.

Roberton, M.A. (1987). Developmental level as a function of the immediate environment. In J. Clark & J. Humphrey (Eds.), *Advances in motor development research* (Vol. 1, pp. 1-15). New York: AMS Press.

Roberton, M.A. (1989a). Developmental sequence and developmental task analysis. In J.C. Skinner (Ed.), *Future directions in exercise and sport science research* (pp. 369-381). Champaign, IL: Human Kinetics.

Roberton, M.A. (1989b). Motor development: Recognizing our roots, charting our future. *Quest, 41,* 213-223.

Roberton, M.A. (1993). New ways to think about old questions. In L. Smith & E. Thelen (Eds.), *A dynamic systems approach to development: Applications* (pp. 95-117). Cambridge, MA: MIT Press.

Roberton, M.A., & Halverson, L. (1984). *Developing children—their changing movement.* Philadelphia: Lea & Febiger.

Roberton, M.A., & Halverson, L. (1988). The development of locomotor coordination: Longitudinal change and invariance. *Journal of Motor Behavior, 20,* 197-241.

Roberton, M.A., & Konczak, J. (2001). Predicting children's overarm throw ball velocities from their developmental levels of throwing. *Research Quarterly for Exercise and Sport, 72,* 91-103.

Roberton, M.A., & Langendorfer, S. (1980). Testing motor development sequences across 9-14 years. In C. Nadeau, W. Halliwell, K. Newell, & G. Roberts (Eds.), *Psychology of motor behavior and sport—1979* (pp. 269-279). Champaign, IL: Human Kinetics.

Roberton, M.A., Williams, K., & Langendorfer, S. (1980). Pre-longitudinal screening of motor development sequences. *Research Quarterly for Exercise and Sport, 51,* 724-731.

Roberts, E.M., & Metcalfe, A. (1968). Mechanical analysis of kicking. *Biomechanics I* (pp. 315-319). New York: Karger.

Robertson, S.S., Bacher, L.F., & Huntington, N.L. (2001). Structure and irregularity in the spontaneous behavior of young infants. *Behavioral Neuroscience, 115,* 758-763.

Robinson, D.N. (1995). *An intellectual history of psychology* (3rd ed). Madison, WI: University of Wisconsin Press.

Robinson, L., Goodway, J., & Williams, E.J. (2007). Developmental trends of overarm throwing performance in young children. *Research Quarterly for Exercise and Sport, 78*(Suppl.), A-48.

Robinson, L.E., & Goodway, J.D. (2009). Instructional climates in preschool children who are at-risk. Part I: Object-control skill development. *Res Q Exerc Sport, 80*(3), 533-542.

Robinson, L.E., Rudisill, M.E., & Goodway, J.D. (2009). Instructional climates in preschool children who are at-risk. Part II: Perceived physical competence. [reports - research]. *Research Quarterly for Exercise and Sport, 80*(3), 543-551.

Rosander, K., & von Hofsten, C. (2004). Infants' emerging ability to represent object motion. *Cognition, 91,* 1-22.

Rosenbaum, P., Walter, S., Hanna, S., Palisano, R., Russell, D., Raina, P., Wood, E., Bartlett, D., & Galuppi, B. (2002). Prognosis for gross motor function in cerebral palsy: Creation of motor development curves. *Journal of the American Medical Association, 288* (11), 1357-1363.

Rosenbloom, L., & Horton, M.E. (1971). The maturation of fine prehension in young children. *Developmental Medicine and Child Neurology, 13,* 2-8.

Rosengren, K.S., Carmichael, C., Schein, S.S., Anderson, K.N., & Gutiérrez, I.T. (2009). A method for eliciting scale errors in preschool classrooms. *Infant Behavior and Development, 32,* 286-290.

Rosengren, K.S., Gutiérrez, I.T., Anderson, K.N., & Schein, S.S. (2009). Parental reports of children's scale errors in everyday life. *Child Development, 80*(6), 1586-1591.

Rosengren, K.S., Rajendran, K., Contakos, J., Chuang, L.L., Peterson, M., Doyle, R., & McAuley, E. (2007). Changing control strategies during standard assessment using computerized dynamic posturography with older women. *Gait and Posture, 25*, 215-221.

Runion, B., Roberton, M.A., & Langendorfer, S. (2003). Forceful overarm throwing: A comparison of two cohorts measured twenty years apart. *Research Quarterly for Exercise and Sport, 74*, 324-330.

Russell D, Palisano R, Walter S, Rosenbaum P, Gemus M, Gowland C, Galuppi B, Lane M. (1998). Evaluating motor function in children with Down syndrome: Validity of the GMFM. *Developmental Medicine and Child Neurology, 40*(10), 693-701.

Russell, D.J., Rosenbaum, P.L., and Gowland, C. (1993). *Gross Motor Function Measure manual* (2nd ed.). Owen Sound, ON: Pediatric Physiotherapy Services.

Russell, D.J., Ward, M., & Law, M. (1994). Test-retest reliability of the Fine Motor Scale of the Peabody Developmental Motor Scales in children with cerebral-palsy. *Occupational Therapy Journal of Research, 14*(3), 178-182.

Russell, DJ, Rosenbaum, PL, Cadman, DT, Gowland, C., Hardy, S., Jarvis, S. (1989). The Gross Motor Function Measure: A means to evaluate the effects of physical therapy. *Developmental Medicine and Child Neurology, 31*, 341-352.

Russell, J. (1987). *Creative dance in the primary school.* Plymouth, UK: Northcote House.

Sacks, B., & Buckley, S.J. (2003). Motor development for individuals with Down syndrome—an overview. *Down Syndrome Issues and Information, 2* (4), 131- 141.

Safrit, M.J., Stamm, C.L., Russell, K., & Sloan, M.R. (1977). Effect of environment and order of testing on performance of a motor task. *Research Quarterly, 48*, 376-381.

Saida, Y., & Miyashita, M. (1979). Development of fine motor skill in children: Manipulation of a pencil in young children ages 2 to 6 years old. *Journal of Human Movement Studies, 5*, 104-113.

Saint-Georges C., Cassel R.S., Cohen D., Chetouani M., Laznik M.C., Maestro S., Muratori F. (2010) What the literature on family home movies can teach us about the infancy of autistic children: A review of literature. *Research in Autism Spectrum Disorders, 4*, 355–366.

Saint-Georges, C., Cassel, R.S., Cohen, D., Chetouani, M., Laznik, M.C., Maestro, S., et al. (2010). What studies of family home movies can teach us about autistic infants. *Research in Autism Spectrum Disorders, 4*, 355–366.

Schaie, K.W. (1965). A general model for the study of developmental problems. *Psychological Bulletin, 64*, 92-107.

Schaie, K.W. (1970). A reinterpretation of age related changes in cognitive structure and functioning. In L.R. Goulet & P.B. Baltes (Eds.), *Life-span developmental psychology— research and theory* (pp. 485-507). New York: Academic Press.

Schaltenbrand, G. (1928). The development of human motility and motor disturbances. *Archives of Neurology and Psychiatry, 20*, 720-730.

Schmidt, R.A. & Lee, T.D. (2011). *Motor control and learning: A behavioral emphasis* (5th Edition). Champaign, IL: Human Kinetics.

Scrutton, D. (1969). Footprint sequences of normal children under five years old. *Developmental Medicine and Child Neurology, 11*.

Seefeldt, V., & Haubenstricker, J. (1982). Patterns, phases, or stages: An analytical model for the study of developmental movement. In J.A.S. Kelso & J. Clark (Eds.), *The development of movement control and coordination* (pp. 309-318). New York: Wiley.

Seefeldt, V., Reuschlein, S., & Vogel, P. (1972). *Sequencing motor skills within the physical education curriculum.* Paper presented to the National Convention of the American Association for Health, Physical Education, and Recreation.

Shaffer, D.M. (1999). Navigating in baseball: A spatial optical tracking strategy and associated naïve physical beliefs. *Dissertation Abstracts International. Section B: The Sciences and Engineering, 59*(8-B), 4504.

Shaffer, D.M., & McBeath, M.K. (2002). Baseball outfielders maintain a linear optical trajectory when tracking uncatchable fly balls. *Journal of Experimental Psychology: Human Perception and Performance, 28*, 335-348.

Shaffer, D.M., Krauchunas, S.M., Eddy, M., & McBeath, M.K. (2004). How dogs navigate to catch Frisbees. *Psychological Science, 15*, 437-441.

Shaffer, D.M., McBeath, M.K., Roy, W.L., & Krauchunas, S.M. (2003). A linear optical trajectory informs the fielder where to run to the side to catch fly balls. *Journal of Experimental Psychology: Human Perception and Performance, 29*, 1244-1250.

Sherrington, C.S. (1906). *The integrative action of the nervous system.* New Haven, CT: Yale University Press.

Shinn, M. (1900). *The biography of a baby: The first year of life.* Boston: Houghton Mifflin.

Shirley, M. (1931). *The first two years—a study of twenty-five babies: Vol. I. Postural and locomotor development.* Minneapolis: University of Minnesota Press.

Shumway-Cook, A., & Woollacott, M. (1985). The growth of stability: Postural control from a developmental perspective. *Journal of Motor Behavior, 17*, 131-147.

Shumway-Cook, A., Anson, D., & Haller, S. (1988). Postural sway biofeedback: Its effect on reestablishing stance stability in hemiplegic patients. *Archives of Physical Medicine and Rehabilitation, 69*, 395-400.

Siegler, R. (2007). Cognitive variability. *Developmental Science, 10*, 104-109.

Sigmundsson, H., Ingvaldsen, R.P., Whiting, H.T.A. (1997). Inter-and intra-sensory modality matching in children with hand-eye co-ordination problems: Exploring the developmental lag hypothesis. *Developmental Medicine and Child Neurology*, vol. 39, 12, 790-796.

Smith, B.A., & Ulrich, B.D. (2008). Early onset of stabilizing strategies for gait and obstacles: Older adults with Down syndrome. *Gait and Posture, 28*(3), 448-455.

Smith, B.A., Kubo, M., Black, D.P., Holt, K.G., & Ulrich, B.D. (2007). Effect of practice on a novel task—walking on a treadmill: Preadolescents with and without Down syndrome. *Physical Therapy, 87*(6), 766-777.

Smith, L.B. (2006). Movement matters: The contributions of Esther Thelen. *Biological Therapy, 1*, 87-89.

Smith, L.B., & Thelen, E. (1993). *A dynamic systems approach to development.* Cambridge, MA: MIT Press.

Smith, L.B., & Thelen, E. (2003). Development as a dynamic system. *Trends in Cognitive Sciences, 7*, 343-348.

Smits-Engelsman, B.C.M., Niemeijer, A.S., & van Galen, G.P. (2001). Fine motor deficiencies in children diagnosed as DCD based on poor grapho-motor ability. *Human Movement Science, 20*(1-2), 161-182.

Smitsman, A.W., & Cox, R.F.A. (2008). Perseveration in tool use: A window for understanding the dynamics of the action-selection process. *Infancy, 13*(3), 249-269.

Smoll, F. (1982). Developmental kinesiology: Toward a subdiscipline focusing on motor development. In J. Kelso & J. Clark (Eds.), *The development of movement control and co-ordination* (pp. 319-354). New York: Wiley.

Soll, D.R. (1979). Timers in developing systems. *Science, 203*, 841-849

Southard, D. (2002a). Change in throwing pattern: Critical values for control parameter of velocity. *Research Quarterly for Exercise and Sport, 73*, 396-407.

Southard, D. (2002b). Control parameters for the development of throwing. In J. Clark & J. Humphrey (Eds.), *Motor development: Research and reviews* (Vol. 2, pp. 26-48). Reston, VA: National Association for Sport and Physical Education.

Sparrow, W. (1989). Creeping patterns in human adults and children. *American Journal of Physical Anthropology, 78,* 387-401.

Speers, R.A., Kuo, A.D., & Horak, F.B. (2002). Contributions of altered sensation and feedback responses to changes in coordination of postural control due to aging. *Gait and Posture, 16,* 20-30.

Spelke, E., & Newport, E. (1998). Nativism, empiricism, and the development of knowledge. In W. Damon & R. Lerner (Eds.), *Handbook of child psychology: Vol. 1. Theoretical models of human development* (5th ed., pp. 275-340). New York: Wiley.

Spelke, E.S., & von Hofsten, C. (2001). Predictive reaching for occluded objects by 6-month-old infants. *Journal of Cognition and Development, 2*(3), 261-281.

Spencer, J., Clearfield, M., Corbetta, D., Ulrich, B., Buchanan, P., & Schoner, G. (2006). Moving toward a grand theory of development: In memory of Esther Thelen. *Child Development, 77,* 1521-1538.

Spirduso, W.W., Francis, K.W., & MacRae, P.G. (2005). *Physical dimensions of aging* (2nd ed.). Champaign, IL: Human Kinetics.

Stallings, L.M. (1973). *Motor skills: Development and learning.* Dubuque, IA: Brown.

Stallings, L.M. (1976). Application of an information processing model to teaching motor skills. *Motor Skills: Theory Into Practice, 1,* 12-22.

Stein, B.E., & Meredith, M.A. (1993). *The merging of the senses.* Cambridge, MA: MIT Press/Bradford Books.

Stodden, D. F., Goodway, J. D., Langerdorfer, S. J., Roberton, M. A., Rudsill, M. E., Garcia, C., & Garcia, L. E. (2008). A developmental perspective on the role of motor skill competence in physical activity: An emergent relationship. *Quest, 60,* 290-306.

Stodden, D., Langendorfer, S., Fleisig, G., & Andrews, J. (2006a). Kinematic constraints associated with the acquisition of overarm throwing. Part I: Step and trunk actions. *Research Quarterly for Exercise and Sport, 77,* 417-427.

Stodden, D., Langendorfer, S., Fleisig, G., & Andrews, J. (2006b). Kinematic constraints associated with the acquisition of overarm throwing. Part II: Upper extremity actions. *Research Quarterly for Exercise and Sport, 77,* 428-436.

Stolze, H.K.-B.-F. (1997). Gait analysis during treadmill and overground locomotion in children and adults. *Electroencephalography and Clinical Neurophysiology: Electromyography and Motor Control, 105,* 490-497.

Stone, J.E. (1996). Developmentalism: An obscure but pervasive restriction on educational improvement. *Education Policy Analysis Archives, 4(8).*

Strohmeyer, H.S., Williams, K., & Schaub-George, D. (1991). Developmental sequences for catching a small ball: A prelongitudinal screening. *Research Quarterly for Exercise and Sport, 62,* 257-266.

Sugar, T.G., & McBeath, M.K. (2001). Robotic modeling of mobile catching as a tool for understanding biological interceptive behavior. *Behavior and Brain Sciences, 24,* 1078-1080.

Sutherland, D., Olshen, R., Biden, E., & Wyatt, M. (1988). *The development of mature walking* (Clinics in Developmental Medicine No. 104/105). Oxford, UK: Blackwell Scientific.

Teasdale, N., & Simoneau, M. (2001). Attentional demands for postural control: The effects of aging and sensory reintegration. *Gait and Posture, 14,* 203-210.

Thelen, E. (1979). Rhythmical stereotypies in normal human infants. *Animal Behaviour, 27,* 699-715.

Thelen, E. (1981). Kicking, rocking, and waving: Contextual analysis of rhythmical stereotypies in normal human infants. *Animal Behaviour, 29,* 3-11.

Thelen, E. (1989). The (re)discovery of motor development: Learning new things from an old field. *Developmental Psychology, 25*(6), 946-949.

Thelen, E. (1989). The developmental origins of locomotion. In M.W. Shumway-Cook (Ed.), *Development of posture and gait across the life span* (pp. 25-47). Columbia, SC: University of South Carolina Press.

Thelen, E. (1995). Motor development: A new synthesis. *American Psychologist, 50*(2), 79-95.

Thelen, E., & Adolph, K. (1992). Arnold L. Gesell: The paradox of nature and nurture. *Developmental Psychology, 28,* 368-380.

Thelen, E., & Bates, E. (2003). Connectionism and dynamic systems: Are they really different? *Developmental Science, 6,* 378-390.

Thelen, E., & Fisher, D.M. (1982). Newborn stepping: An explanation for a "disappearing" reflex. *Developmental Psychology, 18,* 760-775.

Thelen, E., & Smith, L. (1994). *A dynamic systems approach to the development of cognition and action.* Cambridge, MA: MIT Press.

Thelen, E., & Smith, L.B. (1998). Dynamic systems theories. In W. Damon & R. Lerner (Eds.), *Handbook of child Psychology: Vol. 1. Theoretical models of human development* (5th ed., pp. 563-634). New York: Wiley.

Thelen, E., & Ulrich, B.D. (1991). Hidden skills: A dynamic systems analysis of treadmill-elicited stepping during the first year. *Monographs of the Society for Research in Child Development, 56*(Serial No. 223).

Thelen, E., & Whitmeyer, V. (2005). Using dynamic field theory to conceptualize the interface of perception, cognition and action. In J.J. Rieser, J.J. Lockman, & C.A. Nelson (Eds.), *Action as an organizer of learning and development* (pp. 243-280). Mahweh, NJ: Lawrence Erlbaum Associates.

Thelen, E., Bradshaw, G., & Ward, J.A. (1981). Spontaneous kicking in month-old infants: Manifestation of a human central locomotor program. *Behavioral and Neural Biology, 32,* 45-53.

Thelen, E., Corbetta, D., & Spencer, J.P. (1996). Development of reaching during the first year: Role of movement speed. *Journal of Experimental Psychology: Human Perception and Performance, 22,* 1059-1076.

Thelen, E., Corbetta, D., Kamm, K., Spencer, J.P., Schneider, K., & Zernicke, R.F. (1993). The transition to reaching: Mapping intention and intrinsic dynamics. *Child Development, 64,* 1058-1098.

Thelen, E., Fisher, D.M., & Ridley-Johnson, R. (1984). The relationship between physical growth and a newborn reflex. *Infant Behavior and Development, 7,* 479-493.

Thelen, E., Fisher, D.M., Ridley-Johnson, R., & Griffin, N. (1982). The effects of body build and arousal on newborn infant stepping. *Developmental Psychobiology, 15,* 447-453.

Thelen, E., Schöner, G., Scheier, C., & Smith, L.B. (2001). The dynamics of embodiment: A field theory of infant perseverative reaching. *Behavioral and Brain Sciences, 24,* 1-86.

Thelen, E., Ulrich, B., & Jensen, J. (1989). The developmental origins of locomotion. In M. Woolacott & A. Shumway-Cook (Eds.), *Development of posture and gait across the life span* (pp. 25-47). Columbia, SC: University of South Carolina Press.

Thomas, J. (1980). Acquisition of motor skills: Information processing differences between children and adults. *Research Quarterly for Exercise and Sport, 51,* 158-173.

Thomas, J. (2000). Children's control, learning, and performance of motor skills. *Research Quarterly for Exercise and Sport, 71,* 1-9.

Thomas, J., & French, K. (1985). Gender differences across age in motor performance: A meta-analysis. *Psychological Bulletin, 98,* 260-282.

Thomas, J.R., Mitchell, B., & Solmon, M.A. (1979). Precision knowledge of results and motor performance: Relationship to age. *Research Quarterly, 50*(4), 687-698.

Tresilian, J.R., Mon-Williams, M., Coppard, V.L., & Carson, R.G. (2005). Developmental changes in the response to obstacles during prehension. *Journal of Motor Behavior, 37,* 103-110.

Tucker, M.G., Kavanagh, J.J., Barrett, R.S., & Morrison, S. (2008). Age-related differences in postural reaction time and coordination during voluntary sway movements. *Human Movement Science, 27,* 728-737.

Tuller, B., Turvey, M.T., & Fitch, H. (1982). The Bernstein perspective: 2. The concept of muscle linkage or coordinative structure. In J.A.S. Kelso (Ed.), *Human motor behavior: An introduction* (pp. 253-270). Hillsdale, NJ: Erlbaum.

Turiel, E. (1969). Developmental processes in the child's moral thinking. In P. Mussen, J. Langer, & M. Covington (Eds.), *Trends and issues in developmental psychology* (pp. 92-133). New York: Holt.

Turvey, M.T., Fitch, H.L., & Tuller, B. (1982). The Bernstein perspective: 1. The problems of degrees of freedom and context-conditioned variability. In J.A.S. Kelso (Ed.), *Human motor behavior: An introduction* (pp. 239-252). Hillsdale, NJ: Erlbaum.

Ulrich, B. (2007). Motor development: Core curricular concepts. *Quest, 59,* 77-91.

Ulrich, B., & Kubo, M. (2005). Adding pieces to the puzzle: A commentary. *Infant and Child Development, 14,* 519-522.

Ulrich, B., Haehl, V., Buzzi, U.H., Kubo, M., & Holt, K.G. (2004). Modeling dynamic resource utilization in populations with unique constraints: Preadolescents with and without Down syndrome. *Human Movement Science, 23*(2), 133-156.

Ulrich, B.D., & Ulrich, D.A. (1995). Spontaneous leg movements of infants with Down syndrome and nondisabled infants. *Child Development, 66*(6), 1844-1855.

Ulrich, B.D., Ulrich, D.A., & Collier, D.H. (1992). Alternating stepping patterns: Hidden abilities of 11-month-old infants with Down syndrome. *Developmental Medicine and Child Neurology, 34*(3), 233-239.

Ulrich, B.D., Ulrich, D.A., Angulo-Kinzler, R., & Chapman, D.D. (1997). Sensitivity of infants with and without Down syndrome to intrinsic dynamics. *Research Quarterly for Exercise and Sport, 68*(1), 10-19.

Ulrich, B.D., Ulrich, D.A., Collier, D.H., & Cole, E.L. (1995). Developmental shifts in the ability of infants with Down syndrome to produce treadmill steps. *Physical Therapy, 75*(1), 14-23.

Ulrich, D.A. (1985) *Test of Gross Motor Development.* Pro-ED. Inc., Austin, Texas.

Ulrich, D.A. (2000). *Test of gross motor development* (2nd ed.). Austin, TX: PRO-ED,

Ulrich, D.A., Lloyd, M.C., Tiernan, C.W., Looper, J.E., & Angulo-Barroso, R.M. (2008). Effects of intensity of treadmill training on developmental outcomes and stepping in infants with Down syndrome: A randomized trial. *Physical Therapy, 88*(1), 114-122.

Ulrich, D.A., Ulrich, B.D., Angulo-Kinzler, R.M., & Yun, J. (2001). Treadmill training of infants with Down syndrome: Evidence-based developmental outcomes. *Pediatrics, 108*(5), E84.

Utley, A. & Astill, S.L. (2007) Developmental sequences of two-handed catching: how do children with and without developmental coordination disorder differ? *Physiother Theory Pract*, 23, 65-82.

Utley, A., Steenbergen, B., & Astill, S.L. (2007). Ball catching in children with developmental coordination disorder: Control of degrees of freedom. *Developmental Medicine and Child Neurology*, 49(1), 34-38.

Valentini, N., & Rudisill, M.E. (2004a). Motivational climate, motor-skill development, and perceived competence: Two studies of developmentally delayed kindergarten children. [reports - research]. *Journal of Teaching in Physical Education*, 23(3), 216-234.

Valentini, N.C., & Rudisill, M.E. (2004b). An inclusive mastery climate intervention and the motor development of children with and without disabilities. *Adapted Physical Activity Quarterly*, 21, 330-347.

Valentini, N.C., M.E. Rudisill, & J.D. Goodway. (1999). Mastery climate: Children in charge of their own learning. *Teaching Elementary Physical Education* 10 (2): 6–10.

Valsiner, J. (1998). The development of the concept of development: Historical and epistemological perspectives. In W. Damon & R. Lerner (Eds.), *Handbook of child psychology: Vol. 1. Theoretical models of human development.* New York: Wiley.

van Beurden E, Barnett L.M., Zask A., Dietrich U.C., Brooks L.O., & Beard J. (2003). Can we skill and activate children through primary school physical education lessons? 'Move it groove it' – a collaborative health promotion intervention. *Prev Med* 2003 , 36, 493-501.

van der Kamp, J., Savelsbergh, G.J.P., & Davis, W.E. (1998). Body-scaled ratio as a control parameter for prehension in 5- to 9-year-old children. *Developmental Psychology*, 33(4), 351-361.

van der Mars, H., & Butterfield, S.A. (1988). The effects of a performance base curriculum on the gross motor development of preschool-aged children during teacher training: A pilot study. *International Journal of Physical Education*, 25(3), 20-25.

van der Pol, B., & van der Mark, J. (1927). Frequency demultiplication. *Nature, 120,* 363-364.

van Hof, P., van der Kamp, J., & Savelsbergh, G.J.P. (2008). The relation between infants' perception of catchableness and the control of catching. *Developmental Psychology*, 44(1), 182-194.

van Hof, P., van der Kamp, J., Caljouw, S.R., & Savelsbergh, G.J. (2005). The confluence of intrinsic and extrinsic constraints on 3- to 9-month-old infant catching behavior. *Infant Behavior and Development, 28,* 179-193.

van Soest, A.J.K., & Ledebt, A. (2005). Towards a broader scope of biomechanics in developmental studies: A commentary on Jensen (2005). *Infant and Child Development, 14,* 513-518.

Van Waelvelde, H., De Weerdt, W., De Cock, P., Peersman, W., & Smits-Engelsman, B.C.M. (2004). Ball catching performance in children with developmental coordination disorder. *Adapted Physical Activity Quarterly,* 21, 348–363.

VanSant, A. (1990). Life-span development in functional tasks. *Physical Therapy,* 788-798.

VanSant, A. (1995). Development of posture. In D. Cech & S. Martin (Eds.), *Functional movement development across the life span* (pp. 275-294). Philadelphia: Saunders.

VanSant, A. (1997). A life-span perspective of age differences in righting movements. In J. Clark, J. Humphrey, & M.A. Roberton (Eds.), *Motor development: Research and reviews* (Vol. 1, pp. 46-63). Reston, VA: National Association for Sport and Physical Education.

Vercruyssen, M. (1997). Movement control and speed of behavior. In A.D. Fisk & W.A. Rogers (Eds.), *Handbook of human factors and the older adult* (pp. 55-86). San Diego: Academic Press.

Vernazza-Martin, S., Martin, N., Vernazza, A., Lepellec-Muller, A., Rufo, M., Massion, J., & Assaiante, C. (2005). Goal directed locomotion and balance control in autistic children. *Journal of Autism and Developmental Disorders, 35*(1), 91-102.

Vilensky, J.A., Damasio, A.R., & Maurer, R.G. (1981). Gait disturbances in patients with autistic behavior: A preliminary study. *Archives of Neurology, 38*(10), 646-649.

von Bertalanffy, L. (1933). *Modern theories of development.* London: Oxford University Press.

von Bertalanffy, L. (1968). *General system theory.* New York: Braziller.

von Hofsten, C. (1979). Development of visually directed reaching: The approach phase. *Journal of Human Movement Studies, 5,* 160-178.

von Hofsten, C. (1980). Predictive reaching for moving objects by human infants. *Journal of Experimental Child Psychology, 30,* 369-382.

von Hofsten, C. (1983). Catching skills in infancy. *Journal of Experimental Psychology: Human Perception and Performance, 9,* 75-85.

von Hofsten, C. (1993). Prospective control: A basic aspect of action development. *Human Development, 36,* 253-270.

von Hofsten, C., & Fazel-Zandy, S. (1984). Development of visually guided hand orientation in reaching. *Journal of Experimental Child Psychology, 38,* 208-219.

von Hofsten, C., & Rosander, K. (1997). Development of smooth pursuit tracking in young infants. *Vision Research, 37,* 1799-1810.

von Hofsten, C., Feng, Q., & Spelke, E.S. (2000). Object representation and predictive action in infancy. *Developmental Science, 3,* 193-205.

von Hofsten, C., Kochukhova, O., & Rosander, K. (2007). Predictive occluder tracking in 4-month-old infants. *Developmental Science, 10,* 625-640.

von Hofsten, C., Vishton, P., Spelke, E.S., Feng, Q., & Rosander, K. (1998). Predictive action in infancy: Tracking and reaching for moving objects. *Cognition, 67,* 255-285.

Wade, M. (1976). Developmental motor learning. In J. Keogh, (Ed.) *Exercise and Sport Sciences Reviews, 4,* 375-394.

Wagenaar, R.C., & van Emmerik, R.E.A. (2000). Resonant frequencies of arms and legs identify different walking patterns. *Journal of Biomechanics, 33,* 853-861.

Wakefield A.J., Murch S.H., Anthony A., Linnell, J., Casson D.M., Malik M., et al. (1998) Ileal lymphoid nodular hyperplasia, non-specific colitis, and pervasive developmental disorder in children. *Lancet, 351,* 637-641.

Wang, W.Y., & Ju, Y.H. (2002). Promoting balance and jumping skills in children with Down syndrome. *Perceptual and Motor Skills, 94*(2), 443-448.

Ware, E.A., Uttal, D.H., & DeLoache, J.S. (2010). Everyday scale errors. *Developmental Science, 13*(1), 28-36.

Ware, E.Z., Uttal, D.H., Wetter, E.K., & DeLoache, J.S. (2006). Young children make scale errors when playing with dolls. *Developmental Science, 9,* 40-45.

Warren, W.H. (1984). Perceiving affordances: Visual guidance of stair climbing. *Journal of Experimental Psychology: Human Perception and Performance, 10,* 683-703.

Watson, J. (1913). Psychology as the behaviorist views it. *Psychological Review, 20,* 158-177.

Watson, J.B. (1925). *Behaviorism.* New York: People's Institute.

Watson, J.B. (1970). *Behaviorism.* New York: Norton. (Original work published 1930)

Watson, N. (2001). Sex differences in throwing: Monkeys have a fling. *Trends in Cognitive Science, 5,* 98-98.

Webb, D. (2000). Resonant frequences of arms and legs identify different walking patterns. *Journal of Biomechanics, 33,* 853-861.

Webb, D., Tuttle, R., & Baksh, M. (1994). Pendular activity of human upper limbs during slow and normal walking. *American Journal of Physical Anthropology, 93,* 477-489.

Weiss, A., Suzuki, T., Bean, J., & Fielding, R.A. (2000). High intensity strength training improves strength and functional performance after stroke. *American Journal of Physical Medicine and Rehabilitation, 79,* 369-376.

Weisz, S. (1938). Studies in equilibrium reaction. *Journal of Nervous and Mental Diseases, 88,* 150-162.

Welford, A.T. (1960). The measurement of sensory-motor performance: Survey and reappraisal of twelve years' progress. *Ergonomics, 3,* 189-230.

Welford, A.T. (1968). *Fundamentals of skill.* London: Methuen.

Welford, A.T. (1976). *Skilled performance: Perceptual and motor skills.* Glenview, IL: Scott Foresman.

Werner, H. (1957). The concept of development from a comparative and organismic point of view. In D. Harris (Ed.), *The concept of development* (pp. 125-148). Minneapolis: University of Minnesota Press.

Whitall, J. (1989). A developmental study of the interlimb coordination in running and galloping. *Journal of Motor Behavior, 21,* 409-428.

Whitall, J., Getchell, N., McMenamin, S., Horn, C., Wilms-Floet, A., & Clark, J.E. (2006). Perception-action coupling in children with and without DCD: Frequency locking between task-relevant auditory signals and motor responses in a dual-motor task. *Child Care Health and Development, 32*(6), 679-692.

Whiting, H.T.A. (1970). *Acquiring ball skill: A psychological interpretation.* Philadelphia: Lea & Febiger.

Whiting, H.T.A. (1972). Theoretical frameworks for an understanding of the acquisition of perceptual-motor skills. *Quest, 17,* 24-34.

Wickstrom, R. (1970). *Fundamental motor patterns* (1st ed.). Philadelphia: Lea & Febiger.

Wickstrom, R. (1977). *Fundamental motor patterns* (2nd ed.). Philadelphia: Lea & Febiger.

Wickstrom, R. (1983). *Fundamental motor patterns* (3rd ed.). Philadelphia: Lea & Febiger.

Wild, M. (1938). The behavior pattern of throwing and some observations concerning its course of development in children. *Research Quarterly, 9,* 20-24.

Williams, K., Haywood, K., & Painter, M. (1996). Environmental versus biological influences on gender differences in the overarm throw for force: Dominant and nondominant arm throws. *Women in Sport and Physical Activity Journal, 5,* 29-48.

Williams, K., Haywood, K., & VanSant, A. (1990). Movement characteristics of older adult throwers. In J. Clark & J. Humphrey (Eds.), *Advances in motor development research* (Vol. 3, pp. 29-44). New York: AMS Press.

Williams, K., Haywood, K., & VanSant, A. (1991). Throwing patterns of older adults: A follow-up investigation. *International Journal of Aging and Human Development, 33,* 279-294.

Williams, K., Haywood, K., & VanSant, A. (1998). Changes in throwing by older adults: A longitudinal investigation. *Research Quarterly for Exercise and Sport, 69,* 1-10.

Wilson, F. (1998). *The hand.* New York: Pantheon Books.

Wilson, P. H. (2005). Practitioner review: Approaches to assessment and treatment of children with DCD: An evaluative review. *J Child Psychol Psychiatry, 46*(8), 806-823.

Wilson, P.H., & Larkin, D. (2008). New and emerging approaches to understanding developmental coordination disorder. *Human Movement Science, 27*(2), 171-176.

Wilson, P.H., & McKenzie, B.E. (1998). Information processing deficits associated with developmental coordination disorder: A meta-analysis of research findings. *Journal of Child Psychology and Psychiatry, 39*(6), 829-840.

Wilson, P.H., Maruff, P., Ives, S., & Currie, J. (2001). Abnormalities of motor and praxis imagery in children with DCD. *Human Movement Science, 20*(1-2), 135-159.

Wilson, P.H., Thomas, P.R. & Maruff, P. (2002). Motor imagery training ameliorates motor clumsiness in children. *Journal of Child Neurology, 17,* 491-498.

Winders, P.C. (1997). *Gross motor skills in children with Down syndrome.* Bethesda, MA: Woodbine House.

Winstein, C.J., Gardner, E.R., McNeal, D.R., Barto, P.S., & Nicholson, D. (1989). Standing balance training: Effect on balance and locomotion in hemiparetic adults. *Archives of Physical Medicine and Rehabilitation, 70,* 755-762.

Winters, S. (1975). *Creative rhythmic movement.* Dubuque, IA: Brown.

Witherington, D.C. (2005). The development of prospective grasping control between 5 and 7 months: A longitudinal study. *Infancy, 7,* 143-161.

Wohlwill, J. (1970). The age variable in psychological research. *Psychological Review, 77,* 49-64.

Wohlwill, J. (1973). *The study of behavioral development.* New York: Academic Press.

Wolff, P.H. (1987). *The development of behavioral states and the expression of emotions in early infancy: New proposals for investigation.* Chicago: University of Chicago Press.

Wolfson, L., Whipple, R., Derby, C.A., Amerman, P., Murphy, T., Tobin, J.N., & Nasner, L. (1992). A dynamic posturography study of balance in healthy elderly. *Neurology, 42,* 2069-2075.

Woodward, G. (2001). Autism and Parkinson's disease. *Medical Hypotheses, 56*(2), 246-249.

Woollacott, M., & Shumway-Cook, A. (2002). Attention and the control of posture and gait: A review of an emerging area of research. *Gait and Posture, 16,* 1-14.

World Health Organization. (2007). Disorders of psychological development. In *International classifications of diseases (ICD-10)* (pp. F80-F89). *www.who.int/classifications/apps/icd/icd10online/.*

Wu, J., Looper, J., Ulrich, B.D., Ulrich, D.A., & Angulo-Barroso, R.M. (2007). Exploring effects of different treadmill interventions on walking onset and gait patterns in infants with Down syndrome. *Developmental Medicine and Child Neurology, 49*(11), 839-845.

Young, R. (2003). Evolution of the human hand: The role of throwing and clubbing. *Journal of Anatomy, 202,* 165-174.

Zelazo, P. (1983). The development of walking: New findings and old assumptions. *Journal of Motor Behavior, 15,* 99-137.

Zelazo, P., Konner, M., Kolb, S., & Zelazo, N. (1974). Newborn walking: A reply to Pontius. *Perceptual & Motor Skills, 39,* 423-428.

Zelazo, P.Z., Zelazo, N., & Kolb, S. (1972). "Walking" in the newborn. *Science, 177,* 1058-1059.

Zhang, W., & Rosenbaum, D.A. (2008). Planning for manual positioning: The end-state comfort effect for manual abduction-adduction. *Experimental Brain Research, 184,* 383-389.

Zoia, S., Castiello, U., Blason, L., & Scabar, A. (2005). Reaching in children with and without developmental coordination disorder under normal and perturbed vision. *Developmental Neuropsychology, 27*(2), 257-273.

Zoia, S., Pelamatti, G., Cuttini, M., Casotto, V., & Scabar, A. (2002). Performance of gesture in children with and without DCD: Effects of sensory input modalities. *Developmental Medicine and Child Neurology, 44*(10), 699-705.

Zoia, S., Pezzetta, E., Blason, L., Scabar, A., Carrozzi, M., & Bulgheroni, M. (2006). A comparison of the reach-to-grasp movement between children and adults: A kinematic study. *Developmental Neuropsychology, 30,* 719-738.

Zwicker, J.G., Missiuna C., Boyd L.A., (2009) Neural correlates of developmental coordination disorder: A review of hypotheses. *Journal of Child Neurology* 24, 1273-1281.

Index

Note: The italicized *f* and *t* following page numbers refer to figures and tables, respectively.

About the Authors

Kathleen M. Haywood, PhD, is a professor and associate dean for graduate education at the University of Missouri–St. Louis, where she researches life span motor development and teaches courses in motor behavior and development, sport psychology, and biomechanics. She earned her PhD in motor behavior from the University of Illinois at Urbana-Champaign in 1976.

Haywood is a fellow of the National Academy of Kinesiology and the Research Consortium of the American Alliance for Health, Physical Education, Recreation and Dance (AAHPERD). She has served as president of the North American Society for the Psychology of Sport and Physical Activity and as chairperson of the Motor Development Academy of AAHPERD. Haywood is also a recipient of AAHPERD's Mabel Lee Award.

Haywood is also the coauthor of the first, second, and third editions of *Archery: Steps to Success* and *Teaching Archery: Steps to Success* and coauthor of *Life Span Motor Development*, also published by Human Kinetics. She resides in Saint Charles, Missouri. In her free time she enjoys fitness training, tennis, and dog training.

Mary Ann Roberton, PhD, is professor emeritus and past director of the School of Human Movement, Sport, and Leisure Studies at Bowling Green State University in Bowling Green, Ohio. Roberton has been researching and writing about motor development for over 35 years and is well known for her study of developmental sequences in motor development and its application for physical education teachers and physical therapists. In addition to *Advanced Analysis of Motor Development*, Roberton has authored one scholarly book, several book chapters, numerous journal articles, and invited and refereed papers.

In 2011 Roberton received the Hall of Fame Award from the National Association for Sport and Physical Education. She is a fellow of the Research Consortium of the American Alliance for Health, Physical Education, Recreation and Dance (AAHPERD) and was inducted as a fellow into the National Academy of Kinesiology in 2003.

A distinguished faculty member, Roberton was awarded the Faculty Mentor Award in 2000 from Bowling Green State University. Honoring her service to the university and the profession, the Mary Ann Roberton Outstanding Thesis Award and Mary Ann Roberton Outstanding Project Award were established in

1999 by the faculty of the School of Human Movement, Sport, and Leisure Studies at Bowling Green State University. Roberton resides in Madison, Wisconsin. Retired since 2005, she remains active in research and scholarship. In her free time she enjoys swimming, cycling, and reading.

Nancy Getchell, PhD, is an associate professor at the University of Delaware in Newark. She has taught courses in motor development, motor control and learning, research methods, and women in sport. For nearly 20 years, Getchell has focused her research on motor development.

She is a fellow of the Research Consortium of the American Alliance for Health, Physical Education, Recreation and Dance (AAHPERD). She is a member of the North American Society for the Psychology of Sport and Physical Activity, the International Society of Motor Control, and AAHPERD. Getchell also served as the section editor for the Growth and Motor Development section of *Research Quarterly for Exercise and Sport* from 2005 to 2009 and chairperson of the AAHPERD Motor Development and Learning Academy.

In 2001, Getchell was the recipient of the Lolas E. Halverson Young Investigators Award in motor development. She earned a PhD in kinesiology from the University of Wisconsin at Madison in 1996. Getchell resides in Wilmington, Delaware, where she enjoys hiking, playing soccer, and bicycling.

INVENTORY 1983